Legacy
& Promise

150 YEARS OF JESUIT EDUCATION
AT THE UNIVERSITY OF SAN FRANCISCO

Alan Ziajka

with a foreword by USF President Stephen A. Privett, S.J.

University of San Francisco
Association of Jesuit University Presses 2005

Library of Congress Cataloging-in-Publication Data

Ziajka, Alan.
    Legacy & promise : 150 years of Jesuit education at the University of San Francisco / Alan
Ziajka ; with a foreword by Stephen A. Privett.
        p. cm.
    Includes bibliographical references and index.
    ISBN 0-9664059-5-1
    1. University of San Francisco--History. I. Title: Legacy and promise. II. University of San
Francisco. III. Title.
    LD4881.S162Z53 2005
    378.794'61--dc22
                                                                                2005050350

Table of Contents

Foreword

IN 2005 THE UNIVERSITY of San Francisco celebrates 150 years of service to the city and the world. Those 150 years stretch across three centuries during which the world changed more rapidly and dramatically than it had during the previous 3,000 years of recorded history. Some of those changes are recorded here, not in a linear narrative, but through written vignettes and revealing images from the university's history that allow readers to explore topics and themes of interest to them.

Dr. Alan Ziajka has done a masterful job tracing the story of USF from its founding amidst the chaos and confusion of the Gold Rush through two major earthquakes and as many world wars. The USF story surprisingly and intriguingly illustrates the truth of the French axiom, *Plus ça change, plus c'est la même chose* — the more things change, the more they stay the same. Indeed, the past 150 years have seen a great deal of change: from three students to more than 8,000; from a single wooden classroom to a 55-acre campus; from temporary facilities on sand dunes south of Market Street to magnificent St. Ignatius Church near the geographical center of the entire city; from one rigidly prescribed curriculum that gave pride of place to classical Latin and Greek to six colleges that offer graduate and undergraduate degrees in nursing, business, law, education, counseling, the humanities, and the sciences.

If USF has changed over the years, there is a thread of continuity that links past with present and future. The faculty still demonstrates a strong commitment to student learning and a clear focus on students' full development as contributing members of society. The university still educates the sons and daughters of immigrants, no longer Italian, Irish, and German, but Asian and Latin American. USF still offers many students the key to a promising future that they might otherwise be denied. The university's contemporary commitment to promoting a faith that does justice was presaged when the 1951 football team and the 1954–55 NCAA Basketball Championship team broke racial barriers that were firmly in place across the country. True to its Jesuit Catholic tradition, the university continues to offer students, faculty, and staff a rich liturgical life and calls them to reflect on their life choices through prayer and retreat experiences.

USF looks back with pride at its contributions to society — two San Francisco mayors, a United States senator, four California Supreme Court justices, a California lieutenant governor, two Pulitzer Prize winners, an Olympic medalist, a number of athletes in their respective halls of fame, many judges and public servants, countless priests and religious, numerous police and fire chiefs, corporate CEO's, and the current president of Peru. This rich legacy fuels USF's confidence that its contributions to the city and the world have only just begun. This new millennium will see a USF ever more faithful, creative, energetic, and effective in fulfilling its Jesuit Catholic mission of educating minds and hearts to change the world.

Stephen A. Privett, S.J.
President
University of San Francisco

Prologue

ON THE EVENING OF OCTOBER 19, 1905, Jeremiah Sullivan—graduate of St. Ignatius College, first president of the college's alumni association, and San Francisco Superior Court Judge—was the toastmaster for a celebratory banquet marking the 50th anniversary of the founding of the institution. The banquet served as the grand finale to a five-day Golden Jubilee honoring the day, October 15, 1855, when St. Ignatius Academy, the antecedent of the University of San Francisco, first opened its doors to three young men who crossed the sand dunes surrounding an undeveloped Market Street, entered a small wooden building, and became the first students at the Jesuit educational experiment in the City by the Bay.

On the night of the 1905 banquet, Judge Sullivan, and the other dinner speakers, reflected on the growth of the institution from its humble beginnings as a one-room schoolhouse, adjacent to a small Jesuit church and residence, to a magnificent building on Van Ness Avenue that occupied a full city block replete with world-class scientific laboratories, some of the finest libraries in the western United States, and the best-equipped gymnasium in the city. The school was also connected to a majestic church capable of holding 4,000 people. By 1905, scores of the school's alumni had become leaders in the civic, legal, banking, business, and religious communities of San Francisco, and many of the 800 young men attending the school that fall were destined for prominent careers in those same fields. None of the banquet celebrants could

have predicted, however, that in six months the great school and church they had helped build would be completely destroyed by the most devastating earthquake and fire ever to strike an urban area on the North American continent, forcing the leaders of St. Ignatius College (as St. Ignatius Academy was then called) to muster their courage and resolve to ensure the continuity of their institution.

Legacy and Promise will tell the story of the University of San Francisco in a series of 150 vignettes. Rather than serving as a definitive history of the institution during its first 150 years, however, this book will illuminate the university's long and varied history by highlighting many of the important individuals; key social, economic, political, and religious influences; and major national and international

CHURCH AND COLLEGE OF ST. IGNATIUS

St. Ignatius Church and College in 1905, the year of the Golden Jubilee celebrating the 50th anniversary of the founding of the institution. In 1930, during its Diamond Jubilee, St. Ignatius College became the University of San Francisco.

events with which the school's growth and development are intertwined. The University of San Francisco cannot be understood without an appreciation for the Jesuit ideals first articulated by Saint Ignatius of Loyola in the 16th century, the wave of immigrants to the United States in the 19th century, the rapid development of San Francisco following the California Gold Rush of the late 1840s, the earthquake and fire of 1906, and the two world wars and major economic depression of the first half of the 20th century. In ways that are both obvious and subtle, the students, alumni, faculty, administrators, and staff that have formed the nucleus of the university community have been connected to the external world since the institution's founding. The choices these individuals made were both shaped by

and helped to shape the local, national, and international events taking place around them. The complex interaction between individual choices, institutional development, and the history of the city, the nation, and the world is the basis for understanding the legacy and the promise of the University of San Francisco as it celebrates its sesquicentennial.

Part I: Origins

A stained glass window in St. Ignatius Church on the University of San Francisco campus depicts Saint Ignatius of Loyola, the founder of the Society of Jesus.

UNIVERSITY OF SAN FRANCISCO ARCHIVES

THE ORIGINS OF THE UNIVERSITY OF SAN FRANCISCO stretch back to 16th-century Europe with the founding of the Society of Jesus by St. Ignatius of Loyola. Born in 1491, Iñigo Lopez de Loyola was a Basque nobleman and soldier who rejected his original courtly life in favor of one dedicated to faith and service to God and the Catholic Church. He made that decision while recovering from the effects of a French cannonball that shattered his right leg during a battle in Pamplona in northern Spain. While recuperating from his war wound, he reluctantly read the only two books available to him in the castle where he was recovering: a biography of Jesus and *Flos Sanctorum*, a chronicle of the lives of the saints.

Reading these books, and reflecting on their meaning, Ignatius of Loyola radically altered his life. Over the course of the next several years, he underwent a spiritual transformation. After making a pilgrimage to Jerusalem, he traveled and studied throughout Europe, eventually graduating from the University of Paris. He gathered a small group of followers who shared his views, and appealed to Pope Paul III to let his group serve the Church. In 1540, with the Pope's approval, Ignatius of Loyola founded the Society of Jesus, soon to become one of the major religious orders of the Catholic Church. With their headquarters in Rome, the Jesuits originally engaged primarily in social outreach to the less fortunate members of the emerging urban society, especially those in hospitals and prisons. As word spread of the Jesuits' skill in educating the young men who joined their order, however, European leaders began to ask the Society of Jesus to expand their educational offerings to those who were not Jesuits. During the 1540s, the Jesuits founded their first colleges in Europe, and by 1556, the year Ignatius died, the Jesuits were running 46 schools in Italy, Spain, Portugal, France, Germany, and Goa, India, for both Jesuits and lay students. Over the next two centuries, the Society of Jesus established the largest network of educational institutions in the world—in total, 700 schools throughout Europe, Latin America, and Asia. Unlike other religious orders up to that time, however, the Jesuits focused their educational and social efforts on the people living in the developing urban areas of the world. The Society of Jesus also became the first religious

First Jesuit arrives in San Francisco

St. Ignatius Academy founded

State charter awarded to grant college degrees

1849   **1855**   **1859**   **1860**

Gold discovered at Sutter's Mill in California

Abraham Lincoln is elected president

4

order to develop a comprehensive school system for religious and lay students alike seeking a quality education.

In 1789, Georgetown College was founded in Washington, D.C., soon to become the capital city of the new republic of the United States, and over the next 50 years, other Jesuit colleges were established in the Eastern and Midwestern parts of the country. By the 1840s, immigrants from Europe began to flood the western territories. Among those immigrants were approximately 350 Italian Jesuit priests, escaping the persecution and political turmoil that accompanied the unification of Italy. The Jesuits who came west soon established schools and churches for the surviving Native Americans and missions for European immigrants in areas such as the Pacific Northwest. In 1849, the California Gold Rush brought hundreds of thousands of people to California, and during the next decade, the Jesuits began to establish churches and educational institutions in the state. Among these institutions were St. Ignatius Church and St. Ignatius Academy in San Francisco. On October 15, 1855, St. Ignatius Academy, the forerunner of St. Ignatius College and the University of San Francisco, opened its doors for the first time. The founding president was Anthony Maraschi, S.J., a Jesuit priest from northern Italy. The series of vignettes that comprise part I of this book will tell the story of the institution's first 25 years.

In 1540, Pope Paul III approved the formation of the Society of Jesus by Ignatius of Loyola and his followers.

UNIVERSITY OF SAN FRANCISCO ARCHIVES

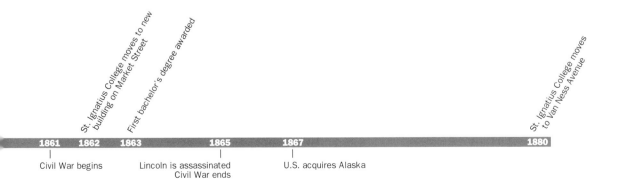

St. Ignatius College moves to new building on Market Street

First bachelor's degree awarded

St. Ignatius College moves to Van Ness Avenue

| 1861 | 1862 | 1863 | 1865 | 1867 | 1880 |

Civil War begins

Lincoln is assassinated
Civil War ends

U.S. acquires Alaska

The California Gold Rush and the Jesuits

ON JANUARY 24, 1848, JAMES MARSHALL REACHED INTO A
stream at Sutter's sawmill in the Coloma valley, about 40 miles east of
Sacramento, and pulled out a few shiny metal flakes. The excitement
created by this discovery launched one of the greatest voluntary migra-
tions in human history: the California Gold Rush. San Francisco, the
port of entry to the gold fields of Northern California, saw its population
swell from 459 people in 1847 to 34,776 by 1852. Hundreds of thousands
more poured through the city on their way to the gold fields, coming
from throughout the United States, Europe, Asia, Latin America,
and Australia.

The gold-seekers reflected a multitude of
cultural, religious, and ethnic backgrounds, and
represented every strata of society. They were
farmers, merchants, shopkeepers, army and navy
deserters, soldiers of fortune, plantation owners
and slaves, the rich and the poor. Groups of
convicts in penal colonies in Australia were set
free to go to California under the stipulation
that they were never to return. The miners
came by sailing ship and steamer through San
Francisco Bay or overland by horse, mule, ox,
covered wagons, and on foot. Thousands died
during the journey and many more succumbed
to the disease and violence that characterized life
in the gold fields. Of the hundreds of thousands
who survived, some made fortunes, but most
did not. In pursuing their dreams, however,
they changed their lives forever and profoundly
altered California and San Francisco.

The California Gold Rush also transformed
the Jesuit presence on the West Coast of North
America, which from 1844 to 1848 was centered
in Oregon Territory. When gold was discovered
in California, many Oregonians, including the
Catholics who were congregants of the Jesuit
mission in that area, left for the gold fields and
the rapidly emerging mining communities of
Northern California. In December 1849, two
Italian Jesuit priests, Michael Accolti, S.J.,
superior of the Jesuit residence at Willamette,
Oregon, and his associate, John Nobili, S.J.,
made a five-day voyage from Astoria, Oregon,
to San Francisco. The City by the Bay was
experiencing rapid growth and virtual civic chaos.
Murder, prostitution, thievery, and gambling
were commonplace. Fortunes were made and
lost in a day through various kinds of specula-
tion. Upon arriving in the city, Fr. Accolti
wrote, "Whether it should be called a madhouse
or Babylon I am at a loss to determine; so great
in those days was the disorder, the brawling,
the open immorality, the reign of crime which

brazen-faced triumphed on a soil not yet brought under the sway of human laws." Another priest, Fr. Antoine Langlois, wrote in 1849, "in spite of the temptations of bar-rooms and saloons on every hand for the multitudes that frequented them…it was possible for a person to save his soul in San Francisco." Jesuits also believed that there was a place for education in this unruly town, and they started the first institution of higher education in the city of San Francisco.

St. Ignatius Academy was officially founded in 1855, though it was renamed St. Ignatius College in 1859 when the State of California issued it a charter to confer college degrees. In 1930, on the occasion of its Diamond Jubilee, the name was changed for the last time to the University of San Francisco. In the city named for Saint Francis of Assisi, there continues a vision and a mission that stretches back to the founding of the Society of Jesus in 1540 by Saint Ignatius of Loyola, that took root in 1855, and that flourishes today at a premier Jesuit Catholic university.

San Francisco in March 1847, ten months before the discovery of gold near Sacramento.

UNIVERSITY OF SAN FRANCISCO ARCHIVES

Michael Accolti, S.J.

THE HISTORY OF ST. IGNATIUS COLLEGE DURING ITS FIRST quarter century is interwoven with the establishment of the Jesuit Order in California, European immigration to the western United States, and the population growth of California and San Francisco as a result of the California Gold Rush. Few individuals better represent the confluence of these historical streams than Michael Accolti, S.J.

Michael Accolti was born into an aristocratic family in the Kingdom of Naples in 1807. In 1832, at the age of 25, he became a member of the Society of Jesus in the Rome province. In 1844, he was sent by the Jesuits to the newly settled territory of Oregon, thus becoming one of the first of approximately 350 Italian Jesuit immigrants who came to America during the 19th century. The immigration of many of these Italian Jesuits, along with thousands of other Italians, was prompted in part by the political upheavals in Italy associated with that country's unification. From 1844 to 1848, Fr. Accolti and another Italian Jesuit, John Nobili, S.J., worked as missionaries in Oregon. In 1848, Fr. Accolti was made superior of the Jesuit residence at Willamette, Oregon. That same year, he and Fr. Nobili received a letter from Fr. Anthony Langlois, a French-Canadian priest working in San Francisco, asking them to help civilize and educate that tumultuous Gold Rush town, whose population was dramatically increasing as tens of thousands of people descended on the city on their way to the gold fields of Northern California. The overwhelming majority of these fortune seekers were young men, and many were Catholics, including a sizeable group from Fr. Accolti's own congregation in

Oregon. Fr. Accolti obtained permission from the superior of the Rocky Mountain Mission, headquartered in present-day Idaho, for he and Fr. Nobili to follow the gold-seekers to Northern California.

The arrival of Fr. Accolti and Fr. Nobili in San Francisco on December 8, 1849, the year before California attained statehood, marked the beginning of a permanent Jesuit educational and religious establishment in the city and in the state. Although Fr. Accolti was ordered to return to Oregon in July of 1850, Fr. Nobili remained in Northern California and founded Santa Clara College in 1851. Fr. Accolti wrote to Rome asking permission to send additional Jesuits to California, but the letter took over a year to get to Rome, and the return letter denied permission to embark on any new apostolic work in the state. By the time Fr. Accolti received the letter, however, many Jesuits were already at work in the Bay Area, prompting some Jesuits to later say: "The California Province was conceived in disobedience and is still running on the same principle." Fr. Accolti sailed back to Rome in late 1853, met with Father General Peter Beckx, and in the following year secured the "adoption" of the California and Oregon mission by the Jesuit province of Turin, Italy. This led to badly needed economic and manpower support for the California enterprise. For example, the Turin provincial ordered Anthony Maraschi, S.J., who was then teaching at Loyola College, Maryland, to head for San Francisco. In 1855, Fr. Maraschi founded St. Ignatius Church and College (described in vignette #3). Although

Fr. Accolti was not in San Francisco when the school was founded, he later served as Fr. Maraschi's assistant for six months before being transferred to Santa Clara College. At Santa Clara, Fr. Accolti was prefect of studies and professor of ethics for four years. He then served as parish priest of Santa Clara, retaining for one year the position of director of studies at Santa Clara College. In 1867, he returned to San Francisco, where he worked at St. Ignatius College and was chaplain at San Quentin Prison. He died on the evening of November 7, 1878, probably of a massive stroke, shortly after leaving for the day from St. Ignatius College. His funeral was held in St. Ignatius Church two days later, after which his body was taken by a Southern Pacific Railroad train for burial in the Santa Clara Mission cemetery.

Saint Ignatius of Loyola, who founded the Society of Jesus in 1540, called for the establishment of Jesuit educational institutions throughout the world. More than 300 years later, in 1850, Fr. Accolti wrote "once that our Society shall, like a vine, have been lawfully planted in California and shall have taken root, it will be easy for it afterwards to spread its branches; hence, when we shall have established one college, it will be an easy matter to put our minds and our hands to the starting of another. Thus will everything be more solid than if we keep many things at the same time before our eyes. Indeed we doubt not that many, nay, very many things for the greater glory of God will, throughout the length and breadth of California, present themselves to be done."

Today on the University of San Francisco campus there is a meeting room dedicated to Michael Accolti, S.J. It is to honor a Jesuit who successfully implemented a mission of Saint Ignatius of Loyola, a mission that continues to this day, and that will guide USF into the future.

Michael Accolti, S.J., who established the Jesuit order in California.

3 The Founding of St. Ignatius Academy

This drawing is of the first site of
St. Ignatius Church and Academy in
1855. The buildings stood amidst
sand dunes on an undeveloped Market
Street, between what would become
Fourth and Fifth streets.

THE UNIVERSITY OF SAN FRANCISCO BEGAN ITS EXISTENCE
humbly as a one-room schoolhouse named St. Ignatius Academy. The
institution's founding president, Anthony Maraschi, S.J., was a Jesuit
from northern Italy, who was teaching "mental philosophy" at Loyola
College, Maryland, when the order reached him in 1854 to depart for
California's distant shores. When Fr. Maraschi arrived
in San Francisco, he applied for and received permission
from Archbishop Joseph Alemany to build a Jesuit church
and school. When Fr. Maraschi asked the archbishop to
designate a spot, His Grace pointed to a stretch of sand
dunes west of the then-central part of San Francisco
and, with a sweep of his hand toward the unoccupied
land, said "any place over there."

THE NATIONAL.

GEO. PEN JOHNSTON, Editor.

MONDAY MORNING, August 16th, 1858.

DAY SCHOOL AT ST. IGNATIUS

Market Street, bet. Fourth & Fifth,

SAN FRANCISCO.

Directed by Fathers of the Society of Jesus.

THE FOURTH ANNUAL SESSION OF
this Institution will commence on the 1st day of September, 1858, with accommodations much better than heretofore.

TERMS:

Rhetoric, Grammar, Composition, Elocution,
Mathematics, Book-Keeping, Arithmetic, Ancient and Modern Languages, History, Geography, Penmanship, Vocal Music—per
month, including Stationery........................... $8 00
Preparatory Department, per month, including
Stationery 5 00
Three lessons in Drawing, per week, of one hour each will
be given for an extra charge of $2 00 per month.

Schools hours from 9 A. M. to 3 P. M. No school on Thurs-
days and holidays. On every Monday tickets are given for
punctual attendance, good conduct, and excellence in recitation, to such as deserved them in the previous week.
Average attendance last session, sixty-five pupils, under
the care of six Professors.
A. MARASCHI, S. J., Principal.

A NIGHT SCHOOL for Book-Keeping, Arithmetic,
and Modern Languages, will be formed as soon as sufficient
attendance is secured.   au16tf

Fr. Maraschi chose a few sand dunes on the south side of Market Street, between Fourth and Fifth streets, and proclaimed, "Here, in time, will be the heart of a great city." Fr. Maraschi borrowed $11,500 and purchased a lot (127 by 275 feet) from Thomas O. Larkin, the first American Consul in Monterey. On this lot, Fr. Maraschi built a church, a Jesuit residence, and a wooden frame building about 26 feet long by 16 feet wide, the first home of St. Ignatius Academy. On October 15, 1855, the school opened its doors to its first class, which numbered three students. To greet those students, there were three instructors: Joseph Bixio, S.J., another Italian Jesuit; John Haley, a lay teacher from Ireland; and Fr. Maraschi.

In testimony to the economic foresight of Fr. Maraschi, the Jesuits sold this original piece of property in 1886 for $900,000 — a hefty profit over its original purchase price. St. Ignatius College moved to two other locations in San Francisco (described in vignette #22) before moving to its current Fulton Street location in

1927. In 2005, the University of San Francisco's main campus occupies 55 acres near Golden Gate Park. Parts of the campus extend west to Stanyan Street, east to Masonic Avenue, north to Anza Street, and south across Fulton Street. In addition, USF offers classes at four Northern California regional campuses, in Santa Rosa, San Ramon, Cupertino, and Sacramento; at a Southern California regional campus in the city of Orange; and at a site in Phoenix, Arizona. USF has sponsored cooperative study-abroad programs throughout the world, including programs in Mexico, Chile, Japan, China, the Philippines, England, Spain, Italy, Hungary, El Salvador, and South Africa. The institution has grown dramatically since its modest begin-ning in 1855.

St. Ignatius Academy ran a series of advertisements in the local press to describe its curriculum, accommoda-tions, tuition, and school hours.

Anthony Maraschi, S.J.

VISION, FAITH, AND DETERMINATION ARE PERHAPS THREE of the most important characteristics needed by an individual seeking to start an enterprise and sustain it during its fledgling years. Anthony Maraschi, S.J., the founding president of St. Ignatius Academy, later to become the University of San Francisco, possessed these characteristics in great abundance.

Anthony Maraschi was born in 1820, in the Italian state of Piedmont. He entered the Society of Jesus in 1841, at the Chieri novitiate in northern Italy. As a scholastic, he began his teaching career in Nice, France, but was forced to flee the city in 1847 in the face of a growing anti-Jesuit movement. After being ordained a priest in Marseilles, France in 1849, Fr. Maraschi came to America. He completed a theology degree at Georgetown College, and briefly taught at that institution before assignment to Holy Cross College in Worcester, Massachusetts, where he taught philosophy and Spanish. He was later sent to teach philosophy at Loyola College in Maryland. In 1854, Fr. Maraschi took his final vows as a Jesuit and was ordered to set sail for San Francisco, arriving on November 1 of that year. When Fr. Maraschi first set foot in the city, it was in the midst of an economic depression following the end of the Gold Rush boom years. Scores of once-lucrative mines had been exhausted, many miners and support workers were unemployed, one-third of San Francisco's approximately 1,000 stores stood vacant, and many companies had gone bankrupt. Economically, it was not the best of times to start an educational enterprise.

During his first six months in San Francisco,

Fr. Maraschi served as an assistant pastor at St. Francis Church and then as an assistant pastor at St. Patrick's Church. During this time, he laid the groundwork for the establishment of a Jesuit church and school in the city. He met with the Dominican Archbishop of San Francisco, Joseph Alemany, to secure approval for a Jesuit institution to be erected among the sand dunes west of the then-downtown section of the city, on Market Street between Fourth and Fifth streets. He borrowed money to purchase a small parcel of land and to build a church, a Jesuit residence, and a one-room schoolhouse. The first St. Ignatius Church in San Francisco was dedicated on July 15, 1855, less than a year after Fr. Maraschi's arrival in the city. With the assistance of Michael Accolti, S.J., and Joseph Bixio, S.J., St. Ignatius Academy opened its doors on October 15, 1855. The enrollment was so disappointing, however, and so few students paid full tuition, that classes were temporarily suspended in February 1856. Undeterred, Fr. Maraschi reopened the academy in the fall of 1856 and was rewarded by a steady increase in enrollment. By 1858, the school had 65 students, necessitating the hiring of additional instructors. In 1859, the Jesuit General in Rome, Peter Beckx, officially recognized the academy. That same year, Fr. Maraschi successfully incorporated the institution under California state law, obtained a charter to issue college degrees, formed a board of trustees, and renamed the institution St. Ignatius College. During the institution's early years, Fr. Maraschi simultaneously served as the college president; college treasurer; and instructor for Latin, Greek, and Spanish. He was also the parish priest for St. Ignatius Church: he preached, heard confessions, visited the sick, kept the church accounts, and supervised repairs and additions to the church and school. In addition, he had general accounting responsibilities for the California and Oregon missions.

In August 1859, Fr. Maraschi received some well-deserved and favorable press in the San Francisco newspaper, *Alta California:* "The Reverend Anthony Maraschi, President of St. Ignatius College, is eminently qualified for the position, being a finished scholar and a man of high moral character. He has labored incessantly to advance the interests of those placed under his charge and the examination of several classes exhibited the complete success which has attended his efforts."

In 1862, Fr. Maraschi turned over the presidency of St. Ignatius College to Nicolas Congiato, S.J. Fr. Maraschi continued, however, to serve as treasurer for the school and college and effectively managed the financial affairs of the institution. The year before he left the presidency, he started a fundraising effort for a new building. The first gift was for $100. Fr. Maraschi secured some other small gifts, borrowed additional money, and oversaw the construction on a new three-story church and school adjacent to the original site. He also obtained bequests to more than 800 acres of land in the East Bay, near Point San Pablo. This land came to be known as "Maraschi's Ranch." Fr. Maraschi lived to see the institution he founded grow and move to another location, on the corner of Van Ness and Hayes streets, and to witness the sale of

the original piece of property he had purchased on Market for a profit of almost $900,000. The sale of this land, plus the sale of "Maraschi's Ranch" for $200,000, enabled St. Ignatius Church and College to eliminate all of its accumulated debt by the turn of the century. Fr. Maraschi died in 1897, after serving in San Francisco for 43 years. Thousands of

Anthony Maraschi, S.J., founder of St. Ignatius Church and Academy in 1855.

people attended his requiem Mass held in St. Ignatius Church, and hundreds more journeyed south with his body to the Santa Clara Mission cemetery on board a special Southern Pacific funeral train.

Today on the University of San Francisco campus a few feet from the northeast corner of St. Ignatius Church, stands a bust of Anthony Maraschi, S.J. It was created by a local sculptor, Harriet Moore, and unveiled in 1985, the 130th anniversary of the institution's founding. In addition, Xavier Hall has a meeting room named after the founding president. The sculpture and the room are dedicated to a man whose vision, faith, and determination were critical to the creation of an institution that has enriched the lives of thousands of people over the course of 150 years.

The First Students

THE OUTLOOK WAS NOT PROMISING FOR THE JESUITS ON
that fall day in 1855. On October 15, they opened the doors for the
first time on their experiment in education in San Francisco:
St. Ignatius Academy. Three students showed up for class,
including Richard McCabe, who later became a "well-
known professional man of San Francisco," and two
others whose names are unknown. Despite that
disappointing start to what eventually became
the University of San Francisco, enrollment
gradually grew to approximately 23 students
by the end of the first academic year, and
to 65 students by 1858, the year before the
institution became St. Ignatius College.

In 1862, a three-story brick building was
constructed on Market Street, between Fourth
and Fifth streets and adjacent to the original
wooden church and school, to accommodate
a further increase in enrollment to 140 students. Among those 140 students was John
Cunningham, the first native San Franciscan
to become a Jesuit. In 1861, most students at
St. Ignatius College were under 18 years of
age. Indeed, John Cunningham was only 6
when he started at the school. Years later, Fr.
Cunningham wrote about his first day at school:
"Ushered into the room, my awe-stricken eyes
beheld my future pedagogue, Mr. John Egan,
who presided over the educational development of some 30 urchins, ranging from five
years of age to thirteen or fourteen. My name

was regis-
tered; I was
assigned a
seat; I was
kissed good-
bye by my
mother, who
warned me not
to eat in class and
to be home early for
dinner…. I recall that
in June, 1861, St. Ignatius
College held its closing exercises
in the open, at the rear of the church.
The year following, we had a wet winter and
our classes were held in the basement of the
church, the floors of which had to be raised

Richard McCabe, the first student
enrolled at St. Ignatius Academy.

UNIVERSITY OF SAN FRANCISCO ARCHIVES

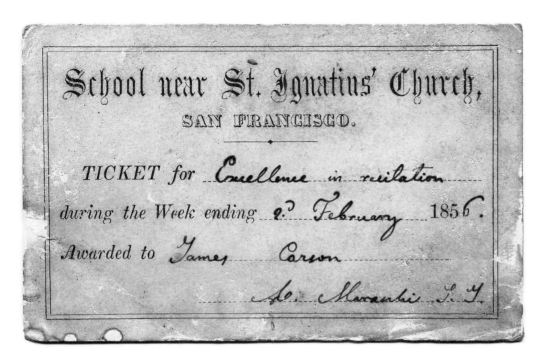

This "ticket for excellence in recitation" as described in the advertisement in Vignette #3, was awarded to James Carson, one of the first students at St. Ignatius Academy in February 1856, four months after the school opened. It was signed by the academy's first president, Anthony Maraschi, S.J., and is one of the earliest artifacts of the institution.

ST. IGNATIUS COLLEGE PREPARATORY ARCHIVES
GIFT OF MRS. ROSIE L. DOMINGUEZ

by planking that we boys might go dryshod to our classrooms."

By 1863, there were 474 students enrolled in all divisions of the institution, although the majority of these were not college-age students. During the early years of the school, a sizable percentage of students were enrolled in elementary classes, corresponding to the present fourth, fifth, and sixth grades; preparatory classes, corresponding to the modern seventh and eighth grades; and grammar (college preparatory) classes, corresponding to the present four years of high school. The elementary school division was eliminated in 1897, the last eighth grade class was dropped in 1918, and the final separation of the high school division from the college division was made in 1959, when St. Ignatius High School became completely independent from the University of San Francisco. Today, both institutions continue to thrive. As of fall 2004, there were 8,274 students enrolled at USF, a significant increase from those first three students walked through the doorway in 1855.

St. Ignatius Church

FROM THE BEGINNING, ST. IGNATIUS CHURCH AND
St. Ignatius Academy were intertwined on a multitude of levels,
including a shared vision and mission, key individuals whose roles
overlapped, and significant
events that concurrently
shaped both institutional
histories. Nevertheless,
St. Ignatius Church has
an identity apart from the
academy that eventually
became the University of
San Francisco.

St. Ignatius Church and College as they
appeared in 1860, drawn from a later
photograph. From 1855 to 1862, the
appearance of the church, school, and
Jesuit residence changed significantly.

UNIVERSITY OF SAN FRANCISCO ARCHIVES

St. Ignatius Church was founded
by the same man, in the same year,
and at the same location as St. Ignatius
Academy. Anthony Maraschi, S.J.,
(whose life is described in vignette #4)
secured the approval of Archbishop
Joseph Alemany to build the first
St. Ignatius Church in San Francisco
among the sand dunes west of what
was then the main part of the city, on
what eventually became Market Street
between Fourth and Fifth streets. That
area of the city was charitably known
as St. Ann's Valley, a desolate stretch
of sand and coastal scrub vegetation.
The first St. Ignatius Church, built for
$4,000, was a small wooden frame build-
ing 75 feet long by 35 feet wide, with a
plain gable roof. The inside walls were

plastered, and on the floor were fitted pews that could seat 400. At the rear of the church was a small seating gallery. St. Ignatius began as a parish church, whose limits were set by Archbishop Alemany in consultation with other pastors in the city. Fr. Maraschi was officially appointed pastor of St. Ignatius Church by Archbishop Alemany on July 14, 1855. Fr. Maraschi continued as pastor after St. Ignatius Academy opened its doors in a small wooden building next door to the church, and the busy Jesuit priest concurrently served as the academy's president, treasurer, and instructor of Latin, Greek, and Spanish, even as the academy grew and became a thriving college in 1859.

The first St. Ignatius Church was dedicated on July 15, 1855, exactly three months before St. Ignatius Academy opened its doors to its first students. Archbishop Alemany performed the dedication ceremony and blessing. He was assisted by Fr. Maraschi and several other Jesuits, including John Nobili, S.J., who along with Michael Accolti, S.J., had been one of the first Jesuits to come to San Francisco in 1849. In 1851, Fr. Nobili became the first president of Santa Clara College. At the dedication ceremony, Archbishop Alemany praised the Jesuits for their work in California and expressed his hope that the founding of St. Ignatius Church was the beginning of a great future for the Jesuits in San Francisco.

A local newspaper covered the dedication ceremony and Mass that followed. The article noted that Archbishop Alemany "delivered an impressive discourse in which he spoke in the most eulogistic terms of the zeal and labors of the Jesuits in propagating the gospel throughout every part of the world, but more especially in California." The writer also observed a "large attendance on the occasion, a considerable portion of whom were ladies," and that the service was "accompanied by very fine music." The article concluded that in the future "Mass will be celebrated in the church every morning except Sunday at 6 and 7 $^{1}/_{2}$ o'clock and on Sundays at the usual hours. Vespers will be sung every Sunday at 5 $^{1}/_{2}$ in the afternoon. The pastor, Father Maraschi speaks the English, French, Spanish, Italian and German languages."

The dedication ceremony and accompanying Mass marked the beginning of the first of five St. Ignatius churches in San Francisco. The ceremony also inaugurated a church identity and history that is separate, yet interwoven, with the history of St. Ignatius Academy, St. Ignatius College, and the University of San Francisco.

The Immigrants (PART I)

7

THE HISTORY OF AMERICA IS THE HISTORY OF IMMIGRATION. Archeological and DNA evidence indicates that the earliest immigrants to America were Asians from Siberia, and that they came across a land bridge spanning the Bering Strait into Alaska 21,000 to 42,000 years ago. The people who reached Alaska around that time would have found their way south across Canada blocked by glaciers until 12,000 years ago. Soon after the glaciers melted, however, these Asian-Siberian immigrants settled all over North America, and within another 1,000 years were in South America, as well. Estimates are that anywhere from 10 million to more than 100 million of these first immigrants, later named Indians by the Europeans, were in the Americas when the first Spanish explorers arrived in the late 15th and early 16th centuries.

Tragically, within 130 years of these first contacts, according to some scholars, approximately 95 percent of the Indians had died of European diseases, such as smallpox and influenza, for which they had no immunities. In the San Francisco Bay Area, the first immigrants arrived between 5,000 and 10,000 years ago, and became divided into four distinct tribes: the Coast Miwoks, the Wintum, the Yokuts, and the Ohlone. These were the tribes encountered by the first Spanish explorers and Franciscan priests who established the California missions and founded San Francisco in 1776.

During the 17th and 18th centuries, hundreds of thousands of Europeans immigrated to America. By the mid-19th century, the tide of immigration from Europe swelled to as many as 250,000 a year, predominantly from Great Britain, Ireland, Germany, and the Scandinavian countries. As early as 1848, the first Chinese immigrants began to arrive in the United States through San Francisco. By 1869, 20,000 Chinese had been brought to California by the Central Pacific Railroad to build the transcontinental railroad. By the mid-1870s, there were approximately 100,000 Chinese immigrants in this country, many of whom eventually settled in San Francisco. In the 1880s, more than 3 million immigrants came to America from Western and Eastern Europe, including a large number of Eastern European Russians, Poles, Russian/Polish Jews, Austro-Hungarians, Czechs, Greeks,

Native American students in a classroom at Sacred Heart Mission in Idaho. The mission was founded by the Jesuits in 1878.

and Italians. Before the American Civil War, a trickle of Italian immigration had begun, but after the war ended in 1865, Italian immigration grew dramatically, rising to 32,000 in 1882, and tripling to 100,000 immigrants per year by 1900. Among the 19th-century Italian immigrants were approximately 350 Jesuit priests, escaping the political turmoil and persecution that accompanied Italian national unification.

Most of the Italian Jesuits migrated to the American West, where they established schools and churches and ministered to the surviving Native Americans in what came to be known as the Rocky Mountain Mission. A Belgian-born priest, Pierre DeSmet, S.J., who had worked among the Native Americans of the Great Plains, was instrumental in convincing Peter Beckx, S.J., the Jesuit Superior General in Rome, to send the Italian Jesuits to minister to the Native Americans in the western United States. By 1896, the schools of the Rocky Mountain Mission enrolled more than 1,000 Native American students from a host of tribes: the Yakimas, Umatillas, Nez Percés,

Cheyennes, Assinoboines, and Crows. These Jesuit institutions consisted of boarding schools for boys and girls and included printing presses, workshops, and farms. Other Italian Jesuits established missions in the Southwest and California. Following the surge of immigration to California after the Gold Rush, Jesuits established churches and educational institutions throughout the state, including St. Ignatius Church and St. Ignatius Academy, the antecedent of the University of San Francisco. The Jesuits of California also worked in hospitals and prisons and provided other social services to the newly arrived immigrants. Thus, the earliest Jesuits in the western United States ministered to the needs of the ancestors of the first Asian immigrants to America and also to the needs of the most recent European immigrants. The work of the Jesuits of San Francisco with the Irish and Italian immigrants of the late 19th century has its counterpart today at the University of San Francisco, where first- and second-generation immigrants from throughout the world now make up a significant percentage of the student population.

The Immigrants (PART II)

TO VARYING DEGREES, MOST AMERICAN INSTITUTIONS of higher education reflect our nation's immigration experience. During the 19th century, St. Ignatius College was the immigration experience. USF's history begins with Italian Jesuit immigrants like Michael Accolti, S.J., who established the Jesuit order in California, and Anthony Maraschi, S.J., who founded St. Ignatius Church and Academy. The first seven presidents of St. Ignatius College were all Italian Jesuit immigrants: Fathers Anthony Maraschi, Nicolas Congiato (who served two terms), Burchard Villiger, Joseph Bayma, Aloysius Masnata, and John Pinasco. Robert Kenna, S.J., who became the eighth president of St. Ignatius College in 1880, was the first St. Ignatius College president to be born in the United States.

Most of the faculty members during these early years were also Italian Jesuit immigrants. Some of the first lay faculty, such as John Haley, Peter Malloy, James O'Sullivan, and Daniel Crowley, were immigrants from Ireland. One of the most prominent spokesmen and recruiters for St. Ignatius Church and College during the second half of the 19th century, James Bouchard, S.J., had a French mother and a Delaware Indian father.

Virtually all of the students at St. Ignatius College, during its first decades, were first- or second-generation Irish or Italian Catholics, a partial reflection of the population of San Francisco. For example, after the Gold Rush of 1849, the Irish came to San Francisco by the thousands, making up nearly one-third of the city's population by the 1880s. Throughout the mid-19th century, and especially in the 1880s

and 1890s, Italians also immigrated to the United States, and to San Francisco, in ever increasing numbers, swelling the population of San Francisco and expanding the enrollment of St. Ignatius College to 650 students by 1880. In the 1880 national census, the population of San Francisco was 233,959, 44.6 percent of whom were foreign born. In that year, San Francisco was the ninth largest city in the United States, but first in the nation, even ahead of New York City, in the percentage of its population that was foreign born. By 1890, the population of San Francisco had grown to 298,997, making it the eighth largest city in the country and tied with New York City for the largest percentage (42.4 percent) of foreign-born residents of any city in the nation. In addition to the Irish and the Italians, large numbers of Germans and

French immigrated to San Francisco in the last decades of the 19th century, some of whom sent their sons to St. Ignatius College, further adding to the European diversity of the institution by the turn of the century.

Today at the University of San Francisco, the tradition of educating the children of first- and second-generation immigrants continues. A survey of freshmen at USF, conducted in the fall semester of 2004, found that more than 8 percent of all first-time freshmen were immigrants to the United States, and more than 43 percent of all first-time freshmen had one or more parents who were immigrants to this country. The current student body, however, is much more ethnically diverse than it was in the 19th century. For the entire USF undergraduate and graduate student population in the fall of 2004, 17.3 percent were Asian, 5.8 percent African-American, 11.5 percent Hispanic, and 7.7 percent international. USF is currently rated as one of the 20 most ethnically diverse universities in the nation. USF is also the most ethnically diverse institution among the 28 Jesuit colleges and universities in the United States. Stephen Privett, S.J, the university's current president, said in his inaugural address of November 18, 2000, "The diversity of our city and our university community closely mirror the rich complexity of our world. The University of San Francisco first served Irish and Italian immigrants who otherwise had no access to quality education. The original roster of student names has expanded over the years from Cleary, O'Brien, Pinasco, and Vanzinni, to include Nguyen, Aquino, Takashi, Gonzales, and Chang…. Providing a quality education to immigrants and the sons and daughters of immigrants will forever be a heart-felt concern of the Jesuit University of San Francisco."

Since the 1920s, Filipino students have been a part of the ethnic diversity of the institution. In 1929, an organization named the Filipino Ignatians was founded in the College of Arts and Sciences. The photo is of the officers of that organization, and appeared in the *Ignatian* in 1929.

UNIVERSITY OF SAN FRANCISCO ARCHIVES

The Charter 9

ALTHOUGH USF IS A JESUIT CATHOLIC UNIVERSITY, tracing its lineage to the founding of the Society of Jesus by Saint Ignatius of Loyola in 1540, its authority to grant college degrees comes from a decidedly secular source: the State of California. The founding president of St. Ignatius Academy, Anthony Maraschi, S.J., understood this when in 1859 he sought to incorporate the academy under California state law and to secure a charter to issue college degrees.

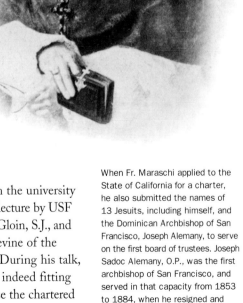

In applying to the governor of California, the superintendent of public instruction, and the board of education for a charter, Fr. Maraschi "humbly prayed the Honorable Lords of Education that the seminary of learning, now of four years existence, be incorporated as a college by the name and title of St. Ignatius College." Fr. Maraschi also sought approval for "a Board of Trustees for the purpose of managing the affairs" of the college. Fr. Maraschi proposed the names of 13 Jesuits, including himself, and the Dominican Archbishop of San Francisco, Joseph Alemany, to serve on the board of trustees. Fr. Maraschi and the archbishop apparently had some political clout, because in less than two months, the governor of California, John Weller; the superintendent of public instruction, Andrew Moulder; and the board of education granted Fr. Maraschi's petition, and St. Ignatius College was incorporated under California state law and granted its state charter. In the charter, the governor and the superintendent of public instruction noted that the college had "an endowment of twenty thousand dollars" and it "also appears that the proposed Trustees are capable men."

In 1959, USF commemorated the 100th anniversary of the issuing of its state charter. A number of special events were held, including an art exhibit in Gleeson Library, an exhibit of pictures and documents from the university archives, a centennial concert, a lecture by USF historian and archivist John McGloin, S.J., and an address by Judge Preston Devine of the San Francisco Superior Court. During his talk, Judge Devine opined that "it is indeed fitting that, on this night when we close the chartered century, the university stands on these noble heights, its lights beaming as symbols to him

When Fr. Maraschi applied to the State of California for a charter, he also submitted the names of 13 Jesuits, including himself, and the Dominican Archbishop of San Francisco, Joseph Alemany, to serve on the first board of trustees. Joseph Sadoc Alemany, O.P., was the first archbishop of San Francisco, and served in that capacity from 1853 to 1884, when he resigned and returned to his native Spain.

who looks from home to hill, its lights within illuminating the minds and hearts of young men and women, in faith kept with God, with its saintly fathers, and with the republic of which it merits well."

Today the original charter from the State of California gives USF all of its state approved "rights, privileges and immunities." The charter is carried in the inauguration of each new USF president as a symbol of his authority. During commencement ceremonies, USF's president refers to this charter when he says "by the virtue of the authority granted by the charter to the University of San Francisco from the State of California, and of the powers vested in me by the Board of Trustees, I hereby confer upon you the degrees certified by your Dean and Faculty." For 150 years, through 27 presidents, this educational mandate from the state has remained unbroken.

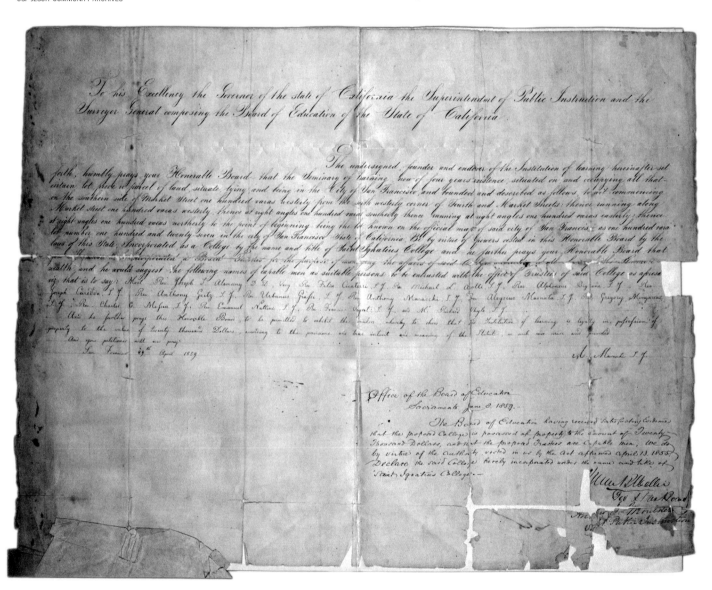

The First College Degrees

FEW MILESTONES IN AN INDIVIDUAL'S LIFE ARE MORE significant than the attainment of a college degree. This achievement can underpin a career, lead to advanced degrees and lifelong learning, and establish an ethical framework and social consciousness to guide one's life decisions. In June of 1863, St. Ignatius College, the antecedent of USF, conferred its first undergraduate college degree.

The recipient was Augustus J. Bowie, who later earned a doctorate in engineering from the Royal Mining Academy in Germany and pursued a successful career as an international mining consultant, superintendent, and author of books on hydraulic mining. In June of 1867, St. Ignatius College granted its first graduate degree to Alexander O'Neill, a physician practicing in San Francisco. Dr. O'Neill obtained his bachelor's degree from St. Ignatius College, received medical training in San Francisco, and returned to his alma mater to receive a master of arts degree.

In May of 2004, during USF's 145th commencement, 1,738 undergraduate, graduate, and professional degrees were conferred on USF students, including 188 JD and 18 master's degrees from the law school. Among the undergraduate degree recipients, 19 percent reported on the graduating student survey that they "plan to attend graduate school soon after graduation" and 56 percent reported that they "plan to attend graduate school sometime in the future." Augustus Bowie began a fine tradition.

From 1996 to 2004, the USF Pre-Professional Health Committee placed 67 USF graduates into medical schools, including such institutions as Yale, UCSF, Stanford, and Johns Hopkins. From 1996 to 2004, 59 percent of USF applicants gained admission to highly competitive medical schools, whereas only 43 percent of all applicants nationwide were admitted to medical schools during this same time period. USF's alumni directory currently lists 187 physicians who hold one or more degrees from USF. Although USF has never had a medical school, it's fair to say that from the time of Dr. O'Neill, USF has lived up to its mission of offering "undergraduate, graduate and professional students the knowledge and skills needed to succeed as persons and professionals, and the values and sensitivity to be men and women for others" (Vision, Mission, and Values Statement, approved September 11, 2001).

Augustus Bowie, first graduate of St. Ignatius College, 1863.

UNIVERSITY OF SAN FRANCISCO ARCHIVES

The First Faculty Members

FROM THE BEGINNING, JESUIT AND LAY FACULTY AND staff have worked together to build the University of San Francisco. In October 1855, the president of St. Ignatius Academy, Anthony Maraschi, S.J., hired the first full-time lay faculty member: John Haley, an instructor from Ireland. Haley joined Fr. Maraschi and Joseph Bixio, S.J., as one of the institution's first three faculty members. Fr. Bixio, another Italian Jesuit, was there on the first day of class in 1855, but left his teaching post at St. Ignatius Academy after a few months. Fr. Bixio served in various positions in California, Virginia, and Australia over the next three decades.

By 1856, an increase in enrollment from the original three students to 23 prompted the employment of a second lay instructor, Peter Malloy, who was also from Ireland. Soon after he was hired, Malloy joined the Jesuits. The 1861 St. Ignatius College Prospectus lists four Jesuit and three lay faculty members. The 1862 catalog lists eight Jesuit and four lay faculty members at St. Ignatius College. The courses taught by the first Jesuit and lay faculty members at USF were both classical

Joseph Bixio, S.J., was one of the first three instructors at St. Ignatius Academy when it opened its doors on October 15, 1855. The other two were Anthony Maraschi, S.J, the academy's president, and John Haley, a lay instructor from Ireland.

UNIVERSITY OF SAN FRANCISCO ARCHIVES

and contemporary. For example, the 1858 St. Ignatius College curriculum included English, Spanish, French, Italian, Latin, Greek, elocution, arithmetic, bookkeeping, mathematics, history, and geography. Tuition was $8 per month.

In October 2004, 344 full-time faculty members, 472 part-time faculty members, and 43 administrators were teaching in 80 separate degree programs at the bachelor's, master's, professional, and doctoral levels at the University of San Francisco. Of the full-time positions, 59 percent were occupied by men, and 41 percent were filled by women. Among USF's full-time faculty, 18 percent were African American, Hispanic, or Asian/Pacific Islander. Eleven of the university's full-time faculty members were Jesuits.

Faculty and other Officers

OF

SAINT IGNATIUS' COLLEGE.

———

REV. A. MARASCHI, S. J., President, Treasurer, Prefect of Studies, Professor of Ancient and Modern Languages, Mathematics and Book-keeping.

REV. A. AFFRANCHINO, S. J., Professor of Ancient and Modern Languages, Arithmetic and Vocal Music.

REV. F. RAFFO, S. J., Chaplain.

REV. U. GRASSI, S. J., Professor of English Literature, Elocution and Arithmetic.

MR. F. SEREGNI, Professor of Drawing and Penmanship.

MR. J. EGAN,
MR. W. H. DOYLE, } Assistant Professors.

The first prospectus of St. Ignatius College, published in 1861, listed the faculty and "other officers" of the school during the 1860-61 scholastic year.

The First College Prospectus and Catalog

A COLLEGE'S PROSPECTUS AND CATALOG COMMUNICATE to the wider world the key features of its institutional history, mission, admission and graduation requirements, policies, and curriculum. These publications may also list the faculty and key administrators and speak to what the institution values in its students. The first prospectus for St. Ignatius College, the antecedent of USF, was published in 1861, six years after its founding, and two years after it received a charter from the state to issue college degrees. The college prospectus was 16 pages long and 480 copies were distributed.

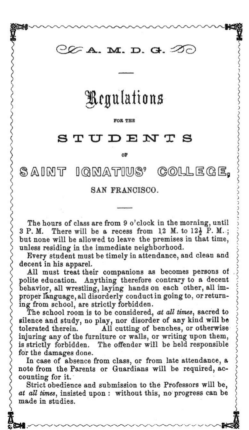

A page from the first prospectus of St. Ignatius College, 1861.

✠ A. M. D. G. ✠

Regulations

FOR THE

STUDENTS

OF

SAINT IGNATIUS' COLLEGE,

SAN FRANCISCO.

The hours of class are from 9 o'clock in the morning, until 3 P. M. There will be a recess from 12 M. to 12½ P. M.; but none will be allowed to leave the premises in that time, unless residing in the immediate neighborhood.

Every student must be timely in attendance, and clean and decent in his apparel.

All must treat their companions as becomes persons of polite education. Anything therefore contrary to a decent behavior, all wrestling, laying hands on each other, all improper language, all disorderly conduct in going to, or returning from school, are strictly forbidden.

The school room is to be considered, *at all times*, sacred to silence and study, no play, nor disorder of any kind will be tolerated therein. All cutting of benches, or otherwise injuring any of the furniture or walls, or writing upon them, is strictly forbidden. The offender will be held responsible for the damages done.

In case of absence from class, or from late attendance, a note from the Parents or Guardians will be required, accounting for it.

Strict obedience and submission to the Professors will be, *at all times*, insisted upon : without this, no progress can be made in studies.

The introductory page tells of the college's founding and incorporation, noting that this "Literary Institution" is "conducted by the Fathers of the Society of Jesus, and is intended for day scholars only." The prospectus describes the curriculum: Latin, Greek, English, French, Spanish, poetry, rhetoric, elocution, history, geography, arithmetic, bookkeeping, mathematics, moral and natural philosophy, and chemistry. The prospectus indicates that other languages, drawing, and vocal music will be taught if required, but for an extra charge. Regular tuition was listed as $8 per month plus a $10 graduation fee.

Several regulations for students were outlined in the first prospectus. It should be noted, however, that in its early years USF enrolled only male students from what would now be considered the upper grades of elementary school through college. The regulations stated, for example, that "every student must be timely in attendance, and clean and decent in apparel." Further, "all must treat their companions as becomes persons of polite education. Anything therefore contrary to a decent behavior, all wrestling, laying hands on each other, all improper language, all disorderly conduct in going to, or returning from school, are strictly forbidden." The "school room," the prospectus continues, "is to be considered, at all times, sacred to silence and study." Finally, "strict obedience and submission to the Professors will be, at all times, insisted upon: without this, no progress can be made in studies."

The first prospectus of St. Ignatius College listed seven faculty members and officers. They included Fr. Maraschi, the president, treasurer, prefect of studies, and professor of ancient and modern languages, mathematics, and bookkeeping; Fr. Raffo, the chaplain; two Jesuit professors; and three lay professors. The prospectus also listed the names of all 144 students enrolled in the college at that time and concluded with a program describing that year's commencement exercises, held on July 17, 1861.

The first college catalog, published for the 1861–1862 academic year, was 18 pages long and paralleled the first college prospectus. It further explicated the institution's educational mission: "The design of the Institution is to give a thorough Classical, Mathematical, and Philosophical Education" and "the most perfect training of the mind." Moreover, "the greatest attention is bestowed on the religious and moral training of the students."

Admission requirements were also outlined in USF's first college catalog: "When a student presents himself for admission," the catalog states, "he is examined by the Prefect of studies, and placed in that class for which his prior attainments may have fitted him. None will be admitted unless he bears a good moral character." The catalog restated the various regulations described in the prospectus and added several requirements regarding students' mandatory attendance at Mass. For example, it was required

that students "attend the holy sacrifice of the mass on Monday, Wednesday, and Saturday," and "that on Sundays and holy days of obligation they be present…to assist at the holy sacrifice of the mass, and the instruction that follows it."

Like the prospectus, the college catalog briefly outlined the classical and practical curriculum. It also listed the faculty, officers of the college, and all current students. Among those students was John Cunningham, the first native San Franciscan to enter the Jesuit Order in California. The catalog described the commencement exercises of June 1862. "On completion of their philosophical studies," the catalog proclaimed, "the degree of A.B. is conferred on all who, on examination, are found deserving of that distinction."

The 2003–2005 general catalog of the University of San Francisco has significant differences and similarities in comparison to the 1861–1862 catalog of St. Ignatius College. In 334 pages, the current catalog lists more than 340 full-time faculty members, describes six separate schools and colleges, outlines degrees offered in more than 75 distinct academic areas, and describes hundreds of courses. The admission requirements, university policies, and academic regulations bear little relationship to those outlined in the 1861–62 catalog. Both catalogs, however, portray the founding of the institution by the Jesuit Fathers in 1855 and make clear the Jesuit values of the school. Although the exact wording has changed with time, some of the same core concepts can be found in both catalogs. These concepts center on the promotion of academic excellence and the development of moral integrity in the students the school serves.

13
A New Home for the Church and College

AS AN INSTITUTION MATURES, IT NEEDS TO ADAPT, SECURE new resources, and plan for the future. By the end of 1861, St. Ignatius Church and College had outgrown the original small wooden buildings on Market Street that it had occupied since 1855. Fr. Maraschi, the founding president of the college, tried to link the three original buildings with an extended roof to provide additional space for a student population that had grown to more than 140. This temporary roofing arrangement proved, however, to be unsatisfactory. Therefore, the Jesuits launched a modest capital campaign that raised approximately $5,000, borrowed $55,000 more from Hibernia Bank (at 1 percent a month interest), and constructed a new three-story brick building on recently purchased property adjacent to the original site.

Nicolas Congiato, S.J., served as the second president of St. Ignatius College from 1862 to 1865, during which time the institution settled into its new home on Market Street.

UNIVERSITY OF SAN FRANCISCO ARCHIVES

Instrumental to the planning of this new home for the Jesuits was James Bouchard, S.J., who was sent from Saint Louis to San Francisco in 1861 to become the new assistant pastor for St. Ignatius Church. Fr. Bouchard, a Delaware Indian, was the first Native American to be ordained a Catholic priest in the United States. As the best public speaker among the San Francisco Jesuits, he announced plans for a new church and college on February 23, 1862, to a large assembly of community members. Speaking from the St. Ignatius Church pulpit, Fr. Bouchard said the Jesuits wanted to "erect a more commodious building and place of worship and also a college for the youth now growing up in our city." He talked of the current debt of the church and college, but stressed

the importance of the new enterprise. "We are but poor Jesuits," Fr. Bouchard proclaimed, "but with God's help, we anticipate no apprehension of failure. Our work here is to promote the honor and glory of God by affording means of worshipping Him in a suitable temple."

The cornerstone for the new St. Ignatius Church and College was laid on Sunday, May 11, 1862. The Archbishop of San Francisco, Joseph Alemany, was away from the city at the time, so he asked the Right Reverend Peter Losa, exiled Bishop of Sonora, Mexico, to represent him and preside over the ceremony. Approximately 3,000 people were present for the event and heard Bishop Losa "solemnly bless" the "foundations of the College of St. Ignatius in the City of San Francisco" and

"duly lay the cornerstone…to the greater glory of God." On Christmas Day, 1862, the new St. Ignatius Church and College opened its doors for worship. The next month, classes resumed. The church and college were soon known as the best in the city. Student enrollment, which had been 144 in 1861, surged to 457 by the end of 1862.

The new three-story brick structure that comprised St. Ignatius Church and College contained large classrooms, scientific labs, and a Jesuit residence. It also included a large assembly hall, which was designed to be a temporary church. The entire building cost approximately $120,000 and attracted the attention of the local press. The San Francisco *Monitor*, for example, noted in October 1862 that the building's height "from where the brick work commences to the top of the cross

in the center is 75 feet," and "the first floor, or basement, a portion of which is now used for public worship, is said to be the most spacious room in the city." The article also noted that the building had a capacity of 3,000 persons, and that the value of the building and the land "will fall very little short of $1,000,000."

With its new building, USF gained something of greater value than mere bricks and mortar. It gained a sense of permanency that it had not previously enjoyed. After seven years of effort to make the Jesuit experiment in San Francisco a success, the founders could proudly point to an institution that was gaining public support, increasing in student enrollment, starting to receive financial gifts, and creating an identity as the first and the best institution of higher education in the city.

St. Ignatius Church and College in San Francisco as it appeared in 1863. The building was located on the south side of an unpaved Market Street, between Fourth and Fifth streets.

UNIVERSITY OF SAN FRANCISCO ARCHIVES

31

Parish Status and St. Ignatius Church

IN 1863, A SIGNIFICANT EVENT OCCURRED IN THE HISTORY of St. Ignatius Church: Archbishop Joseph Alemany removed its parish status. When the church was first dedicated in 1855, parochial limits were not explicitly established. Rather, Archbishop Alemany granted "permission to have a church or congregation, the limits of which will afterwards be designated." By 1862, however, the sand dunes that had originally separated the St. Ignatius Church parish from its nearest northern Catholic parish neighbor, St. Patrick's Church, were gone, replaced by paved streets, street railway lines, homes, and businesses.

For a short time, the archbishop was content to limit the St. Ignatius Church parish to the area between Fourth and Seventh streets and between Market Street and the San Francisco Bay. Notwithstanding these geographic limits, St. Ignatius Church continued to draw parishioners from the other Catholic parishes in the area, due in part to the great oratorical abilities of the priest, James Bouchard, S.J., who gave sermons to increasingly large crowds attending Mass at St. Ignatius Church. Growth in the size of the parish membership was also due to the active efforts of the sodalities of St. Ignatius Church, lay societies set up for religious, outreach, and fundraising activities. The consequent decline in revenue and attendance at the other five Catholic parishes in San Francisco was a major issue for Archbishop Alemany, who saw the other parishes heavily encumbered with mounting debts and in dire need of their parishioners' support. On October 2, 1863, Archbishop Alemany, citing a long-standing disagreement between the Jesuits and himself regarding who should hold the deeds to the church property, removed parish status from St. Ignatius Church.

Archbishop Alemany claimed that according to Church Canon law, buttressed by a decree issued by the Council of Baltimore, the Jesuits had to turn over to him the title of their church property in order to retain parish status. The Jesuits of San Francisco, upon advice from the Jesuit General Peter Beckx in Rome, differed with the Archbishop's position. Felix Sopranis, S.J., was sent from Rome to handle this delicate issue as the personal representative of the Father General. The Jesuits' position was that the Holy See had granted to certain religious orders the right to retain title to their own property and simultaneously retain parish status. Archbishop Alemany saw the issue differently, and after several written exchanges with Fr. Sopranis, issued a decree that essentially ordered the Jesuits to relinquish the parish status of St. Ignatius Church or give up title to their property. The

Jesuits chose to retain title to their property.

On behalf of the leadership of St. Ignatius Church, Fr. Sopranis acknowledged Archbishop Alemany's decree in a formal letter sent to him on October 4, 1863: "Your Grace's communication to Father Maraschi, and the declaration therein contained that St. Ignatius is no longer a parish church, have been received by our Fathers here with that humble submission and reverence which are due to ecclesiastical authority; and, in accordance with this, at every mass today, we have announced to the people that from this day we have no more power of administering baptism, of performing the ceremony of marriage, or of giving the Viaticum and Extreme Unction, as our St. Ignatius is no longer a parish church; notifying them, at the same time, of the extension of limits made by Your Grace to the parishes of St. Patrick, St. Joseph and the Cathedral. All this is right, and neither myself nor any one of the other Fathers has any objection to make as to Your Grace's action."

Despite the loss of its parish status, the consequent loss of revenue from direct parish memberships, and the injunction against performing sacraments such as marriage and baptism, St. Ignatius Church continued to attract large numbers of attendees to its services and to perform various outreach activities to the citizens of San Francisco throughout the 19th century.

In 1993, Archbishop John Quinn approved a recommendation by the Archdiocesan Pastoral Planning Commission that St. Ignatius Church again become a parish church, effective July 1, 1994. With respect to this decision, Charles Gagan, S.J., church prefect, and soon to become church pastor, stated, "As a parish, St. Ignatius Church will be able to participate more fully in the lives of Catholics and the ecclesial life of the archdiocese of San Francisco…. The role

of the parish church is to minister to Catholics through the sacraments; that is the life of the individual Catholic and the life of the Church." The restoration of parish status also meant that St. Ignatius Church and the University of San Francisco were interwoven on another level as USF students, staff, faculty, and alumni could now use St. Ignatius Church for marriage and the baptism of their children, and could more fully connect the church to their lives. The chancellor of USF, John Lo Schiavo, S.J., who had also served on the Archdiocesan

The interior of St. Ignatius Church, as it appeared in 1869.

Pastoral Planning Commission, commented in January 1994: "I have always wished for St. Ignatius Church to become a parish…. Our students come from all over the country and abroad, and the only church they know in San Francisco is St. Ignatius. This is where they go for Mass and this is where they graduate. As a parish, St. Ignatius will bring our alumni that much closer to the university."

Today St. Ignatius Church is a thriving and active parish that serves almost 1,800 families and that affords the university community an opportunity to be fully integrated into the life and faith of the Catholic Church.

15 James Bouchard, S.J.

FATHER JAMES BOUCHARD OF THE SOCIETY OF JESUS HAD a major impact on the development of St. Ignatius Church and College, on the visibility of the Jesuit Order in California, and on the growth of Catholicism in the West during the second half of the 19th century. He also had the distinction of being the first Native American ordained to the Roman Catholic priesthood in the United States.

James Bouchard was born in 1823 in a Delaware Indian village. He was named Watomika — the "Swift-Footed One" — by his Delaware elders. His maternal grandparents, French settlers in the Spanish territory of what is now Texas, were killed by Comanche Indians during warfare with Spanish soldiers. The Comanches took the slain couple's 7-year-old daughter into their tribe, and she was subsequently given to a group of Delaware Indians who had migrated to present-day Kansas. When she was 15, the girl married the young chief of the Delaware tribe, and they had their first son, whom they named Watomika. When the boy was 9, he accompanied his father into warfare with the Sioux Indians, and he saw his father die in battle. The next year, Watomika's Delaware tribe was visited by a Protestant missionary who convinced the 10-year-old boy to journey with him to Marietta College in Ohio for "instruction in the human sciences and Christianity." Watomika never returned to his tribe, and assumed the surname, Bouchard, of his French grandparents.

In 1834, James Bouchard began his formal education in the preparatory division of Marietta College, a nondenominational Christian school for the training of teachers and ministers. He initially studied to become a Presbyterian minister. In 1847, while on a trip to Saint Louis, he strolled into the Jesuit church of St. Francis Xavier, was deeply impressed by the Mass he observed, and began a series of conversations with the assistant pastor of the church, Arnold Damen, S.J. After several weeks of discussion and reflection, James Bouchard converted to Catholicism. In 1847, at age 24, he began training to become a Jesuit priest and was ordained in 1855.

From the beginning of his priesthood, it was clear that Fr. Bouchard was a gifted public speaker. The Jesuits felt that this skill was especially needed in San Francisco, and in 1861, Fr. Bouchard was sent to the city to become the new assistant pastor for St. Ignatius Church. Because of his oratorical skill, he was often the spokesperson for the Jesuit community on major public occasions. His fame as a public speaker quickly spread throughout San Francisco, and his sermons soon were attended by overflow audiences, Catholic and non-Catholic. Indeed, one of the major reasons for building a much larger St. Ignatius Church adjacent to the original wooden structure was to accommodate the crowds that Fr. Bouchard was attracting. Likewise, Fr. Bouchard's oratorical skills had a significant impact on the growth of student enrollment at St. Ignatius College. Florentine Boudreaux, S.J., a contemporary of Fr. Bouchard, wrote about his colleague's impact, concluding that because of Fr. Bouchard's growing fame, "the number of scholars increased so rapidly that the little college became too small."

From 1861 to 1889, Fr. Bouchard gave sermons, dedicated churches, heard confessions, organized support groups of Catholic laypersons (sodalities), and gave public lectures on Catholicism in San Francisco and throughout the West. Using St. Ignatius Church and College as his home base, Fr. Bouchard traveled throughout California, Nevada, Utah, Oregon, Washington, Hawaii, and Vancouver Island, British Columbia. He spoke in cities, towns, and mining camps, in cathedrals, churches, and rustic halls. A reporter for the San Francisco *Monitor* wrote about one of Fr. Bouchard's trips to Los Angeles: "Our City of the Angels will for a long time remember Fr. Bouchard's mission…. He was already well-known to the Catholics of the city, since he had given two missions before…. There is no need of saying that this third one was a success, for it was attended not only by the Catholics of the parish but by many of the Cathedral also."

Likewise, the *San Mateo Times* described one of Fr. Bouchard's trips down the peninsula: "It is needless to add that everyone was pleased with the eloquent and masterly discourse of the learned divine. Those who differed with him in religious belief could not help but admire his freedom from bigotry and prejudice, and the ability with which he handled the various topics on which he spoke. The Reverend gentleman created quite a sensation among the non-Catholics of San Mateo." Nicholas Congiato, S.J., president of St. Ignatius College from 1862 to 1865 and from 1866 to 1869, said Fr. Bouchard deserved the title "Apostle of California."

In January 1880, Fr. Bouchard had the distinction of preaching the last sermon in St. Ignatius Church on Market Street before its move to the new location on Van Ness Avenue. Fr. Bouchard celebrated his last Mass on December 8, 1889, and died on December 27 of that year. Thousands of people attended his funeral Mass at St. Ignatius Church, and several hundred people

accompanied a special funeral train that carried his remains to the Jesuit cemetery in Santa Clara. Patrick Riordan, the second Archbishop of San Francisco, said on the occasion of Fr. Bouchard's death: "To no man in all the West is the Church of God more beholden than to Father James Bouchard of the Society of Jesus. He kept the faith in the mining districts; he sustained the dignity of God's Holy Church in the midst of ignorance and misunderstanding, and everywhere championed her rights. My debt to him, and I speak for my brother Bishops, is incalculable."

James Bouchard, S.J., a gifted public speaker, helped fill the new St. Ignatius Church in San Francisco with large audiences. He also traveled throughout the West giving sermons and public lectures, organizing support groups of Catholic laypersons (sodalities), and recruiting students for St. Ignatius College. His father was a Delaware Indian, and Fr. Bouchard became the first Native American to be ordained a Catholic priest in the United States.

UNIVERSITY OF SAN FRANCISCO ARCHIVES

The Origins of Excellence

THE STUDENTS, FACULTY, AND ADMINISTRATORS OF St. Ignatius College significantly enhanced the reputation of the institution during the time it occupied its second home on Market Street, from 1863 to 1880. The school conferred its first college degree in 1863, the Society of Jesus formally recognized the institution as "a complete college" in 1864, and in that same year, the fledgling college library added to its collection the complete works of the Church fathers, including Saints Augustine, Ambrose, and Jerome.

The first museum of natural history at St. Ignatius College, a collection of minerals and Native American artifacts, given to the school by Joseph Donohoe in 1875.

UNIVERSITY OF SAN FRANCISCO ARCHIVES

36

Two significant areas of accomplishment among the students of this era were forensics (speech and debate) and the dramatic arts. One of the first student organizations was the debating club, initially named the Philodianosian Society and later called the Philhistorian Debating Society. This society was organized in 1863, and its goals included "the improvement of its members in debate, social advancement and general literature." It also sought "to promote in its members the knowledge of history and literature, and to accustom them to speak with ease and fluency." The society held bi-monthly debates on historical and literary topics that the college community and the local press noted for their outstanding quality. Drama also became a major area of accomplishment for students at the school. In June 1863, students put on *Joseph and His Brethren* for the community, the first play performed at the institution. This play marked the beginning of the longest-running drama department, and the oldest continuously performing theater group, the College Players, west of the Mississippi River.

During the 1860s and 1870s, St. Ignatius College also developed an outstanding academic reputation because of the famous scholars it attracted. Joseph Bayma, S.J., a mathematician and scientist of international stature, taught at the college and served as its president from 1869 to 1873. His book *Elements of Molecular Mechanics* was the definitive text of its era on the subject. He also published a three-volume work on rational philosophy and a series of textbooks on college mathematics. Joseph Neri, S.J., and Aloysius Varsi, S.J., also joined the faculty during these years, bringing with them their international reputations in the fields of electricity, physics, and mathematics. Fr. Varsi, for example, was considered one of the top mathematicians of the day. He was also instrumental in raising money for the college and in spearheading social service efforts in the community. Fr. Varsi later served as president of Santa Clara College. Fr. Neri published in scholarly journals, taught chemistry and physics, and gave public lectures on topics such as the electric light, which he first demonstrated to a large audience of San Franciscans in 1874. In 1883, one of Fr. Neri's students, John Montgomery, designed, built, and flew the world's first successful glider.

During the 1870s, the school developed highly acclaimed scientific laboratories, called cabinets in that era, complete with the latest equipment. According to the press, they included scientific "apparatus second to none in the United States." St. Ignatius College also had a priceless ornithological collection and "magnificent" photographic equipment. In 1875, the college received a gift that became the institution's first museum of natural history. The San Francisco *Monitor* recorded the gift: "Our distinguished citizen, Joseph Donohoe, Esq., lately secured [a] collection of minerals and other substances, together with no small collection of objects sculptured by the art of various Indian tribes…and with rare generosity has donated it to St. Ignatius College on Market Street."

Joseph Bayma, S.J., world-renowned mathematician and scientist, taught at St. Ignatius College during the 1860s and 1870s, published some of the most important science and mathematics books of the era, and served as the institution's fifth president, from 1869 to 1873.

Given the academic accomplishments of the faculty and students, and the quality of the college's laboratories and equipment, it is not surprising that the U.S. Bureau of Education rated St. Ignatius College in the top 120 of 500 colleges surveyed in the teaching of chemistry and physics during the decade from 1870 to 1880. This academic legacy is alive and well today at the University of San Francisco and is captured in one of the core values of its Vision, Mission, and Values Statement: a commitment to "excellence as the standard for teaching, scholarship, creative expression and service to the University community."

The Scientists

IN THE 1870S, ST. IGNATIUS COLLEGE, THE ANTECEDENT of USF, had one of the best science programs in the country. In 1876, the Mechanics Institute of San Francisco, the leading professional science association of the era in San Francisco, reported, "We may well congratulate ourselves for possessing within our midst in this young city and state, such facilities for scientific education as St. Ignatius College affords to our rising generation, and such a cabinet of philosophical apparatus, second to none in the United States."

Joseph Neri, S.J., became chairman of the natural sciences department at St. Ignatius College in 1870. Over the next decade, he taught physics and chemistry, published scholarly papers, gave numerous public science lectures, and was the first person to demonstrate electric light to the citizens of San Francisco.

Among the college's stellar faculty members was Joseph Neri, S.J., professor of natural philosophy. In addition to teaching chemistry and physics at the college and publishing in scholarly journals, Fr. Neri frequently gave public lectures to the citizens of San Francisco on science topics. In 1874, Fr. Neri demonstrated the first electric light in San Francisco, using a "mammoth magneto-electric machine" from Paris. The electric light he generated could be seen from 200 miles away. By 1876, this Jesuit scientist had installed three powerful search-lights at St. Ignatius Church and College for night illumination of all of Market Street. It is not an exaggeration to say that Fr. Neri

literally turned on the first electric lights in San Francisco.

In more recent years, science professors at USF have continued Fr. Neri's tradition of cutting-edge science. For example, Arthur Furst, distinguished university professor emeritus of chemistry, is one of the world's leading researchers in cancer and toxicology. He taught at USF in 1944 and again from 1947 to 1981, and though now "retired," he is still active in research and publishing. Fifty years ago, Furst became one of the first scientists in the world to develop an effective chemotherapy drug that could be given orally to fight cancer. He also conducted pioneering studies on the role of metals in causing and treating cancer. His discoveries firmly established him as the world's foremost authority on toxicology. Furst published scores of scientific papers, brought millions of federal dollars to USF, and received numerous awards for his work. He organized USF's Institute of Chemical Biology in 1961 and involved USF students and colleagues in all aspects of his research. Many of his scientific papers have

been, and continue to be, co-authored with students.

Another contemporary USF science professor who has conducted pioneering research in his field is USF physics professor Eugene Benton. Benton is internationally known and highly respected for his innovative experiments on the detection of radiation in outer space and from earth-bound particle accelerators. Since the beginning of the Apollo space program, Benton's experimental devices have been on every manned NASA mission, and on unmanned satellites as well. In 1998, he provided NASA with detectors to monitor radiation exposure of the crew (including Sen. John Glenn) on the flight of the space shuttle Discovery. He also led joint U.S.-Russian experiments on the effects of long-term space radiation on humans aboard the Russian Space Station Mir. Benton has obtained several large NASA grants to support his research, received numerous awards for his work, published a host of scholarly papers, and been invited to lecture at professional conferences throughout the world. Like Furst, Benton has involved USF students, as well as other faculty and staff, in all aspects of his experiments and research.

A magneto-electric machine from Paris, given to St. Ignatius College by Tiburcio Parrott, and used by Joseph Neri, S.J., professor of natural philosophy at the college, to demonstrate the first electric lights in San Francisco in 1874. On July 4, 1876, to commemorate the centennial of the nation's independence, Fr. Neri attached the device to three searchlights mounted on top of St. Ignatius Church and illuminated all of Market Street.

UNIVERSITY OF SAN FRANCISCO ARCHIVES

18 The Jesuits and Social Outreach

THROUGHOUT HIS LIFE, SAINT IGNATIUS OF LOYOLA, founder of the Society of Jesus in 1540, made it clear to his fellow Jesuits that in addition to spiritual and educational activities, they should also engage in social outreach to the less fortunate members of society. Saint Ignatius himself established a house in Rome to care for the city's prostitutes. In the 16th century, the early Jesuit ministries also included caring for the sick, serving food, soliciting alms, celebrating Mass, praying, hearing confessions, and administering the last sacraments to individuals in the prisons and hospitals of Italy and other areas of Europe. Throughout the 19th century, the Jesuits of San Francisco followed these precepts of Saint Ignatius, and they also included lay men and women, organized into sodalities, in their social outreach work. In addition to founding and sustaining St. Ignatius Church and College, the Jesuits established a wellspring of social services to the community that continues to this day.

As early as 1862, Paul Raffo, S.J., of St. Ignatius Church and College, began visiting the sick in San Francisco's hospitals. Joseph Riordan, S.J., historian of the first 50 years of the institution, wrote: "From the earliest days of St. Ignatius, attendance on the city's sick had occupied a great part of the time of one and sometimes several Fathers. But there was good work to be done which could not well be attended by others, and the burden was gladly shouldered, for the spiritual fruit was abundant." The work by the Jesuits in local hospitals continued into the 20th century. For example, Aloysius Stern, S.J., served as chaplain at San Francisco City and County Hospital from 1925 to 1947. Gerald Rader, S.J., succeeded him at that position and spent 15 years in the same ministry.

The Jesuits of San Francisco have a long history of caring for the spiritual needs of the temporary and permanent soldiers stationed at the Presidio. From 1883 to 1907, a Jesuit said Mass each Sunday at the Presidio. For 17 of these years, Ignatius Prelato, S.J., of St. Ignatius College, served as chaplain to the soldiers of the Presidio and to their dependents. In 1888, Jesuits assumed a similar ministry for the soldiers stationed on Angel Island.

During the last eight years of the Army Presidio in San Francisco, Jesuits from USF served as chaplains at the Presidio chapel. They included Daniel O'Sullivan, S.J., who had retired from the USF philosophy department; Thomas McCormick, S.J., former rector of the USF Jesuit community; and Fr. Alberto Huerta, George Kennard, S.J., and Michael Kotlanger, S.J., all from USF.

The social service and outreach activities during the first 50 years of USF's history have their counterparts today. St. Ignatius Church currently offers a wide range of social outreach and justice programs. For example, St. Ignatius Church tithes 8 percent of its parish income to outside organizations that support the poor though its financial outreach fund. Parishioners repair, renovate, and landscape neighborhood schools and centers; construct homes for low-income families; make one-on-one visits to local nursing homes; respond to requests for assistance, clothing, and toiletries; and bring nonperishable food items to Mass to support local food pantries and prepare and serve meals at the San Francisco Interfaith Council Winter Shelter, the Hamilton Family Center, and the St. Anthony's Foundation Dining Room.

The social outreach and service legacy of the 19th-century Jesuits is also seen today on the University of San Francisco campus. University Ministry is involved in a number of social service programs. These include the Arrupe Immersion Experience, in which students build homes, deliver meals to the sick, and seek to learn by living in impoverished areas of San Francisco, Guatemala, or Tijuana, Mexico. In addition, USF students tutor at St. Charles Elementary School in the Mission District; serve meals at St. Anthony's Foundation Dining Room; and collect food, clothing, toiletries, and other items for low-income families at Mercy Housing, for homeless

St. Ignatius Church and College as it appeared in the late 1860s. Then, as now, the institution is a center for social outreach to the community.

and runaway youth at the Larkin Street Youth Center, and for AIDS/HIV victims through Project Open Hand.

USF's Office for Service Learning, in the Leo T. McCarthy Center for Public Service and the Common Good, also carries on the Jesuit tradition of reaching out to the less fortunate. The office helps coordinate and support the various efforts of USF students, faculty, staff, and alumni in identifying and serving the needs of the surrounding community. The office maintains a database of service opportunities for the USF community and also works with faculty to connect service-learning programs to the academic curriculum. Thus, service learning becomes a vehicle for interrelating community service, academic study, and structured reflection. Service learning is, therefore, not just about helping the community; it also seeks to educate students about social issues, to foster critical thinking about those issues, and to develop social responsibility. Reflective of this academic thrust, the USF Core Curriculum, implemented in 2002, requires students to complete a course that emphasizes service learning.

The 16th-century Jesuit legacy of service to others is manifest in various forms at today's University of San Francisco. It is captured in many of the university's programs and is increasingly finding expression in the curriculum. It is also referenced throughout the university's Vision, Mission, and Values Statement, which calls for "social responsibility in fulfilling the University's mission to create, communicate and apply knowledge to a world shared by all people and held in trust for future generations."

The Jesuit Missions at San Quentin and Alcatraz Federal Prisons

USF AND ITS ANTECEDENT INSTITUTION, ST. IGNATIUS College, have a long history of providing social services to the people of San Francisco: in hospitals, schools, homeless shelters, soup kitchens, and prisons. In 1867, for example, Michael Accolti, S.J., who established the Jesuit order in California and assisted Anthony Maraschi, S.J., the first president of St. Ignatius College, became the chaplain of San Quentin Prison. Fr. Accolti's responsibility in caring for prisoners at San Quentin was continued by other Jesuits from St. Ignatius College.

In 1876, Peter O'Flynn, S.J., accepted the chaplaincy for the English-speaking prisoners of San Quentin, while John Piccardo, S.J., also from St. Ignatius College, attended to non-English speaking prisoners. For several years, these two Jesuits paid regular visits to the inmates of San Quentin. These founders of St. Ignatius College thus started a tradition that persists in the mission of their successors in more recent years.

In 1935, Archbishop John Mitty of San Francisco requested that the Jesuit priests of St. Ignatius Church and the University of San Francisco begin to minister to the spiritual needs of the prisoners of the newly opened Alcatraz Federal Prison in San Francisco Bay. Joseph Clark, S.J., professor of physics and geology at USF; James Lyons, S.J., former dean of faculties at USF; and Richard Scannell, S.J., assistant professor of religion, were among the first chaplains at Alcatraz. Other Jesuits from USF, St. Ignatius High School, and St. Ignatius Church continued this chaplaincy until the prison closed in 1963.

Other Jesuits have continued the work of their predecessors at San Quentin prison. Bill Richardson, S.J., conducted Bible classes at San Quentin in the middle 1980s, after his retirement from the USF theology department. Since November 1997, Peter Togni, S.J., associate dean in the College of Arts and Sciences, has made weekly visits to the Catholic Chapel at San Quentin, where he meets with inmates, attends services, and helps young Jesuits and USF students conduct Bible study sessions

During the 1930s, Joseph Clark, S.J., science professor at USF, was among the first Catholic chaplains at Alcatraz Federal Prison in the San Francisco Bay. He built a chapel for the inmates and referred to himself as "Convict" Clark. In 1948, this photo was taken at Alcatraz of Clark and associate warden Paul Madigan.

CALIFORNIA PROVINCE OF THE SOCIETY OF JESUS ARCHIVES

43

Michael Accolti, S.J., who established the Jesuit order in California, was the first in a long line of Jesuits to serve as the Catholic Chaplain of San Quentin Federal Prison. This photo of San Quentin dates from about 1930.

with the inmates. Currently, the Catholic Chaplain at San Quentin is Stephen Barber, S.J., from the Jesuit Community at USF. Fr. Barber oversees the daily workings of Our Lady of the Rosary Chapel at the prison and offers Mass, Devotions, and Rosaries to the inmates. He also provides classes in basic teachings of the Church and pastoral leadership, leads scripture study groups, offers individual and group prayer, and organizes a monthly film club. According to Fr. Barber, "cell ministry" is "first of all trying to humanize what for many can be a very dehumanizing situation. The contact of a human being from the outside to a man who is incarcerated is a link with a human reality outside those walls. At its core, that's the most important thing."

At the end of the spring 2000 semester, USF students donated 1,500 used books to the San Quentin adult education program. In October 2000, Fr. Togni, USF President Stephen A. Privett, S.J., and Santa Clara University President Paul Locatelli, S.J., were part of a task force that went on a fact-finding mission to San Quentin to bring attention to the conditions faced by the prison population. These efforts on behalf of the prisoners of San Quentin reflect the Vision, Mission, and Values Statement of the University of San Francisco, which calls for a "culture of service that respects and promotes the dignity of every person."

The Earthquake of 1868

THREE MAJOR EARTHQUAKES, AND NUMEROUS MINOR ones, have struck San Francisco and the Bay Area since 1855, the year St. Ignatius Church and St. Ignatius Academy were founded. Perhaps more than any other events, the major earthquakes illustrate the historical intertwining between the university and the city.

On October 21, 1868, at 7:53 A.M., an earthquake occurred along the Hayward Fault for about 20 miles, from Warm Springs (now part of Fremont) to the vicinity of Mills College in Oakland. The Richter scale had not yet been developed, but scientists now estimate that the magnitude of the earthquake was 6.8 to 7.0 on that scale. Horizontal displacement was as much as three feet, and every building in the town of Hayward was either severely damaged or completely destroyed. Many buildings in Oakland and across the Bay in San Francisco were also destroyed or damaged. The earthquake killed five and injured approximately 50. Property damage, in 1868 dollars, totaled more than $400,000. The newspaper *Daily Alta California* reported on October 22, "that a dozen brick buildings on made ground" (the 19th-century term for landfill) "are shattered so that they are untenantable, that the cornices of two buildings have been thrown down, and many walls cracked, much plastering loosened and many window panes broken."

The 1868 earthquake caused some damage to St. Ignatius Church. The roof was partially destroyed by a falling chimney, and several plaster ornaments attached to the ceiling fell. There were no injuries, however, to any members of the church or school community. The journal of St. Ignatius College recorded the earthquake: "Today about 8 o'clock the whole city was shaken by a horrid earthquake lasting for the space of forty-two seconds. No one of

Damaged buildings in San Francisco following the earthquake of 1868.

UNIVERSITY OF SAN FRANCISCO ARCHIVES

ours suffered any harm. Two chimneys on the church fell, one upon the roof and the other into the Father's garden. In the church itself, not a little of the plaster of the ceiling fell within the railing of the sanctuary and on the pews, but without injury to any one. Other shocks, less violent, followed during the day." The historian of the first 50 years of St. Ignatius Church and College, Joseph Riordan, S.J., added that the earthquake "had at least the practical effect on laying stress upon the need that existed for an easier and freer exit from the church in case of danger."

The *Daily Alta California* also urged precautionary measures in the event of another earthquake: "The foundations of buildings should, on the made ground, be as solid as possible; and high chimneys should be secured by iron bars, fastened on with bands and running down below to the top of the wall. Brick buildings should be tied together by strong iron rods, their walls should be thick, the best mortar should be used and the height should not exceed three stories."

These and other warnings were largely ignored, however, and by 1906 the earthquake of 1868 had been forgotten by most people of San Francisco.

The 1868 earthquake caused the greatest damage to buildings on "made ground" (the 19th century term for landfill).

UNIVERSITY OF SAN FRANCISCO ARCHIVES

Christmas Gifts

DURING THE CHRISTMAS SEASON OF 1878, THE JESUITS of St. Ignatius Church and College, "in honor of the childhood of our Lord," gathered clothes and put on a Christmas-tree festival for 12 children living in poverty in San Francisco. Also during 1878, Aloysius Varsi, S.J., a mathematics professor at St. Ignatius College, became interested in the work of the Francesca Society of San Francisco. This society, named after Saint Frances of Rome, was "composed of a number of charitable ladies of the city who emulate in their love for Christ's needy ones, the charity of the Saint, their patroness."

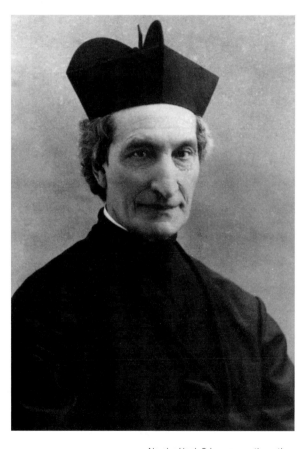

The Francesca society was sponsored by Bertha Welch, one of the wealthiest women in the city at the time. She became a major donor to St. Ignatius Church and College, and USF's Welch field is named in her honor. During the Christmas season of 1878, Fr. Varsi assisted the Francesca Society in securing a large gift of goods from a San Francisco business, Murphy, Grant & Co, to be given to the poor. Fr. Varsi also provided the society with rooms in St. Ignatius Church. In 1880, Fr. Varsi was asked to take over the direction of the Francesca Society. By 1904, St. Ignatius Church and College was annually distributing during the Christmas season clothes to approximately 300 needy children and groceries to some 150 families living in poverty.

Today St. Ignatius Church and the University of San Francisco have continued this tradition of Christmas giving to the poor. During Christmas 2003, for example, St. Ignatius Church provided 600 Christmas gifts to eight Bay Area shelters for women, families, children, and youth. In cooperation with the San Francisco Interfaith Council, St. Ignatius Church also provided approximately 1,000 hot meals to homeless adults and children as part of the Shelter Meal Project during the winter months. Other Christmas community outreach programs by St. Ignatius Church include the December Clothing Drive for the St. Vincent de Paul Society and the

Aloysius Varsi, S.J., was a mathematics professor at St. Ignatius College, prefect of St. Ignatius Church, and director of the Francesca Society, a late 19th century Catholic charity.

UNIVERSITY OF SAN FRANCISCO ARCHIVES

St. Ignatius Church and College in the early 1870s, an institution already well known for academic excellence and service to the community.

Baby Gifts for Jesus Program during which items for newborns are collected at the Christmas Eve Family Mass and donated to new mothers and their babies at Mount St. Joseph/St. Elizabeth Child and Family Services. USF's University Ministry also collected approximately 100 gifts of clothing and toys during Christmas 2003 to be given to various Bay Area shelters. In 2004, University Ministry collected holiday gifts for two local organizations. One was Mercy Housing, which provides support services for hundreds of Bay Area families living in low-cost housing. For this organization, University Ministry collects toys and clothing for children, grocery gift certificates, warm clothing for adults, and baskets of toiletries and personal items. The second organization assisted by University Ministry is the Larkin Street Youth Center, which provides housing, medical care, case management education, and employment services to homeless and runaway youth. For this agency, University Ministry collects clothes, toiletries, backpacks, journals, and art supplies.

These efforts on behalf of the poor during Christmas, and throughout the year, are at one with the 465-year-old Jesuit heritage, linking the institution to a history of outreach to the citizens of San Francisco.

Part II: The Golden Age

THE SECOND LOCATION IN SAN FRANCISCO FOR ST. Ignatius Church and College was on the corner of Van Ness Avenue and Hayes Street, the current site of the Louise M. Davies Symphony Hall. The building occupied a full city block and was dedicated on February 1, 1880. This was actually the third St. Ignatius Church and College in downtown San Francisco. The first small church and school on Market Street, built in 1855, soon proved too small, and in 1862, a three-story building was erected on the same location, adjacent to the original buildings, to accommodate an increase in enrollment in the school and burgeoning membership in the church. Later, further growth in enrollment and membership and rising property taxes on Market Street prompted the Jesuits to acquire the Van Ness site. The new church and college built by the Jesuits later came to be known as "Old St. Ignatius" by the alumni of the early 20th century, and the period from 1880 to 1906, was often referred to as the institution's Golden Age. In 1880, the college opened its doors to 650 students and great reviews in the local press, where it was lauded for its outstanding scientific laboratories, classrooms, and libraries. The attached church was magnificent and could accommodate as many as 4,000 people. In 1903, the college added a new gymnasium, described as the best in the city. The church and college, a block from City Hall, became a center for the educational and cultural life in the City by the Bay. The college's academic reputation spread throughout the state and nation; its drama programs and debating societies were known throughout the Bay Area; and many of its graduates became leaders in law, government, business, and religion. In October 1905, St. Ignatius College celebrated its Golden Jubilee, marking 50 years of educational excellence and service to the community.

The history of St. Ignatius Church and College on Van Ness Avenue came to an abrupt end on April 18, 1906. In the earthquake that struck early that morning and the days of fire that followed, the church and college, along with most of San Francisco, were reduced to almost complete ruin. Initially, the damage to both the college and church from the earthquake itself, though considerable, seemed reparable: walls cracked, plaster fell everywhere, the roof partially collapsed, and marble

St. Ignatius College moves to Van Ness Avenue

St. Ignatius College Alumni Association formed

1865   **1880**   **1881**

Civil War Ends/Reconstruction Begins

statues were thrown to the ground and broken. By far the worst came later that day, however, when fires broke out all over the city and were almost impossible to contain because the earthquake had broken the city's main water pipes and cut off the water supply. The Hayes Valley fire, which destroyed St. Ignatius Church and College, was also called the "Ham and Eggs Fire" because it was started by a woman preparing breakfast in her nearby home after the earthquake. When she lit a fire in a stove connected to an earthquake-damaged chimney, the fire escaped from the chimney and quickly spread to neighboring buildings and to the towers of St. Ignatius Church a block away. Without water, the Jesuit Community and the fire fighters had to watch helplessly as the institution was gutted by a raging inferno.

ST. IGNATIUS CHURCH & COLLEGE, OCT. 15, 1905,

TURRILL & MILLER, PHOTOGRAPHERS SAN FRANCISCO. CAL.

St. Ignatius Church and College on October 15, 1905, the day the institution celebrated the 50th anniversary of its founding in San Francisco.

UNIVERSITY OF SAN FRANCISCO ARCHIVES

Although it is estimated that the San Francisco earthquake and fire of 1906 took more than 4,000 lives (though the official count was 674), none of the 44 Jesuits at St. Ignatius Church and College, nor any of the school's students, were killed, though some were injured. The institution was, however, completely destroyed. What had taken a half-century to develop lay in ashes, and the future was uncertain.

The next series of vignettes will outline the development of St. Ignatius College from 1880 to 1906, portraying its efforts in conjunction with St. Ignatius Church to provide social services to the community, and will describe some of the impact the institution had on the political, educational, cultural, and religious life of San Francisco. This series will close with the earthquake and fire of 1906.

50th anniversary of St. Ignatius College

St. Ignatius Church and College destroyed by earthquake and fire; College relocates to "Shirt Factory" campus

1886	1898	1903	1905	1906

Statue of Liberty dedicated

Spanish-American War
U.S. annexes Hawaii

U.S. acquires Panama Canal Zone

The Institution Moves to Van Ness Avenue

DURING THE 1870S, ENROLLMENT INCREASES AT ST. Ignatius College and rising property taxes on the institution's first location on Market Street precipitated a search by the Jesuits for a new home for the church and college in San Francisco. They finally settled on a location comprising a full city block on the corner of Hayes Street and Van Ness Avenue, the current site of the Louise M. Davies Symphony Hall. The Jesuits sold the original piece of property on Market Street in 1886 for $900,000 (a tidy profit over its original purchase price of $11,500) to the Parrott family, who built the Emporium department store on the property. A plaque on the wall of the old Emporium building on the south side of Market Street between Fourth and Fifth Streets marked the first location of the institution.

In the late 19th century, the term "college" could apply to an institution that educated students from what is today considered the elementary grades, through middle school, high school, and the college levels. This photo of students who attended St. Ignatius College in 1890 reflects this fact.

CALIFORNIA PROVINCE OF THE SOCIETY OF JESUS ARCHIVES

The three-day dedication of the new St. Ignatius Church and College on Van Ness Avenue began on Sunday, February 1, 1880. Joseph Alemany, Archbishop of San Francisco, offered the Mass on that day, and Bishop James Healy of Portland, Maine, known as a great orator, traveled across the country to give the sermon. Bishop Healy's Jesuit brother was then serving as president of Georgetown College, and the bishop was well known in the Jesuit order. After Archbishop Alemany's dedication and Mass, Bishop Healy gave a sermon on the topic, "My House Shall be Called the House of Prayer for All Nations." A contemporary newspaper account described the Mass as a "gorgeous spectacle," the sermon as "outstandingly successful," and the day as "by far the most imposing ecclesiastical gathering ever seen on the coast." It was estimated that as many as 4,000 people were present within the new church for the ceremony, and that another 4,000 people stood outside. Approximately 15,000 people visited the church during this first day of dedication.

On Monday morning following the dedication of the new church, Bishop Healy blessed St. Ignatius College and led a procession of students, faculty, alumni, administrators, and community members from Van Ness Avenue through the new institution. Bishop Healy blessed all the classrooms, the college hall, the library, the laboratories, the museum, and even the corridors. The procession returned to Van Ness, and the students formed into lines, four deep, down Hayes Street, around the corner, and up Van Ness Avenue. The students then marched into the church for a Mass, part of which the students sang, and which was attended by almost as many people as had attended the Sunday Mass the previous day. Celebrating at the Mass was Bishop Healy, assisted by Aloysius Varsi, S.J., Superior of the Jesuits of California and former faculty member at St. Ignatius College. Following the Mass, and probably to their great delight, the students were then given the next day off as a holiday.

The dedication ceremonies for the new church and college continued on Tuesday and culminated in an official reception for the dignitaries who were in attendance. Gov. George Perkins of California was unable to attend but sent a congratulatory letter in which he proclaimed that "the edifice you have raised must rebound to the advantage of Christianity, and future years will consecrate the devotion you have so unfalteringly bestowed on this great work dedicated to science, learning and morality."

Bishop Healy gave the major address on Tuesday evening, the last night of the dedication ceremonies. In his speech, Bishop Healy said, "Yours is a great state and a great city. You have great mountains, great trees and, I might say, a great college…. I would like to impress upon the minds of the young gentlemen present that labor is necessary in every walk of life. What you acquire easily is of little value. Above all,

it is essential to possess an experimental knowledge of Christianity, not that which is culled from catechism but which is felt in the heart. This is the great jewel of education."

St. Ignatius College opened its doors at its new location to 650 students, accompanied by rave reviews in the local press, including the *San Francisco Post* and the *San Francisco Call*.

St. Ignatius Church and College, corner of Hayes Street and Van Ness Avenue, 1880–1906.

UNIVERSITY OF SAN FRANCISCO ARCHIVES

The institution was described as having "scientific laboratories and departments" as "thoroughly equipped as money can make them" and a library that contained "the cream of knowledge on all necessary subjects." The attached church was described as "most magnificent" and could hold, as the dedication ceremony demonstrated, as many as 4,000 people.

Thus began the second major phase in the institution's history, following the first phase of its development on Market Street from 1855 to 1880. Alumni in the early 20th century would fondly refer to this era, from 1880 to 1906, as the "Golden Age of Old St. Ignatius." Today at the University of San Francisco, community members still greatly benefit from the spiritual, ethical, and educational nuggets mined and polished by their predecessors of this era.

23 The Origins of the Alumni Society

IN 1881, THE YEAR after St. Ignatius Church and College moved to its new location on the corner of Van Ness Avenue and Hayes Street, the president of the institution, Robert Kenna, S.J., sent invitations to graduates of the college to come to a meeting to discuss the formation of an alumni association. The result was that in February 1881, the St. Ignatius College Alumni

Robert Kenna, S.J., President of St. Ignatius College from 1880 to 1883, was instrumental in the formation of the alumni society.

UNIVERSITY OF SAN FRANCISCO ARCHIVES

Association was born, becoming the first alumni association at a Catholic college on the West Coast. The first president of the alumni association was Jeremiah Sullivan '70, who later became an associate justice of the California Supreme Court. Other officers included Robert Tobin '72, vice president; Florence McAuliffe '75, secretary; and Alfred Kelly '75, treasurer. All of the officers were prominent in the San Francisco business, banking, and legal communities.

The precursor of modern-day alumni class reunions can be found as early as May 30, 1878, when the graduating classes of 1875, 1876, and 1877 held a banquet at the Maison Doree in San Francisco. Alfred Tobin '76, presided over the event. The dinner was well attended, the alumni were enthusiastic, and the events of college life were recounted in short speeches accompanied by much applause. When it was proposed that college friendships should be renewed by a yearly banquet, there was complete agreement. James Boland '75, was selected to preside at the reunion the following year. After that dinner, however, and following the formal establishment of the alumni association in 1881, the fledgling organization lay dormant for the next 20 years. In 1902, John Frieden, S.J., the college president, decided to revitalize the alumni association in preparation for a major celebration in 1905 commemorating the 50th anniversary of the founding of the institution. Jeremiah Sullivan was again elected president, and John Hicks '71, vice president. Plans were made for an alumni dinner the following year.

On October 8, 1903, a grand alumni reunion dinner was held in the Marble Room of the Palace Hotel. A local newspaper described the evening: "130 graduates of St. Ignatius College enjoyed a most delightful banquet under the auspices of their Alumni Association. The banquet hall was appropriately decorated for the occasion, and there was music by a stringed orchestra throughout the evening. Dr. A.H. Giannini was the toastmaster.... The formal programme opened with a toast to Pope Pius X, the company standing while the toast was drunk. In the same manner, there was a toast to the President of the United States. The Most Rev. Archbishop Montgomery, in an address on 'The Church,' was received with enthusiasm, and he held the attention of the banqueters closely as he spoke about the mission of the Roman Catholic Church." The reporter noted that following the archbishop's address, the president of St. Ignatius College, John Frieden, S.J., gave a speech titled "The Faculty of St. Ignatius College"; Peter F. Dunne, "one of the graduates back in the seventies," toasted "Our Country"; Joseph S. Tobin "talked pertinently" on California; and George A. Connolly spoke about St. Ignatius College. The final address of the evening was by Jeremiah Sullivan, on the topic "The Alumni Association."

The alumni association has been active in the development of USF since the great alumni reunion dinner of 1903. There are currently 81,000 alumni of the University of San Francisco living throughout the world. Over the years, the institution has graduated students who have gone on to become leaders in government, education, religion, social services, business, sports, journalism, and the legal and medical professions. Among the alumni, the school counts two San Francisco mayors, a United States senator, four California Supreme Court justices, a California lieutenant governor, two Pulitzer Prize winners, an Olympic medalist, several professional athletes, 273 Peace Corps volunteers, and the president of Peru. Many of USF's alumni have truly lived up to the Jesuit educational goal to form "men and women for others." These alumni have also planted the seeds for USF to fulfill its current Vision, Mission, and Values Statement, to be "internationally recognized as a premier Jesuit Catholic, urban university with a global perspective that educates leaders who will fashion a more humane and just world."

24 Jeremiah Sullivan

ONE OF THE MOST DISTINGUISHED MEMBERS OF THE San Francisco legal community to have graduated from St. Ignatius College in the 19th century was Jeremiah Sullivan, class of 1870. He was a prominent attorney, superior court judge, and associate justice of the California Supreme Court. Throughout his professional career, he remained active on behalf of his alma mater, and twice served as president of the St. Ignatius College Alumni Society.

Jeremiah Sullivan was born in Litchfield County, Connecticut, on August 19, 1851. When he was eight months old, his immigrant Irish Catholic parents moved the family to a log cabin near the banks of Brush Creek, Nevada County, California, about three miles from the county seat. Jeremiah's father took up placer mining. Among the miners working the claim adjoining his father's was Tom McFarland, a young lawyer who had briefly practiced law in Pennsylvania. After a short mining career, McFarland resumed his law practice, and in 1861 he was elected district judge of the Fourteenth Judicial District of California, which included Nevada County. McFarland was later elected to the

Jeremiah Sullivan, graduate of St. Ignatius College, founding president of the college's alumni association, superior court judge, and associate justice of the California Supreme Court.

CALIFORNIA PROVINCE OF THE SOCIETY OF JESUS ARCHIVES

California Supreme Court and was regarded as one of the ablest members of that court. As a boy, Sullivan was impressed by McFarland's legal career and the legal process. Years later, Sullivan wrote, "As the eldest child on family errands I frequently passed the imposing building in which the District Court was held, and among the day dreams that I cherished was one that some day by hard study I should become one of those lawyers who aided the judges in administering the law."

Ultimately, the Sullivan placer claim failed, and the family moved to San Francisco in 1861. James Bouchard, S.J., the missionary priest from St. Ignatius Church and College (see vignette #15), was instrumental in convincing the Sullivan family to move to San Francisco and to send the family sons to St. Ignatius College. One of the father's main goals had always been to obtain an excellent education for his children.

Jeremiah Sullivan received his bachelor of arts in 1870 and a master's in 1872, both from St. Ignatius College. He began practicing law in San Francisco in 1874, and he also served on the San Francisco Board of Education from 1877 to 1879. In 1880, he was elected superior court judge of San Francisco, a position he held for nine years. He often held court in the same courtroom where his boyhood role model, Tom McFarland, had presided. In 1917, Judge Sullivan began a six-year tenure as president of the Bar Association of San Francisco, serving longer than any president since 1880. From that position, he directed the transformation of the Bar Association of San Francisco from an elite club into an advocacy group. He convinced virtually all of the city's attorneys to join the association, championed legal reforms, and pushed for improvement of the legal profession. In the 1920s, following a legislative battle to create the California State Bar Association, Jeremiah Sullivan was elected its first president. In 1927, he was appointed associate justice of the California Supreme Court. Sullivan died on January 23, 1928.

Throughout his adult life, Jeremiah Sullivan was active in the development of St. Ignatius College. He was the first president of the St. Ignatius College Alumni Association when it was created in 1881, and he was re-elected to that position in 1902. Along with his younger brother, Matthew, Sullivan was instrumental in the founding of the St. Ignatius College School of Law in 1912, the antecedent of today's USF School of Law. Sullivan was also among the first group of professors at the law school. Matthew Sullivan (see vignette #53) was also a graduate of St. Ignatius College, became chief justice of the California Supreme Court, and was the first dean of the St. Ignatius College School of Law.

The Gilded Age and the Golden Age

IT WAS AMERICA'S GILDED AGE. THE DESCRIPTOR, TAKEN from the title of a novel by Mark Twain and Charles Warner, is often used by historians to characterize some aspects of American society during the last two decades of the 19th century and the first few years of the 20th century. Some features of the Gilded Age included opulence in architecture, art, and literature; worship of wealth for its own sake;

A classroom, vintage 1891, from the Golden Age of St. Ignatius College.

CALIFORNIA PROVINCE OF THE SOCIETY OF JESUS ARCHIVES

and marked contrast between the showy extravagance of the rich and the appalling poverty of the poor. In San Francisco, for example, the Big Four who founded the Central Pacific Railroad—Charles Crocker, Mark Hopkins, Collis P. Huntington, and Leland Stanford—amassed giant fortunes and built lavish homes on Nob Hill. Down the hill, however, others were not so fortunate and lived in abject poverty in areas such as the Barbary Coast.

Social and economic inequities did not exist everywhere during the Gilded Age. San Francisco, for example, had a growing middle class based on shipping, manufacturing, fishing, and agricultural production, drawing upon thousands of immigrants who poured into the city in the last two decades of the 19th century. New cable car lines stretched far from the center of the city, opening up areas for housing and business for these immigrants. Moreover, beautification was not overlooked during this era in San Francisco. Golden Gate Park, for instance, developed in the last decades of the 19th century to become one of the premier urban parks in the country.

The Gilded Age of America was the Golden Age of St. Ignatius Church and College in San Francisco. From 1880, when the church and school moved to Van Ness Avenue from its original location on Market Street, to 1906, the year of the San Francisco earthquake and fire, the institution flourished and became a significant educational, cultural, and political force in San Francisco.

Approximately 650 students were enrolled at St. Ignatius College during its first semester at its new home on the corner of Van Ness Avenue and Hayes Street. By 1885, the college catalog listed 840 students, and a faculty composed of 16 Jesuits and nine laymen. The school was still divided into three major divisions: preparatory (equivalent to today's sixth, seventh, and eighth grades), academic (high school), and the college. As the student body grew, efforts were made to cultivate the involvement of former students in their alma mater. In July 1880, the institution's eighth president, Robert Kenna, S.J., took office and promptly pushed for the development of an alumni association (vignette #23). Some of these

St. Ignatius College students had access to state-of-the-art scientific equipment during the institution's Golden Age, as shown in this chemistry lab in 1890.

UNIVERSITY OF SAN FRANCISCO ARCHIVES

alumni became leaders in the political, legal, and business communities of San Francisco during the last two decades of the 19th century and on into the early 20th century.

While wealth accumulated in many quarters of society during the Gilded Age, a newspaper writer for the *Journal of Commerce* praised the Jesuit faculty of St. Ignatius College as educators who served "not for money so much as for love of their work and the Glory of God. It is their vocation and they do not embrace it for the purpose of winning money or a name."

Evidence that the Jesuits sought to provide access to those without means is witnessed by the relatively low tuition charged students during the

By 1900, at the height of its Golden Age, the St. Ignatius College library had expanded to include more than 30,000 books and nearly 8,000 journals — making it one of the best college libraries in the western United States.

UNIVERSITY OF SAN FRANCISCO ARCHIVES

1880s and 1890s. Tuition in this period never exceeded $8 per month for students at the college level, and was even less in the lower grades. This tuition rate was the same as it had been in 1858. Indeed, for three years the Jesuits experimented with a no-tuition policy, made public in 1893: "We fear that many Catholics in this city and state are not aware that, following the rule of their founder where it is possible to do so, the Jesuit Fathers have made of St. Ignatius College a free college…to all young men of good character, the Society of Jesus will give an absolutely gratuitous education — not an ordinary education, but a superior education comprising classics, mathematics, science, philosophy and all cognate matters…. Any young man who may desire to acquire knowledge in its fullest sense has here an opportunity which few in this country possess. San Francisco is, we believe, the only city in the United States which is so blessed, and our young men ought to take advantage of this splendid opportunity offered them. In this respect, the rich have no advantage over the poor, since no other condition is required than a good character and a determination to study."

This no-tuition policy was impossible to maintain permanently, however, and by 1896, the official tuition went back to $8 per month. Even then, however, many students were permitted to attend classes at reduced tuition, or at no cost. The sentiment behind the brief no-tuition policy, and the low tuition that was charged for decades, speaks to a long-held Jesuit goal to provide, if at all possible, education to the least fortunate members of society.

Despite low tuition rates, the economic situation of St. Ignatius Church and College actually improved during its Golden Age. An accumulated institutional debt of more than $1 million was largely eliminated in 1886 by the sale of the institution's original property on Market Street for $900,000 (it was purchased in 1855 for $11,500). That transaction, plus the $200,000 sale in 1901 of more than 800 acres of land in the East Bay that was willed to Anthony Maraschi, S.J., the first president of St. Ignatius College, left the institution debt free at the turn of the century.

26

Educating the Mind During the Golden Age

ST. IGNATIUS COLLEGE OFFERED AN INCREASINGLY WIDE range of educational opportunities for its students and the surrounding community during its Golden Age, the years from 1880 to 1906. The college catalog of 1893–94 provides a good overview of the evolving curriculum of the school and its educational philosophy. The catalog states the institution's goal: "to impart such training as will not only render the student intimately conversant with the social and scientific questions that nowadays agitate the world, but also enable him to excel in any subsequent pursuit, whether professional or commercial."

A physics lab or "cabinet" at St. Ignatius College in 1889.

UNIVERSITY OF SAN FRANCISCO ARCHIVES

The best curriculum to achieve this goal, the catalog continues, is through classical courses, with heavy emphasis on "Latin, Greek, Religious Instruction, English Literature, Mathematics, History, and Elocution." By 1901, the college catalog also announced courses in business, including bookkeeping and stenography. The contemporary St. Ignatius College historian of the era, Joseph Riordan, S.J., wrote: "By the introduction of these classes it was intended to supply the elements of a business education without in any way detracting from the purely classical course which had long been obtained in the college."

Science continued to play a major role in the curriculum of the students who attended St. Ignatius College during its Golden Age. The institution had hardly opened the doors to its new home in 1880 when the press began to comment favorably on what it saw at St. Ignatius College. A writer for the local *Journal of Commerce* commented on the college's outstanding library, laboratories, and scientific programs in specific areas, such as ore assaying, a legacy of the Gold

In 1890, St. Ignatius College had one of the finest mineralogy laboratories in the western United States.

Rush era. The writer noted that this branch of science "is a great study in itself and, by practical example and by tests, it is made interesting and instructive." The article stated that overall, "as a preparatory school for the future chemist, physician, or mining expert, the facilities of St. Ignatius College are unsurpassed in the city." During the Golden Age, the press continuously referred to the science laboratories, or "cabinets" as they were then called, as the best in the western United States. In addition to teaching students about science, the Jesuit faculty of that era continued to bring the latest in scientific information to the citizens of San Francisco through a series of public lectures, experiments, and demonstrations, just as Joseph Neri, S.J., had done in the 1870s with his famous lectures on electricity (vignette #17). From 1880 to 1906, these well-received public lectures included "Wireless Telegraphy" by Nicholas Bell, S.J., "Explosives" by Henry Woods, S.J., and "Discharges in Vacua, Radiant Matter and Radium," by Frederick Ruppert, S.J. In particular,

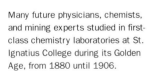

Many future physicians, chemists, and mining experts studied in first-class chemistry laboratories at St. Ignatius College during its Golden Age, from 1880 until 1906.

Fr. Ruppert was well known to the public for a series of public lectures, extending over several years, on various scientific topics.

During its Golden Age, the college's library collection continued to expand to meet students' increasingly diverse academic needs. By 1900, the college library, founded in 1857 with a handful of books, had grown to 30,686 volumes, many of which were rare and extremely valuable. The library also had a collection of 7,927 journals and pamphlets. These holdings were supplemented by another 3,000 books belonging to the church and contributed by the Ladies Sodality of St. Ignatius Church, a women's lay society for religious and fundraising activities.

In 1896, John P. Frieden, S.J., became the 12th president of St. Ignatius College. Fr. Frieden, a native of Luxembourg, held various administrative and teaching positions in the Missouri province of the Jesuit order before coming to San Francisco. He served as the institution's president for 12 years, longer than any of his predecessors. During his administration, several major academic changes took place at St. Ignatius College, including the formal establishment of a graduate school, although a handful of master of art degrees had already been awarded to St. Ignatius College students, beginning in 1867. More significantly, however, Fr. Frieden led the institution through one of its most challenging periods, beginning on April 18, 1906.

Athletics, Drama, and Music During the Golden Age

27

DURING THE GOLDEN AGE OF ST. IGNATIUS COLLEGE, FROM 1880 to 1906, athletics began to play a significant role in the life of the institution, especially with the building of a new gymnasium in 1903. During this era, the college's drama program continued to develop, and by the turn of the century, St. Ignatius College had also developed a music program that included a glee club, a choral group, and an orchestra.

Beginning in 1899, the Gentleman's Sodality, a laymen's society for religious and fundraising activities, began using several rooms in the St. Ignatius College basement as a gymnasium outfitted with exercise equipment. Toward the end of 1902, with the completion of two handball alleys, athletic programs among the students at St. Ignatius were also moving forward. In 1902, the college administration, led by President John Frieden, S.J., decided to build a modern gymnasium for the students.

When the Gentleman's Sodality heard of these plans, the society proposed that a cooperative enterprise be initiated to build the gymnasium, the expenses to be borne by both the Sodality and the college, through the Students' Athletic Association. The idea was favorably received, plans were drawn up, and fundraising efforts were undertaken. In 1903, these plans came to fruition with the building of a state-of-the-art gymnasium for the college, at a cost of $40,000.

The opening of the gymnasium was accompanied by rave reviews in the local press, which described it as "splendid" and the "best equipped in the city." The gymnasium included handball courts; a "bath section" containing showers, "needle" baths, lavatories, and tubs fed by hot and cold water, both salt and fresh; a billiard room; a reading room where "prominent American, Irish and English Catholic journals were kept on file"; two bowling alleys; a pool, or "plunger bath," measuring 50 by 15 feet and 5 to 9 feet in depth; a physician's office; instructors' offices; and a locker room. The gymnasium itself was 10,000 square feet and included a visitors' gallery 12 feet above the floor. There was also a running track, suspended from the roof girders by iron rods and reached by a spiral stairway. The entire gymnasium was "magnificently lighted by large skylights in the roof, and pivoted windows above and below the running track."

Drama also flourished at St. Ignatius College during its Golden Age, extending the successes from the earlier decades in the institution's history. Between 1900 and 1905, for example, the

Edward Allen, S.J., the 11th president of St. Ignatius College, from 1893 to 1896, formed the college's first orchestra in 1898, two years after he left the presidency.

UNIVERSITY OF SAN FRANCISCO ARCHIVES

The St. Ignatius College auditorium served as a theater for many of the highly acclaimed performances by the institution's students during the Golden Age.

elocution classes performed Shakespeare's *Macbeth, Julius Caesar, Richard III,* and *Henry V.* In 1902, students performed *Richelieu,* and in 1904, the theater department presented a sacred drama, *Seducias, the Last King of Juda.* The audiences were large for all of these plays, and included students, faculty, alumni, community members, and for some performances, members of the press, who often commented favorably on what they saw.

Music also had a place at St. Ignatius College during this era. The 1902 college catalog, for example, mentions a glee club, organized by Joseph De Rop, S.J. Fr. De Rop also established the St. Cecilia Choral Society. The St. Ignatius College orchestra was formed in 1898, under Edward Allen, S.J. (the college's president from 1893 to 1896). The orchestra gave annual concerts, which received "high praise" in the local press.

The legacy from USF's Golden Age finds current expression in many areas, including the Koret Health and Recreation Center, the College Players Theatre Group, the bachelor of arts program in performing arts and social justice, and the dance and music programs.

The Koret Health and Recreation Center, built in 1989, houses an Olympic-size indoor swimming pool; fitness machines; weight training, aerobic and martial arts rooms; racquetball and multipurpose courts for basketball, volleyball, and badminton; the Hagan Gymnasium; a deli; student and alumni lounges; and locker rooms. It currently offers a wide range of recreation programs for students, staff, alumni, and community members.

The College Players Theatre Group, now in its 142nd season, is the oldest continuously performing theatre group west of the Mississippi River, and the second oldest in the United States. Every season, the group, which encourages students to experience all aspects of theatrical production, mounts contemporary and classical drama.

USF also offers a bachelor of arts degree in performing arts and social justice. In this program, students receive intensive performing arts training in vocal production, dramatic presentations, dance and movement, and performance design. In addition, students explore various social justice issues through in-depth study, reflection, and experiences, which culminate in the "The Company," a yearlong project by the senior class directed by faculty. Students can also minor in the performing arts, the visual arts, dance, or music.

The dance program, for example, is growing, and students may enroll in ballet courses and in courses such as jazz, modern, ballroom, and flamenco dance. The music program at USF is also expanding: it includes a new orchestra, music appreciation courses; private instruction in voice or instruments; and various student singing groups, such as the USF Voices, which performs popular, choir, and jazz music. The Gospel Choir and University Choir perform classical works. There is a luncheon music program for students and staff, featuring on-campus and off-campus entertainers.

If the faculty and students of St. Ignatius College in 1905 were to return to USF today, they would be proud of the tradition they fostered, a tradition that is alive and well during their institution's sesquicentennial.

The St. Ignatius College Gymnasium, completed in 1903, included an elevated running track suspended from the roof girders by iron rods.

UNIVERSITY OF SAN FRANCISCO ARCHIVES

The Golden Age of St. Ignatius Church

"ST. IGNATIUS CHURCH IS TO BE DECORATED IN A manner and at an outlay that will make it the most notable building of its kind in San Francisco," proclaimed the *San Francisco Chronicle* on April 18, 1890. "The designs for the decorations," the article continued, "belong to the pure classic school of the Italian Renaissance, and the coloring of that age and thought." The period from 1880 to 1906 was the Golden Age of St. Ignatius Church in San Francisco, just as it was for St. Ignatius College.

An interior view of St. Ignatius Church in 1897, highlighting one of the finest church organs in the nation.

UNIVERSITY OF SAN FRANCISCO ARCHIVES

The church and school moved from the original location on Market Street, the institution's home since 1855, to its new home on the corner of Hayes Street and Van Ness Avenue in 1880. The dedication ceremonies for the new church began on February 1, 1880, and concluded on February 3. This was the third St. Ignatius Church in San Francisco and was by far the largest, with capacity for 4,000 people. For a quarter century, St. Ignatius Church on Van Ness was a focal point for the spiritual, artistic, musical, and cultural life of the San Francisco civic center and the surrounding community.

In 1890, Aloysius Varsi, S.J., prefect of the church and a skilled fundraiser, was able to complete a long-term project to decorate the interior of this third St. Ignatius Church with elaborate panels, medallions, rich molding, marble columns, and stained glass windows. Much of the decorative painting in the church was done by Domenico Tojetti, an Italian immigrant painter. The completion of most of the artistic projects was made possible by Bertha Welch, with a gift of $50,000, the first of several donations she made to the church and to the Jesuit Community. In 1895, Mrs. Welch gave another $50,000 toward the purchase of a new organ, described as one of the best in the United States. Indeed, one newspaper called it the "King of Instruments." The organ was delivered to San Francisco in 1896 in four extra-large railroad cars. It was formally initiated on Christmas Day, 1896, by Clarence Eddy, considered the foremost American organist of the era. The contemporary St. Ignatius Church historian, Joseph Riordan, S.J., wrote: "What a treat to lovers of music on that Christmas morning as this artist warmed into sympathy with his instrument and gave birth to harmonies that seemed to transcend the power of man!"

Dionysius Mahoney, S.J., was known as one of the outstanding orators in San Francisco during the Golden Age of St. Ignatius Church. In 1898, Fr. Mahoney also began a monthly publication, the *St. Ignatius Church Calendar*. In 1953, this publication became the *St. Ignatius Bulletin*. Today, this legacy continues in a weekly bulletin published by St. Ignatius Church.

Throughout the Golden Age of St. Ignatius Church, the spiritual works of the Jesuits in San Francisco played a major part in the lives of many Catholics in the city. In December 1904, for example, the Golden Jubilee of the Immaculate Conception of the Blessed Virgin was observed. Albert Biever, S.J., rector of the Jesuit College in New Orleans, came to San Francisco to preach during a weeklong retreat as a preface to the feast of the Immaculate Conception. A contemporary report estimated the number of participants at the retreat in the thousands, with some 3,400 people assembling to hear Fr. Biever's final sermon.

The influence and popularity of St. Ignatius Church during its Golden Age was frequently described by the Jesuits themselves. George de la Motte, S.J., who served throughout the Northwest during the era, wrote in 1905: "San Francisco is an almost Catholic City. Our holy religion is held in honor there and it is not long before one perceives this. We have there

a superb church. This morning at the 8 o'clock Mass there were 1,200 communions and they tell me that this is an ordinary number. I have been impressed by the ardent piety of the communicants."

Another Jesuit of the era, Dennis Kavanagh, S.J., commented on the quality of the services and the priests: "Perhaps the most striking feature of St. Ignatius Church was the solemn services for which it was noted. Who does not recall the male choir of 50 voices under the masterful direction of Father Allen and Father Coltelli? Who does not remember the solemn occasions like the feast of Corpus Christi when 1,600 sodalists, decorated with medal and badge, moved in solemn procession through the aisles? Who does not know how, on days like Good Friday, the church was filled to overflowing two hours before services began? We cannot explain this enthusiasm better than by attributing it to the well known and universally admitted fact that the Fathers connected with the church were remarkable for their eloquence and zeal and self-sacrificing devotion for the cause of religion.... There was a ring of exceptional earnestness in it all which attracted people from all parts of the city."

Today on the University of San Francisco campus, St. Ignatius Church continues to serve the spiritual needs of the school, the community, and the city. The Jesuits of St. Ignatius Church continue to live out the legacy of their predecessors stretching back to the church's Golden Age, to its formative years in mid-19th century San Francisco, and to the founding of the Society of Jesus in 1540.

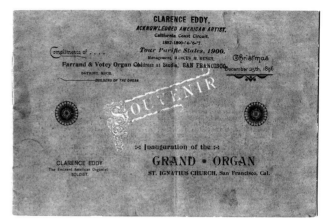

Souvenir ticket to a performance by Clarence Eddy, the foremost organist in the nation during the era, who played the new St. Ignatius Church organ for the first time on Christmas Day, 1896.

UNIVERSITY OF SAN FRANCISCO ARCHIVES

St. Ignatius Church in the Time of National Tragedies

THE HISTORY OF THE UNITED STATES AND THAT OF St. Ignatius Church intersect on a number of levels and at various times. One set of crossroads is marked by American tragedies during which students, staff, faculty, alumni, and the surrounding community come together to pray, to find meaning, and to console one another within the supportive world of St. Ignatius Church.

Four American presidents have been assassinated in the history of the United States. All four of these national tragedies occurred during the history of St. Ignatius Church in San Francisco, and all four events evoked a church response that brought the extended community together for prayer and mutual support.

On April 14, 1865, during the last days of the Civil War, the 16th president of the United States, Abraham Lincoln, was assassinated while attending a play at Ford's Theatre in Washington, D.C. The assassin, John Wilkes Booth, a Confederate sympathizer who initially planned to kidnap Lincoln, was himself killed by Union troops while fleeing into the Virginia countryside. Several days later, 7 million people lined the railroad tracks in the East to view the president's funeral train as it slowly moved from the nation's capitol to Lincoln's home in Springfield, Ill. Three thousand miles away in San Francisco, the Jesuits of St. Ignatius Church, at that time still located on Market Street, draped their church and residence in mourning black and helped organize and participate in a public funeral procession down Market Street that included St. Ignatius College faculty, students, and many citizens of San Francisco.

The 20th president of the United States, James A. Garfield, was shot by Charles Guiteau, a crazed and disappointed office seeker, on July 2, 1881. When the president died on September 19, St. Ignatius Church and College, located on the corner of Van Ness Avenue and Hayes Street, joined in the national mourning. On the day of the funeral for the deceased president, a solemn Mass was held in St. Ignatius Church, including a sermon by Robert Kenna, S.J., president of St. Ignatius College. After the Mass, students, faculty, and members of the Gentleman's Sodality, a laymen's society for religious and fundraising activities on behalf of the church, took part in a public procession down Grove Street.

William McKinley, the nation's 25th president, visited San Francisco in May 1901. On May 4, a grand procession down Market Street was held in his honor. The contemporary Jesuit historian, Joseph Riordan, S.J., wrote about the occasion, "Of all the decorations in the city, those of St. Ignatius College were probably the most tasteful and elaborate. The pupils were arranged on the steps and balconies of the building and gave three rousing cheers when the President passed. To mark his

appreciation, Mr. McKinley stopped his carriage and graciously returned the salute to the young men. He made no effort to conceal his pleasure and turned several times to look back." Four months later, on September 6, these same students returned to St. Ignatius Church to mourn the death of President McKinley, the victim of a bullet fired by Leon Czolgosz as the president opened the Pan-American Exposition in Buffalo, New York.

John F. Kennedy, the nation's 35th president, and the only Catholic to be elected to that office, was shot and killed while riding in an open car in Dallas, Texas, on November 22, 1963. The motives of the assassin, Lee Harvey Oswald, remain unclear, as he himself was murdered two days later by Jack Ruby, a Dallas nightclub operator. After Kennedy's death, his body was flown back to Washington D.C., where, under the gaze of television cameras, three days of national mourning were observed, concluding with his burial in Arlington National Cemetery.

On November 26, students, faculty, staff, alumni, and the extended community of the University of San Francisco came together for a memorial Mass for the slain president in St. Ignatius Church. Charles Dullea, S.J., president of the university, was the celebrant for the Mass, and William Richardson, S.J., professor of theology, delivered the eulogy. Fr. Dullea stated: "Above all this tragedy brings us to our knees in prayer—for our murdered chief, his courageous wife and innocent, bewildered children, his bereaved family, our new president, and our country.... Join with the faculty and students in the family prayer of the household of the faith, in union with Christ, our High Priest."

A tragedy of a different form befell the nation on September 11, 2001, when terrorists attacked the World Trade Center in New York City, the Pentagon in Washington, D.C., and a thwarted attack ended in a Pennsylvania field. As the nation mourned the loss of thousands of lives, the USF community once again came

St. Ignatius Church and College, decorated for the visit of President William McKinley to San Francisco in May 1901. Four months later, St. Ignatius College students mourned his assassination.

UNIVERSITY OF SAN FRANCISCO ARCHIVES

together in St. Ignatius Church to find meaning and comfort and to pray. In his homily, USF's president, Stephen A. Privett, S.J., captured the real and the symbolic meaning of St. Ignatius Church for the extended community in the story of a little girl who is lost in her city until a policeman takes her to her neighborhood church, from where she knows she can find her way home. Fr. Privett continued: "Today, we are lost, frightened and confused, so we come to church in the hope that we may find our way home from here. We leave here today knowing that we are all members of one human family and that guided by God's Spirit, we can care for one another and we can work together to make this world the place that God would have it be, and by so doing, we will find our way home."

For 150 years, five St. Ignatius churches in San Francisco have played a vital role in the lives of the citizens of the city and the students, faculty, staff, and alumni of USF. Over the years, tens of thousands of people have gathered in St. Ignatius Church to pray; to receive religious, spiritual, and family guidance; to hear sermons and homilies; to receive the sacraments; to provide service to the community; to find solace and meaning during times of personal crisis and national tragedy; and as the Jesuits counsel, to find God in all things.

The 50th Anniversary of St. Ignatius Church and College

30

WITH THE APPROACH OF THE 50TH ANNIVERSARY OF THE founding of St. Ignatius Church and Academy in San Francisco, the Jesuit leadership of the institution began to plan for a Golden Jubilee. John Frieden, S.J., president of St. Ignatius College, sought and received a special blessing from Pope Pius X on the work of the Jesuits in San Francisco during their first 50 years in the city. The Holy Father wrote: "To our beloved sons and to their works, for the long line of years to come—we

Visitors and guests joined the members of the Jesuit Community of St. Ignatius Church and College in 1905, during the 50th anniversary celebration of their institution.

UNIVERSITY OF SAN FRANCISCO ARCHIVES

bestow our apostolic benediction." The superior general of the Jesuits, Louis Martin, also sent his congratulations to the Jesuits of San Francisco: "Happy to me beyond measure have been the tidings of the coming of the 50th anniversary of the founding of St. Ignatius College, so dear to me, and of our church, begun under happy auspices by your worthy fellow citizens…. To all, therefore, I send my congratulations; to each, for the part so generously and strenuously played. For, from my heart I pray God, that long and dearly he may cherish church and college; and I beg and beseech you in the Lord, that you will not only live up to but surpass the hopes to which you have given birth."

The Jesuits of St. Ignatius Church and College decided to hold a week of Golden Jubilee events beginning on Sunday, October 15, 1905, 50 years to the day that St. Ignatius Academy welcomed its first three students. On Sunday morning of the Golden Jubilee week, San Francisco's Archbishop George Montgomery presided over a Mass of Thanksgiving in St. Ignatius Church. Present in the sanctuary for this Mass

The Golden Jubilee Mass of Thanksgiving held in St. Ignatius Church on October 15, 1905.

SOCIETY OF CALIFORNIA PIONEERS

was a representative from every Jesuit province and mission in the United States. The sermon, delivered by Reverend Patrick J. Cummins, chancellor of the Archdiocese of San Francisco, addressed the difficulties faced by the first Jesuits in San Francisco as they sought to establish a church and school in the turbulent years following the California Gold Rush. "This great church and the noble college adjoining are the outcomes of humble beginnings," proclaimed Fr. Cummins, yet the "Fathers of the Society of Jesus have been doing work worthy of the best days of their history."

Monday morning of the Golden Jubilee

week began with a Requiem Mass for deceased alumni and faculty of St. Ignatius College. Bishop Edward O'Dea of Seattle, a former student at the college, presided at the Mass. At noon, a banquet was held for the diocesan clergy and the Jesuit community. Tuesday was set aside as a day of honor for former students and included a series of special programs sponsored by the alumni association. On Wednesday, the alumni association hosted the Jesuit visitors on a cruise on San Francisco Bay, and on Thursday, the visitors were taken by train to the peak of Mount Tamalpais. The finale to the Golden Jubilee came on Thursday evening with a gala banquet at the St. Francis Hotel. At the head table was San Francisco Superior Court Judge Jeremiah Sullivan, the evening's toastmaster. Judge Sullivan was a graduate of St. Ignatius College and the first president of the St. Ignatius College Alumni Association. He was joined by Archbishop George Montgomery of San Francisco; John Frieden, S.J., president of St. Ignatius College; and Br. Vellesian Mallon, president of St. Mary's College. Judge Sullivan's opening remarks set the tone for the evening and captured a significant theme of the institution's first 50 years: "Any American citizen who overlooks the portals of the Golden Gate can find much to gratify him both as an American and a Catholic. As he looks out upon the sea, he reflects that, for over 800 miles, it washes the shore of his beloved California. When he looks back on old Yerba Buena, where the Franciscan friars made their first home, he reflects on the wonderful growth of San Francisco. He looks back to the early days of the city where, closely following the discovery of gold, came the followers of Loyola — there they laid the foundation of the great institution of learning whose 50th anniversary we celebrate tonight."

The celebrants of that evening could not have predicted the catastrophe that awaited them in just six months, when their faith, their courage, and their endurance in sustaining the great institution they had built would be called upon as never before.

The Earthquake of 1906

31

DENNIS SULLIVAN, CHIEF OF THE SAN FRANCISCO FIRE Department, came back late to his firehouse on the evening of April 17, 1906, having directed efforts to extinguish a minor city fire. After a few hours of sleep, he was abruptly awakened by a violent shaking of the building. As he rushed to the adjoining bedroom where his wife was sleeping, a wall from the next-door hotel fell through the roof of the firehouse, sending the Sullivans and part of the building crashing to the basement two floors below. Mrs. Sullivan landed on a mattress and suffered minor injuries. Chief Sullivan, however, landed directly on the basement's concrete floor, and became one of the first fatalities of the San Francisco earthquake of 1906.

The initial temblor of the earthquake was recorded at 5:12 on the morning of April 18 and lasted for 40 seconds. There was a pause for 10 seconds, and then a second even more violent shaking lasted for an additional 25 seconds. Several more temblors shook the entire Bay Area throughout the day. Although the Richter scale was not developed until 1935, seismologists estimate that the 1906 earthquake was approximately 8.3 on the 10-point scale — the equivalent of 15 million tons of exploding TNT. It was one of the strongest earthquakes ever to strike North America, and the vibrations were recorded as far away as Birmingham, England. The earthquake ruptured the San Andreas Fault for more than 200 miles, creating a 20- to 40-mile-wide path of destruction from Fort Bragg on the Mendocino Coast to San Juan Bautista near Monterey Bay. In some areas of Northern California, land displacement was

as much as 12 feet. The epicenter was first thought to be located at Point Reyes in Marin County, where a commuter train at Point Reyes Station was flipped off the tracks and onto its side by the force of the earthquake. More recent research, however, indicates that the epicenter was due west of Daly City, just off the coast. Throughout the Bay Area, the damage was extensive: acres of redwood trees in the Santa Cruz Mountains were reduced to kindling, railroad tracks and buildings along the edge of the coast fell into the ocean, and most of the downtown buildings in the cities of Santa Rosa and Palo Alto were leveled. Stanford University suffered enormous damage to most of its buildings, and many structures were reduced to rubble. In San Jose, scores of buildings collapsed, though across the bay, Oakland and Berkeley were little affected.

In San Francisco, the damage from the

The damage to St. Ignatius Church and College was extensive but reparable after the earthquake struck on the morning of April 18, 1906.

earthquake was widespread. Huge splits opened up in many of the city's streets, chimneys and towers collapsed, and frame buildings toppled or leaned severely to one side after the initial temblors. Most of the newly completed city hall collapsed, the victim of the earthquake and of several years of graft-inspired inferior materials and workmanship. Neighborhoods in the city built on landfill that had once been part of the bay, such as in the South of Market area, suffered the greatest damage, and many buildings there were totally destroyed.

On the evening of April 17, approximately 3,000 of the city's citizens had seen Enrico Caruso perform in Bizet's *Carmen* at the Grand Opera House on Mission Street. One of those in attendance was Cora Older, the wife of a prominent San Francisco newspaper editor,

Fremont Older. Mrs. Older, who left instructions for an early morning wake-up call at the main desk of the Palace Hotel where she was staying, recorded her initial reaction to the earthquake: "What my sleepy mind mistook for my call began like the roaring of a monstrous train. The Palace Hotel turned on its axis: the building twisted and moaned. The sound of the earth grew louder and more ominous, then in the living room of our suite a crash as if the walls had collapsed. I found myself out of bed and kneeling in the passageway between the bedroom and the living room."

Although most San Franciscans were still asleep in their beds when the first temblor hit, the 44 Jesuits of St. Ignatius Church and College, on the corner of Van Ness Avenue and Hayes Street, were already up when the earthquake struck. Vincent Testa, S.J., was saying Mass with two Jesuit brothers when the shaking began. He was hit by a falling candlestick, but not seriously hurt. The college president, John Frieden, S.J., was in his room getting ready for the day. Later he wrote, "And so that morning, 13 minutes after five, when the first indications of the earthquake appeared, I crossed myself, made the wonted aspirations, and continued dressing. But in a few seconds I felt that the quake was sharper than any I had ever experienced…. I dropped on my knees, at the foot of my bed, and prayed. Then came that crashing, rumbling intonation, so strangely awful and so terrible that it baffles the power of description — none can comprehend it save those who have experienced it. Yet it was but the herald of the terrific convulsion that followed. The great strata of rock and conglomerate that form the peninsula on which San Francisco stands rotated, tilted, twisted, sank and heaved in veriest agony. The massive buildings of St. Ignatius seemed like a piece of shrubbery in an autumn storm."

None of the Jesuits, lay faculty, or students of St. Ignatius Church and College were killed or seriously injured in the 1906 earthquake. The church and college, however, which were built over an underground stream, suffered considerable, though reparable, damage from the initial temblors: walls cracked; plaster, books, and furniture fell everywhere; and the roof partially collapsed. In the church, marble statues were thrown to the ground and broken, and the Easter decorations from the prior Sunday were a pile of broken candelabra, candles, vases, glass, and flowers. Despite the damage, hundreds of frightened people flocked into St. Ignatius Church immediately after the earthquake. By 6:15 A.M., part of the debris was cleared away, and Henry Whittle, S.J., Father Minister of the Jesuit Community, offered Mass at the main altar, followed by Masses given by President Frieden and two other priests. Several of the Jesuits entered the confessionals and heard confessions steadily until 10 A.M. Immediately after

the earthquake, an emergency hospital was set up in the Mechanics Pavilion, a large auditorium near St. Ignatius Church. The Jesuits quickly responded to urgent calls from the makeshift hospital to minister to the injured and dying victims of the earthquake. Fr. Whittle wrote in his diary that the "sight of the victims, some crushed most horribly, was appalling."

No sooner had the Jesuits and many other San Franciscans begun to respond to the damage and injuries of the initial earthquake that from the rubble-strewn streets of the city, menacing columns of smoke began to rise. The greatest challenge for San Francisco and St. Ignatius Church and College was yet to come.

The Fire that Followed the Earthquake of 1906

BY MID-MORNING, APRIL 18, 1906, ASSISTANT CHIEF JOHN Dougherty of the San Francisco Fire Department faced an imminent catastrophe: the powerful earthquake at 5:12 A.M. had destroyed many buildings throughout San Francisco. City Hall lay in ruins. Dougherty's boss, fire chief Sullivan, was dying under a pile of rubble from a partially collapsed firehouse, and at least 50 separate fires had broken out in the city. The fires resulted from fractured gas lines, crossed and broken electrical wires, overturned stoves, cracked chimneys, and flammable chemicals from spilled and shattered bottles.

To make matters worse, when firemen hooked up their hoses to fight the fires, they found that in almost every case, there was no water pressure. The earthquake had broken the main water lines from the city's two largest reservoirs and had caused more than three hundred fractures to the subsidiary water lines within the city. By late morning of April 18, the numerous fires had coalesced into three major fires: south of Market Street, north of Market Street, and in the Hayes Valley, west of City Hall. South of Market, the raging fire consumed the Emporium, the Hearst Building, the Grand Opera House, the Call Building (the city's tallest structure), the Palace Hotel (the city's most luxurious hotel), and hundreds of other buildings. North of Market Street, the fire destroyed the wholesale produce district before engulfing Chinatown, the financial district, and the retail and hotel district around Union Square.

The Hayes Valley fire, also called the Ham and Eggs Fire, destroyed the major municipal and retail buildings in the civic center before it roared through the Mission District. It was caused by a woman who had prepared breakfast in her Hayes Street home after the earthquake. She lit a fire in her stove, which was connected to an earthquake-damaged chimney. The fire escaped from the chimney and quickly spread to neighboring buildings. This was the fire that destroyed St. Ignatius Church and College. In his diary, Henry Whittle, S.J., Father Minister of the Jesuit Community, recorded how by 11 A.M. this fire "quickly spread in the direction of our college; a fierce wind arising…swept on the fire with irresistible violence." Fr. Whittle described how the fire "broke out in a tower which could not be reached without hose and water, neither of which could be obtained…. The firemen in the tower and our own people there concluded that it was impossible to stop the fire and gave their attention to carrying out the vestments from the church." A wagon was found, and in

Begining of Great San Francisco Fire

addition to the vestments, some church furniture, crucifixes, chalices, and ciboria (covered receptacles for holding the consecrated wafers of the Eucharist) were saved. Meanwhile, the president of St. Ignatius College, John Frieden, S.J., hurriedly gathered up a handful of college documents from the archives that were in his office and a few articles of clothing. Then, as he later wrote, with "satchel in one hand, dragging the archives with the other, I left the house which had become so dear to me, and which I was never to reenter."

The raging fires throughout San Francisco eventually became one giant conflagration that took on a life of its own, fed by thousands of wooden buildings standing adjacent to each other throughout the city. In that uncontrollable inferno, temperatures reached 2,700 degrees Fahrenheit, hot enough to melt marble, iron,

and steel; crumble sandstone; and dissolve glass into liquid. Smoke from the fire rose five miles into the atmosphere, and the flames could be seen from 50 miles away. As Fr. Frieden headed west toward the ocean with thousands of other San Franciscans, and just ahead of the flames, he surveyed the scene behind him. He later wrote, "Two hundred feet from where we halted, even to the San Francisco Bay two miles away, we beheld one vast mass of shifting smoke and lurid flame; it seemed a very ocean set on fire, or a burning desert. Not a business block escaped, nor a home spared. The destruction was complete. Directly in front of us, some 400 feet from where we stood, was 'Old St. Mary's Church,' as it was called — formerly the Cathedral of San Francisco. By this time it was well-nigh destroyed. The tower, though still standing, was wrapped in flames — a few minutes more,

City Hall can be seen in the center of this photo depicting the fire that consumed San Francisco, following the earthquake of April 18, 1906. To the left of City Hall, the towers of St. Ignatius Church are visible through the smoke.

After the earthquake struck at 5:12 A.M. on April 18, 1906, fires broke out all over the city of San Francisco, which the fire department could not effectively fight because the main water pipes throughout the city had been broken by the earthquake. One of those fires swept up Hayes Street and engulfed St. Ignatius Church and College, ultimately gutting the institution.

and it came crashing down."

Faced with an overwhelming fire and virtually no water, the city's firefighters, aided by soldiers from the Presidio and sailors from the U.S. Navy, tried valiantly to contain the raging inferno. Private and public cisterns were tapped but quickly ran dry, and buildings were dynamited by the U.S. Army in a largely unsuccessful attempt to create firebreaks. In many cases, the explosions from the black powder dynamite only served to spread the fires into previously untouched areas. After two days, however, the efforts by the fire crews finally began to achieve some success. By Friday morning, April 20, firefighters had managed to contain the flames in the Mission District at 20th Street by pumping water from an old cistern to a hydrant on the corner of 20th and Church streets. To the west, the fire crossed Van Ness at several points before it was halted by firefighters. By Friday evening, the fire had almost reached the Bay, where crews on land and on fireboats were able to extinguish the flames and save the warehouses beneath the eastern bluffs of Telegraph Hill and all along the wharfs to the south, including the Ferry Building. By Saturday morning, April 21, after three horrendous days, the fire had finally burned itself out, aided by the end of the flame-fanning wind and by a squelching rain.

The Aftermath of the 1906 Earthquake and Fire

THE 1906 SAN FRANCISCO EARTHQUAKE AND FIRE WAS the greatest natural disaster to ever befall a major American city. It was much more destructive than the Chicago fire of 1871. The fire and earthquake destroyed more than 28,000 buildings in San Francisco, leveled 514 city blocks spread over four square miles in the heart of the city, and left 11 million cubic yards of rubble that had to be removed before reconstruction could begin. All but a handful of the buildings from the waterfront north to North Beach, south to Townsend Street, west to Van Ness Avenue, and southwest to 20th Street in the Mission District were turned to rubble and ashes. Within that major part of the city, only two key civic buildings, the United States Mint and the main post office, were saved. Also spared were most of the piers and warehouses on the waterfront and a few small areas near Jackson Square and on Russian Hill and Telegraph Hill. But block after block of homes, businesses, schools, churches, libraries, and civic buildings were gone, leaving only an occasional chimney or charred wall still standing. The number of homeless was 250,000, approximately two-thirds of the city's population. The estimated value of the loss was $500 million, four-fifths of the 1906 property value of San Francisco, or approximately the size of the federal budget in 1906.

Views of the devastation to St. Ignatius Church and College caused by the earthquake and fire of April 18, 1906. As John Frieden, S.J., the president of St. Ignatius College put it, "What it had taken half a century to build up and to equip, lay in ashes."

It is estimated that the San Francisco earthquake and fire took more than 4,000 lives, though the official count was 674. None of the 44 Jesuits at St. Ignatius Church and College, nor any of its lay faculty or students, were killed in the earthquake or fire, though some were injured. The Jesuit educational and religious institution was, however, completely destroyed, including the extensive library holdings consisting of 60,000 volumes; world-class science laboratories; and outstanding museum collections, including the most comprehensive ornithological collection west of the Mississippi. The financial loss was more than $1 million. A few of the items from

the church were saved (vestments, some furniture, chalices, crucifixes, and ciboria) and are held in the present sacristy of St. Ignatius Church. The paintings, statues of pure Carrara marble, most of the furniture, and one of the finest church organs in the country were all destroyed. After the rubble that was once St. Ignatius Church cooled down, the church bell was salvaged; it still rings today in the present St. Ignatius Church.

After the earthquake and fire, John Frieden, S.J., the president of St. Ignatius College, wrote, "How could I be ready to abandon the pile of buildings which obedience had given me in charge with all that they contained? It was like leaving my very self. I was and felt so identified with it all; and now I must make it over to destruction. The 44 Jesuits of San Francisco were homeless. What it had taken half a century to build up and to equip, lay in ashes. The future was a blank." Another contemporary account of the destruction of St. Ignatius Church and College was written by Richard Gleeson, S.J., who was then president of Santa Clara College. He had spent the night at St. Ignatius College just before the earthquake and fire, and he later wrote: "I saw the college and church catch fire and I assure you that it was a sad sight. We could hardly save anything and the church is gone with its many treasures of art. The grand college went next and then the best physical and chemical department in all the Society, at least in America, and with it three splendid libraries with all their treasures. The loss is, in

many regards, simply irreparable."

Coincidentally, on the actual day of the destruction of St. Ignatius Church and College, Louis Martin, Superior General of the Jesuit Order, died in Rome. The previous year, Fr. Martin had sent an encouraging message to the Jesuits of St. Ignatius Church and College on the occasion of their Golden Jubilee celebration (vignette #30).

Today on the University of San Francisco campus, a giant winged bird is engraved on the front wall of University Center. It is the phoenix, a mythological bird that is consumed by fire but rises renewed from the ashes. The phoenix appears on the city seal commemorating the five times the city rebuilt after fires in the 1850s. The phoenix also symbolizes the rebirth of our city and our institution after the earthquake and fire of 1906.

Additional scenes of the destruction to St. Ignatius Church and College caused by the San Francisco earthquake and fire of 1906.

34 Recovery

NEWS OF THE DEVASTATING SAN FRANCISCO EARTHQUAKE and fire of 1906 rapidly reached other American cities and other countries, several of which responded with various forms of aid, including food, medicine, and blankets. Ships loaded with relief supplies were soon on their way to San Francisco. Japan, for example, provided nearly a quarter million dollars in relief assistance. The Empress Dowager of China sent 100,000 taels (Chinese monetary units equivalent to 133,000 ounces of silver) for the relief fund for San Francisco. Within a few days of the earthquake and fire, approximately $8 million in relief funds had been raised, including $2 million appropriated by the U.S. House of Representatives. To administer the funds, the San Francisco Relief and Red Cross Funds Committee was incorporated. James Phelan, former mayor of San Francisco and graduate of St. Ignatius College, was selected as president of the organization and presided over a group of civic leaders to administer the money. U.S. President Theodore Roosevelt entrusted the committee with an additional $10 million in federal relief aid.

The San Francisco Relief and Red Cross Funds Committee had an enormous job, as the earthquake and three days of fire left a quarter million San Franciscans homeless and largely without possessions. Some people found shelter with relatives or friends in the unburned sections of the city or took ferries to the East Bay to escape the devastation. Thousands of people, however, camped out in the city's western and southern parks or at military sites. To assist these citizens, Phelan's committee set up 150 relief stations throughout the city to dispense food, clothing, blankets, and other staples. The U.S. Army sent thousands of tents to San Francisco from military bases throughout the west, some from as far away as Vancouver and San Antonio. Makeshift shelters of rugs and blankets were soon replaced by these tents, and tent cities sprang up around the city, complete with rows of tables for group meals, and including sanitation facilities, set up by the U.S. Army Medical Corps. Within a few weeks, 70,000 people were living in tents and other temporary dwellings in the Presidio alone. Many of the

A tent city set up in Golden Gate Park following the San Francisco earthquake and fire of 1906.

tents were eventually replaced by simple wooden cottages. The extraordinary steps taken to provide food and shelter to the homeless of San Francisco were successful, and there was no mass starvation or outbreak of disease.

Due to the destructive fire that rapidly spread through St. Ignatius Church and College, most of the Jesuits lost all of their personal belongings and had only the clothes they were wearing at the time of the earthquake. St. Ignatius College president John Frieden, S.J., and 11 other priests, initially took shelter in the Convent of the Sisters of the Holy Family, at the invitation of the nuns and at the suggestion of Archbishop Patrick Riordan. The Jesuits occupied the second floor of the building, and the first floor was set aside as an emergency hospital. The convent, on the corner of Hayes and Fillmore streets, was seven blocks west of Van Ness and was spared by the fire. Many of the other Jesuits of St. Ignatius Church and College, after aiding injured and dying citizens, made their way to Santa Clara and stayed at a house offered by friends across the street from Santa Clara College. St. Ignatius

College students of the graduating class of spring 1906 were permitted to complete their work at Santa Clara College.

President Frieden and some of the Jesuit community stayed at the Holy Family Convent in San Francisco until May 22, 1906, when they moved to the home of Bertha Welch on Eddy Street. Welch, a wealthy benefactress who had made major donations to the Jesuits of San Francisco in prior years, offered the Jesuit Community the complete use of her mansion. She had been in New York at the time of the earthquake, and when she heard of the loss of St. Ignatius Church and College, she telegraphed her offer to the Jesuits. Fr. Frieden secured Archbishop Riordan's approval for this relocation and for the establishment of a small temporary chapel in Welch's home to continue the Jesuits' ministry. Soon, 18 Jesuits from the dispersed community moved into the house. From her home, and with her continuing financial assistance, the Jesuits of San Francisco turned to the questions of where, when, and how to rebuild their church and school.

35 Rebuilding

ON APRIL 27, 1906, NINE DAYS AFTER THE HORRIFIC earthquake and fire destroyed approximately two-thirds of San Francisco, including St. Ignatius Church and College, Archbishop Patrick Riordan of San Francisco addressed the first meeting of a citizens committee charged with relief and reconstruction. Archbishop Riordan's words have struck a responsive chord with many San Franciscans for almost 100

Another view of the burned out St. Ignatius Church and College, just before rebuilding commenced following the earthquake and fire of 1906.

MUSEUM OF THE CITY OF SAN FRANCISCO

years. "I am a citizen of No Mean City," proclaimed the archbishop, "although it is ashes. Almighty God has fixed this as the location of a great city. The past is gone, and there is no use of lamenting or moaning over it. Let us look to the future and, without regard to creed or birth, work together in harmony for the upbuilding of a greater San Francisco."

The rubble of what was once the heart of San Francisco had barely cooled before rebuilding began. First, however, some 11 million cubic yards of ruined brick and stone walls, twisted steel, and debris of all types had to be removed. Temporary railroad tracks were laid on key streets throughout the city to enable gondolas and ore carts to haul way the heavy stone, brick, and mortar chunks lifted by steam shovels and cranes. Horses and wagons were also heavily employed in the clearing of debris. Much of

the rubble was deposited in Mission Bay at the foot of Townsend and King streets, or was hauled by barge outside the Golden Gate and dumped into the ocean.

A large number of buildings in San Francisco were rebuilt exactly as they were before the earthquake and fire, but there were significant changes as well. On Market Street, for example, many of the smaller buildings were replaced by much taller structures. South of Market, commercial buildings, small factories, and lower-middle-class apartments were built in areas that had once been slums. Nob Hill was transformed from a wealthy enclave of lavish mansions to luxury apartments and hotels. Civic Center was also redesigned, and a new classically inspired city hall was erected a block away from the one that had been destroyed. Although the new city hall was not dedicated until 1915, and the main library was not completed until 1917, much of the city was rebuilt within a year of the devastation, and virtually the entire city was rebuilt by 1909. Although approximately 28,000 buildings had been destroyed in the 1906 earthquake and fire, by 1909, more than 20,500 buildings had replaced them and formed the heart of a new city.

The Jesuits of San Francisco also moved quickly on their reconstruction plans. John Frieden, S.J., president of St. Ignatius College, conferred with his fellow Jesuits shortly after the earthquake and fire and by early May was ready to contact Archbishop Riordan to discuss a new location for the church and college. The Jesuits decided not to rebuild on the old property on Van Ness Avenue. That section of the city had increasingly become a business area even before the earthquake and fire and was subject to steeply rising property taxes. This had also been the case on the original Market Street location of St. Ignatius Church and College. Not until a California Supreme Court ruling in 1910 were private and parochial schools exempt from property taxes. Instead of going back to Van Ness, the Jesuits considered property near Golden Gate Park, some 20 blocks west of the old location. On May 18, exactly one month after the earthquake and fire, Fr. Frieden wrote to Archbishop Riordan: "Constant increase of taxes on our property on Van Ness Avenue makes it impossible to rebuild there. We ask permission of Your Grace to change the location of the church and college. That portion of the city bounded by Hayes, Stanyan, McAllister and Masonic Avenue seems suitable and free from objection." Archbishop Riordan agreed to this proposal, but he stipulated that

no temporary church or school was to be established at the former Van Ness location, which the Jesuits still owned. Accordingly, on June 1, 1906, Fr. Frieden made a $1,000 deposit on a $100,000 parcel of land bound by Grove, Cole, Shrader, and Fulton streets. At the time, this was to be the permanent location of the new St. Ignatius Church and College. This parcel, which came to be known as the "Frieden Block," needed extensive grading, however, and so a temporary location was still needed if the college was to reopen by the fall semester of 1906.

The Sisters of Mercy, an order of nuns with whom the Jesuits had a long history in San Francisco, offered the Jesuits a parcel of land at the end of Hayes Street to occupy rent-free for two years. After two years, the Sisters of Mercy planned to start construction on a new St. Mary's Hospital at that location. The Jesuits politely declined this offer, however, because they believed they would need a temporary site for more than two years. Instead of this location, Fr. Frieden first leased, and then purchased for $67,500, two lots (measuring 275 by 137.5 feet) owned by Mr. and Mrs. M.H. de Young, on the corner of Hayes and Shrader streets. By early June 1906, plans were developed for the erection of temporary buildings at this location. Like much of San Francisco, St. Ignatius Church and College was indeed going to rise rapidly from the ashes.

Temporary railroad tracks were laid throughout San Francisco following the earthquake and fire of April 1906 to enable ore carts to haul away the bricks, stones, and other rubble to make way for rebuilding.

CALIFORNIA PROVINCE OF THE SOCIETY OF JESUS ARCHIVES

Part III: The Shirt Factory Era

ON SUNDAY, JULY 1, 1906, LESS THAN THREE MONTHS after the San Francisco earthquake and fire destroyed St. Ignatius Church and College, ground was broken for a new location for the institution. The site, on the corner of Hayes and Shrader streets just two steep blocks south of today's campus, was to be only a temporary home. In fact, however, the building erected at this location served the Jesuits, their lay colleagues, and students for more than two decades. The rambling wooden building that comprised St. Ignatius Church and College came to be known as "the shirt factory" because of its resemblance to a number of hastily built structures south of Market Street, some of which actually housed shirt factories.

St. Ignatius College reopened its doors in the shirt factory on September 1, 1906, to 271 students ranging from sixth grade through college. Over the next 21 years, there were many key developments at the institution. In 1907, St. Ignatius College began athletic competition on a regular basis with other Bay Area high schools, colleges, and community organizations using a mixture of high school and college students. The first sports were baseball, rugby, and basketball. In 1911, the *Ignatian* literary magazine was founded and is still published today. The School of Law opened in September 1912, in the old Grant Building on Market and 7th streets, but moved to the shirt factory in 1917. A school of engineering was also started in 1912, and St. Ignatius College was renamed the University of St. Ignatius.

With America's entrance into World War I in 1917 and the subsequent draft, enrollment in the university division declined to less than 100 students. The college participated in a military training program, and 10 of its students were killed in the war. Ten gold service stars on the current service flag of the University of San Francisco commemorate these deaths.

By 1919, owing to a precipitous decline in enrollment, enormous cost overruns on the rebuilding of St. Ignatius Church, and a major recession in the nation and in the Bay Area, the institution's financial situation was dire. The debt rose to more than $1 million, and the church and school teetered on the brink of bankruptcy. The name of the school was changed back to St. Ignatius College in 1919, and the leadership of the church and school, with support from alumni and the community, launched a

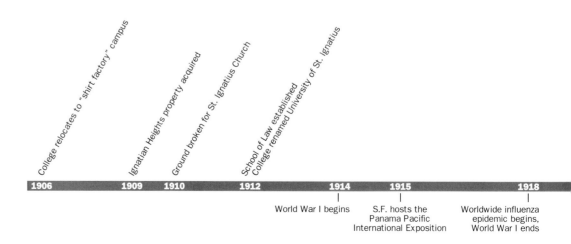

successful fundraising effort to save the Jesuit institution.

By 1924, the debt had been brought under control and enrollment had begun to steadily increase. Numerous changes were also made to the curriculum to reflect changing student and social needs. In 1924, a business program began as a four-year evening certificate option, and by 1925, the College of Commerce and Finance was established, the forerunner of today's School of Business and Management. In that same year, the departments of arts, sciences, and philosophy officially became the College of Arts and Sciences to reflect various program changes, including an increase in the number of elective courses offered to students. In 1926, with a significant increase in student enrollment, work began on a new liberal arts building, the present Campion Hall. In 1927, this new building was dedicated, and St. Ignatius College moved to its present location. By then, the college's drama, debate, and athletic programs had achieved considerable prominence in the western United States.

St. Ignatius Church moved from the corner of Hayes and Shrader streets to its current location in 1914, and the high school division moved from the shirt factory in 1929 to a handsome building on the corner of Turk Street and Stanyan Boulevard, the current site of the Koret Health and Recreation Center. The old shirt factory was eventually torn down, and the site is now the location of the Sister Mary Philippa Health Center, one of the buildings of St. Mary's Medical Center.

The next series of vignettes will detail the many developments at the school and accompanying church over the two decades that comprise the shirt factory era.

The first day of class, September 1, 1906, at St. Ignatius College, when it was housed in a temporary building known as the "shirt factory," a wooden structure hastily nailed together following the 1906 earthquake and fire.

UNIVERSITY OF SAN FRANCISCO ARCHIVES

College renamed St. Ignatius College

Welch Hall completed

Evening classes begin

College of Commerce and Finance established; College of Arts and Sciences formed

Foghorn student newspaper established

College moves to Campion Hall; Women admitted to evening division

1919   **1921**   **1924**   **1925**   **1926**   **1927**

Women given right to vote, Prohibition begins

Charles Lindbergh solo Trans-Atlantic flight

36 Rebirth

ON JULY 2, 1906, THE SAN FRANCISCO *MONITOR* REPORTED on the dedication ceremony held on the previous day for the new site for St. Ignatius Church and College in San Francisco. The event was attended by San Francisco Mayor Eugene Schmitz; the Coadjutor Archbishop of San Francisco, George Montgomery; and many other dignitaries and alumni. "An immense crowd gathered last Sunday afternoon at Shrader and Hayes Streets," the reporter wrote, "to witness the ceremony of breaking ground for the new temporary church and college of the Jesuit Fathers of St. Ignatius. The Fathers are at present domiciled in the beautiful home of Mrs. Welch…but they are anxious to get into a home of their own… [and] for this reason, the project initiated last Sunday with enthusiastic fervor will be pushed with all possible dispatch to conclusion. It is hoped to have temporary structures ready for occupancy by September 1."

A large crowd turned out for the groundbreaking ceremony for a "temporary" St. Ignatius College, at the corner of Shrader and Hayes streets, on July 1, 1906.

UNIVERSITY OF SAN FRANCISCO ARCHIVES

At the dedication, Mayor Schmitz spoke of the connection between the City of San Francisco and St. Ignatius College and Church: "No city can become greater and better than its citizenry and St. Ignatius is to make better citizens. Catholic, Protestant and Jew should support the Jesuit Fathers in this purpose. God does everything for the best and, from the ashes of the past, there will spring up not only a greater and better city but a greater and a better St. Ignatius College and Church."

The president of St. Ignatius College, John Frieden, S.J., drew applause from the audience when he stated that "three months ago, no one would have thought that we would be ready to build a new St. Ignatius upon this site but, undaunted by disaster, we are ready for the new work. We have never lost courage, for we know

that it is God's work and He has provided. If San Francisco is to live, we live with it; if it passes, we pass with it—but not before."

Work on the new buildings took place seven days a week after the groundbreaking ceremony, utilizing some salvaged materials from the former buildings on Van Ness Avenue. On September 1, 1906, as planned, the temporary buildings opened their doors to 271 students. Henry Whittle, S.J., Father Minister of the Jesuit Community, recorded the event in his diary: "We opened the new college today. We were much rejoiced to see a large audience; as the building is not sufficiently complete and, more especially, as we could not as yet procure textbooks for the students, the classes were dismissed to open again next Friday." By early October, the science labs were partially reconstructed with the arrival of 22 cases of science equipment purchased by the Jesuits in Bavaria. President Frieden later wrote, "students and professors alike were jubilant at the sight of the richness of the scientific outfit." Within a year, the destroyed library was also partially restored, with 8,000 new volumes as a result of donations of extra copies of books from Jesuit schools throughout the nation and from private individuals who gave replacement books to the college.

On December 23, 1906, a temporary St. Ignatius Church, housed in the college hall, opened its doors for the first time since the earthquake and fire. Donations made possible five new altars, a pulpit, an organ, a sanctuary carpet, and statues. The pews, the aisles, the vestibule, and the steps were filled with people on that dedication day. Archbishop Patrick Riordan addressed the congregation: "We cannot but deplore the loss of the fine church that is no more, and of the great college so perfectly equipped for imparting a solid education to the young men of this city. Both church and college had a sublime mission in San Francisco, they had nobly fulfilled it; and we grieve because their work of Christian charity and zeal has been so rudely and so unexpectedly arrested. Yet in the midst of our sorrow we do well to remember that the spirit which called into being so magnificent an institution is not dead—even now it lives palpably among you in the men who succeed the heroic souls that have passed away, in the men who are now before you as your priests, your guides, your friends…. In prosperity San Francisco could command their ministrations day and night; and in the season of affliction they have remained faithful to their trust."

Archbishop Riordan's words captured the essence of the historic relationship between the city and the Jesuit institution. That relationship continues today at the University of San Francisco and is succinctly expressed in a Latin inscription on the front wall of University Center: *"Pro Urbe et Universitate"*—"for the city and the university."

A "temporary" St. Ignatius College, known as the "shirt factory," was hastily built during the summer of 1906, following the San Francisco earthquake and fire of that year. It was the home of the institution until 1927.

UNIVERSITY OF SAN FRANCISCO ARCHIVES

37

John Frieden, S.J.

COURAGE, DETERMINATION, AND FAITH ARE PERHAPS THREE of the best words to describe the 12th president of St. Ignatius College, John Frieden, S.J. His tenure as president, from 1896 to 1908, was the longest of any president up to that time. During this period, he oversaw major curriculum changes at the college; helped eliminate a significant institutional debt going back 46 years; cultivated major donors for the institution; was instrumental in building at St. Ignatius College the finest gymnasium in all of San Francisco; helped expand the library, art, and museum collections of the institution; directed the 50th anniversary celebration of the church and college; and most importantly, led the institution through its most difficult period in the wake of the disastrous earthquake and fire of 1906.

John Peter Frieden was born on November 18, 1844, in a small town in the Grand Duchy of Luxemburg. His father, Peter Frieden, a retired school teacher, tutored his son and directed his early education, including six years of elementary school; three years of Normal School; and four years at the Athenaeum, a Jesuit College in Luxemburg. Upon finishing his work at the Athenaeum, John Frieden initially followed in his father's footsteps and taught school for five years. Concurrent with his schooling, John Frieden followed a traditional Catholic religious path, receiving his first communion in 1856 and his confirmation in the same year from Nicholas Adamus, who later became the first Catholic Bishop of Luxemburg.

In 1868, John Frieden decided to become a priest, and he returned to the Athenaeum to study Latin, Greek, and theology. While at the Athenaeum, he learned of the work of a Belgian-born priest, Pierre DeSmet, S.J., who was a pioneer missionary among the Native Americans of the Great Plains of North America, and who was instrumental in convincing the Jesuit Superior in Europe to send Jesuits to the western United States.

In January 1869, Fr. DeSmet returned to Europe and visited the Belgian province of the Jesuits, adjoining Luxemburg. Young Frieden heard of Fr. DeSmet's arrival and his call for missionaries, applied for admission to the Society of Jesus, and became a Jesuit novice in February 1869. He soon left Belgium with Fr. DeSmet and arrived at the Jesuit novitiate near Florissant, Missouri, in July 1869. In 1871, while still a novice, he was transferred to Saint

Louis College, where he taught grammar for three years, and then went to the Jesuit seminary school at Woodstock, Maryland, where he studied and taught philosophy and theology from 1874 to 1881. In April 1880, while at Woodstock, John Frieden was ordained a Jesuit priest by Archbishop James Gibbons of Baltimore. Fr. Frieden next served as prefect of studies and a philosophy professor at Detroit College, becoming the president of that institution in 1885 and provincial of the Missouri province in 1889. In 1896, he was appointed superior of the California mission and president of St. Ignatius College.

The first years of Fr. Frieden's presidency coincided with the latter part of the Golden Age of St. Ignatius Church and College (described in vignettes #25 through #28). A major achievement during his presidency was freeing the institution from long-standing debt. This was accomplished in 1901, when Fr. Frieden sold more than 800 acres of land in the East Bay, near Point San Pablo, for $200,000, and used the money to pay off accumulated institutional debts going back to 1855. The land Fr. Frieden sold had originally been bequeathed to Fr. Maraschi, the founding president of St. Ignatius College. Fr. Frieden also oversaw significant growth in the size of the library holdings, the formation of a college orchestra, the development of a graduate school, and the expansion of the drama program. He played the lead role in building a modern and spectacular gymnasium that the local press described as the "best equipped in the city" and in organizing the institution's Golden Jubilee, celebrating 50 years of the Jesuit enterprise in San Francisco.

Fr. Frieden's leadership of St. Ignatius Church and College during the earthquake and fire of 1906 and during its recovery, rebuilding, and rebirth constitutes his most important legacy. Facing the complete destruction of virtually everything the church and college had built up over its first 50 years, Fr. Frieden managed to harness the human and fiscal resources needed

to reopen the college within five months of the disaster. Moreover, he set the stage for the institution's eventual flourishing at a temporary site in the "shirt factory" two blocks south of the current campus, and ultimately at the present location, part of which Fr. Frieden purchased before he left office in 1908.

Fr. Frieden's faith in the Jesuit experiment

John Frieden, S.J., 12th president of St. Ignatius College, who guided the institution through the difficult period of the San Francisco earthquake and fire of 1906.

UNIVERSITY OF SAN FRANCISCO ARCHIVES

in San Francisco never wavered. After the earthquake and fire, and after the reestablishment of St. Ignatius Church and College, Fr. Frieden wrote: "In 1855 St. Ignatius Church and College began, humbly, on the San Francisco sand hills; fifty one years later, in 1906, we began once again, humbled to the very dust, to do God's work for souls as well as we might. This time we resumed on the ashes. But God's arm is not shortened. He at whose word creation sprang into existence could easily restore the fabric which man had reared. He would sustain the drooping spirits…. He would lend them both energy and foresight to bring order out of chaos and to organize our works anew. Through it all He would bestow endurance and cheerful confidence."

Fr. Frieden left St. Ignatius College in 1908 to become the president of Saint Louis University. On December 2, 1911, while waiting in the office of a potential donor to the university, he suffered a massive heart attack and died 30 minutes later. Three days later, his funeral was attended by 200 ecclesiastics; more than 1,000 students, faculty, and administrators from Saint Louis University; the mayor of Saint Louis; and the former governor of Missouri. The Missouri Jesuit Provincial said the funeral Mass, and the Archbishop of Saint Louis gave the eulogy. Fr. Frieden was buried in the graveyard of the Jesuit novitiate at Florissant, Missouri, where he had entered the Society of Jesus as a novice 42 years earlier, when he first arrived in America.

Bertha Welch

38

NO BENEFACTOR WAS AS CRITICAL TO THE WELL BEING of St. Ignatius Church and College in the late 19th and early 20th centuries as Bertha Welch. She made major financial contributions to the church and college during the institution's Golden Age from 1880 to 1906, supported the Jesuits of San Francisco during their bleakest hours following the earthquake and fire of 1906, and played a major role in the rebirth and rebuilding of the institution.

Bertha Welch offered the Jesuits of St. Ignatius Church and College her mansion on Eddy Street as a temporary home after the destruction of their institution in the earthquake and fire of 1906. The Jesuits stayed there for five months while they built a temporary church and college near Golden Gate Park.

UNIVERSITY OF SAN FRANCISCO ARCHIVES

Bertha Welch was born in Paris in 1849 and married a wealthy New Orleans businessman who made a fortune in sugar production. The Welch family settled in San Francisco in the 1880s, and it included three boys, all of whom attended St. Ignatius College. Following the death of her husband, Welch gave sizeable gifts from her inherited estate to St. Ignatius Church and College and to various Catholic charities in San Francisco. One of the first charities she assisted was the Francesca Society of San Francisco, named after Saint Frances of Rome and dedicated to distributing clothing and food to families living in poverty in San Francisco. Aloysius Varsi, S.J., a mathematics professor at St. Ignatius College, assisted the society for several years and secured rooms for the society in St. Ignatius Church. In 1880, Fr. Varsi took over direction of the Francesca Society and developed a close working relationship with Bertha Welch.

In April 1890, Welch made her first direct contribution to St. Ignatius Church. It was for $50,000, and it enabled Fr. Varsi, who had become church prefect, to add substantially to the art, paintings, stained glass windows, sculpture, and decorations of the church.

Welch soon gave another $50,000 to the church for the purchase of one of the finest church organs in America, referred to by one newspaper as the "King of Instruments." In 1898, the president of St. Ignatius College, John Frieden, S.J., appealed to the Superior General of the Society of Jesus, Louis Martin, to grant to Welch a rare honor: to be designated a benefactor of the

Bertha Welch was the most significant benefactor of the Jesuits of St. Ignatius Church and College from 1890 to 1922.

GIFT OF JOHN YARRINGTON

Society of Jesus and "admitted to a share in all the good works performed by the Jesuit Order." Fr. Martin agreed to this request and wrote to Welch: "Such is your virtue and piety, Madam — such your generosity towards our Society — that we consider in justice due you whatever return we can make. And since in no way can we better show our regard for you than by spiritual favors, we, by that authority which, although unworthy, the Lord has given us in this Society, constitute you a sharer in all and each of the Holy Sacrifices, prayers, fasts and other good works — in a word, in all the affection of our heart, we grant you in Christ Jesus a full participation in them…. He may shower every grace and blessing on you in this life, and with the crown of heavenly glory reward you forever!"

When the earthquake and fire struck San Francisco on April 18, 1906, Mrs. Welch was in New York. When she learned of the destruction of St. Ignatius Church and College, she immediately telegraphed Fr. Frieden, offering the Jesuits her mansion on Eddy Street as a temporary residence. Eighteen Jesuits from the displaced community soon moved into her home,

established a temporary chapel, and lived there for the next five months while they built a temporary church and college on the corner of Hayes and Shrader streets (vignette #36). During this time, Welch moved to her country house in Menlo Park and continued to provide financial support for the Jesuits of San Francisco. In 1920, she donated $200,000 for a faculty building next to the new St. Ignatius Church at its current location on the corner of Fulton Street and Parker Avenue. The building, appropriately named Welch Hall, served as the residence of the Jesuit Community from 1921 to 1959 and as the residence of the St. Ignatius High School Jesuit staff until it was demolished in 1970.

Welch made contributions to many other Catholic institutions in Northern California, including major gifts to the convent for the Sisters of St. Joseph of Eureka, who were in charge of St. Mary's Chinese School in San Francisco's Chinatown; to the Paulist Fathers for their church and residence in San Francisco; to the Helpers of the Holy Souls to establish a house for the sick and poor of the city; and to the Dominican Sisters of Perpetual Adoration to open their chapel and convent in the city and to maintain their headquarters in the old Welch residence.

Bertha Welch died on February 25, 1922, and a requiem Mass was celebrated for her in St. Ignatius Church by Archbishop Edward Hanna of San Francisco. More than 50 priests occupied the church sanctuary, and the pews were filled with family, friends, and the students, staff, faculty, and alumni of St. Ignatius College and St. Ignatius High School. The Catholic newspaper, the San Francisco *Monitor*, covered the funeral, recounted Bertha Welch's life, and proclaimed, "too much praise cannot be given this noble and generous Catholic mother whose purse was ever open to the needs of deserving charities and worthy Catholic causes." Today on the University of San Francisco campus, the large expanse of grass between St. Ignatius Church and Campion Hall, where the Jesuit residence once stood, is named in honor of Berth Welch.

The Shirt Factory

39

IT WAS A CREAKING AND RAMBLING WOODEN BUILDING that looked more like an industrial plant than a Jesuit college campus. The stark and boxlike structure was quickly nailed together on the south side of Hayes Street, between Shrader and Stanyan streets, in the late summer of 1906, following the earthquake and fire that destroyed the magnificent campus on Van Ness Avenue. It was supposed to be a temporary site for St. Ignatius College. In fact, it was the institution's home for 21 years, from 1906 to 1927. During these years, St. Ignatius College was known as the "shirt factory" because of its resemblance to a number of hastily built shirt factories south of Market Street. St. Ignatius Church was also housed on this site until the church relocated in 1914 to its present location, on the corner of Fulton Street and Parker Avenue.

St. Ignatius College chemistry students working in their lab at the "shirt factory," as the college was known from 1906 to 1927.

ST. IGNATIUS COLLEGE PREPARATORY ARCHIVES

During the 1906–1907 academic year, 271 students attended St. Ignatius College. This included all students enrolled in the eighth grade of the grammar department, the high school department, and the collegiate department. The catalog of that year outlined the curriculum for the new academic year in the collegiate department: "To fit the graduates of the College to take up with greater profit the work of professional schools, elective courses for the two undergraduate years are being prepared and will be introduced in the term beginning September, 1907. These will include higher mathematics, mechanical drawing, advanced physics and chemistry, special laboratory work, physiology, biology, modern languages, Latin, Greek and English literature, constitutional and legal history and other branches suitable to prepare one for the study of Engineering, Medicine, or Law."

Most of the students who attended the shirt factory were born and raised in San Francisco and stayed in the city after graduation. Many of the students worked their way through college with part-time jobs, such as driving grocery wagons or delivering parcels. All of the students walked or commuted to school. The Hayes Street trolley was one of the most popular means of transportation to the shirt factory. Edmund Kelley, from the class of 1924, described St. Ignatius as "the poor boy's college. Stanford and Berkeley had better accommodations, but our faculty and subject matter were just as good. Our people became top judges, lawyers, doctors." He also vividly recalled the college building: "Sometimes it was like a haunted house. The most eerie time was coming in at night for a big oral test. You walked up the crickety steps into a dark room. There was one little light over the table where the professors put you through the inquisition." Dr. Albert Shumate of the class of 1927 remembered the roughly built basement library, with shelves covered in chicken wire.

When St. Ignatius Church moved two steep blocks north to its new location, the abandoned church became an all-purpose room: audito-

rium, theater, and basketball court. Edward Strehl of the class of 1928, who played basketball for the college, described how "the pillars were just a few inches from the out-of-bound lines. It was an advantage to the home team, because we knew how to knock opponents into the pillars." Justice Preston Devine, who received a bachelor's degree from the college in 1925 and a law degree in 1927, depicted the shirt factory as a "building unlike any before or since. Its exterior was plain and boxlike, but inside it was indeed as labyrinthine as the maze that imprisoned Theseus. It was the Winchester House built all at one time! Once someone ordered serial numbers to be placed on all the doors and passageways and, after a few thousand had been marked, there were rumors that searching parties had been sent in to find the markers." Justice Devine also noted that "what was laughingly called a heating system consisted of a device looking like a heated pie plate, suspended from the ceiling, creating insufferable heat for those directly below and leaving only fumes and chill for those outside the superheated circle." Another alumnus, retired judge Herman A. van der Zee, who attended St. Ignatius from high school through law school, said simply, "it was the best education available anywhere at the time."

Many students rode the streetcar up Hayes Street to attend classes at the shirt factory.

The 1906–07 Academic Year

On the first day of classes at the reopened St. Ignatius College, September 1, 1906, students posed with their instructors to mark the rebuilding of their school after the earthquake and fire of April 18, 1906.

THE 1906–1907 ACADEMIC YEAR WAS ONE OF THE MOST challenging periods in the history of St. Ignatius College. Following the devastating earthquake and fire of April 18, 1906, all physical aspects of the institution had to be restored: the buildings, the library, the laboratories, the equipment, the books, and all other materials. All of the administrators, faculty, and students of the college survived the earthquake and fire. What persisted, therefore, were human faith, courage, and determination to restore what had been the finest educational institution in San Francisco, and certainly one of the best schools in the nation. The fact that St. Ignatius College was able to reopen less than five months after its total destruction was a remarkable achievement.

The site for a temporary St. Ignatius Church and College, along with a Jesuit residence, was purchased at the corner of Hayes and Shrader streets. A local newspaper captioned the relocation: "The Jesuit Fathers Go West." The cornerstone for the restored institution was laid in midsummer of 1906 with appropriate ceremonies. The construction of the frame buildings progressed rapidly, with the church going up on the corner of Hayes and Shrader Streets and extending halfway down the block toward Fell Street. The Jesuit residence was built to adjoin it on Hayes Street, and the college itself was erected to the west of the residence. The whole frontage on Hayes Street covered about two-thirds of the block. Small groups of the school's students frequently found their way out to the site over the late summer of 1906 to view the progress of the buildings.

The college opened on schedule for the beginning of the fall semester on September 1, though construction and deliveries were still in progress. For example, a bathtub destined for the unfinished Jesuit Community stood unpacked in the middle of the site to greet the arriving students. One student later wrote about his experience when he first entered the new building: "Inside the college, we found a makeshift stairway, which led into a large number of half-furnished class rooms, and which we were able, with some difficulty, to ascend, at the imminent risk of breaking our necks. Whilst we stood around admiring the carpenters making little boards out of big ones, Father Ford, the new prefect of studies, appeared on the scene, and informed us that we might continue our vacation for one week longer" because the textbooks had not yet arrived. Badly needed science and laboratory equipment arrived in early October, and the library holdings were gradually and partially restored over the next several months. Recreation space was provided by a sandlot behind the buildings on the Fell Street side, and by a sand hill on the Hayes Street side that rose steeply to Grove Street. In addition, Golden Gate Park always had its gates wide open on Stanyan Street, inviting students to skip their classes, much to the despair of their professors.

As the 1906–1907 academic year drew to a close in June, the play *The Amanuensis,* adapted for an all-male cast, was staged in the Van Ness Theater and directed by Hubert Flynn, S.J. The theater was a temporary structure erected on Van Ness Avenue, on the site of the St. Ignatius Church and College destroyed by the earthquake and fire. On June 25, 1907, in that same theater, St. Ignatius College held its 48th commencement, presided over by a visiting prelate, Bishop Manuel da Silva of Lisbon, Portugal. During the commencement, six bachelor of arts degrees and five master's degrees were conferred on St. Ignatius College students. In addition, an honorary doctor of philosophy degree was granted to James R. Kelly, president of Hibernia Bank and a major supporter of the Jesuits of San Francisco.

With the help of friends such as James Kelly and Bertha Welch (vignette #38), other Jesuit communities, and many individuals throughout the world, the Jesuit enterprise in San Francisco was restored. The 1907 commencement program expressed the gratitude felt by the Jesuits: "The president and faculty acknowledge with heartfelt thanks the charity with which so many sympathetic friends, forgetful of their own losses, have come to the assistance of the college in its need. The generosity of the provinces and the colleges of the society, not only in America, but also in Europe, fill them with thankfulness. To others, too, not of the Society, both in the United States and beyond the Atlantic, they take this means of expressing their liveliest gratitude."

The Alumni Banquet of 1906

ON NOVEMBER 26, 1906, APPROXIMATELY SEVEN MONTHS after the devastating earthquake and fire of April 1906, and more than two months after St. Ignatius College reopened in its "shirt factory" near Golden Gate Park, the alumni of the college held a grand banquet at Tait's restaurant in San Francisco. The theme for the banquet was the rebuilding of the city and the college after the April catastrophe. Concerns were also raised at the dinner about a series of investigations that were just beginning in San Francisco into graft and bribery charges against some of the city's civic and business leaders.

Several of the banquet speakers addressed the "energetic work of the Jesuit Fathers" in so quickly reorganizing and rebuilding their educational enterprise. In addition to the more than 100 alumni who attended the dinner, honored guests included Archbishop George Montgomery of San Francisco, who spoke about the church in California; John Frieden, S.J., president of St. Ignatius College, who addressed the college's plans for the future; and James Phelan, former mayor of San Francisco and prominent alumnus of the college, who spoke about the city of San Francisco.

Several of the alumni banquet speakers addressed the importance of the city's current investigations into graft and bribery among some of the city's leaders, and the duty of St. Ignatius College graduates to uphold the highest ethical standards in civic life. The 1906 investigations were prompted by the discovery that substandard building materials were used in the construction of the new city hall, the walls of which rapidly collapsed in the 1906 earthquake. Investigations found that many

of the contracts for the building of city hall were procured through bribery.

Fremont Older, editor of the *Evening Bulletin*, for years led the fight against civic corruption in San Francisco. He was supported in his efforts by James Phelan, and in turn, Older strongly endorsed Phelan's successful bid for mayor in 1897. Phelan served as mayor until 1902 and is credited with eliminating a great deal of the corruption that existed in city government. In 1906, Older traveled to Washington, D.C., where he persuaded President Theodore Roosevelt to send federal prosecutors to San Francisco to spearhead a new investigation into civic corruption. The investigations that Older and Phelan helped launch in 1906, and which were discussed at the alumni banquet, eventually led to the indictment of more than 3,000 of the most prominent citizens of San Francisco. Among those convicted were Abe Ruef, a well-known San Francisco attorney, political boss, and legal adviser to Mayor Eugene Schmitz on charges of bribery and influence peddling in securing city-approved franchises

At the alumni banquet of 1906, several of the speakers addressed the widespread graft and corruption among the city's leaders. San Francisco's City Hall, which had taken more than twenty years to complete, symbolized that corruption. Many of the contracts for its building were obtained through bribery, and substandard materials were used in its construction, including newspapers rather than concrete to fill the interior of many of its walls. Consequently, most of City Hall rapidly collapsed during the 1906 earthquake.

COURTESY OF THE BANCROFT LIBRARY
UNIVERSITY OF CALIFORNIA, BERKELEY

city government during what historians label as the Progressive Movement. On the national level, these reforms of the Progressive Movement were championed by President Roosevelt. In San Francisco, two of his strongest allies were Fremont Older and James Phelan. In 1914, Phelan became the first United States Senator from California elected under the new provisions of the 17th Amendment to the United States Constitution, which called for the direct election of senators by the people of a state rather than by the state legislature. In his Senate campaign, Phelan espoused anti-Japanese views, reflecting the widespread racism of the era in California and across the nation.

for the Home Telephone Company, for securing special government privileges for the United Railroads in their operation of the city's cable cars, and for extorting money from various "French restaurants" (prostitution houses) in exchange for expediting their liquor licenses. Ruef was ultimately convicted and served more than four years in San Quentin Prison. San Francisco Mayor Eugene Schmitz was also convicted of extortion in the same "French restaurant" cases, but his conviction was reversed by the state court of appeals. Ultimately, many of the other indictments, including those against 16 members of the county board of supervisors, were dismissed or overturned by higher courts.

The famous graft prosecutions of 1906 through 1912 had a lasting impact on the city government of San Francisco and reflected efforts sweeping across the nation to reform

The Class of 1909

42

BY 1909 SAN FRANCISCO WAS LARGELY REBUILT FROM THE catastrophic earthquake and fire of three years earlier. More than 20,500 new buildings had replaced the approximately 28,000 buildings destroyed in 1906. On June 5, 1909, John Jules Jusserand, the French Ambassador to the United States, presented a gold medal to San Francisco, commemorating the city's rise from the ashes. On October 19, the Portola Festival opened in San Francisco to celebrate the city's recovery from the devastation caused by the earthquake and fire.

The St. Ignatius College class that graduated in 1909 had essentially lived in two worlds. They had received their basic education in the grammar and preparatory departments of the magnificent college that existed on Van Ness Avenue, with its world-class laboratories, outstanding libraries, and state-of-the art gymnasium. They went to school near city hall, they attended Mass in the adjoining St. Ignatius Church, and they played baseball on a field at the corner of Ninth and Brannan streets. In September of 1905, the class of 1909 continued its education at St. Ignatius as college men in the same building where they had received their earlier education, but on the next higher floor. Seven months later, their city, their school, and their lives would be changed forever. Beyond laying waste to their city and their school, the earthquake and fire of April 1906 scattered the class to all areas of the city and state. Many were burned out of their homes and had to seek refuge in one of the camps set up by the military in various parts of the city. However, as a member of the class later wrote: "each and every one was full of hope, and anxious for the time when all should assemble at the New St. Ignatius College, which was shortly in process of construction at Hayes and Shrader Streets."

Despite their hopes, many of the college men who started in 1905 were unable to return to school because of the losses suffered by their families in 1906. Most of the class, however, did return when the college reopened near Golden Gate Park on September 1, 1906, even as workmen were still engaged in nailing together what came to be known as the "shirt factory" (vignette #39). After several weeks, the school began to be partially restored to its former self. The class of 1909 returned to its studies of the classics, Latin, Greek, modern languages, English, history, physics, chemistry, and biology. The class of 1909 sometimes quarreled and competed with the upper classmen, who took classes on the floor above them; occasionally teased the younger boys in the school, who took classes on the floor below them; and played baseball with both groups in the sandlots adjacent to their new school.

The class initiated an annual "Noughty

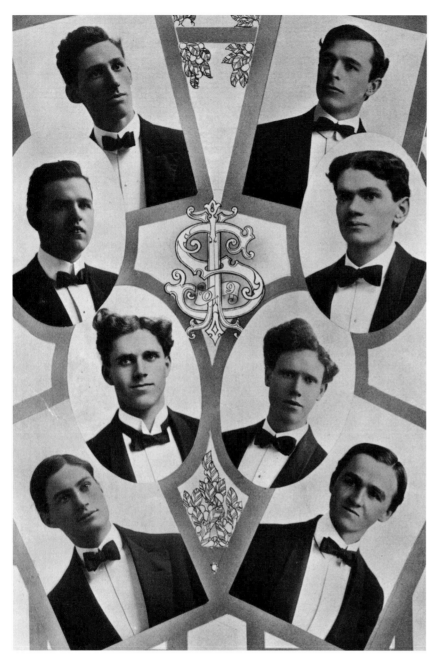

Some members of the St. Ignatius College class of 1909. They originally attended the college when it was located on Van Ness Avenue. After the earthquake and fire of 1906, these students graduated from St. Ignatius College on Hayes and Shrader streets, in what became known as the "shirt factory."

hours of life, which once passed on, can never return again, 'Pickles' Williams gently tickled the somnolent minion of the law with his shoe string, and in accents mild inquired if this were Alameda or Fruitvale. The noble Oaklander eyed him askance for a while, and finally managed to gurgle: 'Say, kid, this is THE city.' With a joyous laugh, at such a sally from one of Oakland's finest, we went on our way."

In their junior year, the class of 1909 witnessed a major curriculum change: specialized courses in engineering, law, and medicine were introduced into the curriculum to prepare the students for entrance into professional schools. The college soon started its own professional schools of law and engineering in 1912. This undergraduate curriculum change was apparently appreciated by the students, one of whom wrote at the time of the 1909 graduation: "Now that we have reached the end of our college career, we wish to extend our heartfelt thanks to all those who have labored so arduously to make us successful in our several walks of life. We feel that they have all done the best for us, and we are now going into the world, filled with determination that the spirit of Noughty Nine shall be ever a credit to them, and that St. Ignatius College shall ever point with pride to the class of 1909."

Nine Night" where the young men went to a theatrical performance in San Francisco or Oakland, sometimes went to a restaurant, and then "rambled along the streets." One such rambling along a street in Oakland was recounted by a member of the class: "We met a policeman snoozing peacefully and upholding at the same time an antique lamp-post. Hurt to the core to see a human being thus wasting the precious

The Origins of Athletics at USF

43

"THE OUTLOOK WASN'T BRILLIANT" FOR THE ST. IGNATIUS freshman baseball team that spring day in 1905. The score stood 6–0 favoring the sophomores, with but four innings more to play. But in the top of the sixth inning, freshman "Wild" Reagan let drive a single, followed by singles by Smith and Conroy to load the bases. "Red" Duffy then tripled to the fence, scoring three runs and putting the freshmen back in the game. With a new lease on life, the freshman pitcher, Jimmy Conroy, mowed down the sophomores in one-two-three order for the rest of the game, and the freshmen scored four runs in the ninth inning on two walks, an error, and a grand slam by "Slats" Malloy, giving the freshmen a dramatic 7–6 victory. "Great was the jubilation of the class that night," a student later wrote, "as they gathered around the bonfire, built in honor of the great triumph on the baseball field, and listened to speeches by 'Babe' Buckley, 'Sis' Ferguson, and 'Red' Duffy."

During the first 50 years of the history of St. Ignatius College, athletics was largely intramural: carried on within the confines of the school's all-male student population. It began when the institution's first president, Anthony Maraschi, S.J., threw out a couple of leather balls to the boys to play with in the yard. Athletics gathered momentum in the last decades of the 19th century as baseball grew in popularity in the nation and at St. Ignatius College, especially after 1869. In that year, the Cincinnati Red Stockings became the first professional baseball team in the nation and traveled to San Francisco on the newly completed transcontinental railroad to play against an amateur team. Baseball was the major intramural game among St. Ignatius College students through the end of the 19th century and on into the early years of the 20th century.

By the end of the 19th century, the college began to play loosely organized and casually arranged contests with other schools. The first recorded game was played on St. Patrick's Day, March 17, 1893, between St. Ignatius College and Sacred Heart College (later to become Sacred Heart Cathedral Preparatory) in rugby. The contest, held on Central Park

The rugby team of St. Ignatius College, composed of college and high school students, played its first game against Sacred Heart College on St. Patrick's Day, March 17, 1893.

Field at the corner of Eighth and Market streets, involved a mixture of college and high school students on both teams. The Sacred Heart team beat St. Ignatius College 14–4.

In the waning years of the 19th century, there was also a movement at St. Ignatius College to develop individual athletic skills within a gymnasium setting. The first step was taken in 1899, when several rooms in the basement of the college were set aside as a small gymnasium. By the end of 1902, two handball alleys had been constructed in the basement of St. Ignatius Church, and in 1903 a magnificent gymnasium was constructed at St. Ignatius College that housed handball courts, two bowling alleys, a pool, and a running track suspended from the roof by iron girders (vignette #27). The athletic program came to an abrupt halt, however, with the earthquake and fire of 1906 that destroyed the new gymnasium, scattered the intramural baseball teams across the city and state, and brought the entire Jesuit educational enterprise in San Francisco to a temporary halt.

Soon after St. Ignatius College reopened at its new location near Golden Gate Park, athletics resumed, starting with intramural sports. Intercollegiate athletics soon followed. In 1907, St. Ignatius College started to play baseball against local colleges, high schools, businesses, and community organizations using a mixture of college and high school students. The college joined the Catholic Athletic League in 1909, and high school and college teams began to compete against other Bay Area teams in rugby, basketball, and track, as well as baseball. The competitors included Santa Clara College, College of the Pacific, and Tamalpais Military Academy. The first issue of the *Ignatian,* the school's yearbook and literary magazine, published in 1911, reported, "the varsity basketball team had a very successful season, losing but one game." The season opened with a 28–16 victory over Tamalpais Military Academy: "The soldier boys put on a good game," according to the *Ignatian* article, "but the speedy work of our team outclassed their grit." After a contest against the College of the Pacific, the *Ignatian* reported that St. Ignatius College sustained its "first and only defeat by the margin of three points." The writer continued, "the game was rather bushy, owing to the umpire. Still U.P. must have recognized our form, as they persistently refused the return game which had been previously agreed upon." During the 1910–11 basketball season, St. Ignatius College beat Santa Clara College 38–31. "The rapid passing of our quintet," reported the *Ignatian*, "repeatedly bewildered the boys from the Mission town," and our "Captain Flood, though suffering from a bad knee, seemed to be all over the court at once and threw some splendid baskets, one of them being a long

shot from an almost impossible angle."

Since the 19th century, athletics have played a major role in the history of the University of San Francisco. Noteworthy achievements were reached by the famous "undefeated, untied, and uninvited" 1951 football team, which was arguably the best college football team that ever played; the development of women's athletics at USF; a soccer program that has produced four NCAA championship teams and the most successful intercollegiate soccer coach, Steve Negoesco, in the history of that sport in America; and the NCAA championship basketball teams of 1955 and 1956, which are credited with greatly enhancing the visibility of USF throughout the nation and the world.

Members of the first St. Ignatius College intercollegiate baseball team in 1907, along with their coach, Joseph Sullivan, S.J. In the back row, left to right are Jack Ryan, Ray Kearney, Fr. Sullivan, Tom Dorland, and "Kid" Reagan. In the front row, left to right, are Vincent Brown, Richard Hyland, Eddie O'Hara, Jerry Mahoney, and Charlie Knight.

The University of San Francisco Seal

THE OFFICIAL SEAL OF THE University of San Francisco has a history that goes back more than 1,000 years. Many of the design elements for the seal can be traced to the tenth century and to the coat of arms of the Spanish noble families of Loyola and Oñaz. In 1261, these two families were united through marriage and became the Spanish noble family of Oñaz y Loyola. The coats of arms of both families were integrated in a new shield.

The coat of arms of the Loyola family consisted of two gray wolves standing on either side of a kettle suspended on a chain from black pothooks. The kettle represented the generosity of the Loyola family in sharing food with others. The wolves were especially popular in Spanish coats of arms and represented the wolves that nursed Romulus and Remus, legendary founders of Rome. The family of Oñaz was represented by seven red bars on a field of gold. The bars symbolized the bravery of seven members of the family who distinguished themselves in battle. In the mid-16th century, Don Martin, a member of the united family, described the history of his family's coat of arms. Martin was the older brother of St. Ignatius of Loyola, founder of the Society of Jesus.

At a meeting of American Jesuit Alumni Associations held in Baltimore in 1889, it was proposed that a badge or button be developed that would identify the wearer as a student or alumnus of a Jesuit college. The idea lay dormant until 1895, when St. Ignatius College of Chicago developed a button to be worn by its students and alumni. The design for the button consisted of an adaptation of the coat of arms of the Oñaz y Loyola family at the time of St. Ignatius. By the turn of the century, several other Jesuit colleges had followed suit and developed their own seals, including Creighton University, St. Louis University,

Detroit College, St. Xavier College of Cincinnati, St. Mary's College of Kansas, and Marquette College of Milwaukee. Each college adapted the original figures and forms of the coat of arms of the Oñaz y Loyola house, changing the coloring and making minor modifications so that each button was distinctive for its particular college.

George Blake Lyle designed a variation of the current USF seal while he was a student at St. Ignatius College. Lyle graduated in 1909, when it was known as the "shirt factory." The seal first appeared on the cover of the 1911 *Ignatian,* the inaugural issue of the yearbook and literary magazine that is still published today. When St. Ignatius College changed its name to the University of San Francisco in 1930, Lyle's design was retained, and only the name of the school was changed on the seal. The current version of the seal has been used on USF documents and papers since that time. In 1979, the president of USF, John Lo

Schiavo, S.J., officially adopted the seal. It is used today on various USF documents and is prominently displayed on the inside front wall of McLaren 252, one of the major locations on campus for special events.

Today, all of the Jesuit Colleges and Universities of America have a seal based on the common design elements traced to the Spanish noble house of St. Ignatius of Loyola. An early 19th-century Jesuit publication, *The Woodstock Letters,* captured the underlying philosophy behind using common elements for all of the seals: "Apart from the fact that its universal adoption would be a tribute of respect to the Society and its Founder, would it not help to draw our students and alumni closer together, foster and promote that benevolence and hearty good fellowship which every student feels for another — in a word, would it not help to create a fellow-feeling among them all — North, South, East and West — as students of one and the same Society?"

The current version of the university seal was designed in 1909 by a St. Ignatius College student, George Lyle, and has appeared on various publications and documents since that year. The seal was slightly modified in 1979.

The *Ignatian*

DURING THE 1910–1911 ACADEMIC YEAR, THE STUDENTS OF St. Ignatius College began publishing a literary magazine, the *Ignatian,* which is still published today. The first editorial stated the magazine's goals: to afford St. Ignatius College students "an opportunity to contribute to a periodical in which their productions will reflect, not only honor on themselves, but also on their school; to cover literary and interesting topics in a style well calculated to hold the reader's attention throughout; and to be a financial and journalistic success in every sense of the word." The editorial concluded that the *Ignatian* will be "a journal of which none may be ashamed and of which they may be justly proud as the official organ of their beloved Alma Mater."

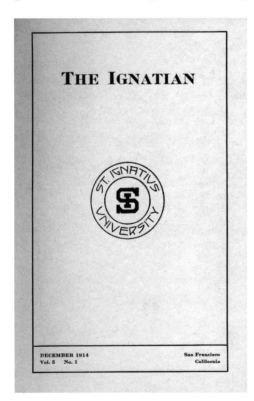

THE IGNATIAN

ST. IGNATIUS UNIVERSITY

DECEMBER 1914
Vol. 5   No. 1

San Francisco
California

The cover of the December 1914 *Ignatian* noted the recent change in the school's name, from a "college" to a "university," prompted in part by the addition of a law school and an engineering school in 1912. One of the magazine's editorials condemned the onset of World War I, which had begun in Europe in August 1914.

The first issue of the *Ignatian* spanned a range of topics. There were seven student poems, two short stories, an essay on the spirituality of thought and will, an article on Robert Lewis Stevenson and his novel *Treasure Island,* and an essay titled "The Dangers of Labor Unions."

The first issue of the *Ignatian* also included a section on the college's alumni association: its founding in 1881 and subsequent history, an overview of the association's meetings and reunion dinners, and highlights of prominent alumni. It noted that Joseph Gleason, who graduated in 1887, became a priest, served as an army chaplain during the Boxer and Philippine campaigns, and was elected to the board of directors of the American Historical Society. Another graduate, Milton Lennon, received a medical degree after graduating from the college, developed a national reputation as a nerve specialist, published numerous articles in medical journals, lectured at the University of California, and became the director of the biology department at St. Ignatius College.

The activities of the various societies of St. Ignatius College were detailed in the first issue of the *Ignatian*. The Loyola Science Academy, for example, was composed of "science enthusiasts" at the college who wanted to foster interest in scientific studies, encourage science research, and deliver public lectures on science topics. The topics for the lecture series during the 1910–11 year included incandescent lighting, radium, magnetism, alternating current, x-rays, and wireless telegraphy. The senior and junior philhistorian debating societies held a series of well-attended and highly publicized debates during the year on topics such as the "New Nationalism of the United States" and the "Fortification of the Panama Canal." The associated students, the *Ignatian* noted, staged two successful plays.

Several pages of the *Ignatian* were devoted to describing the athletic competition during the year for the college teams, including the successful basketball season, which witnessed only one loss for the St. Ignatius team. Mention was also made of the baseball team, which was looking forward to another winning season as the publication went to press.

The *Ignatian* staff congratulated one of the college's students, Vincent Butler, on winning a Rhodes Scholarship to study for three years at Oxford. Not only was Butler the first Rhodes Scholar from St. Ignatius College, the *Ignatian* reported, but he was the "youngest Rhodes Scholar America has ever sent abroad" and is "certainly a worthy representative of California and his Alma Mater."

The editorial pages of the *Ignatian* praised the leadership of the city of San Francisco for its recent victory in Congress in becoming the host city for the Panama Pacific International Exposition, scheduled to open in 1915 and designed to celebrate the opening of the Panama Canal. The editorial also outlined the plans for the building

The first issue of the *Ignatian*, published in 1911, included an artist's rendering of the future St. Ignatius Church, scheduled to open in 1914.

UNIVERSITY OF SAN FRANCISCO ARCHIVES

of the new St. Ignatius Church and College. When completed, the church will be "one of the most beautiful sacred edifices in the city." The editorial writer concluded by pointing out how intimately connected is the history of the Jesuits in San Francisco to the history of the city itself, as witnessed by the earthquake and fire of 1906: "And now seeing San Francisco rapidly recovering its former wealth and prestige, and once more taking its place among the metropolitan cities of the world, the Jesuit fathers, true to their tradition, and having in mind the greater glory of God and the salvation of souls, are building a new church and college, which will surpass any of their predecessors in beauty and magnificence, and will be worthy in every respect to be called the church and college of Greater San Francisco."

46 Breaking Ground for a New St. Ignatius Church

THE JESUITS OF SAN FRANCISCO HELD MARKEDLY DIFFERENT views as to where to build the new St. Ignatius Church following the earthquake and fire of 1906 that destroyed their magnificent church and adjacent college on the corner of Van Ness Avenue and Hayes Street. Some of the Jesuits wanted to rebuild on the same site on Van Ness Avenue, but the majority of the Jesuits, including the president of St. Ignatius College, John Frieden, S.J., opposed rebuilding at this location. Fr. Frieden, along with most of the church and college leadership, felt that rising property taxes on the Van Ness site, along with the increased commercialization of the area, necessitated a move to the western part of the city near Golden Gate Park.

Accordingly, the Jesuits first leased, then purchased, two lots on the corner of Hayes and Shrader streets for a temporary home for St. Ignatius Church and College, which became known as the "shirt factory" (vignette #39). In November 1906, Fr, Frieden also purchased a parcel of land bounded by Cole, Grove, Shrader, and Fulton streets for $102,659. This land came to be known as the "Frieden block" and was intended to be the permanent location for the church and college.

It was soon apparent that the "Frieden block" presented major difficulties. For example, there was a 46-foot difference in height between Grove Street, the southern boundary of the site, and Fulton Street, the northern boundary. This height difference would make building especially difficult and expensive. Therefore, some of the Jesuits, as well as many lay supporters, urged that the permanent church be built across the street, at the corner of Fulton Street and Parker Avenue, on a relatively level parcel of land. In the midst of the debate on where to rebuild St. Ignatius Church, Fr. Frieden took a new position in the Jesuit Province of Missouri. With Fr. Frieden's departure, the opposition to building on the "Frieden block" became so intense that the regional superior of the Rocky Mountain and California Jesuit houses, George De La Motte, S.J., asked 20 of the San Francisco Jesuits for their candid written opinions on the matter. The opinions were varied: some Jesuits wanted to move back to the central part of the city, and others wanted to rebuild in the Mission District, but the majority wanted to stay near Golden Gate Park, but not on the Frieden site.

John Pope, a civil engineer and friend of the Jesuits, entered the debate on where to build

On December 8, 1910, ground was broken for the new St. Ignatius church on the corner of Fulton Street and Parker Avenue

USF JESUIT COMMUNITY ARCHIVES

the permanent St. Ignatius Church. Pope agreed with those Jesuits who felt that the north side of Fulton Street was the best location. Pope addressed a letter to the alumni of the college pointing out the problems with building on the Frieden site: grading and bulkheads alone would cost approximately $40,000, a large retaining wall would need to be built along the entire length of the property, and foundations of great depth would be needed because most of the site was composed of sand to a significantly deep level. By contrast, Pope argued that the land directly across Fulton Street, on the corner of Parker, was relatively level and would provide an impressive 500-foot frontage on Fulton Street, the grading would be cheaper, the foundation would be on solid rock not far from the surface, four major transportation lines (current and proposed) would connect

the new church to the rest of the city, and the location on the crest of a hill would be visually ideal. "The future imposing and noble structure of St. Ignatius Church and College," Pope wrote, "which all of us hope to witness in the concrete very soon, if situated on that superb location, commanding as it does a magnificent view of the surrounding city, hills, bay and ocean, will be a landmark that will ever remain the pride and boast of the people of San Francisco with its towering outlines in views from all parts of the city."

In April 1908, Joseph Sasia, S.J., became the new president of St. Ignatius College and superior of the local Jesuit Community. In September, Fr. Sasia received a letter from Rome granting him permission to rebuild St. Ignatius Church. At first, Fr. Sasia supported the Frieden location, but changed his mind

In 1911, work began on the steel superstructure, towers, and campanile of St. Ignatius Church. Engineers designed the church to withstand enormous stress, a fact ably demonstrated when a strong earthquake rocked the San Francisco Bay Area in October 1989, during which the church suffered virtually no damage.

UNIVERSITY OF SAN FRANCISCO ARCHIVES

in favor of the location advocated by John Pope and many of the Jesuits. Accordingly, between March and December 1909, various parcels of land were purchased by the Jesuits on the corner of Fulton Street and Parker Avenue, and a final decision was made that this site was to be the permanent home of St. Ignatius Church.

After four years of discussion and planning, ground was broken on December 8, 1910, for the new site of St. Ignatius Church. At the open-air ceremony, the St. Ignatius College choir sang the "Litany of the Blessed Virgin," Fr. Sasia blessed the site, said a prayer in Latin, and gave an uncharacteristically brief address. Fr. Sasia, who was known for the great length of

his addresses, had his manuscript swept from the ceremony's temporary platform by a sudden of gust of wind that blew the pages all over the church property and surrounding cemetery. After his shortened address, Fr. Sasia was handed a decorated shovel and commenced to break ground for the new church. The ceremonial shoveling continued with several other Jesuits and laymen, including John Pope, who had pushed diligently for the site. The ground breaking ceremony took place four years and eight months after the total destruction of the previous church on Van Ness Avenue, and 61 years to the day after the arrival of Fr. Michael Accolti, the first Jesuit in San Francisco.

47

The Cornerstone of St. Ignatius Church

THE JESUITS HAVE BUILT FIVE SAINT IGNATIUS CHURCHES in San Francisco. The first church opened its doors in 1855 as a small wooden structure set in the hollow of some sand dunes on what would soon become Market Street, between Fourth and Fifth streets. The second church was constructed next door, fronted on Market Street, and was part of a three-story brick building comprising St. Ignatius

Archbishop Patrick Riordan of San Francisco laying the cornerstone for St. Ignatius Church on March 24, 1912.

UNIVERSITY OF SAN FRANCISCO ARCHIVES

Church and College from 1862 until 1880. The third St. Ignatius Church was a magnificent building with a capacity of 4,000 people on the corner of Van Ness Avenue and Hayes Street. This church, along with its adjacent college, was destroyed in the earthquake and fire of 1906. The fourth church, designed as a "temporary" building on the corner of Hayes and Shrader streets, celebrated its first mass in December of 1906 and was connected to a hastily built St. Ignatius College, known as the "shirt factory."

The cornerstone for the fifth and current St. Ignatius Church was laid on March 24, 1912, at a ceremony attended by the Archbishop of San Francisco, Patrick Riordan; the new president of St. Ignatius College, Albert Trivelli, S.J.; representatives of local Catholic organizations, men and women sodalists (lay supporters and fundraisers of the church); and approximately 5,000 other individuals. The ceremony began with a procession from the temporary church on the corner of Hayes and Shrader streets and headed up two steep blocks to the new church site on the corner of Fulton Street and Parker Avenue. The procession was led by a detachment of police, followed by a full regimental band, 75 girls from the Presentation Convent, the League of the Sacred Heart, the Men's and Ladies' Sodality of St. Ignatius, and Archbishop Riordan, accompanied by several hundred altar boys and many priests. When the procession arrived at the partially completed church (the steel frame and foundation walls were already in place), Archbishop Riordan blessed the ground where the new altar would stand, and then he blessed the church cornerstone, as workmen gently lowered it into place. Fr. Trivelli then read a cablegram from Pope Pius X (later to be a canonized a saint), which stated: "The Holy Father has learned with great pleasure of the laying of the cornerstone of St. Ignatius Church. He sends best wishes for its completion and imparts on this solemn occasion a special and large apostolic blessing."

The major address at the ceremony was given by Rev. Joseph Gleason, St. Ignatius College class of 1887. "We are gathered here today for a very special occasion" he proclaimed, "for the laying of the cornerstone of this building is to commemorate the beginning of another chapter in what is to be erected here to the honor and glory of God. The building of this structure will be an aid to bring back to men the idea that, without faith and without belief, there can be no salvation come to men. The towers of this structure will point ever towards God."

The day after the ceremony, the *San Francisco Call* described the future plans for St. Ignatius Church: "The new building, of which only the steel core has been erected so far, will be one of the most imposing structures of its kind in San Francisco. Two towers, 230 feet high, will adjoin the nave, which will be 72 feet high, the building covering an area of 271 by 158 feet. The style of the architecture will be Italian Renaissance. It is expected that nearly a year will elapse before the edifice is completed."

Six days after the cornerstone was laid, the *San Francisco Star* also commented on the ceremony: "San Franciscans have reason to be proud of the Jesuit Fathers; and with pride, too, they may point to the beautiful temple of worship which soon will crown the heights toward the western sea, the cornerstone of which Archbishop Riordan laid last Sunday. As long as we have such men as the Jesuit Fathers in our midst, lifting up the holy symbol of the Cross as did the missionaries of old, when California was young — lifting up the Cross to charm our sense to lofty thought and pure ideals — as long as we have them, we need not fear for the fate of our country."

After the cornerstone laying ceremony, it would be more than two years before St. Ignatius Church was finally completed. The total building cost was almost $500,000, an extraordinary amount for that era. Although it left the Jesuits deeply in debt for decades, the new church created a priceless symbol of faith in God, faith in the future, and faith in the ultimate success of the Jesuit experiment in San Francisco.

The First Mass in the New St. Ignatius Church

48

AFTER FOUR YEARS OF DISCUSSION AND PLANNING, and another four years of construction, the first Mass in the fifth St. Ignatius Church in San Francisco was celebrated on August 2, 1914. When the new church was finally completed, the total building cost was $477,500, an enormous sum for that decade.

It was the largest church in San Francisco at the time, a position it held until 1971, when St. Mary's Cathedral was erected. Standing on the corner of Fulton Street and Parker Avenue, the church measures 154 feet along Fulton and 263 feet along Parker. Its lofty spires rise to a height of 213 feet, and for decades they were the first edifices seen from ships as they entered the Golden Gate, greeting and bidding welcome to voyagers visiting San Francisco. Indeed, the church was used as a marker on nautical charts for decades. Coincidentally, the newly completed Panama Canal opened to traffic on August 3, 1914, the day after the first Mass was held in the new St. Ignatius Church. Two weeks later, the crew and passengers of the steamship *Arizonan*, the first vessel to arrive in San Francisco via the canal, could see off the starboard bow the new twin spires and crosses of St. Ignatius Church as the ship passed through the Golden Gate.

The architectural style of the church is Italian Renaissance with a façade of Corinthian columns above Ionic columns. The church foundation is concrete, and the exterior material is brick, painted sheet metal, and terra cotta over a steel frame. The extra-thick steel in this frame helped St. Ignatius Church survive the 1989 Loma Prieta earthquake unscathed. The interior of the church is based on early Christian basilica styles and features extensive use of mahogany and white cedar. There are five principal subdivisions within the church: the nave, the east and west aisles, 16 side altar bays, the front portico, and the sanctuary, flanked by two altar bays. The nave is separated from the side aisles by 20 columns, 10 on each side, that rest upon concrete bases approximately four feet high. Another 12 columns grace the sanctuary

The sanctuary of the new St. Ignatius Church, as it appeared at the time of the first Mass on August 2, 1914.

UNIVERSITY OF SAN FRANCISCO ARCHIVES

and are set off by arched wooden panels that separate them one from another. Eighteen clerestory windows and 18 circular windows above the side aisles provide the church with its natural lighting. The seating capacity of the church is 936 in the center pews, 726 in the side pews, and 297 in the gallery, for a total of 1,959.

On the eve of the first service in the new church, the San Francisco *Monitor* captured the importance of the restoration of St. Ignatius Church for San Francisco: "A time is now

The fifth St. Ignatius Church in San Francisco, as it looked between 1914, the year it opened, and 1921, the year Welch Hall was built a few feet to the east of the church. Immediately north of the church is Masonic Cemetery, and further north, across Turk Street, is Lone Mountain, the site of Calvary Cemetery. The San Francisco College for Women was erected on Lone Mountain in 1932. In the distance is the Golden Gate. The Golden Gate Bridge was not completed until 1937.

approaching when San Franciscans will once more gather in a Jesuit church worthy of the great tradition of this country and once more find themselves in a house of worship where, in an unusual degree, art combines with religion to lift man from the sordid realities of life to a sphere of pure and nobler contemplation."

A capacity congregation witnessed the dedication Mass of St. Ignatius Church on August 2, 1914. It was reported by the local press as a magnificent spectacle. Hundreds of candles were lit and shone from the main altar and from the recesses along the body of the church. Surpliced priests and members of various orders and congregations filled the sanctuary. The dedication

began with a procession composed of priests, acolytes, and the presiding prelate, Archbishop Patrick Riordan of San Francisco. The procession went around the outside of the church, then throughout the inside, the Archbishop blessing the edifice as he went. When the procession came to the sacristy, the Bishop of Sacramento, Thomas Grace, began the Mass. The president of St. Ignatius College, Albert Trivelli, S.J., read a cablegram from Pope Pius X, which stated: "On the occasion of the dedication of St. Ignatius Church, the Holy Father earnestly praying that the divine worship may receive splendor and increase, imparts to your Reverence, your fellow religious and the assembled faithful, the Apostolic Blessing." The homilist for the first service, Bishop Edward O'Dea of Seattle, an alumnus of old St. Ignatius College, compared the new church to the rising of the second temple in Jerusalem: "Like it, St. Ignatius Church has gone down in calamity and destruction but it has risen again in appropriate symbolism of Mother Church itself which, like truth, must prevail in spite of every obstacle."

Throughout the day, thousands of individuals visited the new church, admiring it from the inside and outside. As evening came, the church was lit for the first time, and the great twin spires and their crosses could be seen from throughout the city. It was an auspicious day for the Jesuits of San Francisco, who once again had a permanent home. It was also a significant day for the entire California Province; the students, staff, faculty, and alumni of St. Ignatius College; and for the City of San Francisco, with which St. Ignatius Church is historically intertwined.

For Whom the Bell Tolls

49

The St. Ignatius Church bell is pulled from the rubble following the earthquake and fire of April 1906.

CALIFORNIA PROVINCE OF THE
SOCIETY OF JESUS ARCHIVES

THE BELL THAT RINGS TODAY IN ST. IGNATIUS CHURCH FOR its parishioners and for the extended University of San Francisco community also rang for the school and church community in the early years of the institution. One day in August of 1862, Anthony Maraschi, S.J., the founding parish priest of St. Ignatius Church and founding president of St. Ignatius Academy, was strolling through the streets of San Francisco with Burchard Villiger, S.J., who became the third president of St. Ignatius College. The two Jesuits chanced upon the hardware store of Conroy and O'Connor and saw a row of cast steel bells displayed on the sidewalk in front of the store. All of the bells were from England, and the largest of the lot had the inscription "San Francisco" molded into its rim.

Inquiring within, the Jesuits learned that the bell was cast in Sheffield, England, in 1859, and at 6,000 pounds, was the heaviest and largest steel bell produced up to that time in England. The bell was brought around Cape Horn by windjammer in 1860 for use by the Volunteer Fire Company of San Francisco, but the fire company reneged on its order for want of money. Fr. Maraschi decided to buy the bell for his new church and school on Market Street and negotiated a price of $1,350, with unlimited time to pay, from the owners of the hardware store. Fr. Villiger later wrote, "And so we put up a skeleton of a tower of big beams, 30 feet high, in the garden, and placed the bell on its top. We rang it regularly for the college exercises and the Angelus, and its peal resounded for miles around."

Thus the bell began its long history with St. Ignatius Church and College, first in the Jesuits' garden at the original site on Market Street. In 1879, it was moved to the new site for St. Ignatius Church and College, on the corner of Van Ness Avenue and Hayes Street. The bell was placed in a tower of the church on the corner of Franklin and Grove streets. During the 1906 earthquake and fire, the bell crashed through several floors to the basement of the ruined St. Ignatius Church. It was recovered from the smoldering rubble a few weeks later substantially unharmed, however, and was moved by wagon to the Hayes and Shrader streets location, the temporary site of the church and college. There it was tested and installed in a tower of the church. Finally, on July 24, 1914, the historic bell was hoisted to the campanile of the present church, where it summoned San Franciscans to the celebratory first Mass in the new church on August 2, 1914. It still rings there today, sounding the Angelus twice each day, calling people to Sunday Mass, to evening services, and to special church ceremonies. The bells of Mission Dolores are older than the bell of St. Ignatius Church, but they are seldom rung. The bell of St. Ignatius Church is the oldest church bell in constant service in the city of San Francisco.

At noon, on September 11, 2002, the bell summoned the USF community to St. Ignatius Church to attend the Mass of the Holy Spirit as part of the one-year commemoration of the terrorist attacks on the World Trade Center and the Pentagon. In his homily, USF President Stephen A. Privett, S.J., spoke of the human solidarity we feel with the victims of that tragedy, their families, the volunteers and workers who sought to rescue the victims, and the families of those innocent people in Afghanistan who lost their lives in the U.S. bombing after September 11. "We go from this church to our broken world and fractured lives," Fr. Privett said, "and try to put the pieces together, perhaps more slowly and carefully for what we have done here. We leave here in the faith and hope that God's Spirit of unity and reconciliation will animate our lives and this university and connect us to the world at large."

The interconnectedness of the human community is especially salient and poignant during international tragedies when lives are needlessly lost. Likewise, when one's close friend, work colleague, or relative dies, we feel a loss and identification with the deceased. The great 17th-century English poet and minister, John Donne, captured the essence of this identification in his funeral sermon, Devotions Upon Emergent Occasions, with his well-known, yet still moving, line: "Any man's death diminishes me, because I am involved in mankind; and therefore never send to know for whom the bell tolls; it tolls for thee." When the old bell of St. Ignatius Church summons us to a mass during which we mourn those we have lost, we do indeed know for whom the bell tolls.

The Origins of the School of Law

50

THE SEEDS WERE SOWN FOR THE UNIVERSITY OF ST. Ignatius School of Law long before it opened its doors to its first students on September 18, 1912. As early as 1880, Aloysius Brunengo, S.J., initiated a series of lectures at St. Ignatius College for interested students on ethical and natural rights from a legal perspective. By 1900, many of the graduates of St. Ignatius College, including Jeremiah Sullivan, Matthew Sullivan, John Drum, Thomas Hickey, and Joseph Tobin, had become leading members of the San Francisco Bar. These men were all active alumni, were role models for undergraduate students, and began to push for more formal legal education at their alma mater.

In 1909, specialized courses were introduced into the curriculum of St. Ignatius College to prepare students for entrance into law school. This new focus was consistent with a nation-wide trend, which by the early 1900s, saw the medical, legal, and engineering professions demanding greater specialized training and higher educational standards for its members. This demand resulted in a proliferation of schools of law, medicine, and engineering. Many prominent Catholics across the nation and in San Francisco, however, were convinced

In the early 1930s, many of the founders of the University of San Francisco School of Law gathered for a group photograph. They include Eustace Cullinan, Sr., standing fourth from the left; Matthew Sullivan, standing fifth from the right; and Thomas Hickey, standing third from the right. The priest standing in the middle is Edward Whelan, S.J., the president of St. Ignatius College and USF from 1925 to 1932. To the right of Fr. Whelan is James Rolph Jr., the mayor of San Francisco from 1912 to 1931, and a major supporter of the School of Law.

UNIVERSITY OF SAN FRANCISCO ARCHIVES

that the majority of private and public universities were effectively excluding graduates of Catholic institutions from their professional schools. There was considerable historical justification for this perception of discrimination against Catholics.

The roots of anti-Catholicism in America go deep into the nation's history. Throughout the 1820s and 1830s, for example, hostility to immigrants, especially to Irish Catholics and immigrants from other Catholic countries, grew as immigrants poured into Eastern seaport cities, where they competed for jobs and scarce economic and social resources. Newspapers inveighed against Catholic immigrants; riots directed at Irish Catholics broke out in many cities; and a political organization, the Native American Party was formed, calling for the curtailment of immigrants' rights. The party's hostility was directed primarily at the Irish and the Catholic Church. As the number of Irish Catholic immigrants continued to surge on the eve of the Civil War, they increasingly were seen as a threat, and Irish Catholics throughout the nation felt the brunt of religious and ethnic discrimination.

In the 1854 midterm elections, the Native American Party, also known as the Know-Nothings, elected dozens of state legislators and congressmen who ran on an anti-Catholic plank. The hostility toward Catholics continued after the Civil War, especially with the upsurge in immigration from other Catholic countries such as Italy, France, and Poland. Books with anti-Catholic themes abounded; anti-Catholic secret societies were formed; arms and ammunition were collected by these societies and others in anticipation of a supposed Catholic war on Protestants; and forged documents, reputedly issued by the Pope, and calling for the formation of a Catholic army to take over America, were circulated and reprinted in the nation's newspapers.

In California, anti-Catholic prejudice came with many of the gold miners of the late 1840s and 1850s and was widespread. By the early 1900s, help-wanted signs often carried the caveat: No Irish Need Apply. Anti-Catholic attitudes permeated the public schools as well. The Catholic leadership of San Francisco, and the St. Ignatius College alumni who were involved in the creation of the law school, were clearly conscious of this history of anti-Catholicism. Just as the formation of St. Ignatius College and other Catholic colleges across the nation was in part a response to anti-Catholicism, so too, the formation of professional schools connected to Catholic colleges was partly a response to anti-Catholic prejudice. By 1912, many prominent Jesuit colleges, such as St. Louis College, Gonzaga College, and Santa Clara College, had added professional schools and had changed their names to include the word university.

At the commencement exercises of St. Ignatius College, on June 24, 1912, the president of St. Ignatius College, Albert Trivelli, S.J., announced the establishment of a law school and an engineering school, along with a name change for the college, making it a university. The 1911–1912 St. Ignatius College catalog announced this change to the wider world: "Whereas St. Ignatius College has, from its inception, maintained a high standard in the studies of belles lettres and sciences, it has, of late years, introduced incipient courses of law and engineering and it is the purpose of the Faculty to introduce, in the early fall, these two courses in their fullness. Upon formal introduction of these professional branches, the institution will assume the name UNIVERSITY, to which it will then be entitled."

The University of St. Ignatius thus began the fall 1912 semester with an undergraduate College of Letters, Science, and Philosophy; a School of Law; a College of Engineering; and a two-year pre-medical course of study. St. Ignatius High School, officially named as such in 1909, remained connected to the university as a preparatory and feeder school. The College of Engineering was short-lived and closed its program in 1918 for want of students. The School of Law, however, has thrived since its founding.

The First Law Class

51

IN THE EARLY EVENING OF SEPTEMBER 18, 1912, 39 YOUNG men gathered on the fifth floor of the Grant Building, on the corner of Seventh and Market streets in downtown San Francisco. Most of the men were Irish Catholics, first- or second-generation immigrants, and had names like Mahoney, Murphy, Kennedy, and O'Reilly. Many of them were recent graduates of St. Ignatius College and held full-time day jobs. Francis Mannix, class of 1911, was a sports writer for the *San Francisco Bulletin.* An Italian Catholic, Joseph Giannini, a star base- ball player from the class of 1911, worked at the First National Bank. Some of the young men, however, like William Queen and Raymond Feely, were still in their junior year and were completing their bachelor's degrees. What did they all have in common? They comprised the first class of the University of St. Ignatius School of Law, the antecedent of the USF School of Law.

Vincent S. Brown

Paul A. Carew

John M. Deady

Thomas S. Deering

Four graduates from the first class of the School of Law at the University of St. Ignatius appeared in the June 1916 issue of the *Ignatian.*

UNIVERSITY OF SAN FRANCISCO ARCHIVES

Among the 39 students who started law school at the University of St. Ignatius in 1912, 24 graduated within four years, and another seven graduated by 1918: a total of more than 79 percent of the original class. Many went on to long and successful law careers in San Francisco. Two of the graduates, Joseph Golden and Harold Caulfield, would eventually be appointed judges and have distinguished careers on the bench. Raymond Feely (vignette #94) became a Jesuit and later returned to his alma mater and became academic vice president. One of the first-year students who did not readily fit the demographic profile of the rest was Chan C. Wing. In 1918, he became the first Asian American to be admit- ted to the bar in California.

From its founding, the law school had a practical orientation, scheduling classes for students who could not afford to quit their jobs. It sought to meet the needs of an urban, educated, middle-class population of students seeking professional status. In this regard, the University of St. Ignatius School of Law occupied a market niche midway between two types of schools of the era. At one end, the University of California at Berkeley School of Law (Boalt Hall), which was established in 1894, and the Stanford University School of Law, founded in 1893, oper- ated strictly day programs. At the other end of the continuum, the San Francisco

A new City Hall, to replace the one destroyed in the 1906 earthquake and fire, was under construction in September of 1912, when the first law class of the University of St. Ignatius began their studies on the fifth floor of the Grant Building, on the corner of Seventh and Market streets in downtown San Francisco. From the windows of the Grant Building, students had this view of City Hall during the spring semester of 1914. Years later, many of the graduates of that first law class would serve in the courts and offices of City Hall.

Three other graduates of the first law class of the University of St. Ignatius, from the June 1916 *Ignatian*.

Law School and the Oakland College of Law, both proprietary schools, offered evening programs, and accepted anyone who showed up with the money to pay the tuition, irrespective of educational background.

During the first term, the first law class of the University of St. Ignatius read the commentaries of Blackstone, Kent, and Robinson's *Elements of American Jurisprudence*. During their three years of law school, the students took courses covering topics such as elements of law, real and personal property, contracts, personal and domestic relations, torts, criminal law, corporations, probate, equity, constitutional law, international and admiralty law, water rights and mining, public service companies, evidence, and pleading and practice. The law students also received instruction in oratory, logic, psychology, parliamentary law, and ethics.

When not in class or studying, the law students could take breaks at a nearby pub, such as Dierks and von Parten's Bar on Market Street. After classes ended at 9 P.M., students might drop by the Imperial Theatre to watch a silent movie starring America's sweetheart, Mary Pickford.

For its first three years, this first class, and the two classes that followed, took their course work at the Grant Building on Market Street. From their fifth-floor windows, they could watch the construction of the massive dome on the new city hall that was to replace the one destroyed in the 1906 earthquake and fire. It was completed in December 1915. In 1917, the School of Law moved to the "shirt factory," on the corner of Hayes and Shrader streets, where St. Ignatius College had "temporarily" relocated after the 1906 earthquake and fire. In the evenings, the law students took over the rambling and labyrinthine structure that was occupied during the day by the students from the St. Ignatius grammar school, high school, and college.

After graduation from the University of St. Ignatius, or concurrently with their junior year in the university, many of those students began courses at the law school.

Raymond T. Feely

In 1952, at a banquet celebrating the 40th anniversary of the founding of the School of Law, Preston Devine, a prominent alumnus and justice on the California Court of Appeals, highlighted the connection between the opening of the law school and the rebuilding of the city of San Francisco: "This opening, only six short years after the disaster of 1906,

Maurice E. Fitzgibbon

was an example of the enterprising spirit of the college itself. From that moment on, the threads of the college history were destined to be rewoven into the fabric of the rebuilt city of San Francisco."

Jos. M. Golden

The First Law School Faculty

52

THE FACULTY MEMBERS WHO TAUGHT THE FIRST CLASSES at the University of St. Ignatius School of Law were active in politics and associated with the municipal reform movement in San Francisco during the first decades of the 20th century. They were generally products of the large Irish Catholic community, and in many cases, they were graduates of St. Ignatius College. Most were also active in Catholic causes.

The law faculty, all of whom taught on a part-time basis, included several prominent San Francisco attorneys and judges. One notable part-time faculty member, for example, was Superior Court Judge Jeremiah Sullivan, of the class of 1870, who was later elevated to the California Supreme Court (vignette #24).

His brother, Matthew Sullivan, class of 1876, served as the first dean of the University of St. Ignatius School of Law and later was appointed Chief Justice of the California Supreme Court (vignette #53).

Benjamin McKinley, who taught equity and constitutional law, earned bachelor's and

Benjamin McKinley's constitutional law class in 1916, held on the fifth floor of the old Grant Building, on the corner of Seventh and Market Streets. In addition to teaching at the law school, McKinley served as an assistant U.S. attorney in San Francisco.

UNIVERSITY OF SAN FRANCISCO ARCHIVES

master's degrees from St. Ignatius College, was a leader in the Catholic temperance movement, and was appointed assistant U.S. attorney by his cousin, William McKinley, the president of the United States. John O'Gara, who taught a course on evidence, was active in the Democratic Party, was a leader in local reform politics, and was appointed by the Bar Association president, Jeremiah Sullivan, as one of four attorneys to investigate corruption among several police court judges in San Francisco. William Breen, a partner in Matthew Sullivan's law firm, taught a course in probate and later was appointed a probate judge. Joseph Farry taught at the law school and for a period served as the secretary to the Board of Consultors of the University of St. Ignatius. This board was the precursor to USF's Board of Trustees. Stanislaus Riley taught a course on sales and was the assistant attorney general for San Francisco. His claim to fame, however, rests on his efforts to organize a nationwide campaign to recognize Good Friday as a national holiday. He began his campaign in San Francisco, where he organized the Reverend Observance of Good Friday Association, a lay organization that convinced many local business managers to close their businesses on Good Friday afternoon from noon to 3 P.M.

Key individuals in San Francisco city government and politics also served as special lecturers at the law school during its first two decades. Several of the special lecturers were associated with James Rolph, who became the city's mayor in 1912, the same year the law school was founded. "Sunny Jim" Rolph served as mayor for almost 20 years and maintained close ties with the law school and the leadership of St. Ignatius College. In 1913, the mayor's chief adviser and negotiator, Eustace Cullinan, gave the first special lecture at the new law school. It was titled "The Roman Law," and it attracted a large audience of students, faculty, attorneys, and community members.

Another special law school lecturer was Theodore Roche, Matthew and Jeremiah Sullivan's law partner. Roche was later appointed police commissioner by Mayor Rolph. Thomas Hickey, an attorney who occasionally lectured at the law school, was a St. Ignatius College alumnus and chairman of the San Francisco Democratic Convention. In 1928, Hickey seconded the Democratic Party's nomination of Al Smith for United States president, the first Catholic to be nominated for that office.

The December 1912 edition of the *Ignatian,* the University of St. Ignatius literary magazine, waxed eloquent about the new law school faculty. "A glance at the faculty of the College of Law," the magazine proclaimed, "justifies the most roseate expectations of future success. Indeed, if the professors instill into the students the principles and knowledge wherewith they built for themselves such successful careers, it will not be long ere St. Ignatius Law Department will become famous." The expectations of the *Ignatian* were justified; four years later, the April 1916 issue of that magazine reported that the School of Law "boasts the largest attendance of the seven law colleges situated about the Bay." Further, the School of Law "has now a complete curriculum of regular and special courses, and numbers over 150 students."

The prominent men who were the law school's first faculty members and special lecturers served as significant role models for the law students, later helped many of those students secure their first jobs, and instilled in them a pride in and loyalty to their alma mater, the city of San Francisco, and the idea that the law can be a powerful tool for political reform.

Matthew Sullivan

53

FEW INDIVIDUALS IN THE HISTORY OF THE LEGAL
community of San Francisco have commanded more respect than
Matthew Sullivan, a graduate of St. Ignatius College. He was a
prominent attorney, founding dean of the University of St. Ignatius
School of Law, and in 1914 was appointed chief justice of the California
Supreme Court.

Matthew Sullivan, graduate of
St. Ignatius College, prominent
San Francisco attorney, president
of the alumni society, founding dean
of the law school, and chief justice
of the California Supreme Court.

UNIVERSITY OF SAN FRANCISCO ARCHIVES

Matthew Sullivan was born on November 3,
1857, to Irish Catholic immigrants living in
Grass Valley, California. In 1862, his parents,
five sisters, and older brother moved to San
Francisco. Matthew first entered a parochial
school attached to the old Mission Dolores
Church, later attended a public primary school
in the Mission district, and in 1868 entered St.
Ignatius College, from which he received his
bachelor of arts degree in 1876. After graduation, he commenced law studies in the office of
Jeremiah Sullivan, his older brother. Jeremiah,
also a graduate of St. Ignatius College, later
became a superior court judge, faculty member
at the University of St. Ignatius School of
Law, and justice of the California Supreme
Court (vignette #24). After two years of study
in Jeremiah's office, Matthew entered Hastings
Law College on its opening day in 1878. In
1879, he was admitted to the California bar.
When Jeremiah was elected judge of the San
Francisco Superior Court in 1879, Matthew
took over his brother's flourishing law practice.
The law practice continued to thrive, and in
1900 Jeremiah resigned from the superior court
bench and rejoined his brother in establishing
one of the most successful law partnerships in
San Francisco.

The official positions held by Matthew Sullivan from 1893 to 1912 included attorney for the sheriff of San Francisco, assistant to the district attorney of San Francisco, and assistant to the attorney general of the United States. In these positions, Sullivan was successful in prosecuting numerous cases involving civic corruption, and he became involved in various Progressive reform movements to clean up civic government and to elect reform candidates to office. When prosecutor Francis Heney was shot down in court during the trial of political boss Abe Ruef, Matthew Sullivan and Hiram Johnson voluntarily replaced Heney, and won Ruef's conviction. In 1907, Sullivan, along with 15 other citizens, was appointed by Mayor Edward Taylor as a county supervisor to administer the affairs of the city in the wake of the resignation of 16 supervisors who admitted to accepting bribes. In 1912, Governor Hiram Johnson appointed Sullivan to represent California at the Panama Pacific International Exposition, held in San Francisco in 1915, and to manage the $5 million budget for that event.

Throughout his legal career, Matthew Sullivan, along with his brother, Jeremiah, remained active in the affairs of St. Ignatius College and helped found the alumni association, for which Jeremiah served as the first president. In 1905, Matthew was honored with an LL.D. degree on the occasion of the golden jubilee of the college. For years, the Sullivan brothers, along with other alumni who became attorneys and judges, pushed for the establishment of a law school at their alma mater. These efforts came to fruition in 1912 with the establishment of the University of St. Ignatius School of Law. Matthew Sullivan was named the first dean. He also taught classes at the law school, and his name brought enormous respect and prestige to the institution. He also served as president of the alumni association and facilitated the purchase from the Masonic Cemetery Association of 14 acres of cemetery land, where much of USF now stands.

In 1914, Governor Hiram Johnson appointed Matthew Sullivan chief justice of the California Supreme Court, to hold office until the next general election. One week before the election, his associate justices requested him to submit his name to the electorate, and the justices also sent out a public letter, which stated: "The undersigned, justices of the Supreme Court, without the slightest reflecting upon the candidacy of any other man for the position, believe and declare that the best interests of the court demand the election of Hon. Matt. I. Sullivan, present Chief Justice for this term." As a result of this expression of confidence by his judicial associates, 45,000 voters wrote his name on the ballot, and he was elected chief justice. After his retirement from the California Supreme Court, until his death in 1937, Matthew Sullivan remained active in sponsoring legislation beneficial to San Francisco, directing his successful law practice, and championing causes related to his alma mater, which in 1930 was renamed the University of San Francisco.

SEVENTEENTH

ANNUAL COMMENCEMENT

OF

St. Ignatius College,

Held Friday, June 2, 1876.

CONFERRING OF DEGREES.

The Degree of **MASTER OF ARTS** is Conferred on
JAMES I. BOLAND, A. B.,
JOHN T. FOGARTY, A. B.

The Degree of **BACHELOR OF ARTS** is Conferred on
THOMAS BOLAND,
MATTHEW SULLIVAN,
ALFRED TOBIN.

The Degree of **BACHELOR OF SCIENCE** is Conferred on
JOHN W. STATELER,
WILLIAM I. FOLEY.

Matthew Sullivan graduated from St. Ignatius College in 1876 and was among the seven students listed in the announcement of the 17th Annual Commencement Ceremony.

The First World War Begins

54

THE SEVEN MEMBERS OF THE BLACK HAND, A SERBIAN nationalist terrorist group, were hidden in the crowd lining the streets of Sarajevo, the capital of Bosnia, on that fateful Sunday, June 28, 1914. They were waiting for the parade and motorcade of Archduke Franz-Ferdinand, heir apparent to the throne of the Austro-Hungarian Empire. The terrorists were all young men, ages 19 to 27; four were college students. Their goal was to assassinate Archduke Ferdinand, an act they thought would help liberate the southern Slavic regions of Europe, including Bosnia, from the control of the Austro-Hungarian Empire.

As the black convertible sedan carrying Ferdinand and his wife, Sophia, passed along the parade route, one of the terrorists lobbed a grenade at the archduke's car, but it missed, striking another vehicle. The crowd scattered, and the parade came to a halt. When the parade resumed in an hour, the archduke's driver made a wrong turn down a side street, stopping in front of a delicatessen. Standing in front of the delicatessen was Gavrilo Princip, the 19-year-old leader of the terrorist group. Gavrilo hesitated for a moment, stepped forward, turned his head away, and fired two shots from his pistol into the archduke's open car, killing Franz-Ferdinand and his wife.

There were a multitude of underlying causes for World War I: militarism; imperialism; competition among the major European powers for colonies and markets; secret alliances; and perhaps most important, the fever of nationalism. The nationalistic desire of the peoples of the world to belong to autonomous social and political entities called nations had become, by the early 20th century, the most decisive force on the international political stage. In the Balkans, nationalistic forces were catalyzed in 1908 when Austria annexed Bosnia and Herzegovina, still nominally part of the old Ottoman (Turkish) Empire and inhabited largely by Serbs. Soon after this annexation, the Balkan Wars broke out, involving Bulgaria, Serbia, Greece, Montenegro, and Turkey. The major European powers took sides in the conflict, alliances were formed, and when Archduke Ferdinand was assassinated, Austria declared war on Serbia, which had alliances with Russia and France. Germany, which had an alliance with Austria, then

Charles Wiseman graduated from the University of St. Ignatius in 1917 and immediately joined the United States Navy. Many of his letters about his World War I military service were published in the *Ignatian,* the school's literary magazine.

UNIVERSITY OF SAN FRANCISCO ARCHIVES

Wm H. Lasater

Charles P. McVe...

Geo. W. Ross

Three former students from the University of St. Ignatius, as USF was then called, who were killed during the First World War and were memorialized by gold stars on the university's service flag and in the June 1918 issue of the *Ignatian*.

UNIVERSITY OF SAN FRANCISCO ARCHIVES

actually started, it seemed horrible, but far away. The university's literary magazine, the *Ignatian,* in its editorial of December 1914, commented on the plight of Belgium and encouraged donations to its people: "The shame of it all," the editorial declared, "is that the Belgians through no fault of their own have been the sufferers. Mothers torn from their sons, fathers from their children, blooming gardens trampled beneath the feet of a rude soldiery, cottages raised by shell or fire, such is the terrible, heart-rending picture that Belgium presents. The little country, perhaps the wealthiest in all Europe, has been swept from frontier to frontier with the blight of war, leaving behind scenes that nothing, not even time, will ever efface."

As the young men of the University of St. Ignatius returned to school for the fall semester of 1914, little did they know that in less than three years, hundreds of them would be joining thousands of other Americans at war in Europe. The students and young alumni of the University of St. Ignatius, mostly first- and second-generation Europeans, would find themselves fighting alongside or against other young men, also of European ancestry, in the bloodiest war in human history up to that time. The university itself would experience a significant drop in enrollment due to the military draft and the call for volunteers, a harbinger of the precipitous enrollment decline during World War II. During World War I, the institution established a federally sponsored army-training program on campus, a precedent for the army-training program during World War II and for today's ROTC program. In student debates and publications, the institution would for the first time consider issues of war and peace on an international scale, and tragically, 10 young men from the University of St. Ignatius would not return from the "War to End All Wars."

declared war on Russia and France. On August 4, 1914, Germany invaded Belgium, and Britain declared war on Germany.

Six thousand miles away in San Francisco, the students of the University of St. Ignatius were on summer break when war erupted in Europe. Like most Americans, they had known that war in Europe was likely, yet when it

While the War Raged in Europe

ON DECEMBER 28, 1915, MAYOR JAMES ROLPH DEDICATED A new city hall in San Francisco, marking the final major civic restoration in the wake of the 1906 earthquake and fire. The new building was cater-corner from where St. Ignatius Church and College had stood before the 1906 disaster. On February 20, 1915, to celebrate the rebirth of the city and the completion of the Panama Canal, the Panama Pacific International Exposition opened in San Francisco. It was financially managed by Matthew Sullivan, dean of the University of St. Ignatius School of Law. The exposition secured the participation of 25 countries and 29 U.S. states, covered 635 acres of San Francisco's northern waterfront, attracted nearly 20 million people, and was a great financial success for its sponsors.

In Europe, during the same year, World War I reached new levels of brutality: the Germans used poisonous chlorine gas at the second Battle of Ypres, its first use by any warring power; German submarines began a blockade of Britain; torpedoes from a German submarine sank the munitions-carrying British passenger liner *Lusitania* off the coast of Ireland, killing 1,198 people, including 128 Americans; and the Allies suffered 145,000 casualties, mostly Australians and New Zealanders in a failed attempt to invade Turkey's Gallipoli Peninsula.

The University of St. Ignatius literary magazine, the *Ignatian,* pointed out the contrast between life in San Francisco during the year of the Panama Pacific Exposition and the brutality of the war in Europe. "Thanks to San Franciscan's progressiveness and courage," the December 1915 issue of the *Ignatian* proclaimed, "we have one of the most popular, and one of the most successful expositions that will ever go down in the pages of history." The writer was confident "that the year 1915 will loom up with epochal greatness in the long roll-call of centuries, for while the demon of war swept over the battlefields of Europe, plundering every evidence of human achievement in its bloody path, a staggering blow was being dealt in behalf of civilization by an Exposition held on the western shores of a nation over which the Dove of Peace still lingered—a proclamation to the world that happiness and peaceful pursuits still swayed the hearts of men."

While the war raged in Europe, the University of St. Ignatius continued its many peaceful pursuits. Almost a decade earlier, the institution had relocated to the "shirt factory" on the corner of Hayes and Shrader streets. On August 15, 1915, Patrick Foote, S.J., a former student at

The Palace of Fine Arts is the sole survivor of the 32 plaster buildings erected for the 1915 Panama Pacific Exposition, held in San Francisco while World War I raged in Europe. An editorial in the December 1915 issue of the *Ignatian* contrasted the horrors of war in Europe with the peaceful pursuits of the citizens of San Francisco, represented by the Panama Pacific Exposition. The *Ignatian* included this photo of the Palace of Fine Arts and some of the adjacent exposition buildings.

St. Ignatius College when it was located on Market Street, was installed as the institution's 15th president. Fr. Foote was the first former student of the college to be so honored. Students soon identified him with his motto: "Be sociable, be studious, be systematic." The students saw the new president's sociability, expressed in his Christian charity; his studiousness, exemplified by his philosophical writing; and his systematic approach, reflected in his administration of the school's departments. During the 1915 fall semester, the university's debating societies were especially active. More than 40 students, for example, were enrolled in the Philalethic Debating Society, with the war in Europe providing a major source of topics. The Senior Philhistorian Debating Society spent a portion of the semester preparing for a series of debates with the University of Santa Clara. The University of Saint Igantius orchestra and band diligently practiced and performed a number of pieces for the community. The university's engineering students attended the International Engineering Congress held in San Francisco's Civic Center Auditorium, while the law students prepared for their forthcoming moot court. In athletics, the varsity rugby team became the "undisputed champions" of San Francisco, securing victories over teams from the Olympic Club, the College of the Pacific, and other Bay Area institutions. There were also school picnics during the fall, vividly reported by the *Ignatian*. During one such picnic, a "happy crowd of boys motored down the peninsula bound for Woodside, that enchanting spot nestled among the foothills of Redwood City. Football, baseball, swimming and racing were the order of the day. It was a tired but happy crowd of boys that returned up the peninsula that evening under the glow of a rich Indian-summer sunset."

In less than two years, many St. Ignatius students would find such idyllic picnics, along with the other activities of college life, replaced by trenches, barbed wire, artillery, machine guns, mud, and death on the Western Front of Europe.

56

The *Ignatian* Describes America's Entrance Into the War

"WAR IS SYMBOLIC OF ALL that is evil, low, and debased in our nature," declared the *Ignatian*, the literary magazine of the University of St. Ignatius, in its April 1916 issue. "To believe that men of the twentieth century," the editorial continued, "could hurl themselves at one another in the fury of hate, animated by a horrible, sickening lust for blood, augurs poorly for our much-vaunted civilization. Is that civilization a veneer," the editorial asked, "to cover an interior fulsome disease?"

The November 1917 issue of the *Ignatian* published an honor roll of those former students from St. Ignatius College who were serving in the U.S. military during World War I. Heading the list was Brig. Gen. Charles McKinstry, St. Ignatius College class of 1884, the highest ranking officer at the time.

By 1916, the disease of war continued to engulf Europe, and it began to spread to the rest of the world. The human losses on the battlefield were staggering. The Battle of Verdun on the Western Front, from February to July 1916, took 350,000 French lives and almost as many German lives. The Battle of the Somme, from July to September, was the bloodiest in human history. The 140-day offensive by the Allies in France involved 3 million men fighting along a 20-mile front. Virtually no land was gained by either side, but the Allies lost 794,000 men and the Central Powers lost 538,888. More of Europe was also drawn into the war during 1916: Germany and Austria declared war on Portugal, Romania on Austria, and Italy on Germany.

In the United States, the administration of President Woodrow Wilson initially adopted a policy of neutrality toward the warring nations of Europe, urging Americans to be "neutral in fact as well as in name." Even after the sinking of the British passenger liner the *Lusitania* by a German submarine and the consequent loss of 128 Americans, President Wilson stood by his neutrality. "There is such a thing," the president told one audience, "as a man being too proud to fight. There is such a thing as a nation being so right that it does not need to convince others by force."

In the 1916 presidential election, the Democrats campaigned for the reelection of Wilson on the slogan, "He kept us out of war!" Most Americans agreed with Wilson's policy, and he narrowly defeated his Republican opponent, Charles Evans Hughes. The editorial staff of the *Ignatian* endorsed Wilson's policy of neutrality, though it questioned how neutral the administration truly was since it permitted American manufacturers to ship munitions to the Allies. The February 1917 issue called this policy "a peculiar sort of neutrality to be furnishing one side of belligerents with the means of carrying on this gruesome business, while affording no similar aid to their enemies."

Ultimately, Germany's attempt through submarine warfare to stop the flow of war materials from America to Britain was a key factor that propelled the United States into World War I. In January 1917, the German high command resumed unrestricted U-boat attacks on all shipping. In the same month, the British intercepted a coded wireless message from the German foreign secretary, Arthur von Zimmerman, to the German ambassador in Washington, stating that in the event of war, Germany would propose an alliance with Mexico, including the potential recovery by Mexico of its lost territory in Texas, New Mexico,

Ten former St. Ignatius College students were killed during World War I. Many others received the Purple Heart, the U.S. military decoration awarded to servicemen wounded in action.

and Arizona. This message was forwarded by Britain to the United States and buttressed the already successful Allied propaganda efforts against Germany. Stories of atrocities against the Belgian people by the invading German army, promulgated by the British press, had already helped secure considerable American support for the Allied cause. Like many American publications during the early years of the war in Europe, the *Ignatian* carried vivid descriptions of the plight of Belgium at the hands of German troops (vignette #54). Economics also played an important role in America's entry into the war: the flow of American goods, money, and credit to the Allies far exceeded that to the Central Powers, consequently leading to a stronger economic investment in an Allied victory. In the end, however, the resumption of submarine warfare, soon followed by the sinking of three American ships, was the catalyst that caused the United States to sever relations with Germany on February 3 and to declare war on that country on April 6, 1917.

After Congress declared war on Germany, the editorial pages of the *Ignatian* called for unity behind the war effort, notwithstanding its earlier opposition to war and its advocacy of neutrality. "Let us all get behind President Wilson," the magazine urged, "with a determination to do what he asks. Let us show the world that the United States are really united, that they are supporting the Government to a man. When we have done this our part will be finished. The rest we must leave to Him who guides the destinies of men." Over the next 18 months, the destinies of many of the students and recent graduates of the university would be altered forever, and the institution itself would undergo profound changes.

The St. Ignatius Campus During the First World War

57

THE POIGNANT SOUND OF TAPS PLAYED BY A SOLE BUGLER of the University of St. Ignatius Students Army Training Corps floated across the campus at 10 o'clock on that October evening in 1918. The notes he played resonated throughout the halls of the labyrinth building near the corner of Hayes and Shrader streets that comprised the university, then known as the "shirt factory." The sounds of this military composition also symbolized major changes at the University of St. Ignatius, catalyzed by World War I.

Four University of St. Ignatius students who served in World War I: (left to right) Wallace Sheehan, Fred Butler, Joseph Sullivan, and Mark Devine. Their photos appeared in the June 1918 issue of the *Ignatian*.

UNIVERSITY OF SAN FRANCISCO ARCHIVES

The essence of these transformations was captured several months earlier in the June 1918 issue of the *Ignatian:* "It certainly is a fact," one writer noted, "that lively patriotism and the military spirit have come to claim their dominant place at St. Ignatius, where formerly 'school spirit' was the principle of activity. Many of our undergraduates have followed the example of the alumni in joining the colors."

Already undergoing declining enrollment due to the economic conditions in the Bay Area, the university saw even greater declines due to students electing to join the war effort. In 1913, the year before the war began in Europe, enrollment had slipped to 44 students in the undergraduate College of Letters, Science, and Philosophy; 204 students in the high school division; and 148 in the grammar school division (seventh and eighth grades). The new School of Law was the only bright spot on the enrollment landscape, having increased from 39 students in 1912, the year it opened, to 68 students the next year. The College of Engineering, which also started in 1912, never had more than a handful of students, and in 1918 it was discontinued. After the United States declared war on Germany in April 1917 and the Selective Service bill was passed by Congress in May of that year, the number of students at the university who were 18 or older declined to less than 100.

By early June 1917, more than 9 million young American men had registered with local officials whom the War Department authorized to supervise the draft. Before the war ended in November 1918, almost 3 million men had been inducted into the army. In addition, 2 million Americans volunteered for the various armed services. Nearly 400 students or recent graduates from the University of St. Ignatius volunteered or were drafted to serve in one of the branches of the military. In August 1918, the president of the university, Patrick Foote, S.J., announced that the United States Commissioner of Education had requested that as many young men as possible should stay in college to receive government-supervised military training and qualify as officers. This announcement effectively stopped the decline in the institution's enrollment. On September 6, 1918, students were informed that the University of St. Ignatius had been accepted as a unit in the national Students Army Training Corps. This was the predecessor of the Reserve Officer Training Corps (ROTC), which continues today at the University of San Francisco and is administered by the USF Military Science Department.

On September 16, 1918, Lieutenant Arthur Mohr of the United States Army reported to the University of St. Ignatius as the first commanding officer of the Students Army Training Corps. The program was officially announced on October 1, the first military drill occurred on October 7, and by the end of October, the unit was in full operation. The many students who were not of draft age, and who thus could not be part of the military

training program, participated in other war-related activities on campus, including volunteer work with the Red Cross, food conservation programs, and Thrift Stamp, War Saving, and Liberty Bond drives. The campus itself was decorated with service flags, Red Cross information, War Saving notices, Liberty Bond posters, and other war-related information.

Occasionally, a former student briefly returned to campus from a training program in another part of the country. One such former student, Lt. Mark Devine, surprised his one-time classmates when he returned to San Francisco from training at Fort Leavenworth, Kansas, prior to shipping out for France. The *Ignatian* reported that Lieutenant Devine's "return was welcomed by all the fellows with a greeting of Rahs! and cheers," and "he was accorded a place of honor with the faculty" for the day. At the suggestion of one of the Jesuits, "he was unanimously yielded the floor in the Sophomore and Freshman English class, where he delivered an interesting lecture concerning his experiences and his studies at Leavenworth." The writer concluded that "Lieutenant Devine left for 'over there' soon after. Then one day the Fathers at St. Ignatius received the significant little card, stating that he had arrived safely in France." The writer ended with "Over the top, Mark, and the best of luck."

Lt. Devine's luck held out during the war, and he safely returned from Europe. Such was not the case for 10 other former students from the University of St. Ignatius.

Letters from the Front

58

DURING WORLD WAR I, THE students and young alumni of the University of St. Ignatius who served in America's armed forces often portrayed their overseas experiences in graphic detail. This depiction of life during the war was frequently in the form of letters published in the *Ignatian,* the university's literary magazine. The letters told of their military training, the trip on board ships to Europe, boredom, homesickness, the devastated French countryside, trench warfare, artillery attacks, the use of poison gas, and the death of fellow human beings.

Captain Joseph Sullivan, a former star football player, described the fighting in a letter to his brother that was later published in the *Ignatian.* "They threw the picked Prussian Guard divisions against us," Captain Sullivan wrote about one battle, and "they pounded us with artillery and machine-gun barrages till the very air seemed to be so filled with flying lead that there was not room for more. And they showered us with gas, so that our breathing apparatus became null and void." Captain

Richard Queen, St. Ignatius Class of 1912, one of the many servicemen from World War I, whose letters were published in the *Ignatian.* The photo of First Sergeant Queen appears in the June 1919 issue.

UNIVERSITY OF SAN FRANCISCO ARCHIVES

Sullivan and his men were pounded for eight hours in their trenches before receiving orders to attack. When the orders finally came, the battalion rose out of the trenches and charged toward the Germans. The enemy "had direct fire on us with artillery, and it was deadly. He enfiladed us from the flanks and from the left rear as we progressed, and when we reached our objective the battalion was reduced to 200 men under the command of a Lieutenant. The Major was wounded, I was wounded, and Capt. Ed. Leonard, Class of 1917, was dead." Felled by his wound, Captain Sullivan looked around to see men "strewn over the battlefield." Sullivan recovered from his wounds, but he concluded his letter, "I'm sick of war, its havoc, its ruin and destruction."

Another former student, John Carson, described in a letter to his mother, the burial ceremonies for three American soldiers who were killed in battle and interred during a religious and military ceremony: "An altar was improvised and elaborately decorated in the village, and the chaplain of a French regiment conducted the church services in the presence of a large number of troops." Following the church ceremony, the funeral cortege proceeded to a field adjacent to the village, the bodies were placed in front of the grave, and the American flag was placed over the caskets. A French general then arrived, the troops presented arms, and a French band played a funeral march. The chaplain performed a ceremony at the grave, and the French general addressed the troops. At the conclusion of the general's speech, three volleys were fired, taps were sounded, and the general, his staff, and all of the troops marched by the grave, saluting as they passed. "Thus ended," Carson wrote, "one of the most impressive ceremonies that one could ever hope to witness."

Richard Queen, class of 1912, also served in World War I. He was in the second division of the American Expeditionary Forces, a unit that sustained 10 percent of the total American casualties during the war. In May 1918, Sgt.

Queen published a letter in the *Ignatian* that portrayed the front as a "blasted hell" where "shattered trees are trying to bloom." He described how "wild violets, dandelions, and all sorts of summer beauties pop up over night in shell holes which are not gassed. Every dead soldier pushes up verdure and bloom." In June 1918, Sgt. Queen fell victim to a mustard gas attack. He survived the gas, spent more than a month recovering in a French hospital, and was sent back into combat. In one battle, he described lying in a trench a few hundred yards from the German line during a massive artillery attack. "Like a San Francisco earthquake," he wrote, the ground "roared and shook" from the "overwhelming barrage which guns of all calibres from 75s to 355s lay upon the enemy in front of us. None can imagine what the dread barrage is in fact, but one who has fought under it." He survived the war and received several decorations for bravery from the French government. These military decorations notwithstanding, he concluded one letter with "God grant the world will not soon see again a like nightmare to the war!"

St. Ignatius Church Blesses Those Who Served

59

THE ILLUMINATED CROSSES ON THE STEEPLES OF ST. Ignatius Church shown brightly through the thin fog that enveloped the surrounding neighborhood on the evening of May 12, 1918. It was the date of a special church ceremony to bless a service flag for those students and alumni of the University of St. Ignatius who were then fighting and dying in World War I. The nearly 4-year-old church, on the corner of Fulton Street and Parker Avenue, had celebrated its first Mass on August 2, 1914, two days before the major powers of Europe began hostilities in what became the bloodiest conflict in human history up to that time. By April 1917, much of the rest of the world, including the United States, had been drawn into the war. Ultimately, 2 million Americans served in the military during World War I, including 380 students, alumni, and faculty (Frank Lessman, professor of engineering) from the university.

Rev. Joseph Gleason, recipient of a master's degree from St. Ignatius College in 1888, delivered the sermon in St. Ignatius Church on May 12, 1918, during a special ceremony to bless a service flag honoring the students and alumni of the University of St. Ignatius who fought and died in World War I. The photo of Rev. Gleason appears in the *Ignatian*, June 1918.

UNIVERSITY OF SAN FRANCISCO ARCHIVES

The church began to fill with people in the early evening of May 12, long before the scheduled time of the special ceremony. As people arrived, they beheld the sanctuary and altar, decorated with red and white carnations and blue flag lilies. The inside dome above the sanctuary was brightly lighted and draped on both sides by two large American flags. At 8:30, a procession emerged from the sacristy behind the sanctuary. The procession slowly passed in front of the altar rail and moved up the steps to the sanctuary. The procession included 40 acolytes, attired in red cassocks; a line of priests, also in cassocks; two military chaplains, in full military dress uniforms; and two former St. Ignatius students, Lieutenants Vincent Butler and Eugene Conway, both in military uniforms.

When the members of the procession were in their places, the church choir sang "God Bless Our Flag," a hymn composed by Joseph Riordan, S.J., a former student. As the hymn

Exterior view of St. Ignatius Church in 1917, during the nation's involvement in World War I.

Alto, and national chaplain of the Spanish-American War Veterans, moved to the pulpit and gave a sermon on the meaning of the service flag. The actual blessing of the flag was conducted by Fr. Joseph McQuaide, chaplain of the San Francisco Presidio, who, with the assistance of two aides, sprinkled holy water on the outstretched banner while praying for God's protection for all of the young men represented by the stars on the flag.

A writer for the *Ignatian* described what happened after Fr. McQuaide's blessing: "As tears filled the eyes of many onlookers," wrote William Sweigert, "as just pride kindled in the eyes of students, alumni and faculty members, and as the majestic tones of the 'Star-Spangled Banner' brought all to attention, the flag was slowly raised to a place above the altar." This was followed by a choir song, written especially for the occasion by Vincent Hallinan, class of 1919, who years later became one of the most prominent and controversial attorneys in the history of San Francisco. Hallinan's song was set to music by professor Albert Schuh. The service concluded with a Benediction of the Blessed Sacrament.

St. Ignatius Church served during World War I, as it had in the past and would in the future, as the focal point for the extended university community to come together to pray, to offer blessings to those members of the community who were not present, and to assist people in finding meaning in those events that transformed their lives.

ended, a military band, occupying the upper gallery at the back of the church, played John Philip Sousa's "Stars and Stripes Forever." As the last note from this piece died away, eight uniformed soldiers, all graduates of St. Ignatius, marched down the center aisle of the church, carrying an enormous and specially commissioned service flag, which they draped on the altar steps. The banner had a red border, white field, and 378 blue stars, each star representing a student or alumnus who had served in the military up to that point in the war. Three of the blue stars were set in gold, representing the three former students who had already died in the war.

After the service flag was positioned, the church choir sang "Veni Creator," and Rev. Joseph Gleason, St. Ignatius College class of 1887, pastor of St. Thomas Church in Palo

Armistice

60

ON NOVEMBER 11, 1918, AN ARMISTICE ENDING WORLD War I was signed by Germany and the Allies. The human losses from the war were almost beyond comprehension: nearly 10 million soldiers died in combat, another 3 million men were missing and presumed dead, and millions of European civilians died from military actions, disease, and starvation. A pernicious strain of influenza, the Spanish flu, began among the soldiers stationed in Europe at the close of the war. It rapidly spread to the civilian population and became a worldwide epidemic. By 1920, the influenza epidemic had taken nearly 20 million lives. In the United States alone, 500,000 perished, including approximately 3,500 citizens of San Francisco. Among the dead of World War I were 112,432 American servicemen, half of whom died of the influenza that swept through military camps in Europe and America.

The June 1919 issue of the *Ignatian* listed the names of all 380 students, alumni, and faculty who served in World War I, including the names of the 10 young men from the university who died. The editorial of that issue also acknowledged the veterans' return from the war and offered prayers for those young men who would never return: "To our veterans returned to civil life, we extend the hand of welcome, and wish them every success; for our honored dead, while we express our heartfelt sympathy to their dear relatives in their loss, we pray God to crown their heroic deaths with the undying laurels of eternal life."

With the armistice in November, the Students Army Training Corps at the university began to disband, and by the end of 1918, it was completely demobilized. As the veterans began to return to their university, Dionysius Mahoney, S.J., minister of the Jesuit Community, was prompted to note in his diary that the "old order of things is steadily returning." The June 1919 issue of the *Ignation* made several references to the reestablishment of normal college life. "The signing of the World War armistice has had a salutary effect upon the ranks of the Junior Law Class," proclaimed Edward Molkenbuhr, the writer of the "Law School Notes" section of the *Ignatian*. "No longer is the class decimated; it certainly fills one with pride to witness a filled class room and to welcome home and into the fold true American soldiers and sailors, who readily responded to Freedom's call."

future peace was discussed in the pages of the *Ignatian*. The publication's editor-in-chief, Vincent Hallinan, class of 1919 and future St. Ignatius law student, prominent San Francisco attorney, and candidate for U.S. president on the Progressive Party ticket, addressed the failures of the Paris Peace Conference. "For six months now," Hallinan wrote, "has the Peace Conference sat in session. Out of its camouflage of philanthropy there stand only the monuments of perfidy—the greed and avarice of the old nations pitted against the altruism of America." With respect to President's Wilson's efforts at securing a just peace, Hallinan continued, "Stand by your guns, Mr. President! Scorn the demands of brigand nations; dispense the justice and mercy you have spoken so well! This is the time for action and vigilance; uphold the weak and oppressed; America is with you to a man!"

President Wilson's efforts in Europe, however, were largely a failure. Upon his return home, Wilson's plan for a League of Nations was defeated in Congress, a victim of partisan politics. In 20 years, the world would again be plunged into the darkness of a world war. World War II would have even more dramatic consequences than World War I for the students, staff, and alumni of the University of San Francisco.

Folowing the Armistice on November 11, 1918, the *Ignatian* dedicated its June 1919 issue to the young men of St. Ignatius College and the University of St. Ignatius who served and died in World War I. Pictured here are some of the "boys" highlighted in that issue

The return to normal college life notwith-standing, there was still a residual concern among the editorial staff of the *Ignatian* with the quest for a just peace at the close of the war. President Woodrow Wilson's attempt, for example, at the Paris Peace Conference to implement his celebrated Fourteen Points and to establish a League of Nations to ensure

The Financial Crisis of 1919

61

DEBT WAS NOTHING NEW TO THE JESUITS OF SAN FRANCISCO. In 1855, Anthony Maraschi, S.J., the founding president of St. Ignatius Academy, borrowed $11,500 to purchase the institution's first piece of property: less than an acre of shifting sand dunes on what became the south side of Market Street, between Fourth and Fifth streets. He then borrowed an additional $4,000 to build a church, a Jesuit residence, and a small wooden frame building that served as the first home of St. Ignatius Academy. As the institution expanded, its indebtedness grew.

By 1862, the year a three-story brick building for a new church and college was completed adjacent to the original site, the institution was $140,000 in debt. The construction of a magnificent new St. Ignatius Church and College in 1880 on the corner of Van Ness Avenue and Hayes Street raised the institution's indebtedness to more than $800,000, and by 1884, it owed slightly more than $1 million. Most of this debt was eliminated in 1886, however, by the sale of the original piece of land on Market Street for $900,000. In 1901, after a struggle of 46 years, St. Ignatius College finally ended its indebtedness with the $200,000 sale of a parcel of land in the East Bay that had been willed to Fr. Maraschi before his death in 1897.

The destruction of St. Ignatius Church and College in the 1906 earthquake and fire forced the Jesuits to start again down the road of indebtedness. By the end of 1906, the purchase of land on the corner of Hayes and Shrader streets and the building of a temporary church and college on that site put the Jesuits in debt to the amount of $230,000. In 1909, the debt rose another $100,000 from a loan secured by the Jesuits to

purchase a site on the corner of Fulton Street and Parker Avenue for their new church. It was then that finances truly took a turn for the worse. Although the original estimated cost for the church was $300,000, by the time the church was dedicated on August 2, 1914, the overall institutional debt stood at more than $835,000, most of which was from cost overruns on construction of the church. With the enrollment decline before and during World War I, financial matters got even grimmer. By January 1919, the debt had risen beyond $1 million, and a financial crisis was at hand. Each year, $50,000 in interest was due various banks and loan companies. For months, no interest was paid on the principal, and the Jesuits of San Francisco were facing bankruptcy.

In January 1919, Francis Dillon, S.J., provincial of the California Province, decided to assist the Jesuits of San Francisco in their economic crisis. He met with Edward Hanna, the archbishop of San Francisco; Patrick Foote, S.J., the president of the university and rector of the Jesuit Community; and several prominent businessmen and civic leaders. The result of these meetings was

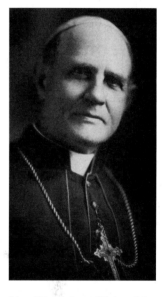

Edward Hanna, the archbishop of San Francisco from 1915 to 1935, was a great supporter of St. Ignatius Church and College. In 1919, he issued a proclamation calling for the citizens of San Francisco to provide financial assistance to the ailing institution. The photo of Archbishop Hanna is from the *Ignatian* of 1927, which dedicated that year's publication to him "for his untiring efforts in behalf of the Fathers of St. Ignatius."

UNIVERSITY OF SAN FRANCISCO ARCHIVES

a public acknowledgment of the financial crisis; the formation of the St. Ignatius Conservation League, headed by Dennis Kavanagh, S.J.; and a public appeal for aid. Members of the St. Ignatius Alumni Society, the Gentlemen's and Ladies' Sodalities, the League of Sacred Heart, the Francesca Relief Society, the Knights of Columbus, and many other organizations promised to solicit funds. The Jesuits of St. Ignatius Church and College were also delegated to make personal appeals for funds.

On April 15, 1919, Archbishop Hanna issued a proclamation calling for the citizens of San Francisco to come to the aid of church and college. "The Jesuit Fathers of San Francisco," the archbishop stated, "have for some time past, been struggling under an insupportable burden of debt, which growing heavier from day to day has assumed such alarming proportions that it has moved the friends of St. Ignatius Church and College to make a supreme effort to relieve the lamentable condition. Something must be done and quickly if we are to preserve the old historic institution. Not only Catholics, but men of every creed, who recognize the need there is, now more than ever, of a religious basis for social as well as individual morality, are interested in the continuance of the work of both Church and College. But in a very special manner, Catholics are interested. For sixty-three years the Jesuit

Fathers have been identified with the Archdiocese of San Francisco, devoting all their energies and resources to the intellectual, moral, and religious betterment of thousands of young men, and receiving no compensation for services other than a meager livelihood." The archbishop's proclamation concluded with his "fullest approval of the efforts" by the friends of St. Ignatius Church and College to raise financial support for their institution. The archbishop called for "all to contribute willingly and generously, according to their means, to so good a cause."

San Francisco newspapers also urged financial support for the church and college in its hour of need. The *San Francisco Call,* in an editorial of June 2, 1919, declared, "St. Ignatius is San Francisco itself." The editorial continued, "every citizen of San Francisco is a son of the old college, and the friends of St. Ignatius now ask those sons to keep death away from its doors. They ask one million dollars to give back to St. Ignatius the strength it had before the fire. In withholding aid, San Francisco kills a part of itself. In giving this money, it gives life to a force that must never die."

The call for financial support for St. Ignatius Church and College was made loud and clear. An answer to that call came soon.

Rescuing St. Ignatius Church and College

62

MANY PROMINENT SAN FRANCISCANS CAME TO THE AID of St. Ignatius Church and College during its time of economic crisis in 1919. The Jesuits faced a debt of more than $1 million and were on the verge of bankruptcy due to unpaid loans associated with rebuilding their college after the 1906 earthquake and fire, a precipitous decline in enrollment prior to and during World War I, and enormous cost overruns associated with building their new church

on the corner of Fulton Street and Parker Avenue. An executive committee, formed to raise funds for the institution during the economic crisis included Edward Hanna, the archbishop of San Francisco; James Rolph Jr., the mayor of San Francisco; James Phelan, United States Senator from California and graduate of St. Ignatius College; and prominent business leaders such as William Crocker, Herbert Fleishhacker, and Daniel Murphy.

Dennis Kavanagh, S.J., a well-known pulpit orator and lecturer from St. Ignatius Church, directed the St. Ignatius Conservation League during its initial and successful efforts in raising money for St. Ignatius Church and College, which was on the verge of bankruptcy in 1919.

UNIVERSITY OF SAN FRANCISCO ARCHIVES

To initiate the fundraising drive, the executive committee organized an alumni banquet on May 12, 1919, at the St. Francis Hotel. Mayor Rolph addressed the 400 individuals present at the banquet, as did Senator Phelan. At the end of his speech, Senator Phelan presented the Jesuits with a check for $10,000. A famous Irish tenor, John McCormick, then sang several songs and contributed an additional $1,000.

Following the banquet, members of the alumni association, the Gentlemen's and Ladies' Sodalities of St. Ignatius Church, and other organizations that were part of the St. Ignatius Conservation League, under the direction of Dennis Kavanagh, S.J., sought contributions in stores, shops, hotel lobbies, theaters, cafes, and door to door in private homes. In three months, more than $200,000 was collected.

The new president of St. Ignatius College, Pius Moore, S.J., gratefully acknowledged the community's generosity in a pamphlet and financial report he issued in 1920. The success of the fundraising campaign was "certainly most gratifying to the Fathers of St. Ignatius," Fr. Moore wrote, "and shows how their appeal in their dire need to the well-known generosity of the San Francisco public, met with a whole-hearted response, not only from the members of our own Faith, but from men and women of every Faith and those of no Faith at all." Fr. Moore concluded that "in relieving a condition brought about primarily by the great disaster of the earthquake and fire of 1906, subsequent business depression, depreciation of real estate values, etc., they were testifying their apprecia-tion of the sixty years of toil and sacrifice entailed by the Fathers in their work for the educational, moral, and spiritual betterment of the community and the up building and formation of intelligent, law-abiding, devoted citizens of the commonwealth."

In August 1919, during the first phase of the fundraising efforts, the Jesuits decided to sell their vacated property on the corner of Van Ness Avenue and Hayes Street, where the church and college had stood before its destruction in the 1906 earthquake and fire. After several months of negotiations, the firm of Heller and Esbery, San Francisco realtors, purchased the property for $311,014. The property was trans-ferred from the Jesuits on February 27, 1920.

A second phase of fundraising was coordi-nated in 1920 by Richard Gleeson, S.J., who succeeded Dennis Kavanagh, S.J., as director of the St. Ignatius Conservation League. This phase included fundraising concerts, dinner dances, and festivals. On January 31, 1921, $6,500 was raised at an event held at San Francisco's Civic Auditorium, billed as "America's Biggest Whist Tournament" and featuring card-playing, bands, and dancing. A "May Festival" held at the Civic Auditorium from May 16 to May 22, 1921, featured speeches by Archbishop Hanna and Mayor Rolph, entertainment, drawings, games, and booths where the attendees could purchase everything from talking dolls and hams to diamond rings and Persian rugs. The festival raised almost $98,000 after expenses. Over the next three years, additional benefit plays, concerts, and dinners were held by the Conservation League. On May 24, 1924, another festival was held, and items such as automobiles, hope chests, washing machines, and a Spanish bungalow were raffled off, enabling St. Ignatius Church and College to repay a long-standing debt to Hibernia Savings Society in the amount of $100,000.

From 1919 to 1925, during the presidency of Pius Moore, S.J., the huge financial debt that had brought the church and college to the brink of financial disaster was reduced from more than $1 million to $150,000. The various fundraising activities during that period, plus the sale of the Van Ness location, brought the debt under control and saved the institution. Within two years, the Jesuits of San Francisco were financially prepared to embark on another venture: the construction of a new college on Fulton Street, the nucleus of the current home of the University of San Francisco.

In 1925, a year after the second festival was held to help pay down the accumulated debt an organization was formed that was to have broad and long-lasting benefits for the college and its affiliated high school. The Loyola Guild of St. Ignatius College and High School was organized by Edwin McFadden, S.J., general director of discipline and later dean of men at the college. The organization was composed of mothers or guardians of past or present students at St. Ignatius College and High School, wives of present or past students, and wives of lay professors. The purpose of the organization was to "foster a deeper acquaintance with all in touch with St. Ignatius College, and to co-operate with its officers to the effect that faculty and parents may work in harmony for the best interests of the school and students."

The first president of the Loyola Guild was Mrs. Frank Silva. Over the 80 years of its existence, the Loyola Guild has been a staunch supporter of the University of San Francisco and St. Ignatius College Preparatory, and it has raised approximately $800,000 for each of those schools, much of it coming from an annual house tour. In 1948, the president of USF, William Dunne, S.J., told its members, "the Guild has become such an integral part of our institution that, to my mind, the words 'University of San Francisco' and 'Loyola Guild' are practically synonymous." In 1950, the Gold Ballroom of San Francisco's Palace Hotel was the location of a Silver Jubilee Banquet honoring the Loyola Guild. At its zenith, the guild had 1,200 members, and according to the organization's current president, Connie Mack, "it was the most prestigious

group to belong to in San Francisco." Although the number of members has declined to approximately 450, many younger members are currently being attracted to the Loyola Guild, and it continues to provide substantial support for USF and St. Ignatius College Preparatory.

James Rolph Jr., (center) the mayor of San Francisco, played an active role in the efforts to rescue the church and college from its financial crisis of 1919. To the mayor's left is Pius Moore, S.J., president of St. Ignatius College; and to his right is Zacheus Maher, S.J., who graduated from St. Ignatius College in 1900, later became the president of Santa Clara University, the president of Loyola University in Los Angeles, and provincial of the California Province of the Society of Jesus.

63 The Sodalities

THE TERM "SODALITY" IS DEFINED BY THE OXFORD ENGLISH Dictionary as an "association or confederation with others; brotherhood, companionship, fellowship." In the Catholic Church, the term "sodality" refers to a lay society for religious and charitable purposes. In 1563, the first sodality was founded in Rome by John Leontius, S.J.

Ignatius Prelato, S.J., stands with some of the young men of the Sodality of St. Ignatius Church, an organization he helped develop during the early years of the Jesuit church in San Francisco. The photo was taken between 1887 and 1888, when the church and college were located on the corner of Van Ness Avenue and Hayes Street in downtown San Francisco.

UNIVERSITY OF SAN FRANCISCO ARCHIVES

In 1859, four years after the founding of St. Ignatius Academy in San Francisco, a student sodality group was formed at the Jesuit institution. The student sodality was "affiliated with a worldwide organization fostering devotion to the Virgin Mother of God and promoting among its members an increase of religious spirit and an active interest in works of charity and social service."

By 1870, the students of St. Ignatius College had a flourishing "Sodality of the Lady," with more than 120 active members under the direction of Ignatius Prelato, S.J. James Bouchard, S.J., one of the early leaders of St. Ignatius Church in San Francisco (vignette #15), announced in 1861 his goal to form a "congregation for the purpose of organizing a Sodality of the Blessed Virgin Mary" for the adult men of the church. Within a week, a group of men became charter members of the St. Ignatius Gentlemen's Sodality

of the Immaculate Conception of the Blessed Virgin Mary, the first association for Catholic lay men in San Francisco. Within a year, the organization had grown to 400 and included many of the most prominent Catholic businessmen, lawyers, and doctors in San Francisco, as well as men from other strata of society, including unskilled laborers.

During the early years of St. Ignatius Church and College, the Gentlemen's Sodality played a significant part in social service activities, major celebrations, Masses, public events, and parades. These included participation in the commemoration of the Silver Jubilee of Pope Pius IX in 1871 and the centennial celebration in 1876 of the founding of San Francisco. The Gentlemen's Sodality also developed a library of Catholic books, papers, magazines, and periodicals; raised money for the church; and attended a special Mass every Sunday morning, during which members wore distinctive gold badges.

By 1900, the Gentlemen's Sodality totaled more than 1,000 members, and on the second Sunday of each month, an average of more than 600 of its members marched in silent procession into the church during special Masses. By the turn of the century, the library of the Gentlemen's Sodality had grown to more than 25,000 volumes. After the 1906 earthquake and fire destroyed St. Ignatius Church, the Gentlemen's Sodality continued to meet and attend special Masses at temporary locations, such as at the home of Bertha Welch, a wealthy supporter of the Jesuits of San Francisco. The organization continued to have a significant presence at the "temporary" location for St. Ignatius Church on the corner of Hayes and Shrader streets, marched in procession when the cornerstone was laid for the new church on the corner of Fulton Street and Parker Avenue, and occupied a large reserved portion of the new church when it was dedicated in 1914.

The Ladies' Sodality was also started by Fr. Bouchard, only a few months after the beginning of the Gentlemen's Sodality. Under Fr. Bouchard's guidance, the Ladies' Sodality became, in the words of the St. Ignatius Church Calendar, "a center of Catholic life and action in San Francisco. One of the outstanding results was zeal for Catholic education; in fact it was the brothers and children of the Sodalists who filled the classes of the lower and higher grades in St. Ignatius College." Within a few years, the Ladies' Sodality exceeded the Gentlemen's Sodality in numbers. Similar to the Gentlemen's Sodality, the women's organization participated in special Masses, church-related ceremonies, social outreach efforts to the poor and the sick, and other support activities. For example, a 3,000-volume library that was part of St. Ignatius Church during its Golden Age from 1880 to 1906 came from contributions made by the Ladies' Sodality.

Although the sodalities were never intended to be major fundraising organizations, the role played by the Gentlemen's and Ladies' Sodalities in organizing and promoting fundraising events during the economic crisis faced by St. Ignatius Church and College in 1919 marked one of the many significant contributions of these lay organizations to the history of the church and school. The Ladies' Sodality, for example, went door to door soliciting money for the campaign to save the church and school from financial ruin (vignette #62). This was a singular effort, however, outside the normal activities of the organization.

By the late 1940s, with the development of other Catholic organizations, membership in the Gentlemen's and Ladies' Sodalities began to decline. The last meetings were held in the mid-1960s. The sodalities, however, served as a foundation for today's Christian Life Community, which sponsors a number of outreach activities that parallel many of the successful works of those dedicated lay men and women who helped support the Jesuits in San Francisco. Likewise, the student sodalities of the 19th and early 20th centuries are the wellspring for the myriad social service activities of today's students at the University of San Francisco.

64 Changing the Institution's Name

DURING THE FIRST FOUR YEARS OF ITS EXISTENCE, FROM 1855 to 1859, the Jesuits' experiment in education in San Francisco was known as St. Ignatius Academy. In 1859, the academy was granted a charter by the State of California to issue college degrees, and it was renamed St. Ignatius College. It should be noted, however, that the term "college" did not necessarily mean what it means today. The Italian Jesuits who founded the institution used the term more in the European sense, equivalent to the French "lycee" or German "gymnasium." In this sense, a college could include classes that corresponded to the present day upper elementary or fourth, fifth, and sixth grades; today's middle school and high school; and the present-day college or university.

Throughout most of the institution's first 50 years, St. Ignatius College educated students at all of those levels, with a majority enrolled in the college preparatory or high school division. In 1897, as a result of the growth of the parish school system in San Francisco, the college discontinued the fourth and fifth grades; in 1917, the sixth grade was dropped, and in 1918, the last eighth grade students attended the school. In 1909, the term "St. Ignatius High School" was used for the first time to designate the college preparatory division; students of high school age comprised the largest student group at the institution until the 1920s.

In 1912, with the establishment of the School of Law and the College of Engineering, and in anticipation of significant enrollment increases, the institution's leadership, under president Albert Trivelli, S.J., renamed the school the University of St. Ignatius. Unfortunately, the optimistic projections of 1912 missed the mark. Although the School of Law was a success, the College of Engineering closed in 1918 for lack of students, and the college division as a whole experienced a precipitous drop in enrollment because of a major economic recession prior to World War I, and due to the war itself, which seriously exacerbated the enrollment decline. By 1919, it was clear to the Jesuit leadership that the name "university" bore little relationship to reality.

In 1919, a report issued by the university's administration, under outgoing president Patrick Foote, S.J., put the nomenclature issue succinctly on the table. In part, the report stated: "Indeed, we never did have a University." The report continued with a tally of the number of students in the college division, "as a matter of fact, it is scarcely worthy of the name of a college at the present moment since it has only

twenty-six students in it!" The report was sent to the Superior General of the Jesuit order in Rome, and on July 5, 1919, the provincial of the California Jesuits, Francis Dillon, S.J., informed Fr. Foote of Rome's decision that the institution should resume its former name, St. Ignatius College.

When Pius Moore, S.J., became president of St. Ignatius College in 1919, one of the first challenges he faced in conjunction with a major economic crisis (vignettes 61 and 62) was how to increase enrollment in what had become a very small college, indeed. Exclusive of the law school, only 41 students were enrolled in the college division of the institution at the opening of the 1921–1922 school year. That same year, St. Ignatius High School, the conjoined college preparatory division of the institution, enrolled 357 students. By the beginning of the 1928–1929 school year, however, 1,100 students

were enrolled in the college division and 710 in the high school. Moreover, by 1929, the institution was on the eve of resurrecting the name "university" for its title and pairing that name with that of the city of San Francisco.

The University of San Francisco as it looked in 1932, two years after it adopted that name. In 1932, the only three buildings on campus were St. Ignatius Church, the Faculty Building (Welch Hall) to the right of the church, and the Liberal Arts Building (Campion Hall) to the right of the Faculty Building. In the background is Lone Mountain, with the newly completed San Francisco College for Women perched on top. The University of San Francisco purchased Lone Mountain from the Religious of the Sacred Heart in 1978.

65 The 1920s and St. Ignatius College

THE 1920S WITNESSED PROFOUND CHANGES IN THE UNITED States, in the City of San Francisco, and at St. Ignatius College. Across the nation, people had widespread access for the first time to the technological wonders of the automobile, the radio, talking movies, and the airplane. The introduction of mass-produced and relatively inexpensive automobiles produced sweeping social changes in courtship patterns, travel opportunities, suburban growth, and individual independence.

During the early 1920s, the rapid introduction of radios into the nation's homes provided instant access to information and popular culture. Likewise, the growth in the movie industry, marked by the introduction of the first talking movie in 1927, fostered popular culture and shared idols. By the end of the 1920s, professional and intercollegiate sports had captured a large following among Americans, and the first modern national celebrities emerged, exemplified by Rudolph Valentino in the movies; Babe Ruth in baseball; and Charles Lindberg, the first solo pilot to fly across the Atlantic Ocean.

By the end of the decade, the proliferation of airlines enabled the rapid transportation of people and mail between America's cities. A new urban culture developed, complete with skyscrapers, mass-produced products, and mass advertising. Dominating the decade was a popular perception of unlimited opportunities and unending prosperity, a perception that came to a crashing end in 1929.

During the decade, women increasingly became independent, pursuing careers and higher education and gaining social freedoms and political influence, their changing status symbolized by the ratification in 1920 of the 19th Amendment to the Constitution, which extended nationwide suffrage to women. Coincidentally, at the same time that women were securing the right to vote, men and women were being restricted in their consumption of alcohol by the ratification of the 18th Amendment, an outgrowth of the Volstead Act, which prohibited the manufacture, sale, or transportation of intoxicating liquor. The amendment became effective in 1920, but was repealed in 1933.

San Francisco fully participated in the social, technological, and economic changes that swept the United States in the 1920s. During the decade, the population of San Francisco increased 25 percent, from 506,676 in 1920 to 634,394 in 1930. This population increase catalyzed the development of the western portions of the city, such as the Richmond and Sunset districts, and the southern areas of the city, including the outer Mission and Potrero districts.

This urban expansion in turn led to the development of new municipal railway lines. For example, the construction of the MUNI

tunnels through Twin Peaks was both a cause and effect of the development of the western and southwestern sections of the city. Shopping areas, businesses, schools, parks, and a greatly enhanced street system also were brought to fruition to accommodate the influx of people, many of whom were driving mass-produced automobiles around the newly developed portions of the city. In 1920, the first transcontinental airmail flight was completed from New York to San Francisco; in 1924, the first "Dawn to Dusk" transcontinental flight was successfully completed at Crissy Field; in 1927, the San Francisco Municipal Airport (Mills Field) was dedicated; and in 1928, daily airline service between Los Angeles and San Francisco was inaugurated. A few blocks from St. Ignatius College, Golden Gate Park increasingly attracted large numbers of people and saw the opening of the M.H. de Young Memorial Museum in 1921, the Steinhart Aquarium in 1923, and Kezar Stadium in 1925.

The social and technological changes in the United States and the population growth and urban expansion of San Francisco are interwoven with developments at St. Ignatius College during the 1920s. The college, from 1920 to 1929, witnessed dramatic changes that laid the foundation for today's institution. Student enrollment significantly increased during the decade, the campus moved to its present location on Fulton Street; and two major buildings (a faculty residence and Campion Hall) were constructed on the new campus.

Curriculum changes also took place during the 1920s, including an increase in the number of elective courses offered, the founding of the College of Commerce and Finance (the antecedent of the current School of Business and Management), and the development of an evening program that enrolled the first women in the institution's history, though the school did not become completely coeducational until 1964. During the 1920s, the law school's reputation grew throughout the city and state; the Jesuits of St. Ignatius Church and College embarked on new community outreach activities; the drama program and debate societies achieved new levels of accomplishment; and the college's athletic programs in baseball, football, and basketball were greatly enhanced, culminating in conference championships in 1928 and 1929 for the basketball team. In 1930, due to efforts by various alumni groups, St. Ignatius College adopted the name of the city itself, and became the University of San Francisco.

In the early 1920s, some of the property in the western portions of San Francisco was beginning to be developed in neighborhoods near St. Ignatius Church, as seen in this photo from the June 1922 edition of the *Ignatian.*

UNIVERSITY OF SAN FRANCISCO ARCHIVES

A New Home for the Faculty

IT WAS A STEEP WALK FROM THE COLD, DRAFTY, AND cramped faculty residence located on the corner of Hayes and Shrader streets in the "shirt factory," up a hill and across Fulton Street to the new St. Ignatius Church. The Jesuit faculty of the college made that walk virtually every day for seven years, from 1914, when the church was completed, until 1921, when they received a gift from their long-term benefactor, Bertha Welch. For 30 years, Welch had been the most significant benefactor of the Jesuits of San Francisco (vignette #38). In 1921, she built them a new residence next door to their church.

The new residence cost $200,000, and Mrs. Welch chose the architect herself for the building and kept a close eye on its construction. In 1920, the Jesuits were trying to raise money to pay off an institutional debt in excess of $1 million (vignettes 61 and 62), and it was noted in a house record that although Welch was "genuinely fond of the Fathers as she had shown abundantly in the past, she was not overly convinced of their business acumen and hence wished to care for certain important details herself."

The *Ignatian* waxed eloquent about the new home for the Jesuits: "Great was the joy," the writer proclaimed, "occasioned by the announcement that the generous benefactress of the Jesuit Order, Mrs. Bertha Welch, is to erect a residence for the community on the lot east of St. Ignatius Church. This gift comes at a time when financial difficulty made it vain to expect an early

The front of the faculty residence, later named Welch Hall, as it appeared in 1928. St. Ignatius Church can be seen just behind the faculty residence to the west. The building was home to the college's Jesuit faculty and administrators from 1921 to 1959. It continued to house the faculty and administrators of St. Ignatius High School until 1969. Welch Hall was torn down in 1970.

UNIVERSITY OF SAN FRANCISCO ARCHIVES

realization of hopes for better living accommodations for the faculty of St. Ignatius College. This gift of Mrs. Welch is by no means the first of her bounty, as those acquainted with the history of St. Ignatius will remember. The members of the Society of Jesus as well as the many friends of the fathers will offer fervent thanksgiving to God for such a favor and beg blessings upon the giver."

Following a simple blessing by Richard Gleeson, S.J., ground was broken for the new faculty residence on September 24, 1920. By the middle of July 1921, the building was completed, and the faculty moved into their new home. In the June 1921 issue of the *Ignatian,* writer George Devine, class of 1923, said the building followed the "general style of the Italian Renaissance" and "recalls an entire block of the Corso in Rome, with its extending balconies and broad windows and evidences of solidity." He noted that Welch's architect "very artistically and with great delicacy adorned the front of the building in a manner restful to the eye. The main entrance surmounted by a cross and two shapely vases, is a little masterpiece of chaste grandeur." Devine looked ahead to "what a glorious sight it will be when three immense buildings crown Ignatian Heights, the College rising in glory to rival the majestic church, and the now completed Faculty Building nestled between the Monument of Religion and the Monument of Learning."

The new faculty building, later named Welch Hall, housed the college's Jesuit faculty and administrators from 1921 to 1959, when a new Jesuit residence, Xavier Hall, was built just north of the church. Welch Hall continued, however,

to house the Jesuit faculty and administrators of St. Ignatius High School until 1969, the year the high school moved to its current location in the Sunset district. Welch Hall was torn down in 1970, and the area once occupied by the building is now an open area of well-manicured grass known as Welch Field. Twice a year, during commencement, when an academic procession marches down a walkway connecting Campion Hall to St. Ignatius Church, it passes directly in front of where Welch Hall once stood. Throughout the year, when the students of today's University of San Francisco picnic, lounge, or play Frisbee or football on Welch Field, they move through a space once occupied by the predecessors of the current faculty, a space memorialized in the name of Bertha Welch, one of the first major contributors to the Jesuits' enterprise in San Francisco.

Another view of Welch Hall as it appeared in the early 1950s, shortly after Gleeson Library (seen directly in back of Welch Hall) was completed. To the left of Welch Hall is St. Ignatius Church, and to the right is Campion Hall.

The Curriculum of the 1920s

THE ST. IGNATIUS COLLEGE CURRICULUM OF THE 1920S reflected the classical roots of Jesuit education; the centuries-old Jesuit focus on moral, religious, and character development; and the impact of contemporary social and economic transformations in the United States and in San Francisco. The various catalogs published by St. Ignatius College during the 1920s addressed major curriculum themes, highlighted numerous co-curricular activities, and underscored the Jesuit philosophy of education.

Throughout the decade, there was relative constancy in the basic curriculum for undergraduate students receiving a bachelor of arts degree. These requirements included substantial course work in Latin, Greek or mathematics, English, public speaking, religion, biology, chemistry, physics, philosophy, and foreign language. In addition to these required courses, the 1920s witnessed a steady increase in the number of elective courses offered to students in areas such as literature, economics, science, law, commerce, and finance. The year 1924 also saw the beginning of an evening program, with courses offered in business management and accounting to working adults.

By 1926, St. Ignatius College had organized its curriculum around several major academic units. The College of Arts and Sciences provided a four-year course of study leading to a bachelor of arts or bachelor of science. The new College of Commerce and Finance offered four years of course work culminating in the degree of bachelor of commercial science. There was also an undergraduate pre-law program to prepare students to enter law school, and a three-year pre-medical course of study in chemistry, bacteriology, biology, and anatomy as a foundation for medical school. The School of Law remained the only post-baccalaureate professional school at the college. The college continued to be connected to St. Ignatius High School, which offered a four-year college preparatory program.

The St. Ignatius College Prospectus of 1921–22 outlined the educational goals of the school. The prospectus stated that the Jesuits "aim at procuring the development of both mind and heart. They recognize moral training as an essential element of education, and therefore, while striving to give the youth committed to their charge higher mental culture, they spare no effort to form them also to habits of virtue." The college catalog of 1925–26 extended this philosophy. "As an integral part of education," the catalog stated, "the Jesuit ideal calls for a systematic effort to develop character; since both experience and common reason sustain the verdict that moral formation—the building up of an enlightened conscience for the right fulfillment of civil, social and religious duties—is never wisely assumed as the normal by product of physical and mental development." In light of this Jesuit goal, the catalog continued, "the acquaintance with facts, the getting of positive knowledge is duly insisted on; but, for the most part, as an instrument employed in a process, not the final purpose to be achieved."

The major documents describing the goals of St. Ignatius College in the 1920s contain concepts similar to those found in today's documents about the University of San Francisco. For example, the current Vision, Mission, and Values Statement of USF, approved on September 11, 2001, declares that the core mission of the university is to promote among its students "the knowledge and skills needed to succeed as persons and professionals, and the values and sensitivity necessary to be men and women for others." The subtext on the institution's Web home page bears a striking resemblance to a phrase in the 1921–22 College Prospectus regarding the institution's aim to "procure the development of both mind and heart." Today, according to the institution's Web home page, USF is committed to "Educating Minds and Hearts to Change the World."

Core Jesuit values are timeless.

Nine faculty members are pictured in this photo from the 1925 *Ignatian*. Two of them, Hubert Flynn, S.J. (center, first column), and Alexis Mei, S.J. (top, second column), later served as dean of the College of Arts and Sciences.

68

The Origins of the School of Business and Management

THE FIRST PROSPECTUS FOR ST. IGNATIUS COLLEGE, published in 1861, listed bookkeeping among the classes available to the young men of San Francisco, the balance of which were of a more classical or traditional nature, such as Latin, Greek, English, rhetoric, history, modern languages, geography, mathematics, and philosophy. The first business-related course at the institution, bookkeeping, provided a practical skill that helped the young graduates of the institution find work in the expanding business and banking world of San Francisco. By 1901, a few other business courses, such as accounting and stenography, were a regular part of the curriculum, to "supply the elements of a business education without in any way detracting from the classical course which had long been obtained in the college."

Opposite: In 1925, the College of Commerce and Finance was established at St. Ignatius College. In the 80 years since its founding, the School of Business and Management has produced graduates who have become business leaders throughout the world. Some of those first graduates began their careers in the financial district of San Francisco, pictured here in the late 1920s. In the background is Treasure Island in the San Francisco Bay, prior to the construction of the Bay Bridge, completed in 1936.

UNIVERSITY OF SAN FRANCISCO ARCHIVES

In 1924, the college began offering evening courses in accounting and business administration to "meet the ever increasing demand for higher and more complete preparation for a commercial career." By the fall semester of 1925, these and other courses formed the basis for the College of Commerce and Finance, the predecessor of today's School of Business and Management. The 1925 issue of the *Ignatian*, described this enhancement of the school: "The addition of the College of Commerce to the other departments was a notable feature of this year's progress," the writer proclaimed, "St. Ignatius is now equipped to furnish instruction in almost every branch of learning, whether it be in the field of the arts or languages, in the realm of science and law, or in supplying the needs of the present day for men capable of guiding the destinies of the great world of commerce and finance."

The college catalog of 1925–26 stated the new College of Commerce and Finance would offer evening courses on Monday, Tuesday, Thursday, and Friday evenings from 7:30 to 9:30 P.M. and would cover four years of college work "suited for success in a business career." The curriculum included elementary and advanced accounting, business law, fundamental and applied economics, business English and arithmetic, advertising and salesmanship, banking, corporate finance, and foreign commerce. Other degree requirements were to be drawn from the College of Arts and Sciences in curriculum areas including English, foreign language, mathematics, public speaking, religion, and philosophy. By the fall of 1926, qualified upper-division students in the College of Arts and Science were permitted to choose elective subjects from the College of Commerce and Finance, applying the credit for those courses to their bachelor's degrees. The College of Commerce and Finance also began introducing lower-division business courses during the day, to be combined with the regular courses in the College of Arts and Sciences.

Entrance requirements for the College of Commerce and Finance, as stated in the catalog, were the same as for a bachelor of science degree in the College of Arts and Sciences, a "less restrictive allowance being made for commercial and vocational subjects among the electives." The regular prerequisite for admission to the College of Commerce and Finance was successful completion of four years of high school. The 1925–26 college catalog did note, "mature persons, however, who have not completed high school, but are otherwise qualified to follow the course profitably, may be admitted as special students."

The first students in the College of Commerce and Finance often found time to participate in the co-curricular life of the institution, including holding office in student government. In May 1928, the College of Commerce and Finance awarded its first bachelor of commercial science degrees to 10 students. The 1928 issue of the *Ignatian* paid tribute to these individuals: "Not only did the men of this senior class do much towards developing the course laid out for the Commerce and Finance Department, but they also gave a great deal of their outside time to further the social and student body activities that fill the yearly calendar of the college." The writer continued, "through their zeal and the interest they took in school affairs, they were appointed as members on all the committees handling school functions, until finally when the elections were held for student body officers for the year 1927–28, despite the fact that they were outnumbered by the Law College,

During the late 19th century, St. Ignatius College offered primarily a classical education, though the curriculum did include some business-related courses to assist students to prepare for careers in the rapidly growing business and banking world of San Francisco. The bookkeeping classroom at the college's Van Ness Avenue location featured a practice bank and post office.

they succeeded in electing one of their number as vice president, the first student body office to be held by a commerce man." The tribute concluded, "this senior class leaves behind it an enviable record. Even though it will pass from the classrooms of the college at graduation, yet it will not be forgotten quite so quickly as other senior classes, because it possesses a certain immortal characteristic — it is the first senior class."

The Evening Division

69

FROM ALMOST THE BEGINNING, THE JESUIT LEADERSHIP of St. Ignatius Academy envisioned an evening program. As early as 1857, just two years after the institution was established, an attempt was made to start a night school. In November of that year, the Jesuits ran an advertisement in the *San Francisco Herald* announcing the academy's intention to offer evening classes. When only two students showed up for the first evening classes, the Jesuits ran another ad in the *San Francisco National.* That advertisement not only displayed the full curriculum for the day program, but also announced that a "night school for bookkeeping, arithmetic, and modern languages, will be formed as soon as sufficient attendance is secured." Sufficient attendance was not secured, however, and the idea of an undergraduate evening division was held in abeyance until the 1920s.

The freshman student officers of the new evening division are listed in the 1928 issue of the *Ignatian,* which includes photos of class president John Riordan, and vice president Margaret McAuliffe, one of the first women admitted to St. Ignatius College.

UNIVERSITY OF SAN FRANCISCO ARCHIVES

Beginning in 1924, individual evening courses began to be offered to undergraduates in subjects such as business management and accounting. Fifty students enrolled in those first classes in the fall semester of 1924. By the fall of 1925, an undergraduate student could begin to fulfill the requirements for a bachelor's degree exclusively at night. These first undergraduate degrees earned through evening classes were awarded in the new College of Commerce and Finance in 1928 (vignette #68). Equally important was the fact for the first time in the history of the 72-year-old institution, women were admitted through the new evening division to an undergraduate degree program, in the fall semester of 1927. Some of the first female students at the college in the late 1920s held offices in student organizations that overlapped both the evening

By the late 1920s, Montgomery Street in San Francisco, pictured here, was known as the "Wall Street of the West." Students from the new evening division at St. Ignatius College, especially in the College of Commerce and Finance, combined their professional careers in downtown San Francisco during the day with classes at night at the Jesuit institution.

UNIVERSITY OF SAN FRANCISCO ARCHIVES

four different economics classes, business English, and business algebra, at $7.50 to $35 per course. The College of Arts and Sciences, through "college extension," offered English, history, languages, mathematics, philosophy, public speaking, and religion to complete a bachelor's degree in commerce and finance. The cost per course ranged from $6 to $25. Finally, a pre-law course of study was offered in the evening division, consisting of a sequence of eight classes, including constitutional history, elementary law, and public speaking and debate. Tuition for this program was set at $50 per semester. By the fall of 1929, 202 students were enrolled in the evening extension program, 124 students were in the College of Commerce and Finance evening program, and 266 law students were pursuing their degrees exclusively at night. Overall, these three student populations comprised 54 percent of the total college enrollment, which in 1929 was 1,099.

The evening division in the 1920s served as the precedent for the University of San Francisco's Evening College, which began in 1951. This college increasingly attracted working adults, many of whom were veterans of World War II and were returning to school under the G.I. Bill of Rights. By 1971, the Evening College was offering a wide range of course work leading to various degrees and was offering nondegree and noncredit courses. During the mid–1970s, the university began to offer off-campus degree programs in the evenings to working adults, initially through the Office of Continuing Education. These degree programs helped underpin the formation of the School of Continuing Education, approved by the board of trustees in 1979. In 1980, the board approved another name change for this unit, which became the College of Professional Studies. Thus, the idea of academic programs offered in the evening was present from virtually the beginning of the institution, came to fruition in the 1920s, and plays a major role at today's University of San Francisco.

and the day divisions. For example, Anne Sullivan was the recorder for the French literary-social club. In 1927, Margaret McAuliffe was elected vice president for the freshman evening college, and Ruth Halpin was elected secretary-treasurer for the freshman class in the College of Commerce and Finance. It was not until 1964, however, that the institution became fully co-educational, and women were admitted to the regular undergraduate programs during the day.

By 1929, St. Ignatius College was publishing an extensive listing of "evening courses for men and women." Students, according to one announcement, may enter the "evening division" to "gain college credit or merely as auditors." For the fall 1929 semester, the Law School listed eight classes in the evening division, including federal procedure, legal ethics, trusts, and philosophy of jurisprudence. The cost per course ranged from $10 to $30, depending on the hours of instruction. The College of Commerce and Finance offered three levels of accounting classes, business law,

The Law School in the 1920s

THROUGHOUT THE 1920S, ENROLLMENT IN THE ST. Ignatius College School of Law, founded in 1912, continued to increase. Enrollment in the School of Law went from 39 students in 1912, to 109 in 1920, and to 266 in 1929. The classes were mostly populated by first- or second-generation Catholic immigrants from Ireland, Italy, and Germany, a reflection of the growth in political and economic power of those ethnic groups in San Francisco.

The student body officers of the St. Ignatius College School of Law in 1925 are depicted in this photo from the 1925 *Ignatian*.

The School of Law's reputation for providing outstanding legal education was also enhanced during the decade. In 1919, the California Supreme Court selected the first Board of Bar Examiners to administer a statewide bar exam to potential attorneys. Graduates did extremely well on the exam. Among the 24 graduates who took the exam in 1922, 23 passed.

The majority of the students who attended the law school during the 1920s went on to successful law careers in San Francisco. Fifteen of those who graduated from 1920 to 1929 were ultimately elevated to the bench in San Francisco or elsewhere in California. George Harris, class of 1926, became the chief judge for the United States District of Northern California. Another graduate who rose to prominence was Preston Devine, class of 1927, who taught at the law school before becoming presiding judge of the California Court of Appeals, Division Four. He served on that court from 1966 to 1974 and was

active in alumni affairs, frequently speaking at university events. In 1927, the first women were admitted to the law school, 37 years before the university's regular undergraduate day program became coeducational. The first women to graduate from the law school were Bertha Ast, who obtained her LL.M. in 1930, and Anne Shumway and Helen Berne who received an LL.B. in 1931.

From 1912 to 1917, the School of Law occupied the fifth floor of the Grant Building on the corner of Market and Seventh streets, and from 1917 to 1927, it shared the

V.C. Hammack, President

J. Duffy, Vice President

R. Fulton, Secretary

L.L. Anderson, Stg. at Arms

G. Kelleher, Treasurer

The law school officers' moderator, Hubert Flynn, S.J., faculty member at the college and later the first dean of the College of Arts and Sciences.

"shirt factory," on the corner of Hayes and Shrader streets, with the students of St. Ignatius High School and College (vignette #51). In 1927, along with the college division, the School of Law moved to Campion Hall, the first academic building on the current campus of the University of San Francisco. In the Grant Building, in the shirt factory, and in Campion Hall, law students attended class exclusively in the evening. A day program was not initiated until 1931. The curriculum included courses in constitutional law, criminal law, contracts, real property, evidence, ethics, pleading, and practice. An essential part of the program was a moot court. Law students were also encouraged to join the institution's debate society where questions of social, historical, civic, and national interest were discussed. According to the St. Ignatius College Bulletin of 1920–21, "students who wish to fit themselves for court speaking will not fail to profit by the excellent training afforded by the debating society" where "practice in public speaking and in Parliamentary Law is thus acquired under the guidance of experienced directors."

In March 1913, six months after the School of Law opened in the Grant Building, the *Ignatian,* proclaimed: "One of the chief sources of gratification to St. Ignatius College has been the number and quality of those whom she has contributed to the legal profession. Many of the bright intellects that grace the bench and bar of this State have been broadened and developed by the instructions they have received from the Jesuit Fathers of this institution." The magazine was referring to the many prominent judges and attorneys that had graduated from St. Ignatius College during the institution's first 58 years, before the creation of a law school. These members of the legal community included Jeremiah Sullivan, justice of the California Supreme Court; Matthew Sullivan, chief justice of the California Supreme Court; Benjamin McKinley, assistant U.S. attorney; and many other distinguished judges and attorneys. With this history to draw upon, the writer for the 1913 *Ignatian* opined: "We can not but wonder, what will be the future of those now attending the College of Law?"

Judging from the law school's growth and success during the 1920s, the immediate future was bright indeed.

The Debaters

FROM ITS EARLIEST YEARS, ST. IGNATIUS COLLEGE emphasized the development of public speaking skills in the educational experience it provided to its students. The first college prospectus, published in 1861, listed rhetoric and elocution among the 15 subjects covered in the curriculum. One of the first student organizations, formed in 1863, was the debating club, initially named the Philodianosian Society and later called the Philhistorian Debating Society. One of the goals of the society was "the improvement of its members in debate, social advancement and general literature."

Two leading debaters from St. Ignatius College in 1927 were Raymond Sullivan (left), who later became an associate justice of the California Supreme Court, and Preston Devine (right), who later became the presiding judge of the California Court of Appeal.

UNIVERSITY OF SAN FRANCISCO ARCHIVES.

Throughout the 19th century, the society held debates on historical and literary topics that the college and the local press noted for their outstanding quality. By the early 20th century, these public debates by the Philhistorian Debating Society increasingly focused on contemporary political issues, especially on the eve of America's entrance into World War I. In 1916, for example, the society held a number of public debates on topics such as whether military training should be made compulsory for the citizens of the United States, and whether Americans should be prohibited by law from traveling on the armed merchant ships of nations engaged in war.

By the 1920s, student debates expanded to include regularly scheduled intercollegiate competition. In May 1920, a debate took place between students from St. Ignatius College and Stanford University on the topic of government ownership of the railroads. For several years, debates between these two schools were major annual events, were well attended, and, with the addition of outside judges, were viewed as an important source of intercollegiate competition. The *Ignatian* covered these debates in great detail and, not surprisingly, was delighted to report on the victories by St. Ignatius College. The June 1922 issue, for instance, proudly proclaimed, "when we realize that out of the comparatively few who attend our College, six men have been chosen each year for the past three years and have received fifteen out of eighteen possible votes; when we compare the two colleges in size and in wealth, we may appreciate what this victory means to us. It means that we have striking evidence of that which we have always known but sometimes refrained from saying; namely, that while we may not be equal in size, in wealth, in magnificent buildings, in great stadiums or amphitheaters to larger institutions of learning, our graduates and undergraduates are in the front rank in the ability to reason clearly, to state facts accurately, to draw correct conclusions from well established principles, and to express their ideas in forceful, eloquent language."

Intercollegiate debates continued throughout the decade. In 1927, a series of debates was held between St. Ignatius College and several other institutions of higher education, including a debate with the University of Idaho on the topic of whether the federal department of education should be put in charge of all primary and secondary education in the United States; a debate with Loyola College of Los Angeles on whether "Mussolini is a benefactor of Italy"; and a debate with the University of Montana on the repeal of the 18th Amendment prohibiting the manufacture, sale, or transportation of liquor. Although the first two of these debates were not formally judged, the third, with the University of Montana, led to a "decision favorable to St. Ignatius." The St. Ignatius debate team on this occasion opposed prohibition and was led by Preston Devine, who later graduated from the St. Ignatius School of Law, and became a distinguished California judge, serving as presiding judge of the California Court of Appeal from 1966 to 1974.

Throughout the 1920s, intramural debates also continued to be held at the college. The Philhistorian Debating Society engaged in weekly debates that were often held in the evening and were open to the public. On the night of April 29, 1925, a freshman named Raymond Sullivan won the prestigious McKinley Gold Medal Debate for "his masterful display of eloquence and forceful arguments" on the negative side of the question, "Resolved: That the United States Navy be increased." Raymond Sullivan graduated from St. Ignatius College, received a degree from the institution's law school, and ultimately became an associate justice of the California Supreme Court.

Although the debating societies no longer exist at USF, oral communication and public speaking continue to be important in the institution's curriculum. The current core curriculum, for example, lists 14 learning outcomes that are part of foundations of communication. Among the outcomes associated with public speaking, students should be able to "understand the importance of oral argument in citizenship and public decision-making" and "understand key concepts from the tradition of rhetoric and use these concepts to assess both their own speaking and that of others." From Fr. Maraschi's first college curriculum to today's core curriculum, the tradition continues.

The Thespians

THEATER HAS A LONG HISTORY AT THE UNIVERSITY of San Francisco. In 1863, when San Francisco's first institution of higher education was still known as St. Ignatius College, students performed their first play for the community, a religious drama called *Joseph and his Brethren.* Throughout the 19th century and into the 20th, the college had an active student theater group that performed classical, sacred, and contemporary plays. These theatrical performances were well attended by students, faculty, alumni, and community members. Not infrequently, members of the local press covered these performances, and invariably wrote positive reviews. The theater group added significantly to the visibility and reputation of the institution.

Finlen

The theater group at St. Ignatius College reached a new level of acclaim in the 1920s, with a number of performances that had exceptionally wide appeal. The most significant of these performances was the 1925 production of *Pageant of Youth,* a dramatic, musical, and dancing extravaganza featuring a cast of approximately 1,000 students and alumni drawn from St. Ignatius College and St. Ignatius High School and from virtually every Catholic school in the Bay Area. The writer of the play was Daniel Lord, S.J., from Saint Louis, and the director was T. J. Flaherty, S.J., of the St. Ignatius College faculty.

Performances of the *Pageant of Youth* were held at the Civic Auditorium in San Francisco. To accommodate the dance groups, lavish scenes, and lighting effects, a special 6,000-square-foot stage was constructed, the largest ever built at the auditorium. The stage also included an arch that was 70 feet wide and 30 feet high. The pageant was depicted in the *Ignatian* as a "musical masque," the "greatest religious, educational, and dramatic production ever presented in San Francisco," and "undoubtedly the greatest activity of the past few years at St. Ignatius." From an artistic standpoint, the *Ignatian* judged the performance "a triumph." The performances "drew many to witness it as many as five successive times, while dramatic critics of all the city's dailies pronounced it a masterpiece."

In 1927, a new venue was added for the theatrical productions of St. Ignatius College with the construction of the Liberal Arts Building (Campion Hall), including the little theater that was a key design element of that building. Under the direction of Alexander Cody, S.J., of the St. Ignatius College English department, a series of plays were performed

Devine

Keil

Ruggles

The *Ignatian* depicted some of the players in the "Pageant of Youth," performed at the Civic Auditorium in San Francisco in 1925 (above and previous page). Thomas Flaherty, S.J., St. Ignatius College faculty member and director of the Pagent of Youth is seen at right.

in the 1927–28 season by the student theater group. These plays represented the continuation of a long-term Jesuit teaching tradition in the field of English. The performances directed by Fr. Cody all played to appreciative audiences, prompting the *Ignatian* to comment, "those responsible for the designing of the Arts and Sciences unit of St. Ignatius College are to be commended for their true wisdom in including a little theater of such complete appointment. Father Cody, too, is deserving of congratulations for his dispatch in putting the new equipment to use."

By the end of the 1920s, the student theater group, now named the College Players, was under the direction of the James Gill, for whom the little theater was named in 1962. For the first time, women were permitted to act in school-sponsored plays and musicals. Ruth Halpin, a student in the new evening division, played a lead role in the 1929 College Players production of *The Hottentot*. During the 1929–30 season, the full schedule of productions consistently played to "a capacity house," according to the *Ignatian*. The initial production of the year, the comedy *White Collar* written by Edith Ellis, was favorably reviewed by George Warren, dramatic editor for the *San Francisco Chronicle*, who wrote that the performance marked a "felicitous beginning of their season." Of the work of James Gill, the *Ignatian* commented, "he stands high in the esteem of those who have worked under him, and has won to himself the utmost confidence of the Players. It is to him that the greater part of the tremendous advance in dramatics at St. Ignatius is due. Through his efforts this year, and the success with which they have attended, the College

looks forward to an entirely new era in this field of activity. With him the College Players hope to perpetuate the reputation which they have won for themselves during the past year."

James Gill died in 1949, after two decades of directing the College Players and helping that theater group develop an outstanding reputation in the community. Some say his presence is still palpable in the theater that bears his name. Like the ghost of Hamlet's father, some claim to have seen him wandering about the theater late at night. Fanciful though those sightings may be, the reality is that Gill contributed mightily to building the College Players Theater Group, the oldest continuously performing theater group west of the Mississippi.

The Emergence of Intercollegiate Basketball

INTERCOLLEGIATE BASKETBALL BEGAN AT ST. IGNATIUS College shortly after the institution joined the Catholic Athletic League in 1909. The first college competitors included Santa Clara College, Tamalpais Military Academy, and the College of the Pacific. The first issue of the *Ignatian*, published in 1911, reported that the varsity basketball team had a very successful 1910–1911 season, "losing but one game, though the sport is comparatively new in the College." During that season, St. Ignatius College beat Santa Clara College twice, by scores of 38–31 and 22–18. In this era, the basketball scores were low because only the set shot and the foul shot were allowed. The one-handed shot, the jump shot, and the dunk shot all were developed decades later.

The 1924 *Ignatian* highlighted the star players from the St. Ignatius College basketball team that won 14 of 18 games.

UNIVERSITY OF SAN FRANCISCO ARCHIVES

Phil Morrisey, captain and star player of the St. Ignatius College varsity basketball teams of 1926 and 1927.

The successful 1910–1911 season was, according to the *Ignatian*, due to coach Orno Taylor, "who labored so earnestly and unceasingly to get the team into shape this year," and to the team captain Robert Flood, who was "a good leader and an exceptional player" and whose "pep spirit was infused into the team he generaled."

During the next few years, St. Ignatius continued to develop its intercollegiate basketball program, notwithstanding the decline in enrollment in the college division of the school. The 1916 issue of the *Ignatian* reported that "basketball this year has been the greatest success ever in the University department. The team has been going like wildfire, and up to March 1, they have lost to but five teams out of fifteen played." During the 1918 season, World War I brought a temporary end to the

basketball program due to the drafting of several of the team's players, including the "trusty team captain, Henry Boyle." The basketball program resumed in 1919, and St. Ignatius finished second in the California-Nevada Intercollegiate Basketball League, losing the last game of the season to Santa Clara 18–17.

The 1920 season witnessed another second-place finish for the team, which lost the deciding game in the California-Nevada Basketball League to Nevada, 47–23. Overall, the season was a great success, however, with St. Ignatius suffering only two league defeats. High points of the 1920 season included the "honor of being the first team to defeat the Los Angeles Athletic Club, ex-champs of the United States," and victories over the College of the Pacific and Santa Clara.

The 1921 season got off to a poor start, with St. Ignatius dropping its first two league games, due partially to injuries. "But smarting under the sting of these two defeats," the *Ignatian* reported, "and imbued with the old St. Ignatius fighting spirit, the team rallied, recovered its old time pep and form and handed quite a few decisive defeats and surprises to the remaining teams." St. Ignatius was twice victorious over Santa Clara, defeated College of the Pacific, and beat St. Mary's. John Connolly, "a former St. Ignatius luminary and demon sport writer," took over basketball coaching duties for the 1922 season, and guided the team to four wins and five losses during regular season play.

Under Coach Connolly, the 1923 team reversed the prior year's record and had five wins and four losses. The high point of the 1923 season was a 31–27 defeat of Santa Clara, which the *Ignatian* described as a "real thriller," and which featured "the clever work of 'Imp' Begley, who opened up a new bag of tricks for the occasion and directly accounted for twenty-one of the points scored by the Varsity." The writer described Begley as the "cleverest and most valuable basketball player in Coast intercollegiate circles."

The 1924 team eclipsed all prior school records by winning 14 of 18 games. The team was now coached by its team captain, Jimmy Needles, and still had "Imp" Begley as its star player, though now in his last year of college. Over the 18 games of the season, the team scored a total of 548 points to their opponents' 349. During the season, Needles, "gave a wonderful exhibition of how basketball ought to be played." With the graduation of its player coach, Needles, and its star player, "Imp" Begley, the team slipped to a record of four wins and eight losses in the 1925 season. An especially satisfying victory for St. Ignatius, however, was against Santa Clara by a score of 29–20. "The Ignatians played superior ball throughout," and "Doc Tierman was the star of the game with five baskets to his credit."

The 1926 season saw Needles back with the team as its head coach. He led the varsity basketball squad to an 8–6 record, including two victories over Santa Clara. The *Ignatian* noted that in one of those games, "Phil Morrisey turned in a more than usually brilliant exhibition at guard, and topped off a fine evening with three perfect goals." Morrisey was back in the 1927 season and captained the team to an 8–7 record, including an upset victory over the University of Nevada in the final game of the season. The *Ignatian* reported this finale: "With the count 26–24, in favor of the Fog, the timer's gun barked and St. Ignatius had taken the third and deciding game of the series from the 1927 champions of the Far Western Conference." This final victory of the season was the herald of the two seasons to follow, during which the St. Ignatius basketball team won two consecutive conference championships.

The St. Ignatius College varsity basketball team of 1920, which lost only two league games on its way to a second place finish in the California-Nevada Basketball League.

The Basketball Champions of 1928 and 1929

THE ST. IGNATIUS COLLEGE BASKETBALL PROGRAM witnessed steady improvement during the 1920s, culminating in the Far Western Conference title in 1928 and the Pacific Coast championship in 1929. The Gray Fog, as the athletic teams were known prior to 1931, won 16 games and lost only five in the 1928 season. The basketball team's conference title at the end of the season was described by the *Ignatian* as "a distinction that represents the utmost in basketball achievement for this section of the country." Noteworthy during the 1928 basketball season was the phenomenal growth in fan support for intercollegiate basketball in California. The *Ignatian* reported, "California has never known the turnout which the indoor sport elicited last winter," and the "Gray Fog varsity contributed more spectacular and breath-taking games this season than any other quintet."

The turning point in the 1928 season was a 30–19 upset victory over the University of California, Berkeley, on the Berkeley campus. Following this win over the Berkeley team, which for years had been the powerhouse of the Pacific Coast Conference, attendance at all future games skyrocketed for St. Ignatius College. At the next game, featuring St. Ignatius against St. Mary's and played at the new Kezar Pavilion in Golden Gate Park, a record-breaking crowd saw the home team defeated 32–31. After this loss, St. Ignatius came back to defeat Fresno State twice at Kezar Pavilion by scores of 43–22 and 31–25. Other notable victories during the season by St. Ignatius on its way to the Far Western

Conference championship were over Loyola College of Los Angeles and Santa Clara.

The 1928 St. Ignatius Far Western Conference championship team was captained by Jack Partridge, described by the *Ignatian* as possessing "that fleeting quality which enabled him to exercise control over his team mates and at the same time to enjoy their respect for him as a leader and esteem for him as a player." Teamwork was critical, however, to the team's success: "While the quintet was composed of individuals of All-State caliber, it was the dazzling teamwork instilled by Coach Jimmy Needles that caught the fancy of the fans. The varsity, being comparatively light in weight and short in stature, relied upon an extremely fast game

in the second game, by a score of 26–13. The team went on to win the Pacific Association Championship and thereby earned a berth in the national championship tournament held that year in Kansas City. In the national tournament, the Gray Fog made it to the third round, but injuries and sickness contributed to the team's defeat at the hands of Phillips University of Oklahoma, by a score of 26–17. The 1929 basketball team was captained by Ray Maloney, the first player from the Pacific Coast to ever be named an All-American. Maloney, playing his third year on the team, was "easily the most outstanding player on the team," according to the *Ignatian,* due to his "consistent shooting and especially for all his manner of handling the team on the court." Overall, he "was a source of inspiration to his

Raymond Maloney, All-American captain of the 1929 St. Ignatius College basketball team.

to score its wins and for this attribute won the support of students of the game. The record of the team and its beauty of action on the floor while making that record installed Jimmy Needles as the ranking basketball mentor for this province."

Following the success of 1928, the 1929 team compiled a record of 17–1 during the regular season. The campaign included victories over Santa Clara, St. Mary's, U.C. Berkeley, Loyola of Los Angeles, and Nevada. The one loss during the regular season was to Santa Clara

teammates." The team was again coached by Needles, who had played guard for the St. Ignatius basketball team seven years earlier, who also coached the football team, and was director for all of the athletic programs.

The basketball program at USF received its first taste of greatness in the 1920s, especially with the championships of 1928 and 1929. The teams of the late 1920s set the standard for future USF teams, such as the national championship teams of 1949, 1955, and 1956 (discussed in future vignettes).

Rugby and the Origins of Intercollegiate Football

BEGINNING IN THE 1890S, ST. IGNATIUS COLLEGE BEGAN to play casual and loosely organized rugby games with other colleges and high schools in the Bay Area. These games, which often included high school and college students playing on the same team, became more formalized in 1909, when St. Ignatius College joined the Catholic Athletic League. The rugby program was briefly dropped in 1910, but in 1911, the college announced that rugby would be restored at both the high school and college levels.

The St. Ignatius College football team in action during the 1924 season, the college's first intercollegiate football team since 1917.

UNIVERSITY OF SAN FRANCISCO ARCHIVES

Starting in 1911, the pages of the *Ignatian* contain numerous references to the institution's rugby team. The 1914 issue, for example, noted the "presence of good timber for a fine rugby team," yet the "constant defeats suffered by the club discouraged the rooters." The 1915 season saw some improvement: "the outstanding feature of the rugby season was the generalship, the perseverance and the iron grip of Coach Nill." The rugby team of that year recorded three victories, two losses, and a tie against teams that included Stanford, Santa Clara, and College of the Pacific.

In 1917, the University of St. Ignatius decided to shift its program from rugby to football. The *Ignatian* recorded this transition: "For well nigh eight years now we have put Rugby teams on the field, and while all were not star aggregations still they made a favorable showing. For the last two years, however, unrest in college athletics on the Coast caused a general upheaval, many of the larger colleges abandoning Rugby for the American game. In the spring the advisability of St. Ignatius falling into line was fully discussed, and at the first meeting of the Associated Students this semester a vote was taken and 'American' came into its own at S.I.U."

The University of St. Ignatius played its first intercollegiate game of "American football" in the fall of 1917 against the Aggies of the California Agricultural College (today U.C. Davis). St. Ignatius won 13–7. The decisive play of the game was when "fullback Boyle scored on a sensational twenty-yard run around right end. It was a pretty piece of sprinting and saved the day for S.I., for we scored no more points." America's entrance into World War I, the decline in enrollment before and during the war, and the financial crisis faced by the school in 1919 all contributed to ending the intercollegiate football program within a year of its inception. The 1924 *Ignatian* reported that "for over five years we have not heard the name of St. Ignatius University coupled with the grand old game of football,"

but that "the College has set its heart on making a good showing in football next year and from the looks of things they undoubtedly will."

In the fall of 1924, football was revived under coach Jimmy Needles, who also coached the successful basketball team. The football team lost all five of its games that season, though the *Ignatian* reported that for its first year, the team "showed remarkable promise." Some of that promise was demonstrated in the last game of the season against the College of the Pacific, when, trailing at halftime 13–0, the St. Ignatius team "put up a desperate fight and tied the score," only to lose by a final score of 17–13. The 1925 football team continued that promise in a brief season that included only three games, finishing with one win, one loss, and one tie. The football schedule greatly expanded in the 1926 season. St. Ignatius College played eight games, winning two, losing three, and tying three. The two victories, both with scores of 6–0, were against the California Agricultural College of Davis and Chico State Teachers College. In the former game, the only score for the Gray Fog occurred when "Guy Dawson carried the ball around end from the 5 yard line." In the latter, Dawson again scored the only points "by scooting 25 yards off tackle to a touchdown."

In 1927, St. Ignatius College moved to its current location on Fulton Street. Concurrent with that move, the football program advanced to a new level of competition, adopted new green and gold school colors, and joined the ranks of colleges and universities across the nation that increasingly viewed football as a major source of alumni support and institutional visibility.

Football in the 1920s

DURING THE 1920S, FOOTBALL EMERGED AS A MAJOR spectator sport in the United States. In October 1925, three-time collegiate All American and professional football player Red Grange became the first athlete to appear on the cover of *Time* magazine. He shared that distinction with such notable people of the decade as Albert Einstein, Sigmund Freud, Leon Trotsky, and Princess Elizabeth of Britain. Across the nation, universities and colleges initiated or greatly expanded their football programs in conjunction with the growing popularity of the sport. Notre Dame's great football success during the 1920s demonstrated to other Catholic colleges the advantage of football in building alumni support, generating publicity, and enhancing revenue. Jesuit colleges such as Georgetown, Fordham, Detroit, and Santa Clara all developed major football programs during the decade.

The 1925 St. Ignatius College football team in action.

UNIVERSITY OF SAN FRANCISCO ARCHIVES

The University of St. Ignatius played its first intercollegiate football game in 1917, tried the sport for one season, and then discontinued the program for seven years. In 1924, St. Ignatius College revived the sport under coach Jimmy Needles, and in 1927, the football program moved to a new level of competition when the institution joined the Far Western Conference. In that same year, the college moved to its current location on Fulton Street and adopted the present school colors of green and gold, replacing its former red and blue. With the exception of the head coach and athletic director, the football and other athletic programs were largely managed by students: coaches, trainers, ticket sellers, and food vendors were all students, supervised by a board of student control.

Until 1931, the St. Ignatius College athletic teams were known as the Gray Fog. Wearing its new green and gold colors, the Gray Fog football team defeated its first opponent of the 1927 season, the University of Nevada 19–0, a "victory that upset all predictions," according to the the *Ignatian*. The St. Ignatius team also defeated Loyola College of Los Angeles 32–7 and beat the Aggies of the California Agricultural College of Davis 7–2. Overall, however, the season ended with only those three victories, with the rest of the season consisting of five defeats and a tie.

In 1928, the St. Ignatius College football team compiled its best record to date with four wins and four losses. Although the 1928 team was composed of almost all freshmen and sophomores, it displayed, in the words of the *Ignatian,* a "brand of football this year that would be a credit to any large institution." St. Ignatius College won the first game of the season, beating the University of Nevada 12–0. In one of the deciding plays of that game, Elmer Sadocchi "received the kickoff on his thirty-five yard line and raced the entire length of the field in a beautiful swerving, dodging manner, to score the first touchdown of the season for the Gray Fog." The team's captain for 1928, Jack O'Marie, won the William S. Boyle Loyalty Award for his play as "one of the outstanding centers on the Pacific Coast" and was "mentioned by almost every sports writer following bay football as being worthy of consideration for an All-American berth."

The team closed out the 1920s with its first winning season ever. In 1929, the Gray Fog, still coached by Jimmy Needles, compiled a record of four wins, three losses, and a tie. Among the many highlights of the season was a 14–7 victory over the Gonzaga University Bulldogs on their home field in Spokane. The *Ignatian* reported that "the defeat of the Northern Jesuit institution was administered decisively and convincingly," and that the Gonzaga team was "pushed up and down the field almost at will." Among the Ignatian players, "Thomas and Bareilles rolled up large yardage totals and Bray and Parina contributed brilliant defensive shows." At the end of the season, team captain and star center Jack

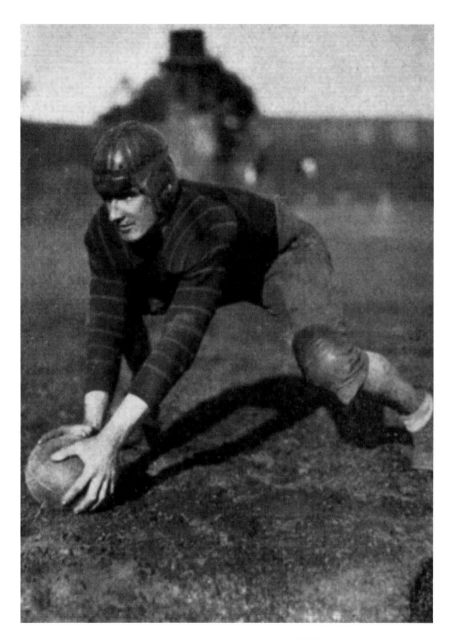

O'Marie, playing in his last year, was again voted the recipient of the William Boyle Award for outstanding play.

In 1951, 22 years after the successful 1929 season, the University of San Francisco's football team defeated every team it played, becoming one of the most famous teams in intercollegiate football history (vignette #105). Some of the building blocks for that athletic success were laid in the 1920s.

Jack O'Marie, two-time winner of the William S. Boyle Loyalty Award for outstanding play, was captain and star center for the St. Ignatius College football team in 1928 and 1929.

77

The Origins of Baseball at USF

From 1912 to 1914, the University of St. Ignatius baseball team played many local amateur and college teams. In March 1913, the team narrowly lost an exhibition game to the Chicago White Sox, 4-2. Joe Giannini (pictured here on the far right of the bottom row) was team leader during these years and eventually made it to the major leagues.

UNIVERSITY OF SAN FRANCISCO ARCHIVES

IN 1869, THE CINCINNATI RED STOCKINGS WERE ORGANIZED as the first professional baseball team in the United States. In that year, the Red Stockings traveled to San Francisco on the newly completed transcontinental railroad to play against an amateur San Francisco team. Although there is no record of any student from St. Ignatius College playing on that amateur team, the national tour of the Red Stockings represented the growing interest in San Francisco and throughout the nation in baseball, which was soon to become the national pastime. During the last decades of the 19th century, there was a proliferation of professional, collegiate, and amateur teams. The poet Walt Whitman wrote about baseball of this era: "It is our game—the American game. It will take our people out-of-doors, fill them with oxygen, give them a larger physical stoicism."

The roots of baseball at St. Ignatius College can be found in the late 19th and early 20th centuries when intramural teams competed on sandlots near the college, both at its Market Street and Van Ness Avenue locations. By 1907, the college had a student-managed baseball program, composed of high school and college players, that competed against other Bay Area teams, including high schools, colleges, and community organizations, such as the Knights of Columbus. Many of these games were described in the pages of the *Ignatian*. The 1912 issue, for example, portrayed a 4–3 victory by the St. Ignatius College varsity team over Santa Clara College. According to the *Ignatian*, it was a "pitcher's battle between Floyd and Purdy and the local lad had a shade the better of it. The game was full of sensational plays, which brought the rooters to their feet on more than one occasion. St. Ignatius took the lead in the first inning with 2 runs and never lost it." The St. Ignatius team of this era played local amateur and college teams. After an 8–3 victory over the Turkey Reds in 1912, the *Ignatian* reported "Joe Giannini, our smiling leader, drove a board out of the right field stands with the bases densely populated," and "Charlie Sullivan fanned enough batters to start a cyclone and was only rapped for five singles."

Major league teams of the era would also occasionally play an exhibition game against a local San Francisco team during spring training. In March 1913, for example, the Chicago White Sox played the recently renamed University of St. Ignatius baseball team. The White Sox beat St. Ignatius 4–2, but the game was close, and the college team "surprised the big leaguers at every turn." Joe Giannini, who briefly made it to the major leagues, got two hits and scored a run, and the St. Ignatius pitcher, "Dutch" Reuter, held the White Sox to just one hit for the first eight innings until the Chicago bats finally came alive in the last inning.

Baseball continued to grow in popularity on the campus of the University of St. Ignatius. The 1914 issue of the *Ignatian* reported that the new season "brought out some fifty aspiring baseballers" for the college and high school teams. In the 1914 season, the university's varsity team competed in a league composed of amateur teams representing local organizations, including the Olympic Firsts, the United Railroads, and the Union Iron Works. Local amateur teams continued to dominate the university's baseball schedule for the next several years. In 1915, for example, the team played clubs such as the Billy Hymes Tigers and the Sperry Flour team. In 1915, the Ignatians beat a team fielded by the San Francisco Police Department, 3–1.

During the 1916 season, the University of St. Ignatius baseball team began to add more local colleges to its schedule. The *Ignatian* reported that the varsity baseball team compiled a record of seven victories, four defeats, and one tie. The Ignatians beat the Weiner Tailors and the Western Electrics, but lost to the University of Santa Clara by a score of 4–0. The *Ignatian* reported that the Santa Clara "game was a pitcher's battle from start to finish, but a fluke home run, the ball taking a bad bound over the fielder's head with two men on base in the first inning, gave Santa Clara a lead that the splendid pitching of Ed Morrissey from then on could not overcome." Another one of the season's games, however, produced a 4–3 victory over Stanford, "that was full of thrills from start to finish." The *Ignatian* reported, "Jimmy Harington's hitting and catching was one of the features of the game. The big catcher hit safely every time he came to bat, and his accurate throwing turned back three runners."

America's entrance into World War I in 1917, a decline in student enrollment, and financial problems at the school all conspired to bring an end to the baseball program at the college level from 1918 to 1923. At the start of the 1923 season, however, the *Ignatian* proudly reported that "the squad, newly equipped and nattily uniformed, has been scooping 'em up and lining' em out for the past month or so, and the boys have been very successful in the majority of games played so far." Baseball had returned to St. Ignatius College.

78

Baseball in the 1920s

NO PROFESSIONAL SPORT IN THE UNITED STATES HAD A greater hold on public consciousness in the 1920s than baseball. One man in particular, Babe Ruth, and his exploits both on and off the baseball diamond, propelled the sport into the national limelight during a decade filled with many great players. At the college level, baseball also grew in popularity during the decade, though at most colleges it lagged behind football and basketball, both of which usually drew larger crowds to games, engendered pep rallies, and brought droves of alumni back to campus. During the 1920s, St. Ignatius College followed this national trend, and baseball was decidedly the third sport behind football and basketball.

Ray O'Connor, captain and star outfielder of the 1929 St. Ignatius College baseball team.

The 1925 issue of the *Ignatian* reported that "for the first time in several years, St. Ignatius College was represented on the diamond by a real, well organized baseball team." During the 1925 season, under coach Johnny Kerr, the team won nine games and lost five against amateur and college teams. A notable victory during the season was a 10–5 trouncing of the Aggies of the California Agricultural College of Davis. The *Ignatian* reported that Bill Barry of St.

Ignatius "pitched a great game and held the slugging farmers to but four safeties," and "George Ghiradelli connected with the longest hit of the game when he hit the ball over the right fielder's head."

In 1926, the team had a five-win, two-loss record against a series of amateur and college teams, though the season began with a 10–2 loss to Santa Clara. The loss was "a bitter pill," but "the varsity took its lesson like men" and came back to beat several amateur teams, including Associated Oil, Blake-Moffitt-Towne, and Union Oil 9. The team closed the 1926 season with a loss to the St. Ignatius Alumni by a score of 5–2. The *Ignatian* described how "Eddie Morrissey, a pitching idol in by-gone days, flashed some of his ancient brilliance and set the collegians of the present day down with ease."

In 1927, the baseball team compiled a record of four wins and one loss in a season shortened by several rainouts. The team was coached by Jack McCarthy and led by star pitcher and team captain Jack Kavanaugh. In the opening game of the season, St. Ignatius beat an amateur team fielded by Edward Brown and Sons. The Ignatian described the work of Jack Kavanaugh, who struck out eight opponents during the game: "The industrialists couldn't see Kavanaugh, who was working in mid-August form, and was being accorded flawless backing by his mates." Against the University of California Dental College team, St. Ignatius was also victorious, 9–5. Tom Carrothers was the star player for the team that day, hitting a run-scoring double and a triple, the latter "being a mute witness as to the stuff his speed is made of."

Tony Lazzeri, native San Franciscan, star second baseman with the world champion New York Yankees, and teammate of Babe Ruth and Lou Gehrig, opened the 1928 season as the head coach of the St. Ignatius baseball team. Before his departure to rejoin the Yankees, Lazzeri worked closely with a new team composed mainly of freshmen and sophomores. Lorenzo Malone, S.J., took over the coaching duties for the balance of the season, which saw the Ignatians compile a disappointing record of two wins and three losses, including two defeats by St. Mary's College. One of the victories, however, was a

15–1 thrashing of Crocker Trust. The *Ignatian* reported that the pitcher, Joe Rock, "had too much stuff for the bankers, flopping thirteen of them on strikes and holding them to four scattered hits." The team also beat a baseball squad fielded by Colgate Cosmetics. The Ignatian pitcher, Jack Partridge, "was in fine fettle this afternoon and with everyone hitting behind him took the decision over the cosmetic men with ease."

In 1929, the St. Ignatius College baseball team was again coached by a former major leaguer. This time it was Frank Pizzola, who had played for the New York Yankees and the Chicago White Sox. Led by its captain and star outfielder, Ray O'Connor, the team had a record of four wins and four losses. One of the victories was a 4–2 win over a semi-pro team named Boss of the Road. The Ignatian reported that the St. Ignatius pitcher, Joe Rock, "besides pitching a beautiful game, got a double with the bases full that scored three runs, winning his own game."

During the 1920s, and for the next seven decades, St. Ignatius baseball teams produced many outstanding players, several of whom played in the major leagues. Most recently, former USF student athlete Jesse Foppert joined the San Francisco Giants. On April 14, 2003, he played in his first major league game against the Houston Astros and pitched two hitless innings. A few days later, he won his first game. Generations of baseball players from St. Ignatius College, which became the University of San Francisco in 1930, could readily identify with those achievements.

The 1929 St. Ignatius College baseball team included ace pitcher Joe Rock, catcher Gerald Vest, and third baseman George Maloney.

The Shirt Factory Presidents (PART 1)

FROM 1906 TO 1927, ST. IGNATIUS COLLEGE EDUCATED young men in a "temporary" facility known as the shirt factory, a rambling wooden building on the corner of Hayes and Shrader streets that was hastily assembled following the 1906 earthquake and fire that had destroyed the Jesuits' magnificent church and college on Van Ness Avenue.

Joseph Sasia, S.J., the institution's 13th president, who served from 1908 to 1911, and (opposite) Albert Trivelli, S.J., the 14th president, who held that office from 1911 to 1915.

UNIVERSITY OF SAN FRANCISCO ARCHIVES

Six Jesuit presidents guided the fortunes of St. Ignatius College while the institution was located in the shirt factory. The first of these men, John Frieden, S.J., who was president from 1896 to 1908, and who led the institution during its immediate recovery after the 1906 disaster, was discussed in vignette #37. Edward Whelan, S.J., who oversaw the move from the shirt factory to its new home in Campion Hall in 1927, will be discussed in vignette #91. The next two vignettes will focus on the four presidents whose tenures were exclusively at the shirt factory, a period in the institution's history marked by the formal transition from a European model of education to an American model. The backgrounds of the four presidents and their administrations symbolize that transition.

Joseph Sasia, S.J., the 13th president, who held that office from 1908 to 1911, was born in northern Italy in 1843. He joined the Jesuits at the age of 25, and three years later, like so many other Jesuits from the Turin province of northern Italy, he was sent to the Jesuit Mission in California. He was ordained a priest in 1877 and served as rector of St. Ignatius Church and president of St. Ignatius College from 1883 to 1887, while the combined institutions were located on Van Ness Avenue. From 1888 to 1891, he was superior of the California Mission, before returning to Italy to become provincial of the Turin province. In 1899, Fr. Sasia came back to California to engage in parish work and to write. In 1907, he was again appointed rector of St. Ignatius Church and president of the college, succeeding Fr. Frieden.

Under Fr. Sasia's leadership, the institution continued its recovery from the 1906 catastrophe in its new home in the shirt factory. The institution also clearly separated the college division from the high school division, symbolized by a separate designation for the latter as St. Ignatius High School in 1909. During Fr. Sasia's administration, St. Ignatius College increasingly participated in intercollegiate sports; developed plans for professional schools of law and of engineering; and witnessed the publishing of the *Ignatian*. Fr. Sasia was also instrumental in the decision to build the new St. Ignatius Church on the corner of Fulton Street and Parker Avenue, and he briefly spoke at the groundbreaking for the church's new home in 1910, the pages of his longer prepared speech being carried away by the wind that whipped through the outdoor ceremony at a most inauspicious time. After leaving the president's office in 1911, Fr. Sasia continued to engage in work at St. Ignatius Church and at Santa Clara, where he died in 1928.

Albert Trivelli, S.J., succeeded Fr. Sasia as the president of St. Ignatius College, serving from 1911 to 1915. Fr. Trivelli, another Jesuit from northern Italy, was born in Billiolo in 1863. He entered the Society of Jesus at the age of 16. In 1882, he immigrated to the United States and spent several years studying philosophy and theology at Woodstock, Maryland, where he was ordained in 1893. Over the next two decades, Fr. Trivelli held a number of positions in the western United States, including minister of the Jesuit novitiate in Los Gatos, California; parish priest in Seattle, Washington, and in Juneau, Alaska; superior of the Jesuit Church in Pendleton, Oregon, and superior of the St. Francis Church and School in Missoula, Montana.

In 1911, Fr. Trivelli was made president of St. Ignatius College. The *Ignatian* noted soon after his inauguration that the new president had already given years of devoted service to various Jesuit endeavors, and that "during the short time he has been President, Father Trivelli has endeared himself to the 'boys' by his keen interest in their endeavors, his quick appreciation of their little difficulties and his ready sanction of their cherished undertakings. We look forward to years of happiness and success with the destiny of St. Ignatius College in the hands of Father Trivelli."

Under Fr. Trivelli's leadership, the school established new professional schools of law and of engineering; changed its name to the University of St. Ignatius; and tried to grapple with a growing economic recession in the Bay Area that negatively affected student enrollment. Under his administration, the fifth St. Ignatius Church in San Francisco was completed and dedicated in 1914, though its construction left the Jesuits in San Francisco with a severe economic burden. Fr. Trivelli left the presidency in 1915 and returned to his former position as superior of the Jesuit Church and School at Missoula, Montana. After a lengthy illness, Fr. Trivelli died at the Jesuit novitiate in Los Gatos in 1922.

Fathers Sasia and Trivelli represented the last of the old guard Italian leaders who administered the Jesuit church, school, and community in San Francisco. Unlike Fathers Sasia and Trivelli, the next two presidents were both born in the United States, but like their predecessors, they both had to face growing financial burdens for their Jesuit institution.

The Shirt Factory Presidents (PART II)

PATRICK FOOTE, S.J., THE 15TH PRESIDENT OF THE University of San Francisco, then known as the University of St. Ignatius, was born in New York City on December 15, 1861, eight months after the beginning of the Civil War. His parents brought their young son to San Francisco and eventually enrolled him at St. Ignatius College on Market Street, in the days when the institution accepted students from the equivalent of elementary school through college. Fr. Foote became the first graduate of St. Ignatius College to become president of the institution.

In 1881, Patrick Foote entered the novitiate of the California Jesuits at Santa Clara College, completed his studies in Rome, and in 1897 was ordained a priest. His first duties were at Santa Clara College and at St. Michael's College in Spokane. He then began his long career at St. Ignatius Church and College, where for many years he directed the Gentlemen's Sodality at the church and taught philosophy and mathematics at the college.

In 1915, Fr. Foote was installed as the institution's 15th president. Shortly after his inauguration, the *Ignatian,* remarked, "our president is a man of whom we are all proud. Everywhere we go his name is mentioned with the swift remembrance of his venerable white hair and odd little glasses. And it is recalled by the graduates, his former pupils, how these odd little glasses he never likes to look through, but to look over rather, as the sight on a gun is used, to fix his luminous yet stern gaze on some poor struggling scholar who is worming about in his chair for a position behind some one else. These and other pleasant memories are recalled, and it is

then that the graduates realize how promising is our outlook for the future."

The impact of World War I, a recession-induced enrollment decline, and a financial crisis were the most significant issues to confront Fr. Foote's administration, which lasted from 1915 to 1919. During Fr. Foote's presidency, 380 students and recent graduates of the college served in World War I, and the college joined the national Students Army Training Corps, the predecessor of the ROTC. Under his leadership, the college's debating societies grew, the new law school expanded, and the varsity rugby team became the champions of San Francisco. The university's financial situation worsened, however, and the institution was on the verge bankruptcy by 1919. After leaving the presidency, Fr. Foote returned to teaching philosophy and mathematics at the college. In 1947, he celebrated his 50th anniversary as a Jesuit priest. Fr. Foote died at the Jesuit house in Los Gatos on September 16, 1948. A requiem Mass was held for him in St. Ignatius Church, followed by his interment in Santa Clara Catholic Cemetery.

Pius Moore, S.J., who succeeded Fr. Foote as the institution's 16th president, and who served in that capacity from 1919 to 1925, was born in Iowa on July 10, 1881. He entered the Society of Jesus in 1900. As soon as he was appointed president of the University of St. Ignatius, he, together with other Jesuits, began work to reduce the enormous financial debt of more than $1 million that jeopardized the future of the institution. With the assistance of prominent alumni, major civic supporters of the church and school, and various organizations that made up the St. Ignatius Conservation League, the institution was able to reduce its indebtedness to $150,000 by the time Fr. Moore left office in 1925.

During Fr. Moore's presidency, the school changed its name from the University of St. Ignatius back to St. Ignatius College. Under Fr. Moore, the College of Engineering was discontinued because of low enrollment, but the other divisions of the institution witnessed steady enrollment increases: from 194 students during the 1919–1920 academic year to 444 students during the 1925–1926 academic year, including, in the School of Law, an increase from 164 to 229 students. An evening division and the College

of Commerce and Finance were also initiated in the last year of Fr. Moore's administration, further underpinning an enrollment increase for the next several years.

After leaving the presidency, Fr. Moore worked among the Japanese of San Francisco, and in 1928 he headed the first group of California Jesuits to go to China. In 1937, he retuned to California to assume the duties of mission treasurer. Just prior to the outbreak of World War II in the Pacific, on December 7, 1941, Fr. Moore made another trip to China, but was caught there and interned with several other Jesuit priests by Japanese troops. In 1943, he was released, returned to the United States, and resumed his duties as mission treasurer. In August 1950, Fr. Moore celebrated his 50th year as a member of the Society of Jesus in St. Ignatius Church. One month later, he suffered a stroke and died on October 12, 1950, at the St. Joseph rectory in San Jose. He was buried in the Jesuit plot at the Santa Clara cemetery.

Fr. Moore's efforts were instrumental to the growth of St. Ignatius College during the balance of the 1920s, and he provided the economic stability necessary for the expansion of the college to a new building on Fulton Street, built under his successor, Edward Whelan, S.J.

(Top) Patrick Foote, S.J., who served as the institution's 15th president from 1915 to 1919, and (bottom) Pius Moore, S.J., who was president from 1919 to 1925.

UNIVERSITY OF SAN FRANCISCO ARCHIVES

8 The Move to Campion Hall

FOR 21 YEARS, THE LEADERSHIP OF ST. IGNATIUS COLLEGE planned to move to a permanent home following the disastrous 1906 earthquake and fire that destroyed their magnificent institution on Van Ness Avenue, and that had forced them to conduct their educational enterprise in a temporary wooden structure, known as the shirt factory. In 1927, their dream of a new college building finally came to fruition.

In September 1926, the Jesuits announced that work was to begin on their new college building on Fulton Street. The structure, initially named the Liberal Arts building, would be next door to the faculty residence that was built in 1921, which in turn stood less than 100 feet from St. Ignatius Church, completed in 1914, on the corner of Fulton Street and Parker Avenue. The official announcement about the building thanked all who had contributed funds to its building, estimated to cost $300,000. The announcement stated that the Jesuits are happy "they are about to start work on the long-desired and much-needed new college building. After years of hard struggle, the debt has been sufficiently reduced to permit them to realize their

The new Liberal Arts building (Campion Hall), as it appeared in 1928, the year after it was completed. The view is of the west side of the building. On the left of the photo is a corner of the faculty residence (Welch Hall), which was demolished in 1970.

UNIVERSITY OF SAN FRANCISCO ARCHIVES

cherished hope," and "gratefully, they hasten to give the good news first to those who have made this beginning possible."

On December 10, 1926, a groundbreaking ceremony was held for the new building. Present at the ceremony were James Rolph Jr., the mayor of San Francisco; Edward Whelan, S.J.; the president of St. Ignatius College; Monsignor Michael Connolly of St. Paul's Parish, representing the Archbishop of San Francisco; Benjamin McKinley, alumnus of St. Ignatius College, professor in the St. Ignatius School of Law, and former U.S. district attorney; and Frank Hughes, class of 1883, president of the alumni association, who officiated at the ceremony. A writer for the *Ignatian*, covered the event and described how Hughes "fittingly expressed the true joy of all the Alumni upon the achievement of this goal and the brilliant future which appeared in store for their Alma Mater," saying this was the "most memorable day in the history of St. Ignatius." McKinley, according to the *Ignatian*, "stirred his audience deeply by an eloquent address in which he eulogized the Fathers of St. Ignatius of past years and the present." Fr. Whelan, who had assumed the presidency of the college in 1925, spoke of how the day "marked the realization of a twenty years' dream" and the "new college, complete in every detail, was to crown Ignatian Heights, a fitting complement to the magnificent temple erected and dedicated to the worship of God." Finally, Mayor Rolph congratulated the faculty and administration of the college on their new building and turned the first shovel of soil, bringing the ceremony to a close.

Thirteen months later, the new Liberal Arts building was completed, and on Sunday, October 9, 1927, the building was officially dedicated, a ceremony presided over by Archbishop Edward Hanna. The dedication began with an academic procession from the church to the new building, passing by the faculty building. In addition to the archbishop, the procession included Fr. Whelan, president of the college, other college administrators, a boy's choir,

priests, the entire Jesuit faculty of the college, and other religious from San Francisco. The archbishop blessed the building and gave a speech on "the sublime work of Catholic education as carried on according to the ideals of the Jesuit system of education."

When the Liberal Arts building opened in the fall of 1927, it housed the entire college: the offices of all the administrators and the faculty of the College of Arts and Sciences, the College of Commerce and Finance, the School of Law, classrooms and lecture halls, laboratories, the little theater, students' lounge and chapel, cafeteria, bookstore, athletic equipment store, libraries, student lockers, and offices for student government. By 1928, 1,090 college students occupied the building for day and evening classes, including 135 women, who were permitted to take classes only in the evening. Remaining in the shirt factory campus were 710 high school students. Space quickly became such a premium in the new building that many of the library books had to be stored in St. Ignatius Church. The church, the faculty residence (later named Welch Hall), and the Liberal Arts building comprised the entire campus until military barracks were constructed on campus during World War II, and the Gleeson Library was built in 1950. The Liberal Arts building was renamed Campion Hall in honor of an English Jesuit, Edmund Campion, who was martyred during the persecution of the Catholic Church in Elizabethan England.

On December 10, 1926, a groundbreaking ceremony was held for the new Liberal Arts building, later named Campion Hall. In this photo from the *Ignatian,* James Rolph Jr., mayor of San Francisco, holds the ceremonial shovel. Edward Whelan, S.J., the president of St. Ignatius College, is behind, and to the right of Mayor Rolph. Monsignor Michael Connolly, standing to the left of Mayor Rolph, represented the Archdiocese of San Francisco at the ceremony.

UNIVERSITY OF SAN FRANCISCO ARCHIVES

The Jesuits in the Community During the 1920s

DURING THE 1920S, THE JESUITS ASSOCIATED WITH ST. Ignatius Church and College continued and expanded the outreach and social service activities to the community that they initiated during the last half of the 19th century and the first two decades of the 20th.

This legacy of social service can be traced to the founder of the Society of Jesus, Saint Ignatius of Loyola, who in the mid-16th century urged his followers to engage in social outreach activities to the less fortunate members of society, especially those in hospitals and prisons.

During the 19th century, several Jesuits from St. Ignatius Church and College assisted in the ministry of the City and County Hospital of San Francisco. During the 20th century, no individuals were more dedicated in the work at this hospital than Aloysius Stern, S.J., and Gerald Fader, S.J. Fr. Stern began his tenure as chaplain at the City and County Hospital in 1925 and ended his work there in 1947. His former altar boy at the hospital, Irwin Schoenstein, gave a sermon about Fr. Stern on the occasion of his Golden Jubilee Mass. Fr. Schoenstein described how "in 1925 at age 50, Father Stern began the most important work of his life when he was appointed chaplain of the City and County Hospital. On

accepting that assignment, he determined to give his all for God's sick and dying. And he did just that, for the next 22 years. He spent all his energies caring for the spiritual needs of a hospital of over one thousand patients."

After Fr. Stern retired to the USF Jesuit community, he continued with his pastoral ministry to people throughout the city who came to see him on a regular basis. Fr. Stern's successor, Fr. Fader, spent another 15 years at the same ministry. After his work at the hospital ended, Fr. Fader became pastor at Our Lady of Guadalupe Church in San Diego, a parish for Mexican nationals. He learned to speak Spanish, and among his many pastoral activities, he facilitated outreach programs by the local Catholic hospital to the neighborhood barrio within his parish.

In 1919, John McCummiskey, S.J., on the faculty of St. Ignatius College, initiated another type of outreach activity at the request of Archbishop Edward Hanna of San Francisco. Fr. McCummiskey began offering special masses to the hearing impaired of San Francisco and Oakland, during which he communicated sermons using sign language. During the 1920s, Louis Egan, S.J., took over this work from Fr. McCummiskey and sustained it until specially trained Diocesan priests were available for the hearing-impaired attendees at masses. Also in 1919, George Fox, S.J., began a series of special retreats for Catholic doctors in San Francisco. By the time of the second retreat, in May of 1920, 62 physicians were present for the first night's exercises, which were open to all medical professionals, Catholic and non-Catholic, in the city. The word got out about the retreat, and by the closing day of the seven-day retreat, on Pentecost Sunday, 92 physicians were present at Mass and 75 physicians received Holy Communion. The Jesuits of St. Ignatius Church never hesitated to offer retreats for other groups of professionals, such as attorneys, who increasingly availed themselves of this service throughout the following years.

In 1925, Pius Moore, S.J., the president of St. Ignatius College, sent a report to Joseph Piet, S.J., California provincial for the Jesuits, outlining the extent and diversity of social outreach activities being performed by the Jesuits of St. Ignatius Church and College. These activities included providing help to several churches, convents, and chapels in the Bay Area, especially for Sunday Masses. At St. Ignatius Church during the 1920s, the thousands of masses celebrated on Sundays, throughout the week, and in conjunction with special devotions such as Novenas or Lenten Talks made a major contribution to the lives of the Catholics of San Francisco. For example, beginning in 1917 and continuing into the 1920s, the Jesuits of St. Ignatius Church held an annual Novena, nine consecutive days of prayers and devotion, on the occasion of the Feast of the Sacred Heart. On average, 800 to 900 members of the community attended these sermons. The thought-provoking and splendidly delivered sermons at St. Ignatius Church, by well-known Jesuits such as Fathers Dennis Kavanagh and Charles Carroll, kept the legacy alive from the first decades of the church's history. In addition to enhancing the spiritual lives of Catholics, the Jesuits of St. Ignatius contributed significantly to the social and intellectual life of the people of San Francisco, a tradition that still flourishes today.

Gerald Fader, S.J., from the USF Jesuit Community, is pictured here counseling a tuberculosis patient at the City and County Hospital of San Francisco in 1955. Fr. Fader continued a tradition that stretched back to Ignatius of Loyola's ministry to the hospitalized of Rome in the mid-16th century and that found expression in San Francisco with the coming of the Jesuits to the city in the mid-19th century.

UNIVERSITY OF SAN FRANCISCO ARCHIVES

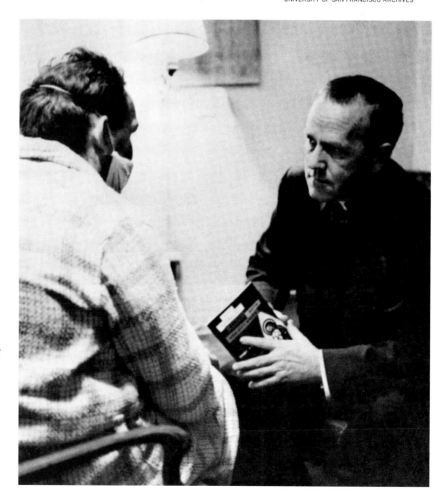

Richard Gleeson, S.J.

AMONG THE MANY JESUITS WHO CONTRIBUTED TO THE development of St. Ignatius Church and College and to the San Francisco community, Richard Gleeson, S.J. was one of the most significant. His efforts in California spanned seven decades and were especially salient for St. Ignatius Church and College beginning in 1918. Fr. Gleeson's importance in the course of the institution's history is symbolized by the fact that the main library on the campus of the University of San Francisco is named in his honor.

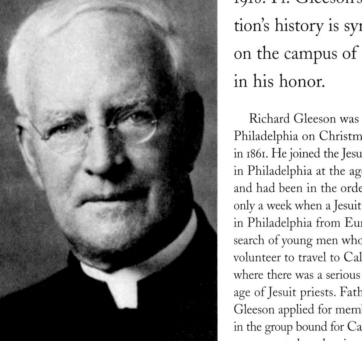

Richard Gleeson, S.J., provincial of the California Jesuits, president of Santa Clara College, director of the St. Ignatius Conservation League, prefect of St. Ignatius Church, and friend of the people of San Francisco.

Richard Gleeson was born in Philadelphia on Christmas Eve in 1861. He joined the Jesuit order in Philadelphia at the age of 15 and had been in the order for only a week when a Jesuit arrived in Philadelphia from Europe in search of young men who would volunteer to travel to California, where there was a serious shortage of Jesuit priests. Father Gleeson applied for membership in the group bound for California, was accepted, and arrived in the Golden State on September 28, 1877. His first assignment was at Santa Clara College, where, after his ordination in 1894, he became prefect of studies. From 1905 to 1910, he was president of that college, though he frequently visited his fellow Jesuits at St. Ignatius College to the north. He was staying at St. Ignatius College on the morning of April 18, 1906, the time of the devastating San Francisco earthquake and fire, which he vividly

described in a later account (vignette #33).

In 1914, Fr. Gleeson was appointed provincial of the California Jesuits, a position he held until 1918. After his tenure as provincial, Fr. Gleeson was assigned to St. Ignatius Church. He arrived in San Francisco just as the 1918 influenza epidemic was raging through the city; the Jesuit Community; and the faculty, staff, and student populations of St. Ignatius. He helped tend to the many individuals associated with the church and college who were struck down by the epidemic, and he also helped minister to the sick in the nearby Japanese community, including assisting Jesuit Brother Matsui to run the Japanese mission in the community.

In 1920, after the epidemic had waned, Fr. Gleeson was put in charge of the St. Ignatius Conservation League, an organization responsible in large part for raising the necessary funds to save St. Ignatius Church and College from financial ruin during its major economic crisis at the end of World War I (vignettes 61 and 62). In 1920, Fr. Gleeson blessed the new

William Monihan, S.J., USF's head librarian, led the efforts to establish a new university library named in honor of Fr. Gleeson. In this photo, Fr. Monihan is meeting with architect Milton Pflueger in 1950 to go over plans for a scale model of the library, the first new construction on the campus since 1927.

faculty residence on the St. Ignatius College campus, which had been funded by Bertha Welch, a long-time benefactor of the Jesuits of San Francisco. During the next two decades, he served as both prefect of St. Ignatius Church and director of the Ladies' Sodality, positions that enabled him to reach out to thousands of the less fortunate citizens of San Francisco and to link them to those who had the means to help. To celebrate his golden jubilee as a Jesuit, a Mass was held in his honor on November 13, 1927, followed by a reception and dinner at the Palace Hotel on Market Street. Thousands of Fr. Gleeson's friends gathered at the hotel to honor him, including San Francisco Mayor James Rolph Jr.

Following a series of long illnesses, Fr. Gleeson died on December 23, 1945, one day before his 84th birthday, surrounded by his fellow Jesuits at the University of San Francisco, and on the day that his portrait by local artist Arthur Cahill was to be unveiled in the little theater of the Liberal Arts Building (Campion Hall). Fr. Gleeson's funeral was held four days later in St. Ignatius Church and was attended by hundreds of friends, religious from other orders and congregations, diocesan clergy, and Jesuits from throughout California.

In 1937, on the occasion of Fr. Gleeson's 60th anniversary as a Jesuit, a group of his friends pledged to raise the money necessary to build a library on the University of San Francisco campus in his memory. After his death, those efforts were intensified under the leadership of William Monihan, S.J., university librarian. On December 3, 1950, the Richard A. Gleeson Library was dedicated at the University of San Francisco. To this day, it remains the heart of the university, serving as a lasting tribute to a man who gave so much to the university and to the people of San Francisco.

Part IV: Surviving Depression and War

T HE STOCK MARKET CRASH OF OCTOBER 1929 USHERED IN a worldwide depression that had major effects on the nation, the city of San Francisco, and the university that would soon adopt the city's name. Like the city itself, the Jesuits' experiment in education faced major economic challenges during the 1930s — finances were a constant source of concern, and enrollment was flat during most of the decade. The institution began the decade, however, on several optimistic notes, including a celebration of its 75th anniversary, a new name, and a U.S. Supreme Court decision paving the way for a major land acquisition that encompassed part of an old Masonic cemetery and extended the campus north to Golden Gate Avenue, east to Masonic Avenue, and west to Parker Avenue. The shortage of cash during the Depression did, however, prevent USF from purchasing that portion of the cemetery that ran all the way to Turk Street and from building on the land that it did acquire.

The co-curricular programs that had flourished during the 1920s, including athletics, drama, and debate, survived the economic woes of the 1930s, though desperately needed improvements for the library, science equipment, and classroom facilities were financially impossible. Graduates of the university found the job market terrible, and alumni contributions were minimal.

Concurrent with the beginning of a national economic recovery by 1939, World War II erupted in Europe and Asia, finally engulfing the United States, as well, on December 7, 1941. During the war, the University of San Francisco saw its enrollment plummet to fewer than 400 students as most of the student body volunteered for the armed forces or were drafted. Former USF students fought all over the globe and in every branch of the service. Many were wounded, and more than 100 former USF

ROTC Annual Review, April 17, 1941. The "Armory" center sits atop the old cemetery reservoir. A cemetery monument is at right. Standing (left to right) are Robert Griswold '43, Ezio Paolini '42, and James Switzer '43.

UNIVERSITY OF SAN FRANCISCO ARCHIVES

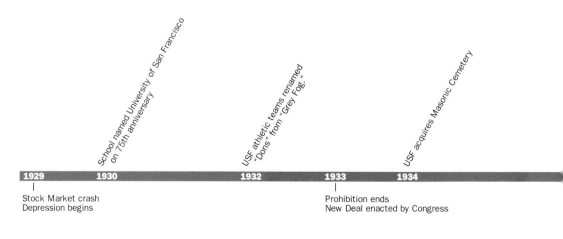

School named University of San Francisco on 75th anniversary

USF athletic teams renamed "Dons" from "Grey Fog."

USF acquires Masonic Cemetery

| 1929 | 1930 | 1932 | 1933 | 1934 |

Stock Market crash
Depression begins

Prohibition ends
New Deal enacted by Congress

students lost their lives. At USF, monthly deficits soared, and had it not been for the establishment of a military training program on campus and a modest but ultimately crucial fundraising campaign, the institution might have closed its doors before the war finally ended on August 16, 1945. Once again, however, the university survived external threats largely through the resourcefulness of its leaders, including its president, William Dunne, S.J. With the end of the war, a new era of expansion and challenges was at hand. The sacrifices of those who did not return from the war, however, were not forgotten by the nation or by San Francisco's Jesuit institution of higher education.

The major developments at USF during the 1930s and early 1940s, during depression and war, will be the subject of the next several vignettes.

The University of San Francisco as it appeared in 1930, the year the institution changed its name from St. Ignatius College. A corner of the faculty residence (Welch Hall) can be seen between Campion Hall and St. Ignatius Church.

UNIVERSITY OF SAN FRANCISCO ARCHIVES

1937	1939	1941	1945
Golden Gate Bridge opened	World War II begins	United States enters World War II	World War II ends U.N. Charter signed in San Francisco

The Crash of 1929

AS THE FALL SEMESTER OF 1929 GOT UNDERWAY, THE administration, faculty, students, and alumni of St. Ignatius College could look back to the prior decade with a great sense of accomplishment. Their institution had gone from the brink of bankruptcy in 1919 to economic stability in 1929; the campus had moved from a temporary wooden structure into a permanent home that boasted two new buildings; enrollment in the college division had dramatically increased from 194 students in 1919 to 1,099 in 1929; a new College of Commerce and Finance and an evening program had been successfully launched; the law school had grown in reputation and in enrollment; new curriculum areas had been developed; and the college's drama, debate, and athletic programs were flourishing, highlighted by the basketball team's capture of the 1929 Pacific Coast championship.

The success and growth of St. Ignatius College during the 1920s paralleled that of the city of San Francisco and the nation as whole. Innovations in technology, expansion in numerous industries, significant population growth, and high employment appeared to guarantee unending prosperity, limitless opportunities, and optimism about the future. Then came the stock market crash of October 1929. Within a matter of days, $30 billion was lost, and the economy of the United States and much of the world was shaken to the core. Although only a relatively small percentage of the U.S. population was directly affected by the stock market crash, the market's collapse set in motion economic forces that soon led to massive layoffs, business closings, and bank failures that eliminated the life savings of tens of thousands of people. In 1930, the United States saw 26,000 businesses close, followed by another 28,000 in 1931. By 1932, almost 3,500 banks had gone under, eliminating billions of dollars in uninsured deposits. Twelve million people, or nearly 25 percent of the labor force, lost their jobs, and those who kept their jobs saw their real earnings fall by 33 percent. The economic collapse of the U.S. economy ushered in what soon became known as the Great Depression.

Like the rest of the cities in the United States, the stock market collapse and the depression that followed had a major impact on San Francisco. Unemployment in the city soon rose to 20 percent. Among the hardest hit segments of the labor force in San Francisco were those associated with the maritime shipping industry, such as longshoremen. The early years of the Depression witnessed increased activism on the part of unions, including the Longshoreman's Association. In 1933 and 1934, there were a series of strikes by that union and others, followed by escalating violence. On both sides of the strikes were the parents of USF students. On July 5, 1934, a confrontation between strikers and police led to two deaths and more than 60 injuries in a day that came to be known as Bloody Thursday. Throughout the nation, the 1930s became a time of increased labor unrest and reaction and overreaction by police and management. As labor-management relations deteriorated, as unemployment soared, and as people's economic lives were threatened, the optimism of the 1920s gave way to the pessimism of the 1930s.

Throughout the 1930s, public works projects helped reduce the nation's massive unemployment. In San Francisco, the 1930s witnessed the building of two great publicly funded bridges that connected the city to the eastern and northern sections of the Bay Area. The San Francisco Oakland Bay Bridge was completed in 1936, and the Golden Gate Bridge was finished in 1937. To celebrate the completion of these two bridges, to provide a psychological boost to the city, and to stimulate the economy, San Francisco decided to host a world's fair by the end of the decade. These plans came to fruition in 1939 with the Golden Gate

International Exposition, which ran from February 19 to October 29. Sunday, October 14, was set aside as USF Day at the world's fair.

The main gateway to the University of San Francisco in 1931, up the steps from Fulton Street. If visitors to the campus in 1931 passed through this gate, they would first come to the Jesuit residence (Welch Hall). To their left would be St. Ignatius Church, and to their right, the Liberal Arts Building (Campion Hall). Until 1950, these were the only three permanent buildings on campus.

UNIVERSITY OF SAN FRANCISCO ARCHIVES

St. Ignatius College Becomes the University of San Francisco

AS ST. IGNATIUS COLLEGE BEGAN TO PREPARE FOR ITS 1930 Diamond Jubilee, an event marking 75 years of Jesuit education in San Francisco, the college's leadership began to receive suggestions that the name of the institution should be changed to the University of San Francisco. Exactly who first proposed the name change is not known, though apparently a group of alumni were initially behind the fledgling movement to have their alma mater take on the name of their city.

As word spread about a possible new name for the college, support and opposition to the change emerged. When Jesuit Superior General Wladimir Ledochowski first heard of the possible name change, he was opposed. By August 1930, however, word was received that the superior general of the Jesuits had changed his mind. The provincial of the California Jesuits, Joseph Piet, S.J., communicated this change of heart to the president of St. Ignatius College, Edward Whelan, S.J., in a letter that stated, "Father General expressly ceases all opposition to the change of name from St. Ignatius College to the University of San Francisco and he adds in a letter to me a prayer that both our Holy Father St. Ignatius and the patron of the city of San Francisco may intercede for the school that it may do still more than it has been doing and has done previously to promote the greater glory of God."

As support grew to change the institution's name to the University of San Francisco, the college's leadership thought it prudent to solicit the views of the civic and religious leaders of San Francisco. Archbishop Edward Hanna of San Francisco endorsed the name change, as did two other California prelates: Bishop Robert Armstrong of Sacramento and Bishop John MacGinley of Fresno. The five-term mayor of San Francisco, James Rolph Jr., also responded positively to the proposed name change. Mayor Rolph had been a long-time supporter of the institution; was a close friend of the dean of the law school, Matthew Sullivan; and had received an honorary degree from St. Ignatius College. In January 1930, he wrote to President Whelan about his views on the matter. "There should be here a University of San Francisco," the mayor wrote, and added that "the name should be appropriated by your Order before other far-seeing educators adopt the name. If the name is changed, nothing will be lost in the character of the institution and, in my opinion, its influence will be greatly increased."

Other Bay Area institutions of higher education opposed the Jesuit school taking on the name of the city of San Francisco. An editorial in the student newspaper of the University of California at Berkeley, for example, argued that "San Francisco may not be happy at being adopted by St. Ignatius," and that it was unfair for the Jesuit school to usurp the name "since the City of San Francisco might wish at a later date to establish a public university." Likewise, the student newspaper of San Mateo Junior College was critical of the name change in an editorial that stated: "The name of the City of San Francisco belongs to the people of the city as a whole; it does not belong to a sectarian institution as is St. Ignatius or to any other body that represents a particular creed." The St. Ignatius College student newspaper, the *Foghorn,* responded that students attending the school were from all creeds, that there were no barriers along sectarian lines, and that the name change was consistent with the views of the citizens of San Francisco.

After carefully weighing the pros and cons of changing the name of the institution to the University of San Francisco, President Whelan's advisers agreed "to begin immediately to call our college the University of San Francisco." On October 10, 1930, two days before the institution officially began its Diamond Jubilee week of celebrations, Articles of Incorporation

for the University of San Francisco were filed with the California Secretary of State in Sacramento and in the County Clerk's Office in San Francisco. As the *Ignatian* put it, "the change of name, which had been discussed and planned long in advance by faculty and alumni heads, could have been announced at no more appropriate time than at the Diamond Jubilee."

The city and school that had been intertwined for three quarters of a century were now linked by name as well as by history.

The week of the Diamond Jubilee, celebrating the 75th anniversary of the founding of St. Ignatius Church and College, was held from October 12 through October 19, 1930. It was used as the occasion to announce that the name of St. Ignatius College was to be changed to the University of San Francisco. The last day of the Diamond Jubilee included a parade of civic, religious, and fraternal leaders and organizations. Seated in the rear seat of this parade car are James Rolph Jr., mayor of San Francisco, and Cardinal Patrick Hayes of New York, who delivered the sermon at an outdoor Mass following the parade.

UNIVERSITY OF SAN FRANCISCO ARCHIVES

86 The Diamond Jubilee

IN 1930, ST. IGNATIUS COLLEGE CELEBRATED ITS 75TH year of Jesuit education in San Francisco. This Diamond Jubilee, comprising a host of civil and ecclesiastical events, was planned under the direction of the institution's president, Edward Whelan, S.J., with the assistance of staff, faculty, alumni, and civic leaders.

The Diamond Jubilee began on May 19, 1930, with the annual commencement exercises held in San Francisco's Dreamland Auditorium. San Francisco Archbishop Edward Hanna presided over the commencement exercises, during which 95 undergraduate and law degrees were awarded to the Diamond Jubilee Class. Three days later, a ceremony was held at the site of the first St. Ignatius Church and College on Market Street, then the location of the Emporium department store. At the ceremony, the Society of California Pioneers unveiled a brass plate, attached to the archway leading into the store, commemorating the founding of St. Ignatius Church and Academy in 1855. John Lerman, past president of the Pioneer Society, spoke of the debt that San Francisco owed to the Jesuits and of his respect for the institution's founding president, Anthony Maraschi, S.J., whom he knew personally. "Here 75 years ago with the turning of the first shovel full of sand," Lerman declared, "was witnessed the birth of a great institution, nurtured in its infancy by the fostering care of saintly Fr. Maraschi."

On July 14, the celebration continued with a luncheon for civic leaders held at the Palace Hotel. At the luncheon, Mayor James Rolph lavished praise on the institution's preparations for its 75th birthday and committed the City of San Francisco to support the celebration. "We are delighted at the opportunity," the mayor proclaimed, "to do something and do it big for St. Ignatius." At the luncheon, Archbishop Hanna added his thoughts on the institution's celebration: "If the City of San Francisco owes an eternal debt of gratitude to St. Ignatius College, if the cities surrounding San Francisco owe the same debt, if the whole State and the Pacific slope owe what they can never repay, may I in all humility say that the Archbishop owes it still more. St. Ignatius through 75 years, has furnished the Archbishops of San Francisco with a steady force of intelligence — the power that works through the community may not only be successful but may be an exemplification of the teachings of Christ."

October 12 through October 19, 1930, was designated as Diamond Jubilee week. It began on Sunday, October 12, with a Mass of Thanksgiving in St. Ignatius Church, presided over by John Collins, S.J., a visiting bishop from New York. The next day, students of the college and high school, faculty, and many alumni held a Diamond Jubilee rally in the St. Ignatius High School stadium. Darrell Daly, representing the alumni association; Wallace Cameron, student body president of St. Ignatius College; and Morris Murphy, president of St. Ignatius High School, all made speeches. Two rooting sections cheered

the speakers, and the newly organized college Glee Club sang several selections.

On October 14, the Alumni Association hosted a luncheon at the Elks Club for visiting educators and alumni. Speakers included Matthew Sullivan, graduate of St. Ignatius College, former Chief Justice of the California Supreme Court, and dean of the law school. That evening the festivities moved to Civic Auditorium, where the university's honor literary society, Kappa Lambda Sigma, hosted a series of lectures, featuring among others, Herbert Bolton, historian at the University of California, and Zacheus Maher, S.J., graduate of St. Ignatius College and president of Loyola University, Los Angeles.

On October 15, visiting clergy and educators from across the country were given a sightseeing tour of San Francisco, followed in the evening

by a concert on the lawn between the faculty residence and the brightly lit St. Ignatius Church. On Thursday morning, a requiem Mass was offered in St. Ignatius Church by Fr. Whelan for deceased faculty, staff, and alumni of the college. That evening, Archbishop Hanna, Mayor Rolph, and Fr. Whelan all spoke at a Jubilee banquet held at the Palace Hotel and attended by an overflow audience of 1,200 guests. The next evening witnessed another event in Civic Auditorium for representatives from colleges, universities, and other institutions from throughout the United States and Europe who were attending the celebration. The visitors heard speeches about the educational work of the Jesuits in San Francisco and related topics from scholars such as James Walsh from New York and John McMahon, a member of the San Francisco Bar. On

The Diamond Jubilee celebration included an open-air Mass on campus before a colossal altar. The Mass was held at the St. Ignatius High School Stadium, the current site of Negoesco Stadium, adjacent to what is now the Koret Health and Recreation Center of the University of San Francisco.

UNIVERSITY OF SAN FRANCISCO ARCHIVES

Archbishop Edward Hanna of San Francisco was the principal celebrant at the outdoor Mass on October 19, 1930, celebrating the 75th anniversary of the founding of St. Ignatius Church and College.

constructed altar under an enormous canopy. The mass was attended by 30,000 people and featured Archbishop Hanna as the principal celebrant, with Cardinal Patrick Hayes of New York giving the sermon. Cardinal Hayes' sermon was broadcast live by a local radio station: "San Francisco, spiritual of name and spiritual in birth, rightly glories today in three-quarters of a century of St. Ignatius College" declared Cardinal Hayes. "It has earned for itself a prestige and a place of honor among outstanding scholastic foundations being bone of the bone, flesh of the flesh, spirit of the spirit, of that intrepid, erudite and apostolic order of the teachers, the Jesuits."

For 75 years, the Jesuits had served the citizens of San Francisco. It seemed altogether fitting, therefore, that the Golden Jubilee Celebration was the occasion for the announcement that the Jesuits' experiment in education would hence-forth incorporate the city's name and become the University of San Francisco.

October 18, a Jubilee Ball was held for students at the Fairmont Hotel.

The Diamond Jubilee week concluded on October 19. The day began with a parade of civic, religious, and fraternal organizations of San Francisco, marching from the Panhandle section of Golden Gate Park to the stadium of St. Ignatius High School. At that location, an outdoor Mass was held at a specially

The Cemetery

IN 1930, THE YEAR THAT THE UNIVERSITY OF SAN Francisco celebrated its Diamond Jubilee, the U.S. Supreme Court made a decision that was to have a major impact on the development of the university. After years of litigation, the Supreme Court ruled that the old Masonic Cemetery, consisting of approximately 28 acres of land located directly to the north of the new Liberal Arts Building (Campion Hall) on Fulton Street, could be sold to any prospective bidder.

Looking toward the eventual expansion of their institution, the Jesuits had sought for years to buy this cemetery, which extended from Parker to Masonic Avenue and from Turk to Fulton Street, not including the property already owned by the Jesuits and where St. Ignatius Church, the faculty residence, and the Liberal Arts Building stood. Although burials had not been permitted on this property since 1903, there was strong opposition on the part of 17 cemetery lot owners to the removal of the estimated 19,000 bodies interred within the cemetery limits.

After years of litigation and negotiations, approximately 14 acres of the Masonic Cemetery, situated just north of Campion Hall and St. Ignatius Church, was purchased by USF in 1934. This photo was taken on October 14, 1930, during USF's diamond jubilee celebration.

SAN FRANCISCO HISTORY CENTER, SAN FRANCISCO PUBLIC LIBRARY

When the removal issue was brought before the San Francisco Board of Supervisors in 1928, an ordinance authorizing the removal of the bodies was passed, with the support of the Masonic Cemetery Association, owner of the property. This association was eager to sell the property and argued that the land had become a "menace to health, a wilderness frequented by vagabonds and a barrier to fire apparatus." The cemetery lot owners fought the ordinance in the federal circuit court, which issued an injunction against the ordinance. This injunction was appealed all the way to the U.S. Supreme Court, the appeal being handled by Matthew Sullivan, graduate of St. Ignatius College, former Chief Justice of the California Supreme Court, and dean of the St. Ignatius School of Law. On March 10, 1930, the Supreme Court dissolved the injunction and upheld the ordinance, thus clearing the way for the Jesuits to buy the cemetery.

After several years of negotiations, the Masonic Cemetery Association agreed to sell the entire cemetery to the Jesuits for $690,000. With the beginning of the national depression in 1929, however, and with the Jesuits' growing financial burdens, USF was able to purchase only approximately half of the cemetery property (the land south of Golden Gate Avenue) at a cost of $290,000, with an option to purchase the rest of the land by 1934. Unfortunately, the Jesuits could not raise the funds necessary to exercise this option, and the land between Golden Gate Avenue and Turk Street was sold to private developers. The deeds to the property south of Golden Gate Avenue finally passed to the Jesuits in March 1934.

On Easter Sunday, April 1, 1934, St. Ignatius Church announced to its congregation "with gratitude to God, that, during the past week, the lower half of the Masonic cemetery, for which we have been for so long negotiating, has finally been actually acquired by the university. It now owns that part of the cemetery between Parker Avenue and Masonic Avenue and South of Golden Gate Avenue projected. As the purchase price, $290,000, was considerably in excess of the actual funds collected in the 1931 drive, our debt has been increased and this makes our immediate problems, already aggravated by the impossibility of so many of our students to meet tuition, more urgent."

In the months following the purchase, the unclaimed headstones and tomb monuments at the Masonic Cemetery were removed and used for seawalls and landfill along the San

Francisco Bay, and most of the bodies interred in the cemetery were carefully exhumed and transported to the Woodlawn Cemetery in Colma. Many of the bodies were missed by the removal crews, however, because the deceased had often been buried in inexpensive 19th-century wooden coffins. The bodies had sometimes moved from their original location under marked tombstones in the wake of earthquakes and other land movements, and many of the caskets and cemetery mausoleums were buried under tons of dirt removed from the excavation site of the San Francisco College for Women on Lone Mountain.

In later decades, when foundations were constructed for new buildings on campus, overlooked bones were frequently unearthed. When contractors were excavating the foundation for Gleeson Library in 1950, one of their large earthmovers crashed through the roof of a buried mausoleum, and caskets containing bodies were churned up by the tractor operator. In 1966, when space for the foundation for Hayes-Healy Residence Hall and adjacent garage was dug, the first work crew came upon so many bones that they quit, and a less squeamish crew had to be hired. Undoubtedly, the remains of a few 19th-century citizens of the City of San Francisco are still resting just below the surface of today's University of San Francisco.

The Origins of the *Foghorn*

IN 1926, THE ASSOCIATED STUDENTS OF ST. IGNATIUS College undertook the publication of a monthly student-directed and student-financed newspaper. Five issues were published during that first year under the temporary title *Ignatian,* the same name as the college's literary magazine, which published its first issue in 1911. Andrew Black, the editor of the *Ignatian* in 1927, agreed to let the staff of the newspaper borrow the name until a decision was made on a permanent title. The first-year student newspaper was edited by Edward McQuade, a junior who later worked at the *San Francisco Examiner.* Raymond Feely, S.J., a faculty member in the College of Arts and Sciences, served as the moderator for the student newspaper. Fr. Feely became the university's first academic vice president in 1951.

The management of the first student newspaper of St. Ignatius College included (from top to bottom) Edward McQuade, editor; James Smyth, business manager; and John Lounibos, associate editor.

UNIVERSITY OF SAN FRANCISCO ARCHIVES

During its first year of publication, the student newspaper carried articles about St. Ignatius College, feature columns, and a sports section. One especially popular column, written by Will Connolly, who later became a sports columnist for the *San Francisco Chronicle,* was called "The Thinker"; in this column, "anything and everything was discussed that might conceivably interest the student mind."

During the 1920s, editorials in the school newspaper criticized Russian communism, tried to engender school spirit, and were highly critical of most movies, especially the new "talkies." The sports section in 1926 was written by James McGee, who later covered the San Francisco Giants for the *San Francisco*

News-Call Bulletin, and Wilson O'Brien, who later became city editor of the *San Francisco Examiner.*

In 1927, the *Ignatian* became the *Ignatian News* and was published every other Thursday. Will Connolly was the editor for the *Ignatian News* that year, and he also served as the yearbook editor and the manager of the college's publicity bureau. James McGee became editor in 1928, followed by Edward Sullivan, who eventually became a Hollywood writer. Under Sullivan, the name of the school newspaper was changed for the final time: to the *Foghorn,* the name it carries to this day.

St. Ignatius College changed its name to the University of San Francisco in 1930 (vignette #85). The *Foghorn,* with Mervin Hauser as its editor, defended this name change against attacks from other Bay Area student newspapers, such as the student newspaper at the University of California at Berkeley. Throughout 1930, the year of the Diamond Jubilee, the *Foghorn* covered every major school event: the 75th anniversary celebration, social events, dances, plays, games by USF's athletic teams wearing their new green and gold colors, and human interest features. One serial feature, "Memoirs of Vaccaro," followed a former St. Ignatius College student body president on his vagabond travels across Europe. During that year, the paper's financial status improved under business manager Jack Hanley, and the newspaper became a member of the National Scholastic Press Association.

Over the next three decades, except for 18 months when publication was disrupted by World War II and the resulting shortage of newsprint, the *Foghorn* continued to experiment with different formats, page layouts, editorial policies, columns, and special features. Editorials increasingly addressed not just campus issues, but also controversial political and social topics at the local, national, and international levels. Along the way, many of the paper's editors and writers developed the skills that later translated into notable careers in journalism.

One of the best known of these individuals was Pierre Salinger, who entered USF in 1946 and simultaneously became a reporter for the *Foghorn* and the *San Francisco Chronicle.* After graduation, Salinger became night editor of the *Chronicle.* He later became the press representative for Adlai Stevenson's presidential campaign in California, joined the staff of *Collier's* magazine, was the press secretary for President John F. Kennedy, and was ABC News bureau chief in Paris. Other notable *Foghorn* editors and writers have included Kevin Starr, former USF professor of communication arts and State Librarian of California; Leo McCarthy, former California lieutenant governor; former *San Francisco Chronicle/Examiner* columnist Warren Hinkle; and current *San Francisco Chronicle* reporter Carl Nolte.

In 1961, the American Newspaper Publishers' Association named the *Foghorn* the best college newspaper in the nation for its "forceful reporting" of campus news and bestowed upon the *Foghorn* staff the Pacemaker Award. It was the first time the award had been given in 15 years. In the same year, the Associated Collegiate Press Association awarded the *Foghorn* the All-American rating for the 15th consecutive year. After the *Foghorn* staff received the Pacemaker Award, congratulatory notes poured in from alumni, friends, and public figures such as Edmund G. Brown, the governor of California; William Randolph Hearst; and Pierre Salinger. The California Senate passed a resolution praising the *Foghorn* staff. The resolution read in part, "the members of the Senate extend their congratulations and commendations to the University of San Francisco *Foghorn*, its editorial and management personnel and the remainder of the staff for a well-earned award and recognition for its efforts." The president of USF, John Connolly, S.J., wrote that the "The *Foghorn* has been a credit to the University for all of its thirty-five years."

The *Foghorn* won its second Pacemaker Award in the 1995–1996 academic year.

Pierre Salinger (top, in a 1960 photo) was a reporter for the *Foghorn* and the *San Francisco Chronicle* while a student at USF. He became an editor at the *Chronicle,* worked for *Collier's* magazine, was press secretary for President John F. Kennedy, and was ABC Bureau Chief in Paris. Kevin Starr (bottom, in a 1998 photo) was editor of the *Foghorn* when it won a Pacemaker Award as the best college publication in the nation. He later became a professor in the communication arts department at USF. He went on to become University Professor at the University of Southern California and the State Librarian of California. He is the author of *Americans and the California Dream* and numerous other books and articles on California's intellectual and cultural history.

UNIVERSITY OF SAN FRANCISCO ARCHIVES

89 Go Dons!

THE BEGINNING OF THE 1930S WITNESSED BOTH CHANGE and continuity in the athletic programs at the University of San Francisco. Under Head Coach Jimmy Needles, the 1930 football team compiled its best record ever, with six wins and three losses. One of the starting tackles for the team was Isaiah Fletcher, the first of many African Americans to play on a varsity intercollegiate team for the University of San Francisco. This was decades before most universities and colleges began to integrate their teams or their campuses.

Tom Rice (above) played football (he was an All-Coast tackle) and rugby for USF from 1936 to 1939. In the 1950s, he was a professional wrestler (pictured here) under the name of the Red Scorpion, the Red Phantom, and the Masked Marvel. He was a major supporter of his alma mater, and for decades he devoted much of his time to university advancement, where he was known as "the generator." Earl Booker (right), who received a bachelor's degree in history from USF in 1941, won the Intercollegiate Boxing Championship in 1936.

UNIVERSITY OF SAN FRANCISCO ARCHIVES

After two straight Pacific Coast championships, the 1930 basketball team, also coached by Needles, slipped to a respectable record of nine wins and four losses. Nevertheless, the 1930 edition of the *Ignatian* waxed eloquent about coach Needles, who had been coaching the basketball team for six years: "Year after year he has produced one of the finest squads in this section of the country. Again during this past year, although he himself may not consider the season among his good ones, he turned out a team whose record was the equal of any college aggregation on the Coast. Playing against some of the most severe competition in the country, he has successfully preserved his teams on a high plane. In the true sense of the word he has proven himself a great coach. The

individual stars he has trained, and the records of his teams bear unassailable testimony to this fact." The writer concluded, "as a football coach Needles ranks high; but as basketball coach there is none like him. He is at the top."

The baseball program lay dormant during 1930, but was revived in 1931 under a former baseball star of the professional Pacific Coast League, Gene Valla. "The return of the national pastime to the Heights was greeted with wholehearted welcome," the 1931 *Ignatian* reported. According to the writer, "more than fifty candidates turned out for the squad on the first day of practice." Unfortunately, after a year of inactivity, the team compiled a disappointing record of two wins, seven losses, and a tie. Ever optimistic,

however, the *Ignatian* opined that "although Coach Valla's victories this season were few, every member of the team feels confident that he will turn out a championship team next year." After another disappointing season in 1932, the *Ignatian* concluded the "Rome wasn't built in a day," and that it "takes time and patience to build a ball team."

The occasional hiatus by a USF team during the 1930s was often the result of financial considerations, the current talent pool, and student interest during the end of an era of largely student-organized and operated athletic teams. Various sports programs, however, were instituted or revitalized at the University of San Francisco during the early part of the 1930s. For example, the track team, which began minimal intercollegiate competition in the late 1920s, had become a formidable opponent by 1932, compiling its best record to date, including a victory in the Sacramento Intercollegiate Relays. Likewise, the varsity

tennis program that began in 1928 with just three intercollegiate matches was playing a robust schedule by 1932. The University of San Francisco began a boxing program in 1931, and in its first intercollegiate competition, the team won five out of seven bouts against St. Mary's. Boxing was considered a "manly" sport at the largely all-male school, and many members of the boxing team went on to fight professionally. The USF soccer team played its first intercollegiate competition in the fall 1930, losing 5–0 to the Bears of the University of California at Berkeley. One year later, however, the soccer team had become a Pacific Coast power, compiling a record of four wins, one loss, and two ties and ending up tied with Stanford for the 1931 Pacific Coast Soccer League championship.

In November 1931, USF's student body president, George Ososke, received a letter from the San Francisco Junior Chamber of Commerce critical of the university's use of

The 1931 USF soccer team, in its second year of intercollegiate competition, tied Stanford University for the Pacific Coast League championship.
UNIVERSITY OF SAN FRANCISCO ARCHIVES

(Above) During the 1930 football season, the USF football team defeated Loyola University of Los Angeles 14–0 at Wrigley Field in Los Angeles. (Bottom) Three of USF's star players were Jack Gaddy, left, Isaiah Fletcher, center, and Louis Prusinovski, right.

the term "Grey Fog" to designate its athletic teams. The Junior Chamber of Commerce felt that the name did not give a positive image to the city and potentially hurt advertising. The *Foghorn* published a series of letters addressing the issue of a possible name change for the athletic teams, followed by a contest to come up with a new name. Student interest in the contest for a new name for the athletic teams was minimal and only a few names were submitted, including Vigilantes, Golden Gaters, Seagulls, Seals, and Sea Lions. These and other possible names were voted on by a committee composed of four undergraduates, four alumni, and four administrators, selected by USF President Edward Whelan, S.J. In January

1932, the *Foghorn* announced the new name for the university's athletic teams: the Dons. Jack Rhode, a sophomore in the College of Arts and Sciences, and sports editor for the *Foghorn*, had the honor of having his suggestion chosen as the official athletic nickname for the university.

Hubert Flynn, S.J. and the College of Arts and Sciences

FROM 1925 TO 1934, DURING A CRITICAL PERIOD IN THE development of the University of San Francisco, Hubert Flynn, S.J., served as the first dean of the College of Arts and Sciences. Before and after his tenure as dean, he taught English, classics, religion, and philosophy; advised numerous student organizations; and was a beloved student adviser and advocate. During the 1920s and 1930s, few individuals had a greater impact on students and colleagues at the university than did Fr. Flynn.

Hubert Flynn, S.J., first dean of the College of Arts and Sciences, long-term faculty member, and beloved adviser to students and their organizations, meets with students at the entrance to Campion Hall, 1930.

UNIVERSITY OF SAN FRANCISCO ARCHIVES

Hubert Flynn was born in San Francisco on October 1, 1879. He attended Mission Dolores grade school from 1885 to 1889 before enrolling at St. Ignatius College, then located on the corner of Van Ness Avenue and Hayes Street, and which included grammar school, high school, and college divisions. He continued through high school at St. Ignatius College, graduating in 1894. Following graduation, he entered the Jesuit Novitiate in Los Gatos, California, where he remained until 1900. That year, he began work at Gonzaga College on a bachelor's degree in philosophy, followed by a master's degree in philosophy from that same institution in 1903.

From 1904 to 1907, Fr. Flynn taught at St. Ignatius College, and from 1907 to 1908, at Gonzaga College. In 1908, he began four years of theological studies at Saint Louis University. He was ordained a Jesuit priest in 1911. In 1912, Fr. Flynn began a one-year assignment teaching philosophy at Gonzaga, followed by a similar one-year assignment at St. Ignatius College. From 1915 to 1921, he taught at the Jesuit Novitiate

The sophomore class in the College of Arts and Sciences in 1926, the year after the college was officially formed. In the front row on the far left is John Barrett, the class president, and in the middle of the front row is John Gearon, S.J., one of the college's professors.

at Los Gatos, at Loyola College in Los Angeles, and at the University of Santa Clara before returning to St. Ignatius College.

From 1921 to 1925, Fr. Flynn developed and taught courses in English, classics, and philosophy at St. Ignatius College, and wrote and printed numerous detailed course descriptions, lecture notes, and syllabi. During this period, the pages of the *Ignatian* were replete with photos and notes about Fr. Flynn's efforts as a faculty adviser to a host of student organizations, including the student body government of the law school, debating societies, and various literary clubs and organizations. He was also a strong supporter of the institution's athletic programs. Fr. Flynn knew virtually every student on campus by name and was genuinely interested in every student's well being, reflective of the Jesuit ideal of *cura personalis* — care of the person as a unique individual.

In 1925, the departments of arts, sciences, and philosophy were officially integrated to become the College of Arts and Sciences. This merger reflected various program changes, including an increase in the number of elective courses offered to students. Latin, however, was still required to graduate with a bachelor of arts degree. Fr. Flynn was named the first dean of the College of Arts and Sciences. He

served in that capacity from 1925 to 1934, a period of significant growth in the college. Student enrollment in the undergraduate college during this period went from 98 students in 1925 to 676 in 1934. Fr. Flynn oversaw major curriculum developments in the college during this period and strongly influenced the enhancement of the debating societies, the drama program, and athletics. He helped develop an evening program, beginning in 1925, and the institution's first summer session, in 1932.

In 1934, Fr. Flynn stepped down as dean to return to teaching for a year at the University of Santa Clara. He returned to USF in 1935, where he began a nine-year tenure teaching and advising students and their organizations. In 1944, Fr. Flynn celebrated his Golden Jubilee as a Jesuit. On that occasion, the president of the alumni association, Timothy Fitzpatrick wrote, "Father Flynn is one of the outstanding educators in the history of the Jesuits of San Francisco…and his achievements have earned him universal admiration and affection." Fitzpatrick continued, "Dean Flynn is also fondly remembered as the distinguished and beloved professor of philosophy, his special field, at Santa Clara University and Loyola at Los Angeles, as well as at the University of San Francisco where he is at present Professor of Ethics." Moreover, his "profound scholarship and great talents both in English literature and the classics are so marked that even his natural modesty and graceful native humor have been unable to hide them. The student who had Father Flynn as teacher has been highly privileged."

Fr. Flynn died in San Francisco on September 17, 1945, but his legacy continues at the University of San Francisco. At commencement every year, the Father Flynn Award is given to the graduating senior who has, throughout the entire undergraduate curriculum, maintained the highest grade point average. In addition, every year at the Fr. Hubert "Hub" Flynn Athletic Hall of Fame Dinner, former USF student athletes and teams are inducted into the USF Hall of Fame.

Edward Whelan, S.J.

91

HE WAS THE LAST PRESIDENT OF ST. IGNATIUS COLLEGE, and after the institution changed its name in 1930, the first president of the University of San Francisco. Edward Whelan, S.J., did much more, however, than serve as president of the school when it changed its name. He oversaw the move of the institution from its location in the "shirt factory," on the corner of Hayes and Schrader streets, to its current location on Fulton Street; presided over the building of the Liberal Arts Building (Campion Hall), the first academic building on the new campus; played a critical role in the purchase of property that significantly increased the size of the campus and ensured its eventual growth; and successfully guided the institution through the first years of a major worldwide depression.

Fr. Whelan, during his second year as president of St. Ignatius College, spoke at the groundbreaking ceremony for the new Liberal Arts Building (Campion Hall), on December 10, 1926. Seated in the far left of the photograph is James Rolph Jr., mayor of San Francisco. Next to Mayor Rolph is Monsignor Michael Connolly of St. Paul's parish, representing the Archbishop of San Francisco.

UNIVERSITY OF SAN FRANCISCO ARCHIVES

Edward Whelan was born in San Francisco on September 20, 1887. He attended the Crocker Grammar School in San Francisco and St. Ignatius College, where he completed the seventh and eighth grades, high school, and two years of college. Beginning in 1907, he studied for the priesthood at the Jesuit Novitiate in Los Gatos, California. From 1910 to 1913, he attended Gonzaga College in Spokane, Washington, where he received a master's degree in philosophy. From 1913 to 1919, he taught English, Greek,

Three views of the "new" wing to Campion Hall, which opened in 1931, the year before Fr. Whelan left the presidency of USF: a second floor hallway (above) an exterior shot from the west (bottom), and the student lounge (opposite top).

UNIVERSITY OF SAN FRANCISCO ARCHIVES

and history at the Santa Clara College High School, followed by four years of theological study in Burgos, Spain, where he was ordained a Jesuit priest in 1921. In 1925, he became president of St. Ignatius College.

During the first years of his administration, Fr. Whelan helped develop a new College of Commerce and Finance and an evening division, which admitted women to the institution for the first time in its history. These additions, plus growth in the undergraduate College of Arts and Sciences and the School of Law, propelled the enrollment of the institution from 444 students in 1925 to 1,099 in 1929. The institution's move to its current location on Fulton Street, the building of Campion Hall, the fundraising and legal efforts necessary to extend the campus to Golden Gate Avenue, and the institution's spectacular Golden Jubilee Celebration are all significant university milestones, for which Fr. Whelan deserves enormous credit. Fr. Whelan was also an accomplished orator and frequently gave speeches to community organization and to various Bay Area institutions. For example,

the director of the educational and religious department at San Quentin State Prison, H. A. Shuder, wrote to Archbishop Edward Hanna of San Francisco after a presentation by Fr. Whelan at that prison, "Fr. Whelan came over and gave us one of the finest addresses it has ever been my pleasure to hear, and I want to tell you this because of my appreciation of him and his message."

Fr. Whelan stepped down as president of the University of San Francisco in 1932 and immediately took over as superior of the Jesuit retreat house in Los Altos. In 1934, he was named the rector of Loyola High School in Los Angeles, which was financially reeling from the effects of the Depression. He managed to stabilize that institution's economic difficulties, and in 1942, he was made president of Loyola University, also in Los Angeles. He performed the same economic feat at that institution as he had at Loyola High School. Having guided Loyola University through its economic crisis and through World War II, Fr. Whelan took over the leadership of the Jesuit retreat house in Azusa, California, where from 1949 to 1952 he directed retreats, gave speeches in the community, and provided advice to priests and religious throughout the archdiocese. Fr. Whelan was next sent to St. Henry's

parish in Brigham City, Utah, to direct a parish and to care for 2,000 Navajo Indian children who were housed in military barracks erected during the war at the Intermountain Indian School. In 1955, he returned to the University of San Francisco to work in development relations.

In September 1955, Fr. Whelan celebrated his Golden Jubilee as a Jesuit in St. Ignatius Church. In his sermon honoring Fr. Whelan, John Laherty, S.J., asked the following question about Fr. Whelan: "What was behind all this indefatigable work, energy, and zeal of fifty years?" Fr. Laherty then answered his own question: "During all these successful years, Father Whelan had one characteristic which swept away all difficulties. He was and is today a selfless man. He got the cue from his Father Ignatius way back in his novitiate days when he studied himself in his examination of conscience." Fr. Laherty concluded, "Selflessness is the keynote of the spiritual legacy left us by St. Ignatius of Loyola, and Farther Whelan is an outstanding legatee of that great legacy."

During the last years of his life, Fr. Whelan served as the superior and pastor of Our Lady of Sorrows Church in Santa Barbara and as the Spiritual Father at the Montecito Jesuit Novitiate in Montecito, California. Fr. Whelan died at the Jesuit infirmary in Los Gatos on October 9, 1971.

For the University of San Francisco, Fr. Whelan's legacy of achievements during one of the institution's most challenging periods is profound. His views on Jesuit education also resound today. In a sermon Fr. Whelan gave in 1928, the third year of his presidency, he noted how the Jesuits endeavor to educate students "intellectually and at the same time morally." For the Jesuits, Fr. Whelan insisted, "the training of the mind must go hand in hand with the training of the heart; that it is but labor lost if the minds of the young are well trained as far as intellectual attainments are concerned, but whose moral training is sadly overlooked." The spirit of Fr. Whelan's words are echoed in USF's dedication to "educating minds and hearts to change the world."

Surviving the Great Depression

BY 1936, THE WORLDWIDE DEPRESSION, USHERED IN BY the stock market crash of 1929, had deepened, and educational institutions in the United States, such as the University of San Francisco, struggled to survive economically. Although USF had managed by 1934 to purchase approximately half of the 28 acres of cemetery property offered by the Masons due north of Campion Hall for $290,000, the school was unable to purchase the other half of the land, and it was left considerably in debt for the property it did purchase (vignette #87).

Despite the Depression of the 1930s, USF managed to find the economic resources to sustain its athletic programs, including varsity football, basketball, baseball, rugby, boxing, soccer, golf, and tennis. Pictured here is the 1937 USF varsity tennis team.

UNIVERSITY OF SAN FRANCISCO ARCHIVES

The economic consequences of the Depression significantly reduced fundraising among alumni and friends, put a moratorium on further expansion of the campus, and precluded construction on the land that had been acquired. Fortunately, enrollment declined only slightly during the first years of the Depression from its high water mark of 1,099 students in 1929 to 1,077 in 1936. By 1939, as the nation began to recover from the Depression, enrollment at USF increased to 1,481 students in all divisions.

Edward Whelan, S.J., successfully guided the institution from 1925 to 1932, including during the first years of the Great Depression. When he left office in 1932, he was replaced by William Lonergan, S.J., who was born in San Francisco in 1883, attended St. Ignatius College when it was located on the corner of Van Ness Avenue and Hayes Street, and joined the Jesuits in 1904. He came to the presidency of USF from a position on the editorial staff of *America*, the national Catholic weekly. His tenure as president was short and controversial due in part to the perception of many that he was opposed to the growth in the number of non-Catholics who were attending USF. His presidency came to an end in the middle of the spring semester of 1934, when he resigned and returned to his editorial position at *America*. He died two years later at age 52.

In April 1934, Harold Ring, S.J., replaced Fr. Lonergan as the president of USF. Harold Ring was born in San Francisco in 1893, attended St. Ignatius High School and College, and was ordained a Jesuit priest in 1926. He served as prefect of discipline at the University of Santa Clara from 1927 to 1930, and rector of Loyola High School in Los Angeles from 1930 to 1934.

When Fr. Ring was appointed president of USF in 1934, one of his first stated goals as president was to "consolidate the advances of former years, and to strengthen in our students that morale which is the driving force in all good work." He was also concerned about the impact of the Depression on the employment of recent graduates of USF. He repeatedly contacted USF's alumni about helping graduates of their alma mater find jobs in the middle of the worst depression in the nation's history. In a letter that Fr. Ring wrote to all USF alumni in April 1936, he concluded, "The USF graduates must face a rather cold world on May 25th. We ask your counsel and assistance in their difficult task of finding employment. Placement bureaus are very actively working with the Alumni Office. Please help our hard-working secretary, Mr. Frank Hughes, in placing these young men." In another letter to the alumni in June 1937, Fr. Ring wrote about how the young graduates "are now confronted with the very practical problem of employment. Many of them are without influential contacts." Fr. Ring then asked, "Will you not help us make the going easier for these young men? If you know of vacancies, telephone the Alumni Office; put in a good word to employers; consult the school for recommendations. The young men will be deeply appreciative of your interest; they are really in need of your help."

The Depression notwithstanding, the university continued to support many of its co-curricular programs during the 1930s. The 1937 edition of *The Don,* the university yearbook, is replete with descriptions of its debate, drama, and athletic programs. Under the leadership of its faculty adviser, Russell Berti, the varsity debate team engaged in debates with San Francisco State, San Jose State, St. Mary's College, U.C. Berkeley, Stanford, and Santa Clara. The College Players, under the stellar direction of James Gill, witnessed an outstanding 1937 season with well-received performances of "The Tavern," the "Music Master," "Seventh Heaven," and "Criminal at Large." During the 1936–1937 season, the USF football team played 10 games, compiling a record of four wins, four losses, and two ties, against nationally ranked powerhouses such as Texas A&M University. The varsity basketball team that year won 10 of its 17 games, including contests with the College of the Pacific, San Jose State, Santa Clara, and Loyola of Los Angeles. The university also continued to support varsity baseball, rugby, boxing, soccer, golf, and tennis.

The absence of funds for needed academic improvements did, however, weigh heavily on Fr. Ring. In a 1936 letter to the alumni, he wrote, "Our students and faculty must carry on their work under the difficulties of restricted library, laboratory, and class room space. The rich endowments of many of our sister private and public institutions have encouraged us to think that we too shall some day emerge from our present difficulties and be able to offer our students adequate library, laboratory, and gymnasium facilities. The present endowment of USF consists solely of the endowment of man; that is, the religious teachers who give their services without other compensation than their sustenance and the lay teachers who carry on so efficiently in the face of so many sacrifices."

By the end of the 1930s, USF had recovered from the slight enrollment decline it suffered during the Depression. These photos depict USF students in 1940 in front of Welch Hall (top) and in the library in Campion Hall (bottom).

UNIVERSITY OF SAN FRANCISCO ARCHIVES

As the nation and the university began to emerge from the Depression, there was a glimmer of hope that the fortunes of USF might improve. Soon, however, the world would be plunged into a war that would further test the institution "in the face of so many sacrifices," economic and human.

On the Eve of War

IN JULY 1938, WILLIAM J. DUNNE, S.J., BECAME THE 20TH president of the University of San Francisco, a position he held for 16 years. Fr. Dunne's presidency, the longest in the history of the institution, was inextricably intertwined with international events.

The same year he became president, Adolf Hitler annexed Austria, took over a third of Czechoslovakia, and instigated the Kristalnacht "riots," during which Jewish shops, homes, and synagogues in Germany were looted and burned, and 30,000 Jews, the first of 6 million from throughout Europe, were sent to concentration camps.

The USF class of 1941 was the last to graduate before the United States entered World War II. In this photo, some members of that class pose in front of Welch Hall on the USF campus.

UNIVERSITY OF SAN FRANCISCO ARCHIVES

On September 1, 1939, Hitler invaded Poland, Britain and France declared war on Germany, and World War II began in Europe. In Asia, Japan continued its territorial expansion, begun in 1931 with its occupation of Manchuria. By 1937, Japan had seized Shanghai, Peking, Tietsin, and Nanking. During 1938 and 1939, Japanese troops took over Shansi Province, Canton, and Hankow. Chiang Kai-shek, head of the Chinese Nationalist Party (Kuomintang), united with his former enemies the Chinese Communists, led by Mao Zedong, to fight the Japanese invaders. Ultimately, the war in Europe and in Asia involved the United States and dramatically affected the students, faculty, and administrators of USF.

As war was breaking out in Europe and Asia,

the citizens of San Francisco were preparing for a world's fair to celebrate the building of the San Francisco-Oakland Bay Bridge in 1936 and the Golden Gate Bridge in 1937. The Golden Gate International Exposition opened on February 18, 1939, on Treasure Island, the largest man-made island in the world. Ironically, the theme for the exposition was "Peace in the Pacific."

Like its forerunner, the Panama Pacific International Exposition of 1915, the Golden Gate International Exposition of 1939 was held during the first months of war in Europe. The exposition featured halls and temples patterned on Cambodian, Malaysian, and ancient Mayan and Incan structures; a 400-foot Tower of the Sun topped by a gilded rising Phoenix; a statue of the goddess Pacifica, complete with cascading fountains; an art exhibit of European masters valued at $40 million; and a carnival area with ferris wheels, roller coasters, assorted entertainment, and exhibits.

October 14, 1939, was designated by the exposition organizers as "USF Day." On that day, approximately 2,500 USF students, staff, and alumni, as well as thousands of visitors, attended the festivities on Treasure Island. The actual events honoring USF began at 2 P.M., when the school band, "resplendent in their new Dons uniforms," marched on to the island and gave a concert next to the Tower of the Sun. This was followed by the USF Glee Club giving a concert in the San Francisco Building. In the evening, USF students staged a rally and variety show, illuminated by colored lights. Next on the agenda was a fireworks display, followed by a dance in the California Building and a midnight bonfire. The Golden Gate International Exposition closed for the first time on October 29, 1939, and the international visitors to the fair returned to what had become in many cases their war-ravaged countries. The fair reopened on May 25, 1940, and closed for the last time on September 29, 1940. By then, France had fallen to the Germans, and Japanese forces had begun to occupy French Indochina.

Four months after Fr. Dunne became president, USF played a football game against a powerful team from Saint Mary's College, against whom the Dons had not scored a touchdown since 1932. On that fateful October afternoon in 1938, in the mud of Kezar Stadium, the Dons ended a six-year drought when USF quarterback Cliff Fisk threw a 45-yard touchdown pass to Bill Telesmanic. The next day, the *San Francisco Chronicle* carried a photo of Telesmanic and two other Dons, Danny Fisk and Dante Benedetti, celebrating the touchdown. USF eventually lost the game 13–6, however, and the caption under the photo read "The Joy That Died." The photo's caption was hauntingly predictive, as all three young men pictured in the photo were killed in World War II. Danny Fisk died in a military training flight in Northern California; Dante Benedetti was killed while flying a combat mission during the Battle of Guadalcanal in December of 1942; and in that same month, Bill Telesmanic was killed in a plane crash in the North African theater. Five years later, in 1947, Fr. Dunne delivered a sermon in St. Ignatius Church during a memorial Mass for these three men and the other 103 former USF students and faculty who died during the war.

Three USF football players celebrating a touchdown pass against Saint Mary's College in October 1938. In the middle is Bill Telesmanic, who caught the pass; on the left is Danny Fisk; and on the right is Dante Benedetti. The celebration was short-lived, however, as USF lost 13–6, and the *San Francisco Chronicle* carried the photo under the caption "The Joy That Died." All three young men later died during World War II.

UNIVERSITY OF SAN FRANCISCO ARCHIVES

Raymond Feely, S.J., and the USF Credo

BY THE END OF THE 1930S, DEMOCRACY WAS IN FULL retreat around the world. In Europe by 1939 only 10 out of 27 nations remained democratic, permitted free elections, and allowed a reasonable level of freedom among their citizens. In 1938, Raymond Feely, S.J., a faculty member at the University of San Francisco, traveled through Europe, where he conducted a political and economic survey of the continent.

Raymond Feely, S.J., USF faculty member, dean of faculties, regent of the law school, first academic vice president, author of the USF Credo, and originator of the first required college course in the United States on communism.

Fr. Feely, an authority on communism, Nazism, and fascism, had taught political science at USF for five years, and had written and lectured in various public forums on totalitarian regimes. He correctly predicted that if Hitler moved into Czechoslovakia, neither England nor France would attempt to stop him, and that if Hitler invaded France, that country would quickly fall. For Fr. Feely, the German-Soviet nonaggression pact of 1939 was also not the shock that it was for many people throughout the world. Fr. Feely believed that the two systems that governed Germany and the Soviet Union, Nazism and communism, were essentially cut from the same cloth, notwithstanding apparent ideological differences.

Few men in the first half of the 20th century were more closely identified with St. Ignatius College and USF than Fr. Feely. Born in San Francisco in 1895, Raymond Feely attended Immaculate Conception Grammar School in San Francisco before enrolling in St. Ignatius High School, from which he graduated in 1910. He graduated from St. Ignatius College in 1914, and from the institution's law school in 1916, having been a member of the first law class, which matriculated in 1912. After law school, he went into private practice, and three years later he was offered a position at the prestigious law firm of Roche, Sullivan, and Sullivan. He declined, however, saying he had a better offer: to join the Jesuits. He was ordained a Jesuit priest in 1930.

From 1931 to 1939, Fr. Feely taught philosophy, religion, and political science at the University of San Francisco. In 1934, he became a regent of the USF School of Law, and in 1939 he was appointed dean of the faculties, a position he held until 1951, when he was appointed USF's first academic vice president. As academic vice president, he inaugurated a course titled "The Dynamics and Tactics of World Communism," making USF the first American university to require such a course for all of its undergraduates. The course gained national publicity in *Time* magazine, which described its requirements as follows: "Students will read everything from *Das Kapital* to transcripts of the Hiss trial. They will interview local C.P. members and FBI men, and write detailed term papers on local Communist-front activities and how they work." In 1956, Fr. Feely suffered a major heart attack and was forced to cut back his work schedule. He returned to teaching political science at USF until 1963 when ill health forced his retirement. He died on November 17, 1965, at St. Mary's Hospital in San Francisco. At his requiem Mass, California Governor Edmund G. Brown proclaimed, "Fr. Feely in his long and distinguished life truly served mankind and the cause of freedom. He truly performed God's work on earth."

On February 24, 1940, while war was raging in Europe and Asia, Fr. Feely published a document called the USF Credo, which later appeared in the USF catalog. The USF Credo soon received national publicity and was reprinted in the publications of many other Jesuit colleges and universities. In the USF Credo, Fr. Feely outlined what he viewed as basic beliefs in American Democracy and Jesuit education in contrast to the totalitarian political and economic systems that were sweeping across the world. Among its key statements, the USF Credo argued, "the struggle today is to capture the mind of youth. Foreign dictatorships seek to perpetuate their shackles through youth movements. The American youth is exposed to these pernicious poisons which have the potency to destroy our hard won liberties." Fr. Feely then expressed his views on the belief system of USF: "It believes in God. It believes in the personal dignity of man. It believes that man has natural rights, which come from God and not from the State. It therefore is opposed to all forms of dictatorship, which are based on the philosophy that the 'total man' (totalitarianism) belongs to the State. It believes in the sanctity of the home — the basic unit of civilization." Fr. Feely went on to state that both labor and management have rights and obligations, and that "liberty is a sacred thing," and that USF "is vigorously opposed to all forms of 'racism' — persecution or intolerance because of race."

Less than two years after the publication of the USF Credo, many USF students and young alumni were fighting totalitarian regimes thousands of miles from their hilltop campus in the city named for St. Francis of Assisi.

> *"…[USF] believes in God. It believes in the personal dignity of man. It believes that man has natural rights, which come from God and not from the State. It believes in the sanctity of the home — the basic unit of civilization. It is vigorously opposed to all forms of 'racism'…"*

World War II and USF

AFTER GERMANY INVADED POLAND ON SEPTEMBER 1, 1939, an event that marked the beginning of World War II in Europe, the United States watched for more than two years as the Nazis overran Western Europe, attacked the Soviet Union, and conquered North Africa. During the same time, Japan extended its conquest of Asia, including China and much of Southeast Asia. The United States isolation from the war ended, however, on December 7, 1941, when the Japanese launched a surprise attack on the U.S. naval base at Pearl Harbor. The next day, President Franklin Roosevelt gave his famous "Day of Infamy" speech before Congress, which then declared war on Japan. On December 11, 1941, Germany and Italy declared war on the United States, and World War II became a global conflict.

Members of the USF class of 1942 receiving training in their ROTC unit.

UNIVERSITY OF SAN FRANCISCO ARCHIVES

In San Francisco, thousands of people flocked to Ocean Beach immediately after news arrived of the attack on Pearl Harbor and stared out to the horizon, probably looking for Japanese ships and planes in what many believed was going to be the imminent invasion of California. For the first time in history, a blackout was called for the city, and all lights were to be turned out by 6:15 P.M. St. Ignatius Church canceled the evening services that had been scheduled for Monday, December 8, and the illumination of the church towers was discontinued for the war's duration. During the war, St. Ignatius Church, with its tall spires, was on all of the maritime maps, however, helping captains guide their ships into San Francisco Bay. For servicemen, those spires were the last objects seen after leaving the Golden Gate, and the first objects seen coming home to San Francisco.

With the beginning of the war, the University of San Francisco underwent profound changes. Enrollment dropped precipitously as the young men of the university volunteered for the armed forces or were drafted. Before the attack on Pearl Harbor, enrollment in all divisions of the institution stood at 1,337. By the beginning of the spring semester of 1945, enrollment in all divisions had declined to 321. The onset of the war also forced a change in the academic calendar. Beginning in the fall semester of 1942, the traditional two-semester schedule was replaced with a trimester system in which the traditional six-week summer session was lengthened to a regular semester. In the law school, upon the recommendation of Raymond Feely, S.J., law school regent, classes were taught in short and intensive nine-week sessions. These changes were made to accelerate student completion of their programs in light of their expected service commitments, and to help students gain the opportunity to go to officer's candidate school when they reported for active duty. St. Ignatius High School, with which USF was joined until 1959, graduated its students six months early so they could complete at least a semester of college before being drafted. The completion of at least one semester of college would increase their chances of attending officer's candidate school.

Given the dramatic enrollment decline and the consequent budget shortfall during the war, USF President William Dunne, S.J., traveled to Washington to seek retention of the ROTC program and the addition of other military training programs for the university. Fr. Dunne's efforts began to bear fruit in July 1943, when the U.S. government established an Army Specialized Training Program (ASTP) at USF. This program, for the training of engineers, brought 300 students from all over the country to the university, adding to the institution's geographic diversity. Many former ROTC students were also reassigned to USF for further training. On the north side of the campus, along Golden Gate Avenue, eight temporary buildings, including barracks, offices, and an infirmary, were hastily built. These buildings survived well past the end

of the war for classroom use, and only with the construction of the Harney Science Center in 1965 and University Center in 1966 were the barracks finally removed from campus. The accelerated ASTP program, with its heavy demand on intense science courses, initially helped stabilize USF's uncertain financial situation. In March 1944, however, the government announced the discontinuation of the ASTP

Members of a USF ROTC unit stand at attention in front of St. Ignatius Church in 1942.

UNIVERISTY OF SAN FRANCISCO ARCHIVES

This aerial photograph of USF was taken on July 24, 1943, by the U.S, Army Air Force. In the upper left are St. Ignatius Church, Welch Hall, and Campion Hall, the only permanent buildings on campus at the time. In the upper right, perched on the top of Lone Mountain, is the San Francisco College for Women. The eight one-story buildings in the middle of the photograph (along Golden Gate Avenue) are barracks, offices, and an infirmary for approximately 300 students in the Army Specialized Training Program (ASTP).

U.S. ARMY AIR FORCE

program nationwide due to the desperate need for overseas manpower. At USF, the program was officially closed in 1944, and the students were ordered to active military service. The termination of this program further added to the economic woes of the university. By 1944, revenue had declined enormously, and USF was running a monthly deficit of $6,000 to $7,000.

In light of USF's mounting financial problems, a committee of alumni and friends was formed by Fr. Dunne to raise money for the struggling institution. The committee was headed by William McCarthy, former San Francisco postmaster, fire commissioner, and county supervisor; Florence McAuliffe, former president of the San Francisco Bar Association; and Daniel Murphy, an executive with Crocker Bank. This was the same trio that had helped secure the purchase of the Masonic Cemetery that would underpin the eventual post-war expansion of the university. The resulting

fundraising campaign brought in $150,000, a modest sum even by 1940s standards, but a sufficient amount to help ease the university through a challenging economic period.

While USF was struggling to survive economically and alumni and friends of the university were sacrificing financially to ensure its continuation, hundreds of its young men were fighting overseas, and more than 100 of those young men made the ultimate sacrifice.

The Last Full Measure

96

THE CRUISER U.S.S. *SAN FRANCISCO* SLICED THROUGH the cold dark waters of Lengo Channel near the South Pacific island of Guadalcanal in the late evening of November 13, 1942. The United States had entered World War II less than a year earlier, following the Japanese attack on Pearl Harbor in Hawaii. The cruiser was the flagship of a battle group of U.S. warships composed of five cruisers and eight destroyers, commanded by Rear Admiral Daniel Callaghan, native San Franciscan and graduate of St. Ignatius High School and the U.S. Naval Academy.

An ROTC unit at the University of San Francisco prepares to go overseas during World War II. One hundred thirty-six former students of St. Ignatius High School, St. Ignatius College, and the University of San Francisco "gave the last full measure" during the war.

UNIVERSITY OF SAN FRANCISCO ARCHIVES

A career naval officer, Admiral Callaghan had once served as naval adviser to President Franklin Roosevelt. On the night of November 13th, Admiral Callaghan's objective was to intercept a Japanese navy task force that was heading for Guadalcanal to bombard the U.S. Marines who were fighting the Japanese for control of that strategically important island.

As the U.S. battle group moved through the waters near Guadalcanal, flashes of lightning illuminated the nearby Solomon Islands and revealed low-flying clouds under a moonless sky. Officers and men aboard the ships peered out from darkened bridges, waited in plotting rooms, stood at gun stations on deck, or sweated below deck in crowded engine rooms. Suddenly, the Japanese task force was spotted on radar by the U.S.S. *Helena*, one of the few American ships equipped with this new technology. The sighting was relayed to Admiral Callaghan, who gave the order to head straight toward the middle of the Japanese formation, composed of two battleships and six destroyers. As the range quickly closed between the two naval formations, visual contact was made, and the battle was joined.

In the ensuing hellish fight at close range, torpedoes and gun salvos frequently found their marks, inflicting destruction on both groups of ships and death to many of the sailors on board.

221

Rear Admiral Daniel J. Callaghan, USN, graduate of St. Ignatius High School and the U.S. Naval Academy, naval adviser to President Franklin Roosevelt, and commander of a U.S. naval task force that successfully repulsed a larger Japanese force near the island of Guadalcanal in November 1942. Admiral Callaghan lost his life in the battle and was posthumously awarded the Congressional Medal of Honor, the nation's highest military award.

Two American cruisers and four destroyers were sunk, while the Japanese lost a battleship and two destroyers. Hundreds of men on both sides were killed. A cascade of shellfire from three different Japanese ships rained down on the *San Francisco* as it passed through the center of the Japanese task force with its guns blazing. The command bridge of Admiral Callaghan was raked with shells, and the admiral, his staff, the ship's captain, and nearly every man on the bridge were killed. The Japanese ships were repulsed, however, and the marines on Guadalcanal were saved from a deadly enemy bombardment and from Japanese efforts to land reinforcements on the island.

Admiral Callaghan was posthumously awarded the Congressional Medal of Honor, the nation's highest military award. Although heavily damaged, the cruiser *San Francisco* was repaired, fought in later battles during the war, and returned to its home port of the City by the Bay, where its crew received the Presidential Unit Citation, the nation's highest tribute to a ship and its company. The city of San Francisco memorialized its cruiser by placing a section of its shell-riddled superstructure, a mast, bell, and flag in a monument at Land's End, 200 feet from the water's edge, where it can still be seen today.

Daniel Callaghan was memorialized by the University of San Francisco as one of 136 former students of St. Ignatius High School, St. Ignatius College, and the University of San Francisco who lost their lives fighting in World War II. A combined USF and St. Ignatius High School service flag (the two schools were joined until 1959) was displayed above the altar of St. Ignatius Church during the war. The flag included white stars representing faculty, students, and alumni who served, and gold stars representing those who lost their lives. By the end of the war, the flag had more than 3,000 white stars and 136 gold stars. They were added to the 370 white and 10 gold stars from World War I.

Continuing the tradition from that earlier conflict (vignette #59), the service flag was blessed at special ceremonies held in St. Ignatius Church on Sunday, May 24, 1942, and on George Washington's birthday, February 22, 1944. At both ceremonies, William Dunne, S.J., president of USF, delivered sermons. The 1944 ceremony was announced as a "religious patriotic service of remembrance," beginning with an academic and military procession. James Lyons, S.J., chaplain of the local military unit then undergoing training at USF, sang Mass, and the enlarged service flag was rededicated to those, who in Abraham Lincoln's immortal phrase from another war, gave "the last full measure."

Letters Home

97

THROUGHOUT WORLD WAR II, AN ALUMNI PUBLICATION called the *Don Patrol* kept the University of San Francisco community informed about many of its young men who were serving overseas. The publication reported on the promotions and decorations received by former students, provided information about those killed or missing in action, and often quoted from servicemen's letters from the front. The August 1943 issue noted that up to that point in the war, 1,900 former USF students were in the military, 15 had been killed, and five were missing in action. In that issue, Lt. Bill Anderson, a former USF student serving in the Army Air Corps in the Pacific, wrote, "It really looks like USF is all out for the armed forces, both in person and in spirit. We are flying P-38s and have been doing pretty well by ourselves."

The same issue also reported on five Jesuits from USF who were serving overseas as chaplains. One of those Jesuits, Fr. Jerome Sullivan, was a "Lieutenant aboard a battle-wagon somewhere in the Pacific." Later in the war, Fr. Sullivan was given a commendation for "superior ability and leadership" by the commander of the battleship, U.S.S. *Pennsylvania.* The commendation cited Fr. Sullivan for "attending to the spiritual needs of the sick and wounded with understanding and care," including celebrating "Catholic Mass each day on this ship whether at sea or in port, whether actually in combat or at rest," for "maintaining high morale of the officers and crew," and for taking "part in the toughest amphibious operation for this ship" when the "going was hardest."

Many of the young men from the University of San Francisco who were serving in the military also wrote letters to their former teachers and priests. Later, many of these letters were reprinted in the *St. Ignatius Church Bulletin.* One of the most popular of those letter recipients was Alexander Cody, S.J., English professor at USF and priest at St. Ignatius Church. The letters written by his former students provide glimpses into the lives of young men during World War II while in training, on the front, and at those times that permitted a degree of reflection and introspection. Due to wartime security concerns, the exact location of the letter writer was generally not revealed, and even the name of the writer often was omitted. Occasionally, an initial or two does provide the needed clue to identify the writer.

"I am certainly appreciative of the fine sentiments both you and Father Feely sent my way," former student Tom Stack wrote to

Lt. Tom Stack, a former USF student, served in the Army Air Corps in Europe during World War II and described some of his experiences in letters he wrote to Alexander Cody, S.J., English professor at USF and priest at St. Ignatius Church.

Fr. Cody on March 18, 1945. "It's truly gratifying to know that the spirit of the Hilltop, fraternal as well as spiritual, has followed its loving constituents across the face of the globe and miles above it." Stack, a Lieutenant in the Army Air Corps stationed in Europe, vividly described to Fr. Cody his feelings about flying combat missions. "The first time aloft on a combat mission had me jittery and duly apprehensive, but everything worked out O.K. I prayed hard, though short, before we stepped aboard, and equally as hard when we turned down the bomb run." Throughout his tour of duty, his faith sustained his confidence that he would survive the war. "It's faith I have, Father, strong and true, and I firmly believe that I shall see

this through. It's a confidence that smooth the jitters and all nervousness. I can work right along smoothly and accurately while the flak is bursting so close you can smell it. I'm scared to death, true, but confident that everything will be O.K. It's a feeling that doesn't breed relaxation and carelessness, but it does inspire confidence." Stack concluded his letter by thanking Fr. Cody for his prayers: "You'll never know how much they can help. I'll be seeing you one of these days." Stack's confidence was well founded, because a month later he again wrote to Fr. Cody: "You should have a very special 'thank you' handed your way from me, Father, for the wonderful job you've done knocking at heaven's door for me. And to top it off, your intercession must have had a Class A priority, for look at me now, an ex-combat, war-weary veteran of some 35 sorties, on his way home! How does that sound to you, Father? Boy, is sure feels good!"

Another serviceman in the medical corps wrote to Fr. Cody from the Italian front: "The war is causing a lot of casualties which we are trying to heal as fast as possible. There have been a few strafing attacks on combat units next to us and air activity overhead, but we are doing all right." Not all of his patients were as fortunate, however, as in the following example he gives: "One of my patients is a Catholic Chaplain who had his leg blown off while trying to bury a dead soldier on the front lines. A booby trap was attached to the dead man." From the South Pacific, a different soldier also writes about the chaplains attached to his unit: "During this campaign we were very fortunate to have both our Catholic and Protestant Chaplains along at all times. They always would show up just when we needed them the most. They were very helpful in taking care of the prisoners of war, and their first aid treatment was wonderful at all times." The soldier then writes, "Our greatest privilege was having Mass and General Absolution both on the boats and on the Island during the campaign. The attendance was excellent and many have returned to the Faith. I had a couple dozen rosaries along and passed them out in the first few days to the boys who asked for them. I was sorry I did not have more. The Chaplains came along, however, and replenished my supply."

From Europe, another service man, B.R., wrote to Fr. Cody about his disappointment that "the squadron hasn't a Catholic Chaplain. It is impossible to go to Mass or to receive the Sacraments," he explained, "especially when we are on the move, as we are now. Two weeks ago I went to Mass in Luxembourg. The sermon was in German. The Church had all windows blown out, shrapnel holes in the ceiling, and part of one wall missing. But I was glad to be able to go." The young man concluded by asking

Fr. Cody "to remember me in your prayers."

On the front lines and at home, to provide strength in the face of death and to provide solace to those who grieved the loss of others, faith played a critical role for many young men from USF during World War II.

A pamphlet published by the University of San Francisco in 1945 highlighted the school's educational aims, reprinted the USF Credo, included a number of historical photos of the institution, and with World War II coming to an end, included a two-page spread on the university educating for war and peace.

98 The Flag Seen Around the World

IN FEBRUARY 1945, JOE ROSENTHAL, FORMER STUDENT at the University of San Francisco, and photographer for the Associated Press, was covering the invasion of Iwo Jima by the United States Marines in the final year of World War II. The bleak, eight-square-mile volcanic island of Iwo Jima, located 650 miles southeast of Tokyo, had become a high priority in the United States' war effort against Japan. The island lay near the midpoint of the American bomber route from the Mariana Islands to Japan, and it was the only island in that part of the Pacific large enough to accommodate an airfield for fighter escorts for the U.S. bombers and to serve as an emergency landing strip for damaged bombers.

Japan, which considered Iwo Jima one of its homeland islands, also recognized its strategic importance and was defending the island against an invasion with 22,000 troops entrenched in an underground network of tunnels, caves, and concrete pillboxes built deep inside the island's rock crust.

Following a naval bombardment and attack by carrier-based planes, the marines began their amphibious assault on Iwo Jima on February 19, 1945. After the first wave of marines was ashore, the Japanese defenders unleashed a deadly rain of artillery, mortar, and machine gun fire. The Japanese fire resulted in 2,400 marine casualties within a few hours, making it the most lethal single day of the war in the Pacific. Joe Rosenthal landed at noon on the first day of the invasion and risked his life to take photos during the horrendous combat. Rosenthal would later comment that "not

getting hit was like running though rain and not getting wet."

Rosenthal began the fourth day of the deadly battle for the island by slipping on a wet ladder and falling into the ocean as he was disembarking from a naval ship to a landing craft on his way to cover the fighting. He was fished out of the ocean along with his camera, which was inside a waterproof bag and was undamaged. On his way to the island, he heard from a sailor that there was going to be a flag-raising ceremony on Mount Suribachi, on the southern tip of the island. The mountain was in the process of being secured by the marines, after days of intense fighting. Upon landing, Rosenthal, and two marine combat photographers, with weapons ready, started up the steep trail to the top of the mountain.

By the time Rosenthal reached the top of Mount Suribachi on the afternoon of February 23, one flag raising had already taken place. The first flag raised on the mountain was considered too small, however, so five marines and a navy corpsman were ordered to raise a larger flag, which had been rescued from a sinking ship at Pearl Harbor following the Japanese attack on December 7, 1941. Rosenthal arrived at the top of Mount Suribachi in time to capture that second flag raising on film. Some have subsequently claimed that the resulting shot was "staged," but it was not. The photo did, however, become one of the most famous photos of World War II and appeared in hundreds of newspapers and magazines around the world. It became a symbol for the United States' war effort and won for Joe Rosenthal the Pulitzer Prize in photography. A columnist for the *New York Times* called it "the most beautiful picture of the war." For weeks after its release on February 25, 1945, reprints of the photo were sold faster than they could be produced.

After the flag raising captured by Rosenthal's camera, the battle for Iwo Jima raged another month and ultimately resulted in more than 26,000 American casualties, including nearly 6,800 killed. Among the dead were three of the six men who helped raise the flag in the scene immortalized by Rosenthal. Of the 22,000 Japanese defenders, only 216 survived, two of whom hid out for four years and surrendered in 1949. Throughout the war, only 353 United States servicemen were awarded the Congressional Medal of Honor, the nation's highest military decoration. Of those, 27 were awarded for the four weeks of battle on Iwo Jima, a record for any battle in U.S. history.

During World War II, 405,399 U.S. servicemen lost their lives in combat or in service-related deaths. Of these, 106 were students, alumni, or faculty from the University of San Francisco. Today at the University of San Francisco, a bronze plaque mounted in the foyer of War Memorial Gymnasium lists the names of all

On February 23, 1945, Joe Rosenthal, AP photographer and former USF student, took what was arguably the most famous photograph of World War II, showing the raising of the American flag on Iwo Jima in the midst of the battle against the Japanese for that strategically important island. Rosenthal won the Pulitzer Prize for photography in 1945 for the photo.

AP/WIDE WORLD PHOTOS

106, etched in bold relief. The university also maintains a service flag emblazoned with 136 gold stars, representing all of the men from St. Ignatius High School and USF who died in World War II. Joe Rosenthal's photo was the model for the sculpture in Arlington National Cemetery commemorating all of the nation's soldiers who served in the war.

The End of World War II

BY THE SPRING OF 1945, WORLD WAR II WAS COMING TO an end. In Europe, Hitler's "thousand-year Reich" was virtually over, destroyed by months of Allied bombing and now overrun by Allied armies from the west and the east. On April 30, Hitler took refuge in a Berlin bunker and committed suicide. What was left of the German government and military leadership surrendered on May 7. On August 6, 1945, in a blinding flash of death, destruction, and horror, an atomic bomb was dropped by a United States B-29 bomber on Hiroshima, Japan. The bomb initially killed 100,000 people and reduced the city to smoldering rubble. Almost 100,000 more people from Hiroshima later died from burns and radiation. Three days later, a second atomic bomb was dropped on Nagasaki, with equally destructive results, and the loss of an additional 75,000 lives outright. Burns and radiation later caused 75,000 more deaths among the people of Nagasaki. On August 16, the Japanese surrendered, and World War II was over.

In San Francisco, thousands of people poured into the streets on August 16, 1945, to celebrate the end of the war. The celebration soon turned into a riot: store windows were broken, street cars were derailed, fights erupted, and it took the city and military police several days to restore order. By September 1945, thousands of men were processed out of the armed services in San Francisco and throughout the United States. In many cases, they returned to cities and towns that had dramatically changed as a result of the war.

San Francisco and the Bay Area witnessed a dramatic population increase during World War II along with a major expansion of industry, shipping, and housing. Most of the returning veterans had undergone profound transformations as a result of their war experiences. The men who returned to USF, for example, were usually older, more serious, and eager to complete their education and get on with their lives and careers. Some were already married and had families to support.

To help servicemen return to civilian life, Congress passed, and President Franklin Roosevelt signed, the Servicemen's Readjustment Act of 1944, better known as the G.I. Bill of

Rights. It was arguably one of the most important pieces of legislation in the history of the nation. It entitled former military personnel to guaranteed loans for buying homes and setting up businesses, provided unemployment insurance, and most important for the nation's colleges and universities, allocated funds to cover educational expenses. Thousands of individuals who had previously been deterred from attending college because of cost now had a major portion of their education subsidized by the federal government. This one law had a monumental educational and social effect on the nation and on its institutions of higher education, including the University of San Francisco.

As World War II was coming to an end, international law also took a turn that had profound implications for the future of the world. After months of discussion and planning, representatives from the United States, China, Great Britain, and the Soviet Union agreed to invite the nations of the world to a conference in San Francisco to establish a United Nations. From April 15 to 24, 1945, 282 delegates from 46 nations, accompanied by more than 1,000 staff assistants, came to San Francisco to attend the United Nations Conference on International Organization. The University of San Francisco invited this distinguished group of international representatives to attend a Mass of the Holy Spirit in St. Ignatius Church on April 24, 1945. At the Mass, the president of USF, William Dunne, S.J., blessed the conference, scheduled to open the next day. The university also held a special ceremony marking the United Nations meeting, during which it bestowed an honorary Doctor of Laws degree on George Bidault, chairman of the French delegation to the United Nations Conference and French Minister of Foreign Affairs. Minister Bidault was an alumnus of a French Jesuit college.

On April 25, 1945, the United Nations Conference held its first session in the San Francisco War Memorial Opera House.

Opening addresses urged the conference delegates to draw up a world charter for an organization of "peace-loving nations." After two months of discussion and debate, the United Nations Charter was signed on June 26,

The service flag of the University of San Francisco, honoring those former students who fought and died during the two world wars, was displayed during special memorial ceremonies held in St. Ignatius Church.

UNIVERSITY OF SAN FRANCISCO ARCHIVES

William Dunne, S.J., president of the University of San Francisco, to the right, shakes hands with Harry S. Truman, president of the United States, during the founding of the United Nations in San Francisco in April 1945. Standing between Fr. Dunne and President Truman is Edward Stettinus, secretary of state of the United States, and later the country's representative to the United Nations.

1945, and printed in English, French, Spanish, Russian, and Chinese. The actual signing of the document began with representatives from China, Russia, Great Britain, and France, followed by the rest of the nations in alphabetical order, beginning with Argentina. After more than four hours of signing, President Harry S. Truman appeared at the conference door as planned, marched down the aisle of the War Memorial Opera House, and to thunderous applause, signed the charter on behalf of the United States. In the history of San Francisco and of the world, it was a significant day,

indeed, though the charter's ideals of world peace and understanding are yet to be fully realized.

In February 1946, the *Don Patrol,* an alumni publication that chronicled the lives of many former USF students who fought in World War II, published its last issue. The president of USF, William Dunne, S.J., addressed a lengthy letter to the returning veterans in that issue, concluding: "Now you are to resume your normal lives. Some of you will return to the University to complete your undergraduate education, others will proceed to graduate studies. All of you will return to find a common task. You must complete the job you began in the Southwest Pacific, in Asia, in Europe, for the calm which came over the battlefield will prove but a lull unless it is made permanent by the individual lives of each of you. The ideals which led you in battle must now find the Peace. As in War, so in Peace — we will be with you. God bless you."

Part V: From the Postwar Era through the 1960s

FOLLOWING THE END OF WORLD WAR II, VETERANS returned to the nation's colleges and universities in vast numbers, thanks in large part to the G.I. Bill of Rights. The student population grew rapidly at the University of San Francisco, and several new programs and buildings were planned and completed between 1945 and 1969. The buildings included Gleeson Library; War Memorial Gymnasium; Xavier Hall, a new residence for the Jesuit Community; Kendrick Hall, the new home of the School of Law; Harney Science Center; University Center; Cowell Hall, the new location for the School of Nursing; and Phelan, Gillson, and Hayes-Healy residence halls.

During the postwar era, the College of Arts and Sciences, the School of Law, and the College of Business Administration all witnessed rapid increases in student enrollment and major curriculum changes. In 1947, USF started a department of education for the certification of teachers, which developed into the School of Education by 1972 with the addition of numerous graduate programs. In 1948, a nursing program was initiated at USF in cooperation with St. Mary's Hospital, and by 1954 it had developed into an autonomous School of Nursing. A full-fledged graduate division and an evening college were also initiated at USF in the immediate postwar era to accommodate changing educational, professional, and social needs.

The immediate postwar years saw a revival of the athletic programs at the university, and the institution developed a West Coast and national reputation in several sports. In basketball, USF won national championships in 1949, 1955, and 1956, and players such as Bill Russell and K.C. Jones became household names. The 1951 USF football team was one of the best intercollegiate football teams that ever played—it had an undefeated and untied season and would have gone on to a postseason bowl game were it not for prevailing national racism that precluded the team and its star African American players, Ollie Matson and Burl Toler, from postseason participation. The 1950 USF soccer team also faced racism, but nevertheless went to the first intercollegiate soccer bowl game ever played, and emerged as co-national champions. From 1945 to 1960, the USF soccer

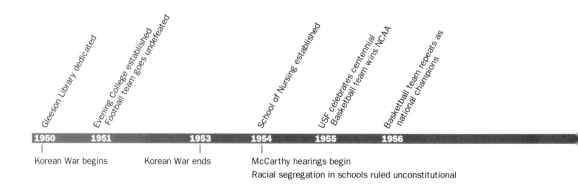

Gleeson Library dedicated

Evening College established
Football team goes undefeated

School of Nursing established

USF celebrates centennial
Basketball team wins NCAA

Basketball team repeats as national champions

| 1950 | 1951 | 1953 | 1954 | 1955 | 1956 |

Korean War begins   Korean War ends   McCarthy hearings begin

Racial segregation in schools ruled unconstitutional

team, under coach Gus Donoghue, won 11 conference championships, and under Steve Negoesco, who took over as head coach in 1962, the soccer team brought back 13 conference championships and four national titles. Negoesco led his teams to more victories than any other coach in the history of the game in the United States.

Three presidents guided the fortunes of the University of San Francisco from 1945 to 1969: William J. Dunne, S.J., whose tenure stretched back to 1938; John F.X. Connolly, S.J.; and Charles W. Dullea, S.J. These Jesuits worked mightily to secure the fiscal and human resources needed to support the university's expansion. They oversaw numerous academic changes at the institution and they shared in the growing reputation of USF as a leading institution of higher education. In 1964, women were admitted for the first time to the regular day division of the university, though women had been pursuing degrees at night in law, business, and the arts since the late 1920s, in nursing beginning in 1948, and in education since the early 1950s. Fathers Connolly and Dullea presided over the institution during the 1960s, a turbulent era for the nation's colleges and universities, and USF was not immune to the social, political, and cultural upheaval sweeping the nation. The next several vignettes will tell the story of the university from the postwar era through the 1960s, and will highlight many of the talented faculty members, administrators, staff, alumni, and students who contributed to the development of the Jesuit institution.

An ROTC Color Guard leads graduates from Campion Hall past Welch Hall to St. Ignatius Church for Baccalaureate Mass during the 90th commencement ceremonies for USF, held on June 5, 1949. The immediate postwar years witnessed phenomenal enrollment growth at the university, fueled in large part by the G.I. Bill of Rights, one of the most significant pieces of legislation in the history of the nation.

UNIVERSITY OF SAN FRANCISCO ARCHIVES

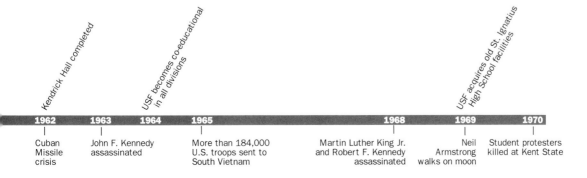

Kendrick Hall completed

USF becomes co-educational in all divisions

USF acquires old St. Ignatius High School facilities

1962	1963	1964	1965	1968	1969	1970
Cuban Missile crisis	John F. Kennedy assassinated		More than 184,000 U.S. troops sent to South Vietnam	Martin Luther King Jr. and Robert F. Kennedy assassinated	Neil Armstrong walks on moon	Student protesters killed at Kent State

Coming Home

VETERANS OF WORLD WAR II BEGAN TO RETURN IN LARGE numbers to the nation's colleges and universities during the fall of 1945. Many were coming back to school with the financial support made possible by the G.I. Bill of Rights. The University of San Francisco began to witness significant changes on campus as a result of the veterans' return. In the spring semester of 1945, student enrollment in all divisions at USF stood at a mere 321. By the fall of 1945, as a result of the first wave of returning veterans, student enrollment had jumped to 762, a 137 percent increase. One hundred thirty-eight of the new students attended USF under the G.I. Bill.

In the early fall of 1945, the *Foghorn* commented on the return of the veterans to campus. "The men here of the Hilltop form a nucleus of a greater post-war USF," wrote *Foghorn* editor James Donohue. "By next spring, most of the war veterans will be back at school. They will be looking for scholastic, social and athletic organizations and activity. They will expect us to have gotten these functions started. We have an obligation to these returning heroes, as well as to ourselves, to fulfill. Let us not fail them or us."

Another *Foghorn* editor, Rinaldo Carmazzi, also emphasized the importance of restoring the campus to its prewar activity and to "giving the vets a deserved salute." By late November 1945, Carmazzi already began to notice progress in reestablishing the institution and preparing for the future: "There's a trace of more sobriety, a deeper appreciation of the opportunities afforded by the school, and a stronger determination to make the most of these advantages. The value of this new perspective lies not only in knuckling

down to scholastic pursuits, but also a desire to make all university organizations perform up to their highest ideal of purpose. We believe herein lies the key to our school's future success as a top-flight institution. With student groups embracing every field of endeavor, the interest and enthusiasm for expansion should be limitless."

In January 1946, James Lyons, S.J., USF's dean of freshmen, described for the *Foghorn* the "traditions of the Dons." He expressed his ardent hope that the precious traditions of the university had not been permanently disrupted by the war, and that all students, administrators, and faculty will work at "building the greater University for the days of peace."

By the spring of 1946, some of the old USF traditions were revived, such as competitive athletics. Student clubs and organizations also began to stage a comeback after the hiatus caused by the war. One of the more successful new student organizations was the International

Relations Club under Paul Eisler. Because many of the returning students found it necessary to take part-time jobs, and many also had families, the time necessary to participate in extracurricular activities was often limited.

Other changes denoted the postwar university, as well. By the fall semester of 1947, 134 students, from across the United States and from other countries, were living on campus in six of the eight barracks left over from the Army Specialized Training Program (ASTP) held at USF during the war. Through extensive remodeling, however, the former barracks had been converted into more comfortable rooms, housing two students in double bunks, and now included an infirmary, chapel, and dining room. This extra housing was desperately needed, because by the beginning of the 1947 fall semester, enrollment at USF had further increased, to 2,086.

Despite the return to a semblance of normalcy at the University of San Francisco during the years immediately following the end of hostilities, memories of World War II were never far away. On November 14, 1947, at the annual Memorial Mass held in St. Ignatius Church, the entire student body, faculty, and administration gathered to honor those members of the university community who had died during the war. The Mass was celebrated by James Lyons, S.J., student chaplain, and the sermon was delivered by William Dunne, S.J., president of USF. The faculty, in academic regalia, led the procession into the church. As the

procession entered, the church was filled beyond capacity with students from all of the university's divisions. Displayed in the sanctuary during the Mass was a bronze plaque on which were listed the names of 106 USF faculty, students, and alumni who had been killed during World War II. The plaque was given a solemn blessing during the Mass and was later installed over the fireplace in the student lounge of Campion Hall. The plaque is now on the wall of the foyer of the War Memorial Gymnasium, a reminder of the sacrifices made by those who never came home from the war.

John Giambastiani, S.J., dean of students, meets with students who were veterans of World War II.

101 Building Plans

UNIVERSITY OF SAN FRANCISCO PRESIDENT WILLIAM Dunne, S.J., was deeply concerned about the future of the institution as the fall semester of 1946 got underway. On one hand, the university's registrar, William Dillon, reported that the semester was beginning with the largest enrollment in USF history, due in large measure to the return of the veterans from World War II under the G.I. Bill of Rights. Total enrollment had reached 2,086 students, including 324 students in the law school. Overall, 1,461 students were veterans under the G.I. Bill of Rights. The previous enrollment high at the university was in the fall of 1941, just prior to the attack on Pearl Harbor, when enrollment reached 1,337.

On the other hand, although this dramatic enrollment increase was reassuring for the future of the university, the school's space for classrooms, library holdings, and laboratories had not substantially changed since 1927, when the Liberal Arts Building (Campion Hall) was constructed. The university was terribly overcrowded.

On a short-term basis, the critical need for classrooms to accommodate the enrollment upsurge was partially addressed by the hasty construction of government-surplus prefabricated units on campus. These Quonset huts provided space for 12 additional classrooms and for other activities. They were made available through the Veterans Educational Facilities Program and marked USF as the first California institution of higher education to receive assistance from this federal agency. Robert McCarthy, a local contractor who had erected barracks on the campus for the military training program during the war on a cost-only basis, came back to construct the prefabricated government units.

McCarthy's crew began work in October 1946 and had the classrooms ready by the beginning of the spring semester. Although these units helped ease the classroom shortage, a full plan for the development of the university on a long-term basis was desperately needed.

Fr. Dunne outlined his concerns about USF, especially the need for long-range planning, in a report he sent to Joseph King, S.J., provincial of the California Jesuits, in February 1946. One of Fr. Dunne's primary issues was the lack of an adequate physical plant, a problem that would increasingly handicap the university in trying to attract high school students. Fr. Dunne contended that USF's facilities were in many cases inferior to those of local high schools.

Among the highest planning priorities, according to Fr. Dunne, was a university library to replace the inadequate facility on the top floor of Campion Hall. Space was so limited in Campion Hall that many of the most valuable library holdings were stored in a loft in St. Ignatius Church.

The second priority was a new faculty residence to replace Welch Hall, which had become inadequate for the growing number of faculty needed to serve the burgeoning student population.

President Dunne's report also addressed finances. Notwithstanding the Depression, the precipitous enrollment decline during the war, a heavy debt left over from the building of St. Ignatius Church, and the purchase of a portion of the old Masonic cemetery, the university found itself in reasonably good financial shape in 1946, according to the president's report. During the prior quarter-century, the major debts had been largely offset by more than $3 million in gifts, leaving an accumulated debt of only $170,000 for the institution.

Fr. Dunne proposed in his report that USF should secure a loan of some $770,000 to help "solve the great problems that confront us." Fr. Dunne continued, "I do not believe that we can solve them by waiting. We believe that the erection of two buildings would so encourage the people of San Francisco that we shall be put in a better position to gather further funds for one or two other buildings that are most vitally needed such as a college gymnasium and a science building."

After issuing his report to the provincial, Fr. Dunne took steps to launch a major building campaign at the university. Toward that end, the president established the university's first Board of Regents, which in turn embarked on a major development effort and the preparation of the first master building plan in the university's history. Moreover, the president and other administrators at USF developed a document titled "The Future of Your University," which was distributed to alumni to secure their support to help raise the money needed to expand the university. In the document, issued in 1947, the university's master plan was summarized, and

Fr. Dunne called upon USF's alumni to help raise $5 million for the construction of a new library, a faculty residence, a new wing to Campion Hall, a gymnasium, a law building, a building for the college of business, a science building, a student union, a residence for undergraduate students, and various student scholarship endowments.

In his appeal to alumni, Fr. Dunne wrote, "within eight years we shall commemorate our Centenary. Now is the time to look to the future. Explain our lack of prosperity how we will, we have no answer for the inertia on Ignatian Heights. Long ago, we should have made more progress. Yet, I see no reason why in the next eight years we should not accomplish everything for which we have hoped."

From 1927 to 1950, the only permanent buildings on campus were St. Ignatius Church, Campion Hall, and Welch Hall. To accommodate the burgeoning student population following World War II, barracks from the war years were used, as depicted in this aerial photo of USF taken during the war. The barracks are the eight long buildings on the campus in the lower left of the photo.

UNIVERSITY OF SAN FRANCISCO ARCHIVES

102 The First Board of Regents

THE UNIVERSITY OF SAN FRANCISCO HAD A BOARD OF trustees from almost the beginning of its history. In 1859, when the institution's first president, Anthony Maraschi, S.J., incorporated St. Ignatius College and secured a charter from the state of California to issue college degrees, he also established a 14-member board of trustees to "manage the affairs" of the college (vignette #9). To this day, the president and other executive officers are responsible to the board of trustees, which oversees the administration of all areas of the university: academic affairs, business and finance, student life, faculty affairs, fundraising, legal matters, and the university's mission.

Two members of the first USF Board of Regents, Dr. Edmund Morrissey, left, and Vincent Compagno, right, are pictured at a fundraising event in 1947, the year that William Dunne, S.J., president of USF, established the board. In the upper right of the photo is Richard Egan, an actor and 1943 graduate of USF.

UNIVERSITY OF SAN FRANCISCO ARCHIVES

By contrast, when William Dunne, S.J., the university's 20th president, created the first board of regents in 1947, he sought a group of professional and business leaders to assist him for a limited period of time to help in a specific area: to plan the physical growth of the university and to find the resources to make that growth possible. The first USF Board of Regents, which existed until 1954 and served as a precedent for other Jesuit schools on the West Coast, did its job very well, indeed.

Fr. Dunne called the first meeting of the board of regents for May 12, 1947. The meeting was held in the California Room of the Palace Hotel in San Francisco, and William McCarthy was elected chairman of the 18-member board. McCarthy had helped marshal the fundraising activities to purchase the old Masonic cemetery that comprised most of the campus in 1947. He had previously served as San Francisco's first postmaster, a fire commissioner, and a county supervisor. The board of regents that McCarthy headed was formally inducted at the 88th commencement exercises of USF, held at the War Memorial Opera House on June 1, 1947. Wearing their newly designed regalia, the board sat in reserved places in the sanctuary of St. Ignatius Church for the baccalaureate Mass preceding the commencement exercises.

Soon after their formal induction, the regents went to work on a master building plan for USF and a fundraising plan to bring the master plan to fruition. The first activities by the new board of regents, with the enthusiastic backing of Fr. Dunne, were noted in the *San Francisco Chronicle* in September of 1947: "San Francisco's oldest center of culture and learning is building toward new eminence among universities of the West. The University of San Francisco, soon to complete a century of service, is inaugurating a pre-centennial program of expansion that embraces plant, faculty and curriculum. On the 22-acre Hilltop site that commands a spectacular sweep of ocean, strait, and city, the Jesuit Fathers have launched a construction project of magnificent proportions. The $5,000,000 project is to be financed by the university's 8,000 active alumni. It will provide accommodations for an anticipated student body of 5,000 — library, faculty residence, gymnasium, dormitories, student union, and spacious buildings to house the separate colleges of liberal arts, law, sciences and business administration."

By 1949, the board of regents had increased the fundraising goal from $5 million to $15 million. In September 1949, a dinner was held to mark the kickoff of the Greater University of San Francisco Fund campaign. At the dinner were 200 alumni and university leaders who were to solicit gifts from other alumni and friends of the university in the following year. This fundraising drive would serve as the initial step toward an ultimate goal of $15 million by 1955. According to the *USF Alumnus* of September 1949, this fundraising "embraces wide solicitation of the general public as well as those identified with the University." Hon. Timothy Fitzpatrick, member of the board of regents and chair of the university fundraising group, spoke at the dinner. "If we go at this project with our full enthusiasm," Fitzpatrick said, "we are sure to be successful in building by 1955 an institution which may not be the largest but surely the finest metropolitan university in the land. That prospect is of itself enough to elicit the finest effort of everyone identified with our beloved University."

The foundation was laid in the late 1940s for a host of building projects and fundraising campaigns that carried the university through the next two decades. These successful projects began with the dedication of Gleeson Library in December 1950. Many buildings followed the library: War Memorial Gymnasium, 1958; Xavier Hall, the Jesuit Residence, 1959; Kendrick Hall, the law school building, 1962; Harney Science Center, 1965; University Center, 1966; and Cowell Hall, the nursing school building, 1969. In addition, three major residence halls were constructed during the 1950s and 1960s: Phelan Hall, 1955; Gillson Hall, 1965; and Hayes-Healy Hall, 1966. It took 20 years, but Fr. Dunne's vision and the board of regents' master plan for a greater University of San Francisco was largely realized.

Gleeson Library and the Geschke Learning Resource Center

FOR YEARS, THE JESUITS AND THEIR LAY COLLEAGUES had dreamed of a new library as the centerpiece of a greater University of San Francisco. From virtually the first day that the Liberal Arts Building (Campion Hall) opened in 1927, it was clear that space allocated on the top floor of that building for a library was inadequate. Many of the most valuable holdings of the library, for example, had to be stored in a loft in St. Ignatius Church.

In 1937, a group of friends of Richard Gleeson, S.J., former provincial of the California Jesuits, prefect of St. Ignatius Church, and major fundraiser for USF and for thousands of impoverished San Franciscans, began to raise money to build a library at USF in his memory. The Depression and World War II, however, put those plans on hold. After the war ended, USF President William Dunne, S.J., and his newly appointed board of regents, made construction of Gleeson Library the highest priority in a new master plan for the university and for a major new building campaign. Concurrently, William Monihan, S.J., university librarian, traveled throughout the nation to study other university libraries, consult with architects, develop construction plans, and raise money to build the new library.

On May 15, 1949, years of planning and fundraising came to fruition when ground was broken for Gleeson Library, the first major new building on campus in more than 20 years. Milton Pflueger of San Francisco was chosen as the architect for the project, and the construction was to be done by Barrett and

Hilp, local contractors. The groundbreaking ceremony included speeches by Fr. Dunne and by James Farraher, a member of the board of regents. San Francisco Archbishop John Mitty was represented at the ceremony by the Right Reverend Harold Collins, who blessed the new library site. The entire Jesuit and lay faculty were in attendance at the ceremony, wearing academic regalia.

The groundbreaking was followed 19 months later, on December 3, 1950, by the dedication of the completed library. At the dedication, Fr. Dunne gave a brief talk, describing the new library as the "first unit in the overall plan for a Greater University of San Francisco;" Archbishop Mitty blessed the new building; and the bishop of Reno, Thomas Gorman, gave a major address, in which he suggested that one distinct feature of the new library "might be the gathering and preservation of the manuscript records of Catholic San Francisco in the making of whose history yesterday's college and today's university have had and will have no mean part."

The final cost for Gleeson Library was

Gleeson Library as it looked in 1950, the year it was dedicated.

$1,143,130. Almost $575,000 of this came from the estate of Delia Walsh, and another $200,000 came from contributions to the Gleeson Library fund started by Fr. Monihan. The five floors of the new library were to have a maximum capacity of more than 800,000 volumes and a seating capacity of 2,250 students. From its opening in 1950 to the building of Kendrick Hall in 1962, Gleeson Library also housed the School of Law and various administrative offices.

In 1957, the Gleeson Library Associates was formed at the suggestion of Albert Shumate, M.D., a dedicated alumnus of USF. The organization, directed for more than three decades by Fr. Monihan, supported the library and presented an annual summer symposium that attracted world-class scholars to the campus for lectures, discussions, and elegant dinners for friends and supporters of the library and the university. Topics ranged from "Venice Through the Ages" to "Egypt: People of the Sun." The *San Francisco Examiner* described the USF Summer Symposium as "an intellectual staple of San Francisco life."

In September 1997, a major addition was made to the Gleeson Library: the Geschke Learning Resource Center. The center was named for Charles and Nancy Geschke, long-time supporters of the university. For years, Geschke served on the USF Board of Trustees, and in 2003 he was named its chairman. In attendance at the dedication ceremony for the new center were the Geschkes; trustees, faculty, staff, students, and alumni; Tyrone Cannon, dean of the Gleeson Library; Paul Birkel, former library dean; Louis Giraudo,

In 1997, the Geschke Learning Resource Center was added to the Gleeson Library. Pictured cutting the dedication ribbon are (from left) Louis Giraudo, chairman of the USF Board of Trustees; Mrs. Nancy Geschke; USF President John Schlegel, S.J.; and Charles Geschke, co-founder of Adobe Systems and future chairman of the USF Board of Trustees.

chairman of the USF Board of Trustees; and John Schlegel, S.J., the president of USF. The 36,000 square feet of space of the new center included enhanced areas for reference, circulation, periodicals, and government documents; improved access for disabled students; group study rooms; new computer technology; and the William Monihan, S.J. Atrium, comprising 5,000 square feet of open space encircled by glass walls and balconies. The atrium was designed as a living room for students and faculty, and as a venue for select special events.

Today, Gleeson Library and the Geschke Learning Resource Center holds more than 680,000 books and 130,000 journals, subscribes to nearly 2,200 periodicals, and has more than 900,000 other materials, including microforms, government documents, CD-ROMs, videos, and audios.

The library also includes the Donohue Rare Book Room, started by Fr. Monihan, and housing the university's special collections, such as the Sir Thomas More Collection, the Albert Sperisen Collection of Eric Gill, and the L. Frank Baum Collection. In addition, the university's archives are located in Gleeson Library. The Thacher Gallery, on the main floor, features a variety of media and artists that span age, race, and gender; includes exhibitions that explore aesthetic, community, and social justice issues; and fosters interfaith and multicultural dialogue on issues of art and society.

From the time of its dedication, Gleeson Library has served as the heart of the academic enterprise at USF. Since 1997, when a graduating student survey was first conducted at USF, graduate and undergraduate students have consistently ranked library services as the highest among all USF services and facilities. Gleeson Library and the Geschke Center continue to have a lasting impact on the university and the community it serves.

The Year of the Champions, 1949

104

AT THE CLOSE OF THE 1947–1948 BASKETBALL SEASON, during which the USF team compiled a disappointing record of 13 wins and 11 losses, the team gave its coach, Pete Newell, a briefcase on which were engraved the words: "That's OK. We'll get 'em next year." How prophetic. In the 1948–1949 season, the team won 21 games and lost only five, received a belated bid to play in the National Invitational Tournament (N.I.T.), and traveled to New York City as 21–1 underdogs to take the coveted national crown.

The 1949 USF basketball team, winners of the National Invitational Tournament (NIT), considered the national championship of the era.
UNIVERSITY OF SAN FRANCISCO ARCHIVES

Beginning on March 12, 1949, during a phenomenal series held in Madison Square Garden, the Dons won four straight games, including a final 48–47 victory over Loyola of Chicago to become the national champions. The Dons sports information director, Pete Rozelle, who later became the commissioner of the National Football League, wrote "probably no team in the twelve-year history of the National Invitational Basketball Tournament has so captured the fancy of the Gotham cage fanatics as Pete Newell's amazing University of San Francisco Dons."

Don Lofgran, USF's star forward and center, who scored 75 points during the four-game series, was given the Most Valuable Player Award in the tournament. He and his teammates, including team captain John Benington, Joe McNamee, Frank Kuzara, René Herrerias, Ross Giudice, Don Giesen, Jack Hanley, Hal DeJulio, and Frank Sobek; coach Newell; and team chaplain Carlo Rossi, S.J., returned to San Francisco to a joyous civic welcome and a series of celebrations, on and off campus. The Chamber of Commerce hosted a testimonial luncheon for the team at the Fairmont Hotel, and coach Newell was given a 1949 Chevrolet. A special issue of the *Foghorn* recorded all the details in what was up to that point the most illustrious event in the athletic history of the institution.

Basketball was not the only sport to bring national recognition to USF in 1949. The tennis team, under coach George Kraft, won the National Collegiate Athletic Association (NCAA) championship that year, led by Art Larsen and Sam Match. The nine-man tennis squad compiled a perfect 10–0 record on its way to winning two Northern California championships and the national title. In the prior year, the USF tennis team had been edged out of a national championship by a single point by William and Mary College, although Harry Likas, who graduated in 1948, won USF's first individual NCAA championship title that year.

USF's golden year of athletics also saw the soccer team, under coach Gus Donoghue, win the West Coast championship of the American Collegiate Soccer Association and to compete in the first annual intercollegiate soccer bowl game. The Dons tied Penn State in the game, and the teams were declared co-national champions. The USF soccer team was led by All-American players Robert Lee, defensive left half, and Steve Negoesco, a fullback who later became the most honored and successful soccer coach in the history of USF and all of intercollegiate soccer in the United States.

The fourth athletic title for USF in 1949 was claimed by the rifle team, which won the William Randolph Hearst trophy for universities in the United States Sixth Army region. Al Crow, star Don rifleman that year, was picked for a berth on the All-American Rifle Team.

Although the 1948–1949 USF football team compiled a dismal record of two wins and nine losses, under its new head coach Joe Kuharich, a scan of that year's team roster reveals the names of several young players, such as Ollie Matson and Gino Marchetti, who by 1951 would form the nucleus of a team that was possibly the greatest intercollegiate football team ever, and that set a new standard for moral integrity in intercollegiate sports.

Harry Likas won USF's first individual NCAA title in 1948. The next year, the USF tennis team won the NCAA championship.

UNIVERSITY OF SAN FRANCISCO ARCHIVES

Football and Values in 1951

105

THE UNITED STATES WAS STILL A LARGELY SEGREGATED society in 1951, 175 years after the Declaration of Independence boldly proclaimed to the world that "all men are created equal." Neighborhoods, restaurants, public and private accommodations, and schools at every level across the nation were segregated by law and custom. The supreme law of the land, as interpreted by the U.S. Supreme Court, permitted separate public schools for white and black children. The famous Supreme Court decision in Brown v. Board of Education declaring segregated schools to be "inherently unequal" was still three years down the legal road.

Ollie Matson was fullback for the undefeated USF football team of 1951. He was the nation's leading intercollegiate rusher and scorer in football during that season, was selected to be a member of *Look* Magazine's All-American team, won silver and bronze medals in track at the 1952 Olympics, had a spectacular career in professional football, and was inducted into the Pro Football Hall of Fame.

UNIVERSITY OF SAN FRANCISCO ARCHIVES

In the South, segregation was virtually absolute everywhere and was upheld by city ordinances, state laws, and violence. In the North, segregation was also widespread and buttressed by social mores and on occasion by force. In July 1951, while the local police stood by and watched, a white mob of more than 2,000 people violently prevented a black couple from moving into an all-white neighborhood in Cicero, Illinois, a suburb of Chicago. Change, however, was slowly coming to the nation.

In 1947, Jackie Robinson signed a contract with Branch Rickey, general manager of the Brooklyn Dodgers, to become the first African American baseball player in the major leagues in 61 years, and the next year, President Harry Truman officially integrated the armed forces by executive order. A small minority of institutions and areas of the nation were also ahead of most of the country in racial integration. Jackie Robinson, for example, attended integrated public schools in Southern California and played varsity baseball and football for integrated teams at the University of California, Los Angeles.

The University of San Francisco was also decades ahead of most of the nation and fielded its first integrated football team in 1930. The 1951 football team, with its shoulder-to-shoulder African American and white players, was relatively rare by contemporary 1951 intercollegiate standards, but reflected a long-term values system on the hilltop campus. The finale to the 1951 football season revealed just how unique that values system was in the United States.

The USF football team of 1951 was arguably the best intercollegiate team ever. The team, coached by Joe Kuharich, compiled a perfect record of nine wins, with no losses or ties. The team saw nine of its starting players drafted directly into the National Football League, five of whom went on to play in the NFL Pro Bowl, with three of those eventually inducted

The USF football team on offense during the 1951 season. Carrying the ball is halfback Roy Barni, who later played for the Chicago Cardinals and the Philadelphia Eagles professional teams.

into the Pro Football Hall of Fame. No other collegiate team ever had this many of its players so honored. Ollie Matson, one of the two African American players on the team, won silver and bronze medals in the 1952 Olympics before launching his spectacular career in professional football, culminating in his induction into the Pro Football Hall of Fame. Burl Toler, the other African American on the team, was drafted by the Cleveland Browns, but was

prevented from playing professional football by a knee injury. Instead, he became the first African American to become an NFL game official. Toler later obtained a master's degree in educational administration from USF and in 1968 became the first African American junior high school principal in San Francisco's history when he was named principal of Benjamin Franklin Junior High, after having taught at that school for several years. In addition to Ollie Matson, Gino Marchetti and Bob St. Clair had great NFL careers and were voted into the Pro Football Hall of Fame. Several other players from the team also played in the NFL: quarterback Ed Brown, halfbacks Joe Scudero and Roy Barni, and linemen Lou Stephens, Ralph Thomas, Merrill Peacock, Dick Stanfel, and Mike Mergen. Bill Henneberry, the backup quarterback for the team, later became director of athletic development at USF. Pete Rozelle, the team's sports information director, eventually became the commissioner of the National Football League.

Despite the Dons' perfect football record in 1951, the team was not invited to any post-season bowl games, which should have been a given for a team with USF's spectacular season. The College of the Pacific, for example, which the Dons had beaten 47 to 14, was invited to the Sun Bowl. Other teams with inferior records also went to bowl games. The reason the USF team was not invited soon became clear: racism. In the benighted days of 1951, teams with black athletes simply were not invited to play in post-season bowl games. Finally, the

organizers of the Orange Bowl did express an interest in having the Dons play, but only if they left their two black players behind. The team players adamantly refused this offer and became known as the team that was "undefeated, untied, and uninvited." The University of San Francisco ended its football program after the 1951 season. The program had been losing approximately $70,000 per year, and the president of the institution, William Dunne, S.J., reluctantly announced the termination of the football program after the 1951 season for financial reasons.

On September 29, 2001, the 1951 USF football team was honored at a dinner celebrating the 50th anniversary of its famed season. That night, the team players, their families and friends, and more than 400 others came together to acknowledge its record on the football field and to applaud the moral values represented by the team. The current president of USF, Stephen Privett, S.J., captured the essence of the team's legacy during his dinner speech: "These men exemplified the values that remain at the core of our identity as a Jesuit Catholic university. I refer to dedication to a common good, rather than the interests of any one individual, respect for the dignity and worth of every human being, and an unwavering commitment to excellence on the field, in the classroom, and in their personal and professional lives. The men who we celebrate this evening paid a price for their integrity. They refused a bowl bid rather than compromise their values. They sacrificed glory for honor and character."

The USF football team of 1951 was undefeated on the gridiron and had nine of its players drafted by the National Football League. Three of those players (Ollie Matson, Gino Marchetti, and Bob St. Clair) were eventually inducted into the Pro Football Hall of Fame. Despite fielding perhaps the best collegiate football team of all time, the Dons were not invited to play in any postseason bowl games unless they left their African American players (Ollie Matson and Burl Toler) at home. The team refused, stood on principle, and transcended the segregated and racist temper of the times.

UNIVERSITY OF SAN FRANCISCO ARCHIVES

IAccreditation

ACCREDITATION IS A RIGOROUS PROCESS OF EXTERNAL
peer review used for more than 100 years in the United States to ensure
academic quality among colleges and universities, to provide access by
institutions of higher education to federal aid and federal programs,
and to foster employer confidence in the college degrees submitted by
applicants for employment. Accreditation is critical for institutions of
higher education: it communicates to the world that an association
of peers has evaluated the academic quality and financial stability of a
school and found the school to be capable of achieving its educational
mission. Today, there are three types of accreditation organizations:
regional, national, and specialized or professional. The University of San
Francisco is currently accredited by a host of national and professional organizations as well as a major regional accreditation agency,
the Western Association of Schools and Colleges (WASC).

In 1950, a course on the history of
San Francisco was first offered by the
eminent historian John McGloin, S.J.,
standing in the back of the classroom.

UNIVERSITY OF SAN FRANCISCO ARCHIVES

On November 2 and 3, 1950, the Western
College Association (the forerunner of the
Western Association of Schools and Colleges)
paid its first official visit to the University of
San Francisco. A committee of six California
educators read reports prepared by administrators,
met with faculty and staff, and visited a sam-
pling of classes. The dean of faculties at USF,
Raymond Feely, S.J., was the key administrator
who prepared for the WCA visit. Fr. Feely became
USF's first academic vice president the next year.
In April 1951, the secretary-treasurer of the
WCA, Charles Fitts, wrote to USF President
William Dunne, S.J., noting that USF had
been approved for complete accreditation. The
final report by the WCA stated that USF's

programs were carefully planned, that faculty were actively involved in planning and curriculum development, and that the "religious commitment of the institution did not limit freedom of learning or scholarship and that there was considerable adaptation of the content of courses to the needs and problems of students in the modern world." The WCA committee underscored its view that there was no interference with academic or scholarly freedom at USF — not an insignificant concern in American higher education in the early 1950s. Senator Joseph McCarthy of Wisconsin, through his senate subcommittee, was engaged in a witch hunt for communists in virtually all of the nation's institutions. Colleges and universities came under McCarthy's scrutiny, and "loyalty oaths" and investigations of individuals' political backgrounds were required at many schools, though not at USF.

Throughout the 1950s, USF was formally visited by the WCA accreditation teams on a regular basis, and the institution saw its accreditation reaffirmed and extended for the maximum period of five-year intervals throughout the decade. On July 1, 1962, the Western Association of Schools and Colleges (WASC) replaced the WCA, and the new accrediting body reaffirmed USF's accreditation throughout the 1960s. In 1971, accreditation was again reaffirmed, and in 1974, USF was approved to offer a program in business administration in Tokyo, the first of USF's fully accredited overseas programs. In 1976, however, WASC raised concerns about the contractual degrees that USF was starting

In 1950, the same year that USF was first accredited by a regional accrediting agency, Gleeson Library opened its doors. William Monihan, S.J. (right), university librarian, is pictured with George Laird, S.J. (left) director of buildings and grounds, when Gleeson Library was dedicated on December 3, 1950.

UNIVERSITY OF SAN FRANCISCO ARCHIVES

to offer through its Office of Continuing Education and the Institute for Professional Development (IPD), an external educational provider and marketing organization. Although accreditation was reaffirmed in 1977, WASC required several interim self-studies, reports, and fact-finding visits over the next four years addressing its concerns with the regulation of the IPD programs and with other matters, including the university's fiscal condition. The university discontinued the IPD programs, but WASC's concerns about the university's financial situation and fiscal planning remained, and WASC issued a warning about these concerns in 1981. In the same year, WASC also raised questions about the academic quality of the bachelor's degrees offered by the new USF College of Professional Studies. An interim visit occurred in the spring of 1984.

From 1981 to 1984, the fiscal situation at USF significantly improved, new academic regulations were implemented by the College of Professional Studies, and in 1984 USF issued a self-study report that WASC considered exemplary. As a result, WASC removed the warnings, and the next comprehensive visit took place in December 1988. After the 1988 visit, however, WASC deferred reaffirmation of accreditation and issued a warning, citing various concerns with off-campus programs in the College of Professional Studies. A special visit was made by WASC in 1991, the concerns were addressed, the warning was removed, and accreditation was reaffirmed. The next official visit was in the fall of 1997. The report in preparation for that visit was coordinated by Susan Prion, assistant to the provost, and was structured around USF's Vision and Plan 2005, which focused on six areas: USF's Jesuit and Catholic identity; the learning community; pluralism; the university community; the broader community; and human, physical, and financial resources. In March 1998, the WASC commission reaffirmed USF's accreditation, with a fifth-year visit scheduled in the fall of 2002 to consider issues of assessment of learning outcomes and planning, and selected issues in the College of Professional Studies. Robert Niehoff, S.J., vice president for planning and budget, associate provost for academic affairs, and liaison officer to WASC, coordinated the university's response to the WASC fifth-year visit in November 2002. The WASC visiting team issued a positive report about USF, and confirmed that the next preparatory review was scheduled for the fall of 2007, and the next educational effectiveness review was scheduled for the fall of 2008. Gerardo Marín, associate provost for academic affairs and liaison officer to WASC, is currently coordinating the university's preparation for the next WASC visits.

In addition to WASC, the University of San Francisco is accredited by several professional accrediting bodies. In 1935, the USF School of Law joined a small number of select schools when it was approved by the American Bar Association (ABA). In 1937, the law school was also accredited by the California State Bar

and the Association of American Law Schools (AALS). For more than 65 years, these accreditations have been regularly reaffirmed. The California State Board of Education first sent a committee to report on USF's education programs in 1950. The following year, as a result of that visitation, the teacher-training program was approved for five years, the longest time frame that could be granted. Periodically, this approval is reaffirmed by the California Commission on Teacher Credentialing. In 1953, USF's College of Business Administration, now the School of Business and Management, became one of just a handful of schools to be accredited nationally by the American Assembly of Collegiate Schools of Business (AACSB). In 1981, AACSB granted separate accreditation for USF's graduate programs in business. The undergraduate and graduate business programs at USF were re-accredited by AACSB International — The Association to Advance Collegiate Schools of Business in 1988 and again in 2001. Today, USF is one of only 370 schools of business in the nation that is accredited by AACSB International at both the undergraduate and graduate level. The School of Nursing baccalaureate program was first accredited by the National League for Nursing in 1958, the year the first class of nurses graduated. The master of science in nursing was accredited by the same organization in 1994. In addition, the School of Nursing is periodically visited and accredited by the California Board of Registered Nurses. In 2003, the School of Nursing was fully accredited by still another agency: the Commission on Collegiate Nursing Education (CCNE).

Historically, the University of San Francisco has achieved high marks from external accreditation bodies. This positive evaluation continues to our own time and substantiates what generations of USF students know to be the case regarding the quality of education provided by their institution.

The Postwar Development of the College of Arts and Sciences

IN THE BEGINNING, THE LIBERAL ARTS COMPRISED VIRTUALLY the entire curriculum at St. Ignatius Academy. The first documented curriculum, in 1858, three years after the school's founding, included English, Spanish, French, Italian, Latin, Greek, elocution, arithmetic, mathematics, history, geography, and bookkeeping. For an extra fee, drawing lessons were also available. The next year, the institution was renamed St. Ignatius College and it began to issue college degrees under the authority of a charter granted by the State of California. Moral philosophy, natural philosophy, and chemistry were added to the curriculum.

During the 1860s and 1870s, physics, chemistry, and mathematics blossomed at St. Ignatius College under internationally respected professors such as Joseph Bayma, S.J., Joseph Neri, S.J., and Aloysius Varsi, S.J. (vignettes #16 and #17). By 1900, the college's science programs, equipment, museums, and laboratories were considered by many international visitors, national and local agencies, and the popular press to be among the finest in the nation. In addition to the sciences, the curriculum continued to emphasize the liberal arts, including the classical languages, religion, philosophy, English, history, and public speaking. Theater arts and debate also flourished.

Economic setbacks and enrollment declines caused by the disastrous earthquake and fire of

1906, a major recession, America's entrance into World War I in 1917, and cost overruns in building St. Ignatius Church led to the near bankruptcy of the institution in 1919. St. Ignatius College recovered, however, during the mid-1920s. Desperately needed funds were raised, enrollment increased, and the separate

Edmund Smyth, S.J., dean of the College of Arts and Sciences from 1955 to 1967. He developed a reputation for knowing the name of every student in the college.

UNIVERSITY OF SAN FRANCISCO ARCHIVES

departments of arts, sciences, and philosophy were combined in 1925 to become the College of Arts and Sciences under its first dean, Hubert Flynn, S.J. By the fall of 1929, there were 507 students in the day division and 202 students in the evening division of the College of Arts and Sciences. The total enrollment at St. Ignatius College in 1929 was 1,099. Enrollment at USF dipped slightly during the Depression; it rebounded to 1,448 students by the fall of 1941, only to fall again during World War II. By the spring semester of 1945, the total enrollment at USF stood at 321, of whom a mere 86 students

P. Carlo Rossi, S.J., USF professor of languages from 1940 to 1975, helped build the modern languages department in the College of Arts and Sciences during the postwar years. In 1949, he was awarded the Order of the Southern Cross for furthering cultural relations between Brazil and the United States. At the award ceremony are (from left) Jose Fabrino de Oliveira Baiao, Consul General of Brazil; William Geiger, director of the Department of Public Health in San Francisco and former recipient of the award; Fr. Rossi; and William Dunne, S.J., president of the University of San Francisco.

UNIVERSITY OF SAN FRANCISCO ARCHIVES

were enrolled in the College of Arts and Sciences.

The end of World War II triggered a major upturn in enrollment at USF, helped in no small measure by the G.I. Bill of Rights. Under the leadership of Alexis Mei, S.J., the first postwar dean of the College of Arts and Sciences, enrollment dramatically increased in the college, to 1,062 students by the fall of 1948, out of a total of 3,044 students registered at USF. The curriculum witnessed both change and continuity. In the liberal arts in 1948, a student could major in English, French, German, Greek, Italian, Latin, Portuguese, Spanish, classical languages, economics, philosophy, history, or political science. In the sciences, majors included biology,

chemistry, mathematics, and physics. All students were required to take English, a modern or classical language, natural science, American history, and public speaking. Four years of philosophy were also required. Every Catholic student had to be enrolled in one religion course each semester. To obtain a bachelor of arts degree, students needed to enter the college with four years of high school Latin and complete an additional four courses of Latin in college. For a bachelor of science degree, students were exempt from the Latin requirement. Overall, the College of Arts and Sciences, according to the USF General Catalog 1948–1949, did "not aim to provide a specific vocational training but rather by its integration of knowledge, its training in analysis, and its cultural scope to prepare a student for any field in our complex civilization."

The many foreign languages that USF students could pursue in the immediate postwar years were a reflection of the internationalizing of the curriculum following World War II. This curriculum focus was also a result of the efforts of P. Carlo Rossi, S.J., professor of languages, who together with his colleagues, professors Luigi Sandri and Giacinto Matteucig, built a highly respected and innovative modern languages department at USF. Fr. Rossi wrote textbooks on French language instruction and on Brazilian Portuguese language instruction, directed the Luso-Brazilian Institute on campus, and received a special civilian award from the Brazilian government for his work.

During the immediate postwar years, there was an influx of many new faculty members and students. Among the new faculty members was Desmond FitzGerald, who began as an assistant professor of philosophy in 1948, while finishing his doctorate at U.C. Berkeley. FitzGerald taught at USF for 50 years, longer than any other professor. As an emeritus professor at USF, he continues to teach at the Fromm Institute for Lifelong Learning. Ashbrook Lincoln was another U.C. Berkeley graduate who began teaching at USF immediately after the war. Lincoln's field was history, and he published and taught in his academic field at USF from 1946 to 1988.

Another long-term professor who began at USF in the postwar era was Robert "Sarge" MacKenzie. Mackenzie taught government from 1946 to 1979 and helped coach the football team in the years immediately after the war. Timothy McDonnell, S.J., began his career at USF in 1946 as an assistant professor of government and retired 46 years later after having served as vice president for university development and as the first and only regent of the USF School of Nursing. Lloyd Burns, S.J., was an assistant professor of classics from 1947 to 1969, and in 1984, he was granted emeritus status by the university. For decades, Fr. Burns also served as alumni chaplain and touched the lives of hundreds of the university's graduates.

Edmund Smyth, S.J., succeeded Fr. Mei as dean of the College of Arts and Sciences in 1955 and held the position for the next 12 years. Fr. Smyth developed a reputation for knowing the name of every student in the college and for insisting that students meet with him at least twice a year to discuss their academic progress. Fr. Smyth also taught in the history department prior to and after his tenure as dean and served as academic vice president in the late 1960s.

Other notable faculty members who began their careers in the College of Arts and Sciences during the 1950s included Ralph Lane, who started teaching in the sociology department in 1958, retired 30 years later, and is currently an emeritus professor. Among Lane's many accomplishments was his work in helping to create the Students Western Addition Project (SWAP). Other emeriti faculty who began their careers at USF during the 1950s included John Gleason, who began a 32-year career in the English department in 1956; David Walsh, S.J., who taught mathematics for 30 years, beginning in 1958; Robert Cunningham, who taught philosophy from 1955 to 1991; Robert Seiwald, a professor in

the chemistry department from 1957 to 1989; John Fischer, S.J., who taught mathematics from 1954 to 1982, chaired the mathematics department for 17 of those years, and was instrumental in bringing the computer science program to USF; and George McGlynn, who retired in 1998 as a professor of exercise and sport science after a 39-year career. In 1959, John Collins began a 32-year career at USF

USF students relax and study in Campion Hall lounge during the fall semester of 1949.

UNIVERSITY OF SAN FRANCISCO ARCHIVES

as a teacher, director, writer, and student mentor. Many of his students went on to professional theater, film, and television careers. He was named professor emeritus in June 1991.

When the University of San Francisco celebrated its centennial in 1955, it could proudly look back to its faculty and programs in arts and sciences over the preceding 100 years as the wellspring for its growing reputation for academic excellence within the tradition of Jesuit education.

The Postwar School of Law

THE UNIVERSITY OF SAN FRANCISCO SCHOOL OF LAW, like the rest of the schools and colleges, was dramatically affected by the return of the veterans at the end of World War II. During the immediate postwar years, almost 90 percent of USF law students received educational benefits under the G.I. Bill of Rights. Enrollment in the school, which had dropped to 50 by the spring of 1945, more than doubled to 109 by the fall of 1945.

Two years later, enrollment had soared to 357, and as the fall semester of 1948 got underway, enrollment reached 450, more students than could be accommodated in the crowded classrooms and packed law library on the third floor of Campion Hall. Many classes had to be held in former barracks along Golden Gate Avenue, which had been used for military training programs during the war. The demographics of the law school student population also changed from the prewar years. The students were older, with almost two-thirds over age 25. More than 50 percent were married, and fewer than 60 percent were Catholic. As in the prewar years, however, the overwhelming majority of law students grew up in the Bay Area, and many attended USF as undergraduates.

In 1949, the California State Bar created a Special Survey Board to assess legal education in the state's institutions of higher education. The USF School of Law was one of many schools that the survey board noted was suffering from severe overcrowding to the detriment of its educational mission. This finding helped push USF administrators to move the School of Law in the fall of 1950 to the third floor of the newly constructed Gleeson Library, a "temporary"

location until a new law school could be built. This new university library, and a future law school building, were both high priorities in the university's first master plan, articulated by USF President William Dunne, S.J., and by the university's newly appointed Board of Regents (vignettes 101 and 102).

The move of the law library from the third floor of Campion Hall to the third floor of the Gleeson Library was orchestrated by Elizabeth Anne Quigley, the head law librarian. During the move, an outside company used a winch to lower boxes of law books from the third floor of Campion Hall, and teams of law students, organized by Quigley into a human chain, passed the boxes across campus to the new Gleeson Library. In 1962, she organized another move by the law library, this time to its new home in Kendrick Hall. Overall, there were few individuals who had more of an impact on the postwar School of Law than did Elizabeth Anne Quigley. Beginning her USF career in the law library in 1946, she served the school for 37 years and oversaw the growth of the library holdings from 14,000 volumes to more than 150,000 volumes. Quigley also assisted nine different deans and acting deans to maintain ABA and AALS accreditation standards regarding library holdings, and she worked with thousands of students until her retirement as head law librarian in 1983.

In addition to overcrowding, the postwar School of Law faced challenges on several other fronts. Edward Hogan was dean in 1945, a position he had occupied for more than a decade. Hogan's failing health, however, necessitated a search for a replacement, a lengthy process that finally ended in the fall of 1951, with the selection of Vernon Miller, formerly dean of Loyola University School of Law in New Orleans. Miller's tenure began in the wake of ongoing struggles with the ABA over accreditation issues, and was further complicated by a first-time bar passage rate among USF law students that had steadily declined in the immediate postwar years to 38 percent in the fall of 1951.

The new academic vice president of USF, Raymond Feely, S.J., a graduate of the law school, a former law school faculty member, and a prior regent of the law school, increasingly put pressure on the new dean to immediately raise admissions standards and enact more rigorous grading policies. Miller also strongly believed in raising standards, but he favored a more gradual approach. Even though the bar passage rate began to increase, averaging 61 percent from the fall of 1952 to the fall of 1953, Fr. Feely and Miller continued to disagree on a number of issues regarding admissions and grading policies in the law school. Finally, Miller left USF at the end of the 1953–1954 academic year to become dean of the Columbus School of Law at Catholic University, declining to accept a contract extension offered to him by Fr. Dunne.

Ironically, the year after Miller left, the first law class to spend its entire law school career under his leadership achieved an overall passage rate of 91 percent on the state bar exam. From 1953 to 1958, when students admitted under Miller's more rigorous standards graduated, the law school attained a three-year average pass rate of 82 percent, among the highest of California's law schools.

With Vernon Miller's departure, Associate Dean A. Russell Berti was named acting dean of the USF School of Law, a position he occupied for three years, while a nationwide search was conducted for a new dean. Acting Dean Berti was a graduate of St. Ignatius High School,

The USF School of Law, class of 1949, and some of their professors are pictured on the stairs of Campion Hall. In the front row, from left to right are Professors William deFuniak, E.L. Merica, and Charles Knights, Dean Edward Hogan, and Professor C.F. Stanley. In the second row, second from the left, is librarian Elizabeth Anne Quigley.

attended St. Ignatius College when it was housed in the shirt factory on the corner of Hayes and Shrader streets, and graduated from the law school. He taught English at St. Ignatius College, organized the Saint Ives Law Society for pre-law undergraduates, became a law professor at USF, and was appointed associate dean of the law school in 1950 to take on many of the responsibilities of Dean Hogan, who was in ill health. During the course of his USF law school career as a professor, associate dean, and three-time acting dean, A. Russell Berti left a salient mark on the development of the USF School of Law through his teaching, curriculum development, writing, and administrative duties. In 1987, he was named Alumnus of the Year by USF's Alumni Association.

Frank Walsh, a USF law school faculty member, was named the new dean in 1957, becoming at age 33 the youngest law school dean in the country. He left the post in 1970 to take a position at the Federal Communications Commission. His long tenure was marked by steady enrollment increases, reaching 494 by fall 1970. This enrollment expansion was especially pronounced in the day division, which by fall 1962 surpassed enrollment in the evening division for the first time since 1932. Among the current full professors of law at USF who began their careers at USF during the 1960s are Thomas McCarthy, now considered one of the foremost authorities on intellectual property law in the nation, and Robert Talbot, a specialist in evidence, trial practice, and criminal law.

During Walsh's tenure in the 1960s, the nation's civil rights struggles and the Vietnam War raised the consciousness of many Americans to issues of justice at home and abroad. Attorney General Robert Kennedy's 1962 speech during the dedication ceremonies of Kendrick Hall, the new home of the School of Law at the University of San Francisco, addressed the civil rights issue, and his speech at USF during the presidential campaign of 1968, less than two months before his assassination, highlighted the nation's growing moral debate over the Vietnam War. Students who attended law school during the 1960s, at USF or elsewhere, could not help but be exposed to the social and ethical issues raised during that turbulent decade in the nation's history.

The 1960s were punctuated by calls by many USF law students for an end to the Vietnam War; for greater diversity among faculty and students; for student representation on decision-making committees; for more need-based student financial aid; and for a curriculum that had greater relevance to contemporary social issues. By the 1960s many USF law students, supervised by law school faculty, began providing legal services to community members in need. These legal aid programs were the precursors of the Street Law program begun in 1976 under Tom Nazario. These legal aid services also reflected USF's Jesuit legacy of reaching out to provide support to the surrounding community.

Elizabeth Anne Quigley, law school librarian (third from the left), is pictured among several librarians from the Gleeson Library in the early 1950s. The School of Law was housed on the third floor of the Gleeson Library from 1950 to 1962.

UNIVERSITY OF SAN FRANCISCO ARCHIVES

The Postwar Development of the College of Business Administration

109

THE ANTECEDENT OF THE CURRENT SCHOOL OF BUSINESS and Management at the University of San Francisco can be found at St. Ignatius College during the 1920s. In 1924, the college began a four-year evening program leading to a general business certificate, followed the next year by the establishment of the College of Commerce and Finance. The 1925–1926 college catalog described the curriculum as "suitable for success in a business career." The courses included accounting, economics, banking, advertising, business ethics, taxes, law, foreign commerce, corporate finance, and auditing.

When these courses were integrated with a sequence of required courses in the College of Arts and Sciences in 1926, students were eligible for a bachelor of commercial science degree. The first 10 of these degrees were awarded in 1928 (vignette #68). The prior year, the first three women began as students in the evening division of the College of Commerce and Finance, and by the fall of 1929, there were 123 men and eight women pursuing evening degrees in commercial science. Despite the Depression, enrollment in the College of Commerce and Finance at USF held steady during the 1930s, grew significantly at the close of the decade, and by fall 1941, on the eve of World War II, enrollment had increased to 255 students, out of a total USF enrollment of 1,448.

After World War II, enrollment skyrocketed at USF, many students attended the institution under the G.I. Bill of Rights, and the College of Commerce and Finance was renamed the College of Business Administration under its

Roy C. Hall, first dean of the College of Business Administration, played a major role in the postwar development of the college.

UNIVERSITY OF SAN FRANCISCO ARCHIVES

first dean, Roy C. Hall, who played a critical role in the development of the postwar business programs. The 1946–1947 catalog stated that among the aims of the business college was to "understand the broader fundamental social relationships in the industrial system." Moreover, the "City of San Francisco is the University's laboratory," and "the lifelong inter-relation of City and University has created a unique opportunity for students to correlate the work of the classroom with the policies and practices of business firms."

By the fall of 1948, there were 835 students in the College of Business Administration out of a total USF enrollment of 3,044. In 1953, the College of Business Administration became one of a small number of schools to be nationally accredited by the American Assembly of Collegiate Schools of Business (AACSB), a distinct and superior accreditation it has maintained to this day. Among the more prominent graduates of the business school in the 1950s was Dominic Tarantino, who received a bachelor's in accounting in 1954, eventually rose to become chairman of Price Waterhouse World Firm Limited; was given numerous professional awards, including the Gold Medal for Distinguished Service by the American Institute of CPA's; served on the USF Board of Trustees, including chairing it from 1999 to 2003; was honorary chair of the 2003 business school expansion project; and continues to be a major supporter of his alma mater.

During the 1950s and 1960s, the college continued to grow and to develop new curricula. Richard Mulcahy, S.J., served as the college's dean from 1956 to 1962. Before and after his term, he taught economics at USF, eventually retiring as a professor of economics emeritus. Fr. Mulcahy had a doctorate in economics from U.C. Berkeley; was an internationally known economist; taught many of the successful stock-brokers, bankers, and financiers in San Francisco and New York; and worked on the floor of the Pacific Stock Exchange before he joined the Jesuits. Vincent Wright, who was dean from 1963 to 1967, oversaw the development of the college's first MBA program.

Among the business faculty members who began their careers at USF during the 1950s and 1960s and who later retired as honored emeritus professors after helping to build the curriculum and teach thousands of students were Joseph Simini, professor of accounting; Eamonn Barrett, professor of labor relations management; Edward Nolan, professor of organizational psychology; Edwin Shapiro, professor of quantitative methods; and William Regan, professor of marketing. Regan also

served as the dean of the college from 1967 to 1974 and was responsible for hiring many new business faculty members. By the fall of 1975, there were 630 full-time undergraduate students and 667 graduate students in the College of Business Administration. The undergraduate areas of emphasis included accounting, finance, industrial relations, international business, marketing, management science, and social issues in administration. In addition, the college offered a bachelor of arts degree in rehabilitation administration and three master's degrees: in business administration, personnel administration, and rehabilitation administration.

Harold Walt became dean of the College of Business Administration in 1974, following Regan's return to the faculty. Walt came to USF from the presidency of William Pereira and Associates, architects of the Transamerica Building. Walt brought an important external business perspective to the college, but he also had to endure budget cuts that reduced the faculty to nine full-time positions. Following Walt, Edward Lynch, S.J., served as acting dean from 1977 to 1978.

During its first 50 years, the USF business school underwent major curriculum changes, enrollment increased dramatically, and the student population became more diverse. The school never lost sight, however, of its guiding principles, which included educating leaders to assume positions of responsibility in society, relating the theory and research of the classroom to the realities of the surrounding social and business world, incorporating the latest breakthroughs in technology into the curriculum, and applying Jesuit social and ethical values to the students' professional lives.

During the 1953-1954 academic year, accounting student Dominic Tarantino served as ASUSF President. After graduation, he pursued an accounting career, rising to become chairman of Price Waterhouse World Firm Limited. He later served on the USF Board of Trustees, chairing it from 1999 to 2003. He has been a major supporter of his alma mater.

UNIVERSITY OF SAN FRANCISCO ARCHIVES

The Founding of the School of Education

110

THE RETURN OF VETERANS AT THE END OF WORLD WAR II had major social consequences for the United States. The number of births, for example, went from 2.5 million in 1940, to 3.6 million in 1950, and to slightly more than 4 million in 1955 — a 57 percent increase in 15 years. This increase in births dramatically affected the nation's schools, especially in California. Increasingly, California's schools became overcrowded, and credentialed teachers were in short supply.

To meet this need, the California State Department of Education sought out top-quality institutions of higher education that did not have teacher preparation programs and asked those schools to consider adding teacher-training programs to their curriculum. The University of San Francisco was one of the schools that repeatedly received these requests, and in the spring of 1947, USF started a department of education, chaired by Paul Harney, S.J. In January 1948, the State Department of Education approved USF's granting of secondary school teaching credentials in content areas including foreign languages (French, Latin, and Spanish), English, life sciences and general science, physical science, and social studies. During the 1949 commencement exercises, the first class to be granted secondary teaching credentials at USF, a class composed of 22 men, walked across the graduation stage.

In addition to Fr. Harney, other founding professors of the USF department of education included John Martin, S.J.; Edward Griffin, who became the second department chair in 1956; professors John Devine and Henry Hall; and Thomas Reed, S.J., who later became principal of St. Ignatius College Preparatory, and who also served on the San Francisco Board of Education from 1973 to 1978.

By the fall of 1949, these founding professors had developed a program leading to a master's in education in addition to a secondary teaching credential program. In 1951, the department of education added the secondary school administration and supervision credentials to its repertoire. By 1955, the junior college credential was approved, and in 1964, a counseling and guidance credential was added. In that same year, the regular undergraduate programs at USF became coeducational, and for the first time both women and men began to pursue undergraduate liberal arts programs with the goal of obtaining a credential at the secondary or elementary school levels.

In 1966, Katherine Bishop, a former public

Edward Griffin, the first dean of USF's School of Education, which was established in 1972, 25 years after USF's Department of Education began preparing teachers for California's schools.

UNIVERSITY OF SAN FRANCISCO ARCHIVES

The School of Education moved from Campion Hall to the Rossi Wing of Lone Mountain in 1979, the year after USF acquired the Lone Mountain campus from the Religious of the Sacred Heart. Pictured here is the garden behind Lone Mountain's Rossi Wing.

1998; Robert Lamp, who began a 27-year career at USF in 1968; Thomas McSweeny, professor of education from 1961 to 1984; and Anthony Seidl, who, beginning in 1966, taught at USF for 24 years.

In 1972, due to enrollment increases and the development of several new master's programs in the department of education, the board of trustees voted to establish the School of Education. Edward Griffin made the transition from department chair to first dean of the school. He was followed in that capacity by Allen Calvin, who served as dean from 1974 to 1978. Under his leadership, the School of Education developed a doctoral program. In 1975, the first students commenced work on the doctor of education degree, which came to include concentrations in curriculum and instruction, educational psychology/counseling, organization and leadership, private education leadership, and multicultural education. The doctoral program grew rapidly in enrollment, and its graduates played a significant role in California educational leadership.

During Allen Calvin's administration, the School of Education also expanded its off-campus programs to facilities in local school districts, eventually offering credential and master's programs at regional USF campuses throughout Northern California and Southern California. Dean Calvin also initiated a multi-cultural program, first directed by Jose Llanes, followed by John Tsu. The program offered a bilingual/cross-cultural specialist credential in Spanish, Cantonese, Filipino, and Japanese; a master's in multicultural education; and a doctor of education in multicultural education. The multicultural programs attracted a large number of new students and a significant amount of federal grants.

Calvin also hired Donald Erickson to direct the newly created Center for Research on Private Education. Erickson was an eminent scholar on private education and educational administration, was vice president of the educational administration division of the

school administrator, became the director of a new program exclusively designed to prepare credentialed elementary school teachers. Notable education professors who began their careers at USF during the 1960s and who retired as emeritus professors include Larry Bishop, who taught from 1967 to 1996; William Van Burgess, whose tenure ran from 1968 to 1990; James Counelis, professor of education from 1969 to

American Educational Research Association, and had been a tenured full professor at the University of Chicago and at Simon Fraser University in Vancouver, British Columbia. The School of Education also developed an Evaluation Institute, and Michael Scriven was hired from U.C. Berkeley to become the institute's founding director. Scriven was a world-class scholar on evaluation, helped create the field of educational evaluation in the 1960s, and had published scores of books and articles on educational evaluation and related topics.

In 1976, Michael O'Neill, soon to become the third dean of the School of Education, launched the Institute for Catholic Educational Leadership (ICEL), a program that coordinated academic offerings and community service programming for educators in Catholic and private education from throughout the nation. The program was intended to meet the needs of Catholic and private school administrators, religious and secular, and did indeed draw some of its students from the ranks of non-Catholic private school administrators. The institute offered a doctorate in education with a concentration in private education leadership, a master's in private school administration, community service symposia and conferences, workshops for diocesan teachers and administrators, and various research initiatives. ICEL also offered Summer West, a six-week summer session of academic courses and workshops for master's and doctoral students from throughout the nation and the world who were preparing to assume leadership roles in Catholic and private schools. In 2001, ICEL celebrated its silver jubilee, marking 25 years of service to the community. After Michael O'Neill became dean, the two key figures leading ICEL for more than two decades were Edwin McDermott, S.J., and Mary Peter Traviss, O.P. In August 2004, Brother Raymond Vercruysse, of the Congregation of Christian Brothers, assumed the directorship of ICEL.

In 1978, the year Allen Calvin left the dean's office to return to teaching and Michael O'Neill

Katherine Bishop was the first director of the teacher education credential program for elementary school teachers.

became the new dean, the School of Education had 1,063 students. This represented more than 15 percent of the total student enrollment at USF. The school offered myriad programs at the master's and doctoral levels and was authorized to offer a range of credentials by the California Commission for Teacher Preparation and Licensing, including credentials for multiple-subject instruction for elementary school teachers, single-subject instruction for secondary teachers, bilingual/cross-cultural education, early childhood education, special education, administrative services, pupil personnel services, reading, and speech pathology. In its mission statement, the School of Education articulated both interpersonal and broad social goals: "to establish a learning environment which promotes an individual's growth as a person who is also an educator; stimulate an educator response towards creating a better human community; and prepare educators who have the courage to take risks responsibly."

Over its first 30 years, the USF School of Education grew from 22 to more than 1,000 students; developed a range of credential and graduate degree programs; and articulated a mission that encompassed educational, developmental, and social goals.

The Origins of the School of Nursing

THE ORIGIN AND DEVELOPMENT OF THE USF SCHOOL OF Nursing is intertwined with the history of health care in America, the professionalization of nursing, and social changes in the role of women in colleges and in society. The success of Florence Nightingale's reformation of the British medical system and her employment of female nurses in the Crimean War in the 1850s, the need for nurses during the American Civil War, and the development of hospitals during the 19th century to replace the traditional home-based health care also underpinned the development of nursing in the United States. Finally, Catholic women's religious orders played a significant role in fostering hospital-based training programs for nurses in the United States. For example, a contingent of the Sisters of Mercy came from Ireland to San Francisco in 1854 and established St. Mary's Hospital, including a training program for nurses. This was during the same time period that the Jesuits were founding St. Ignatius Church and College in San Francisco.

By the end of the 19th century, there was a growing movement to link nursing to academic training in institutions of higher education. Pioneering institutions for such training were Teacher's College at Columbia and the University of Minnesota. In 1907, a nurse-training program was started at the University of California Hospital in San Francisco, and in 1918, U.C. Berkeley offered a baccalaureate degree for nurses. In 1900, the Sisters of Mercy opened an educational training school for Catholic and lay nurses, which was approved in 1917 by the California State Board of Nursing.

Over the next several decades, the Sisters of Mercy engaged in a series of discussions with the Jesuits about establishing a formal relationship with St. Ignatius College to offer nursing education. It was not until 1947, however, that William Dunne, S.J., president of the University of San Francisco, approved the concept of USF partnering with St. Mary's Hospital to provide nursing education. In 1948, a department of nursing was formed within the College of Arts and Sciences. The aim of the USF nursing curriculum, according to the 1951 catalog, was "to provide the necessary academic credit which, coupled with a three-year basic curriculum in Nursing in an accredited hospital, permits a student to obtain the degree of Bachelor of Science in Nursing. The degree is intended to furnish an academic background for the professional nurse and equip her for administrative duties."

Mary de Paul, S.M., headed the USF nursing program during its first years as a department within the College of Arts and Sciences, while she simultaneously directed St. Mary's Hospital and its nursing program. The administrative offices for the program were located at St. Mary's Hospital across the street from USF, on the corner of Fulton and Shrader streets, but students took their basic arts and science courses in Campion Hall or in temporary postwar buildings from the government, called Quonset huts, located on the north side of the campus, along Golden Gate Avenue. Many of the nursing students lived in a dormitory on the south side of Hayes Street, directly across from the hospital. Coincidentally, the dormitory was on the same site as the old "shirt factory" campus of St. Ignatius College.

In 1954, USF established an autonomous School of Nursing. Mary Martha, S.M., was appointed acting dean of the School of Nursing and was soon followed by Mary Beata Bauman, S.M., the first permanent dean. She held this position until 1970, and under her leadership, the School of Nursing attained full accreditation by the National League of Nursing (NLN) and approval by the California State Board of Nurse Examiners, articulated its unique mission within the context of Jesuit

education at USF, developed an integrated curriculum, expanded its clinical opportunities, increased its number of lay faculty, began to focus on nursing research and publication, initiated continuing education programs for practicing nurses under its own provider number, and saw a steady growth in enrollment: from 20 students in 1954, to 101 in 1957, and to 360 by 1969. In 1964, USF became completely coeducational, though women in the School of Nursing could vote and hold office in student government before 1964. In 1957, Jane Summerfield, a nursing student, became the first female reporter for the *Foghorn*. USF graduated its first male nurse, John Meenaghan, in 1967.

Mary Martha, S.M., first acting dean of the School of Nursing, and Timothy McDonnell, S.J., first regent of the School of Nursing.

UNIVERSITY OF SAN FRANCISCO ARCHIVES

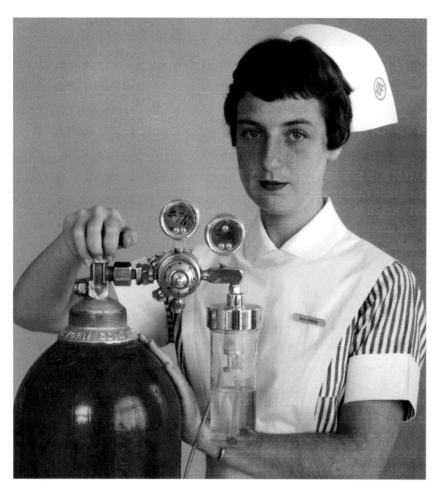

In 1954, when the USF School of Nursing was established, starched blouses, pinafores, and caps were required of nursing students, and nurses had not attained the status they enjoy today as healthcare leaders. Over the past 50 years, the USF School of Nursing has significantly contributed to the enhancement of the profession.

UNIVERSITY OF SAN FRANCISCO ARCHIVES

Among the nursing faculty members who began their careers at USF during the 1950s and 1960s and who retired as professors emeritae were Frances Carter, who taught for 31 years, from 1957 to 1988; Lois Dunlop, whose 17-year career began in 1964; Mary Sylvia Grandsaert, S.M., whose teaching career at USF ran from 1953 to 1967; Eleanor Hein, whose 26-year year career began in 1967; and Mary Martha Kiening, S.M., who taught at USF from 1952 to 1976. Joan Green, professor emerita of nursing, began her teaching career at USF in 1960, was the first nursing faculty member to obtain a doctorate, and before her retirement in 1995 served in numerous administrative capacities, including assistant, associate, and acting dean of the School of Nursing and associate vice president for academic affairs.

In the spring of 1969, Cowell Hall opened

its doors as the new home for the School of Nursing. The dedication was on May 25, 1969, and included remarks by Timothy McDonnell, S.J., the first regent of the School of Nursing. The principal address was by Sister Mary Beata, who was in her 13th year as dean. The building was named for Samuel Cowell, San Francisco businessman and philanthropist, whose foundation contributed $450,000 toward the construction costs. Other contributions were made by the U.S. Department of Health and by Crown Zellerbach Foundation.

In 1971, Mary Geraldine McDonnell, S.M., succeeded Sr. Bauman as dean of the School of Nursing. Under Sr. McDonnell, the School of Nursing was re-accredited for a full eight-year period by the NLN; saw the installation of the Beta Gamma Chapter of Sigma Theta Tau, the national nursing honor society; witnessed a revamping of the undergraduate curriculum congruent with the new requirements of the California Board of Registered Nurses (BRN); and increasingly incorporated new technologies into the curriculum. Among the faculty members who began their careers at USF in the 1970s, contributed mightily to the development of the School of Nursing, and are still teaching in the school are Betty Carmack; Jane Vincent Corbett; Mary Brian Kelber, R.S.M.; and Mary Ellene Egan, R.S.M. Among the many outstanding graduates of the USF School of Nursing during the 1970s was Sheila Burke, class of 1973, now a trustee of USF and undersecretary for American museums, programs, and national outreach at the Smithsonian Institution in Washington, D.C. Prior to her position at the Smithsonian, Ms. Burke served as chief of staff for U.S. Senator Bob Dole and was executive dean of Harvard's John F. Kennedy School of Government.

By the time Sr. McDonnell retired in 1981, student enrollment in the School of Nursing stood at 600, and it had a highly regarded curriculum taught by outstanding faculty. The School of Nursing also had articulated a mission at one with Jesuit values and the legacy of USF, founded on compassionate service to others.

A Graduate Division

THOUGH ST. IGNATIUS COLLEGE AWARDED ITS FIRST graduate degree in 1867, it was not until the fall of 1949 that a full-scale graduate division was launched at the University of San Francisco. The first dean of the graduate division was John Martin, S.J., and the first three master's degrees were in biology, chemistry, and history.

The USF professors who developed and taught the first courses in 1949 in the new graduate division established the foundation for the graduate programs that were to follow. In biology, the department first offered courses for a master's degree in the fields of physiology, vertebrate zoology, invertebrate zoology, and genetics. These courses were developed and taught by professors Edward Kessel, the biology department chair and a world renowned expert on the flat-footed common fly; Harold Harper, whose book on physiological chemistry went through 23 editions and was published in 26 languages; William Hovanitz, a highly respected researcher on genetics; and Robert Orr, author of numerous books on mammals of North America, California, and the Bay Area.

The new master's degree in chemistry included course work in the fields of biochemistry, inorganic chemistry, organic chemistry, and physical chemistry. These courses were developed and taught by professors William Maroney, department chair; Arthur Furst, who later became the world's foremost authority on toxicology and the recipient of numerous awards and federal grants (vignette #17); and Charles "Mel" Gorman, who received the university's first annual distinguished teaching award in 1964, and who published extensively in the area of the history of science.

The master's degree program in history offered graduate courses in four areas: North American history, Latin American history, medieval European history, and modern European history. The first graduate history courses were taught by professors Peter Dunne, S.J., the first department chair of history and author of 10 books and some 60 articles; Ashbrook Lincoln; Earle Stewart; and John McGloin, S.J., author of several books, including *Jesuits by the Golden Gate: The Society of Jesus in San Francisco, 1849–1969.*

From 1949 to the late 1960s, graduate enrollment and programming increased significantly. Enrollment went from 10 graduate students in the fall of 1949 to 520 in the fall of 1968. Many of the students used their master's degrees from USF to advance to doctoral programs at other institutions. Several new graduate degree programs were started in education during this time period, and were augmented by graduate programs in political science in 1951, English

John Martin, S.J., served as the first dean of USF's graduate division, which was established in 1949, and offered master's degrees in biology, chemistry, and history.

UNIVERSITY OF SAN FRANCISCO ARCHIVES

In 1949, the same year that the graduate division was launched at USF, Raymond Feely, S.J., (left) celebrated his 10th year as dean of faculties. In this photo, USF President William Dunne, S.J., (right), congratulates Fr. Feely on his 10th anniversary as dean. In 1951, Fr. Feely became USF's first academic vice president. Standing between Fr. Dunne and Fr. Feely is USF professor Harold Harper, a leading authority on physiological chemistry and one of the developers of the master's degree in biology in the new graduate division.

UNIVERSITY OF SAN FRANCISCO ARCHIVES

and theology in 1962, and business administration in 1964. By the fall of 1978, there were 1,512 students pursuing graduate work at USF, and the graduate division had expanded to include additional programs in education, economics, international economics, government, toxicology, religious education, and applied spirituality (in the summer only). By 1978, the McLaren College of Business had added a master's degree in personnel administration and one in rehabilitation administration to its MBA offerings. During the 1978–1979 academic year, the university made a decision to economize, reduce duplication of services, and administer the myriad graduate programs within the separate schools and colleges. Therefore, a distinct graduate division was fazed out of the university's organizational structure.

During the first 50 years of the institution's history, 28 master's degrees were granted by St. Ignatius College. During the 2003–2004 academic year alone, more than 1,200 graduate degrees were awarded. Today, the University of San Francisco enrolls more than 2,500 graduate students, plus more than 700 law students. The university currently offers 34 separate master's degree programs in the College of Arts and Sciences, the Masagung Graduate School of Management, the School of Nursing, the School of Education, and the College of Professional Studies; four different doctorate programs in the School of Education; and the juris doctor and two separate master of law programs in the School of Law. The minor experiment in the second half of the 19th century in graduate education has become a major underpinning for the institution at the beginning of the 21st century.

The Evening College

AT THE UNIVERSITY OF SAN FRANCISCO, AS AT OTHER higher education institutions across the nation, many of the World War II veterans who returned to college under the G.I. Bill of Rights held jobs during the day to support themselves and their families. Only during the evening hours were these veterans at liberty to pursue higher education. USF had considerable experience in evening programming, stretching back to the founding of the School of Law in 1912 (vignette #51). In the mid-1920s, the newly formed College of Arts and Sciences began to offer a wide range of general education courses in the evening, and the new College of Commerce and Finance initiated evening courses in areas such as business management and finance (vignette #68).

During the late 1940s, the number of course offerings, degree and certificate options, and enrolled students steadily increased in the evening division. Beginning in the 1948 fall semester, for example, the College of Business Administration offered an evening program

For decades the lighted spires of St. Ignatius Church, seen here in the 1950s, have guided evening students to their destination—a first-rate education at the University of San Francisco.
UNIVERSITY OF SAN FRANCISCO ARCHIVES

leading to a bachelor of science degree in business administration, with majors in accounting, finance, foreign trade, industrial relations, marketing, and general business. Three-year certificate programs in the evenings were also available in these same business areas. A full range of courses in the liberal arts was also available in the evening, as were specialized courses in pre-law, teacher training, and nursing. As had been the case since 1912, a law degree could be attained completely through evening course work. The faculty members teaching in the evening division were largely drawn from the day division and the faculty of St. Ignatius High School, plus various Bay Area professional organizations.

By the fall of 1951, the total enrollment in the evening division, including the law school, reached 1,394 students, in comparison to 1,432 day students. Significantly, in the fall of 1951, the number of undergraduates in the evening division exceeded the number of undergraduates during the day for the first time in the institution's history. Moreover, the number of undergraduate evening students increased 18 percent from 1950 to 1951, while the number of undergraduate students during the day declined by the same percentage. The evening division permitted women to enroll in courses, whereas the day division did not accept women until 1964. Beginning in 1951, the evening division, directed by George Lucy, S.J., followed by Gerald Sugrue, S.J., began to be referred to by some as an evening college.

The first USF catalog to refer to a dean of an evening college, however, was published for the 1976–1978 academic years, when Robert Maloney, S.J., was so designated. Lawrence Romani served as the student academic adviser under Fr. Maloney. By 1978, the evening college, under Fr. Maloney, focused on three major areas: in the liberal arts, where bachelor's degrees were offered in Spanish, economics, English, government, history, philosophy, psychology, sociology, and sociology with a concentration in social welfare; in the sciences, where a bachelor's degree in mathematics was offered; and in business administration, where a bachelor's of science was offered in several areas of emphasis, including accounting, finance,

During the 1950s, the new Gleeson Library successfully accommodated the educational needs of a growing number of evening students on the USF campus.

industrial relations, international business, marketing, management, and transportation. Business certificates were also offered in these same content areas.

The Labor Management School, founded in 1947 by George Lucy, S.J., was another example of evening programming at USF during the years immediately following World War II. The school was designed to educate students in labor and management issues and for several years was directed by Andrew Boss, S.J., who sometimes served as a mediator in local labor disputes. From 1947 to 1969, the Labor Management School enrolled approximately 5,000 students in its evening courses, including students from approximately 200 business firms and 500 unions. By the mid-1970s, however, interest in the Labor Management School waned, and the school closed.

By 1978, organizational and administrative change was on the horizon for the evening college, and the respective colleges increasingly assumed responsibility for evening programming. As was the case with the graduate division, mounting financial problems at USF in the 1970s were the driving force in the demise of the evening college, as ways were sought to consolidate administrative efforts. As this process unfolded, the number of students in the evening college began to plummet as the student count was credited to each separate college that offered the evening courses. In 1981, the evening college, as it had come to be known for 30 years, ceased operations. Simultaneously, another administrative unit arose to offer a different selection of undergraduate and graduate degrees in the evenings and on weekends. This unit began in 1975 as the Office of Continuing Education, was upgraded to the School of Continuing Education in 1979, and finally was recast in 1980 as the College of Professional Studies.

Throughout its 30-year history, the evening college published a newsletter titled *The Night Owl*. The publication carried feature stories

George Lucy, S.J., director of both the evening division and the Labor Management School, is shown here with four trade-union leaders from Germany who visited USF in 1950.

about the history of the university, Jesuit education, evening college students, alumni, and faculty; articles about local and state politics, business, and entertainment; program updates, schedules, and other administrative information; and lists of students who were graduating from the evening college. In May 1981, the last issue was published, and it included a farewell to students from the outgoing dean, Theodore Taheny, S.J., who thanked the staff, faculty, and diverse students he had worked with over the years. He also outlined the goals that had been set by the evening college: to provide professional competence in academic disciplines, to deepen a sense of principles to be honored and lived, to work in the service of life and living, and to succeed in fulfilling the Jesuit goal of forming "men and women for others." Fr. Taheny concluded, "This City and this campus, its classrooms and laboratories, the questions you framed, the answers discovered — all came together to make the Evening College a home for your minds, a Cathedral for your hearts." According to Fr. Taheny, "dedicated lay faculty and staff, Jesuit teachers and administrators shared one common goal in the Evening College: your education."

William Dunne, S.J.

IF GREAT LEADERSHIP IS MARKED BY SUCCESSFULLY guiding an institution through a prolonged period of challenges and crises, then the 20th president of the University of San Francisco, William Dunne, S.J., merits the term great. Fr. Dunne served as USF president for 16 years, longer than any other man. From 1938 to 1954, he guided the institution through the end of a major economic depression, a world war that drained the university of nearly all of its students, a consequent economic crisis due to the Depression and the war, an upsurge in enrollment following the war that seriously taxed the physical resources of the university, the beginning of the most significant building campaign in the history of the school, and a host of institutional changes ranging from the creation of a board of regents to the development of significant new academic programs.

William Dunne was born in San Francisco on December 9, 1897, and he grew up near the corner of Geary Boulevard and Parker Avenue, close to the site of the future campus he would one day lead. He attended Richmond Grammar School before transferring in 1909, at the beginning of the sixth grade, to St. Ignatius Grammar School, which was then still part of St. Ignatius College. During his time at St. Ignatius High School, William Dunne was greatly influenced by the Jesuit scholastics he met in the classroom and during extracurricular activities. He decided to join the Jesuits when he was 18 and was formally admitted to the Society of Jesus at Sacred Heart Novitiate in Los Gatos, California, on July 15, 1915.

After four years at Los Gatos and three years

at Mt. St. Michael's College and Gonzaga University in Spokane, Washington, Fr. Dunne received his bachelor's and master's degrees. In 1922, he was assigned to Seattle College to teach philosophy. At that school, he also directed dramatics and coached baseball, basketball, and tennis. From 1925 to 1929, he studied theology in France, and in 1928, he was ordained a Jesuit priest in Lyons. Fr. Dunne returned to the United States in 1929, where he taught for one year at Seattle College, followed by assignment as minister and then rector, to the Sacred Heart Novitiate in Los Gatos. Simultaneously, he completed work for a doctorate from the Gregorian University in Rome in sacred theology, which he was awarded in 1939. In 1938, at age 40, Fr. Dunne was appointed rector of the Jesuit community and president of the University of San Francisco.

From the beginning of his presidency, Fr. Dunne faced severe economic problems stemming from an accumulated debt from the building of St. Ignatius Church, completed in 1914; a shortage of funds caused by the longest economic depression in the nation's history; and in the third year of his presidency, the beginning of a world war that led to an enrollment decline that almost closed the university. Initially, Fr. Dunne helped offset the student decline by traveling to Washington, D.C., to secure an on-campus military training program at USF, known as the Army Specialized Training Program (ASTP). When that program was discontinued in 1944, however, enrollment dropped to less than 400 students. In the face of a major financial deficit, Fr. Dunne successfully launched a fundraising effort that kept the doors open at the university through the end of the war in 1945.

After the war, the university faced a new challenge: an unprecedented enrollment increase catalyzed by the return of the veterans under the G.I. Bill of Rights. Facing a severe space shortage, and looking toward the long-term growth of the university, the president established the first board of regents in the institution's history to help develop a master plan for the university, to raise money, and to launch a major building campaign that first bore fruit in the completion of the Gleeson Library in 1950 and that provided the underpinning for other buildings on campus, such as Phelan Hall, completed after Fr. Dunne left office in 1954. In that year, university enrollment stood at slightly more than 3,000 students, a record. Fr. Dunne was also committed to the development of new academic programs, and under his administration, USF began a department of education for the training of teachers, initiated a graduate division, greatly expanded the university's evening division, and launched the School of Nursing. In 1950, USF passed its first university-wide accreditation visit.

After leaving the presidency of USF in 1954, Fr. Dunne served at the Jesuit retreat house at Los Altos for a year, followed by a two-year stint as pastor of a Jesuit parish in Utah, where he tended to the needs of Navajo youth at a government school. In 1957, he was invited to become executive secretary for the college department of the National Catholic Education Association (NCEA) in Washington, D.C., where he advised on legislation concerning Catholic colleges. He also served on the executive committee of the Western College Association. In 1964, he was awarded the John Carroll Medal by Georgetown University for

William Dunne, S.J., 20th president of the University of San Francisco, served in that capacity longer than any other man. During his administration, from 1938 to 1954, USF successfully adapted to worldwide economic depression and war, accommodated a postwar upsurge in enrollment, witnessed a major building campaign, and launched a host of new academic programs.
UNIVERSITY OF SAN FRANCISCO ARCHIVES

In 1979, Fr. Dunne, president emeritus of USF, met with Pete Rozelle (left), class of 1950, former USF sports information director, and commissioner of the National Football League. Also pictured is Al Alessandri (right) who graduated from USF in 1950 and later served as president of the alumni association, vice president for university relations, and special assistant to the president at USF.

outstanding service to education. In that same year, Fr. Dunne was reassigned to the Jesuit retreat house at Los Altos.

In 1965, Fr. Dunne celebrated his golden jubilee as a Jesuit at St. Ignatius Church, and he returned to USF as director of estate planning and adviser to successive USF presidents. In 1972, Fr. Dunne received an honorary doctorate of humane letters from USF and was given the title president emeritus, the only former USF president to hold that honor. An endowed scholarship for students, based on academic achievement and community service, was also created in his name. Following a long illness, Fr. Dunne died on Christmas Day, 1980, at age 83. At his resurrection Mass, held in St. Ignatius Church, the president of USF, John Lo Schiavo, S.J., eloquently highlighted Fr. Dunne's life and his outstanding contributions to the Society of Jesus, to the community, to higher education, and to USF. In the words of Fr. Lo Schiavo, "because of his own brilliant academic career, his proven

talent for administration, his sterling eloquence and his great love for his hilltop school, Bill Dunne seemed perfectly fitted to be president of USF—and time proved that appearance to be a reality."

Today, Fr. William Dunne's legacy continues in many forms. Among those reminders of his efforts on behalf of USF is the Fr. William Dunne Award, the university's highest individual honor, bestowed annually upon a member of the USF community for extraordinary service to USF and the community at large. It reflects the values and mission of the university that Fr. Dunne represented in his own life.

The Basketball Triumphs

IN THE FALL OF 1954, USF BASKETBALL COACH PHIL
Wolpert surveyed a team that looked promising, having compiled a
record of 14 wins and 7 losses in the prior season. Even coach Wolpert,
however, could not have predicted the phenomenal achievements this
team and its successors were about to compile over the next three seasons.

The 1954–1955 team started the season with
two of the greatest players the game has ever
seen: Bill Russell and K.C. Jones. That team
finished the season with a 26–1 record and
headed to the first round of the NCAA
competition in Corvallis, Oregon, where it
defeated the University of Utah 78–59, and
Oregon State 57–56. The Dons then went
on to Kansas City, where they defeated the
University of Colorado in the semifinal contest,
62–50. This victory set the stage for the national
championship game against defending champion, La Salle College. On March 19, 1955,
USF defeated La Salle 77–63 to become the
NCAA national basketball champions. Three
days later, the team was given a ticker-tape
parade through downtown San Francisco,
led by the mayor of San Francisco, Elmer
Robinson, and the president of USF, John
Connolly, S.J. The parade culminated in a
victory luncheon at the Fairmont Hotel
attended by more than 1,000 supporters.
United Press named Phil Wolpert coach of
the year, and Bill Russell was selected as a
first-team All-American and was voted the
Most Valuable Player in the NCAA tournament after setting a new scoring record.

Just as the undefeated 1951 USF football
team was far ahead of most of the nation in
fully integrating its team, the 1954–1955 USF

The 1954–55 Dons exiting their flight
with championship trophy in hand
after winning the NCAA tournament.
Coach Wolpert is at the far left, at
the top of the stairs.

UNIVERSITY OF SAN FRANCISCO ARCHIVES

basketball team became the first major college
or university basketball team to win a national
title with three African American players (Bill
Russell, K.C. Jones, and Hal Perry) among its
five starters. Many college teams throughout
the nation, especially in the South, did not
integrate their teams until the late 1960s or
early 1970s. The segregated nature of various
regions of the nation was underscored by a

trip that USF took to Oklahoma City to play in a tournament during the 1954–1955 season. Upon arrival in the city, the team's black players were denied hotel accommodations. The team voted unanimously, however, to stay together in an unoccupied college dorm, thus buttressing a growing sense of team unity in the face of discrimination.

The 1955–1956 basketball team continued the victory parade from the prior season with many of its returning veterans, and some new faces. Gene Brown, Carl Boldt, Warren Baxter, and Mike Farmer joined returning players such as Bill Russell, K.C. Jones, and Hal Perry to win every game in the regular season. The year climaxed with the national championship game held in Evanston, Illinois, when the

Dons won their second straight NCAA championship, defeating Big Ten champion Iowa 83–71, despite playing without K.C. Jones, who had been declared ineligible for the tournament because he played one game as a freshman four years earlier. Once again, the team was honored by a victory parade upon its return to San Francisco. On April 5, more than 150 green-and-gold bedecked cars traveled from USF to city hall for a reception hosted by the mayor and followed by a victory banquet at the Sheraton-Palace Hotel attended by 1,200 guests.

During the summer of 1956, the basketball team accepted an invitation to travel on a good will tour to Central and South America as part of the United States International

Bill Russell (left) and K.C. Jones (right) in action during the 1955–1956 NCAA championship season.

Educational Exchange Program. The team put on exhibition games in numerous countries, including Venezuela, El Salvador, Panama, and Paraguay. Wherever the team traveled, it received glowing reports on its sportsmanship, good will, and exemplary conduct on and off the court. The embassy staff in Paraguay, for example, wrote, "the visit of the Dons to Asuncion was a real success and the Americans conducted themselves like true American Ambassadors of Sport."

The USF basketball team opened the 1956–1957 season without several of its former star players, including Bill Russell, K.C. Jones, and Hal Perry, who had completed their educations at USF. Nevertheless, led by stars from the prior season, such as Mike Farmer, Eugene Brown, and Carl Boldt, the Dons won the first 10 games of the season, to extend their streak to a record 60 games. The Dons were finally defeated, however, by the Olympic Championship team, led by former Dons Bill Russell and K.C. Jones. Although this was only an exhibition game, the spell had been broken, and the USF team lost its next four regular season games, defeats compounded by injuries and illnesses. The team did compile a 20–5 season record, won the Far West Regional Tournament, and went to the national NCAA tournament, where it was defeated by Kansas, a team led by the legendary Wilt Chamberlain. The Dons did finish third in the NCAA, however, after defeating Michigan State, 67–60.

The NCAA basketball championships of 1955 and 1956, along with the record-breaking winning streak that extended into the 1956–1957

season, provided a major stimulus to the fund-raising campaign then in progress to build a gymnasium on campus. Indeed, at the March 1955 victory luncheon at the Fairmont Hotel, it was announced that $300,000 had been raised for a new gymnasium. During the luncheon, an additional $25,000 was pledged. The proceeds from the 1956 victory banquet also went to the campaign to build a new gymnasium. The basketball triumphs served as the wellspring for efforts that culminated in the dedication of the War Memorial Gymnasium in November 1958. Moreover, the USF basketball teams of this era set a new standard of athletic accomplishment with a fully integrated team and created an unparalleled level of recognition for the University of San Francisco throughout the nation and the world.

A reluctant piglet, Daphne, was recruited by Mrs. Pinky Russ, a Dons' booster, as a good luck mascot before the 1957 NCAA Far Western Regional semifinal game against California, which USF won, 50-46. Despite Daphne's best efforts, however, the Dons attempt at a third-straight NCAA championship came up short, when Kansas, led by Wilt Chamberlain, defeated USF in the semifinals.

UNIVERSITY OF SAN FRANCISCO ARCHIVES

The Centennial Celebration

THE UNIVERSITY OF SAN FRANCISCO, THE OLDEST institution of higher education in the city, celebrated a special birthday in 1955: one century had passed since the institution's founding. St. Ignatius Academy, the antecedent of USF, first opened its doors on October 15, 1855. In the fall of 1954, John Connolly, S.J., the newly appointed president of USF, established an advisory committee to plan a series of celebratory events to be held during October 1955. Other regularly scheduled and special university events during 1955 and 1956 were also adapted to the centennial celebration.

The anniversary year began with a centennial graduation on Sunday, June 11, 1955, during which 313 students received their degrees. The graduation exercises were held in the War Memorial Opera House on Van Ness Avenue, and Judge Preston Devine, who had received both his undergraduate and law degrees from St. Ignatius College, was the featured commencement speaker. On October 10, 1955, the San Francisco Board of Supervisors unanimously adopted a resolution that honored USF's centennial milestone and noted that the institution has "spread the fame of San Francisco throughout the world by the activities of its students and graduates in the field of sports, law, medicine, military science, and religion." The local press also highlighted the USF centennial celebration. The *San Francisco Chronicle* published a feature article on the history of St. Ignatius College on Market Street. "A Catholic institution in a heavily Catholic city, USF has always had its own traditions, its campus lore," the article stated, but "last week, a century after its founding, USF was still on the move with an expansion program on the boards."

Several religious services marked the centennial week during October 1955. On October 13, a special Mass was sung in St. Ignatius Church by William Tobin, S.J., rector of the Jesuit community at USF and a graduate of St. Ignatius High School. The sermon for that Mass was given by Charles Casassa, S.J., president of Loyola University of Los Angeles and a graduate of St. Ignatius College. The next day, a university memorial Mass for deceased USF students and faculty was offered by Fr. Connolly. The centennial week came to a close on Sunday, October 16, with a Mass in St. Ignatius Church, presided over by San Francisco Archbishop John Mitty. During the Mass, Francis Corkery, S.J., president of Gonzaga University gave the sermon, noting that the university's first century is "a story of vision, courage, zeal, and sacrifice. It is written where all may read: in the souls of men and in the fabulous story of the civic and spiritual growth of this great metropolis."

The centennial celebration continued with the dedication of Phelan Hall on October 23.

The university cheer girls celebrate the institution's centennial in front of the Golden Gate Park Conservatory.

The seven-story building, with accommodations for 386 students and a 1,000-person-capacity dining room (now McLaren 250, 251, and 252), was the institution's first student residence hall. At the dedication ceremony, Fr. Tobin blessed the new building; Fr. Connolly gave a short dedication speech; William O'Brien, class of 1924, gave the main address; and Noel Sullivan, class of 1912, unveiled a portrait of his uncle, James Phelan, graduate of St. Ignatius College, three-time mayor of San Francisco, and U.S. Senator from California. The Maraschi Club, composed of USF students of Italian heritage, also organized a display of the paintings of the Italian-born artist Domenico Tojetti, a major portrait artist of San Francisco and the chief artist and decorator for the Jesuits of San Francisco from the late nineteenth century through 1906.

The anniversary celebration continued into 1956. On January 24, KGO-TV made USF the focus of its "Success Story" program, sponsored by Richfield Oil Company. USF was chosen "because of its scholastic reputation, NCAA championship basketball team and development programs." On February 1, a centennial banquet was held at the Fairmont Hotel. The 1,500 attendees heard addresses by Charles Sweigert, St. Ignatius Class of 1897; George Christopher, mayor of San Francisco; and Goodwin Knight, governor of California. Governor Knight paid tribute to the Jesuits of San Francisco. "This is a centennial of men rather than of mortar," the governor said, "and the happiest note is struck when we think of the men who have taught and who have been taught within the walls of this university." Other celebratory events in early 1956 included a special luncheon at the Sheraton-Palace Hotel hosted by the Society of California Pioneers to honor former USF President Edward Whelan, S.J., and current USF President,

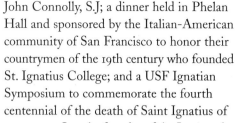

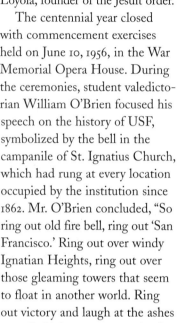

John Connolly, S.J; a dinner held in Phelan Hall and sponsored by the Italian-American community of San Francisco to honor their countrymen of the 19th century who founded St. Ignatius College; and a USF Ignatian Symposium to commemorate the fourth centennial of the death of Saint Ignatius of Loyola, founder of the Jesuit order.

The centennial year closed with commencement exercises held on June 10, 1956, in the War Memorial Opera House. During the ceremonies, student valedictorian William O'Brien focused his speech on the history of USF, symbolized by the bell in the campanile of St. Ignatius Church, which had rung at every location occupied by the institution since 1862. Mr. O'Brien concluded, "So ring out old fire bell, ring out 'San Francisco.' Ring out over windy Ignatian Heights, ring out over those gleaming towers that seem to float in another world. Ring out victory and laugh at the ashes out of which you grew mighty."

The University of San Francisco had indeed grown mighty since its humble beginning as a small one-room schoolhouse, initially enrolling three students and set on less than an acre of land amidst the sand dunes of an undeveloped Market Street. In the fall semester of 1956, USF registered 3,854 students, its highest enrollment up to that date. The 22-acre campus near Golden Gate Park was in the middle of a major building campaign, recently witnessed the completion of Gleeson Library and Phelan Hall, and would soon see a new gymnasium under construction. Several new academic programs had been successfully launched in the past five years, accreditation agencies gave USF high marks, and the national championship basketball team brought the school international visibility. The legacy of the institution's first century held great promise for the second century.

Soccer with Gus Donoghue and Steve Negoesco

ON NEW YEAR'S DAY IN 1950, THE UNIVERSITY OF SAN Francisco soccer team met Penn State in Saint Louis for the first annual intercollegiate soccer bowl game in the United States. The Dons had spent the prior three nights sleeping on cots in the living room and dining room of a Saint Louis college fraternity house because none of the city's hotels would provide accommodations for the team's black player, Olufumni Osibogun, an exchange student from Nigeria. Much of the United States was still segregated by Jim Crow laws or social mores from the post-Civil War era. The team elected to stay with its black player rather than acquiesce to racist attitudes, a harbinger of the moral stand taken by the USF football team the next year.

On the day of the game, USF and Penn State battled to a 2–2 draw, and the teams were declared co-national champions. For coach Gus Donoghue, who was named 1950 Coach of the Year by the San Francisco Football Association, it was a triumphant conclusion to an undefeated season and one more achievement in his illustrious career at USF.

Gus Donoghue was born in Scotland in 1911, where he learned the game of soccer. He came to San Francisco in 1925, and at the age of 14, he enrolled at St. Ignatius High School and continued on to St. Ignatius College, which in 1930 became the University of San Francisco. The soccer program began at USF in 1931, and in its second year, the Dons tied Stanford for the championship of the Pacific Coast Soccer League. From 1932 to 1936, the USF soccer team won five consecutive conference championships. For the first four of those years, Gus Donoghue was the team captain, and he was named All-American in 1933, 1934, and 1935. He was also the student body president one year.

After graduation, Donoghue earned a master's degree from U.C. Berkeley, taught high school, and served in the Navy during World War II. After the war, he returned to USF, where he taught history, coached the soccer team, earned a doctorate in history from Stanford, and in 1953 was named director of admissions, a position he held for 20 years until his retirement in 1973. During his career as USF's soccer coach, from 1946 to 1960, Donoghue compiled a record of 121 wins, 12 losses, and 14 ties. His teams once amassed 44 consecutive victories and captured 11 straight Northern California Intercollegiate Soccer

Gus Donoghue captained the USF soccer team to four consecutive Pacific Coast Soccer League championships from 1932 to 1936, was a three-time All-American player, and was elected student body president. After Navy service during World War II, Donoghue returned to USF to teach history, serve as director of admissions, and coach the soccer team to 11 consecutive Northern California Intercollegiate Soccer Conference titles and a co-national championship.

UNIVERSITY OF SAN FRANCISCO ARCHIVES

The 1950 USF Soccer team was declared co-national champions after tying Penn State in the first annual intercollegiate soccer bowl game. In this photo, Coach Gus Donoghue is standing in the back row on the far left, and star player and future coach Steve Negoesco is fourth from the left in the middle row.

UNIVERSITY OF SAN FRANCISCO ARCHIVES

Conference titles. Donoghue was later inducted into the National Soccer Coaches Association of America Hall of Fame.

The triumphant 1949–1950 Dons' soccer season under Donoghue marked the first year that the USF soccer team shared a national championship, and the second year in a row in which the team had won the Northern California Conference title. On the road to the California title, the team defeated long-time athletic rivals Santa Clara, U.C. Berkeley, Stanford, U.C.L.A., and City College of San Francisco, among other teams. The 1950 championship team included center forward Dick Baptista, the squad's leading scorer; Olufumni Osibogun, a defensive ace and exchange student from Nigeria; and two athletes who had been voted as All-American players the previous year. One of those All-Americans was Bob Lee. The other was a recent arrival from Romania, Steve Negoesco.

Negoesco was born in New Jersey in 1925, but after his mother died, his father took him to live with an uncle in Romania, where he

was first introduced to the game of soccer. When the Nazis took over Romania during World War II, 15-year-old Negoesco, already a soccer star, was imprisoned in a labor camp in Germany. He survived partly through his soccer skills, which so impressed some of his German guards that they helped him escape. After the war, he played soccer in Romania before returning to the United States and enrolling at USF. He helped lead the Dons to their first co-national championship in 1950, and he twice received All-American honors. After graduating in 1951, Steve taught biology in junior high school while simultaneously helping to develop youth soccer on the West Coast and in the Bay Area. He founded the San Francisco Junior Soccer League, coaching as many as 11 teams in a single year.

In 1962, Steve Negoesco became soccer coach at USF, leading the Dons to 13 West Coast Conference (WCC) championships and to the national championship games seven times. His teams won four national titles, in 1966, 1975, 1976, and 1980, and his teams took runner-up honors in 1969 and 1977. The Dons won a fifth national championship in 1978, but the title was rescinded because of an infraction by a team member who did not play a moment in the championship series. Negoesco recruited many of the players he had coached in the San Francisco youth program for the USF team. Indeed, on his first national championship team of 1966, 13 of the 18 players had played soccer as children under coach Negoesco. He also heavily recruited from around the world, and USF's soccer teams always had a strong international cast. During his career, more than 30 of his players were selected as All-Americans. Coach Negoesco also insisted on academic achievement among his players, more than 90 percent of whom graduated from USF, and many of who were consistently on the USF honor roll. Many of his players went on to become physicians, attorneys, educators, and corporate leaders. Not surprisingly, several became intercollegiate soccer coaches, and more than 20 of his former USF student athletes became professional soccer players.

On October 24, 1995, Steve Negoesco, at age 70, became the first Division I soccer coach to win 500 games, when the Dons defeated Stanford 2–1. By the time he retired at the end of the 2000 season, after 39 years as soccer coach, his teams had posted a record of 544 wins, 182 losses, and 66 ties, an unsurpassed record that included more victories than any coach in the history of intercollegiate soccer competition in the United States. Steve Negoesco was succeeded as head soccer coach by Erik Visser, a graduate of USF, a player on two of coach Negoesco's championship teams, a member of his coaching staff, and the head coach of the women's soccer team from 1985 to 1990. In January 2003, Steve Negoesco was inducted into the National Soccer Coaches Association Hall of Fame.

After his retirement from coaching, Negoesco remained on the USF staff as director of soccer, where, among other duties, he developed summer camps, helped coach the women's soccer team, and cultivated alumni support for the athletic programs at USF. In addition to being inducted into the National Soccer Hall of Fame in 2003, Negoesco also received the NSCAA Bill Jeffrey's Award, named after the late Penn State Coach, which recognizes lifetime service to intercollegiate soccer. In 1988, Negoesco also received the annual Fr. William Dunne Award from the University of San Francisco, the highest individual honor bestowed on a member of the USF community for extraordinary service to USF and the community.

Service to others is a defining value at USF and is expressed in the university's current Vision, Mission, and Values Statement as a "culture of service that respects and promotes the dignity of every person." Steve Negoesco reflects that core value in his service to thousands of young people at USF and in the broader community. As a lasting tribute to Steve Negoesco, the USF soccer stadium is named in his honor.

Eric Visser, on the right, played on two of Steve Negoesco's national championship teams, and succeeded him as head soccer coach. In 2004, Visser's team won the West Coast Conference Championship, and he was named WCC Coach of the Year and NSCAA Far West Region Men's Coach of the Year.

UNIVERSITY OF SAN FRANCISCO ARCHIVES

Steve Negoesco is the all-time leader among NCAA soccer coaches in games won, with 544 victories over 39 seasons, including 13 West Coast Conference championships and four national titles. He also played on the 1949 USF soccer team that won a co-national championship. In 2003, he was inducted into the National Soccer Hall of Fame.

UNIVERSITY OF SAN FRANCISCO ARCHIVES

John F.X. Connolly, S.J.

JOHN CONNOLLY, S.J., SERVED THE UNIVERSITY OF SAN Francisco as its 21st president, was later chosen to be the provincial of the California Province of the Society of Jesus, and then returned to USF as vice president for university relations. While president of USF, from 1954 to 1963, he guided the university through an unprecedented period of campus development. During his presidency four major buildings opened on campus: Phelan Hall, the first student residence; Xavier Hall, a new Jesuit residence; War Memorial Gymnasium; and Kendrick Hall, the home of the School of Law.

John Connolly, S.J., served as the 21st president of the University of San Francisco from 1954 to 1963, and as provincial of the California Province of the Society of Jesus from 1963 to 1968. During his presidency, USF underwent a major building campaign, increasingly reached out to the community with social programs, and celebrated its centennial.

UNIVERSITY OF SAN FRANCISCO ARCHIVES

John Connolly was born in San Francisco on July 28, 1915. After attending St. Anne's School and St. Ignatius High School, he entered the Society of Jesus in 1933. He studied for the priesthood at Sacred Heart Novitiate in Los Gatos from 1933 to 1937; attended Gonzaga University from 1937 to 1940, where he obtained his bachelor's and master's degrees; and was ordained a Jesuit priest at St. Mary's Cathedral in San Francisco in 1946. From 1943 to 1947, Fr. Connolly pursued additional graduate work in theology at Alma College in Los Gatos, where he received his Licentiate of Sacred Theology (S.T.L.). Fr. Connolly served as an instructor at St. Ignatius High School from 1940 to 1943, as minister and assistant to the rector at USF from 1947 to 1949, and as rector of the Sacred Heart Novitiate from 1949 to 1954. In 1954, Fr. Connolly was named the 21st president of the University of

San Francisco, succeeding William Dunne, S.J.

When Fr. Connolly assumed the presidency on August 12, 1954, he became, at age 39, the youngest president in the history of the university up to that time. During the beginning of his second year as president, USF celebrated its centennial, which included the opening of Phelan Hall. Fr. Connolly later dedicated an additional wing to Phelan Hall, which became home of the McLaren School of Business. He also broke ground for War Memorial Gymnasium, dedicated in 1958, and Xavier Hall, completed in 1959.

In 1960, Fr. Connolly initiated the Second Century Program, a campaign that raised more than $5.5 million for the university, and that included the construction of Kendrick Hall in 1962 and Harney Science Center in 1965. During his administration, the Institute of Chemical Biology was founded by Professor Arthur Furst, and the institute began to conduct pioneering research on cancer, toxicology, brain chemistry,

and nutritional disorders. Much of this published research was funded by major federal grants and was used by research centers worldwide.

Under Fr. Connolly's stewardship, USF undertook broader community responsibilities, encouraged faculty research on social issues, and sponsored conferences on farm labor and aging. In 1961, the university launched a series of Police-Community Relations Institutes, held annually through 1967. A powerful speaker, Fr. Connolly frequently gave talks at meetings of community organizations and at citywide special events. Fr. Connolly was awarded Peru's Order of Merit of the Grand Cross for his work with students from Latin America. In January 1962, he presented a New Year's message on world peace broadcast on television station KTVU.

Fr. Connolly left the presidency in 1963 to become provincial of the California Province of the Society of Jesus, a position he occupied for five years. In 1968, he returned to USF as vice president for university relations, and the next year he was named to the newly created position of chancellor of the university. On September 16, 1969, the day he was to take office as chancellor, he suffered a major heart attack and died in the chapel of Xavier Hall, where he had broken ground 10 years earlier. He was 54. A requiem Mass was held two days later in St. Ignatius Church, followed by interment in the Jesuit cemetery in Santa Clara.

Throughout his administration, Fr. Connolly urged USF students to become actively engaged in the community, setting the stage for many social outreach programs. On September 18, 1958, Fr. Connolly delivered a speech to the San Francisco Chamber of Commerce in honor of USF's 104th year as the first institution of higher education in the city. As president of USF, he reflected on the original mission of the institution in 1855, to teach young men the "rudiments of philosophy, theology, the classical languages, and mathematics." Fr. Connolly then asked whether or not because of its more recent social and community concerns and outreach programs, USF had "somehow lost sight of the essence of a university?" To this rhetorical question, the president emphatically said that it had not. To the contrary, Fr. Connolly argued, "in offering increased services to the community, universities need not repudiate their original and timeless mission. A university may be rightly understood only against the background of its own age and environment. While preserving the cultural heritage of the past, it must adapt itself to the needs of the day. It must do more than that— it must anticipate the needs of future days."

In his own work as president of USF, John Connolly, S.J., did much to anticipate the future needs of the university he served, to greatly enhance its mission, and to help articulate its Jesuit vision.

USF President John Connolly and USF basketball legend Bill Russell hold the ceremonial shovel at the groundbreaking for the War Memorial Gymnasium, completed in 1958, the 4th year of Fr. Connolly's presidency. To the left of Bill Russell is Francis Callahan, S.J., vice president for development; to the right of Fr. Connolly is George Christopher, mayor of San Francisco; and kneeling is Wilma Hastings, a USF nursing student and cheer leader.

UNIVERSITY OF SAN FRANCISCO ARCHIVES

Xavier Hall, seen here under construction in 1958, was completed during Fr. Connolly's presidency. It served as the home of the Jesuit Community from 1959 until 1999, when Loyola House was built on Lone Mountain as the new home for the Jesuits. Xavier Hall later became a residence hall for students and the home for the visual arts department and its classroom studios. In 2003, the university announced that Xavier Hall will be remodeled and renamed the Alfred and Hanna Fromm Lifelong Learning Center.

UNIVERSITY OF SAN FRANCISCO ARCHIVES

The 1960s and USF

IT PROVED TO BE ONE OF THE MOST TUMULTUOUS DECADES in United States history. The 1960s were punctuated by political assassinations, civil rights struggles and urban riots, a costly overseas war that led to demonstrations and death at home and abroad, and international tension that brought the world to the brink of nuclear annihilation.

Senator Robert Kennedy spoke to a capacity crowd in USF's War Memorial Gymnasium on April 19, 1968, during his California campaign for the nation's presidency. He called for an end to the Vietnam War and for action on behalf of the poor. Less than two months after his speech at USF, he was assassinated.

During the 1960s, the University of San Francisco was affected by events on the national and international fronts, though the campus never experienced the level of violence and student strikes over the Vietnam War that rocked other college campuses such as Columbia, the University of Wisconsin, San Francisco State University, and U.C. Berkeley. A small number of USF students, including students in the law school, were highly vocal, however, in their criticism of society's ills and called for an end to the Vietnam War, greater rights for the nation's minorities, and curriculum changes.

The decade began with the election of John F. Kennedy as the nation's first Catholic president. During his administration there was a build up-of tension with Cuba that culminated in the Cuban missile crisis and a narrowly avoided nuclear conflict with the Soviet Union; an escalation of the Cold War denoted by the building of the Berlin Wall; a rapid build-up of nuclear arms; and the initial deployment of U.S. military advisers in Vietnam. The United States was also engaged in a space race with the Soviet Union, and the Kennedy administration pushed for a program that put the first American, John Glenn, into orbit around the Earth in 1961 and culminated in Neil Armstrong's walk on the moon, the first for humankind, by the close of the decade.

On the domestic front, widespread racial tensions, demonstrations, and demands for civil rights led Kennedy to propose sweeping civil rights legislation in 1963. Before Congress acted on that legislation, however, Kennedy was shot and killed, on November 22, 1963, while riding in an open car in Dallas, Texas. Kennedy's successor, Lyndon Johnson, successfully pushed through Congress the most significant civil rights legislation since Reconstruction, as well as laws affecting health care and education for disadvantaged children and families.

During the Johnson administration, the nation also became increasingly mired in what many Americans perceived as an unjust war in Vietnam. As the death toll mounted in Vietnam, demonstrations increased at home against the war, especially on college campuses. In the face of massive opposition to the Vietnam War, Johnson chose not to seek reelection in 1968. Senator Robert Kennedy of New York, John Kennedy's brother and former U.S. attorney general, emerged as one of the leading Democratic contenders for the presidency, campaigning for an end to the Vietnam War and for increased civil rights and social programs at home. On June 5, 1968, Robert Kennedy was shot and killed in Los Angeles.

Two months earlier, the leading civil rights leader in the nation, Rev. Martin Luther King Jr., was also assassinated in Memphis, Tennessee. In the face of demonstrations on the home front that increasingly turned violent, and with the Democratic Party in disarray after a riot-plagued Democratic Convention in Chicago in the summer of 1968, former vice president Richard Nixon, the Republican candidate, was elected president. In October 1969, more than a million people across the nation publicly demonstrated against the war in Vietnam.

Beginning in 1962, some USF students answered President Kennedy's call for participation in the Peace Corps, and to this day USF is ranked as one of the top schools in the nation for its size with respect to the number of students who volunteer for the Peace Corps. Like

the rest of the nation, USF students, faculty, and staff were stunned by President's Kennedy's assassination in 1963, and four days after his death, the USF community filled St. Ignatius Church for a memorial Mass. On April 19, 1968, Robert Kennedy visited USF as part of his presidential campaign in California. He addressed a capacity audience in War Memorial Gymnasium, calling for action on behalf of the nation's poor and disadvantaged and an end to the Vietnam War. Less than two months later, the USF community also mourned the loss of Robert Kennedy to an assassin's bullet.

In the immediate community, USF students

In April 1960, Vice President Richard Nixon stopped at USF during his campaign for the presidency to speak at a faculty and student convocation and to receive a framed copy of the USF Credo. Nixon is pictured here with USF President John Connolly, S.J. (left) and School of Nursing Regent Timothy McDonnell, S.J. (right). Nixon lost the presidential election to John F. Kennedy, and two years later he was defeated by Edmund G. Brown in his bid to become California's governor. Nixon ran again for the presidency in 1968 and this time was successful. He was reelected in 1972 but resigned two years later in the wake of the Watergate hearings.

were active in the 1960s in providing service to others. In 1962, for example, the Student Western Addition Project (SWAP) was founded, under the guidance of USF sociology professor Ralph Lane. By 1968, SWAP had become the largest student organization on campus, with approximately 250 members. The students' goal was to serve underprivileged groups in the Western Addition of San Francisco, including providing special education and tutorial programs for children in local schools, recreational activities for families, and assistance to senior citizens.

An offshoot of SWAP, called Whites Against Racism (WAR), tried to sensitize the student community to racist attitudes and policies prevalent in the broader community. A small number of students also traveled to the South to help register African American voters. Other students helped organized a boycott in 1969 of the local Safeway market in support of Cesar Chavez, founder of the United Farm Workers (UFW) of California, who was trying to unionize migrant farm workers in response to the deplorable employment and living conditions they faced working for the farming industry in California. The non-unionized

grape industry became the first focus of a statewide boycott by the UFW. In 1969, a busload of USF students traveled to Delano, in central California, the UFW headquarters, to demonstrate their support for Cesar Chavez.

By the late 1960s, especially after the Tet offensive of 1968, the Vietnam War increasingly caused activity on the USF campus. A group of about 25 students publicly burned their draft cards, and a fledgling resistance movement was begun by a small student group called the Radical Student Union. A few fires were set in the ROTC offices on campus to protest the war, though both the administration and student leaders were convinced that the fires were set by individuals with no affiliation to USF. Beginning in the spring of 1969, a weekly open-air microphone was set up in Harney Plaza for students who wanted to speak about the Vietnam War, race relations, or any other issue. The president of USF from 1963 to 1969, Charles Dullea, S.J., and his successor, Albert Jonsen, S.J., encouraged study, analysis, and debate by students, faculty, and outside speakers on the issues of the day.

In addition to a limited number of protest activities at USF during the late 1960s, the decade also witnessed the full integration of men and women into the traditional undergraduate program in 1964, some growth in the minority student population, and the formation of the Black Student Union in 1968. The core curriculum was also modified during the decade. In 1966, students were still required to take 16 units of theology

John Lo Schiavo, S.J., the dean of students in 1963, surveys the center of campus from atop Xavier Hall. Temporary structures, including World War II Quonset huts, still occupied part of the campus.

and 21 units of philosophy to graduate. By 1968, the number had been reduced to 12 units in each of those content areas. The number of sociology majors increased dramatically during the 1960s, and Michael Harrington's seminal book, *The Other America,* was a touchstone work for many liberal arts students. In 1966, ROTC training was still mandatory for all male students at USF. By 1968, ROTC training was voluntary. In 1964, the Honors Program was added to the curriculum, an academic gem in the crown of new programming efforts at the university.

On the international level, the sweeping changes called for in the Catholic Church by the Second Vatican Council, which opened in Rome in 1962, dramatically affected Catholics throughout the world, in the United States, and at USF. In the years immediately following the Second Vatican Council, there was a major upsurge in interest in the field of theology among many of the nation's schools, and the USF theology department grew in stature, aided in no small measure by Albert Zabala, S.J., and his summer theology programs that brought world-class scholars to USF, and hundreds of priests, nuns, seminarians, and laity to the school to pursue graduate degrees in religious education, theology, and scripture.

The campus was also transformed by the construction of several major buildings during the 1960s. In 1962, during the administration of John Connolly, S.J., Kendrick Hall, the new home of the law school was completed, thanks to the gift of Charles Kendrick, chairman of the USF Board of Regents. During the presidency of Charles Dullea, S.J., from 1963 to 1969, five major buildings on campus were opened. These included the Harney Science Center for the College of Arts and Sciences, dedicated in 1965, as a result of a donation of Charles Harney, a USF regent. In the same year, another former USF regent, George Gillson, provided the funding for Gillson Residence Hall, providing housing for 325 men and women students. In the following

year, both University Center and Hayes-Healy Residence Hall opened, the latter as a memorial by John and Ramona Hayes-Healy to their parents. Finally, in 1969, the Samuel Cowell Foundation donated the funds to construct a new home for the School of Nursing, named for a prominent San Francisco businessman and philanthropist. During the decade, the surplus barracks and Quonset huts left over from World War II began to disappear from campus as new buildings were constructed.

In 1962, the Student Western Addition Project (SWAP) was founded, under the guidance of Ralph Lane, USF sociology professor. Pictured here is the 1968 SWAP steering committee. Sitting on the curb (left to right) are Bob Downey and Neil MacIntyre. The six students standing directly behind Downey and MacIntyre are (left to right) John Howe, Mary Spohn, Leanna Burke, Charlie Martinez, Margie Ryan, and Bob Giddings. Standing in back (with his hand on the Fillmore Street sign) is Chuck Riffle.

UNIVERSITY OF SAN FRANCISCO ARCHIVES

120 A New Home for the School of Law

IT WAS THE MOST IMPORTANT SINGLE DONATION IN THE history of the University of San Francisco up to that time: a $1 million gift in 1960 toward the construction of a new building for the School of Law. The donor, Charles Kendrick, had studied law, was admitted to the California Bar in 1902, started several successful companies in the 1920s, became a prominent San Francisco businessman and patron of the city, contributed to the building of the War Memorial Opera House and Veterans Building, served on the Mayor's Emergency Relief Committee during the Depression, was chairman of the board of trustees of Mills College, and was vice-president of the California School of Fine Arts.

In 1959, Charles Kendrick began working with USF President John Connolly, S.J., to organize the President's Council of Advisors, and he was elected its first chairman. In that capacity, Kendrick became increasingly impressed with the accomplishments of the university's graduates and the institution's contributions to the city, was drawn to the Jesuits' value system and educational philosophy, and developed a close friendship and respect for Fr. Connolly. He strongly believed that USF should continue to be the city's preeminent university. One of the main goals of the Council of Advisors was to develop a strategy to raise the estimated $5.5 million needed to build a new home for the School of Law. The council, and its chief fundraiser, Thomas Jordan, agreed that the first major gift was critical and would set the pace for the gifts to follow. In the spring of 1960, Charles Kendrick called Fr. Connolly to tell him he knew someone willing to give a $1 million lead gift toward the fundraising

effort. That "someone" was, of course, Kendrick himself.

In May of 1961, the groundbreaking ceremony was held for Kendrick Hall. Fr. Connolly; Kendrick; and Francis Walsh, dean of the School of Law, took turns holding the ceremonial shovel. In September 1962, on the 50th anniversary of the founding of the law school, the new building was completed. The weekend of September 28 witnessed a host of celebratory events, including a convocation honoring law professors Joseph Farry, William Breen, and James Burns for their long years of service; a dinner by the Law Society; and the dedication ceremony for the building, including a blessing by San Francisco Archbishop Joseph McGucken; and a speech by Herman Phleger, former legal adviser to the State Department and local attorney.

The finale to the celebration occurred in the Grand Ballroom of the Fairmont Hotel, where 1,200 people came to hear a speech by Robert

F. Kennedy, attorney general of the United States. Racial tensions in Mississippi, however, kept Kennedy in Washington that weekend, and he had to deliver his speech by telephone and public address system hook-up to the hotel audience. In his speech, Kennedy criticized the prominent attorneys of Mississippi and the American Bar Association for remaining silent in the face of obstruction by local officials to federal court ordered integration and enforcement of civil rights. Kennedy argued that moral courage was the highest ideal of the legal profession, and was confident that "the graduates who come out of Kendrick Hall in the long years of its future will be lawyers courageously dedicated to the broadest horizons of citizenship and service. We will be waiting for them. We need them."

Following Kennedy's speech, Fr. Connolly thanked Charles and Kathryn Kendrick for the gift that made the new building possible. In his reply, Kendrick noted, "when I became a regent of the University of San Francisco, I grew quickly aware that the Jesuit Fathers earnestly and sincerely labor to improve mentally and spiritually the human material that comes into their hands. For 50 years, the university has been successfully educating lawyers although, comparatively speaking, it has never had a properly equipped law school. Nevertheless, the quality of its education is attested by the important place occupied by its graduates on the Bench and Bar of California. Here was the inspiration for the gift that made this new law school a reality."

Thirty-seven years after the dedication of Kendrick Hall, in March 1999, another ceremonial groundbreaking took place, for a major addition to the school: the Dorraine Zief Law Library. Arthur Zief, a 1947 graduate of the law school, named the new library after his wife, Dorraine. His $3.2 million gift also underpinned a new student lounge, named for Zief's son, Arthur, and an entry plaza named after Zief himself. The Dorraine Zief Law Library opened in August 2000 as a state-of-art facility,

On May 23, 1961, a groundbreaking ceremony was held for Kendrick Hall. Shown here are John Connolly, S.J. (left), president of the University of San Francisco, and Francis Walsh (right), dean of the School of Law. Charles Kendrick (center), chairman of the president's council of advisers, made a $1 million gift to the university, the foundation for the successful campaign for the construction of the building that bears his name.

UNIVERSITY OF SAN FRANCISCO ARCHIVES

with data and power outlets at every seat, multimedia classrooms, and space for more than 300,000 legal and interdisciplinary volumes.

In the spring of 2002, the Koret Foundation, one of the largest Jewish-sponsored charitable trusts in the United States, awarded $3.25 million to the School of Law toward the renovation of Kendrick Hall. The grant helped construct a three-story atrium connecting Kendrick Hall to the Zief Library, technologically advanced classrooms, a new rotunda outside the classrooms, and a student information center. The current dean of the School of Law,

In January 2004, the University of San Francisco School of Law dedicated its new Koret Law Center, named for the project's principal donor, the Koret Foundation. The University of San Francisco School of Law now includes a fully reconstructed Kendrick Hall (originally built in 1962) and the Dorraine Zief Law Library, which opened in 2000.

ARCHER DESIGN INC

Jeffrey Brand, addressed the importance of this grant in "helping the University of San Francisco School of Law to grow, to train skilled, ethical lawyers, and to help us focus on new generations of lawyers concerned with societal responsibility and social justice."

On the evening of January 29, 2004, more than 800 people attended the dedication ceremony of the Koret Law Center. The first part of the dedication ceremony was held in St. Ignatius Church and featured speeches by Martin Murphy, chairman of the Kendrick campaign; Charles Geschke, chairman of the USF Board of Trustees; Stephen Privett, S.J., president of USF; Susan Koret, chairman of the Koret Foundation board; and Anthony Kennedy, Associate Justice of the United States Supreme Court. A few moments before the audience moved from the church across Fulton Street for the ribbon-cutting ceremony and reception at the Koret Law Center, Dean Brand noted in his closing remarks how far the law school had come since "its humble beginnings in 1912," and quoted from California Supreme Court Justice Raymond Sullivan, graduate of the USF law class of 1930: "knowledge and wisdom, courage and imagination, and understanding and love, these are the

hallmarks of the University of San Francisco School of Law."

From the first major gift by Charles Kendrick, through the contributions of Arthur Zief, the Koret Foundation grant, and the support of many other individuals and charitable organizations, the buildings that comprise the University of San Francisco School of Law symbolize a commitment to producing socially responsible lawyers who not only know the law, but also know how to use the law to foster social change grounded in ethical precepts. In that sense, the mission of the School of Law, "pursuing excellence and educating for justice," is at one with the broader mission of the University of San Francisco, as articulated in its most recent Vision, Mission, and Values Statement: to educate "leaders who will fashion a more humane and just world."

Becoming Coeducational (PART I)

121

THEY WERE INTREPID PIONEERS EMBARKING ON A challenging educational journey: the first women to enter St. Ignatius College, the heretofore all-male Jesuit institution of higher education in San Francisco. The year was 1927, and the women included Margaret McAuliffe, Anne Sullivan, and Ruth Halpin, the first women in the evening division in the new College of Commerce and Finance; and Anne Shumway, Bertha Ast, and Helen Byrne, the first female law students.

The undergraduate day division of the school would not become coeducational until 1964, but in 1927, Shumway was elected vice president of the first-year law class; McAuliffe was elected vice president of the freshman evening division; Ruth Halpin starred in several performances by the College Players theater group; and Anne Sullivan served as an officer in the French literary social club and was active in student government. By 1930, there were 20 women studying law (out of a total law school enrollment of 265), and there were eight women among the 110 students in the evening division. Ten years later, there were 137 women studying in the evening division or in the law school out of a total student enrollment of 1,337. By the fall of 1944, World War II had reduced the total student enrollment to a meager 196 full-time day students and 135 evening division students, of whom seven were women law students and 58 were women in the evening division. An emergency fundraising campaign

launched by William Dunne, S.J., president of USF, in 1944 kept the institution from having to close its doors for want of tuition revenue (vignette #95). Approximately 20 percent of the tuition revenue that was generated in 1944, however, came from female students.

With the end of World War II, enrollment dramatically increased at USF. Among the 2,024 students who swelled the classrooms of USF during the 1946 fall semester, 93 were women. In 1948, a department of nursing was established in the College of Arts and Sciences, and by 1954, the program had become the independent School of Nursing (vignette #111),

Two of the first female students to attend St. Ignatius College, in 1927. Anne Sullivan (left), was one of the first women in the evening division in the new College of Commerce and Finance. She was an officer in the French literary social club and was active in student government. Anne Shumway (right), was a student in the School of Law and was elected vice president of her first-year law class.

UNIVERSITY OF SAN FRANCISCO ARCHIVES

During the 1955-1956 academic year, nursing student Ellen Tully served as ASUSF Secretary, the first female ASUSF officer in the history of the institution. Pictured with Ellen Tully is Thomas Klitgaard, ASUSF President.

In 1951, Fr. Feely became academic vice president, and he, along with many other administrators and faculty members at USF, pushed for the inclusion of women in the undergraduate day division of the university. For many years, administrators and faculty at USF pursued this goal in the face of opposition from several quarters, including the San Francisco College for Women on neighboring Lone Mountain and the Catholic hierarchy in Rome.

Enrollment increases in the number of women in the nursing program, coupled with a gradual increase in the number of women in the evening college, the department of education, and the law school, helped increase the number of female students at USF during the 1950s. By the fall of 1960, there were 942 women on campus out of a total enrollment of 4,115.

Despite petitions by USF faculty and administrators for the admittance of female undergraduate students to the day division of the College of Arts and Sciences and to the School of Business Administration, petitions supported by a large segment of USF alumni and even nuns in local Catholic high schools, the Catholic hierarchy in Rome continued to oppose full coeducational status for USF as the fall semester of 1963 got underway. The Jesuit-run University of Santa Clara, 50 miles to the south, was, however, granted the right to admit women to all of its programs in 1961.

further adding to the number of female students at USF.

In 1948, the dean of faculties, Raymond Feely, S.J., began to advocate the inclusion of women in all the programs at the university. He argued that undergraduate women in arts and sciences and business administration, Catholic and non-Catholic, should have an opportunity to receive a distinctive Jesuit education. Moreover, Fr. Feely noted that women were already admitted to the nursing program, law school, evening programs, and summer session; and that men and women "urgently needed formal instruction in religion, philosophy, and the Christian approach to social problems."

Becoming Coeducational (PART II)

122

JOHN CONNOLLY, S.J., THE PRESIDENT OF THE UNIVERSITY of San Francisco from 1954 to 1963, repeatedly raised the issue of the inclusion of women in the day division of the school with John Mitty, the archbishop of San Francisco. For years, the archbishop failed to support that inclusion. In 1961, Fr. Connolly again wrote to the archbishop, pointing out how the existing Catholic women's colleges in the Bay Area were completely inadequate to meet the growing demand for undergraduate Catholic education for young women. "The University of San Francisco for some years now has been coeducational in all branches except the undergraduate day division," Fr. Connolly wrote, "and after careful study and the experience of some years, it now seems clear that we should extend coeducation to the undergraduate day division. We have received hundreds of requests for this: 300 in 1957 alone, and many more in increasing numbers since then."

In 1961, Archbishop Mitty finally gave his approval to USF to become a fully coeducational institution. Authorities in Rome, however, still balked at the idea. When Fr. Connolly became provincial of the California Province in 1963, he persisted with the Jesuit authorities in Rome, with the full backing of his successor, the new president of USF, Charles Dullea, S.J. Finally, in October 1963, the announcement was made that USF had received permission from Rome to accept women in all divisions of the university, and in 1964, USF became fully coeducational. Among the 475 women undergraduates who enrolled at USF during the 1964 fall semester, 235 were enrolled in the School of Nursing, 232 were in

In 1964, Frances Anne Dolan was selected as USF's first dean of women. Twenty-three years later, she retired as vice president for student development. For almost a quarter century, she bought a superb leadership style to the university's student affairs administration. In recognition of her many achievements, the university established a scholarship fund in her name to assist student-athletes complete their degrees.

UNIVERSITY OF SAN FRANCISCO ARCHIVES

the College of Arts and Sciences, and eight women enrolled in the School of Business Administration. Among the 4,724 students attending USF that fall in all divisions, 1,310, or almost 28 percent, were women. William Perkins, S.J., dean of men, noted as the fall semester got under way, "the place women have in the world requires all the opportunities of a Catholic university education. As a society becomes better educated, women cannot be left out of the picture."

Frances Anne Dolan, formerly assistant dean of women at the Jesuit-run Marquette University in Milwaukee, was selected in August 1964 to be USF's first dean of women. She was on hand, therefore, to greet the first fall class of women in the regular day division in the history of the institution. Anne Dolan was later elevated to vice president for student development, and from that position she oversaw the inauguration in 1976 of the first women's

intercollegiate athletic teams at USF, in basketball, volleyball, tennis, and softball. Overall, the first women undergraduates in the day division were outstanding, according to a report issued by Dolan in June of 1965: "Our women students came to us with excellent high school academic records and fine College Board scores. The number of applicants made it possible for the admissions office to be quite selective, so that our women students were academically strong." For example, the report noted, "of the fifteen students selected for the honors seminar, seven were women." USF President Charles Dullea, S.J., also described how well the women fit into the academic life of USF, and indeed raised the caliber of the student body academically. Years later, Fr. Dullea remarked, "The fellas called the women the DAR—Dammed Average Raisers."

In 1966, Hayes-Healy Hall was built, providing the first residence hall for approximately

In 1964, men and women registered together for classes in the regular day division for the first time in the history of the University of San Francisco.

As a result of going coeducational in 1964, USF drew large audiences of male and female students to special events such as this hootenanny.

350 women students on campus. The hall was the result of a donation from Ramona Hayes-Healy and John Healy, as a memorial to their parents, Mr. and Mrs. Joseph Hayes and Mr. and Mrs. Richard Healy. In the first years of coeducation at the undergraduate level at USF, women students faced strict curfews and dress codes, as did men, though less severe. In 1968, for example, the general regulations for the university included the following: "Women students are expected to be appropriately dressed when on campus. Mini-mini skirts and pant dresses are not acceptable campus wear. Women students may not wear sports clothes (slacks, jeans, stretch-pants, capris, Bermudas) in or around any campus building, including the lounge areas of the women's residences, or when attending basketball games. Sports clothes are appropriate when participating in active sports and when going to or returning from the area of active sports. 'Short' shorts, jeans, and cut-offs are not acceptable at any time." For men, the rules simply stated that "blue work Levi trousers and Bermuda shorts should not be worn in class, in the library, or in the dining room of the University Center." By the end of the 1960s, the last vestiges of dress codes were eliminated from the university's regulations.

By the fall of 1978, women comprised 50.3 percent of the student population at USF, which in that year stood at 6,931. By the fall semester of 2004, there were 8,274 students at USF, 62 percent of whom were women.

From the first women pioneers in 1927 to today, the dramatic increase in the percentage of women at USF, and at colleges and universities across the nation, is attributable to several factors. These include historical and social changes in the role of women in our nation, including the expanding role for women in the labor force during World War II; the women's liberation movements of the 1960s and 1970s; federal and state legislation prohibiting discrimination against women; and the consequent opportunities for women in professions for which higher education is critical, such as business, law, medicine, and other professions that had once been largely the exclusive domain of men. Most important of all, however, has been the powerful role of individual women, such as the first women at St. Ignatius College in 1927, as agents in producing attitudinal, political, educational, and social change in the United States.

Community Outreach Programs in the 1960s

STUDENTS AT THE NATION'S COLLEGES AND UNIVERSITIES experienced a renewed call for social activism during the 1960s. The challenge to young people for service to others at home and abroad was issued by John F. Kennedy in his inaugural address of January 20, 1961. Kennedy's touchstone phrase was often quoted by young and old: "And so, my fellow Americans — ask not what your country can do for you — ask what you can do for your country." Several community outreach programs were initiated at the University of San Francisco during the 1960s. These programs reflected the appeal by the nation's first Catholic president and the legacy of community service in San Francisco by the Jesuits and their lay colleagues and students from virtually the founding of the institution in 1855.

Marisa Dryden, USF philosophy major and member of the SWAP executive committee, tutors students in a Western Addition neighborhood study hall in 1964.

UNIVERSITY OF SAN FRANCISCO ARCHIVES

One of the most notable examples of community service at the University of San Francisco during the 1960s was the Student Western Addition Project (SWAP), under the guidance of sociology professor Ralph Lane. This program, aimed at disadvantaged families in the Western Addition neighborhood adjacent to USF, included long-range efforts to provide health education and assistance, educational tutoring, and neighborhood cleanup.

The project was initiated in 1962 when two students, John Dervin, the student body president, and Joe Spieler, sophomore class president, approached professor Lane about increasing student service to the community. At approximately the same time, Lane was asked by consultants from the Western

Addition District Council to supply volunteers from USF to help improve conditions in their community. Out of discussions with representatives from the agencies associated with the district council was born SWAP, along with a commitment for direct USF student involvement in helping the citizens of the Western Addition. A representative from the district council had originally suggested that the name of the USF project should be the Western Addition Student Project, or WASP. Professor Lane noted, however, that neither USF nor the neighborhood and its citizens were White Anglo Saxon Protestants.

During the spring of 1963, under Dervin's and Spieler's leadership, and with guidance from Lane, the first three SWAP projects were undertaken. These projects included a survey of health attitudes among Western Addition citizens for the Westside Health Center; backyard cleanup projects and assistance to families to improve rundown buildings; and the establishment of a study hall and special tutoring project by USF students for grade-school pupils, held at Bethel African Methodist Episcopal Church on Laguna Street.

By 1964, 11 student service projects were under way. The original study hall project expanded to the Buchanan YMCA and included junior and senior high school students. Other USF students arranged guest talks by minority group executives to youth organizations in the Western Addition, developed recreational projects, and conducted surveys of family use of public health services. Twelve USF College Players conducted a drama project at a junior high school, providing instruction to students on acting, production, lighting, and costume design. By 1969, there were approximately 250 USF students involved in SWAP.

The foundation for another USF community service project was laid in 1964, when Congress passed the Economic Opportunity Act authorizing Upward Bound. The goal of Upward Bound was to prepare youth from disadvantaged communities to gain admission

to college and successfully complete a postsecondary education. The focus of the program was on skill development, motivation, and self-esteem for potential first-generation college students.

In 1966, Jack Curtis, a USF sociology professor, submitted USF's first grant program for Upward Bound. The grant was approved, and USF inaugurated its first Upward Bound Project for 39 low-income high school students from ethnically diverse backgrounds whom their school counselors had recommended as potential college students. Funded by the Federal Office of Economic Opportunity and by USF, the first students spent six weeks living on the USF campus during the summer, attending special classes and lectures by USF faculty, and receiving advice on applying for college.

Upward Bound still exists at USF and nationwide. The program at USF is currently directed by Janice Dirden-Cook, who began as a teacher in the program in 1975. It is administratively housed in the School of Education and has expanded considerably since

Charles Dullea, S.J., president of USF from 1963 to 1969, pictured here with Jack Curtis, sociology professor, and a student coordinator of the United Crusade on campus, was strongly supportive of the efforts by faculty, staff, and students to provide a wide-range of community support services.

UNIVERSITY OF SAN FRANCISCO ARCHIVES

the 1960s. During the 2002–2003 academic year, for example, the USF Upward Bound program served 126 participants in a summer residential program as well as in an after-school program during the regular year. The current participants are drawn from the ninth and tenth grades from 12 public high schools, three charter high schools, and one Catholic high school in San Francisco.

During the 1960s, the School of Law also initiated a local community service project, the Urban-Problems Legal Clinic. By 1969, it had enlisted many law students, under faculty supervision, to provide legal assistance, linkage to law centers, and the drafting of legal documents for those unable to afford legal services. The legal aid program of the 1960s was the antecedent of the USF Street Law Program initiated by Professor Tom Nazario in 1976. That program initially involved law students working with three cooperating high schools. Under faculty supervision, the law students served as student instructors to teach a "Street Law" course to predominantly inner-city youth that emphasized practical knowledge of the law and how the legal system can work on one's behalf.

In 1998, Nazario received USF's annual Sarlo Prize that recognizes teaching excellence exemplifying the ethical principles underlying the university's vision, mission, and values. By 2002, the USF Street Law program had grown to include 91 law students teaching approximately 3,000 students at 54 schools throughout the San Francisco Bay Area. The *Street Law* textbook that accompanies the course has become one of the best-selling law textbooks in the nation.

On March 1, 2002, the USF Street Law program celebrated its 25th anniversary. The featured speaker for the event was Robert F. Kennedy Jr., son of the former attorney general and slain presidential candidate, and nephew of President John F. Kennedy. The Robert F. Kennedy Memorial fund had helped underpin many of the 39 street law programs nationwide, including the program at USF. At the ceremony, Kennedy praised Nazario's work in developing the Street Law project as "the best memorial to my dad." Nazario had earlier been the recipient of the Robert F. Kennedy Fellowship for his work in community legal education. In his talk, Kennedy said "the Street Law project is about saving one person at a time." He noted that his father "believed in community. Not in large government programs, but in individuals who can care enough to improve another person's life." While Kennedy was at USF for the celebration, Jeffrey Brand, dean of the USF School of Law, presented him with the Marshal P. Madison Distinguished Visiting Professor Award for his work as an attorney in the area of environmental protection, and for his work with law students in directing the Pace University Environmental Litigation Clinic. Dean Brand referred to Kennedy as a "shining example of 'Educating for Justice'" in representing his father's legacy. Attorney General Robert Kennedy had spoken to the USF community 40 years earlier at the dedication of Kendrick Hall (vignette #120), telling his audience "responsibility is the greatest right of citizenship and service is the greatest of freedom's privileges."

Arts and Sciences Programs and Faculty in the 1960s

THE COLLEGE OF ARTS AND SCIENCES WITNESSED THE development of several new programs and institutes during the 1960s, as well as the addition of numerous outstanding faculty members. The programs included the Institute of Chemical Biology, the Honors Program in the Humanities, and one of the first computer science programs at a university on the West Coast.

Arthur Furst (standing), founder of USF's Institute for Chemical Biology in 1961, achieved international acclaim and obtained numerous federal grants and private foundation gifts for his pioneering research and publications on the environmental causes of cancer. He is credited with establishing the field of toxicology.

UNIVERSITY OF SAN FRANCISCO ARCHIVES

Since its founding by Arthur Furst in 1961, the Institute of Chemical Biology has achieved national and international acclaim for its cutting-edge research in areas including the causes of cancer, toxicology, and environmental problems. More than 230 scientific publications and technical reports have been generated by USF science faculty, typically with the assistance of undergraduate and graduate students, who are frequently cited as co-authors in scientific publications. Over the years, many of the students who worked on projects in the institute have gone on to become university professors, researchers, and medical doctors. The research of the institute has been supported by millions of dollars from government contracts and grants, and gifts from private foundations and corporations. Under the current director, James Brown, professor of biology and environmental science, there are a host of ongoing research projects involving faculty and students, including a project that is monitoring biotic and abiotic resources in polluted environments.

In the spring of 1964, the College of Arts and Sciences launched the Honors Program in the Humanities, under John Martin, S.J.,

with the assistance of several Jesuit and lay faculty. The program, designed for academically outstanding students, and still offered today, includes a series of seminars, limited to 15 students, beginning in the freshman year, which focus on the study of Western European thought. From its inception, the program has concentrated on the classical expressions of Western civilization and has sought to enhance students' analysis and critical thinking about major works of literature and art, ideas and movements, and individuals from antiquity to the present. Course topics have spanned history, literature, psychology, philosophy, theology, painting, sculpture, music, drama, politics, and sociology. Representative figures include Homer, Plato, Augustine, Chaucer, Shakespeare, Machiavelli, da Vinci, Twain, Dickinson, Darwin, Marx, Freud, and Faulkner. By 1969, 20 students had graduated

from the program, and by 2003 the total had reached approximately 300. John Elliott, professor of theology and religious studies, directed the program from 1967 to 1980. Today, the program is under the leadership of Alan Heineman, professor of English.

The bachelor of science in computer science was initiated in 1966, under the leadership of professor James Haag. The curriculum emphasized systems and applications programming, business and data processing, numerical analysis, computer logic, computer-assisted instruction, and various programming languages. By 1970, the year the academic program became a full department, it was serving 57 majors as well as students in the School of Business Administration, the School of Nursing, and other students in the College of Arts and Sciences. Students had access to a newly installed computer, the

In 1966, USF began to offer a bachelor's degree in computer science, and four years later, 10 USF students were awarded a bachelor's degree in computer science. By 1970, USF had also installed a state-of-the-art mainframe computer— the RCA Spectra/70. It was one of the first computers at a West Coast university, required special air conditioning, filled several rooms in Harney Science Center, and had all of one megabyte of internal memory. Students used the computer for various projects, including assisting the San Francisco School Board to reassign public school students to reduce school segregation.

RCA Spectra 70.

In May 1970, 10 USF students received bachelor's degrees in computer science, one of the first groups of students in the United States to be awarded this degree. Today, the computer science department offers bachelor's and master's degrees. Students in the department, and in other disciplines, obtain hands-on experience in the department's laboratories, a new 128-node parallel computing cluster, and multimedia classrooms, including a state-of-the-art computer classroom in Harney Science Center. This facility, which opened in the fall of 2002, was a gift of USF alumnus Alfred Chuang and was named after a now-emeritus professor of computer science, Michael Kudlick, who inspired Chuang during his student days at USF.

Among the many notable faculty members who began their careers at USF during the 1960s was Eugene Benton, currently a professor of physics, and a highly respected international researcher stemming from his work on radiation detection in outer space (vignette #17). The late Frank Beach taught in the history department from 1957 to 1961, and returned to the institution in 1966 to resume a career that spanned the next 28 years, during which he served as department chair for 18 years and acting academic vice president from 1975 to 1976. Kathleen Gallagher, currently associate professor of visual and performing arts, began her USF career in 1968, and was instrumental in developing the school's dance program. USF emeriti professors whose careers began in the 1960s include Clifton Albergotti, physics professor, whose 35-year USF career began in 1964; Philip Applebaum, also in physics, who taught from 1961 to 1994; Francis Buckley, S.J., whose teaching and writing in the department of theology and religious studies spanned 42 years, from 1960 to 2002; Jack Curtis, who taught sociology from 1963 to 1986 and was instrumental in starting the Upward Bound Project; David Derus, professor of English from 1968 to 1992; John Elliott, a Lutheran priest, who taught in theology and religious studies from 1967 to 2001, was the first protestant minister to hold a full-time faculty position in the department, and who directed the Honors Program in the Humanities; Rabbi David Davis, who also taught theology from 1969 to 1997, was the first Rabbi to hold a faculty position in the department, and who directed the Judaic Studies program during this time period; Elisabeth Gleason, professor of history from 1969 to 1997, a widely published historian, and past president of the American Society for Reformation Research; Hamilton Hess, professor of theology and religious studies from 1967 to 1988; George Lerski, professor of history and anti-Nazi war hero from Poland, who taught from 1966 to 1982; William Mathes, whose 27-year career in the history department began in 1966; Lawrence Murphy, professor of psychology from 1965 to 2000; Patrick Smith, whose career as a professor of English ran from 1966 to 1995; Lucy Treagan, biology professor from 1962 to 1987; Yuan-Li Wu, who taught economics from 1960 to 1988; and Andrew Woznicki, who in 1967 began a 30-year career of teaching and writing in the philosophy department.

In 1967, Edward Smyth, S.J., who had served as the dean of the College of Arts and Sciences since 1955, stepped down from that position to return to teaching, though he soon became the new vice president for academic affairs. Fr. Smyth was replaced as dean by Richard Vaughan, S.J., former director of the psychology department. In 1969, Fr. Vaughan left USF to become the first Jesuit vice provincial of California for education.

From the beginning, part of the strength of the College of Arts and Sciences has been its willingness to experiment with innovative curricula, while maintaining a traditional liberal arts foundation, grounded in timeless Jesuit values and presented by an outstanding faculty.

Charles W. Dullea, S.J.

ON JANUARY 9, 1963, THREE DAYS AFTER HE TOOK OFFICE
as the 22nd president of the University of San Francisco, Charles
W. Dullea, S.J., held a press conference. At his side was a man who
had considerable experience at such events. The man was his father,
Charles W. Dullea Sr., former police chief of San Francisco. These
two men represented a family of native-born San Franciscans who
were committed to service to their community. One of Fr. Dullea's
brothers, John, was also a Jesuit priest, and the other, Edward, was an
attorney in San Francisco and a graduate of the USF School of Law.

Charles Dullea, S.J., 22nd president
of the University of San Francisco,
helped shape a new era for the university, which included the admission
of women to the undergraduate
day division for the first time, the
construction of five new buildings
on campus, the development of several new academic and community
outreach programs, and a dramatic
increase in student enrollment.

UNIVERSITY OF SAN FRANCISCO ARCHIVES

At the press conference, Fr. Dullea praised the
efforts of his predecessor, John Connolly, S.J.,
who, after nearly nine years as president of USF,
had been named provincial of the California
Province of the Jesuits. Building on the successes
of Fr. Connolly, the new president outlined
his ideas for the future of the university he was
chosen to serve. Fr. Dullea's vision included a
faculty of outstanding scholarly prestige and
accomplishment, a student body committed to
academic excellence, and an enriched physical
environment composed of state-of-the art
buildings to support the educational enterprise.
Throughout the next six years, during one of
the most tumultuous periods in the nation's
history, Fr. Dullea worked mightily to bring
his vision to reality.

Charles Dullea was born in San Francisco
in 1916, attended Most Holy Redeemer School
in San Francisco, and won a prized eight-year
scholarship to attend St. Ignatius High School
and the University of San Francisco. He
entered the Jesuit novitiate in Los Gatos in
1934; studied philosophy from 1938 to 1941 at

Mount St. Michael's College in Spokane,
Washington; taught philosophy, English,
speech, modern drama, and debate as a
scholastic at USF during World War II; and
completed a licentiate of sacred theology
(S.T.L.) at Alma College in Los Gatos. In
1947, Fr. Dullea was ordained to the priesthood
in St. Mary's Cathedral by San Francisco
Archbishop John Mitty. From 1949 to 1954,
Fr. Dullea served on the staff of the Jesuit
curia in Rome, until his appointment as rector
of Bellarmine College Preparatory School in
San Jose. In 1958, Fr. Dullea was named rector
of the Jesuit Community at the University of
San Francisco, a position he kept after he was
selected as president of USF in 1963.

"Becoming President of the University of
San Francisco in the year 1963," Father Dullea
wrote in the March-April 1963 *USF Alumnus,*
"is somewhat like being thrust into a canoe
that is about to shoot the rapids. The experience
will be exhilarating and the accomplishment
greatly satisfying should one survive the hazards
of the course." Over the next six years, Fr.

Dullea did much more than merely survive the experience of stewarding USF; he helped shape a dramatic new era for the institution. It began in 1964 with the admission of women to the undergraduate day division for the first time in the institution's history and included several major fundraising campaigns; the construction of five major buildings on campus; and the acquisition of the old St. Ignatius High School property, comprising 6.1 acres of land directly west of the campus on Parker Avenue. Enrollment increased 53 percent, from a total of 4,438 students in the fall of 1963 to a total of 6,804 by the fall of 1969. Several new academic and community outreach programs were also initiated under Fr. Dullea's stewardship, including the Honors Program in the Humanities, the Student Western Addition Project (SWAP), the School of Law's Legal Aid Program in the community, and the Upward Bound Project for low-income high school students from ethnically diverse backgrounds.

The buildings that went up during Fr. Dullea's administration comprise a sizable percentage of the center of the current USF campus. The Harney Science Center, named after USF regent and benefactor Charles Harney and his wife, was completed in 1965. Gillson Hall, also completed in 1965 and honoring USF regent and major contributor George Gillson, houses approximately 325 male and female students on alternate floors. Hayes-Healy Hall, a residence hall, was completed in 1966 (vignette #122), and Cowell Hall was built in 1969 as the new home for the School of Nursing (vignette #111). In 1966, University Center was completed.

On June 6, 1969, Fr. Dullea announced his retirement from the presidency of USF. He soon departed for Rome, where he spent seven years as superior of the Pontifical Biblical Institute and completed his doctoral studies in theology. He turned his doctoral dissertation into a book, *A Catholic Looks at Billy Graham*, a favorable treatment of the Protestant evangelist's life and work. In 1977, Fr. Dullea returned to USF as special assistant to the vice president for university relations as well as assistant director of the St.

Ignatius Institute. For 22 days in January 1977, Fr. Dullea was named interim president of USF by the board of trustees. It proved to be an uneventful "second term" for Fr. Dullea. In 1977, he was named chancellor of the University of San Francisco. For the next 14 years, Fr. Dullea engaged in a series of development and university relations activities with the San Francisco community and assisted the president, John Lo Schiavo, S.J., in a number of important tasks. For example, Fr. Dullea worked tirelessly to bring to fruition the Koret Health and Recreation Center, which was dedicated in 1989. He served as chancellor emeritus, from 1991 to 1999, prior to his retirement to the Jesuit Community in Los Gatos. Fr. Dullea died at the Sacred Heart Jesuit Center in Los Gatos on June 8, 2004. A funeral Mass was held on June 15 in St. Ignatius Church on the USF campus, where Fr. Dullea had given countless homilies before. His brother, John Dullea, S.J., was the main celebrant and homilist for the Mass.

A powerful swimmer his entire life, Fr. Dullea was known for swimming in the frigid waters of San Francisco Bay, including across the Golden Gate span seven times and to Alcatraz Island three times. Given Fr. Dullea's athletic prowess and his labors in helping cultivate the support needed to build the Koret Health and Recreation Center, it is fitting that the Olympic-size pool that is the centerpiece of the Koret Center is named the Charles W. Dullea, S.J. Natatorium.

On his third day in office, USF President Charles Dullea, S.J., held a press conference. Present was a pro at such events—Charles Dullea Sr., former police chief of San Francisco and the new president's father.

UNIVERSITY OF SAN FRANCISCO ARCHIVES

Harney Science Center, made possible by a gift from Pauline and Charles Harney (a former USF regent), was one of the many USF buildings completed during the presidency of Charles Dullea, S.J. In this 1965 photo, members of the construction crew are reviewing blueprints for the building, which soon housed desperately needed science laboratories, classrooms, and faculty and administrative offices.

UNIVERSITY OF SAN FRANCISCO ARCHIVES

Part VI: From 1970 to 2005

DURING THE EARLY 1970S, THE UNITED STATES
witnessed a continuation of many of the problems from the 1960s while several
new challenges arose for institutions of higher education. The Vietnam War
continued until 1973, and in its wake the nation faced a huge war-related national
debt, recession, and runaway inflation. Compounding the economic problems that
affected all segments of the nation, institutions of higher education also faced a decline in the
number of traditional undergraduate students as the last cohort of children born immediately after
World War II moved through the nation's schools. Colleges and universities were caught in a cycle
of rising prices, national recession, and declining enrollments. The University of San Francisco was
especially hard-hit by these external forces.

Albert Jonsen, S.J., who served as president from 1969 to 1972, and William McInnes, S.J., who
was president from 1972 to 1976, grappled with the mounting financial and enrollment crisis at USF.
In the face of significant budget deficits, Fr. McInnes instituted major budget cuts, wage freezes, and
a large tuition increase, and he began the process of cutting staff and faculty. As was the case at many
other colleges and universities that were facing similar economic problems and potential layoffs, the
faculty decided to unionize, and in 1975 the USF Faculty Association was born. Fr. McInnes resigned
in 1976 and was replaced the next year by John Lo Schiavo, S.J., who began a 14-year tenure as
president. During his administration, enrollment began to increase, the budget was balanced, and
a major capital campaign was successfully completed. USF acquired the Lone Mountain Campus,
the Koret Health and Recreation Center was built, and the College of Professional Studies and
the Center for the Pacific Rim were established, along with several other programs.

When Fr. Lo Schiavo retired from the presidency in 1991 to become chancellor, the institution
was on a solid financial base, and his successor, John Schlegel, S.J., was able to capitalize on the
university's fiscal and human strengths to move the institution forward in several areas. From 1991 to
2000, USF saw a significant increase in its enrollment and the diversity of its students and benefited
from the largest and most successful fundraising campaign in the university's history. During Fr.

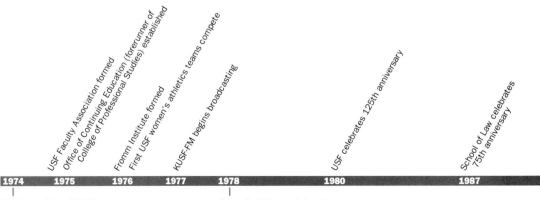

USF Faculty Association formed
Office of Continuing Education (forerunner of
College of Professional Studies) established
Fromm Institute formed
First USF women's athletics teams compete
KUSF-FM begins broadcasting
USF celebrates 125th anniversary
School of Law celebrates
75th anniversary

| 1974 | 1975 | 1976 | 1977 | 1978 | 1980 | 1987 |

President Richard M. Nixon resigns   Camp David Accord signed

Schlegel's tenure, several buildings were renovated; the Gleeson library was transformed by the addition of the Geschke Learning Resource Center; the Dorraine Zief Law Library was built; the Jesuits moved to a new home on Lone Mountain, Loyola House; and renovations were completed on a new building for the School of Education purchased from the Sisters of the Presentation, a religious order with which USF also arranged a lease/purchase option on another building destined to be the new home for the College of Professional Studies. A major housing project for faculty and staff, Loyola Village, was initiated on the north side of Lone Mountain, though it ultimately became primarily a student residence. In 2000, Fr. Schlegel left USF to become president of Creighton University, and Stephen A. Privett, S.J., provost and academic vice president of Santa Clara University, was chosen as the 27th president of the university.

During the first year of his presidency, Fr. Privett and his leadership team, with insights from trustees, alumni, faculty, and staff, crafted a new Vision, Mission, and Values Statement. The vision, to make USF a "premier Jesuit Catholic, urban University with a global perspective" that "educates minds and hearts to change the world" has found expression in a multitude of values-based programs, on campus and around the world. At USF, the activities of the new Leo T. McCarthy Center for Public Service and the Common Good exemplifies this emphasis on social justice programming, as do a multitude of international programs sponsored by the university and its schools and colleges. During Fr. Privett's administration, the institution has also witnessed continuing growth in student enrollment and student diversity, the establishment of the Koret Law Center, the creation of the Ralph and Joan Lane Center for Catholic Studies and Social Thought, the completion of facilities for a new fine arts program, a new budgeting and planning process, the development of a master plan outlining major renovations throughout the campus over the next decade, and the initiation of a core network infrastructure project to dramatically enhance student learning and administrative services through technology.

The transformation of USF over the last 35 years from an institution struggling for its economic survival to an internationally respected institution of higher education in the finest Jesuit tradition will be highlighted in the last series of vignettes.

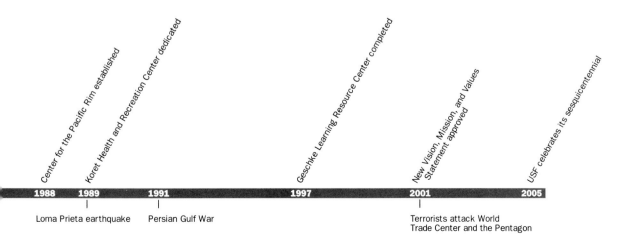

The 1970s and USF

THE SOCIAL AND POLITICAL UPHEAVALS IN THE UNITED States during the 1960s continued into the first years of the next decade. In May 1970, the United States extended the Vietnam War into Cambodia; many college campuses across the nation were shut down by student protest strikes; police and students clashed on major campuses; four students were shot to death by National Guardsmen at Kent State University in Ohio; and two black students were killed and 11 others wounded by highway patrolmen at Jackson State University in Mississippi.

The front page of the *Foghorn* on May 8, 1970, announced the response of the USF Student Senate to the extension of the Vietnam War into Cambodia and the killing of four students by National Guardsmen at Kent State University in Ohio.

UNIVERSITY OF SAN FRANCISCO ARCHIVES

Although there was no violence on the USF campus following the Cambodian invasion, Albert Jonsen, S.J., the president of USF, agreed to student requests to suspend classes for two days following the killings at Kent State and to hold a series of teach-ins addressing the Vietnam War.

In August 1970, a one-ton bomb, set by radical protestors, exploded on the Madison campus of the University of Wisconsin, blasting a crater in a science building and killing a physicist. The next year, thousands of anti-war protestors descended on Washington, and more than 12,000 people were arrested by police and military units.

Faced with mounting protest at home, growing opposition from allies abroad, a staggering war–related national debt, and a Congress that was beginning to repeal some of the legislation that had supported the Vietnam War buildup, the Nixon administration sought a way out of the Vietnam nightmare. After months of negotiations held in Paris, the Vietnam War finally ended with the signing of peace accords in January 1973. The last American troops left Vietnam in March 1973, and in June, U.S. bombing of Cambodia ended, marking a halt to 12 years of American combat in Southeast Asia.

The war claimed the lives of 1.3 million Vietnamese and 58,000 Americans. Officially, one USF graduate, Lt. Arthur Timboe, was among those killed, and several former USF students were wounded. In April 1975, a group of USF faculty members and administrators, led by sociology professor Michael Howe, and including more than 200 USF students, volunteered

SAN FRANCISCO FOGHORN

Vol. 64, No. 25   May 8, 1970   751-3118

Protesting Ohio killings

STRIKE IS ON

By Ron Fontana
Foghorn Managing Editor

A general strike in support of the ASUSF demands, in sympathy for the students murdered at Kent State University, and in opposition to the United States' involvement in Cambodia has been called for today in action by the

pus be exposed. In no way shall this investigation be understood as a disciplinary action.

2. We demand that the University agree to hire minority faculty, administrative and staff members for Spring Semester, 1971. That the departments and deans give the student body a pro-

The senate first passed a motion for a strike in protest of the Kent State University murders, the illegal invasion of Cambodia, and the disciplinary hearing of the students involved in the incident of March 6.

Senators Tony Geraldi and Bill Topf moved to change "murder" to "kill-

Shut it down

"It's better for us to fight for something we want and lose than fight for something we don't want and win."
—Eugene Debs

At the beginning of its meeting Tuesday night, the Student Senate voted (14-1) to call a general strike of the University on Friday to protest the

Many colleges and universities across the nation were shut down by student strikes following the killing of four students by National Guardsmen at Kent State University during a Vietnam War protest on May 4, 1970. USF President Albert Jonsen, S.J., agreed to suspend classes on May 8 so that students, staff, and faculty could attend a series of on-campus teach-ins addressing the Vietnam War.

to help organize an airlift of Vietnamese war orphans to the Bay Area. For several weeks, USF became a focal point of efforts in the Bay Area to shelter, feed, and secure medical attention for several thousand Vietnamese children whose parents had died in the war.

The University of San Francisco faced a financial crisis during the early 1970s induced in part by a major national recession related to the enormous expenditures of the Vietnam War; rapid inflation, punctuated by a sharp increase in oil prices resulting from the OPEC oil embargo; and a nationwide decline in undergraduate college enrollment as the baby boomers passed out of the nation's schools. During the relatively short presidency of Albert Jonsen, S.J., from 1969 to 1972, the university had to grapple with budgetary and enrollment problems connected to these nationwide factors. In the late spring of 1972, Fr. Jonsen resigned from the presidency, to be replaced by William McInnes, S.J., the first president chosen by the board of trustees rather than by the Jesuit Provincial of California.

Fr. McInnes attempted to balance the budget with a wage freeze, a tuition increase of 11 percent, and major budget reductions in virtually all departments. The School of Law was especially hard hit by the new budget, and a group of law students filed suit against the university, charging breach of contract. During the summer of 1973, USF law students pursued their legal action against Fr. McInnes and the university. In the fall of 1973, an out-of-court settlement was reached that restored some of the budget cuts to the School of Law. To add to the issues confronting Fr. McInnes, faculty members at the university, facing potential layoffs, took steps to form a faculty association. A new era of faculty and administration relations had begun at USF.

In 1976, Fr. McInnes resigned from the presidency, to be replaced in 1977 by John Lo Schiavo, S.J., who began a 14-year term as president of USF, second in length only to that of Fr. William Dunne. During the first three years of Fr. Lo Schiavo's administration, the university budget was brought under control; enrollment began to increase, and USF acquired the Lone Mountain campus.

Albert Jonsen, S.J., and William McInnes, S.J.

WHEN 38-YEAR-OLD ALBERT R. JONSEN, S.J., WAS appointed president of the University of San Francisco on July 1, 1969, he was the youngest man to ever lead the institution. Fr. Jonsen had been an assistant professor of philosophy and theology at USF before assuming the presidency, having had no prior administrative experience. Fr. Jonsen came from a family with a long history in San Francisco. His great-grandfather came to the city in 1852, and his grandfather graduated from St. Ignatius College in 1883 and later taught penmanship and arithmetic as he worked his way through Hastings Law School. His uncle, William Sweigert, graduated from the St. Ignatius College School of Law and became a federal judge.

Major challenges were in great abundance during the administration of Albert Jonsen, S.J., the 23rd president of USF (right), and William McInnes, S.J., the 24th president of the institution (opposite).

Albert Jonsen was born in San Francisco, entered the Society of Jesus in 1949, was ordained a priest in Saint Mary's Cathedral in 1962, and obtained bachelor's and master's degrees from Santa Clara and Gonzaga universities. He was the first Catholic priest ever to receive a doctorate in religious studies from Yale University. In 1967, Fr. Jonsen was recruited by Albert Zabala, S.J., of the USF theology and religious studies department, to teach theology and philosophy at the institution. Two years later, the Jesuit provincial, Patrick Donohoe, S.J., thought that Fr. Jonsen would be a good choice to enhance communication with students, and selected him to succeed Charles Dullea, S.J. as the next president of USF.

During his inauguration, the first formal inauguration ever held for a USF president, Fr. Jonsen was given a series of "challenges" by

the inaugural speakers: Michael Whelan, student body president; Ralph Lane, representing the faculty; Al Alessandri, president of the alumni association; Richard Cooley, president of Wells Fargo Bank; Joseph Alioto, mayor of San Francisco; and Philip Lee, chancellor of the University of California at San Francisco. Challenges were indeed in great abundance during Fr. Jonsen's presidency.

Fr. Jonsen became president at a time when many of the nation's colleges and universities were witnessing considerable turmoil as a consequence of the Vietnam War and increased demands by African Americans and Hispanics for greater responsiveness to their recruitment and programmatic goals. Although disruptions at USF were limited in number, Fr. Jonsen faced a student demonstration in the university dining room that led to some broken windows, a sit-in by the Black Student Union, a march by a small group of students into the president's office, and some incursions by outside groups protesting the Vietnam War. Throughout the turmoil, Fr. Jonsen kept local law enforcement agencies off the campus; consistently met with student groups; and even invited John Burton, the local anti-war Congressman, to speak at a student anti-war rally.

Under Fr. Jonsen's leadership, the university moved toward an affirmative action policy, actively recruited minority students and faculty, established an ethnic studies program, and increased the number of programs connected to the surrounding community. Fr. Jonsen also appointed Herman Gallegos, a leading Hispanic social activist, to the board of trustees.

On other fronts, Fr. Jonsen's presidency witnessed curriculum reform that included a reduction in the number of courses required in philosophy and theology, the acquisition of the old St. Ignatius High School building (Loyola Hall), and the upgrading of the department of education to the School of Education. He also approved greater autonomy for the School of Law, which developed its own budget, fundraising program, and faculty appointment and promotion procedures. Fr. Jonsen also pushed to reorganize the board of trustees to include lay members.

Following a directive from the Jesuit superior general in Rome to all the Jesuit institutions in the nation, Fr. Jonsen also oversaw the legal separation of USF from the Jesuit community. The goal of the separation was to avoid jeopardizing federal financial aid to students and federal grants to faculty. The separation was not, however, unanimously supported by the trustees, still composed primarily of Jesuits.

To add to Fr. Jonsen's challenges, the nation was entering a major recession that hit especially hard in the Bay Area, highlighted by cutbacks in defense spending, the aerospace industry, and social programs from the Lyndon Johnson presidency. Simultaneously, national inflation precipitated a rapid rise in costs in the Bay Area and at USF, especially in faculty and staff salaries. Enrollment at USF was also declining. The university's financial situation worsened, and by June 1971, the deficit was nearly $900,000 out of a total operating budget of $12.4 million.

In March 1972, citing a desire to return to a career in theological education, Fr. Jonsen resigned from the presidency to accept an invitation by the board of trustees of the Graduate Theological Union (GTU) of Berkeley to become that institution's next president. Fr. Jonsen ultimately decided not to accept the GTU presidency, however, when he learned that the trustees had bypassed the top administrators at the school in making their offer directly to him.

Briefly without a job, Fr. Jonsen was offered and accepted a faculty position at the UCSF School of Medicine teaching bioethics, where he became a pioneering scholar in this new field. He was chief of the division of medical

USF's deteriorating financial situation proved to be the most challenging issue facing William McInnes, S.J., the institution's 24th president.

UNIVERSITY OF SAN FRANCISCO ARCHIVES

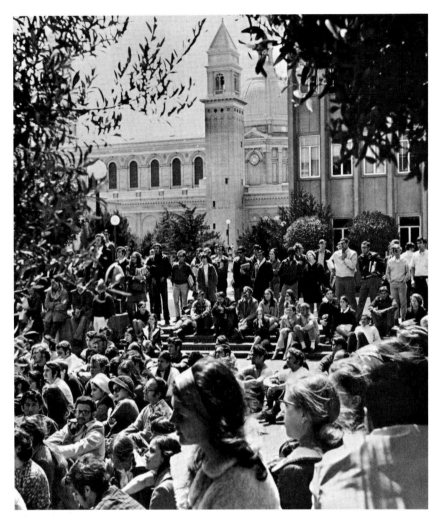

On May 7, 1970, the ASUSF Senate moved outdoors where a crowd of students gathered in Harney Plaza to hear speakers denounce the U.S. "incursion" into Cambodia during the Vietnam War and to express sympathy for four students killed by national guardsmen at Kent State University three days earlier.

UNIVERSITY OF SAN FRANCISCO ARCHIVES

ethics at UCSF for 15 years, left the Jesuit order, and married. He later became chairperson of the department of medical history and ethics in the School of Medicine at the University of Washington, a position he held for 12 years. As an emeritus professor, Albert Jonsen is currently teaching in the Fromm Institute for Lifelong Learning at USF and serves as co-director of the Program in Medicine and Human Values at the California Pacific Medical Center.

In August 1972, following a six-month search by the board of trustees, William McInnes, S.J., the president of Fairfield University, a Jesuit institution in Connecticut, was selected to become USF's new president. This marked the first time the selection was made by the board of trustees rather than by the Jesuit provincial.

Fr. McInnes was born in Boston in 1923 and received bachelor's and master's degrees from Boston College and his doctorate from New York University. He entered the Society of Jesus in 1946, was ordained a priest in 1957, and completed his theology work at Weston in 1959.

Fr. McInnes spent four years at Boston College as an associate professor and associate dean of business administration, and nine years as president of Fairfield University. At Fairfield, Fr. McInnes was known for his support of education for people of all ages and for his advocacy of a broader interaction between the university and the community. The Fromm Institute for Lifelong Learning was established at USF during the presidency of Fr. McInnes (vignette #130). Fr. McInnes also invited Sr. Gertrude Patch, president of Lone Mountain College, to several dinners at USF for informal discussions. These overtures may have helped create the climate conducive to the purchase of Lone Mountain by John Lo Schiavo, S.J., USF's next president.

Fr. McInnes brought to the president's office a reputation for balancing budgets and for fiscal responsibility. In March 1973, Fr. McInnes submitted a budget to the board of trustees for the 1973–1974 year that sought to address the university's mounting deficit. The board approved the budget, which called for a wage freeze, a tuition increase of 11 percent, and major budget reductions to be proportioned among all units of the university. For the School of Law, the new budget included a freeze in faculty hiring, the termination of financial aid for special-admission students, reduced financial aid for existing students, a decrease in the number of elective courses, and a curtailment in library services. The School of Law faculty organized its own independent union to respond to the cutbacks. USF's Student Bar Association immediately prepared a lawsuit against the university, and when no concessions were forthcoming, a group of law students filed suit, charging breach of contract.

Concurrently, the dean of the law school,

C. Delos Putz Jr., confronted Fr. McInnes with the potentially negative impact of severe budget cuts on its forthcoming accreditation visits by the American Bar Association and the Association of American Law Schools. Another related source of controversy with the law school was the decision by Fr. McInnes to rescind an agreement made by Fr. Jonsen to permit the School of Law to engage in independent fundraising activities. In the ensuing out-of-court settlement between the law students and USF, some financial aid was restored, a promise was made to increase the number of full-time faculty, the number of elective courses was maintained, and the law school was permitted to engage in independent fundraising, with the proceeds to go directly to the law school.

At the same time that Fr. McInnes was facing challenges from the School of Law, the entire university faculty, facing an unacceptable salary increase from a president whom they perceived as being unwilling to negotiate, and sensing the possibility of layoffs, began to organize a faculty association. In December 1975, the university sent out preliminary dismissal notices to all 111 nontenured faculty members and 42 of its 120 administrators. In June 1976, after months of difficult negotiations, a collective bargaining agreement was signed with the new USF Faculty Association (vignettes #128 and #129).

Overall, the university's financial situation continued to be the major issue facing the institution. From the fall of 1970 to the fall of 1976, total USF student enrollment declined more than 14 percent. During the 1975–1976 fiscal year, USF ran a deficit of $491,000, with a $2.5 million cumulative debt. For the 1976-1977 fiscal year, the budget cuts proposed by Fr. McInnes projected a balanced budget, a $700,000 surplus, and a reduction in the university's cumulative debt by $800,000. The proposed budget cuts, however, created major turmoil within the university. In October 1976, at the request of the board of trustees, Fr.

McInnes resigned from the presidency.

The nation's economic problems during the 1970s, including runaway inflation, coalesced with enrollment declines and budgetary deficits to make USF a challenging institution to lead. In 1976, the institution began to look for its third president in seven years.

During the 1970s, USF saw an increase in the number of ethnic minority students on campus, a fact reflected in the growth of student organizations such as the Black Student Union (top), La Raza (middle), and the Philippine Club (bottom).

UNIVERSITY OF SAN FRANCISCO ARCHIVES

128

The Origins of the Faculty Association at USF (PART 1)

BY THE 1970S, THE NATION'S CENTURY-OLD ORGANIZED labor movement had gained a significant percentage of adherents among faculty members in higher education. More than 20 percent of all full-time teaching faculty members in higher education in the United States were represented by collective bargaining agents by 1974.

The causes for faculty unionization were varied: the inflation of the early 1970s and the consequent perception by many faculty members that collective bargaining agents were needed to negotiate salaries to keep pace with rising prices; job insecurity, especially among untenured faculty members, who witnessed declining college enrollments and shrinking federal dollars in the early 1970s after the unprecedented growth in student enrollment and federal dollars during the 1960s; a decline in the influence of faculty members over decision making in institutions of higher education, especially in large and increasingly complex state systems; and the spread of the activism of the 1960s on college campuses from students to other groups such as clerical workers and faculty members.

A nationwide survey of college and university faculty members conducted in 1975 indicated that 72 percent of the nation's faculty members would vote for unionization if an election were held on their campus. Concurrent with the growing acceptance of collective bargaining among faculty in higher education, jurisdiction of the National Labor Relations Board (NLRB) was extended in 1970 to include private colleges and universities with annual gross revenue in excess of $1 million. The NLRB was authorized by Congress in 1935 to ensure employees

the right to bargain collectively.

Against this national backdrop and in a city with a long history of unionization, events at USF during the 1970s coalesced to precipitate the formation of a faculty association. As early as 1971, the president of USF, Albert Jonsen, S.J., in an address to representatives of the American Association of University Professors (AAUP) and members of the university community, predicted a logical and inexorable thrust toward unionization of the faculty, although he personally believed that collective bargaining among faculty was inappropriate in a university setting and would be detrimental to the education process. Fr. Jonsen said he was favorable to unions in general, and to collective bargaining among certain categories of university employees, such as service employees, but that collective bargaining among faculty would serve to dissolve the participatory framework among administrators and faculty in university governance; would inevitably lead to collective bargaining over inappropriate items; and would increasingly create rigidity and formality in the relations between administration and faculty. Fr. Jonsen believed that a university senate was the proper forum for addressing faculty concerns, including issues of salaries and benefits. He pointed to the increasing role of the faculty welfare

San fRancisco foghorn

Vol. 70 No. 11   September 26, 1975

Faculty decides to unionize

Commons manager

photo by Denis Solis

Tepper aims to please students

by Chuck Reilley

Possessed with a desire to please and to create a good impression, Barry Tepper, the energetic, 30-year-old manager of the University Commons wants to know what students think. "Responsiveness," says Tepper, "is our main goal. We want to make USF residents feel comfortable and at home."

Disgruntled possessors of sensitive palates may be surprised and even shocked by Tepp er's remarks. Those with a cynical sense of humor point out that the USF Commons is hardly the most popular eatery in San Francisco.

Nevertheless, Tepper, like a good captain, defends his ship. "I am definitely proud of the food we serve here. When compared with other colleges cafeterias, we rank in the top five-ten per cent."

He goes on to enumerate the many advantages and benefits available to his patrons: infinite servings of salads, soups, desserts and beverages; seconds on all hot entrees.

Despite an annual food cost of almost half a million dollars, the cafeteria serves thousands of meals per week at a reasonable cost to the clientele.

Inflation is not Tepper's only problem. Students who waste food drive costs up. Those costs, in turn, diminish the amount which can be spent for better quality.

Many who demand steak are only willing to pay for spaghetti. The Commons strives to obtain and serve high quality items, pleasing to both the palate and the pocketbook.

Although he is concerned

D.P.

Non-law faculty voted 3-1 in favor of unionizing, on Wednesday, September 24 at the University of San Francisco.

Out of the eligible 248 faculty members 203 voted, which is about an 80 percent turn out. There were 155 votes in favor of unionization and only 48 against it.

Votes were counted immediately after the voting took place. Present at the counting were William Gromesch, Michael Lehmann and Ralph Lane, plus two members from the National Labor Relations Board.

The major issues voted on dealt with faculty compensation, University governance and the allocation of University resources.

It was important that as many non-law faculty members voted, due to the fact that the outcome would be decided according to a majority vote. In other words, if only 50 persons voted only 26 were necessary to win.

Professors began a strong

New ASUSF theme:
WE MEAN IT !

by Steve Purhill   a vote, but the quality and mat-   3) President Castoria has set
ASUSF President Louie   urity of our participation this   up a comission to look into the

The vote by the USF faculty to unionize was proclaimed in a *Foghorn* headline on September 26, 1975.

committee of the university senate, for example, in addressing faculty issues at USF.

Although USF had established a university senate as early as 1950 to "act in an advisory capacity to the President" on all matters, including faculty salaries and benefits, the senate was tripartite, with representatives from the ranks of faculty and librarians, students, and administration. In the face of growing economic difficulties at USF during the early 1970s, as a result of falling enrollment and escalating costs, some faculty members began to perceive faculty influence as weakened by the tripartite structure of the university senate. Moreover, when Fr. Jonsen's successor, William McInnes, S.J., called for a wage freeze for the 1973–1974 academic year to help reduce the growing budget deficit at the university, the law school faculty responded by organizing a faculty association, and the clerical staff at USF joined the AFL-CIO. By 1974, the only full-time group of employees on campus, aside from administrators, who were not organized for purposes of collective bargaining was the approximately 230 non-law school full-time faculty members.

In 1975, the faculty welfare committee, which for years had advised various presidents on matters related to the faculty, had mixed results in its dealings with the university's president. In February 1975, for example, the faculty welfare committee recommended a 5 percent across-the-board salary increase for faculty and the inclusion of a dental plan in the benefits package for faculty members. Fr. McInnes accepted the dental plan recommendation but said the salary increase would have to be less than 2 percent because of the institution's financial problems. He did, however, suggest a contingency plan whereby any tuition dollars in excess of the university's projected revenue for the year would be applied to faculty salaries. At a meeting in April 1975 with Fr. McInnes, a group from the faculty welfare committee composed of Michael Lehmann, Edward Muenk, Joseph Simini, and Giacinto Matteucig indicated that the president's counterproposal was unacceptable. These faculty members understood Fr. McInnes to say that he was not legally bound to negotiate with the faculty welfare committee, and that if the faculty didn't like the situation, they could go to collective bargaining. Although Fr. McInnes later denied having said this, the impasse over salary increases, and the perception by members on the faculty welfare committee that they lacked the power to negotiate for faculty interests, were important catalysts in the formation of a faculty union.

In April 1975, the faculty welfare committee sent a letter to the board of trustees protesting the president's failure to accept the faculty welfare committee's salary recommendation, claiming that the president refused to negotiate with the committee and stating that the non-law faculty may be compelled to resort, "however reluctantly, to collective bargaining." At the same time, Michael Lehmann and Joseph Simini distributed cards to faculty members to obtain signatures to petition the NLRB for authorization to permit the USF non-law faculty association to represent faculty and librarians in collective bargaining. By the end of April 1975, approximately 70 percent of the full-time faculty who would potentially be in the bargaining unit had signed the cards authorizing such representation. The following September, a vote was taken, and 155 faculty members voted for representation by a faculty association, and 48 voted against it. On October 2, 1975, the NLRB certified the USF Faculty Association to represent all full-time faculty members (excluding law school faculty) and all non-administrative full-time professional librarians for purposes of collective bargaining. A new era had dawned in the development of faculty and administration relations at USF.

129

The Origins of the Faculty Association (PART II)

IN SEPTEMBER 1975, THE FULL-TIME FACULTY AT THE University of San Francisco, excluding the law school faculty, voted to authorize the USF Faculty Association (USFFA) to represent their interests in collective bargaining. Among the 203 faculty members who cast ballots, 76 percent voted in favor of unionization.

Michael Lehmann was the founding president of the USF Faculty Association.

As plans were being formulated for the first round of negotiations between the new USF Faculty Association and the administration, the university announced on December 12, 1975, that due to the worsening financial situation at USF, termination notices had been sent to all 111 nontenured faculty (about 40 percent of the total faculty), and 42 administrators (about 33 percent of that group). The annual deficit had risen to almost $500,000, and the cumulative debt was $2.5 million. Although USF President William McInnes, S.J., expressed his hope that massive layoffs could be avoided, he said that contractual obligations required early notice of termination. For Fr. McInnes, the sending of termination notices to nontenured faculty members and administrators was a necessary legal step. For the overwhelming majority of faculty members, the threat of layoffs confirmed the necessity of a faculty union.

In January 1976, the USF Faculty Association elected permanent officers consisting of an executive board and policy board. Michael Lehmann, associate professor of economics, was elected the association's first president. The 1976 election also brought Alan Heineman, Clifton Albergotti, Edward Muenk, and Millianne Granberg on to the executive board. The Faculty Association also contracted with

Donald MacIntyre served as USF's vice president for academic affairs during the first round of negotiations between the University of San Francisco Faculty Association and the administration.

Victor Van Bourg, a well-known labor attorney in San Francisco, to represent the union in the forthcoming negotiations. During the long and difficult negotiations over the next six months, numerous impasses were broken by a series of negotiated compromises. The major issues included the proposed lay-offs of nontenured faculty; arbitration of disputes over tenure and promotion; grievance procedures; faculty participation in academic affairs, including curriculum, program, and personnel matters; faculty participation in areas of student affairs, business and finance, and university relations, including fundraising; salary and retroactive pay increases; the existence of a union shop; and teaching-load requirements.

At the end of April 1976, after weeks of protracted negotiations, a tentative settlement was reached, and the exact language in the agreement was hammered out by the end of June. The final agreement recognized the USFFA as the exclusive collective bargaining agent for all full-time faculty members (excluding law school faculty) and for all nonadministrative full-time professional librarians; mandated the collection of association dues from each faculty member's salary; provided for a consultative

role by the faculty on matters of curriculum and programs; left other areas such as student affairs, business and finance, and university relations to the purview of the administration; instituted grievance and arbitration procedures for tenured faculty who were denied promotion, disciplined, discharged, or laid off; established procedures for applying for tenure and for arbitration by faculty who were denied tenure; stipulated a 24-unit contact hour teaching load per academic year; called for a 15 percent across-the-board salary increase; specified the salaries associated with each step in each rank; called for administration consultation with faculty regarding standards for advancement in rank, as well as in the evaluation of probationary faculty members, appointments, promotions, tenure, nonretention, and sabbaticals; and maintained existing faculty benefits.

The number of faculty who were actually subject to layoffs was reduced to 20 during the course of negotiations, and each of those lay-offs was decided on an individual basis: one was reinstated, for example, by receipt of a grant, three were considered for administrative positions, two left on their own accord, several were denied tenure, and seven were laid off with the closing of the English Language Center. Of the seven faculty members in the English Language Center, three were restored to full-time tenure track positions after a grievance, and the other four rejected offers to be rehired as part-time instructors. The agreement was to be in effect for five years, though it could be reopened annually on matters of compensation, workload and productivity, curriculum and program issues, and personnel procedures and standards. On June 30, 1976, amid a series of champagne toasts, the university's first collective bargaining agreement between faculty members and the administration was signed at a special ceremony hosted by Donald MacIntyre, vice president for academic affairs.

Since 1976, the collective bargaining road between the USFFA and the administration has not always been smooth, and yet through the many years of sometimes-difficult negotiations, strikes have been avoided, and people of intelligence and goodwill have emerged to ensure the unbroken continuity of the Jesuit educational enterprise in San Francisco.

In 1988, Alan Heineman, professor of English and director of the Honors Program in the Humanities in the College of Arts and Sciences, was elected president of the USFFA. There has not been a significant contract dispute since 1988, the year a major settlement was reached, and faculty and administration relations have steadily improved over the past two decades. During the 30 years since the formation of the USFFA, the economic position of USF faculty members has become one of the best in the state of California.

In 1983, the USF Part-Time Faculty Association was formed to engage in collective bargaining. Reflective of the present state of administration and faculty relations, USF President Stephen A. Privett, S.J., publicly congratulated the USF Part-Time Faculty Association on its 20th anniversary and wrote that "part-time faculty contribute to the vision and mission of the university in many ways.

Most significantly, their teaching, interaction with students, service on committees and scholarship exemplify their dedication and loyalty. The Part-Time Faculty Association continues to assist in building a collaborative culture in labor relations that focuses on the common good for all."

Alan Heineman, professor of English and director of the Honors Program in the Humanities in the College of Arts and Sciences, was elected president of the University of San Francisco Faculty Association in 1988.

UNIVERSITY OF SAN FRANCISCO ARCHIVES

The Fromm Institute for Lifelong Learning

WHEN WILLIAM McINNES, S.J., WAS SELECTED AS THE 24th president of the University of San Francisco in 1972, he brought to the institution a reputation for supporting education for people of all ages and for nontraditional college programming. He was also known for fiscal responsibility and balancing budgets. His role in establishing the Fromm Institute for Lifelong Learning, an educational program for retirees at USF, was in keeping with the first part of that reputation, but his decision to grant the institute classroom space, administrative offices, and various support services free of charge seemed to some to be at odds with his reputation for fiscal responsibility, especially at an institution reeling from financial problems, as USF was in the early 1970s. Twenty-seven years later, however, when the Friends of the Fromm Institute pledged $10 million to the university, in addition to the sizable gifts to USF by Alfred and Hanna Fromm over the past decades, Fr. McInnes' decision seemed fiscally responsible, indeed.

Alfred Fromm, representing the fourth generation of a family of Bavarian vintners, immigrated to the United States in 1936 to escape Nazi Germany. He founded Fromm and Sichel, one of the largest distributors of fine wines in the world. His company became the international distributor for Christian Brothers' wine and brandy and for the Paul Masson line of wines. Fromm also became a leading philanthropist in the Bay Area, and he took on leadership roles in organizations such as the San Francisco Opera Association, the San Francisco Conservatory of Music, the Jewish National Fund, and the Eleanor Roosevelt Memorial Foundation. His wife, Hanna, also a refugee from Nazi Germany, held a degree in choreography and music from the University of Essen in Germany, had a lifelong interest in education, and also served on many boards, including the National Council on Aging, the American Red Cross, the Community Music Center, and the National Board of Fine Arts Museums.

One day in 1975, Hanna asked Alfred what

he wanted to do in retirement, to which he replied, "I'd like to go back to school but not with my children or grandchildren. I would like to study along with persons of my own age, and be taught by persons of my own age." By 1976, Alfred and Hanna Fromm had decided that their interests in contributing to the community and their desire for lifelong learning should be parlayed into an educational program for retirees. Her research indicated that only Harvard and the New School for Social Research offered academic programs for retirees. In looking for a university that would become the third higher education institution to offer such programming, USF came to her attention. "The university really selected us," Mrs. Fromm later noted, "They — that is Fr. William McInnes, who was president at the time — was greatly taken by our idea. It was innovative, and the university was looking for innovation. USF offered to be the host institution, we gratefully accepted, and the rest is history. It has been a wonderful relationship."

In 1976, when the Fromms held their first open house and registration at USF for an academic institution for older individuals, they expected to have perhaps 50 people show up. Amazingly, some 500 people were there to fill the 75 allocated student slots. One tearful 60-year-old man became number 76 when he successfully pleaded to be allowed into the first classes so he could keep up with his five children who were enrolled in college.

The institute rapidly established a reputation for an outstanding curriculum in a range of academic areas, including history, politics, art, music, literature, psychology, philosophy, creative writing, and the sciences. The courses were taught by highly respected professors emeriti from Bay Area institutions. Over the years, faculty members have included individuals such as Thomas Blaisdell, former assistant secretary of commerce and professor emeritus of political science at U.C. Berkeley; Leslie Lipson, also professor emeritus of political science at U.C. Berkeley; Elisabeth Gleason, former president of the American Society for Reformation Research and professor emerita of history at USF; and Albert Jonsen, former president of USF and professor emeritus of ethics in medicine at the University of Washington.

The institute is endowed by significant contributions by the Fromm family over the years as well as by community support, including from many Bay Area corporations and foundations. Any retired person who is at least 50 may enroll in the Fromm Institute for a modest membership fee or per-session charge. Scholarship assistance is available to those who cannot afford the fees, and no one in the history of the Fromm Institute has ever been turned away because of inability to pay.

Alfred Fromm died in July 1998, and Hanna Fromm passed away in January 2003. Their memory and their work live on, however, at the University of San Francisco. All aspects of the program continue to be managed by Robert Fordham, the long-time program director, and now executive director, of the Fromm Institute for Lifelong Learning. In the spring semester of 2003, for the first time

In 1976, Alfred and Hanna Fromm translated their lifelong interest in contributing to the community and their ideas about lifelong learning into an educational program for retirees at USF.

THE FROMM INSTITUTE FOR LIFELONG LEARNING

Students from the Fromm Institute for Lifelong Learning walk near Harney Plaza in this photo from 1991. The institute's student population grew from 76 in 1976 to 971 in 2004. Currently, the median age of Fromm Institute students is 71.

in its history, Fromm Institute students took a class with regular USF undergraduates: a course taught by politics professor Robert Elias on law, politics, and the national pastime, baseball. In the fall of 2003, Fromm Institute students joined a freshman seminar on intergenerational communication offered by Lisa Wagner, associate professor of psychology at USF.

On October 24, 2003, the university announced that the former Jesuit residence on campus, Xavier Hall, will be remodeled and renamed the Alfred and Hanna Fromm Lifelong Learning Center. The institute's founders, Alfred and Hanna Fromm; the Friends of the Fromm Institute; family; students; philanthropists; and the Fromm Institute Board of Directors have pledged $10 million to USF, approximately one-third of which will go to the renovation and remodeling of Xavier Hall. In addition to housing the Fromm Institute, the building will include

the current undergraduate residence hall, classroom studios for USF's fine arts majors, space for interfaith worship, and a day-care center—a truly intergenerational learning environment.

Lone Mountain

THE EARLY SPANISH EXPLORERS AND SETTLERS IN THE area called the 488-foot rise of land El Divisidero, or "lookout point." It is an apt description for what is now the Lone Mountain Campus of the University of San Francisco. The campus offers a 360-degree view of the surrounding world: downtown San Francisco and the East Bay communities; a large portion of San Francisco Bay; the Golden Gate and the Marin Headlands; the Pacific Ocean, including the Farallon Islands on a clear day; and some of the southern portion of the city, punctuated by Mount Sutro.

In 1861, Lone Mountain was a Catholic Cemetery for gold miners, silver barons, wealthy businessmen, and politicians. Today, it is the site of the Lone Mountain campus of the University of San Francisco.

UNIVERSITY OF SAN FRANCISCO ARCHIVES

An aerial photo of Lone Mountain and the San Francisco College for Women during the 1930s.

The first archbishop of San Francisco, Joseph Alemany, purchased Lone Mountain in 1860, and the eastern slope soon became Calvary Cemetery. During the late 19th century, the spectacular views from Lone Mountain were shared by gravediggers, mourners, and other visitors to the 23-acre cemetery. Successful gold miners, silver barons, wealthy businessmen, and politicians were all laid to rest on Lone Mountain until 1900, when the city supervisors outlawed any more burials within the city limits. Following the earthquake of April 18, 1906, many San Franciscans journeyed to Lone Mountain to stand amid the gravestones and watch two-thirds of their city burn to the ground. The Masonic Cemetery, just south of Lone Mountain, housed the remains of an additional 19,000 deceased San Francisco residents, often from more modest backgrounds than those buried on Lone Mountain (vignette #88). The main campus of the University of San Francisco, as well as the Lone Mountain campus, are built over these former cemeteries.

In 1929, Archbishop Edward Hanna of San Francisco proposed that a Roman Catholic Women's College be opened in San Francisco. The honor went to the Religious of the Sacred Heart, an order of Catholic nuns that had come to the United States from France in 1818. The original site for their college in the Bay Area was in Menlo Park, and in 1930 the order acquired Lone Mountain from Archbishop Hanna. By then, many of the bodies buried on Lone Mountain had been removed for reburial in Holy Cross Cemetery in Colma.

The Religious of the Sacred Heart contracted to have the remaining bodies buried on Lone Mountain removed to Colma and to begin grading the crest of Lone Mountain. The contractor had to remove a significant portion of the mountaintop to create a flat building area and also had to cover a groundwater spring. In 1932, the Sacred Heart sisters erected a magnificent Spanish Gothic building, topped by an iron cross, 115 feet above the mountain's crest. From Turk Street at the southern base of Lone Mountain, 105 curving stone steps, modeled after the Spanish Steps in Rome, were built to lead up to the building. The sisters named their school the San Francisco College for Women.

For 37 years, young Catholic women received a first-rate liberal arts education at the college, studying literature, art, music, theology, history, science, languages, and mathematics. Students also participated in basketball, volleyball, tennis, and archery. In the east wing of the building, a beautiful oak-beamed library housed more than 100,000 volumes, many donated by Monsignor Joseph Gleason, an alumnus of St. Ignatius College. The library also included numerous letters written by former U.S. presidents, an autographed and unpublished poem by Henry Wadsworth Longfellow, a series of numbered lithographs by Salvador Dali, sermons by Pope Leo the Great, wills from the reigns of English kings from James I to George I, various papal bulls, and one of the most complete collections of bookplates in the nation. By 1960, nearly 800 women were enrolled at the college, many supported by the generosity of alumnae of the institution. By the mid-1960s, however, the popularity of women's colleges in the United States had begun to decline, and enrollment at the San Francisco College for Women was especially hard-hit when USF became completely coeducational in 1964. In 1969, in the face of a severe enrollment decline and a consequent financial crisis, the college became coeducational, changed its name to Lone Mountain College, and introduced an experimental curriculum in place of the traditional liberal arts focus. Enrollment continued its downward spiral, however, alumnae support withered, and the institution faced insurmountable financial problems by the mid-1970s.

In 1977, Lone Mountain College president Berndt Kolker approached the new president of USF, John Lo Schiavo, S.J., about a secured loan of $700,000 to help the college through the spring semester of 1978. The loan agreement included an option to purchase the entire 23-acre campus, including its buildings and equipment, after the spring semester ended. In June 1978, following a series of discussions among the leaders of USF and a financial analysis regarding the current and projected USF need for additional classroom space, offices, and student housing, Fr. Lo Schiavo, with the unanimous backing of the USF Board of Trustees, announced that USF would purchase Lone Mountain for $5.8 million. Fr. Lo Schiavo described the purchase as "the most significant expansion decision in our 123-year history."

Although USF had recently faced its own financial problems, Fr. Lo Schiavo's administration had taken major steps in addressing those financial problems; enrollment was increasing; and alumni, friends, and foundations had by the time of the acquisition pledged $1.6 million toward the purchase price. Fr. Lo Schiavo wrote to the USF community: "I see a renewed enthusiasm and optimism which will fulfill a dream of many of our pioneer benefactors, Jesuit fathers, and long-term faculty who have believed that USF all along was destined to become one of the pre-eminent educational institutions in the West. The Lone Mountain acquisition, while a substantial challenge, will bring us close to touching that realization."

Today, the Lone Mountain campus of the University of San Francisco houses classrooms; faculty offices; the conference center; the Center for the Pacific Rim; residence hall rooms for undergraduate and graduate students; and a multitude of administrative offices, including those of the president, chancellor, provost, and vice presidents for university advancement, planning and budget, and international relations. In 2002, the university completed work on Loyola Village, a 136-unit residential complex for students, faculty, and staff, located at the northeast base of Lone Mountain.

The first phase of another major campus renovation project began on Lone Mountain in April 2004 with the demolition of the old auditorium and ballroom. The auditorium, unusable for the past decade because of its lack of accessibility, will be rebuilt into three floors of administrative space, two of which will house USF's Information Technology Services. The ballroom will be converted into two floors of double-occupancy residence rooms for students. During the summer of 2004, 21 classrooms in Lone Mountain were reconfigured and 15 classrooms had technological upgrades to facilitate project and multimedia presentations. Major renovations are also scheduled in the summer of 2005 for the center wing of Lone Mountain to accommodate many of the administrative offices currently housed in Campion Hall.

On the northeast crest of Lone Mountain is situated Loyola House, built in 1999, and currently housing 24 members of the USF Jesuit Community. From that crest, the Jesuits can look east to downtown San Francisco, where their institution originated and grew in the 19th century, to the south, where the college relocated following the earthquake and fire of 1906, and to the north to the Golden Gate, through which Michael Accolti, S.J., founder of the Jesuit order in California sailed in 1849, followed five years later by Anthony Maraschi, S.J., founding president of St. Ignatius Academy, the antecedent of USF. From this "lookout point," the Jesuits and their many lay colleagues and friends can also reflect on the Jesuit legacy, stretching back to the efforts of Saint Ignatius of Loyola in mid-16th-century Europe, and on the promise of Jesuit education today.

On the Radio with KUSF

132

BEGINNING IN 1922, COLLEGES AND UNIVERSITIES throughout the United States started to add campus radio stations to their list of educational endeavors and to secure federal licenses to broadcast to their surrounding communities. In that first year alone, the federal government granted broadcast licenses to 40 institutions of higher education, and by the end of the decade, more than 100 colleges and universities were on the air.

The distinctive logo of KUSF-FM.

KUSF 90.3 FM

During the 1940s, USF President William Dunne, S.J., began to investigate the possibility of establishing a radio station on campus, but it was not until the late 1950s that the institution took direct steps toward that end. Spearheading this effort was Fred Spieler, S.J., a physics professor who wrote a proposal, secured the funding, and obtained equipment to start USF's first radio station.

In October 1960, USF received permission from the Federal Communications Commission (FCC) to construct a non-commercial, educational FM radio station on campus. The station was to be built on the roof of Phelan Hall, and plans were made to start broadcasting in December 1961. During the spring of 1961, however, the university received a large number of requests from prospective students wishing to reside on campus during the coming fall. Therefore, the administration decided to add a new floor to Phelan Hall and to relocate the radio station.

Because of the added expense for the relocation of the station, as well as the station's projected annual cost, the university decided to defer the project, and USF returned its broadcasting license to the FCC. The sudden death of Fr. Spieler in 1961 in an automobile accident further delayed the initiative, and it was not until 1963, that an AM radio station with the call letters KUSF finally began broadcasting. The station was funded by the Associated Students of USF (ASUSF), and was operated and managed entirely by undergraduate students.

In 1970, Steve Runyon, an undergraduate economics major, was selected as the student general manager of KUSF, which at that time was still a campus-limited AM station. Now designated as KDNZ 880 AM, that station currently provides students with an opportunity to gain experience in radio broadcasting, provides campus news and events information to the USF community, and supplies a diverse range of music and entertainment.

As general manager of KUSF-AM, Runyon realized that for the station to achieve its greatest potential, it had to obtain an FM frequency and reach all of San Francisco. In 1973, after unsuccessful negotiations to share an FM frequency with a San Francisco Board of Education radio station, USF was offered an FM station by the president of Simpson Bible College of San Francisco, who wanted to discontinue his own college's radio station because the students wanted to play rock and roll, hardly appropriate programming for a bible college. Runyon had six weeks to finalize a deal with Simpson College, purchase its transmitter and antenna, and complete the FCC paperwork to secure the transfer. Although this transfer process normally takes two years, Runyon met the deadline, and succeeded in obtaining a license from the FCC for a non-commercial FM radio station at USF. On April 25, 1977, the first show was broadcast on KUSF 90.3 FM from a 3,000-watt transmitter. Runyon built the station from scratch with seed money from the ASUSF, the National Science Foundation, and the Father Fred Spieler Trust. The new station broadcast on the same frequency as Fr. Spieler originally intended; thus, after more than a decade's hiatus, the priest's dream was finally fulfilled. Runyon was the station's first general manager, and he still manages it today.

KUSF-FM went on the air in April 1977 with a six-hour per day broadcasting schedule. By 1981, the station was broadcasting 24 hours per day in stereo to San Francisco and much of the Bay Area from its limited space on the ground floor of Phelan Hall. Administratively, KUSF is under the purview of the College of Arts and Sciences, and Edward Stackpoole, S.J., was the first of many deans to support the efforts of KUSF. From its inception, KUSF-FM has served as a training ground for students interested in broadcasting, providing them with a laboratory, work experience, and a potential connection to academic departments at USF, such as media studies. Many USF students who have volunteered at KUSF have gone on to careers in radio broadcasting, television, media relations, and the recording industry. USF faculty members can broadcast on "USF Forum," a program that addresses issues and ideas related to faculty members' academic interests and seeks to educate the broader community. Additionally, for more than 27 years, KUSF's "Podium Series" has broadcast presentations and lectures by prominent

national and international figures that have spoken on the USF campus. The station also maintains one of the most extensive record and audio material libraries in the Bay Area, a collection buttressed in 1983 by a donation from Carlo Rossi, S.J., of hundreds of rare recordings.

Over the 27 years of its operation, KUSF's broadcasting has undergone significant changes, though much of its original philosophy has remained constant. In its first years, KUSF was a fairly traditional college station, broadcasting cultural, ethnic, foreign language, and fine arts programs on weekends and evenings only.

Some of the earliest shows that are still on the air include the "Hamazkayin Armenian Hour," the "Polish Cultural Hour," the "Turkish Cultural Hour," and "Chinese Star Radio," which features news, music, and social justice issues broadcast in Cantonese. More recent multicultural programming includes "Radio Goethe," a German language and music show; "Havaye Tazeh," which focuses on issues and news for the Iranian community; "Kidoideira," which carries news and music from Brazil; "Music Masala," providing music and news from India; "San Francisco Jewish Radio" in

KUSF 90.3 FM broadcast its first show on April 25, 1977, from the station pictured here on the ground floor of Phelan Hall. From its inception, KUSF provided a training ground for students who later successfully pursued careers in the recording industry, radio broadcasting, television, and media relations. The station broadcasts a wide range of music, cultural, and social justice programs to the Bay Area, and affords faculty and special speakers at USF an opportunity to share their ideas with a large and appreciative audience.

UNIVERSITY OF SAN FRANCISCO ARCHIVES

Steve Runyon (standing) has been the general manager of KUSF since 1970, when he was an undergraduate economics major at USF, and the station, seen in this 1975 photo, was a campus-limited AM station. Today, KUSF-FM broadcasts 24 hours a day to San Francisco and much of the Bay Area, has won numerous awards for broadcasting excellence, and has an international reputation.

Russian; "Studio Finland;" "Synagogue of the Air," which carries sermons and music from the Sabbath services at San Francisco's Congregation Emanu-El; and "God's People on the Air," a Cantonese language program for Bay Area Chinese Catholics, produced in cooperation with the Archdiocese of San Francisco.

In more recent years, KUSF has also developed a reputation in the community for broadcasting avant-garde music. In 1980, a group of students convinced a reluctant Steve Runyon to experiment with a late-night punk-rock program called "Harmful Emissions," and the station was one of the first to air the now-famous groups the B-52s and Metallica. KUSF has received gold records from groups that got their first exposure on the station, such as R.E.M. and The Bangles. Today, KUSF's disc jockeys play everything from classical music to heavy metal, hard-core punk, world beat, and drum'n bass, and the station has come to be known for its innovative programming. The importance of KUSF as a radio station and as an idea can be seen in the worldwide popularity of t-shirts sporting the station's distinctive skull-and-crossed-microphones logo.

Virtually from the beginning, KUSF has also broadcast programs that carry a social justice theme. For example, for almost 20 years, the station has broadcast a weekly program titled "Disability and Senior News Report," which addresses current issues of importance to senior citizens and individuals with disabilities. Another program, "Community Crusade of the Month," features one or more local community-service organizations involved in social justice advocacy and support. Likewise, a weekly program, "Contact," discusses issues pertinent to the poor, disadvantaged, and marginalized in the community. The "Podium Series" frequently broadcasts lectures on social justice topics, including those given by the many Nobel Peace Prize recipients that have appeared at USF. The current president of USF, Stephen A. Privett, S.J., praised KUSF's "commitment to educating students to social responsibility through direct exposure to injustice and discrimination by broadcasting a significant group of important social justice programs."

Over its 27 years, KUSF has received numerous accolades and awards from a variety of individuals and organizations. Former San Francisco Mayor Willie Brown described KUSF as a "premier resource for community service." The station has been officially honored in San Francisco with a "KUSF Day" three times in the last 15 years; it was honored four times by the San Francisco Board of Supervisors with the Certificate of Honor for community work; it has been named the best radio station in the San Francisco Bay Area by local media, including *SF Weekly*, the *Bay Guardian*, and *San Francisco* magazine; and it has been named the best college radio station in the nation by such publications as *Esquire*. Additionally, American Women in Radio and Television has honored KUSF with its KUDO Award for the best cultural diversity programming on Bay Area radio.

For 150 years, the University of San Francisco has been known for its innovative educational programming and for its values-based outreach to the community. KUSF both reflects and has significantly contributed to that legacy.

The Building of the Koret Health and Recreation Center

133

ON OCTOBER 19, 1987, DURING A CELEBRATION OF THE construction of the university's Koret Health and Recreation Center, University of San Francisco President John Lo Schiavo, S.J., donned a welder's mask and helped seal a time capsule to be placed in the lobby of the new building. Among the capsule's contents were a copy of the original charter of St. Ignatius College from 1859, a brick from the institution's building on Van Ness Avenue that was destroyed in the earthquake and fire of 1906, photographs of the college's original gymnasium built in 1903 and gutted in the 1906 disaster, a 1929 class yearbook, a 1959 alumni magazine, and a 1987 catalog of classes.

At the celebration, Deputy San Francisco Mayor Peter Henschel read Mayor Dianne Feinstein's proclamation declaring "USF Building on Our Tradition" day, and congratulating the university on its contributions to the city of San Francisco. The mayor's proclamation was also placed in the time capsule, to be opened by the university's future leaders in 2055, during the institution's bicentennial celebration.

Many of the individuals who were crucial to building the Koret Health and Recreation Center attended the ceremony. In addition to Fr. Lo Schiavo, present at the celebration were Charles Dullea, S.J., USF's chancellor, campaign chairman, former president of the university, and long-term advocate for the center; Susan Koret, widow of philanthropist Joseph Koret, whose foundation gave the lead gift for the center; and Melvin

Guests at the opening of the Koret Health and Recreation Center on September 17, 1989, were greeted by a statue of Jesse Owens, the great African American athlete who won four gold medals at the 1936 Olympic games held in Germany.

UNIVERSITY OF SAN FRANCISCO ARCHIVES

327

Swig, chairman of the USF Board of Trustees and major contributor to the campaign to build the center. The campaign raised more than $16 million, and other major contributors included Gordon Getty, philanthropist, composer, and USF graduate; the James Irvine Foundation; Angelo Sangiacomo, USF class of 1948; and the USF Jesuit Community. Hundreds of other friends and benefactors of USF contributed to the campaign that made the Koret Health and Recreation Center a reality. As the distinguished guests; campaign committee members; mayoral candidates; and hundreds of alumni, faculty, staff, students, and university friends looked on, Fr. Lo Schiavo spoke of the day's significance: "This Center is being built upon the traditions of excellence in USF's past and present. Today, we are commemorating our traditions and celebrating the impact they'll have on our future with the Koret Center."

By the time of the October 1987 ceremony, the foundation had been laid for the building, and some of the walls had been built. Over the next two years, the structure rose on the corner of Turk and Stanyon streets, the former site of

St. Ignatius High School, later known as Loyola Hall. Construction of the building was delayed for several months, however, and building costs were significantly increased, when it was discovered that serpentine rock, a source of natural asbestos, existed at the site. The construction crews had to be fitted with special equipment, and a series of community meetings was held to address neighbors' fears that harmful asbestos would be released into the atmosphere. The completed building was finally dedicated at another gala ceremony on September 17, 1989. It was attended by thousands of alumni, students, faculty, staff, and community members. The throngs of people who toured the center saw a 120,000-square-foot facility featuring one of the largest indoor pools in Northern California and only the second Olympic-size pool in the city of San Francisco. The visitors also observed weight training, aerobics, and martial arts rooms; a cardiovascular alley with fitness machines; five racquetball courts; four multipurpose courts for basketball, volleyball, and badminton; lounges and locker rooms; and an alumni lounge and university club providing space for dining and meetings. Adjacent to the building, the day's guests saw Negoesco Soccer

Stadium, completely regraded and landscaped, home to USF's championship soccer team and named after Stephen Negoesco, the most victorious coach in the history of USF and intercollegiate soccer in the United States.

Today, the Koret Health and Recreation Center offers a multitude of programs for students, staff, alumni, and the community, under the supervision of Chuck White, director of the recreational sports department and the Koret Center. In addition to use of the facilities, individuals can participate in intramural sports, such as men's and women's basketball, volleyball, flag football, indoor soccer, and softball; outdoor programs, such as sailing, skiing, camping, white-water rafting, and kayaking; club sports, including fencing, martial arts, rugby, golf, and snow boarding; aquatics, including swimming classes and programs for all ages and skill levels; and fitness and wellness programs, featuring state-of-the art cardiovascular equipment and options that range from personal training to CPR, from massage to yoga.

Since its completion in 1989, the Koret Health and Recreation Center has fulfilled several goals: to continue USF's tradition of educating a sound mind in a sound body, to keep the institution competitive with other universities by offering complete physical-fitness facilities, and to serve as an important resource for recruiting and retaining students. In front of the entrance to the Koret Health and Recreation Center, is a statue of Jesse Owens, the great African American athlete who stunned Nazi Germany and the world by winning four gold medals at the 1936 Olympic games held in Germany. The statue was commissioned by Fr. Lo Schiavo and completed by a German sculptor, Edith Peres-Lethmate. The sculpture symbolizes USF's long tradition of outstanding athletic programs, including the full participation of members of all ethnic groups in athletic and other programs decades before most institutions were willing to grant that right.

Students and guests celebrated the opening of the Koret Center pool on September 17, 1989. The Olympic-size pool, officially named the Charles W. Dullea, S.J., Natatorium, after the late USF president and chancellor who spearheaded the drive to build it, is the largest in San Francisco. It measures 50 by 22.5 meters, holds more than a million gallons of water, and has a depth from 3.5 to 13.5 feet. Holding the banner in front of the pool are Chuck White, director of the Koret Center, and Denise Swett, ASUSF business manager. To the left of Fr. Lo Schiavo is Melvin Swig, chairman of the USF Board of Trustees.

UNIVERSITY OF SAN FRANCISCO ARCHIVES

The Origins of the College of Professional Studies

THE ROOTS OF THE COLLEGE OF PROFESSIONAL STUDIES are deeply embedded in the fertile institutional history of the University of San Francisco. Various attempts were made by the leadership of St. Ignatius College during the 19th century to start a "night school" for those students who could not attend the day program. With the exception of the School of Law, however, which began exclusively as an evening program in 1912, attempts at evening programming were unsuccessful until 1924. In that year, evening courses in business management and accounting were launched, followed in the next five years by a full array of courses in arts, sciences, and business leading to a bachelor's degree in commerce and finance.

By 1929, more than 50 percent of the 1,099 students at St. Ignatius College were enrolled in an evening "extension program" in the College of Arts and Sciences, in the evening division of the College of Commerce and Finance, or in the School of Law, which continued to operate exclusively at night until 1932. Most of these evening students, both men and women, worked during the day. Women were not permitted to enroll in the day division until 1964. During the Depression, and during the war years from 1941 to 1945, evening programming remained important to the university.

With the end of World War II, USF increasingly enrolled working adults, many of whom were veterans with families and were returning to college under the G.I. Bill of Rights. In 1952, the university made the decision to organize and administer the plethora of evening course offerings and degrees, with the exception of those within the School of Law, under a single entity called the Evening College. The Evening College gradually expanded during the next two decades, and by 1978, a large number of majors were available to students seeking a bachelor's degree in the arts, sciences, or business. From 1978 to 1981, the College of Arts and Sciences and the McLaren College of Business increasingly began to assume responsibility for evening programming in their respective academic areas, and the Evening College finally closed its doors in 1981 (vignette #113). During the final years of the Evening College, a new administrative and academic unit was started at USF to offer a different selection of undergraduate degrees in the evenings and on weekends, mostly to working adults who had undertaken some college work

The School of Continuing Education was the immediate antecedent of the College of Professional Studies. Pictured here is the cover from one of the school's brochures from 1979, depicting the site of its main administrative offices in the Pacific Wing of Lone Mountain.

but had not completed a degree. This unit, which began in 1975, was first known as the Office of Continuing Education.

By the mid-1970s, USF was reeling from financial problems stemming from a sharp decline in enrollment, national inflation, and a recession (vignette #126). In 1975, a group of faculty members, led by Hartmut Fischer, assistant professor of economics, approached USF President William McInnes, S.J., with a proposal to start a weekend division, to be offered in eight-week modules, for students of varying ages and educational backgrounds to earn college credit. The potential students included individuals who were working and who wanted to further their education without interrupting their careers; employees of businesses willing to pay tuition support to encourage their employees to continue their education; students who wanted to combine work experience with university education; women trying to combine family responsibilities and employment with education; transfer students from other Bay Area colleges; and qualified high school seniors who wanted advanced credit.

In the proposal, all of these potential student groups would attend classes at a lower price than the regular tuition rates. The weekend division courses were advertised in brochures and on the radio during the spring semester of 1975, and Michael Howe, instructor in the sociology department, offered the use of his office and secretary to answer phone inquiries about the new courses in the weekend division. During the peak of the marketing effort for the weekend courses, however, Howe became involved in organizing an international airlift for Vietnamese war orphans, and the marketing efforts for the weekend division did not yield sufficient student inquiries to justify going ahead with the weekend courses. The foundation was laid, however, to begin to offer courses and programs during the following fall on weekends and in the evenings for non-traditional students, under the Office of Continuing Education.

Howe was the first director of the Office of Continuing Education, and in 1977, he was named its dean. Hartmut Fischer, who began as the associate director in charge of the weekend division of the office, was named associate dean. From 1975 to 1979, the Office of Continuing Education developed undergraduate degrees in applied economics, human relations and organizational behavior, public administration, and public service. The degree programs were premised on a cohort model, in which a group of learners began and ended an entire degree program as a community of learners. The office also developed an assessment center, permitting undergraduate students to apply for college credit for experiential learning acquired prior to admission to the program. To earn college credit applicable to a degree, a student had to develop a portfolio of essays to support prior learning experiences and have those documented experiences evaluated and awarded college credit by faculty members with appropriate content expertise. At the undergraduate level, the Office of Continuing Education also included supplementary curriculum and philosophy programs, which offered courses in general education needed to complete a degree. The cohort model, the experiential learning component, and the delivery of the programs in the evenings and on weekends placed USF on the cutting edge of adult education in

the United States. The Office of Continuing Education also administered a cooperative bachelor of fine arts program with the Academy of Art College in San Francisco, and offered master's degree programs in environmental management and occupational toxicology, human relations and organizational development, public administration, and public service.

In 1975, USF's administration was approached by John Sperling, who was also developing a non-traditional approach to adult learning and needed an institutional base. Sperling's newly formed company, the Institute for Professional Development (IPD), was contracted to help develop and market USF's continuing education programs in Northern and Southern California. For accreditation reasons, however, and because USF personnel thought they could do a better job themselves, the university terminated the contract with IPD in 1978. John Sperling later founded the Apollo Group, moved to the

Colin P. Silverthorne, chairman of the USF psychology department, was named acting dean of the School of Continuing Education in 1979. The next year he became dean, and the school's name was changed to the College of Professional Studies (CPS). Under Dean Silverthorne's leadership, CPS grew in number of students, the range of its programs expanded, and several new off-campus sites were added.

desert hills of Arizona and founded the University of Phoenix, now the largest for-profit university in the country.

In 1979, Mike Howe and Hartmut Fischer proposed that the Office of Continuing Education be elevated to the status of an independent college and renamed the Thomas More College of Professional Studies. As acting dean, Hartmut Fischer presented the proposal for an independent college to the USF Board of Trustees in September 1979. The board approved the proposal but settled on a different name: the School of Continuing Education. Howe was named dean of the school and Fischer became associate dean. During the fall of 1979, however, Howe resigned from the university and Fischer was appointed associate vice president for academic affairs at USF. Colin Silverthorne, chairman of USF's psychology department, was named acting dean in December 1979. In the spring of 1980, Silverthorne proposed that the name of the school be changed to the College of Professional Studies. The president of the university, John Lo Schiavo, S.J., and the USF Board of Trustees, accepted this change.

During the 1981–1982 academic year, the College of Professional Studies made its first appearance in the general catalog of the University of San Francisco. In addition to Dean Silverthorne, key administrators during this first year included Stan Buller, who directed the undergraduate degree programs in applied economics, public administration, and the graduate program in public administration; David Fox, who directed the undergraduate program in human relations and organizational behavior; Joseph Petulla, who was in charge of the graduate program in environmental management; Harlan Stelmach, director of the general education division; Martin Lonergan, who managed the philosophy program; Allan Berenson, in charge of supplementary curriculum; and Brenda Schildgen, director of the writing program. These program directors developed courses and curricula, hired adjunct faculty, assessed the programs, and engaged in a multitude of functions related to the marketing of the programs and the advising of students. The college also included an advising staff and an experiential learning center to provide undergraduate students with an opportunity to document learning through jobs or other life experiences that were equivalent to classroom learning. In conjunction with a special seminar, a team of experiential learning associates assisted students in developing written portfolios of learning experiences to be evaluated for the awarding of college credit by faculty members with appropriate content expertise. Overall, one of the goals of the college was to "integrate experiential and classroom learning" to "meet the unique needs of a working adult student population."

During the early 1980s, the College of Professional Studies, under Dean Silverthorne, continued to grow in its number of students, the diversity of its programs, and the range of its off-campus sites. The off-campus regional offices were initially located in Sacramento, Fresno, Cupertino, and in Covina in Southern California. In 1986, San Ramon was added as a regional office. In 1983, the college also assumed responsibility through its Office of Special Programs, under Alan Ziajka, for the administration of the university-wide summer session and intersession; special programs including public lectures, seminars, and conferences; and non-credit continuing education offerings. The USF Conference Center, directed by Maryann Noble, also fell within the purview of the College of Professional Studies. At the undergraduate level, degree programs included applied economics, public administration, and organizational behavior. By 1985, a bachelor's degree in general studies for prospective teachers, in conjunction with a credential from the School of Education, had been added to the curriculum, though that program lasted only for two years. The college also initiated a bachelor's degree in information systems management. At the graduate level, master's degrees were offered in the evenings and on weekends in health systems leadership, human relations and organizational development, public administration, public administration with a specialty in health services administration, and environmental management.

In 1983, Michael O'Neill, former dean of the School of Education and founder of the Institute for Catholic Educational Leadership, began the Institute for Nonprofit Organization Management in the College of Professional Studies. The institute developed a master's degree in nonprofit administration, one of the nation's first master's degrees in the field. The institute also developed two certificate programs, initiated a robust research agenda, including a landmark study of ethnic philanthropy, developed a comprehensive database on California nonprofit organizations, and secured more than 60 grants from national and local foundations that by 2004 reached a sum of over $7 million, including two from the Kellogg Foundation totaling more than $2.3 million. It became the most successful fundraising institute in the history of the university. The institute also organized major conferences and brought a number of prominent speakers to campus, including John W. Gardner, Secretary of the U.S. Department of Health, Education, and Welfare under President Lyndon Johnson, and later founder of Common Cause.

In 1985, Brenda Schildgen developed a master of arts degree in writing, offering graduate students a unique opportunity to study techniques, styles, genres, writing, and editing under the close guidance of professional authors. The graduate program also sponsored special writing seminars, workshops, and conferences. By 1987, however, the university had decided to move the master's program in writing, as well as the master's program in environmental management, founded by Joseph Petulla, to the College of Arts and Sciences. In 1986, special programs, summer sessions, and the conference center were moved from the College of Professional Studies to the Office for the Vice President for Academic Affairs. In 1987, Colin Silverthorne resigned as dean and returned to

his faculty position in the psychology department.

During the 1980s, the College of Professional Studies became a pioneer in higher education by offering undergraduate degree completion programs for working adults by means of an evening and weekend cohort delivery system that included opportunities for students to earn college credit by developing a portfolio of documented content-related experiences. The college provided university-level education to adult learners who wanted to advance their careers and complete their college degrees, often begun years earlier. By 1986, the College of Professional Studies had graduated more than 4,000 students from its undergraduate and graduate programs. As enrollment began to increase rapidly during the 1980s, it became apparent that the needs of a large number of working adults were indeed being successfully met. At the same time, the university's need for an important source of new revenue was being addressed, helping the institution stabilize its financial situation after the challenging economic decade of the 1970s.

The Administration of John Lo Schiavo, S.J.

135

HOW DOES ONE MEASURE THE SUCCESS OF A UNIVERSITY president? Among the potential yardsticks is the institution's financial stability during the president's term of office, successful fundraising campaigns, endowment growth, development and implementation of outstanding academic programs, growth in student enrollment, creation of a capable management team, attainment of educational goals consistent with the university's mission, and enhancement of an institution's reputation for integrity and ethical values. By these measures, the presidency of John Lo Schiavo, S.J., a 14-year span from 1977 to 1991, and second only in length to the presidency of William Dunne, S.J., was successful indeed.

John Lo Schiavo, S.J., has been associated with the University of San Francisco for more than half a century and with the greater Bay Area for most of his life. He was born in San Francisco in 1925, graduated from Star of the Sea Grammar School and St. Ignatius High School, joined the Society of Jesus in 1942, and later earned bachelor's and master's degrees in philosophy from Gonzaga University, and an S.T.L. in theology from Alma College in Los Gatos, California.

Fr. Lo Schiavo's formal association with USF began in 1950, when he became an instructor of philosophy, a position he held for two years, and that he briefly resumed in 1956. In 1961, he also taught theology at USF. His education career path lay in administration, however, and Fr. Lo Schiavo served as vice principal of Brophy College Preparatory School in Phoenix, Arizona,

from 1958 to 1961, as USF's dean of students from 1962 to 1966, and as the university's vice president for student affairs from 1966 to 1968. This was followed by a seven-year tenure as president of Bellarmine College Preparatory School in San Jose. During much of the time at Bellarmine, he simultaneously served on the board of trustees at USF, including chairing the board from 1970 to 1973. In 1975, Fr. Lo Schiavo was appointed rector of the Jesuit community at USF. When Fr. Lo Schiavo assumed office as the 25th president of the University of San Francisco in January 1977, he was well aware of the institution's great legacy in San Francisco and the greater Bay Area, as well as the many challenges it faced.

Chief among the challenges at USF when Fr. Lo Schiavo became president was the institution's financial situation, including a

During the 14-year presidency of John Lo Schiavo, S.J., USF was significantly transformed: financial stability was restored, enrollment grew, Lone Mountain was acquired, the Koret Health and Recreation Center was built, and a multitude of new academic programs were successfully launched.

UNIVERSITY OF SAN FRANCISCO ARCHIVES

1975–1976 fiscal year deficit of $1.7 million and an endowment of only $4.6 million. Moreover, the financial accounting system was in such disarray that the new president found it impossible to obtain an accurate monthly statement of expenditures and revenue. Fr. Lo Schiavo hired Elwood "Woody" Hancock as the new vice president of business and finance to establish an accurate accounting system, a goal he soon achieved. Fr. Lo Schiavo also sought to raise money for the institution, and with the assistance of Al Alessandri, vice president for university relations, the university launched the REACH capital fund campaign. When the campaign ended in 1982, it had brought in $26.8 million, making it the largest and most successful fundraising effort in the history of the institution to that time. The returns from that campaign enabled USF to add a wing to Kendrick Hall and to purchase the Lone Mountain College property (vignette #131). Another capital campaign, which raised an additional $18 million in the mid-1980s, underpinned the construction of the Koret Health and Recreation Center in 1989, a state-of-the art facility to serve students, faculty and staff, alumni, and the surrounding community (vignette #133). Fr. Lo Schiavo's presidency was also marked by significant growth in the university's endowment, from $4.6 million in May 1976 to $38.7 million by May 1991, and by the elimination of the long-standing cumulative debt of the university. Beginning in 1980, every annual budget under Fr. Lo Schiavo was balanced, and by the time he left office in 1991, USF was on a solid financial base, a far cry from the institution's situation in 1976.

Ricky Curotto, completing his third term as President's Ambassadors Chairman, was honored at the organization's annual banquet on May 13, 1982, by USF President John Lo Schiavo, S.J. Curotto, who holds both a bachelor's degree and law degree from USF, has been associated with the university for over 50 years as a student, alumnus, trustee, and in fundraising leadership positions. He is a recipient of the USF's Alumni Association Distinguished Service Award and was inducted into the USF Athletic Hall of Fame. Curotto currently serves as chair of the trustee development committee. During The Campaign for USF, Ricky Curotto and his wife, Therese, gave a $2 million lead gift to improve and expand the athletic facilities and offices in the War Memorial Gymnasium.

Four academic vice presidents served under Fr. Lo Schiavo: Donald MacIntyre; Joseph Angilella, S.J.; William O. Binkley; and John Clark, S.J. With their support, and with the initiative and efforts of many deans, other administrators, and faculty members, a host of new academic programs was developed during Fr. Lo Schiavo's presidency (discussed in future vignettes). Among the more salient of those programs, however, were the hospitality management and telecommunications programs in the McLaren School of Business; the Swig Judaic Studies, Asia Pacific Studies, and sports and fitness management programs in the College of Arts and Sciences; and the environmental management and nonprofit organization management programs in the College of Professional Studies. Fr. Lo Schiavo was especially instrumental in the development of the College of Professional Studies during its fledging years in the early 1980s, and he initiated the efforts that led to the development of the Center for the Pacific Rim, which coordinates the university's Pacific Rim academic programs, research initiatives, and fundraising efforts. Several other academic programs were developed or enhanced under the stewardship of Fr. Lo Schiavo, the university's mission and goals statement was significantly revised, and the university as a whole had its accreditation reaffirmed by the Western Association of Schools and Colleges (WASC) in 1991, after a series of concerns were raised by WASC during the 1980s. During the final months of Fr. Lo Schiavo's presidency, Maureen Pryor was named executive director of campus ministry. She was the first woman and non-Jesuit to hold that position in the history of the university. She had served as associate director of campus ministry for the preceding two years.

No issue at USF during Fr. Lo Schiavo's presidency gained more local and national attention than did the president's decision to suspend the university's Division I intercollegiate basketball program in 1982, and then to reinstate it in 1985. Fr. Lo Schiavo, a former all-city basketball player at St. Ignatius High School, and a man vastly knowledgeable about the rich basketball heritage of USF, felt he had no alternative but to suspend the institution's basketball program after repeated warnings about recruitment and other violations of rules established by the National Intercollegiate Athletic Association (NCAA). These warnings predated Fr. Lo Schiavo's administration and extended into his term of office. Fr. Lo Schiavo's decision to suspend the basketball program, premised on ethical principles, was strongly supported by the board of trustees and the executive officers of the university. After the decision was announced in July 1982, hundreds of letters poured into the university, more than 90 percent of which supported the president's action. Editorials were also published throughout the nation regarding Fr. Lo Schiavo's decision, the vast majority of which were highly laudatory. In 1985, Fr. Lo Schiavo restored the basketball program under new leadership and more stringent guidelines. More than 25 years later, Fr. Lo Schiavo's decision to suspend the university's basketball program was still being referenced in articles addressing the topic of ethics and sports.

In February 1990, Fr. Lo Schiavo announced his retirement as president, though it would not be until June 1991 that his successor, John

Schlegel, S.J., would assume office after a lengthy nationwide search. Following in the footsteps of Fr. Charles Dullea, Fr. Lo Schiavo became the chancellor of the University of San Francisco, and he continues to serve the university today as an adviser to the president, as a key administrator for special projects, and as a significant leader in alumni relations and fundraising activities. During and after his presidency, his many national and local awards have brought visibility to the university. These awards include the Torch of Liberty Award from the Anti-Defamation League of B'nai B'rith, the Unity Medal from the United American Hebrew Congregation, and the Koret Foundation prize for contributions to higher education. He has also received honorary doctoral degrees from Hanyang University in Seoul, Korea, and from the University of San Francisco. In April 2004, Fr. Lo Schiavo received the USF Alumni Association's first Lifetime Achievement Award. The award was named in his honor, and future recipients of the John Lo Schiavo Lifetime Achievement Award will be individuals who exemplify the Jesuit ideals of courage, integrity, and selflessness and have acted on their convictions for the benefit of others irrespective of personal sacrifice.

In a letter to the USF community announcing his retirement from the presidency, Fr. Lo Schiavo addressed the university's legacy and promise for the future. "Catholic education is more relevant today than ever before," he wrote, "the need for moral and ethical standards in every sector of modern society has never been more evident…the USF of the future must resolutely continue its Catholic mission in the Jesuit tradition, if it is to provide the unique services to society which it has faithfully served for the past 135 years."

"We look forward to welcoming you to San Francisco in 1987," said USF President John Lo Schiavo, S.J., to Pope John Paul II, when Fr. Lo Schiavo and 80 other presidents of Jesuit institutions from throughout the world met with the Pope in Rome in 1985.

UNIVERSITY OF SAN FRANCISCO ARCHIVES

San Francisco Mayor Dianne Feinstein presents USF President John Lo Schiavo, S.J., with a proclamation declaring the week of October 13-19, 1980, as "University of San Francisco Week" throughout the city during the university's 125th anniversary celebration.

UNIVERSITY OF SAN FRANCISCO ARCHIVES

136

Twenty Years in the College of Arts and Sciences 1969–1989

BY THE EARLY 1970S, THE POSTWAR BABY BOOM THAT had buttressed college enrollments during the 1960s was coming to an end. Like many higher education institutions throughout the nation, the University of San Francisco witnessed a significant enrollment decline from 1969 to 1979. At USF, the College of Arts and Sciences was especially hard hit by the drop in enrollment. Overall, USF went from a total of 6,804 students in 1969 to 6,339 in 1979, a decrease of almost 7 percent. Traditional undergraduate enrollment in the College of Arts and Sciences during that same decade declined even more precipitously, from 2,788 in the fall of 1969 to 1,742 in the fall of 1979, a decrease of more than 37 percent. Against this backdrop of dramatically shrinking enrollments, faculty in the College of Arts and Sciences led the effort to form a faculty association at USF (vignettes #128 and #129), and administrators struggled to balance budgets, cut costs, and find new student markets.

Lloyd Luckmann, professor of political science at USF, served as dean of the College of Arts and Sciences from 1969 to 1975.

UNIVERSITY OF SAN FRANCISCO ARCHIVES

In 1969, Lloyd Luckmann, USF class of 1931, holder of both a doctorate and a law degree and professor of political science at USF for three years, became the new dean of the College of Arts and Sciences. He guided the college from 1969 to 1975, a challenging period in the institution's history. In 1975, Edward Stackpoole, S.J., an Oxford graduate and associate professor of English at USF since 1961, became the dean of the college, just as the USF Faculty Association was forming. Fr. Stackpoole served as dean for five years, was assistant vice president for academic affairs for one year, became rector of the Jesuit Community at USF, taught in the master's degree program in writing in the College of Arts and Sciences, and retired as professor emeritus of English in 1999. After retirement, he taught as an adjunct professor in the writing program in the College of Professional Studies.

Other notable faculty members who began their careers in the College of Arts and Sciences during the 1970s included Frederick Amory, who retired in 1994 as associate professor emeritus of English after a 21-year career at USF that included receipt of the Distinguished Research Award from the faculty association and the university; Joseph Angilella, S.J., who began his career at USF in 1979, served as vice president for academic affairs from 1979 to 1983, taught sociology until his retirement from the department in 2002, and is currently minister of the USF Jesuit community; Paul Bernadicou, S.J., who began a 30-year career in 1970 in the department of theology and religious studies and left as professor emeritus to become the rector of the Jesuit Community at Loyola Marymount University; and Cornelius Buckley, S.J., who taught history from 1973 to 2000 and left as professor emeritus of history.

Other prominent arts and sciences faculty who began at USF in the 1970s included Paula Campbell, who retired in 2000 as professor emerita of visual and performing arts, after a 25-year career at USF; Carol Chihara, professor emerita of biology, whose career of teaching and research at the institution began in 1975; Joseph Eagan, S.J., who taught in the theology and religious studies department from 1975 to 1993 and is currently associate professor

Edward Stackpoole, S.J., former associate professor of English, was dean of the College of Arts and Sciences from 1975 to 1980. After his tenure as dean, he served as assistant vice president for academic affairs, taught in the master's degree program in writing in the college, and became rector of the Jesuit Community at USF.

UNIVERSITY OF SAN FRANCISCO ARCHIVES

emeritus; William Jordan, professor emeritus of biology and environmental sciences, whose teaching and research career spanned the years 1973 to 2001; Richard Kozicki, who began a 23-year career in 1970 that included receipt of the Distinguished Teaching Award, and who is now professor emeritus of politics; and Michael Kudlick, professor emeritus of computer science, whose 23-year career at USF began in 1973, was highlighted by receipt of the Distinguished Teaching Award from the faculty association and the university in 1980, and who had a state-of-the art classroom named in his honor in 2002. Other notable faculty who began teaching in the 1970s at USF in the College of Arts and Sciences included Mary Neill, O.P., recipient of the Distinguished Teaching Award in 1979, and who retired in 1997 as associate professor emerita of theology and religious studies after 25 years of teaching; and Thomas Zavortink, professor emeritus of biology, who taught at USF from 1975 to 2001.

In the 1969–1970 academic year, the College of Arts and Sciences had 15 departments offering curricula leading to a bachelor's degree. In the arts, these included communication arts, economics, English, government, history, languages, philosophy, psychology, sociology, and theology. In the sciences, the departments were biology, chemistry, computer science, mathematics, and physics. The

Michael Kudlick taught in the computer science department for 23 years, won the Distinguished Teaching Award, and had a state-of-the art classroom named in his honor.

UNIVERSITY OF SAN FRANCISCO ARCHIVES

The growth in student diversity during the 1980s at USF is reflected in the 1989-1990 Chemical Society in the College of Arts and Sciences. From left to right, the students pictured here are Makoto Takahashi, Joe Leonetti, Ronald Limsin, Regina Matamoros, Stephanie Grzybicki, Luong Truong, Samson Berhane, Natalie Limson, and Ramsey Deeik.

Desmond FitzGerald taught philosophy at USF from 1948 to 1998, the longest teaching stint in the history of USF. As a professor emeritus, FitzGerald now teaches for the Fromm Institute for Lifelong Learning.

World English Center (WEC) began in 1974 under John Teeling, S.J., and in 1983, Edward Justen, S.J., became the director. The center was designed to enhance the English-language skills of international students prior to admittance to USF. Over the first 10 years of the WEC's operation, approximately 5,000 international students received English instruction, two-thirds of whom matriculated at USF. The WEC became the Intensive English Program (IEP) in 1987 and soon came under the direction Leila Kellow. By 1979, military science and physical education had been organized as distinct liberal arts departments, theology was expanded to include religious studies, and an ethnic studies program was added to the curriculum. In the sciences, computer engineering emerged during the 1970s as a separate program, though closely allied with physics. Although enrollment declined among traditional undergraduate students in virtually all of the departments during the 1970s with the exception of communication arts, growth in other areas of the university, including the evening college in the early 1970s, the College of Continuing Education in the late 1970s, and the School of Education throughout the decade, helped offset some of the consequent revenue decline for the university.

The College of Arts and Sciences was guided by three deans from 1979 to 1989: David Harnett, an historian with a Ph.D. from Harvard; William O. Binkley, who briefly served as acting dean of the college while he simultaneously held the post of academic vice president; and Carl Naegele, who had served as professor of physics and associate dean in the college before becoming dean. During this period, the undergraduate enrollment in the college continued its downward trend, from 1,742 students in the fall of 1979 to 1,221 students in the fall of 1989, another 30 percent decrease. Graduate enrollment in the college, however, increased slightly during this period, from 142 students in the fall of 1979 to 178 in the fall of 1989. Overall, enrollment at USF during these 10 years declined from 6,339 students in the fall of 1979 to 6,028 students in the fall of 1989, a decline of 5 percent. By that fall, however, the university was accelerating its graduate programming, and the College of Arts and Sciences, under Dean Naegele, increasingly explored the feasibility of offering select programs at the master's level. In 1987, for example, a marketing study was conducted for a potential master's program in Asia Pacific Liberal Studies; and in 1989, a marketing study was conducted on a potential master's degree in Sports and Fitness Management, a program initiative first proposed by George McGlynn, professor of exercise and sport science.

Over the next several years, these and other graduate programs were successful in bringing new students to the college. Moreover, by 1987, the master's program in writing, under Brenda Schildgen, and the master's program in environmental management, under Joseph Petulla, had been moved from the College of Professional Studies to the College of Arts and Sciences. In addition, freshman enrollment in the college began to increase during the last two years of Naegele's administration, from 238 first-time and transfer freshmen in the fall of 1987 to 321 by the fall of 1989. The College of Arts and Sciences also witnessed the development of several special institutes and programs during the 1970s and 1980s that continue to enrich the university community. These programs include the Judaic Studies Program, the St. Ignatius Institute, the Davies Forum, and the Center for the Pacific Rim (vignette #137).

The heart of the College of Arts and Sciences has always been its outstanding faculty. One way of recognizing achievements by faculty members is through the annual awarding of

the Distinguished Teaching Award and the Distinguished Research Award by the USF Faculty Association and the university. During the 1980s, College of Arts and Sciences faculty who won the Distinguished Teaching Award included Mary Neill, O.P., associate professor of theology and religious studies; Michael Kudlick, professor of computer science; Thomas Gruhn, professor of chemistry; Maureen O'Sullivan, professor of psychology; and Scott McElwain, professor of politics. From 1980 to 1989, recipients of the Distinguished Research Award in the college included Eugene Benton (twice), professor of physics; John Soderquist, professor of chemistry; Kevin Starr, professor of communication arts; James Brown, professor of biology; Jeffrey Lang, professor of mathematics; and John Elliott, a Lutheran minister and professor of theology and religious studies. Elliott won three distinguished faculty awards: for research in 1982 and in 2001, and for teaching in 1991.

Throughout the history of the College of Arts and Sciences, faculty members have been called upon to assume administrative leadership positions in the college and in the university, in addition to teaching and conducting research. The dean of the College of Arts and Sciences, for example, has usually come directly from the faculty. Following that tradition, the decade of the 1990s opened with a new dean for the college, Stanley Nel, professor of mathematics, who had also served as the associate dean for the sciences in the college. (Developments in the College of Arts and Sciences under dean Nel and his successor, Jennifer Turpin, will be highlighted in vignette #141.)

Beginning in 1969, Elisabeth Gleason taught history at USF for 28 years, published numerous books and articles, served as president of the American Society for Reformation Research, and was the first recipient of USF's Sarlo Prize, recognizing teaching excellence that exemplifies the ethical principles underlying the university's vision, mission, and values.

UNIVERSITY OF SAN FRANCISCO ARCHIVES

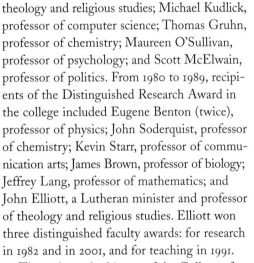

John Elliott, a Lutheran minister, taught theology and religious studies at USF for 34 years. He received the Distinguished Teaching Award and twice won the Distinguished Research Award.

UNIVERSITY OF SAN FRANCISCO ARCHIVES

Special Institutes and Programs

DURING THE 1970S AND 1980S, THE COLLEGE OF ARTS AND Sciences at the University of San Francisco developed a wide range of special institutes and programs designed to highlight the university's Jesuit and Catholic mission, cultivate external financial support, attract new students after years of declining enrollment, and enrich the university's programming for the broader community. Four programs that reflect these goals and still flourish today are the Judaic Studies Program, the St. Ignatius Institute, the Davies Forum, and the Center for the Pacific Rim.

Melvin Swig, businessman, developer, and philanthropist, funded the Swig Judaic Studies Program at USF in 1977. Swig joined the USF Board of Trustees in 1983 and became its chairman in 1985.

In 1977, Melvin Swig, a leading San Francisco businessman, developer, and philanthropist, funded the Swig Judaic Studies Program at USF. The new president of USF, John Lo Schiavo, S.J., became a close personal friend of Swig, and strongly supported the creation of the program. Fr. Lo Schiavo recommended that the Committee on Trustees of the USF Board of Trustees invite Swig to join the board. Swig accepted the board's offer in 1983, and he was named board chairman in 1985. Rabbi David Davis, who helped develop the program, was honored as the first occupant of the Swig Chair, becoming the first rabbi to occupy a full-time position in a theology department of any American Catholic university. Over the years, the Swig Judaic Studies program brought world renowned scholars to USF, including award-winning author Chaim Potok; Nobel Prize-recipients Saul Bellow and Elie Wiesel; Erik Erikson, winner of the Pulitzer and National Book awards; and Abba Eban, ambassador from Israel. In addition to sponsoring such visiting scholars, the Swig

Judaic Studies program also offered a variety of courses in Judaica through the department of theology and religious studies. The program also sponsored numerous community events, lectures, and seminars, and cooperated with various Jewish organizations in the Bay Area for educational programming. For example, the university has for years enjoyed a close relationship with Temple Emanu-el, a few blocks from the campus. In 1991, Melvin Swig, Fr. Lo Schiavo, and Rabbi Davis received the first Unity Medal given by the Union of American Hebrew Congregations in recognition of their life-long contributions to racial and religious harmony. In 1997, Andrew Heinze, professor of history, became director of the Swig Judaic Studies Program. He has continued to expand the educational endeavors of the program, including organizing immersion programs to Israel, developing new courses, and bringing prominent speakers to campus. In April 2000, for example, Cardinal Edward Idris Cassidy, president of the Vatican Commission for Religious Relations with the Jews, and Rabbi Norman Solomon, fellow in Modern Jewish Thought at the Oxford Centre for Hebrew and Jewish Studies, were guest speakers at the inaugural symposium of the Swig Judaic Studies Program Flannery-Hyatt Institute for Faith Understanding at USF. Under Professor Heinze's direction, the event sought to bring together representatives of the Jewish and Christian faiths for dialogue and mutual understanding. In the fall of 2003, Heinze was awarded USF's Ignatian Faculty Service Award.

The St. Ignatius Institute was founded in 1976 by Joseph Fessio, S.J. The institute was designed to provide an integrated curriculum based on the Great Books and authors of Western Civilization, with an emphasis on works in the Catholic tradition. Students in the St. Ignatius Institute lived together in the same residence hall, engaged in off-campus outings and spiritual retreats, and had special opportunities to study abroad during their junior year. From almost the beginning,

however, the leadership of the St. Ignatius Institute was embroiled in controversy with the leadership of the university and with many members of the Jesuit Community over a host of issues, including the integration of the institute with the rest of the university, the meaning of Catholicism in the context of a university setting, and the appropriate use of outside contributions to the institute. In 1987, John Lo Schiavo, S.J., then president of the university, removed Fr. Fessio as director of the institute. In 2001, Stephen A. Privett, S.J., USF's current president, likewise removed the director and associate director of the St. Ignatius Institute and replaced them with Paul Murphy, assistant professor of history (vignette #149). Professor Murphy has continued to develop the St. Ignatius Institute into a premier Great Books program grounded in Christian humanism and the Catholic tradition. The main curricular areas in the program are literature, philosophy, theology, fine arts, and history, with courses offered in a seminar/lecture format. Murphy has also expanded the study abroad options; has developed a synergistic relationship between the institute and the Catholic Studies Program, which he also directs; and has fully integrated all aspects of the program with the university.

The Davies Forum was organized and planned in the fall of 1981 by administrators and faculty in the College of Arts and Sciences. It was initially underwritten by part of a $1 million endowment from the noted San Francisco philanthropist Louise M. Davies, and was named in her honor. Two-thirds of her endowment was earmarked for the Davies Forum, and one-third was given to the St. Ignatius Institute. Mrs. Davies — who was deeply concerned about the frequent absence of ethics in public life during the 1970s — wanted to build a program that would raise ethical and moral questions with students, helping them define their own values as they moved into adulthood and assumed leadership positions in society. When her gift was announced publicly in

March 1982, Mrs. Davies noted, "We seem to have lost our ideals of a more just and ethical society." One goal of the Davies Forum, therefore, was to help produce future leaders who were committed to personal responsibility, public service, and ethical leadership.

Since its inception, the Davies Forum has included a semester-long seminar for advanced undergraduate students, taught by a USF professor, and a public lecture given by a national or international leader, designated as a Davies Fellow, drawn from the fields of government, religion, education, or business. In addition to a public lecture, Davies Fellows also participate in faculty colloquia and lead classroom discussions. The general theme of the Davies Forum is "A Search for Values in Contemporary America." The inaugural Davies Forum, under the direction of John Dywer, associate dean, College of Arts and Sciences, was offered in the spring semester of 1983. The first topic was "Perspectives on Nuclear Arms," a theme that coincided with a national debate on weapons systems and the release of the American Bishops' Pastoral Letter, "The Challenge of Peace: God's Promise and Our Response." The first seminar for students was coordinated by Clifton Albergotti, USF professor of physics, and the Davies Fellow was San Francisco Archbishop John Quinn, who spoke at USF the week before he traveled to Chicago for the meeting at which the American Bishops gave final approval to their famous pastoral letter. Over the years, other Davies Fellows have included Pierre Salinger, Dean Rusk, Betty Frieden, Jesse Jackson, and Ralph Nader. The Davies Forum is currently under the direction of Michael Bloch, associate dean for social sciences, College of Arts and Sciences.

In 1987, USF President John Lo Schiavo, S.J., spearheaded an effort to develop a Center for the Pacific Rim. Underpinning Fr. Lo Schiavo's

Barbara Bundy, the first executive director of USF's Center for the Pacific Rim, meets with Edward Malatesta, S.J., co-founder of USF's Ricci Institute for Chinese Western Cultural History.

UNIVERSITY OF SAN FRANCISCO ARCHIVES

decision to establish the center was the Jesuits' centuries-old connection to Asia, made even more relevant by the university's strategic geographic position in San Francisco as a gateway to the Pacific, the accelerating global economic influence of the Asian countries, the large number of Asian immigrants in California, and the growing number of Asian students at USF and alumni in Asia.

Fr. Lo Schiavo appointed a committee to study the feasibility of creating the center, and based on the committee's recommendation, the center was approved by the Board of Trustees in 1988. Barbara Bundy, former president of Dominican College, was chosen to be the first executive director, a position she still holds. Over the years, the Center for the Pacific Rim has grown enormously in its national and international prestige. Within the College of Arts and Sciences, and for the benefit of the university at large, the center currently administers graduate and undergraduate interdisciplinary Pacific Rim studies programs; presents lectures, seminars, conferences, and other special outreach activities for the community; and seeks to educate the extended USF community about the Pacific Rim region, including producing an online journal, *Asia Pacific: Perspectives.*

The Master of Arts in Asia Pacific Studies, the first evening program of its kind in the United States to serve working professionals, includes multidisciplinary coursework in the history, philosophy, politics, religions, literature, arts, societies, cultures, and economics of China, Japan, and Korea in the broader context of the Pacific Rim, which includes South and Southeast Asia, Australasia, Pacific Russia, and North and South America. Language options in the degree program include Japanese, Korean, and Mandarin. The center also administers a 12-unit graduate certificate in Asia Pacific Studies and a BA/BS-Master of Arts in Asia Pacific Studies, as well as coordinating an undergraduate minor in Asia Pacific Interdisciplinary Studies. The center also oversees

the Kiriyama Chair for Pacific Rim Studies, established in the College of Arts and Sciences through a $2 million endowment from the Reverend Seiyu Kiriyama, president of the Agon Shu Buddhist Association in Japan. The Center for the Pacific Rim is the only USF department that has two fully endowed chairs, one for teaching and one for research. The research arm of the center is the Ricci Institute for Chinese Western Cultural History, cofounded by the late Edward Malatesta, S.J., an international expert on the history of Catholicism and the Jesuits in China. The core of the institute's collection is an 85,000-volume Jesuit East Asian library. Albert Chan, S.J., retired senior research fellow at the institute and internationally recognized expert on the Ming Dynasty, was largely responsible for developing the Jesuit East Asian library and bringing it to USF from China. The library is ranked among the top 20 of its type in North America. The Ricci Institute administers the Charles W. Stewart Chair for Chinese-Western Cultural History and sponsors a unique Internet resource, the Ricci 21st Century Database on the History of Christianity in China. The Center for the Pacific Rim, including its Ricci Institute, offers approximately 30 public lectures, seminars, and conferences, both at USF and in China, on Pacific Rim issues.

138 Women's Athletics

THE 1970S WITNESSED INCREASED DEMANDS FOR GENDER equality throughout American society. In intercollegiate athletics, a catalyst for change was the passage in 1972 of Title IX, a federal law requiring parity between men's and women's athletic programs at the nation's colleges and universities. In 1976, twelve years after the University of San Francisco became completely co-educational, the institution fielded its first four women's athletic teams: in basketball, volleyball, tennis, and softball. In 1978, women's cross-country was added, followed by soccer in 1985, and golf in 1990. Rifle was introduced in 1984 as a co-educational sport.

Valerie Gillon celebrates after the Lady Dons basketball team won its second straight West Coast Conference Tournament in 1996. She was the WCC Tournament MVP in 1995 and 1996, the WCC Scholar-Athlete of the Year in 1996, and is a member of the USF Hall of Fame.

UNIVERSITY OF SAN FRANCISCO ARCHIVES

In 1976, the first female athletic scholarship was awarded to Suzanne Enos, a basketball and volleyball player. By the following year, there were three full scholarships available for female student-athletes. Anne Dolan, who had been appointed USF's first dean of women in 1964 and had been elevated to vice president for student development by the time the women's intercollegiate athletic program was inaugurated, worked hard to ensure the success of the program in its early years. After she retired, she established a scholarship fund in her name to assist student-athletes to complete their degrees.

Sandee Hill, who came to USF in 1979 to serve as associate director of athletics, has had a major impact on the development of women's athletics at USF. She has pursued gender equity for women's athletics, played a key role in the selection of coaches for the women's teams, served as the athletic department's business manager, sought scholarships for women athletes, and seen more than 2,000 women play intercollegiate sports while attending USF. She is currently senior associate director of athletics. In 1979, Hill's first year, there were 19 full scholarships earmarked for female student-athletes, but by the 2004–2005 academic year, the number of scholarships for female student-athletes had grown to 57, in large part through her efforts. In 1997, through Hill's work, and also that of Bill Hogan, USF's current executive director of athletics, USF received a perfect score from the NCAA review team on gender equity. To honor her service to students, Hogan instituted an award in Sandee Hill's name to go to an outstanding graduating student-athlete.

In 1978, a young woman from Sunnyvale by the name of Mary Hile led the Lady Dons basketball team to its first AIAW regional championship, which qualified the Lady Dons to play in the AIAW National Basketball Tournament. By the time she graduated in 1981, Hile had become a USF basketball legend. She was a two-time Academic All-American and was twice selected as a finalist for the Wade Trophy, awarded to the nation's top collegiate player. Among male or female players, Hile became the leading scorer in USF history, with 2,324 points. In 1986, she was the first woman inducted into the USF Athletic Hall of Fame, and her jersey is retired along with those of basketball greats Bill Russell, K.C. Jones, Bill Cartwright, Mike Farmer, and Phil Smith, and coaches Pete Newell and Phil Wolpert. Brittany Lindhe, who was later coached by Hile, was the second female basketball player to have her jersey retired. Hile currently holds 11 USF career records, nine single-season records, and five-single-game records. She also excelled in the classroom, receiving the Anne Dolan Award in 1979 and 1981 as USF's outstanding female student-athlete. After graduation, Hile played professional basketball in Italy for a year, was an assistant basketball coach at Long Beach State for three years, and spent one year each at the University of Hawaii and at Chaminade University as assistant coach and assistant athletic director, respectively.

By the opening of 1987–1988 season, Hile had returned to USF and joined her husband, Bill Nepfel, as co-head coach of the Lady Dons basketball team. Hile-Nepfel was named sole head coach following the 1999–2000 season, when Bill Nepfel was appointed USF's assistant athletic director for compliance and academic services. During her 17 seasons as USF's head or co-head basketball coach, her teams have won three West Coast Conference regular season championships and three West Coast Conference tournament titles and have qualified for three NCAA tournament berths.

During the 1995–1996 season, the Lady Dons made a dramatic run to the Sweet Sixteen with upset victories over 16th-ranked Florida and over 13th-ranked Duke. Although the Lady Dons were eventually defeated in the tournament, they became the first team in West

By the time she graduated in 1981, Mary Hile had become the leading scorer in USF history among female or male student-athletes, was a two-time All-American, and had won numerous other awards. In 1987, Mary Hile-Nepfel returned to USF as co-head coach of the Lady Dons basketball team with her husband Bill Nepfel. Their teams won three West Coast Conference regular season championships, three West Coast Conference tournament titles, and qualified for three NCAA Tournament berths. In 2000, Mary Hile-Nepfel was named sole head coach of the Lady Dons basketball team.

UNIVERSITY OF SAN FRANCISCO ARCHIVES

Kari McCallum was an all-conference MVP in women's cross-country and tennis and also played on the basketball and soccer teams. In 1992, she graduated from USF with a nearly straight-A average and received the Anne Dolan Award as the outstanding woman student-athlete of the year. She was inducted into the USF Athletic Hall of Fame in 2001.

UNIVERSITY OF SAN FRANCISCO ARCHIVES

Brittany Lindhe is one of two USF women basketball players to have their jerseys retired and is the second leading scorer in program history. She was selected to four All-West Coast Conference First Teams during her career, led the Lady Dons to three straight WCC Tournament Titles, and to three consecutive NCAA berths. She was a catalyst for the Lady Dons run to the NCCA Sweet 16 in 1996, was named the WCC's Female Student-Athlete of the Year in 1999, and inducted into the USF Hall of Fame in 2005.

UNIVERSITY OF SAN FRANCISCO ARCHIVES

Coast Conference history to advance to the third round of the NCAA tournament. At the conclusion of the season, the Lady Dons were ranked 16th in the nation in the USA Today/CNN Coaches poll, the first team to achieve such national ranking in the history of women's athletics at USF.

At the end of the 2001–2002 season, the Lady Dons appeared in the Women's National Invitation Tournament, the first NIT appearance in USF women's basketball history. Hile-Nepfel was twice selected to share with her husband WCC Coach of the Year honors. Her teams have amassed more victories than under any other coach in USF history, and she has coached 13 players who earned 25 All-West Coast Conference First Team honors, including Brittany Lindhe, the only four-time First Team selection honoree in league history. She and her staff also helped produce five West Coast Conference Freshmen of the Year. Throughout her years as head coach, Hile-Nepfel has ensured the academic success of her players and has seen many of her players selected to the West Coast Conference All-Academic team. Hile-Nepfel and her teams have also been active in community service, raising awareness and money, for example, in the fight against breast cancer; volunteering for clinics for the Special Olympics; and holding youth clinics throughout the Bay Area.

A touchstone for the pairing of athletics and academics in women's athletics is found in the career of Kari McCallum, who graduated from USF in 1992 with a nearly straight-A average. She played basketball, soccer, and tennis, and ran on the cross-country team. In tennis and in cross-country, she was an all-conference MVP and received the Anne Dolan Award as the outstanding woman student-athlete in 1992, and she was inducted into the USF Athletic Hall of Fame in 2001.

Women athletes at USF have excelled at other sports, as well. For three successive years, beginning in 2001, the Lady Dons' golf team has received NCAA tournament bids, and one of its players, Susie Laing, was named to the All-League First Team in 2002 and 2003. In 2001, the women's golf coach, Sara Range, was selected as WCC Coach of the Year by her peers. In women's tennis, Hilary Somers was named the 2003 West Coast Conference Coach of the Year after her team compiled a record of 15 wins and 6 losses and attained a fifth-place finish in the WCC tournament, the best finish for the USF women's tennis team in more than 10 years. In July 2003, Helen Lehman-Winters was named to head the men's and women's cross-country team and to serve as the first coach of the USF women's track team, beginning in the 2004–2005 season.

In October 2004, she was named West Coast Conference Coach of the Year; the first time in USF history a cross-country coach received this honor. In the same month, her cross-country team produced its best showing in program history in the 2004 West Coast Conference Championships: the women finished second and the men placed fifth. In the spring of 2004, the women's volleyball team made its first NCAA tournament appearance, following an outstanding season of 23 wins and only 8 losses, under new coach, Jeff Nelson. In September 2004, Brittanie Budinger, one of that team's star players, and the most dominant player in the history of the USF women's volleyball program, had her jersey retired. She was the first player in volleyball, the third woman in the school's history, and only the ninth individual at USF to earn this honor.

Today, women's intercollegiate athletics NCAA Division I teams include basketball, soccer, volleyball, golf, tennis, cross-country, track, and rifle. The University of San Francisco has recently renewed its commitment to female and male student-athletes in its new athletic initiative, "Reaching New Heights on the Hilltop," which was unanimously approved by the USF Board of Trustees on September 24, 2002. The program calls for a $2.6 million incremental increase over five fiscal years for athletic programs, including a greater number of scholarships for student-athletes and the addition of a women's track and field program. This increase in spending for athletics will come primarily from fundraising. The plan also includes an expectation for competitive success, and is strongly supported by USF President Stephen A. Privett, S.J.

On April 8, 2003, Robert Niehoff, S.J., USF's associate provost and vice president for planning and budget, was the featured speaker at the annual USF women's sports awards banquet. During the prior season, Fr. Niehoff had served as the chaplain for the women's basketball team. During his speech, Fr. Niehoff reflected on his experiences with the team during the year, including the appreciation he had developed for the time commitment of the players as they sought to balance practice, travel, games, and school work; the importance for the players of values such as faith, trust, teamwork, and confidence; and the responsibility the players bore in representing USF to the surrounding world. Fr. Niehoff thanked the players for representing the university and its values so effectively. "You have made great sacrifices and accomplished a great deal, individually and as teams," Fr. Niehoff said, "and know that you, too, have a critically important role in USF's mission to educate 'minds and hearts to change the world.' Thank you for helping USF to do that better."

Senior outside hitter Brittanie Budinger helped power the USF volleyball team to its best season ever and an NCAA tournament berth in the spring of 2004. She was the first volleyball player, the third woman in the university's history, and the ninth individual at USF to have her jersey retired.

UNIVERSITY OF SAN FRANCISCO ARCHIVES

Susie Laing, a star player on the Lady Dons' golf team, was named to the All-League First Team in 2002 and 2003.

UNIVERSITY OF SAN FRANCISCO ARCHIVES

The Athletic Tradition (PART I)

THE TRADITION BEGAN SOMETIME DURING THE FIRST years of St. Ignatius Academy, from 1855 to 1859, when Anthony Maraschi, S.J., the founding president of the institution tossed a couple of leather balls into a sand lot to give the few dozen boys who comprised the student body a bit of recreational relief from their rigorous academic studies. After the Civil War, baseball began its march up the road to becoming the national pastime, and it soon became popular in San Francisco, including at the renamed St. Ignatius College. Through the end of the 19th century, and into the early years of the 20th, baseball was a popular intramural sport among the boys and young men of St. Ignatius College, a school that encompassed education from upper elementary grades through college.

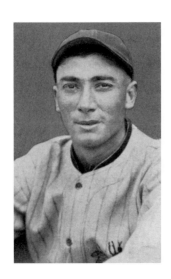

Tony Lazzeri, star second baseman for the world champion New York Yankees, teammate of Babe Ruth and Lou Gehrig, and native San Franciscan, coached the St. Ignatius College baseball team in the opening months of the 1928 season before he rejoined the Yankees. Lazzeri was later inducted into the National Baseball Hall of Fame.

UNIVERSITY OF SAN FRANCISCO ARCHIVES

In 1907, St. Ignatius College started to play baseball on a regular basis against other Bay Area high schools, colleges, community organizations, and businesses, using a mixture of high school and college students. By World War I, baseball had further expanded to include a host of Bay Area colleges in its schedule. The war, a decline in student enrollment, and financial problems at the school all coalesced, however, to bring a halt to the baseball program until 1924. During the remainder of the 1920s, the college baseball team resumed a full schedule against other colleges and even saw a few of its players make it briefly into the major leagues (vignette #79).

By 1909, various Bay Area teams, including St. Ignatius College, Santa Clara College, and the College of the Pacific, had formed the Catholic Athletic League, and high school

and college teams also began to compete in rugby and basketball. The basketball program grew in popularity during the second decade of the 20th century. It was briefly suspended during World War I, but roared back during the 1920s under Jimmy Needles, who was first a star player, then a player-coach, and finally head coach for the team. His era produced two West Coast basketball championships for St. Ignatius College, in 1928 and 1929. In 1936, Jimmy Needles coached the U.S. Olympic basketball team to a gold medal.

By 1917, the college's initial interest in rugby had waned and was replaced by American football, reflecting a trend in intercollegiate athletics throughout the nation. Because of World War I and financial problems at the school, football was suspended from 1918 until 1924, when it was revived under Needles, who,

as noted, also coached the basketball team.

In 1927, St. Ignatius College moved to its current location on Fulton Street, replaced its red and blue colors with green and gold, and brought its football program to a new level of competition when it joined the Far Western Conference. The football program, like the rest of the athletic programs at the college, was largely managed by students, with guidance from the head coach and the athletic director. In the late 1920s, the college's track team also began intercollegiate competition on a limited schedule, and the varsity tennis team played its first three intercollegiate matches in 1928. Until 1931, all of the college's athletic teams were known as the Gray Fog. In that year, a sports writer for the *Foghorn*, Jack Rhode, came up with a new name that has lasted to this day: the Dons.

St. Ignatius College changed its name to the University of San Francisco in 1930. Despite the depression of the 1930s, the USF basketball, football, baseball, track, and tennis teams continued throughout the decade with full schedules against West Coast college teams, sometimes facing teams from other regions of the nation, as well. During the 1930s, varsity rugby was still played at USF, golf was initiated, and boxing made a brief appearance as an intercollegiate sport. The

USF soccer program began in the fall of 1930, and the next year the Dons tied Stanford for the Pacific Coast Soccer League championship. From 1932 to 1936, the USF soccer team won five straight conference championships. During four of those years, the team was captained by All-American player Gus Donoghue, who returned to coach the team in 1941.

World War II brought a temporary halt to the USF athletic programs, but after the war, the athletic programs were revived and soon entered a golden age, beginning with the 1948–1949 season (vignette #105). During that year, the USF basketball team, coached by Pete Newell and led by star player Don Lofgran, won the National Invitational Tournament (NIT), held in New York City. USF's first national intercollegiate championship was chronicled by sports information director Pete Rozelle, who later became the commissioner of the National Football League. In 1949, the USF tennis team, coached by George Kraft, and starring Art Larsen and

Coach Pete Newell (right) and Don Lofgran (left) celebrate USF's 1949 NIT basketball championship. Lofgran was voted the NIT tournament's most valuable player.

UNIVERSITY OF SAN FRANCISCO ARCHIVES

During the 1920s, Jimmy Needles (behind the wheel) was a star player, player-coach, and eventually head coach for the St. Ignatius College basketball team. In 1928 and 1929, his teams won the West Coast basketball championship. Needles was also head coach for the college's football team pictured here, and in 1936, he coached the U.S. Olympic basketball team to a gold medal in Berlin, Germany.

UNIVERSITY OF SAN FRANCISCO ARCHIVES

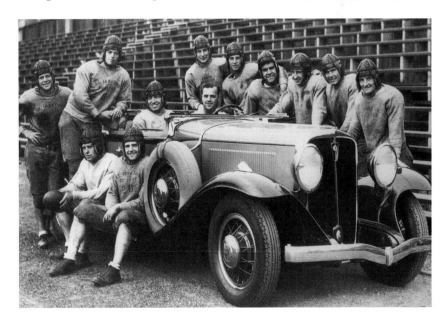

(Above) The 1954-1955 USF basketball team won the NCAA Championship and began a 60-game winning streak that led to another NCAA Championship during the 1955-1956 season. The winning streak extended partway into the next season, and established a new NCAA record up to that time. It is still the second longest winning streak in NCAA history. Pictured here is the 1955 Championship team. In the top row, left to right, are coach Phil Wolpert, K.C. Jones, Dick Lawless, Gordon Kirby, Bill Bush, and team manager, Ray Healy. In the middle row, left to right, are Tom Nelson, Stan Buchanan, Bill Russell, Jerry Mullen, Jack King, and Bob Wiebusch. In the bottom row, left to right, are Hal Perry, Steve Balchios, Rudy Zannini, and Warren Baxter.

(Right) Mike Farmer joined Bill Russell, K.C. Jones, and Hal Perry on the 1955–1956 USF basketball team, which had an undefeated season and won its second straight NCAA Championship. He helped take the 1956–1957 team to the final four in the 1957 NCAA Championship Tournament, was an All-American in 1958, played seven seasons in the NBA, had his USF jersey retired, helped coach the women's basketball team, and has remained active in athletic development.

Sam Match, won the National Collegiate Athletic Association (NCAA) championship. The prior season, tennis player Harry Likas won USF's first individual NCAA championship. Another athletic title was claimed for the Dons in 1949, when the USF rifle team won the William Randolph Hearst Trophy as the best in the western region. During the 1949–1950 season, the USF soccer team won the Northern California Conference title for the second year in a row, went to the first Intercollegiate Soccer Bowl game ever played, and emerged as co-national champions.

The USF football program reached the pinnacle of its success in 1951, when, under coach Joe Kuharich, and led by Ollie Matson, Burl Toler, Gino Marchetti, and Bob St. Clair, the team compiled a perfect undefeated season, only to be denied a post-season bowl bid because of racism: the team was not permitted to bring its two African American players (Matson and Toler) to the one bowl game it was tentatively invited to play in, and the team voted to reject the offer. For financial reasons, the football program was discontinued the following year (vignette #106). The football program was revived briefly in the late 1960s on a limited scale, but once again it proved too expensive to run; football was eliminated for good in 1970.

By the mid-1950s, the USF basketball program had developed into the best in the nation, and the team, coached by Phil Wolpert and led by future NBA greats Bill Russell, K.C. Jones, and Mike Farmer, won two consecutive NCAA national championships, in 1955 and 1956, and set a new college basketball record, extending into the 1956–1957 season of 60 straight victories (vignette #115). The success during these years helped the school raise the money to construct War Memorial Gymnasium in 1958 and provided national and international visibility for the university. The basketball triumphs of 1955 and 1956 coincided with the celebration of the 100th anniversary of the founding of the university during the 1955–1956 academic year. The fusion of the academic and the athletic traditions of the University of San Francisco could not have been better timed.

The Athletic Tradition (PART II)

THE UNIVERSITY OF SAN FRANCISCO'S ATHLETIC TRADITION was further enhanced as it began its second century in 1955. The basketball team captured its second consecutive national championship at the close of the 1955–1956 season and ran its winning steak to a record-setting 60 games before its first defeat midway through the 1956–1957 season (vignette #139). At the close of that season, the team won the Far West Regional Tournament and went to the NCAA tournament, where it finished third.

Although 1956 was the last year the basketball team captured an NCAA championship, it has subsequently had many outstanding seasons and produced a host of star athletes. Between the 1955–1956 season and the 2003–2004 season, the team won 13 West Coast Conference titles and secured NCAA Tournament berths 13 times. From 1962 through 1966, under coach Pete Peletta, the Dons won three straight conference championships. During the 1970s, the team, coached by Bob Gaillard, and led by star players Phil Smith and Bill Cartwright, won seven conference championships. Smith, who played from 1971 to 1974 and was named All–West Coast Conference player for three years in a row and an All-American in his senior year, and Cartwright, who played from 1975 to 1979 and was a three-time All-American and the leading scorer in men's basketball history, both had their numbers retired by USF. Both had illustrious professional basketball careers after leaving USF.

The most recent trip to the NCAA tournament by the USF basketball team was in the 1997–1998 season, when coach Philip Mathews led

Bill Cartwright was the USF men's basketball team all-time leading scorer, was a three-time All American from 1976 to 1979, played for 16 years in the NBA, led the Chicago Bulls to three NBA titles, and became head coach for the Bulls.

UNIVERSITY OF SAN FRANCISCO ARCHIVES

his team to victory in the West Coast Conference Tournament and to an NCAA tournament berth, the first NCAA tournament appearance for the school since basketball was resumed in 1985–1986 following a three-year suspension of the program (vignette #135). Overall, the USF men's basketball program has produced 18 All-American players and 23 of its athletes have gone on to careers in the NBA. In April 2004, Jessie Evans, a highly successful basketball coach from the University of Louisiana at Lafayette, was named USF's new basketball coach. During the 2004-2005 season, he led the team to a record of 16 wins and 13 losses, and to its first postseason invitation (to the NIT) since 1998. The team got its first

Phil Smith led the USF men's basketball team in scoring from 1971 to 1974, was an All-American in 1974, and led the Golden State Warriors to their only NBA championship in 1975.

UNIVERSITY OF SAN FRANCISCO ARCHIVES

The 1969 USF soccer team compiled a regular season 11-0-2 record, won the Western Regionals, were victorious in the NCCA semi-finals, and reached the NCCA finals where they were finally defeated. The team won the NCAA national championship in 1966, 1975, 1976, and 1980. Stephen Negoesco (standing at the far right in the second row) was their coach during these years.

UNIVERSITY OF SAN FRANCISCO ARCHIVES

post-season victory in 26 years when it defeated Denver 69–67 in the first round of the NIT before losing to Cal State Fullerton in the second round.

The USF soccer team continued its winning tradition from the 1930s into the beginning of the university's second century. The team, under Gus Donoghue, won its 11th consecutive conference championship in 1958. In that year, the team was undefeated and untied during the regular season. The USF soccer team under coach Steve Negoesco won 13 conference championships and four national titles during his coaching career, which spanned 1962 to 2000. In 1988, a soccer stadium was constructed on campus and named in Coach Negoesco's honor (vignette #115). One of his former star players, Erik Visser, took over as head coach, and led the team to another West Coast Conference Championship in 2004. In November 2004, Visser was named WCC Coach of the Year, and in December of that year, he was named the National Soccer Coaches Association of America (NSCAA) Far West Region Men's Coach of the Year. The team's star forward, Aaron Chandler, was named WCC Player of the Year, and the team was ranked 14th in the nation.

Women's athletics at USF got its start in 1976 with the initiation of basketball, volleyball, tennis, and softball (vignette #138). The program blossomed under the leadership of Sandee Hill, associate director of athletics, and its basketball program gained regional and national visibility under co-coaches Mary Hile-Nepfel (previously a star player for the Lady Dons basketball team) and Bill Nepfel. From 1987 to 2000, this husband and wife team led women's basketball teams at USF to three West Coast Conference titles, three NCAA tournament berths, and had one Sweet Sixteen appearance. At the end of the 2000–2001 season, Mary Hile-Nepfel took her team to its first NIT post-season appearance.

Dante Benedetti coached

the USF baseball team for 29 years, ending his coaching career in 1980, after accepting one dollar per year in payment for his services. Benedetti, a successful restaurant owner in San Francisco, had grown up in North Beach playing baseball with Joe DiMaggio. Benedetti is a member of the USF Athletic Hall of Fame, and in 1985, the USF baseball diamond was named in his honor. By the end of the 1990s, USF baseball was again becoming competitive in WCC play. In the 2003 season, it missed the playoffs by one game and recorded 17 conference victories, the second highest number of conference wins ever. Several of USF's baseball stars of the last five years have gone on to professional baseball careers. During the 1999 season, Taggert Bozied set eight school records in baseball, led the nation in home runs, with 30, and was the first West Coast Conference player ever to win the Triple Crown, when he led the conference in home runs, RBIs, and batting average. He was drafted by the San Diego Padres and is currently in their farm system. Jesse Foppert, a star at USF in 2001, was drafted by the San Francisco Giants and pitched his first regular major league game in April 2003. In June 2004, a record four former USF baseball players (Kevin Rose, Joe Jacobitz, Armand Gaerlan, and Derek Tate) were selected in the Major League Baseball draft. In 2005, the USF baseball team set a single-season school record for victories, going 38–18 for the season and finishing a game back of Pepperdine in the WCC after narrowly losing to the Waves in the final game of the season.

There have been many other recent achieve-

ments by USF athletic teams and individuals. Former USF golfer Todd Fischer qualified for the PGA tour in 2003. During his career at USF in the early 1990s, he was selected four times as an All–West Coast Conference player. In 1991, he won the West Coast Conference individual title, and in 1992, he won the Western Intercollegiate Championship and the Pacific Coast Amateur Championship. The men's and women's golf teams recently both made appearances in NCAA tournaments. Sara Range, the women's golf coach, was named Coach of the Year in 2001, led her teams to two West Coast championships, and qualified for the NCAA regional championships in three consecutive seasons, from 2001 to 2003. In October 2004, Helen Lehman-Winters, head coach for the men's and women's cross-country team, was named WCC Coach of the Year, concurrently leading her team to its best showing in program history in the 2004 WCC Championships. In the spring of 2004, the women's volleyball team, coached by Jeff Nelson, and led by star player Brittanie Budinger, made its first NCAA tournament appearance, and Budinger became only the ninth individual in USF history to have her jersey retired.

The University of San Francisco currently offers 104 athletic scholarships to the 208 student-athletes at the institution. Fifty-seven are for female athletes and 47 are for men. The USF athletic program continues to take great pride in the academic accomplishments of its student-athletes and in their participation in the full range of campus activities, including volunteer and community service work. During the 2003–2004 academic year, USF student-athletes set two new school academic records: 85 individuals were named to the West Coast Conference Academic Honor Roll by maintaining a grade point average between 3.0 and 4.0, and 16 were selected to WCC sport all-academic teams, an honor which requires a minimum 3.2 grade point average and designation as a key player in competition.

Today, the University of San Francisco's NCAA Division I teams include men's basketball, soccer, baseball, golf, tennis, cross-country, and rifle, and women's basketball, cross-country, golf, soccer, rifle, tennis, volleyball, and track. The athletic program is part of the Division of University Advancement, under Vice President Dave Macmillan; the executive director of athletics is Bill Hogan, who has held that position since 1991. On September 24, 2002, the USF Board of Trustees approved a new athletic mission and goals statement, "Reaching New Heights on the Hilltop," arguably the most important document in the history of USF athletics. The goals articulated in the document include the following: to comply with the letter and spirit of all university, conference, and NCAA rules and guidelines; to set high standards for winning at the conference and national level, including an overall first- or second-place finish in the West Coast Conference Commissioner's Cup; to enhance the visibility of the institution through athletics; to increase the number of undergraduates actively engaged in athletic teams and support services; to use athletics as a force for community building; and to enhance the funding for the athletic programs. Finally, the new statement calls for the continuing development of Jesuit values in student-athletes through academic achievement, active engagement in the university community, and leadership in the service of others. Today's USF student-athletes exemplify these values that extend back to the founding of the institution in the mid-19th century. The tradition continues.

Co-Champions of the West Coast Conference, the 1995-1996 Lady Dons basketball team became the first women's team in WCC history to advance to the third round of the NCAA tournament. The team was ranked 16th in the nation in the USA Today/CNN Coaches poll, the first nationally ranked team in the history of women's athletics at USF. In the front row, left to right, are athletic trainer Tresa McIlnay, graduate assistant coach Mark Nagel, co-head coach Mary Hile-Nepfel, co-head coach Bill Nepfel, assistant coach Tami Adkins, and student assistant Donna Spragan. In the middle row, left to right, are Amy Voilard, Jamie Shadian, Brittany Lindhe, Renee Demirdjian, Audra Souther, Andrea Kagie, Michele Matthews, Deana Itow, and student assistant Dan Pardi. In the top row, left to right, are Julie Murdent, Tinna Nielson, Valerie Gillon, Sarah Wanless, and Chelsea Richardson.

UNIVERSITY OF SAN FRANCISCO ARCHIVES

Enhancing the College of Arts and Sciences 1990–2005

AS THE FALL SEMESTER OF 1990 GOT UNDERWAY AT THE University of San Francisco, total enrollment in its College of Arts and Sciences stood at 1,496 undergraduate and graduate students — 289 fewer students than in the fall of 1980. By the fall of 2004, however, enrollment in the college was 3,269, an increase of 119 percent in 14 years. During the same 14-year period, overall student enrollment at USF had increased from 6,331 to 8,274, a 31 percent gain. The enrollment growth during the 1990s and into the first years of the 21st century can be attributed to many factors: a modest national increase in the number of potential college-age students; a robust American economy, at least through 2000; and outstanding recruitment efforts by the admission staff at USF. Within the College of Arts and Sciences, the enrollment increase could also be traced to new leadership, aggressive recruitment of new students, a plethora of outstanding new faculty, and an expansion of attractive new majors, minors, and special programs and institutes.

In October 1990, Stanley Nel was named dean of the College of Arts and Sciences. A Rhodes Scholar, Nel did his undergraduate and graduate work at the University of Cape Town in South Africa, specializing in applied mathematics, mathematical physics, and cosmology. He joined USF in 1983 as an assistant professor of mathematics, was promoted to associate professor with tenure, chaired the mathematics department, was promoted to full professor, and served as associate dean for the sciences before becoming the college's dean.

Under Nel's stewardship, and in cooperation with academic services and the admission office, the College of Arts and Sciences developed and implemented an aggressive student recruitment program that dramatically increased the college's enrollment. Their efforts included faculty phone-a-thons to accepted students to increase the percentage of students who actually enrolled, science outreach programs for local high school students and their teachers, science open houses on the USF campus, and beginning in 1994, an annual Bay Area Math Meet, a day-long mathematical problem-solving contest for high school students.

During Nel's tenure as dean, several new programs were instituted in the college and the existing programs strengthened to attract new students. At the undergraduate level, programs initiated between 1990 and 2003 included bachelor's degrees in environmental studies, Latin American studies, media studies, performing arts, a dual degree in physics and engineering with the University of Southern California, a cooperative bachelor's degree in the fine arts and in architecture with the California College of Arts and Crafts, a joint degree in politics and a juris doctor with the USF School of Law, and a dual degree teacher preparation program combining a bachelor's degree with a master's degree and a teaching credential from the USF School of Education.

Existing undergraduate degree programs were enhanced through a rigorous academic program review process. By 2003, the undergraduate degree programs, in addition to the new programs, included biology, chemistry, communication studies, computer science, economics, English, environmental science, exercise and sport science, fine arts, French, history, mathematics, philosophy, physics, politics, psychology, sociology, Spanish, theology and religious studies, and visual arts. The college developed in several new areas as well, with the addition of the Center for Latino Studies in the Americas, the Catholic Studies Program, and the Leo T. McCarthy Center for Public Service and the Common Good (vignette #149). Moreover, a host of international programs were initiated in the college under Nel's administration (vignette #148). Finally, several living-learning communities were initiated or strengthened in the College of Arts and Sciences. These communities included the Martín-Baró Scholars Program, the Erasmus Project, and the Phelan Multicultural Program.

The Martín-Baró Scholars Program exemplifies the university's and the college's focus on social justice and service to others. In the fall of 2002, 33 freshmen from diverse ethnic backgrounds entered the university as Martín-Baró Scholars, a program sponsored by the James Irvine Foundation and directed by Gerardo Marín, formerly senior associate dean in the College of Arts and Sciences, and now associate provost for the university. The Martín-Baró Scholars Program was based in a living-learning community of socially involved scholars in the spirit of Ignacio Martín-Baró,

one of the Jesuits killed in El Salvador in 1989. In addition to living in the same residence hall during their freshman year, the students participated in an integrated course specially designed to explore issues of social justice and diversity through reflective service learning. The students also received academic and social support and advising from peer and faculty mentors and engaged in a variety of social justice activities. After a successful first year, the Martín-Baró Scholars Program was continued into the students' sophomore year, and other program components were added. A second group of Martín-Baró scholars entered USF as freshmen in the fall of 2003, and a third group in the fall of 2004.

The Erasmus Project, named after the Renaissance humanist Erasmus of Rotterdam,

Stanley Nel (left) served as dean of the College of Arts and Sciences from 1990 to 2003, a period of significant growth in student enrollment, faculty recruitment, and program development in the college. Here he is introducing fellow South African and Nobel Peace laureate Desmond Tutu, Anglican Archbishop of Cape Town, who keynoted an Interfaith Conference for Youth held in June 1995 at USF, part of the United Nations 50th anniversary celebration. In 2003, Nel was appointed USF's first vice president for international relations.

In 2003, Jennifer Turpin became the first female dean in the history of the College of Arts and Sciences. She began at USF in 1991 as an assistant professor of sociology, published extensively, helped found the women's studies program at USF, chaired the sociology department, and was promoted to full professor while serving as associate dean in the college.

UNIVERSITY OF SAN FRANCISCO ARCHIVES

Roberta Johnson, professor of political science, received a Woodrow Wilson fellowship to pursue her Ph.D. at Harvard; was a Fulbright professor at the University of Indonesia; published numerous articles, book chapters, and books; and received the USF College of Arts and Sciences Service Award in 2003. In 2005, she completed her 20th year of teaching at USF.

UNIVERSITY OF SAN FRANCISCO ARCHIVES

brings together sophomores from the College of Arts and Sciences, the School of Nursing, and the School of Business and Management in a community of learners that live on the same residence hall floor, take at least one course in common, participate in community service, and develop a mentoring relationship with faculty members who have offices on the same floor. The Phelan Multicultural Program is a living-learning community collaboratively run by the College of Arts and Sciences, the Office of Residence Life, and Multicultural and International Student Services. Each year, 24 students spend a year building a multicultural community in and out of the classroom. In both the fall and spring semesters, the students take a core or elective course in common that focuses on cross-cultural communication, critical thinking, and examination of social issues. Members of the community also engage in a weekend retreat each semester and attend weekly seminars led by guests from USF and the surrounding community.

All undergraduate students at the University of San Francisco are required to complete the new core curriculum, largely taught by full-time faculty members in the College of Arts and Sciences. In the spring of 1998, Jim Wiser, USF's provost and academic vice president, authorized the joint university general education

curriculum committee to recommend revisions to the university's general education curriculum. By 2002, the new core curriculum was implemented and learning outcomes were identified by faculty in their respective disciplines. The new core curriculum provides students with choices in selecting courses in the following core curriculum areas: visual and performing arts, the humanities, social sciences, math, and the natural sciences. All students are also required to complete foundation courses in speaking and writing, a service-learning course, and a cultural diversity course. The service-learning and cultural diversity requirements are directly derived from the current Vision, Mission, and Values Statement of the university (vignette #150).

At the graduate level, several new programs were also developed under Nel's administration. The master's program in Asia Pacific liberal studies saw its first 20 students begin in the fall of 1993, and the first 24 students in the new master's program in sports and fitness management began in the spring of 1992. In addition to these new graduate programs, the existing programs were strengthened, including the master's degrees in economics, theology, writing, biology, chemistry, computer science, and environmental science.

As with all the schools and colleges at the University of San Francisco, the faculty

members are at the heart of the teaching, research, and service to students that take place in the college. When Nel became dean, there were approximately 100 full-time faculty members in the College of Arts and Sciences. By the fall of 2003, that number had grown to 186. With the addition of new faculty positions, coupled with departures and retirements, Nel had an opportunity to significantly rebuild the college's full-time faculty base. The current faculty in the college is exemplary by any measure: research productivity, curricular reform, and teaching excellence. From 1990 to 2005, faculty members in the College of Arts and Sciences who have won the Distinguished Research Award include Frederic Amory and Rachel Crawford in English, Andrew Woznicki in philosophy, Thomas Zavortink and Daneb Karentz in biology, Elisabeth Gleason and Elliot Neaman in history, John Colbey and Jeff Curtis in chemistry, Gerardo Marín in psychology, Robert Elias and Shalendra Sharma in politics, Tristan Needham in mathematics, Stephen Roddy and Noriko Nagata in modern and classical languages, Bruce Wydick in economics, John Elliott in theology and religious studies, and Horatio Camblong in physics.

With regard to the Jesuit legacy and value system of USF, faculty service to the institution and to the community is acknowledged in a different annual award first given in 1992. The Ignatian Service Award recognizes extraordinary commitment to students, the university, and the community. College of Arts and Sciences faculty members who have won this award include Lois Lorentzen in theology and religious studies, Pamela Balls Organista in psychology, Thomas Lucas, S.J., in visual and performing arts, Andrew Heinze in history, Kevin Chun in psychology, and Hartmut Fischer in economics.

Since 1990, faculty members in the College of Arts and Sciences who have won the Distinguished Teaching Award include James Brown in biology, John Elliott and Lois Lorentzen in theology and religious studies, Richard Davis and Rhonda Parker in communication arts, Richard Kozicki,

Shalendra Sharma, and Brian Weiner in politics, Jennifer Turpin in sociology, Tami Spector and Claire Castro in chemistry, the late Robert Makus in philosophy, Tracy Seeley in English, and Thomas MacDonald in environmental studies. Since 1997, the university has also awarded the Sarlo Prize to recognize teaching excellence that exemplifies the ethical principles underlying the university's vision, mission, and values. College of Arts and Sciences faculty members who have won this award include Elisabeth Gleason in history, the late Robert Makus in philosophy, Francis Buckley, S.J., in theology and religious studies, Patricia Schulz in biology, Jack Lendvay in environmental science, and Alexandra Amati-Camperi in visual and performing arts.

At the end of the spring semester of 2003, Nel left the dean's position to become USF's vice president for international relations, a new position designed to oversee international student recruitment, alumni and major donor cultivation, and program development for USF students studying abroad. After a nationwide search, Jennifer Turpin, associate dean for arts and humanities in the College of Arts and Sciences for the prior five years, was selected to be the new dean. Turpin, one of the many faculty members hired during Nel's administration, began at USF in 1991 as an assistant professor of

Gerardo Marín (second from the right) is currently associate provost and professor of psychology and Latin American Studies at USF, having started his career at USF in 1982 as an assistant professor of psychology and rising through the College of Arts and Sciences to become its senior associate dean. He has written more than 135 books and articles on topics related to Hispanics, including cultural norms, risk behaviors, and culturally appropriate methodology; obtained various federal and private grants; was instrumental in the development of numerous new academic programs, including the Center for Latino Studies in the Americas and the Martín-Baró Scholars Program; and has developed many international programs. In 2005, he received an honorary doctorate from Péter Pázmány Catholic University in Budapest, Hungary. In this 1998 photo, Marín is pictured with four other arts and sciences faculty members who served on the governing board of the Center for Latino Studies in the Americas, including (left to right) the late Esther Madriz, sociology; Eduardo Mendieta, philosophy; Michael Stanfield, history; and Lois Lorentzen, theology.

UNIVERSITY OF SAN FRANCISCO ARCHIVES

On April 4, 2004, more than 350 students, community volunteers, and faculty members from the USF computer science department in the College of Arts and Sciences organized the first "flash mob supercomputer" event in history. The supercomputer created in USF's Koret and Recreation Center linked approximately 670 computers to two portable generators and performed 180 billion mathematical operations per second. The event was reported by more than 200 media outlets worldwide, including the *New York Times,* which described the event in a front-page story.

USF MAGAZINE, SPRING 2004

sociology. She was a founding member and coordinator of the women's studies program at USF, published extensively, received tenure and promotion to associate professor, and served as chair of the sociology department before becoming associate dean. As associate dean, she oversaw the development and implementation of the new core curriculum, the conversion of courses from three to four units, and the undergraduate and graduate writing programs, among other responsibilities. She was promoted to full professor while serving as associate dean. Turpin's selection as dean of the College of Arts and Sciences marked the first time in the history of the university that a woman has occupied that position. Her associate deans currently include Michael Bloch, Brandon Brown, Dean Rader, and Peter Tongi, S.J.

Since becoming dean, Turpin has overseen the creation of several new programs in the college, including master's degree programs in international and development economics, financial analysis, and Internet engineering; bachelor's degree programs in international studies, Japanese studies, and Asian Studies; and the Environmental Living and Learning Community. This new living-learning community, implemented in the fall of 2004 by the environmental studies department, is housed in Gillson Hall, and requires students to include one course in their academic program each semester that focuses on environmental issues. The program also mandates community service and provides for field visits throughout the Bay Area.

In 2004, the college also received a $1 million gift from Joan and Ralph Lane to endow a center for Catholic social thought at USF. The Joan and Ralph Lane Center for Catholic Studies and Social Thought will be directed by professor Paul Murphy and associate director Julia Dowd. In addition to the Lanes' gift, the family of Chancellor John Lo Schiavo, S.J. agreed that its fully endowed chair, the Joseph and Anna Lo Schiavo Chair, be located within the Lane Center for Catholic Studies and Social Thought. With these two gifts, USF will be able to focus the insights of Catholic social thought on contemporary problems to the benefit of the university community and society at large.

The current programs and curricula offered by the College of Arts and Sciences are rooted in the Jesuit tradition of academic excellence and values-based education stretching back five centuries. For 150 years, the arts and sciences curriculum in the city's Jesuit institution of higher education has reflected that tradition and served as the nucleus for student learning. Over the last decade, the rapid growth of courses in the college that embrace a service learning component is a contemporary manifestation of the Jesuit tradition of combining education with service to others. The upsurge in international programs in the college in recent years is also consistent with a long history of Jesuit education and values carried around the world. The reflection of that history at USF is captured in the Vision, Mission, and Values Statement that calls for educating "leaders who will fashion a more humane and just world."

From Kendrick Hall to Angkor Wat, the Quest for Global Justice

142

DURING THE EARLY 1970S, THE UNIVERSITY OF SAN Francisco was seriously affected by a decline in the number of traditional college-age students, the erosion of federal support for higher education, and national economic problems marked by runaway inflation and a major recession. Like many higher education institutions, USF saw its overall enrollment decline, its costs increase, and its deficit swell. USF's School of Law was not immune to the university's overall difficulties, even though law school enrollment continued to increase. Older students, representing the last of the population cohort

The entire faculty of the USF School of Law was included in this 1971 photo. In the front row, left to right, are Dean C. Delos Putz, Stan Darling, and Raymond Coyne. In the second row, left to right, are Francis Walsh, Jack Bonanno, James Cox, Cherie Gaines, and Elizabeth Anne Quigley. In the back row, left to right, are Eldon Reiley, Joseph Henke, J. Thomas McCarthy, and Ted Rhodes.

UNIVERSITY OF SAN FRANCISCO ARCHIVES

born immediately after World War II, were at a prime age to return to graduate and professional schools, attorneys commanded high salaries, and many students saw the law as a major vehicle for changing society. Enrollment in the USF School of Law burgeoned, from 504 students in the fall of 1970 to 769 students in the fall of 1976, a 53 percent increase. During that same period, enrollment for the entire university declined 14 percent, from 6,799 to 5,818.

In the spring of 2004, a group of law students and USF law professor Constance de la Vega traveled to the United Nations Commission on Human Rights in Geneva to present oral and written statements on several international human rights issues, including the trafficking of women and children, domestic violence, arbitrary detention, the rights of migrant workers, and the juvenile death penalty. Pictured here (kneeling from left) are USF law students Sarah Canepa and Jen Naegele, and (standing from the left) Boalt Hall law student Lynsay Skiba, USF law students Jacqueline Brown Scott, Jean Covington, Nikki Belushko, and Professor de la Vega.

USF LAWYER, FALL 2004

In 1971, C. Delos Putz, a 33-year-old assistant dean at New York University's School of Law, was selected to be the new dean of the USF School of Law. Putz immediately set about creating economic stability for the law school by developing the school's first independent budget. With a separate budget, the law school became responsible for balancing its own expenses and revenue and for deducting a specified amount to return to the university as overhead. Various financial issues, including university cutbacks in student services and student financial aid, elimination of separate fundraising by the law school, and a proposed major increase in the size of the law school's overhead contribution, served as major points of disagreement between Putz and the new USF president, William McInnes, S.J. Demands by law students for restoration of services culminating in a student law suit against the university, coupled with pressure from the American Bar Association and the Association of American Law Schools, the school's accreditation bodies, helped to restore some of the budget cuts and persuaded the university to permit separate fundraising by the law school.

Despite budgetary problems, Putz's tenure was characterized by a significant increase in the number of faculty members to accommodate the increases in student enrollment in the law school. Putz and his faculty enhanced the law school's curriculum and increased its services to the community, an outgrowth of the school's growing social consciousness. Putz also authorized student representation on a number of important school committees and supported minority special admissions programs. In 1973, Putz appointed Ken Lloyd as the admissions director of the law school. Under Lloyd's stewardship, the special admissions program flourished. When he started as admissions director in 1973, students of color represented 16 percent of the entering law school class, and women represented 12 percent of the class. When Lloyd retired in 1994, 26 percent of the entering class were students of color, and 50 percent were women.

In 1975, Putz resigned to return to teaching and was replaced by Paul McKaskle, who had been director of litigation at the Western Center on Law and Poverty in Los Angeles before coming to USF to teach law in 1971.

One of McKaskle's goals was to establish a solid financial base for the school through external fundraising, including raising the necessary funds to add a new wing to the overcrowded Kendrick Hall. Toward this end, he worked with Tom Jordan, the chief development officer for the law school, to create an independent board of counselors to advise the dean and raise external support. The founding chairman of the board was George Helmer, a graduate of USF and its law school, former adjunct law professor at USF, and a highly respected attorney and partner in a San Francisco law firm. Helmer led a successful campaign that raised more than $1 million to help build an additional wing to Kendrick Hall, and he also created an endowed scholarship fund for law students.

David Ratner, a law professor at Cornell University for 18 years and a national authority on securities law, took over the deanship in 1982. Under Ratner, the law school's endowment grew significantly, major curriculum changes were instituted, Kendrick Hall was renovated, and library facilities were improved. In September 1987, Ratner presided over the 75th anniversary of the founding of the School of Law, a celebration marked by a jubilee dinner and dance at the Fairmont Hotel. As part of the celebration, Ratner commissioned the publication of *The University of San Francisco School of Law History* by Eric Abrahamson, and he dedicated a new moot court classroom featuring photographic portraits of 150 alumni who became judges.

From the first law class that began in 1912 through the school's 75th anniversary in 1987, 150 graduates of the USF School of Law were elevated to the bench. By 2004, that number had grown to 229. Among the current judges is Ming Chin, associate justice of the Supreme Court of California. He was appointed to that post in 1996 after serving as the presiding justice of the First District Court of Appeal, Division Three, in San Francisco. Justice Chin, a first-generation Chinese American, is only

the second justice of Asian descent to serve on the seven-member state high court. He received his bachelor's degree in 1964 and his law degree in 1967, both from USF, and has remained active in the affairs of his alma mater. He served as a member of the USF Board of Trustees, as president of the alumni association, as a member of the law school board of counselors, and as an adjunct professor of law. He has been honored as both the university's alumnus of the year and as the law school's alumnus of the year.

In 1989, Jay Folberg, a law professor at the Northwestern School of Law at Lewis and Clark College, a judge pro tem in the Oregon trial courts, the first director of Oregon Legal Services, and the author of several books and articles on mediation and alternative dispute resolution, was appointed dean of the law school. During the 10 years he served as dean, the law school witnessed a successful effort to add a new library to the school when Arthur Zief, a 1947 graduate of the law school, contributed $3.2 million to the construction of a new library named for his wife, Dorraine Zief (vignette #120). Also noteworthy during Folberg's tenure was an accelerating California bar exam pass rate for USF law students. The pass rate reached 85.2 percent in February 1998, the third highest in the state. During Folberg's tenure, international programming at the law school proliferated. Through the work of USF law professors Dolores Donovan and Jeffrey Brand, along with the assistance of alumnus Judd Iversen, the law school engaged in activities to assist the development of the rule of law with justice in Cambodia, Vietnam, and Indonesia. For example, faculty exchange programs were created with Indonesian and Vietnamese law schools, the latter being the first of its kind since the end of the Vietnam War. These activities were carried out through the Center for Law and Global Justice, which Brand and Iversen created. Through 2004, the center raised nearly $10 million in grants to support its work, which included creating

Ming Chin earned a bachelor's in political science from USF in 1964 and a law degree from USF in 1967. In 1996, he was appointed Associate Justice of the California Supreme Court. He has served on the USF Board of Trustees, was president of the Alumni Association, and was honored as Alumnus of the Year by the both the university and the law school, where he has taught as an adjunct professor.

UNIVERSITY OF SAN FRANCISCO ARCHIVES

Jeffrey Brand, a professor in the USF School of Law since 1987, became its dean in 1997. As dean, he oversaw the continued expansion of the Center for Law and Global Justice, which he helped establish as a faculty member; witnessed the launching of the J. Thomas McCarthy Institute for Intellectual Property and Technology Law; and was instrumental in securing a $3.25 million gift from the Koret Foundation to help launch the School of Law's Koret Law Center.

UNIVERSITY OF SAN FRANCISCO SCHOOL OF LAW

an independent law school, working with land mine victims, and addressing issues related to massive human rights abuses in Cambodia; training judges in Vietnam; and assisting with commercial arbitration and legislative drafting in Indonesia.

In September 1999, Jeffrey Brand, a professor in the USF School of Law since 1987, became the law school's new dean, a position he still holds. Prior to joining the faculty at USF, he served as a public defender in Contra Costa County, an administrative law judge for the Agriculture Labor Relations Board, and a partner in a law firm specializing in employment law and civil rights litigation. After joining the law faculty, he helped establish the Center for Law and Global Justice, directed the Academic Support Program, worked on various international law projects, and was named the Distinguished Law Professor of the year four times. As dean, Brand oversaw the continued expansion of the Center for Law and Global Justice and the growth of international global justice projects by the School of Law (vignette #147). Brand also witnessed the launching of the J. Thomas McCarthy

Institute for Intellectual Property and Technology Law. The institute was named for Thomas McCarthy, whose 36-year career at USF was marked by such outstanding and cutting-edge publications that he became the most influential trademark attorney in the United States. Brand was also instrumental in securing a $3.25 million gift from the Koret Foundation that led to a major renovation of Kendrick Hall and the launching of the School of Law's Koret Law Center (vignette #120).

Brand has also extended the efforts of recent law school deans at USF to integrate the law school with the rest of the university. Toward that end, Brand serves on numerous university-wide task forces and committees and is frequently called upon by members of the extended USF community to address the Jesuit values and mission of USF. At a conference of faculty and administrators from the Jesuit colleges and universities in the Western United States held on the USF campus in October 2001, Brand articulated his belief that "the law school of a Jesuit university has a special responsibility to help students develop a thirst for justice and to provide opportunities to quench that thirst." In his talk, Brand addressed some of the distinctive qualities of the USF School of Law that reflect its Jesuit legacy: ethical training throughout the curriculum, the street law program where law students talk to high school students about their legal rights and responsibilities, service learning and community service, and programs that provide legal service to other countries and promote international justice. Brand concluded "this is the time to acknowledge our collective purpose and responsibility, to celebrate it and to commit ourselves to promoting justice in a meaningful way. We do it because it is our mission and we do it because it is the right thing to do."

Going International: The School of Business and Management

143

DURING THE EARLY 1970S, THE COLLEGE OF BUSINESS Administration, like the rest of USF, felt the impact of a major national recession, high inflation, and declining student enrollment. From the fall of 1970 to the fall of 1973, enrollment decreased from 865 to 728 undergraduate and graduate students in the business college. On a positive note, however, USF received a major grant in 1973 from the Irvine Foundation to remodel the west end of Phelan Hall on the USF campus. It was given to honor Norman Loyall McLaren, a long-term trustee of the Irvine Foundation and a regent of USF.

In 1974, the McLaren Center was dedicated, and the College of Business Administration moved into the new center. Norman McLaren died in December 1977, and the USF Board of Trustees changed the name of the College of Business Administration to the McLaren College of Business at its 1978 winter meeting.

Bernard "Bernie" Martin became dean of the McLaren College of Business in 1978, and three years later he oversaw efforts that led to separate accreditation for the graduate program in business by the American Assembly of Collegiate Schools of Business (AACSB). Today, USF is one of only 370 schools of business in the nation that is accredited at both the graduate and undergraduate levels by AACSB International — The Association to Advance Collegiate Schools of Business. Several new programs were developed under Martin's stewardship of the college, including undergraduate programs in information systems and hospitality management and two joint degree graduate programs: a JD/MBA in cooperation with USF's School of Law, and an MS in Nursing/MBA with USF's School of Nursing. From 1978 to 1986, the year Martin left the dean's position, enrollment increased from 1,221 to 1,550 undergraduate and graduate students. The student body also became more diverse in the process, with international students currently constituting more than 20 percent of the business student population.

In 1986, Gary Williams became dean of the McLaren College of Business, a position he continues to hold. In 1991, the college was renamed the McLaren School of Business, and in 1999, the name was changed again, to the

Bernard "Bernie" Martin served as dean of the McLaren College of Business from 1978 to 1986, and oversaw the accreditation of the school's graduate programs by AACSB, the development of several new undergraduate and graduate programs, and a significant increase in the number and the diversity of business students.

UNIVERSITY OF SAN FRANCISCO ARCHIVES

School of Business and Management, to reflect its broader scope of activities. By 2004, several additional changes had taken place in the academic programs within the school. In 2003, a major donation by Putra Masagung, a 1974 graduate of the business school, led to a capital campaign involving more than 3,000 donors in building a new wing for the business school, a state-of-the art facility that opened in 2004. In recognition of Masagung's lead gift, the graduate programs are now offered within the Masagung Graduate School of Management. In recognition of a major closing gift, the new business school facility was named Malloy Hall for donor Thomas E. Malloy, class of 1961, and his wife, Sharon. The undergraduate programs in the school remain within the McLaren College of Business.

Under Williams, the undergraduate and graduate business programs at USF were successfully re-accredited by AACSB International in 1988 and again in 2001, a reaffirmation good until 2011. In addition, the school greatly increased its fundraising and major donor activities; significantly expanded its alumni support and programs; and developed a wide range of advisory boards, drawing upon the resources of more than 130 executives from national and international firms. The school also developed a series of strategic plans and established several new academic programs, including a professional MBA for executives and a joint MBA/MA in Asia Pacific Studies with the College of Arts and Sciences. New curricula developed at the undergraduate and graduate levels emphasized global management and leadership, ethics, technology, and communication skills. USF's business program, for example, was one of the first in the United States to require its students to subscribe to an Internet e-mail service to facilitate communication among faculty, students, and staff.

MBA areas of emphasis currently include finance, international business, management, marketing, telecommunications, and entrepreneurship.

From 1980 to 2005, numerous School of Business and Management faculty members received university-wide recognition. In 1981, Oren Harari was selected to receive the Distinguished Teaching Award. Other business faculty members who have won the Distinguished Teaching Award include David Scalise in 1986, Nicholas Imparato in 1990, and Cathy Goldberg in 2005. Professors Philip Taylor and Stephen Huxley received the Distinguished Research Award in 1988, and 12 years later, Huxley won the university's Sarlo Prize, which recognizes excellence in teaching based on the moral values underlying USF's identity. In 1988, Leslie Goldgehn became the first female faculty member in the business school to be granted tenure. Professor David Weiner received the Ignatian Faculty Service Award in 1993, an honor that recognizes an exceptional commitment to the service of students, the university, and the community at large. Heather Hudson, professor of telecommunications management and director of the telecommunications program, which she founded, won the Distinguished Research Award in 1990. Thomas Costello, an administrator with faculty responsibilities who started at USF in 1990, was instrumental in expanding the highly acclaimed hospitality management program at USF, and currently serves as its director. In 1996, he won the university's Ignatian Service Award. In 1997, Professor Kathleen Kane also won the Ignatian Faculty Service Award. In 2005, Eugene Muscat, senior associate dean for external affairs, won the Center for Instruction and Technology Award for Innovation, through his development of online undergraduate courses on family business in cooperation with other Jesuit institutions.

Beginning in the mid-1980s, the business school greatly expanded its opportunities for students to study abroad and to gain an international business perspective. The school also placed a significant emphasis on becoming an important center for international management education. In light of USF's commitment to involvement in the Pacific Rim, the business school became a leader in executive education in Asia. For example, the school developed an Executive MBA program for key managers at China Resources Holdings Co., Ltd., and at Guangdong Enterprises, Ltd., with offices in Hong Kong, Guangzhou, and Beijing. Most of the students in these programs were executives from mainland China, and when they came to USF to participate in commencement activities in St. Ignatius Church, it was, for most of the new graduates, the first time in their lives they had entered a church.

The international programs in the School of Business and Management are currently complemented with an on-campus MBA program for executives that emphasizes global management education. A two-week international study tour is required of students as part of this program. Over the years, USF students have gone to the former Soviet Union, Estonia, Russia, Mexico, Chile, Japan, Hong Kong, mainland China, Korea, Malaysia, Singapore, Australia, the United Kingdom, Germany, and the Czech Republic. In 2000, the EMBA program was merged with the MBA program for executives and was implemented on the main campus and at USF's North Bay Campus in Santa Rosa. This graduate degree program was supplemented with a series of non-degree short programs for students and international executives. In 2003,

the School of Business and Management welcomed more than 200 executives from 13 countries to USF into its non-degree business programs.

Over the decades, USF's business school has altered its program and curriculum numerous times to adapt to changes in the national and international business community. Since 2000, the school has distinguished itself with the development of a small number of academic centers including the new venture, family business, and telecommunications centers. In 2004, the school offered its first online course in cooperation with two other Jesuit schools (Loyola University of Chicago and Fordham University). The basic features of the school's mission, however, have remained constant: to provide students with the learning experiences, knowledge, and skills needed for professional success; to create opportunities to use the city of San Francisco and, increasingly, locations around the world as laboratories for translating classroom theory into business practice; to foster service to others; and to establish an ethical framework for decision making in business and in the broader social world.

Malloy Hall, the new home for the School of Business and Management, was dedicated in September 2004.

Expanding the Range of Care: the School of Nursing 1981–2005

BY THE BEGINNING OF THE 1980S, THE SCHOOL OF NURSING at the University of San Francisco had grown significantly since its fledgling years from 1948 to 1954, when it was a small department within the College of Arts and Sciences chaired by Mary de Paul of the Sisters of Mercy. During those early years, the USF department of nursing was administratively and academically connected to St. Mary's Hospital for the preparation of nurses seeking a bachelor of science in nursing. Indeed, Sr. Mary de Paul concurrently directed the USF department of nursing and St. Mary's Hospital and the nursing program.

In 1954, USF established an independent School of Nursing, although the first three deans, spanning the years 1954 to 1980, were all from the Sisters of Mercy Order, and the connection with Saint Mary's Hospital remained strong. Under the leadership of Sisters Mary Martha,

Nicole Telles, a student in the USF School of Nursing, examines a one-day-old infant at home in the arms of his grandmother in the Guatemalan village of San Lucas Toliman. This nursing research project was under the direction of Linda Walsh, USF associate professor of nursing.

UNIVERSITY OF SAN FRANCISCO ARCHIVES

Mary Beata Bauman, and Mary Geraldine McDonnell, and with the support of a dedicated group of faculty members, the school achieved full accreditation from the National League for Nursing and the California State Board of Nurse Examiners. The school also developed an integrated curriculum, effectively adapted that curriculum to changing requirements within the nursing profession, expanded the range of clinical experiences for students, increased the number of lay faculty, began to stress faculty research and publications, and witnessed an increase in student enrollment from 101 in 1957 to 638 in 1981 (vignette #111).

In 1981, Fay Bower became the first lay dean of the School of Nursing. Under her tenure, over the next seven years, there was increased emphasis on faculty research and scholarship along with a growing expectation that faculty members hold doctoral degrees. Under Bower, numerous curriculum changes were introduced, designed to respond to changes in health care throughout the nation and to more effectively introduce freshmen to the field of nursing. In 1984, the school started its first graduate program, leading to a master of science in nursing. This was soon followed by a joint program with the McLaren School of Business leading to a master of science in nursing/master of business administration.

During Bower's administration, the School of Nursing increasingly became integrated with the academic life of the university, symbolized by her selection to chair the university-wide task force established in 1987 to prepare for an accreditation visit by the Western Association of Schools and Colleges and by her appointment as acting vice president for academic affairs in 1989, after William O. Binkley stepped down from that position. When John Clark, S.J., was selected to be USF's new academic vice president in 1989, Bower became coordinator of university planning. In 1991, she was selected to be president of Clarkson College, a small private professional school in Omaha, Nebraska.

With Bower's departure from the dean's office, nursing professors Antoinette Bargagliotti and Louise Trygstad successively served as acting deans until the selection of a new permanent dean, Norma Chaska. Under Acting Dean Bargagliotti, the school expanded its degree completion programs to various off-campus locations in the Bay Area. Chaska continued this effort, and USF nursing students were also provided an increasingly wide range of off-campus clinical educational opportunities, such as at Stanford University Hospital, where their clinical experiences were supervised by Stanford University staff and faculty. There was also a restructuring of the School of Nursing under Chaska, including the creation of academic departments, each headed by a faculty member who received three units of release time for serving as the chair. The first three department chairs were Jane Corbett, Marjorie Barter, and Roberta Romeo. During the early 1990s, the school also began to focus, at the graduate level, on preparing men and

women for advanced practice nursing, as family nurse practitioners and clinical nurse specialists. Chaska required that the graduate program at USF combine these two roles so that students would be able to take the American Nursing Association exams for both the family nurse practitioner and clinical nurse specialist certifications. Under Chaska, the school was accredited for the first time by the Commission on Collegiate Nursing Education (CCNE) for its baccalaureate and graduate programs.

Jane Corbett, professor in the School of Nursing, won both the Distinguished Research Award and the Distinguished Teaching Award from USF and the USF Faculty Association.

UNIVERSITY OF SAN FRANCISCO ARCHIVES

From 1980 to 2004, numerous School of Nursing faculty members received university-wide recognition. In 1984, Jane Corbett received the Distinguished Research Award from among all the faculty members at USF. Ten years later, she also won the Distinguished Teaching Award. Other School of Nursing faculty members who have won the Distinguished Teaching Award in the past two decades include Judith Barrett, in 1983; Betty Carmack in 1989; and Gregory DeBough, in 2002. Among the nursing faculty members who began their careers at USF in the 1980s and who retired as professors emeritae were Louise Trygstad, whose 16-year career began in 1985 and included a stint as acting dean and as associate dean. Roberta Romeo, associate professor of nursing emerita, who taught from 1991 to 2003, also received the Ignatian Faculty Service Award that recognizes exceptional commitment to the service of students, the university, and the community at large.

In October 1994, Sheila Burke, who received a bachelor's degree in nursing from USF in 1973, delivered the keynote address at USF's first Presidential Forum on Health Care in America. At that time, Burke was chief of staff to U.S. Senate Republican Leader Robert Dole. She later became executive dean and lecturer in public policy at Harvard University's John F. Kennedy School of Government. She is currently Undersecretary of the Smithsonian Institute in Washington, D.C., and a member of the USF Board of Trustees.

John Lantz became dean of the USF School of Nursing in 1998. Under his leadership, the school was successfully re-accredited, developed a more community-based curriculum, formed new partnerships with several Bay Area agencies, refined undergraduate and graduate admission standards, developed a new graduate program for students who have a non-nursing baccalaureate degree, and increased student enrollment.

In 1998, John Lantz, the new dean of the School of Nursing, became the first male to occupy that position in the history of USF. Under Lantz's leadership, the School of Nursing faculty has developed a more community-based curriculum, and it has formed several new partnerships with Bay Area agencies, including Catholic Healthcare West. Lantz has also secured grants to improve the learning resource center (skills lab) and to hire nursing graduate students as teaching assistants. He has also helped redefine the standards for student admission to both undergraduate and graduate programs and has implemented strategies for improving undergraduate student test scores on required nursing exams. Lantz oversaw the development of a successful new graduate program, the master's entry option (MEO) for students who have a non-nursing baccalaureate degree (or higher) and who seek RN licensure as well as graduate preparation in advanced practice nursing. During Lantz's tenure, the School of Nursing was re-accredited by the California Board of Registered Nurses and the Commission on Collegiate Nursing Education, and student enrollment, which had declined to 353 undergraduate and graduate students by the fall semester of 2000, rebounded to 650 undergraduate and graduate students by the fall semester of 2004.

Today, the School of Nursing at USF continues to offer the bachelor of science in nursing degree, as it has for more than 50 years. The degree program can be taken as either a four-year baccalaureate degree or as a completion program for transfer students from two-year programs. For 20 years, a master of science in nursing has been offered at USF, and it currently includes options in advanced practice and clinical systems management; a master's entry option, as noted earlier; and joint master's degree programs in nursing and business administration (MSN/MBA), public administration (MSN/MPA), and information systems (MSN/MSIS). The school also offers continuing education programs for practicing nurses and post-master's degree certificate programs. Notwithstanding myriad program and curriculum changes over the past 50 years to adapt to changing national health care standards, professional requirements, and community needs, the School of Nursing has adhered to a core set of Jesuit values. These precepts include compassionate, personalized care for others, the highest standards for life-long learning, leadership in service to the community, and critical reasoning and ethical decision making within professional settings.

From Classroom to Community: the School of Education 1978–2005

145

ENROLLLMENT AT THE USF SCHOOL OF EDUCATION grew dramatically from 1972 to 1978: from 302 students in the fall of 1972 to 1,063 students in the fall of 1978. This growth necessitated major academic, organizational, budgetary, and scheduling changes.

Following the resignation of Dean Allen Calvin in 1978, it fell to the school's third dean, Michael O'Neill, a faculty member in the School of Education and founding director of the Institute for Catholic Educational Leadership, to implement those changes. O'Neill instituted the doctoral program schedule still in use today: doctoral classes are held on the USF campus every other weekend, on Friday night, and all day Saturday. One result of this schedule was the development of general courses in research methodology and statistics to be taken by students in all the doctoral concentrations. Both O'Neill and Calvin mandated that no doctoral programs were to be held at regional sites. In contrast to Calvin, however, O'Neill limited the number of new doctoral students to 125 per year. He also strengthened the entrance requirements and insisted that all doctoral candidates be required to take a statistics course, a course in basic research, and another in advanced research design.

For the on-campus master's and credential programs, O'Neill's tenure also saw the program directors and faculty members agree to a common schedule, which produced a two-block (late afternoon and early evening) weekday format. The result of this scheduling change was the elimination of low-enrollment and duplicate courses. It also permitted students from one

program to take elective courses in other programs. O'Neill also reorganized the off-campus master's and credential programs, placed Dan Muller in charge of those programs, and designated him assistant dean for external programs. Given the financial difficulties faced by USF during the 1970s, O'Neill was charged with streamlining staffing patterns and the budgeting process. During his tenure, there were several major budget cuts and significant personnel reallocation within the School of Education. With the school's program directors, O'Neill also implemented one- and five-year planning systems. He also insisted on national

Paul Warren, dean of the USF School of Education from 1989 to 2002, oversaw the development of several new degree and credential programs, including a dual degree program with the College of Arts and Sciences for students pursuing a bachelor's and master's degree, plus a teaching credential.

UNIVERSITY OF SAN FRANCISCO ARCHIVES

searches for all new tenure-track faculty positions and major administrative positions, and he required that the final list of candidates include people of color and women. In addition to a more rigorous hiring process, O'Neill implemented a more comprehensive system of faculty and staff evaluation. He also converted four of the eight faculty positions in the multicultural program from largely grant-funded term positions to tenure-track status, and he required a national search for the four tenure-track positions.

During O'Neill's tenure, several new programs were developed in the school, including a master of arts in teaching English as a second language and a specialist credential in school psychologist services. During the three years O'Neill served as dean, the School of Education moved from Campion Hall to the Rossi Wing of the Lone Mountain Campus; developed a closer working relationship with various USF service offices; enhanced its relationships with local school districts; developed an advisory council composed of district superintendents, representatives from the California State Department of Education, businesses, and local schools; instituted the first school catalog, newsletter, and student handbook; and reactivated the Education Alumni Society.

Michael O'Neill resigned from the dean's position in the early summer of 1981 and was replaced by Wayne Doyle, the director of the school's organization and leadership program. Tragically, Doyle was diagnosed with cancer shortly after assuming the dean's position and died within a year. During that time, William Garner, who had joined the education faculty in 1979, served as acting dean. In October of 1983, he was named permanent dean.

The School of Education continued to develop new programs during Garner's administration, and he increasingly attempted to refocus the school on teacher education. Most significantly, he initiated a master of arts degree with an emphasis in educational computing and a 15-unit certificate program

in educational computing. He hired Mary Furlong as an assistant professor to help run the education computing programs and to direct the teacher education program. In conjunction with the new degree and certificate emphasis, Garner and Furlong developed the Center for Instruction and Technology (CIT) in the fall of 1983 as a model classroom environment for students in teacher education. In 1984, with $5,000 seed money from the university, the CIT lab opened in the basement of the Lone Mountain campus with nine Commodore computers. By 1987, the center had Apple IIe, Apple MacIntosh, and Hewlett-Packard 150 computers.

The school's certificate program in educational computing was designed for classroom teachers, school administrators, and doctoral students and included courses in the instructional use of computers, issues and trends in educational computing, programming languages, and computer management of school instruction systems. During its early years, several research grants were awarded to the center, including one from the Markle Foundation to support research on the use of technology for older adult learners. Initially, classes such as "Computers for Kids over Sixty" were taken by more than 200 senior students. This program, directed by Mary Furlong, was renamed SeniorNet and rapidly expanded to become a national network of seniors and brought significant media coverage to USF. Another grant from Apple Computer provided the center with state-of-the-art multimedia equipment. Over the next decade, the CIT collaborated with Information Technology Services (ITS) and with the Office of Human Resources at USF to offer training to the university's employees and assistance to faculty members with course development.

In December 1987, Garner resigned as dean but continued to direct the CIT, first with Mike Benedict, and later with John Bansavich. In 1994, Garner supervised the move of CIT, with the assistance of Harold Hansen, USF's

In 1983, William Garner, dean of the School of Education, and Mary Furlong, assistant professor of education, developed the Center for Instruction and Technology (CIT) as a model classroom for teacher education students. Pictured in this 1994 photo, left to right, are Professor Furlong; Michael Benedict, co-director of the CIT; William Garner, former dean, professor of education, and co-director of the CIT; Robert Paterson, executive director of information technology services; and Paul Warren, who became dean of the School of Education in 1989.

chief engineer of plant services, to its current location in the School of Education building, formerly the campus of Presentation High School. In 1993, Garner secured $100,000 from the university to reestablish the CIT in the new School of Education building, and in 1999 he helped obtain a $750,000 federal grant to assist education faculty members to improve their technology skills and to integrate technology into the credential curriculum. Garner currently directs the master of arts program in educational technology, and the CIT is now under the purview of Information Technology Services and directed by John Bansavich.

Dorothy Messerschmitt, who began her career at USF in 1978 and is currently professor of education, served as acting dean of the school from 1987 to 1989. Other education faculty members who began their careers at USF during the 1970s and 1980s and who retired as professors emeriti were Allen Calvin, Henry Clay Hall professor of education and former dean, who served from 1974 to 2001; Edwin McDermott, S.J., who taught and directed the Institute for Catholic Educational Leadership from 1978 to 1999; Alan Cohen, who began an 18-year teaching career in 1977;

Anita De Frantz who taught in the school from 1977 to 2000; Emily Girault whose 18-year career started in 1975; and Joan Hyman, who taught for 18 years at USF, from 1977 to 1995. Three faculty members in the School of Education have won the Distinguished Teaching Award. They are Susan Evans, Patricia Busk, and Alma Flor Ada. In 1992, USF initiated the annual Ignatian Faculty Service Award, which recognizes outstanding commitment to students, the university, and to the community. To date, four School of Education faculty members have received this award: Larry Bishop, Allen Calvin, Sr. Mary Peter Traviss, and Elena Flores.

In 1985, Emily Girault and Brian Gerrard, associate professors of education, developed the Catholic Schools and Family Counseling program to provide counseling services for elementary school children and their families in the Mission District of the Archdiocese of San Francisco and to train master's and doctoral candidates. Since the program's founding, thousands of children and their families have received help from the School of Education. In 1988, the program received a grant from the Stanley S. Langendorf Foundation, one of several foundations that lent their support to the project.

The School of Education Building, formerly Presentation High School, was acquired by USF in 1991. It houses the School of Education faculty and administrative offices, classrooms, the Center for Instruction and Technology (CIT), and a theater that seats 500 people.

In 1989, Paul Warren, former professor and dean of education at Boston University, became the dean of the School of Education at USF. He held this position until his retirement in 2002, setting a record for longevity as dean of the school. Among Warren's accomplishments were the development of a dual degree program with the College of Arts and Sciences for students seeking a five-year program culminating in bachelor's and master's degrees, plus a teaching credential. Warren also helped create the Center for Teaching Excellence and Social Justice, under the direction of internationally known writer and educator Herb Kohl. The center was designed to prepare educators to reform schools in urban settings and to make the promotion of social justice a major focus of the School of Education.

In 1993, the School of Education became the first school in the state to offer an alternative learning specialist (LH) credential approved by the California Commission on Teacher Credentialing (CTC). Directed by Susan Evans, professor of education, the program enabled students to earn the LH credential in one year while teaching in a special education

classroom with full pay. This innovative program represented a collaborative effort between USF and Bay Area school districts. During Warren's administration, the School of Education also developed the Home Link Program, a community outreach project at Plaza del Sol, a housing project in the Mission District. At the project, USF graduate students in education staffed a resource center that offered tutoring, computer-assisted instruction, and moral support to children and youth living in the project. The resource center was also used in the evenings to teach English as a second language to local families.

Beginning in 1990, Warren hosted an annual awards ceremony for students from neighborhood elementary, middle schools, and high schools to recognize outstanding local students, their teachers, and their parents. In 1994, when the Cross-Cultural Language and Academic Development (CLAD) credential became available in California, the USF School of Education received approval from the CTC to offer it as an option to the basic credential at the multiple subjects (elementary school) level. Rosita Galang, professor of education, prepared the documents to secure state approval, and she coordinated the CLAD program at USF.

In 1997, the school initiated a cross-cultural credential for Catholic schoolteachers, which was developed in cooperation with St. Ignatius College Preparatory School, a high school that had been connected to USF until 1959. The program, delivered at the St. Ignatius campus in the Sunset District, was designed to offer Catholic schoolteachers the opportunity to earn a California single- or multiple-subject credential. In 1997, USF began to participate in the America Reads Program, a federal program to train college students to tutor elementary school students in reading. Kathleen Jonson, assistant professor of education; Susan Murphy, associate dean and director of financial aid in academic services; Alan Ziajka, assistant dean in academic services; Janice McAlister, student employment administrator; and Edgar Callo, assistant coordinator of the learning center, developed a collaborative project to meet the federal program guidelines. To deliver the program, USF worked in collaboration with the San Francisco Unified District's Reading Recovery program, selected Catholic elementary schools, nonprofit children's centers, school principals, primary teachers, and reading specialists. Initially, 18 USF students participated in the program as tutors, a number that grew to more than 80 students by 2004.

Today, the School of Education enrolls approximately 1,000 students and offers a wide range of doctoral, master's, and credential programs on the USF campus and at regional campuses in Cupertino, Santa Rosa, Sacramento, and San Ramon. These academic programs include the full-range of multiple-subject, single-subject, service, and specialist credentials; master's programs in counseling, Catholic school leadership and teaching, educational technology, international and multicultural education, learning and instruction, multicultural literature for children and young adults, organization and leadership, teaching English as a second language, and teaching; and doctoral programs

in Catholic school leadership, learning and instruction, international and multicultural education, and organization and leadership. Among the various programs, the special education program, headed by Susan Evans, has been especially successful in securing federal grants, having received $3.6 million in federal grant awards since 1997.

The various degree and credential programs in the School of Education are complemented by several community-based service and applied research centers and institutes. These agencies include the Center for Child and Family Development, founded by the late professor Larry Palmatier, which provides counseling services to low-income families in San Francisco's Mission District and the city's schools; the Center for Instruction and Technology, noted previously; and the Center for Multicultural Literature, developed by Professor Alma Flor Ada, which sponsors special programs, colloquia, and conferences for educators, students, and children that focus on the rich literary heritage of a multicultural society.

From 2002 to 2004, Larry Brewster served as acting dean for the School of Education, while he simultaneously served as dean of the College of Professional Studies. In 2004, Walter Gmelch, dean of the College of Education at Iowa State University, was selected in a nationwide search to be the new dean of the School of Education at USF.

Although the USF School of Education has grown enormously since its parent, the department of education, conferred secondary teaching credentials upon 22 students in 1949, the core set of Jesuit values at the heart of the enterprise have been maintained for educators and students. These values are centered on social justice; the importance of values-based education; and the commitment to education as a lifelong experience that integrates the moral, spiritual, personal, social, and academic realms.

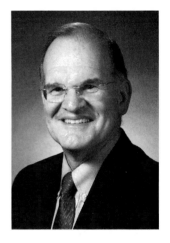

Walter Gmelch became dean of the School of Education in 2004. Prior to coming to USF, Gmelch was dean of the College of Education at Iowa State University and interim dean at Washington State University. He has conducted research and published extensively on the topic of leadership and has been selected as a Kellogg National Fellow, a Fulbright Scholar, and Danforth Fellow.

UNIVERSITY OF SAN FRANCISCO ARCHIVES

146

Transforming the College of Professional Studies 1987–2005

THE COLLEGE OF PROFESSIONAL STUDIES AT THE University of San Francisco witnessed a host of programmatic and organizational changes from 1987 to 1999 under five successive deans and acting deans. In 1987, David Fox, former associate dean of the College of Professional Studies, became the new dean, replacing Colin Silverthorne, who had resigned earlier that year. Fox selected Stan Buller to be associate dean for academic programs and Denise Lucy to be associate dean for student and corporate development.

In 2001, the College of Professional Studies moved into its new building on the corner of Masonic Ave. and Turk Blvd. USF is leasing the 20,000-square-foot building from the Sisters of the Presentation, who occupy a portion of the third floor. The building includes three classrooms, one conference room, and workspace for most of the college's faculty and staff.

In 1989, the first six full-time faculty members were hired by the college, and three more full-time faculty positions were added by 1991. This change from the former practice of utilizing only adjunct faculty was prompted by WASC accreditation concerns and was designed to bring the college closer to the mainstream of the university. Fox strengthened the admission and graduation standards for CPS students, reorganized the college into academic departments, and sought collaborative programs with the other schools and colleges at USF. As a result of one such collaboration, CPS and the College of Arts and Sciences developed a four-year on-site degree completion program with Pacific Bell. In 1991, Fox resigned from the dean's position and was replaced briefly by an acting dean, Robin Pratt, an associate professor in the college. Following a national search, Bettye Taylor, formerly the dean of the Graduate School at Lesley College, was named dean of the College of Professional Studies in 1992.

Under Taylor, the college's student affairs and off-campus administration were reorganized, with each regional campus director reporting to Stan Buller, now the associate dean for student affairs. The responsibility for the hiring, orientation, and development of adjunct faculty was given to Carol Taylor, associate dean for academic affairs. The college also developed its first alumni society. Margaret Barrett, associate director of the Office of Student Enrichment Programs at USF and a graduate of CPS, was the founding president of the CPS Alumni Society.

In September 1996, the College of Professional Studies opened its North Bay campus in Santa Rosa. The founding director of the center was Maryann Noble, and during its first year, the center served 100 CPS and School of Education students enrolled in nine undergraduate and graduate programs. In the 1995–1996 academic year, the college celebrated the 20th anniversary of its founding as the Office of Continuing Education. By 1998, the college administered five regional campuses. In addition to the North Bay Regional Campus, campuses were located in Sacramento, directed by Michael McAdams; in San Ramon, directed by Jan Wilson; in Cupertino (the South Bay Regional Campus), directed by Adele Salle; and in Oakland, under associate director Cora Augusta-Dupar. John Murphy served as the director of the San Francisco Regional Center.

In 1998, Taylor resigned as dean and was replaced by BJ Johnson and David Robinson, S.J., as acting co-deans. Johnson served as acting co-dean while simultaneously serving as dean of academic services. She held both positions for one year, while a search was conducted for a new CPS dean. During this year, Johnson and Fr. Robinson strengthened the regional campuses and enhanced their technological and administrative links to the main campus. When Johnson returned to her position as dean of academic services, the responsibility for the administration, budget, and supervision of the regional campuses moved with her to academic services.

In May of 1999, after a nationwide search, Larry Brewster, dean of Professional Studies and Academic Affairs at Menlo College, was named the new dean of the College of Professional Studies. After he became dean, plans were finalized to move the College of Professional Studies to a new location on campus, a building on the corner of Turk Street and Masonic Avenue, owned by the Sisters of the Presentation. USF had just entered into a long-term lease/buy agreement for the building, which for two decades had been the home of Lincoln University.

Under Brewster, the college was significantly reorganized, curriculum changes were instituted, the number of full-time tenured faculty members increased from four to seven, and one new faculty position was added for a total of nineteen full-time faculty positions. In the fall of 2003, the full-time tenured faculty members were David Fox, Sylvia Flatt, Sharon Wagner, Jack Gillespie, James Shaw, Michael O'Neill, and Maurice Penner. Increasingly, the full-time faculty members in the college are involved in decision-making, teaching courses in the regions, and in mentoring adjunct faculty. An academy was created to offer workshops for adjunct faculty. The college was also reorganized around programs rather than departments; an operations division, under long-term CPS administrator Margaret Roberts, was created to coordinate the management of budgets, scheduling, registration, publications and reports, enrollment management, and special events; and a student services division was developed, under Sherry McCoy and Claudia Gillingwater, to improve student services and advising. In recent years, the college has become more integrated with the university, and it has developed systems and procedures to align itself with the other schools and colleges in areas such as scheduling and billing.

During Brewster's administration, significant program changes were made at the

Larry Brewster became dean of the College of Professional Studies in 1999. Under his leadership, the college was successfully reorganized, several new full-time faculty positions were added, and programs were initiated at the undergraduate and graduate levels to respond to fluctuating enrollment patterns and new academic goals.

UNIVERSITY OF SAN FRANCISCO ARCHIVES

undergraduate and graduate levels to respond to enrollment changes and new academic goals. At the undergraduate level, coursework was integrated between the public administration and law enforcement leadership programs, and an emphasis in nonprofit administration was added to the public administration program. Moreover, the college achieved, through its core curricular model, the long-term goal of requiring all undergraduate students to satisfy the same general education requirements as all other USF students. At the graduate level, two new master's programs were added, in information systems and in organization development, and coursework was integrated between public administration and health services administration. The college also developed a joint master's degree in nursing and information systems with the School of Nursing.

In 2001, the International Institute of Criminal Justice Leadership was founded. It is currently under the direction of Anthony Ribera, former police chief of San Francisco. The institute provides training and research in law enforcement leadership for international, national, and local law enforcement personnel, and it sponsors an annual symposium that raises thousands of dollars each year for student scholarships.

The college has also increasingly incorporated the university's Jesuit identity into its program offerings. For example, under David Robinson, S.J., the interdisciplinary studies program has integrated its courses in autobiographical literature, advanced expository writing, and social ethics into the Ignatian Humanities Program, in which students explore their lives, values, careers, families, communities, and the global dimensions of personal and professional decision-making from a Jesuit perspective. Increasingly, service learning is integrated into the curriculum so that students can develop sensitivity to the role of the professional as an agent of change in the world.

Today, the College of Professional Studies offers a range of undergraduate and graduate programs. At the undergraduate level, students are pursuing degrees in applied economics, information systems, organizational behavior, and public administration. The public administration degree includes optional emphases in nonprofit administration and law enforcement leadership. Undergraduate students can earn up to 30 units of undergraduate college credit through the experiential/portfolio development process and can meet their general education requirements through a variety of courses and programs offered through the extended education program. At the graduate level, CPS students are earning master's degrees in organization development, nonprofit administration, information systems, public administration, and public administration with an emphasis in health services administration. In cooperation with the School of Nursing, the College of Professional Studies offers a program in which students enrolled in the master's of nursing program can also earn a master's in public administration with an emphasis in health services administration. At both the undergraduate and graduate levels, students are pursuing their educational goals in the evenings, on weekends, and on a year-round basis. Courses are held on the main USF campus and at regional campuses in Santa Rosa, Sacramento, San Ramon, and Cupertino. These regional campuses provide comprehensive academic advising, library services, and technological support.

One of the goals of the founders of St. Ignatius Academy, the antecedent of the University of San Francisco, was to provide educational experiences for nontraditional students at alternative times of the day and night. This goal has been achieved in the College of Professional Studies, and in all the schools and colleges at USF. Indeed, the Jesuit ideas expressed in the current Vision, Mission, and Values Statement of USF resonate with the students, faculty, and administrators of all of the institution's programs: to offer undergraduate, graduate, and professional students the "knowledge and skills needed to succeed as persons and professionals, and the values and sensitivity necessary to be men and women for others."

The Administration of John P. Schlegel, S.J.

IN 1991, JOHN P. SCHLEGEL, S.J., CAME FROM THE MIDWEST to lead the University of San Francisco through the last nine years of the 20th century. During his tenure as the university's 26th president, the institution witnessed an enrollment increase of nearly a thousand students; a significant increase in the diversity of the student body; the development of a multicultural action plan; the framing of a strategic plan that carried the university through a successful re-accreditation process; a major development campaign that brought $92 million to the university; the purchase, lease, renovation, or construction of several buildings; and an award-winning campus landscaping effort.

John Schlegel was born in Dubuque, Iowa, in 1943; entered the Society of Jesus in 1963; and was ordained a Catholic priest in 1973. He earned bachelor's and master's degrees from Saint Louis University, a theology degree from the University of London, and a doctorate in international relations from Oxford University. In 1969, he obtained a faculty position at Creighton University in Omaha, Nebraska, and later served as an acting department chair and as assistant academic vice president at that institution. Beginning in 1982, he moved rapidly through the administrative ranks of three other Midwestern Jesuit universities. He served as academic dean and dean of the College of Arts and Sciences at Rockhurst College, as dean of the College of Arts and Sciences at Marquette University, and as executive and academic vice president at John Carroll University. In December 1990, following a lengthy nationwide search, Fr. Schlegel was selected as president of the University of San Francisco, succeeding John Lo Schiavo, S.J. He assumed office in June 1991 and was inaugurated on October 26 of that year.

Just three months after Fr. Schlegel took office, he launched the Multicultural Action Plan (MAP), an initiative to enhance the cultural, ethnic, and racial diversity of USF.

From 1991 to 2000, John P. Schlegel, S.J., guided the University of San Francisco as its 26th president. During his term of office, the university witnessed significant growth in student enrollment and diversity, the development of a multicultural action plan, successful re-accreditation, a major development campaign, and a multitude of building and landscaping projects.

UNIVERSITY OF SAN FRANCISCO ARCHIVES

Louis Giraudo, chairman and CEO of Pacific Coast Bakery, was appointed chairman of the USF Board of Trustees in 1992. During the board meeting of September 15, 1992, USF President John Schlegel, S.J., gave him his gavel—made of sourdough.

The plan called for the establishment of a fund to enhance multiculturalism; the active recruitment of minority faculty, staff, and students; the development of special programs and forums to stimulate discussion of issues related to diversity; and the incorporation of additional multicultural perspectives into the curriculum. In 1993, the James Irvine Foundation awarded USF a $500,000 grant to fund the Multicultural Action Plan. The grant included support for two minority scholars per year to teach at USF while they completed their doctoral dissertations; funds for the Learning Resource Center to enhance the academic skills of all students; and a budget to be used at the discretion of Fr. Schlegel to strengthen MAP's overall impact on campus. The foundation's minority scholars program was directed by Gerardo Marín, associate dean in the College of Arts and Sciences, while the grant itself fell under the administration of Phaizon Wood, director of multicultural

services at USF. Fr. Schlegel also authorized the establishment of the Creating Community Committee to sponsor university-wide programs by student groups, faculty, and staff addressing issues related to cultural, ethnic, and religious diversity; gender; and disability. Fr. Schlegel's own commitment to multicultural and interfaith understanding was symbolized by a book, *Building Wisdom's House,* which he co-authored in 1997 with William Swing, the Episcopal Bishop of California; Stephen Pearce, senior rabbi of Temple E-Manuel in San Francisco; and Bonnie Kahn, a San Francisco writer and sociologist.

In 1992, Fr. Schlegel publicly launched the most ambitious fundraising campaign in the history of the university up to that time. The goal of the "Building a Bold Tomorrow" campaign, under the direction of David Macmillan, vice president for university advancement, was $75 million. The chairman of the board of trustees, Lou Giraudo, was very supportive of the campaign, and Fr. Schlegel and Giraudo enjoyed a strong friendship. When the campaign ended in 1996, foundations, corporations, alumni, and friends had donated a record $92 million to help finance new academic programs, student financial aid, faculty support, building construction and renovation, and campus landscaping.

During Fr. Schlegel's administration from 1991 to 2000, the size of the USF endowment grew from $38.7 million to $149 million. Among its many benefits, this endowment growth made substantial funds available for student financial aid and the amount budgeted for financial aid increased 190 percent. This expanded financial aid helped to increase the size of the student body and its diversity. Through the efforts of BJ Johnson, dean of academic services; William Henley, associate dean and director of admissions; and Susan Murphy, associate dean and director of financial aid; and aided by their respective staffs, student enrollment went from 6,853 in the fall of 1991 to 7,366 by the fall of 2000. During the same time period, the population of students at USF who came from ethnically diverse backgrounds, including international students, increased from 35 percent to 45 percent.

During Fr. Schlegel's administration, the USF campus underwent a significant physical transformation. Landscaping was one of the president's passions, and at USF that passion was expressed in a host of landscaping projects, which enhanced the beauty of the campus. In 1997, USF received a National Landscape Honor Award as the best urban campus in the nation. Building renovation, construction, and purchases also marked Fr. Schlegel's presidency. The Gillson, Phelan, Lone Mountain, and Hayes-Healy residence halls were all renovated; the Gleeson Library was transformed by the addition of the Geschke Learning Resource Center (vignette #104); and many new computer labs and technology-enhanced classrooms were added to the campus.

The executive offices of the university were moved to a renovated Rossi Wing of the Lone Mountain campus, thus freeing space for a more centrally located Priscilla A. Scotlan Career Services Center and for expanded student operations in University Center. The Pacific Rim Conference Center was completed in 1995, due in large part to a $1.5 million federal grant secured by Fr. Schlegel, with the assistance of Barbara Bundy, executive director of the Center for the Pacific Rim. In 1999, Loyola House, a Tuscan-style Jesuit residence on Lone Mountain, was completed, and Xavier Hall, the Jesuits' residence since 1959, was made available for much needed student housing. The purchase and renovation of Presentation High School, the new home for the USF School of Education, a project initiated during Fr. Lo Schiavo's presidency, was completed under Fr. Schlegel. In 1995, the elegant Handlery

Dining Room was added to a number of other enhanced facilities on Lone Mountain. In 1999, ground was broken for the Dorraine Zief Law Library, a state-of-the art addition to the USF School of Law, which opened its doors two months after Fr. Schlegel left office (vignette #120).

Toward the end of Fr. Schlegel's presidency, a long-term lease/buy option was signed with the Sisters of the Presentation on a building they owned on the corner of Turk Street and Masonic Avenue, a structure that became the new home for the College of Professional Studies, after Fr. Schlegel left office. Plans were also laid for the Anza Street faculty and staff housing project behind Lone Mountain. Lacking sufficient faculty and staff demand to purchase the new units, however, the complex — named Loyola Village — opened in 2002 as a residence hall largely for students, with a handful of rental units set aside for staff.

During Fr. Schlegel's presidency, the university developed a new strategic plan, named The 2005 Plan, which focused on six areas: USF's Jesuit and Catholic identity; the learning community; pluralism; the university community; the broader community; and

In 1997, John P. Schlegel, S.J., president of USF, signed an agreement with Juan Lafarga Corona, S.J., president of Mexico's Sistema Universidad Iberoamericana-ITESO, to develop academic exchange programs.

John W. Clark, S.J., served as provost and academic vice president of USF from 1988 to 1997, a period of significant growth in student enrollment, new program development, and enhanced relations between the USF Faculty Association and the administration.

human, physical, and financial resources. The 2005 Plan served as the basis for a successful re-accreditation visit in 1997 by the Western Association of Schools and Colleges (WASC). The WASC visiting team issued a highly laudatory report that reaffirmed the university's accreditation for the maximum 10 years.

In February 1997, John W. Clark, S.J. resigned from his position as provost and academic vice president of USF after nine years at the institution. Before coming to USF, Fr. Clark had served as Jesuit Provincial of the California Province and academic vice president at Loyola Marymount University in Los Angeles. Among his many achievements while at USF, Fr. Clark played a major role in building positive relations between the USF Faculty Association and the administration. In September 1997, after a nationwide search, James Wiser, senior vice president and dean of faculties at Loyola University of Chicago, was named USF's new vice president for academic affairs. Wiser, a widely published scholar in political theory, had served as dean of the College of Arts and Sciences, chairman of the Department of Political Science, and as a political science professor at Loyola of Chicago, where he was recognized as Teacher of the Year in Loyola's honors program. During Wiser's second year at USF, Fr. Schlegel added the designation of provost to his title.

In November 1999, Fr. Schlegel announced to the USF community that he was returning to the Midwest to assume the presidency of Creighton University in Omaha, Nebraska, where he had begun his career in higher education 30 years earlier. In his farewell convocation address on March 23, 2000, Fr. Schlegel hearkened back to his inaugural address of October 26, 1991, where he stated that "my deepest hopes for the University of San Francisco into the next century — are that it remains committed to its rich tradition as Catholic and Jesuit, that it continues to play its role as provider of morally educated leadership for this wonderful city, that it continues to empower the marginalized, to temper the conventional trends of the day with the proven wisdom of the past; that it not hide its light under a bushel but shine forth as a beacon on the Hilltop; that it be open as an intellectual, cultural, and moral crossroads; that as a bridge it connects all those elements of society that are separated." He closed the convocation by thanking the board of trustees, faculty, students, and staff for making his hope at the start of his administration a reality by the end of his administration. "USF has become a bridge, a crossroads, and a beacon," the outgoing president stated, with a "wonderful future to claim."

A Global Perspective 148

THE UNIVERSITY OF SAN FRANCISCO HAS HAD AN international character since its founding in 1855. The first seven presidents of the institution were Italian Jesuit immigrants; most of the first faculty members were immigrants from Italy or Ireland; and during the university's first decades, virtually all of the students were first- or second-generation Irish or Italian, a partial reflection of the immigrant population of San Francisco. In the last decades of the 19th century, large numbers of Germans and French immigrated to San Francisco, many of whom enrolled at St. Ignatius College, further adding to the institution's European diversity on the eve of the 20th century.

Today at the University of San Francisco, the tradition of educating the children of first- and second-generation immigrants continues. In the fall of 2004, almost 9 percent of all first-time freshmen were immigrants to the United States, and more than 42 percent of all first-time freshmen had one or more parents who were immigrants to this country. The current student body, however, is ethnically much more diverse than it was in the 19th century. Among the entire USF undergraduate and graduate student population of 8,274 students at the beginning of the fall semester of 2004, 41 percent identified their ethnic background as Asian, African American, Hispanic, Native Hawaiian/Pacific Islander, or multiethnic. Almost 8 percent of the student population is international, including nearly 400 students from Asia: China, Hong Kong, India, Indonesia, Japan, Korea, the Philippines, Taiwan, or Thailand. USF is currently one of the 20 most ethnically diverse universities in the United States, according to several national publications, and it is also the most ethnically diverse of the 28 Jesuit colleges and universities in the United States.

USF currently has almost 81,000 living alumni, of whom more than 2,900 are international. The university consistently reaches out to these international alumni through special events, programs, and visits by executive officers. The *USF Magazine* frequently carries articles that have an international focus.

The University of San Francisco sponsors a wide range of international programs, including undergraduate and graduate programs in cooperation with Péter Pázmány Catholic University in Budapest, Hungary. These USF students are standing at Hosek Ter (Hero's Square) in Budapest. Pictured here (left to right) are Jessica Gueco, Nicole Duran, Crystal Lewis, and Melissa Segado.

SHARON LI, UNIVERSITY OF SAN FRANCISCO

During their spring break, USF students (left to right) Marcie Rodriguez and Celestine Johnson work to enhance the lives of families in the Guatemalan village of San Lucas Toliman.

The Lawyer, a magazine published by USF's School of Law, devoted the entire spring 2002 issue to the globalization of legal education. One article in the issue focused on the commitment of USF President Stephen A. Privett, S.J., to values-based international education. "If on-campus diversity provides USF with a learning resource absent from many other universities," stated Fr. Privett, "so does engaging other cultures on their own turf and their own terms. Both campus diversity and experiencing other cultures contribute to our humanizing of education." Consistent with this global perspective, Fr. Privett recently joined student groups traveling and studying in South Africa and India.

Although there has always been an international stream flowing though USF's institutional life as witnessed by the European immigrants who founded, staffed, and attended the institution during its first 50 years; by the large percentage of current students who are international; and by the school's current multitude of study abroad and international programs, this international stream has been transformed into a river of moral commitment channeled toward the promotion of international justice. This commitment is articulated in the current USF Vision, Mission, and Values Statement, which calls for the university to take a "global perspective that educates leaders who will fashion a more humane and just world."

The schools and colleges comprising the University of San Francisco offer students and faculty a multitude of international experiences that enrich the learning community and fulfill the university's mission. The USF School of Law, for example, through its Center for Law and Global Justice, has engaged at various times in human rights and economic development activities around the world. These programs include human rights internships for USF law students at the University of Central America in San Salvador; judicial training programs in association with Hanoi Law University, the Ho Chi Minh City University Law School, the People's Supreme Court, and the United Nations Development Program in Hanoi, Vietnam; and legal education, human rights, economic development and rule-of-law projects in Phnom Penh, Cambodia, the Eastern Islands of Indonesia, and East Timor. The law school has also engaged in faculty and student exchange programs with Ho Chi Minh City College of Law in Vietnam and the East China University in Shanghai. It offers summer study abroad programs at Trinity University, Dublin, Ireland; at Charles University, Prague, the Czech Republic; and at Péter Pázmány Catholic University in Budapest, Hungary. The law school currently provides students with internships at the State University of Rio de Janeiro and at the United Nations Commission on Human Rights in Geneva, the law school's international human rights clinic.

It has also been instrumental in developing two justice centers for legal aid in Cape Town, South Africa; and an educational outreach scholarship program connected with the Tibetan government in exile in India. Finally, the law school offers two master's of law programs for foreign practicing lawyers in comparative law and intellectual property.

USF's School of Business and Management has recently provided numerous international opportunities for faculty and students to develop a global perspective on business and management, including cooperative MBA programs with the Korean Advanced Institute for Science and Technology in Seoul; with the Helia Business School in Helsinki, Finland; and with Peking University in Beijing, where USF was a founding member of the Consortium of Jesuit Universities. The USF School of Business and Management also has a joint academic project with the Estonia Business School in Tallinn, Estonia, and a cooperative agreement with Universidad Adolfo Ibanez, in Santiago, Chile. The school sponsors study tours for business students to Universidad Iberoamericana in Mexico City and to Frankfurt, Germany; and over the years, the school has also organized study tours to the United Kingdom, Russia, Estonia, the Czech Republic, Chile, Japan, Hong Kong, Ecuador, Costa Rica, Chile, Japan, mainland China, Korea, Malaysia, Singapore, and Australia.

USF's College of Arts and Sciences also offers a wide range of international programs that help fulfill the institution's mission. These have included in the last few years the numerous initiatives developed by the Center for the Pacific Rim (vignette #137); the Maria Elena G. Yuchengco Philippines Studies Program, which offers courses on Filipino society, culture, history, and politics to students of Filipino and non-Filipino descent; undergraduate and graduate programs in cooperation with Péter Pázmány Catholic University, in Budapest, Hungary; cooperative M.S. programs in environmental management with Ateneo de

Manila University in Manila, the Philippines; Xiamen University in Xiamen, China; and in Bangkok, Thailand; an M.S. in financial analysis in Bangkok, Thailand; cooperative undergraduate programs with Ateneo de Manila University and with Universidad Centroamericana in San Salvador; and cooperative undergraduate programs with Universidad Ibereoamericana in Tijuana and Puebla, Mexico, and with Universidad Jesuita Alberto Hurtado in Santiago, Chile. In addition, the college has recently sponsored travel study programs or service learning opportunities in South Africa, England, Austria, Peru, Chile, Belize, and India.

The School of Education, in cooperation with the College of Arts and Sciences, also

Since 1997, the University of San Francisco has cooperated with Universidad Ibereoamericana in Mexico in an undergraduate exchange program. Pictured here are USF students at Puebla, Mexico, one of the program locations.

UNIVERSITY OF SAN FRANCISCO ARCHIVES

In 2004, a group of USF students from the Erasmus Project, a living learning community that participates in community service, traveled to India. Pictured with the students are David Batstone, professor of theology and religious studies (back row, second from left) and Michael Duffy, associate director, University Ministry (back row, far right).

offers an M.A. in teaching English as a second language in cooperation with Xiamen Educational College in Xiamen, China. In addition, the USF School of Nursing offers a clinical program for prospective nurses in Guatemala and a continuing education program for practicing nurses in London. Finally, University Ministry offers an international social justice program, the Arrupe Immersion Experience, in which students build homes, deliver meals to the sick, and seek to learn by living in poverty areas in Guatemala, in Tijuana, Mexico, in Belize, and in Peru.

USF students currently study abroad at a large number of locations around the world as exchange students for the same costs as if they were on the USF campus. They are also entitled to the same financial aid (except for federal work study). These opportunities include Ateneo de Manila University, in the Philippines; five locations through Universidad Iberoamericana, in Mexico (Mexico City, Leon, Torreon, Puebla, Tijuana); ITESO, in Guadalajara, Mexico; Universidad Catolica de Quito, in Quito, Ecuador; Universidad Jesuita Alberto Hurtado, in Santiago, Chile; Pontificia Universidade Catolica do Rio de Janeiro, in Brazil; Universite Catholique de Lille, in Lille, France; University College, in Dublin, Ireland; Universidad Comillas, in Madrid, Spain; Universidad de Deusto, in Bilbao, Spain; Sophia University, in Tokyo, Japan; and Universidad Ramon Lull, in Barcelona, Spain.

During the 2004–2005 academic year, 600 USF students participated in USF-sponsored study abroad, exchange, intern, or social justice programs, or studied abroad through cooperative arrangements with other American universities or organizations, coordinated through the central USF study abroad office, under the direction of Margaret Barrett, who has witnessed a dramatic increase in the number of USF study abroad students since the mid-1990s. During the past seven years, the university's study abroad students have been consistently surveyed regarding their oversees experiences. More than 90 percent of those surveyed "strongly agreed" that their study abroad experience helped them "appreciate and understand a different culture" and "develop greater tolerance for different people and ideas."

Many of USF's on-campus programs have a strong international focus, reflective of extensive faculty involvement in international research, teaching, and service. USF's core curriculum also has an international dimension, and asks students to "assume a level of social responsibility, and communicate and apply knowledge to a world shared by all people and held in trust for future generations" and to "demonstrate an understanding of the effects of global interdependence." These objectives, along with the USF mission statement, serve as a touchstone for all of USF's programs, including the myriad degrees and certificates the university offers that have a specific international focus. Given this international focus, it is not surprising that USF has sent 273 volunteers into the Peace Corps since 1961, to serve in 84 different countries. Year after year, USF is among the top 10 colleges and universities of its size in the nation with regard to the number of active Peace Corps volunteers.

Reflective of USF's international focus, 12 Nobel Peace Prize laureates from throughout the world have spoken to the campus community over the past few years. These distinguished individuals have included Bishop Desmond Tutu (South Africa); John Hume, Mairead Corrigan Maguire, and Betty Williams (Northern Ireland); Elie Wiesel and Jody Williams (United States), Rigoberta Menchú (Guatemala), Adolfo-Pérez Esquivel (Argentina), and Oscar Arias Sánchez (Costa Rica). In September 2003, the Dalai Lama, the exiled leader of Tibet and 1989 Nobel Peace Prize laureate, received a USF honorary doctorate and shared his views on international peace and justice with the community. In April 2005,

Kim Dae-jung, former president of South Korea and 2000 Nobel Peace Prize laureate, was awarded an honorary doctorate by USF. In May 2005, Shirin Ebadi, the 2003 Nobel Peace Prize laureate, and the first Muslim woman and first Iranian to receive that honor, spoke at USF and received an honorary doctorate.

In the final analysis, the international commitment of USF is linked, in the words of the USF Vision, Mission, and Values Statement, to a "culture of service that respects and promotes the dignity of every person" and to a 465-year-old Jesuit legacy of international education, service to others, and to the promotion of justice throughout the world.

The Habitat for Humanity building project in Mexico is one of many service learning opportunities for USF students.

UNIVERSITY OF SAN FRANCISCO ARCHIVES

The Administration of Stephen A. Privett, S.J.

THE IMAGES OF THE SIX SLAIN JESUIT PRIESTS FROM El Salvador, displayed on large banners in the sanctuary of St. Ignatius Church, were clearly visible to the 1,200 people who gathered for the inaugural Mass of Stephen A. Privett, S.J., 27th president of the University of San Francisco. It was November 17, 2000, and the date of the new president's inaugural Mass had been purposely chosen to coincide with the eleventh anniversary of the assassination of the Jesuit priests, their female employee, and her daughter, at the University of Central America in El Salvador. Throughout the two days of ceremonies, including the Mass and the installation, the commemoration of the Jesuit martyrs was interwoven with the inauguration's overall theme, Educating for a Just Society.

During the inaugural Mass of Stephen A. Privett, S.J., the images of six slain Jesuit priests (Ignacio Ellacuría, S.J., Segundo Montes, S.J., Juan Ramón Moreno, S.J., Amando López, S.J., Ignacio Martín-Baró, S.J., and Joaquin López y López, S.J.) from the campus of the Universidad Centroamericana (UCA) in San Salvador were carried to the sanctuary of St. Ignatius Church. The Jesuits' housekeeper, Julia Elba Ramos, and her daughter, Celina, were also killed by El Salvadorian soldiers.

In his inaugural address, Fr. Privett spoke of his fellow Jesuits: "These renowned and gifted scholar-teachers dedicated considerable talents and their entire academic careers to serving as the moral compass in a country where the vast majority of poor Salvadorans were the victims of a mindless violence and terror, savagely directed toward maintaining the privileged status of a small but wealthy and powerful elite. These university martyrs whom we remember today pointed out to an entire nation the narrow and steep pathway home that they walked, but too few were willing to follow. They exercised their human and academic responsibilities with the requisite rigor and the marshalling of compelling evidence that is the heart of the academic enterprise. May their passion for the truth and their courage in its telling continue to be a model and an inspiration for all of us at the Jesuit University of San Francisco." Throughout his administration, Fr. Privett has offered a moral compass to guide the university community toward social justice at home and abroad, seeking to achieve, in the words of what became the touchstone phrase for the new administration's overarching mission: to educate minds and hearts to change the world.

Stephen Privett was born in St. Mary's Hospital, across the street from the University of San Francisco, on December 8, 1942. He went to school in Los Angeles and entered the Society of Jesus in 1960. He earned a bachelor's degree in philosophy and classics from Gonzaga University, a master's degree in divinity from the Graduate Theological Union in Berkeley, and a doctorate in Catechetics from the Catholic University of America, where his dissertation focused on the Hispanic community in the Catholic Church. Early in his career, Fr. Privett taught at the Jesuit High School in Sacramento and served as principal of Bellarmine College Preparatory in San Jose. In 1985, he joined the faculty of Santa Clara University, and through his service, teaching, and publications was promoted to associate professor and granted tenure. Fr. Privett received the Sears Roebuck Foundation Award for teaching excellence and campus leadership at Santa Clara University, where he was named academic vice president in 1991 and provost in 1997. In March of 2000, the USF Board of Trustees, led by Lou Giraudo and Dominic Tarantino, recruited Fr. Privett to become the next president of USF, replacing John Schlegel, S.J., who had been named the new president of Creighton University. Fr. Privett assumed the presidency on September 15, 2000.

During the first months of Fr. Privett's administration, a leadership team composed of the president, provost, vice presidents, deans, chief information officer, general counsel, and associate provost drafted a Vision, Mission, and Values Statement, which was widely circulated to the USF community for comment and changes. Fr. Privett shared the draft with hundreds of alumni in a series of town hall meetings that took him from USF to Washington, D.C., with stops in Los Angeles, Palo Alto, Sacramento, Marin County, and Berkeley along the way. The dialogue about the final form of the statement, involving all segments of the university community, continued until it was approved by the USF Board of Trustees on September 11, 2001, as discussed in the next vignette.

Concurrent with the holding of the town hall meetings, the Privett administration faced one of its first serious issues: the future direction of the St. Ignatius Institute. From the first days of his administration, Fr. Privett was aware that this important USF academic program was directed by non-faculty members and that it had separated itself from the mainstream of university life. For example, the institute ran its own study abroad program and held liturgies for its students off campus, during which no Jesuits from USF were allowed to preside. After consultation with the executive committee of the board of trustees, individual trustees, and the executive officers of the university administration, Fr. Privett—acting through Stanley Nel, dean of the College of Arts and Sciences—changed the administrative leadership of the St. Ignatius Institute, and appointed Paul Murphy, assistant professor of history, as the new director. This decision created considerable controversy in the USF community, manifested in pointed questions, comments, and some pickets at the town hall meetings; the departure of some faculty from the institute, though not from the university; and a well-organized media and letter-writing campaign from a group that

Stephen A. Privett, S.J., became the University of San Francisco's 27th president in 2000. By late 2004, his administration had witnessed the development and implementation of a new Vision, Mission, and Values Statement for the university; continuing growth of a diverse student body; major campus improvements, renovations, and technology upgrades; several new academic programs and institutes; and the successful launching of the largest fundraising campaign in the history of USF.

UNIVERSITY OF SAN FRANCISCO ARCHIVES

opposed the president's decision, an effort that reached the Archbishop of San Francisco and the Vatican. In the final analysis, the hierarchy of the Catholic Church supported the president's decision, and contrary to the critics' assertions that the president intended to close the institute, it is currently growing, and its students are fully integrated into the university community.

Continuing growth in student enrollment, and further increases in the diversity of the student population during the Privett administration have helped the university both to maintain its financial stability and to fulfill its mission to enroll a diverse student body. Under the direction of BJ Johnson, dean of academic services, enrollment has increased over ten percent during the last four years, from 7,366 in the fall of 2000 to 8,274 in the fall of 2004. Moreover, the percentage of minority and international students has increased from 45 percent to 48 percent during that same time period.

Significant organizational changes have taken place during Fr. Privett's presidency. The divisions of academic affairs and university life, for example, were combined into one division and renamed the provost division. This division, under Provost and Academic Vice President Jim Wiser, includes academic services, directed by Dean BJ Johnson; the Gleeson Library/Geschke Center, under Dean Tyrone Cannon; international relations, managed by Vice President Stanley Nel; and university

life, administered by Vice President Margaret Higgins. The six deans of the USF schools and colleges also report to the provost. They currently include Jennifer Turpin, College of Arts and Sciences; Jeffrey Brand, School of Law; Gary Williams, School of Business and Management; John Lantz, School of Nursing; Walter Gmelch, School of Education; and Larry Brewster, College of Professional Studies. Gerardo Marín, associate provost, also reports to the provost. The division of planning and budget, headed by Vice President Robert Niehoff, S.J., falls within the provost division as well, though in March 2005, Fr. Niehoff was selected to be the new president of John Carroll University, a Jesuit university in Cleveland, Ohio. This division includes the budget office, managed by Michael Harrington; institutional research, directed by Alan Ziajka; sponsored projects, under Pamela Miller; and instructional technology services, supervised by Tracy Schroeder, the university's chief information officer. The other two major divisions of USF are business and finance, under Vice President Charles Cross, and university advancement, directed by Vice President David Macmillan.

To date, the Privett administration has witnessed several major campus improvements, including the completion of the Koret Law Center at the School of Law; the completion and dedication of Loyola Village, a new residence for students that had originally been designed under Fr. Schlegel's presidency as a residence for faculty and staff; the renovation of Gillson Hall; the completion of new studios and offices for the fine arts program; and the completion of a new wing (Malloy Hall) for the School of Business and Management. The new campus master plan calls for a major renovation of Campion Hall, the oldest academic building on campus; significant remodeling of the Lone Mountain campus; renovation of University Center and Xavier Hall, with the latter to be renamed Fromm Hall after the founders of the Fromm Institute (vignette

The University of San Francisco announced the establishment of the Leo T. McCarthy Center for Public Service and the Common Good at a press conference on November 30, 2001. The McCarthy Center "is about creating a better society for all—through teaching, faculty scholarship, publications, and forums," USF President Stephen A. Privett, S.J., said at the press conference. Pictured (left to right) are USF student Liz Holstein (daughter of donors Robert and Loretta Holstein), Fr. Privett, former Lt. Governor of California Leo T. McCarthy (a USF graduate and donor to the Center), donors Joan and Ralph Lane (USF sociology professor emeritus), and former San Francisco Mayor Art Agnos.

UNIVERSITY OF SAN FRANCISCO ARCHIVES

#130); and a host of other changes to the university campus over the next decade. Under the Privett administration, the university is also implementing a core network infrastructure project in conjunction with the master plan. Originally under the direction of the university's first chief information officer, the late Abe Baggen, the core infrastructure project, now directed by Tracy Schroeder, the new CIO, is designed to create a fiber optic/wire backbone for USF's telecommunications and data networks for the next decade. The project will involve the majority of campus buildings and will entail significant space planning. The goal is to greatly enhance student learning and administrative services through technology, as called for in the Vision, Mission, and Values Statement of the university.

During the Privett administration, the university began its most ambitious fundraising campaign to date. Under the direction of David Macmillan, vice president for university advancement, The Campaign for USF: Educating Minds and Hearts to Change the World seeks to raise $175 million. By the fall of 2004, in its "quiet phase," $110 million had already been raised, including $30 million for

scholarship endowments, $10 million from the Friends of the Fromm Institute for Fromm Hall and other campaign projects, $10 million for the School of Law's Koret Law Center, $18 million for the building of a new wing for the School of Business and Management and for the renovation of the McLaren Center, and numerous other gifts and pledges. Overall, the campaign will enhance all aspects of campus life, including student scholarships and academic program endowments; faculty research and faculty chair endowments; technology upgrades; a new science building, a renovated Campion Hall, and a renovated Memorial Gymnasium; as well as a wide range of other major projects that will help fulfill the strategic initiatives of USF's Vision, Mission, and Values Statement.

Symbolic of the university's commitment to social justice during the Privett administration, the trustees of the university voted in June 2003 to extend healthcare benefits to all adults legally-domiciled with USF employees. This policy change eliminated marriage as a prerequisite for healthcare benefits and established USF as the first Jesuit university in the nation to make a healthcare commitment to same-sex

James Wiser, the current provost and academic vice president of USF, came to the university in January 1998 from his position as senior vice president and dean of faculties at Loyola University of Chicago. A political scientist by training, Wiser received his master's and doctoral degrees from Duke University and his bachelor's degree from the University of Notre Dame. In his tenure at USF, he has successfully worked with faculty, deans, and other administrators to develop new academic programs; institute a new core curriculum; integrate the efforts of academic and non-academic units to enhance student learning; and ensure the academic and fiscal integrity of the university. He has developed a well-deserved reputation as a consensus builder, whose door is always open to colleagues and students.

In September 2003, the Dalai Lama made an historic visit to the University of San Francisco. He spent several days on campus where he met with students, faculty, and staff; gave two public presentations; and was awarded an honorary doctorate. He was escorted around campus by USF President Stephen A. Privett, S.J. (left) and John R. Treacy, S.J. (right), rector of the Jesuit Community.

Shirin Ebadi (center), the 2003 Nobel Peace Prize laureate, and the first Muslim woman and first Iranian to receive that honor, spoke at USF in May 2005 and was presented an honorary doctorate by Maureen Clark (left), vice chair of the USF Board of Trustees, and USF President Stephen A. Privett, S.J.

UNIVERSITY OF SAN FRANCISCO ARCHIVES

partners, non-married other-sex partners, and financially dependent family members such as parents or siblings. The USF Faculty Association voted in February 2004 to support this new healthcare policy. Although some argued that extending healthcare benefits to same-sex partners violated Catholic doctrine, two experts on Catholic teachings, William Bassett, USF professor of law, and Peter Togni, S.J., associate dean of arts and sciences and assistant professor of theology and religious studies, concluded that Catholic church documents going back as far as 1931 support the extension of healthcare benefits to legally-domiciled adults as a matter of social justice. For Fr. Privett, the extension of health care benefits to this population was an ethical imperative, supported by Catholic doctrine.

Among the many programs initiated during the administration of Fr. Privett, the Leo T. McCarthy Center for Public Service and the Common Good perhaps best exemplifies the inaugural theme of educating for a just society. Indeed, a conversation at Fr. Privett's inauguration between the new president and Leo McCarthy, graduate of USF and former

Lieutenant Governor of California, led to a major gift by McCarthy that now underpins the center. The center has also received major support from Ralph Lane, emeritus USF faculty member in sociology, and from his wife, Joan; from the late Robert Mills Holstein, a prominent attorney, and his wife, Loretta; and from the federal government, assisted by Congresswoman Nancy Pelosi. The center, under the direction of Patrick Murphy, associate professor of politics, is designed for USF students from a variety of academic programs who are interested in public service. It combines direct social experience, coursework consistent with students' public service interests, and special programs featuring distinguished public servants. The center also serves as a catalyst for campus-wide discussions about social justice issues, policy analysis, and scholarly research.

In May 2004, Ralph and Joan Lane gave a second $1 million gift to USF to endow a Center for Catholic Studies and Social Thought, to be named in their honor. The center will focus the insights of Catholic social thought on contemporary social problems and will be fully integrated into the university community. The family of former USF president and current chancellor, John Lo Schiavo, S.J., has agreed to have a fully endowed chair, named for Joseph and Anna Lo Schiavo, located at the center.

The guiding principles for the program initiatives during Fr. Privett's administration are found in the current University of San Francisco Vision, Mission, and Values Statement, the subject of the final vignette.

Vision, Mission, and Values

THE MORNING OF SEPTEMBER 11, 2001, DAWNED BRIGHT and clear in San Francisco, in New York City, and in Washington, D.C. USF President Stephen A. Privett, S.J., was preparing to meet with the USF Board of Trustees regarding the approval of a new Vision, Mission, and Values Statement for the university. The board meeting was to be followed at noon by the Mass of the Holy Spirit, an annual event held in St. Ignatius Church to bless the start of the academic year, with the homily to be delivered by Fr. Privett.

Just before the board meeting was to begin, word reached the president and the trustees of the terrorist attacks on the World Trade Center in New York City and the Pentagon in Washington, D.C., followed shortly by news of the crash of another terrorist-hijacked plane in the fields of Pennsylvania. There was discussion among the USF leadership about closing the university after early reports indicated that other locations in the nation, such as the Golden Gate Bridge, might be at risk from further terrorist attacks. The university stayed open, but the plan for the day was dramatically changed. Fr. Privett discarded his prepared homily for the Mass and hastily wrote a few notes for a new homily about the day's tragedy.

By noon, St. Ignatius Church was completely filled with more than 2,000 students, faculty, staff, and community members. In his homily, Fr. Privett addressed the day's events: "Today violence has rocked this country in ways previously unknown to us, and sent shock waves around the world. What is a one-time occurrence for us is woven into the fabric of daily life for our brothers and sisters in Africa,

"The University of San Francisco will be internationally recognized as a premier Jesuit Catholic, urban university with a global perspective that educates leaders who will fashion a more humane and just world."

VISION, MISSION AND VALUES STATEMENT OF THE UNIVERSITY OF SAN FRANCISCO, APPROVED BY THE USF BOARD OF TRUSTEES, SEPTEMEBER 11, 2001

Northern Ireland, Palestine, Iraq, and the former Yugoslavia. Today we see first-hand the consequences of violence and hatred, unrestrained by reason or compassion. Today we acknowledge that hatred and violence are inherently destructive and lead only to darkness and death…. Let us determine not to return hatred with hatred or violence with violence, but to draw deep from the wellspring of our humanity and produce living waters that offer more abundant life to all men and women, not just a privileged few."

393

Reflecting a deeply held Jesuit values system, the USF Vision, Mission, and Values Statement calls for students and graduates to be "men and women for others." As part of USF's Arrupe Immersion Experience, the students pictured here used their spring break to help build a Habitat for Humanity home in Guatemala and to cook and serve meals for workers in Mexico.

the evening of September 11, John Savard, S.J., director of University Ministry, led a candle-light vigil in Harney Plaza for students. Other events and forums were held on campus over the next several days to discuss the tragedy, and University Ministry started a fund to help the families of firefighters who lost their lives in the aftermath of the terrorist attacks.

The Vision, Mission, and Values Statement, initially drafted by the president's leadership team, reflected nearly a year of discussion among trustees, faculty, staff, students, and alumni, who had an opportunity to discuss the statement directly with the president during a series of coast-to-coast town hall meetings (vignette #149). The final version

Fr. Privett concluded his homily by referring specifically to the language of the Vision, Mission, and Values Statement, which the board had passed that morning: "Can anyone today argue that we do not need persons who will fashion a more just and humane world? Does anyone not see the world's need for men and women who live their lives for others and not simply for themselves? Is it even possible to talk of faith in God that does not do justice in this world? Can any of us question the necessity of promoting a common good that transcends the interests of particular groups or individuals? Is there any doubt that reasoned discourse and persuasion, not coercion and violence, are the only tools with which to make a better world?"

After the noon Mass, campus support activities continued throughout the day, with students, faculty, and staff meeting in lounges, residence halls, and other sites around campus to discuss the day's events and to support each other. On

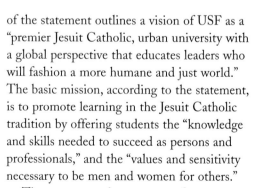

of the statement outlines a vision of USF as a "premier Jesuit Catholic, urban university with a global perspective that educates leaders who will fashion a more humane and just world." The basic mission, according to the statement, is to promote learning in the Jesuit Catholic tradition by offering students the "knowledge and skills needed to succeed as persons and professionals," and the "values and sensitivity necessary to be men and women for others."

The statement advances a set of 10 core values, including the precepts that faith and reason are complementary, that persons of any faith and those with no religious belief at all are full members of the community, and that truth and evidence should be followed to their logical conclusions. The statement proposes that learning should be social and humanizing rather than competitive, that the common good arrived at by reasoned discourse is superior to coercive decision-making, and that "diversity of perspectives, experiences, and traditions" is essential for quality education. Reflecting a deeply held Jesuit value system, the statement posits that excellence is the standard for "teaching, scholarship, and creative expression," and that there is a social responsibility to "create, communicate, and apply knowledge" within a "world shared by all people." The statement stresses that there is a moral dimension to every significant human choice, that no individual or group should prosper at the expense of others, and that the university should reflect a "culture of service that respects and promotes the dignity of every person." The statement's strategic initiatives are to recruit a diverse and outstanding faculty and staff committed to the university's mission and core values, to enroll and support diverse and academically oriented students who will become socially responsible leaders, and to provide the resources for technology and facilities to "promote learning throughout the university." In 2004, a fourth strategic initiative was added to the original listing: "Continue to strengthen the university's financial resources to support its educational programs."

Since the approval of the Vision, Mission, and Values Statement on September 11, 2001, a primary goal of the university has been to translate the words of the document into action. The continuing growth of a diverse and academically talented student population and a committed faculty and staff; the allocation of resources necessary to promote learning through enhanced technology and improved facilities; the initiation of new programs, such as the Leo T. McCarthy Center for Public Service and the Common Good and the Ralph and Joan Lane Center for Catholic Studies and Social Thought; the extension of health

care benefits to all adults legally domiciled with USF faculty and staff; and the growth of international programs that reflect a global perspective, are some examples of the university's efforts to translate rhetoric into reality. The future of USF is closely tied to successfully demonstrating to its various publics that it does, in fact, offer students a rigorous Jesuit Catholic curriculum "that educates leaders who will fashion a more humane and just world."

In the summer of 2003, Fr. Privett took 16 members of USF's leadership team, including the deans, vice presidents, and the chief information officer, to El Salvador to experience first hand that country's social, political, and economic challenges. The group gained a better sense of the nation's tragic and brutal recent past, which witnessed a 12-year civil war that left more than 75,000 poor campesinos and their supporters dead; and saw the assassination of the country's Archbishop, Oscar Romero, S.J.; and the murder of six Jesuit priests, their housekeeper and her daughter. Fr. Privett, who had personal experience in El Salvador, sought to enhance the leadership team's understanding of what it means to be involved in Jesuit education and to fulfill USF's mission to educate leaders with a global perspective who will work for social justice.

In the summer of 2003, USF President Stephen A. Privett, S.J., took members of the USF leadership team to El Salvador to better understand the country's tragic past and current challenges. In the back row, left to right, are Charles Cross, vice president, business and finance; Jeffrey Brand, dean, school of law; Jim Wiser, provost; Larry Brewster, dean, college of professional studies; and Gerardo Marín, associate provost. In the middle row, left to right, are David Macmillan, vice president, university advancement; Margaret Higgins, vice president, university life; Tracy Schroeder, chief information officer; Robert Niehoff, S.J., vice president, planning and budget; and Kevin Yonkers-Talz, program host in El Salvador. In the front row, left to right, are John Lantz, dean, school of nursing; Donna Davis, general counsel; Tyrone Cannon, dean, Gleeson Library/Geschke Center; Stanley Nel, vice president, international relations; BJ Johnson, dean, academic services; Lizz Kaune, program host in El Salvador; and Fr. Privett.

UNIVERSITY OF SAN FRANCISCO ARCHIVES

Epilogue

CORE ELEMENTS OF THE VISION, MISSION, AND VALUES Statement of the University of San Francisco can be found in Jesuit values that stretch back to the 16th century, when Saint Ignatius of Loyola sent his followers throughout the world to establish educational institutions and promote Jesuit and Catholic ideals. The result of these first Jesuit efforts was the largest network of schools and colleges in the world, amounting to 700 educational institutions by the 18th century. In 1789, Jesuit education came to the new republic of the United States with the founding of Georgetown College. By 1855, the seeds of Jesuit education were planted in San Francisco with the establishment of St. Ignatius Academy, the forerunner of the University of San Francisco.

During its 150 years, the university's leaders and community members have repeatedly demonstrated faith, reason, creativity, and moral courage to face challenges and crises. In 1855, the challenge was to build and sustain an experiment in Jesuit education amidst the turbulent economic and social forces at work in San Francisco in the wake of the California Gold Rush. Despite a minuscule original student enrollment and rising debt that extended over several decades, St. Ignatius Academy (renamed St. Ignatius College in 1859) gradually expanded its student base, built a reputation for academic excellence, and developed a network of social service and community outreach activities in San Francisco buttressed by its connection to St. Ignatius Church. In 1880, St. Ignatius Church and College, facing rising taxes on the Market Street location and increasing enrollment, risked further indebtedness to build a magnificent institution on Van Ness Avenue, a block from City Hall, that soon became a center of educational and cultural life in San Francisco. The college's academic reputation spread throughout the state and nation, and many of its graduates became leaders in law, government, business, and religion. This golden age of St. Ignatius Church and College came to an abrupt end on April 18, 1906, when an earthquake and fire destroyed the institution and two-thirds of San Francisco.

The Jesuit leadership of St. Ignatius College faced the crisis caused by the earthquake and fire with courage and commitment. They rebuilt a temporary home near Golden Gate Park, known as the shirt factory, which opened just five months after the devastation. For 21 years, the institution at this location successfully adapted to local, national, and international forces and events. The college added a law

An aerial view of the University of San Francisco in 2005. From 1970 to 2005, USF witnessed extraordinary change: student enrollment grew from less than 6,800 to more than 8,300 students; the number of full-time faculty members increased from 230 to 348; the institution significantly increased in acreage and number of buildings; and the university developed a multitude of new on-campus, regional, and international programs.

school, experimented with new programs, launched an intercollegiate athletics program, and managed to survive the drain on human resources caused by World War I and major debts from the rebuilding of the church, exacerbated by a national and local recession. By 1919, the institution was $1 million in debt and on the verge of declaring bankruptcy. The college leadership called upon alumni and the community for help, and they were successful in the first major fundraising campaign in the institution's history. So successful, in fact, that the school began to purchase property in the 1920s and early 1930s on the current site of the University of San Francisco.

St. Ignatius College was renamed the University of San Francisco in 1930. The Depression of the 1930s, followed by World War II, brought new challenges to USF. Enrollment decreased slightly during the Depression years and

resources were limited, but the real crisis came during the war, when enrollment fell dramatically and the monthly debt skyrocketed. Once again, the university leadership confronted the crisis by first securing federal support through an officer-training program, and when that ended, by appealing directly to alumni and friends for financial support to save the school.

With the end of World War II, the school faced pressure to rapidly expand facilities, classrooms, and housing for the burgeoning enrollment at USF, induced in part by the G.I. Bill of Rights. Changes in the student population also called for more programming for professionals and working adults with families. Again, the institution responded effectively, launching a major building campaign and initiating many new programs. Growth continued into the turbulent 1960s, which saw the emergence of new demands for ethnic and gender equality, social change, and curriculum reform. USF rose to the challenge and successfully addressed problems that proved insurmountable at many other institutions of higher education. The early 1970s brought the nation's economic problems, including recession and inflation, directly to USF, and when paired with a significant decline in the number of traditional college-age students, USF faced another major economic crisis. Three successive USF administrations struggled with a host of economic and enrollment issues, and it was not until the early 1980s that solid financial stability was restored, enrollment began to increase, and the stage was set for the expansion of the 1990s that has continued into our own time.

Recent years have been punctuated by a new set of issues and challenges, including defining an identity for a Jesuit Catholic institution in a world marked by international economic and social injustice, violence, and war. The Vision, Mission, and Values Statement speaks to those global issues and advances a blueprint for change. Its words reflect a legacy of educational excellence and social justice in San Francisco that has prevailed for 150 years and Jesuit values that have endured for 465 years — a promise to use reason and faith, mind and heart, to seek a better world now and in the future.

Outside the office of University Ministry on the USF campus is a bronze plaque portraying Saint Ignatius of Loyola (1491-1556), founder of the Society of Jesus. The inscription A.M.D.G. stands for the Latin phrase *Ad Majorem Dei Gloriam* ("For the greater glory of God"), the motto of the Jesuits.

Presidents of the University of San Francisco

The Presidents of St. Ignatius Academy (1855–1859), St. Ignatius College (1859–1912), the University of St. Ignatius (1912–1919), St. Ignatius College (1919–1930), and the University of San Francisco (1930 to present):

1855–1862: ANTHONY MARASCHI, S.J.

1862–1865: NICOLAS CONGIATO, S.J.

1865–1866: BURCHARD VILLIGER, S.J.

1866–1869: NICOLAS CONGIATO, S.J.

1869–1873: JOSEPH BAYMA, S.J.

1873–1876: ALOYSIUS MASNATA, S.J.

1876–1880: JOHN PINASCO, S.J.

1880–1883: ROBERT E. KENNA, S.J.

1883–1887: JOSEPH C. SASIA, S.J.

1887–1893: HENRY IMODA, S.J.

1893–1896: EDWARD P. ALLEN, S.J.

1896–1908: JOHN P. FRIEDEN, S.J.

1908–1911: JOSEPH C. SASIA, S.J.

1911–1915: ALBERT F. TRIVELLI, S.J.

1915–1919: PATRICK J. FOOTE, S.J.

1919–1925: PIUS L. MOORE, S.J.

1925–1932: EDWARD J. WHELAN, S.J.

1932–1934: WILLIAM I. LONERGAN, S.J.

1934–1938: HAROLD E. RING, S.J.

1938–1954: WILLIAM J. DUNNE, S.J.

1954–1963: JOHN F.X. CONNOLLY, S.J.

1963–1969: CHARLES W. DULLEA, S.J.

1969–1972: ALBERT R. JONSEN, S.J.

1972–1976: WILLIAM C. McINNES, S.J.

1977–1991: JOHN LO SCHIAVO, S.J.

1991–2000: JOHN P. SCHLEGEL, S.J.

2000–PRESENT: STEPHEN A. PRIVETT, S.J.

Acknowledgments

THE WRITING OF THIS book was a three-year labor of love pursued largely in the early morning hours before I transitioned to my day-job as the director of institutional research at the University of San Francisco. The book never would have succeeded, however, without the help of many Jesuits, their lay colleagues, and many other individuals.

First, Michael Kotlanger, S.J., the archivist of the University of San Francisco, provided the archival material, including letters, newspapers, photographs, and other primary documents, that made this book possible. He also read every word of this manuscript in its preliminary form and offered many invaluable insights and corrections. John Lo Schiavo, S.J., chancellor and former president of USF, read the manuscript as well, giving special attention to factual details about the institution's history over the past 50 years. Edward Stackpoole, S.J., former dean of the College of Arts and Sciences, past rector of the USF Jesuit Community, and professor of English emeritus at USF, gave me complete access to the archives of the USF Jesuit Community and offered many valuable contributions to the book along the way.

Stephen Privett, S.J., the current president of USF, supported the project in numerous ways from its inception. In addition to writing a wonderful foreword to the book, he provided many valuable contributions to the text and gave me the needed administrative, financial, and moral support to see the project through to completion. Likewise, Robert Niehoff, S.J., vice president for planning and budget at USF and future president of John Carroll University, supported this project from the beginning, read every vignette in its draft form, and greatly contributed to my knowledge of the Society of Jesus. Thomas Lucas, S.J., associate professor of visual and performing arts, also provided several important insights and corrections to the book. Daniel Peterson, S.J., the archivist of the California Province of the Society of Jesus, supplied critical biographical information about several of USF's former presidents from the vast resources he maintains at the offices of the California Province in Los Gatos, California. He also supplied several rare photos for this book. Renate Otterbach, my senior research analyst in the Office of Institutional Research, was invaluable in helping to gather and analyze much of the current data about USF that I have integrated into this book. The many other Jesuit and lay colleagues who contributed material to this book are acknowledged in the notes that follow. I am also grateful to the USF Jesuit Community for its financial support in publishing this book.

On the editorial side, I am indebted to Jim Muyo, director of publications in university advancement at USF, for his keen editorial suggestions and corrections. He also provided overall production and design management for the project. In this effort, he was greatly aided by Thomas Henke, senior graphic designer at USF. The overall design of the book is Mr. Henke's vision. Angie Davis, editor of *USF Magazine,* also lent her editorial expertise to the project.

Paul Totah, author of *Spiritus 'Magis': 150 Years of St. Ignatius College Preparatory,* deserves a special acknowledgment. He generously shared the photos he gathered for his book with the USF design staff, and many of those photos appear in *Legacy and Promise.* He was also a constant source of support for my book, even as he was completing his own.

My wife, Judy Ziajka, and my daughter, Anna, edited early versions of many of the vignettes contained in *Legacy and Promise.* My son, Anton, with Anna's help, designed a handsome precursor to this book, including photographs, which he downloaded from USF's sesquicentennial Web site. Their initiative greatly encouraged my efforts when the project was at an early stage.

It has become a cliché to claim that one stands on the shoulders of giants, but in this case it seems appropriate to make that declaration. Two deceased Jesuit historians, Joseph Riordan, S.J., and John McGloin, S.J., provided in their earlier histories of USF the foundation I needed to embark on this work. In my 22 years as an administrator at the University of San Francisco, I have often heard it said that with the decline in the number of Jesuits in the United States and throughout the world, it is critically important for lay people to increasingly help carry out the mission of the Society of Jesus. I would like to think that this book will help serve that goal, and that it will contribute to the legacy and the promise of the Jesuits of the University of San Francisco. It is to those Jesuits who founded the academy 150 years ago as a one-room school house amid the sand dunes of San Francisco, who guided the college through the numerous crises and opportunities described in this book, and who, with the help of their lay colleagues, made the university one of the premier institutions of higher education in the world, that this book is dedicated.

Alan Ziajka
University of San Francisco
June 1, 2005

Notes

THE BOOKS, MAGAZINE AND JOURNAL ARTICLES, NEWSPAPERS, catalogs, yearbooks, reports, individuals, and other primary and secondary sources that informed *Legacy and Promise* are referenced in the following notes. To cite every source of information in the text itself would leave the vignettes unduly cluttered with footnotes. For the complete citation for the publications listed in the notes, see the bibliography.

Introduction to Part I Among the many books written about the origins and development of the Society of Jesus, one of the best is *Landmarking: City, Church, & Jesuit Urban Strategy* by Thomas Lucas, S.J. The development of the Society of Jesus during its first decades is described in *The First Jesuits* by John O'Malley, S.J. The success of the Society of Jesus in employing sound leadership principles throughout its history is chronicled in *Heroic Leadership: Best Practices from a 450-Year-Old Company that Changed the World* by Chris Lowney.

Vignette #1 For the first vignette, and many to follow, I have drawn upon *The First Half Century: St. Ignatius Church and College*, written by Joseph Riordan, S.J., and published in 1905. Also indispensable has been *Jesuits by the Golden Gate: the Society of Jesus in San Francisco, 1849–1969* by John McGloin, S.J., the late historian and archivist at USF. His book was published in 1972. The quote from Fr. Langlois is from page 20 of Fr. Riordan's book, and the quote from Fr. Accolti is from page 1 of Fr. McGloin's book. The California Gold Rush is described in numerous books. Three of the best accounts are in *Americans and the California Dream, 1850–1915,* by Kevin Starr, pages 50–68; *Fire and Gold: the San Francisco Story,* by Charles Fracchia, pages 36–44; and *The Age of Gold: The California Gold Rush and the New American Dream,* by H.W. Brands.

Vignette #2 The life and times of Michael Accolti, S.J., are described in detail in *The First Half Century: St. Ignatius Church and College* by Joseph Riordan, S.J., pages 22–28, and in *Jesuits by the Golden Gate: The Society of Jesus in San Francisco, 1849–1969* by John McGloin, S.J., pages 1–3, 12–20, and 175–177. Many of the missionary activities of the Jesuits in the West during the 19th century are described in "Across the Rockies: Italian Jesuits in the American West," which appeared in the November 2000 issue of the magazine *Company,* written by Gerald McKevitt, S.J., pages 17–21.

Vignette #3 The founding of St. Ignatius Academy is described in *The First Half Century: St. Ignatius Church and College* by Joseph Riordan, S.J., pages 69–101, and in *Jesuits by the Golden Gate: The Society of Jesus in San Francisco, 1849–1969* by John McGloin, S.J., pages 12–21. The role played by Joseph Bixio, S.J., in the founding of St. Ignatius College is described in "Joseph Bixio, Furtive Founder of the University of San Francisco," which appeared in the spring 1999 issue of the journal *California History,* written by Cornelius Buckley, S.J., pages 14–25.

Vignette #4 The life of Anthony Maraschi, S.J., is described in *The First Half Century: St. Ignatius Church and College* by Joseph Riordan, S.J., pages 69–112 and 319–323, and in *Jesuits by the Golden Gate: The Society of Jesus in San Francisco, 1849–1969* by John McGloin, S.J., pages 2–50 and 156–161. The quote from the *Alta California* appears on page 14 of Fr. McGloin's book.

Vignette #5 The work of Joseph Riordan, S.J., who wrote *The First Half Century: St. Ignatius Church and College,* has been indispensable in documenting the first students at the institution. Also useful has been *Jesuits by the Golden Gate: The Society of Jesus in San Francisco, 1849–1969* by John McGloin. S.J. The quote from John Cunningham appears on page 45 of Fr. McGloin's book. Current enrollment data was supplied by Fred Baldwin, database manager in Academic Services at USF.

Vignette #6 The history of the founding of St. Ignatius Church is described in *The First Half Century: St. Ignatius Church and College* by Joseph Riordan, S.J., pages 73–104; in *Jesuits by the Golden Gate: The Society* of Jesus in San Francisco, 1849–1969 by John McGloin, S.J., pages 7–12; and in *The Fifth St. Ignatius Church in San Francisco, California, 1910–1950* (an unpublished USF master's thesis) by Terrance Mahan, S.J., pages 3-12.

Vignette #7 The story of the first immigrants to America is effectively told in two different articles that appeared in the magazine *Discover:* "Coming to America," by David Meltzer, which appeared in October 1993, pages 90–97, and "The Latest on the Earliest," by Jared Diamond, which appeared in January 1990, page 50. Recent research on the sophisticated culture and enormous size of the Native American population in the Western Hemisphere on the eve of the Spanish explorations and the decimation of that population because of European diseases is summarized by Charles Mann in "1491," which appeared in the March 2002 issue of *Atlantic Monthly*, pages 41–53. The missionary activities of the Jesuits in the West during the 19th century are described in "Across the Rockies: Italian Jesuits in the American West," by Gerald McKevitt, S.J., which appeared in the November 2000 issue of the magazine *Company*, pages 17–21. The classic works on European immigration to America are Oscar Handlin's the *Uprooted* and Marcus Lee Hansen's *The Atlantic Migration 1607–1860*. Page Smith's *The Rise of Industrial America: A People's History of the Post Reconstruction Era* effectively places 19th-century immigration patterns, especially the Chinese experience, within the broad sweep of American history.

Vignette #8 The ethnic composition of St. Ignatius College during the second half of the 19th century is indicated by Joseph Riordan, S.J., in his book *The First Half Century: St. Ignatius Church and College,* pages 378–384. Immigration statistics for San Francisco during this same time period are available from the U.S. Census Bureau at its Web site, www.census.gov. The ethnicity of USF students in the fall semester of 2004 is portrayed in table 17 of the document *USF Registration Statistics, Fall Semester 2004,* published by the Office of the Registrar and compiled by Fred Baldwin, database manager, Academic Services. The annual UCLA-CIRP freshman survey is administered by the staff of Academic Services, under the direction of Dean BJ Johnson. Fr. Privett's inaugural address is available from the President's Office through the USF Web site home page, at www.usfca.edu/president/speeches/inaug_address.html.

Vignette #9 The best resource for information on the institution's state charter is *Jesuits by the Golden Gate: The Society of Jesus in San Francisco, 1849–1969,* by John McGloin, S.J. The appendices of his book, pages 286–288, contain a copy of the original petition for a state charter submitted by Fr. Maraschi, as well as the full charter signed by the governor, the president of the board of education, the surveyor general of the State of California, and the superintendent of public

instruction. The quote from Preston Devine appears on page 249 of Fr. McGloin's book.

Vignette #10 For timely information on undergraduate and graduate degrees conferred at our most recent commencement ceremonies, I am indebted to Kevin Wilson, associate registrar, Academic Services. Likewise, James Ostrowski, USF's law school registrar, furnished the most recent information on degrees conferred by our law school. Michael Kotlanger, S.J., USF's archivist, furnished details on Bowie's life after graduating. The Office of Institutional Research houses information on the USF graduating student surveys from May 1997 to the present, as well as data on USF students who have pursued professional degrees in the health-related professions since 1996.

Vignette #11 The faculty members of St. Ignatius College during its early years are described in *The First Half Century: St. Ignatius Church and College* by Joseph Riordan, S.J., pages 81–86, and in *Jesuits by the Golden Gate: The Society of Jesus in San Francisco, 1849–1969* by John McGloin, S.J., pages 13–144. The varied career of Joseph Bixio, S.J., is portrayed in the article "Joseph Bixio, Furtive Founder of the University of San Francisco," by Cornelius Buckley, S.J., that appeared in the Spring 1999 issue of *California History*, volume LXXVII, No. 1, pages 14–25. Current information regarding full-time faculty and part-time faculty at USF is located in the Office of Institutional Research.

Vignette #12 The original prospectus and catalog of St. Ignatius College are housed in the university archives, located in the Gleeson Library/Geschke Center, administered by Michael Kotlanger, S.J., university archivist.

Vignette #13 Details on the second St. Ignatius Church and College in San Francisco are furnished in *The First Half Century: St. Ignatius Church and College* by Joseph Riordan, S.J., pages 112–114, and in *Jesuits by the Golden Gate: The Society of Jesus in San Francisco, 1849–1969* by John McGloin, S.J., pages 22–42.

Vignette #14 The parish issue for St. Ignatius Church during its early years is framed in *The First Half Century: St. Ignatius Church and College* by Joseph Riordan, S.J., pages 103–104; in *Jesuits by the Golden Gate: The Society of Jesus in San Francisco, 1849–1969* by John McGloin, S.J., page 26; and in *The Fifth St. Ignatius Church in San Francisco, California, 1910–1950* (an unpublished USF master's thesis) by Terrance Mahan, S.J., pages 164–168. The restoration of parish status to St. Ignatius Church is described in *USFnews*, vol. 3, no. 56, January 18, 1994.

Vignette #15 The life and times of James Bouchard, S.J., is described in *Eloquent Indian: the Life of James Bouchard, California Jesuit,* by John McGloin, S.J. The book, published by Stanford University Press in 1949, was an outgrowth of Fr. McGloin's doctoral dissertation. The newspaper quotes are from pages 268–284 of that book. Other details on Fr. Bouchard can be found in *The First Half Century: St. Ignatius Church and College* by Joseph Riordan, S.J. pages 286–287.

Vignette #16 The history of St. Ignatius College during the 1860s and 1870s is described in *The First Half Century: St. Ignatius Church and College* by Joseph Riordan, S.J., pages 92–215, and in *Jesuits by the Golden Gate: The Society of Jesus in San Francisco, 1849–1969* by John McGloin, S.J., pages 28–31. The achievements of Jesuit science professors Joseph Bayma, S.J., Joseph Neri, S.J., and Aloysius Varsi, S.J., are described in *Spiritus Magis: 150 Years of St. Ignatius College Preparatory* by Paul Totah, whose book also details the life of John Montgomery, a former St. Ignatius College student who developed and flew the world's first glider.

Vignette #17 An extensive article on the life and work of Arthur Furst, written by Angie Davis, appeared in the fall 2001 issue of *University of San Francisco Magazine*, pages 12–17. Professor Benton's research and awards have been highlighted frequently throughout the last decade in numerous issues of *USFnews*, the USF community newsletter. Extensive articles appeared on 2/13/95, 2/26/96, and 10/15/96. For the life and times of Joseph Neri, S.J., there is probably no better source than *The First Half Century: St. Ignatius Church and College*, by Joseph Riordan, S.J., pages 159–193.

Vignette #18 *The First Jesuits* by John O'Malley provides a good overview of the social outreach activities of Saint Ignatius and his immediate Jesuit followers in 16th-century Europe. The efforts of the 19th-century Jesuits of St. Ignatius Church and College are described in *The First Half Century: St. Ignatius Church and College* by Joseph Riordan, S.J., pages 126, 148, and 199, and in *Jesuits by the Golden Gate: The Society of Jesus in San Francisco, 1849–1969* by John McGloin, S.J., pages 175–188. Fr. McGloin extends the history of the San Francisco Jesuits well into the 20th century. Michael Kotlanger, S.J., USF's archivist, also supplied several important details about the social service efforts of USF's Jesuits over the past 50 years. The current efforts in the community by St. Ignatius Church parish, under Charles Gagan, S.J., pastor, are described in the St. Ignatius Church pamphlet, *Programs and Services Guide*. Jani White, assistant director, University Ministry, supplied information about some of the more important current social activities of University Ministry, under the direction of John Savard, S.J., executive director.

Vignette #19 The 19th-century efforts by the Jesuits on behalf of the prisoners at San Quentin Prison are described by Joseph Riordan, S.J., in his book *The First Half Century: St. Ignatius Church and College,* pages 148 and 203. Nigel Hatton reported on Peter Togni, S.J., and his ministry to the inmates at San Quentin Prison

in the winter 2000 issue of *University of San Francisco Magazine,* page 24. Stephen Barber, S.J., the current Catholic Chaplin at San Quentin, was interviewed by Jack Smith for publication in *Catholic San Francisco,* February 13, 2004, and is available though the publication's Web site, catholic-sf.org/021304.html.

Vignette #20 The earthquake of 1868 is described in *The San Francisco Almanac* by Gladys Hansen, pages 192–193, and in a series of articles that appeared in the January 21, 1990, issue of the *San Francisco Chronicle.* The impact of the 1868 earthquake on St. Ignatius Church is detailed in *The First Half Century: St. Ignatius Church and College* by Joseph Riordan, S.J., pages 153–154 and in *Jesuits by the Golden Gate: The Society of Jesus in San Francisco, 1849–1969* by John McGloin, S.J., page 27. The quotes from the *Daily Alta California* appear in Fr. Riordan's book on page 154.

Vignette #21 *The First Half Century: St. Ignatius Church and College* by Joseph Riordan, S.J., pages 258–259, is the source of quotes and details regarding 19th-century Christmas giving by the Jesuits of St. Ignatius Church and College. Melanie Bailey, assistant for parish programs, furnished the current information regarding Christmas outreach activities by St. Ignatius Church. Likewise, Jani White, assistant director, University Ministry, supplied the information pertaining to the work of University Ministry during Christmas 2003 and 2004. The citizens of San Francisco owe a debt of gratitude to Charles Gagan, S.J., pastor of St. Ignatius Church, and to John Savard, S.J., executive director, University Ministry, and to their Jesuit and lay colleagues for sustaining and enhancing the charitable ministry of their predecessors.

Vignette #22 Events surrounding the institution's move from Market Street to Van Ness Avenue are described in *The First Half Century: St. Ignatius Church and College* by Joseph Riordan, S.J., pages 215–243, and in *Jesuits by the Golden Gate: The Society of Jesus in San Francisco, 1849–1969* by John McGloin, S.J., pages 43–71.

Vignette #23 The institution's first alumni events are described in *The First Half Century: St. Ignatius Church and College* by Joseph Riordan, S.J., pages 344–351.

Vignette #24 The life and times of Jeremiah Sullivan are recounted in *The Bulletin of the Museum of the City of San Francisco, Diamond Jubilee Edition,* September 8, 1925; *Who's Who in America, Volume I, 1987–1942; The University of San Francisco School of Law: A History 1912–1917,* by Eric Abrahamson, pages 19–20; and *Jesuits by the Golden Gate: The Society of Jesus in San Francisco, 1849–1969,* by John McGloin, S.J., pages 55, 69, and 86.

Vignette #25 America's Gilded Age is described in most standard texts on United States history, including *The United States: An Experiment in Democracy* by Avery Craven and Walter Johnson, pages 438-504. A good summary of the Gilded Age in San Francisco appears in *Historic San Francisco* by Rand Richards, pages 127–139. The Golden Age of St. Ignatius College is described in detail in *The First Half Century: St. Ignatius Church and College* by Joseph Riordan, S.J., pages 233–335, and in *Jesuits by the Golden Gate: The Society of Jesus in San Francisco, 1849–1969* by John McGloin, S.J., pages 54–71.

Vignette #26 The educational accomplishments of St. Ignatius College during the Golden Age are described in *The First Half Century: St. Ignatius Church and College* by Joseph Riordan, S.J., pages 306–315, and in *Jesuits by the Golden Gate: The Society of Jesus in San Francisco, 1849–1969* by John McGloin, S.J., pages 54–71. The quote from the Journal of Commerce appears on page 56 of Fr. McGloin's book.

Vignette #27 Athletics, drama, and music at St. Ignatius College during the Golden Age are described in *The First Half Century: St. Ignatius Church and College* by Joseph Riordan, S.J., pages 343–359, and in *Jesuits by the Golden Gate: The Society of Jesus in San Francisco, 1849–1969* by John McGloin, S.J., pages 56–71. For information about USF's current performing arts programs, I am indebted to several faculty members in visual and performing arts at USF: Thomas Lucas, S.J., Rick Davis, Kathileen Gallagher, Alexandra Amati-Camperi, and Peter Novak.

Vignette #28 The history of St. Ignatius Church during its Golden Age is described in *The First Half Century: St. Ignatius Church and College* by Joseph Riordan, S.J., pages 289–298; in *Jesuits by the Golden Gate: The Society of Jesus in San Francisco, 1849–1969* by John McGloin, S.J., pages 43–53; and in *The Fifth St. Ignatius Church in San Francisco, California, 1910–1950* (an unpublished USF master's thesis) by Terrance Mahan, S.J., pages 16–17. The quote from Fr. Kavanagh appears on page 52 of Fr. McGloin's book.

Vignette #29 Information about the assassinations of four United States presidents can be found in numerous books and articles. Especially comprehensive accounts appear in Page Smith's *Trial by Fire: A People's History of the Civil War and Reconstruction*, pages 568-580, and in his *The Rise of Industrial America: A People's History of the Post Reconstruction Era*, pages 454, 457, and 903–904. The responses by the Jesuits of St. Ignatius Church to the assassinations of Presidents Lincoln, Garfield, and McKinley are described in *The First Half Century: St. Ignatius Church and College* by Joseph Riordan, S.J., pages 139, 252, and 338. The Mass at St. Ignatius Church and related activities following the assassination of President Kennedy are described in the *San Francisco Foghorn* of November 26, 1963 and in the *University of San Francisco Alumnus*, February–March 1964. Fr. Privett's complete homily of September 11, 2001, is available through the USF Web site, at www.usfca.edu/president/homilies/9_11_01.html.

Vignette #30 Events surrounding the institution's Golden Jubilee are described in *The First Half Century: St Ignatius Church and College* by Joseph Riordan, S.J., pages 363–364, and in *Jesuits by the Golden Gate: The Society of Jesus in San Francisco, 1849–1969* by John McGloin, S.J., pages 68–71.

Vignettes #31, #32, and #33 The earthquake and fire of 1906 is described in *The San Francisco Almanac* by Gladys Hansen, former archivist of San Francisco, page 195; in *Denial of Disaster: The Untold Story and Photographs of the San Francisco Earthquake and Fire of 1906* by Gladys Hansen and Emmet Condon; in *Fire and Gold: The San Francisco Story* by Charles Fracchia, pages 99–127; in *Historic San Francisco: A Concise History and Guide* by Rand Richards, pages 171–189; in *San Francisco: Magic City* by Cora Older, pages 1–8; in *The Great Earthquake and Firestorms of 1906* by Philip Fradkin; and in numerous other books and articles. The impact of the 1906 earthquake and fire on St. Ignatius Church is detailed in *Jesuits by the Golden Gate: The Society of Jesus in San Francisco, 1849–1969* by John McGloin, S.J., pages 72–80, and in numerous documents, such as the personal reminiscences of John Frieden, S.J., president of St. Ignatius College in 1906, that are housed in the USF archives and maintained by Michael Kotlanger, S.J., USF's archivist, who also added several important details to the 1906 story.

Vignettes #34, #35, and #36 The recovery and rebuilding of San Francisco following the 1906 earthquake and fire are described in *The San Francisco Almanac* by Gladys Hansen, page 195; in *Fire and Gold: The San Francisco Story* by Charles Fracchia, pages 129–130; in *Historic San Francisco: A Concise History and Guide* by Rand Richards, pages 191–198; and in numerous other books and articles. The Web site for the Museum of the City of San Francisco, www.sfmuseum.org, contains an excellent collection of photos of the damage caused throughout the city by the earthquake and fire, including photos of the gutted St. Ignatius Church and College, as well as photos of the city's recovery. The impact of the 1906 earthquake and fire on St. Ignatius Church and College is detailed in *Jesuits by the Golden Gate: The Society of Jesus in San Francisco, 1849–1969* by John McGloin, S.J., pages 81–88. The quote from Archbishop Riordan appears on page 81 of Fr. McGloin's book. The recovery of the church and college is described in numerous other documents, such as the personal reminiscences of John Frieden, S.J., president of St. Ignatius College in 1906, that are housed in the USF archives and maintained by Michael Kotlanger, S.J., USF's archivist, who also added several important details regarding the institution's recovery, rebuilding, and rebirth.

Vignette #37 The life and times of John Frieden, S.J., are described in *The First Half Century: St. Ignatius Church and College* by Joseph Riordan, S.J., pages 315–366, and in *Jesuits by the Golden Gate: The Society of*

Jesus in San Francisco, 1849–1969 by John McGloin, S.J., pages 63–78 and 82–98. Important information about Fr. Frieden's life is also found in a paper he wrote about his experiences during the 1906 earthquake and fire and in other documents housed in the USF archives, expertly presided over by Michael Kotlanger, S.J.

Vignette #38 The life of Bertha Welch and her contributions to St. Ignatius Church and College are described in *The First Half Century: St. Ignatius Church and College* by Joseph Riordan, S.J., page 329, and in *Jesuits by the Golden Gate: The Society of Jesus in San Francisco, 1849–1969* by John McGloin, S.J., pages 82–85, 107–108, and page 129. Important information about Welch's life is also found in the *Monitor* of April 1922 and in other documents housed in the USF archives and available through Michael Kotlanger, S.J.

Vignette #39 St. Ignatius College, when it was known as the shirt factory between 1906 and 1927, is described in *Jesuits by the Golden Gate: The Society of Jesus in San Francisco, 1849–1969* by John McGloin, S.J., pages 89–112. Important information about the institution during this era was also obtained from primary documents housed in the USF Jesuit community, and furnished by Edward Stackpoole, S.J., former rector of the Jesuit community and USF professor emeritus of English.

Vignette #40 The 1906–1907 academic year at St. Ignatius College is described in *Jesuits by the Golden Gate: The Society of Jesus in San Francisco, 1849–1969* by John McGloin, S.J., pages 96–97. Valuable information about the institution during this year was also obtained from documents furnished by Edward Stackpoole, S.J., former rector of the Jesuit community and USF professor emeritus of English. Important details about the year were also found in *The Senior*, a student publication of the era furnished by USF's archivist, Michael Kotlanger, S.J.

Vignette #41 The alumni banquet of 1906 is described in *Jesuits by the Golden Gate: The Society of Jesus in San Francisco, 1849–1969* by John McGloin, S.J. pages 97–98. Important information about the 1906 investigations into civic corruption can be found in *San Francisco: The Story of a City* by John McGloin, S.J., pages 267–277; in *Fire and Gold: The San Francisco Story* by Charles Fracchia, pages 103–132; and in *Boss Ruef's San Francisco: The Story of the Union Labor Party, Big Business, and the Graft Prosecution* by Walter Bean.

Vignette #42 Details about the city of San Francisco in 1909 can be found in *The San Francisco Almanac* by Gladys Hansen, pages 44–45. The St. Ignatius College class of 1909 is described in *The Senior*, a student publication of the era furnished by USF's archivist, Michael Kotlanger, S.J., who also supplied several other important details about that class.

Vignette #43 Information on the origins of the athletic program at USF can be found in *Jesuits by the Golden Gate: The Society of Jesus in San Francisco, 1849–1969* by John McGloin, S.J., page 99. Valuable information about our institution's athletic history was also supplied by USF's archivist, Michael Kotlanger, S.J., in the form of student publications such as the *Ignatian* and the *Senior*, photos and game tickets, and other sources of USF sports memorabilia. I could not resist opening this vignette using a few words from the famous baseball poem, *Casey at the Bat* by Ernest Thayer.

Vignette #44 Documents related to the university seal were obtained from the USF archives, courtesy of the university's archivist, Michael Kotlanger, S.J. These documents included the 1911 issue of the *Ignatian*, where Lyle's design first appeared; the *Woodstock Letters*, a Jesuit publication from the early 20th century; and a brief report on the seal written by Michael Mathes, former history professor at USF. Fr. Kotlanger also provided many valuable insights into the history of the USF seal. Jim Muyo, the university's director of publications, also provided a file of helpful information regarding the USF seal.

Vignette #45 The first issue of the *Ignatian*, published in 1911, is housed in the USF archives, and maintained by the USF archivist, Michael Kotlanger, S.J.

Vignette #46 The events leading up to the ground breaking for the new St. Ignatius Church are described in *Jesuits by the Golden Gate: The Society of Jesus in San Francisco, 1849–1969* by John McGloin, S.J., pages 113–133, and in *The Fifth St. Ignatius Church in San Francisco, California, 1910–1950* (an unpublished USF master's thesis) by Terrance Mahan, S.J., pages 42–43.

Vignette #47 The ceremony during which the cornerstone was laid for the new St. Ignatius Church is described in *Jesuits by the Golden Gate: The Society of Jesus in San Francisco, 1849–1969* by John McGloin, S.J., pages 95–96; and in *The Fifth St. Ignatius Church in San Francisco, California, 1910–1950* (an unpublished USF master's thesis) by Terrance Mahan, S.J., pages 52–54. The quotes from Rev. Gleason, Archbishop Riordan, and the *San Francisco Star*, appear on pages 95 and 96 of Fr. McGloin's book.

Vignette #48 The first Mass and dedication ceremony for the new St. Ignatius Church is described in *The Fifth St. Ignatius Church in San Francisco, California, 1910–1950* (an unpublished USF master's thesis) by Terrance Mahan, S.J., pages 60–63, and in *Jesuits by the Golden Gate: The Society of Jesus in San Francisco, 1849–1969* by John McGloin, S.J., pages 114–117. The quotes from the *San Francisco Monitor*, Fr. Trivelli, and Bishop O'Dea appear in Fr. McGloin's book, pages 115–116.

Vignette #49 The history of the bell in St. Ignatius Church is described in *The First Half Century: St. Ignatius Church and College* by Joseph Riordan, S.J., pages 118–122; in *Jesuits by the Golden Gate: The Society of Jesus in San Francisco, 1849–1969* by John McGloin, S.J.; pages 84–85; and in *The Fifth St. Ignatius Church in San Francisco, California, 1910–1950* (an unpublished USF master's thesis) by Terrance Mahan, S.J., pages 159–163. Fr. Privett's complete homily of September 11, 2002, is available through the USF Web site at www.usfca.edu/president/homilies/9_11_02.html.

Vignette #50 Information about anti-Catholicism in America can be found in numerous books and articles. An especially comprehensive account appears in Page Smith's *The Rise of Industrial America: A People's History of the Post Reconstruction Era*, pages 580-586. The origins of the USF School of Law are described in *The University of San Francisco School of Law: A History, 1912–1987* by Eric Abrahamson, pages 11–22; and in *Jesuits by the Golden Gate: The Society of Jesus in San Francisco, 1849–1969* by John McGloin, S.J., pages 100–102.

Vignette #51 The first class at the School of Law is described in *The University of San Francisco School of Law: A History, 1912–1987* by Eric Abrahamson, pages 11–13. The quote from Justice Devine's speech appears in *Jesuits by the Golden Gate: The Society of Jesus in San Francisco, 1849–1969* by John McGloin, S.J., page 101.

Vignette #52 The first faculty members at the School of Law are described in *The University of San Francisco School of Law: A History, 1912–1987* by Eric Abrahamson, pages 30–34. The quote about the law school faculty appears in the *Ignatian*, December 1912, page 42, and the quotation regarding law school attendance is in the *Ignatian*, April 1916, page 48.

Vignette #53 The life and times of Matthew Sullivan are described in *The University of San Francisco School of Law: A History, 1912–1987* by Eric Abrahamson, pages 16–19; in *Jesuits by the Golden Gate: The Society of Jesus in San Francisco, 1849–1969* by John McGloin, S.J., pages 158–163; and in *The History of San Francisco*, edited by Lewis Byington, pages 1–3. The quote about Chief Justice Sullivan's election appears in Byington's book, page 3.

Vignette #54 Among the hundreds of books and articles about the origins of World War I, Barbara Tuchman's *The Guns of August* is one of the most accessible. The assassination of Archduke Ferdinand and his wife is vividly described in *The Century* by Peter Jennings and Todd Brewster, pages 53 and 54. The impact of the war on the University of St. Ignatius is described in *Jesuits by the Golden Gate: The Society of Jesus in San Francisco, 1849–1969* by John McGloin, S.J., pages 103 and 104; and in all the issues of the *Ignatian* published between 1914 and 1918. The quote about the plight of Belgium appears in the December 1914 issue of the *Ignatian*, page 32.

Vignette #55 The Pan-Pacific International Exposition is described in numerous books and articles. One of the best descriptions can be found in *Fire and Gold: The San Francisco Story* by Charles Fracchia, pages 142–143. The 1915 issue of the *Ignatian* provides a wealth of information about life at the University of St. Ignatius during that year. The quotes about the university appear in the 1915 issue of the *Ignatian*, pages 47 and 54.

Vignette #56 For details on America's entrance into World War I, Page Smith's *America Enters the World: A People's History of the Progressive Era and World War I*, pages 467-525, is outstanding. The 1916 and 1917 issues of the *Ignatian* provide valuable commentary on the institution's attitudes about the looming war. The quote about the evils of war appears in the April 1916 issue, page 40; the quote regarding America's peculiar neutrality is on page 77 of the February 1917 issue; and the quote on calling for support for President Wilson appears in the November 1917 issue, page 46.

Vignette #57 The impact of the war on the University of St. Ignatius is described in *Jesuits by the Golden Gate: The Society of Jesus in San Francisco, 1849–1969* by John McGloin, S.J., pages 103 and 104, and in all of the issues of the *Ignatian* published between 1914 and 1918. The quote about the patriotism and military spirit on campus appears in the June 1918 issue, page 76, and the description of Lt. Devine's return to campus is on page 79 of that issue.

Vignette #58 Numerous letters from students and young alumni of the University of St. Ignatius, who served in all branches of the military during World War I, were published in the June 1918 and June 1919 issues of the *Ignatian*. The letter from Joseph Sullivan appears in the June 1919 issue, pages 11–16, and the letter from Richard Queen is found on pages 33–37 of the same issue. The letter from John Carson is in the 1918 issue, pages 46–49.

Vignette #59 The special church ceremony in 1918 to bless the service flag is described in *Jesuits by the Golden Gate: The Society of Jesus in San Francisco, 1849–1969* by John McGloin, S.J., pages 103–104, and in the June 1918 issue of the *Ignatian*, pages 16–18. The quote from William Sweigert appears on page 18 of that issue.

Vignette #60 The impact of the armistice on the University of St. Ignatius is described in *Jesuits by the Golden Gate: The Society of Jesus in San Francisco, 1849–1969* by John McGloin, S.J., page 104, and in the June 1919 issue of the *Ignatian*. A complete list of all the former students who served in World War I, including the names of the 10 who died appears on pages 57–66 of that issue. The quote regarding extending a welcome to the returning veterans is on page 58 of that issue, the quote about the filled classrooms in the School of Law can be found on page 79, and Hallinan's editorial on President Wilson's efforts appears on pages 54–55. Michael Kotlanger, S.J., USF's archivist, also supplied several important details about the 1918 influenza pandemic in San Francisco.

Vignette #61 The financial crisis of 1919 is described in *Jesuits by the Golden Gate: The Society of Jesus in San Francisco, 1849–1969* by John McGloin, S.J., pages 105–107; and in *The Fifth St. Ignatius Church in San Francisco, California, 1910–1950* (an unpublished USF master's thesis) by Terrance Mahan, S.J., pages 70–77. The quote from the *San Francisco Call* appears on page 105 of Fr. McGloin's book, and the proclamation by Archbishop Hanna is found on page 80 of Fr. Mahan's thesis.

Vignette #62 The successful efforts in securing support for St. Ignatius Church and College during the financial crisis of 1919 are described in *Jesuits by the Golden Gate: The Society of Jesus in San Francisco, 1849–1969* by John McGloin, S.J., pages 105–107, and in *The Fifth St. Ignatius Church in San Francisco, California, 1910–1950* (an unpublished USF master's thesis) by Terrance Mahan, S.J., pages 77–91. The quote from Fr. Moore appears on page 105 of Fr. McGloin's book. Details on the formation and development of the Loyola Guild are in the 1926 issue of the *Ignatian*, page 141; in Fr. McGloin's book, page 221; and from information supplied by Mira Schwirtz, *USFnews* writer and editor, who interviewed Connie Mack, current president of the Loyola Guild.

Vignette #63 The sodalities at St. Ignatius Church are described in *The First Half Century: St. Ignatius Church and College* by Joseph Riordan, S.J., pages 163 and 209, and in *The Fifth St. Ignatius Church in San Francisco, California, 1910–1950* (an unpublished USF master's thesis) by Terrance Mahan, S.J., pages 120–123.

Vignette #64 Background information on the names of the Jesuit educational institution before it became the University of San Francisco can be found in *Jesuits by the Golden Gate: The Society of Jesus in San Francisco, 1849–1969* by John McGloin, S.J., pages 12, 100, 106, and 152.

Vignette #65 The 1920s is described in most standard texts on United States history, including *The United States: An Experiment in Democracy* by Avery Craven and Walter Johnson, pages 656-686. A good summary of the 1920s in San Francisco appears in *The San Francisco Almanac* by Gladys Hansen, pages 47–49, and in *Fire and Gold: The San Francisco Story* by Charles Fracchia, pages 138-145. The 1920s at St. Ignatius College is detailed in *Jesuits by the Golden Gate: The Society of Jesus in San Francisco, 1849–1969* by John McGloin, S.J., pages 108–112, and in all issues of the *Ignatian* published during that decade.

Vignette #66 Background information on the first faculty building on the USF campus, including Welch's statement about the Jesuits for the house records, can

be found in *Jesuits by the Golden Gate: The Society of Jesus in San Francisco, 1849–1969* by John McGloin, S.J., pages 107 and 108. The article by George Devine, from which the quotes about the faculty building are drawn, appears in the *Ignatian*, June 1921, pages 8–15.

Vignette #67 Information on the curriculum of the 1920s is found in various St. Ignatius College Bulletins published from 1919 to 1930 that are housed in USF's archives and maintained by Michael Kotlanger, S.J., USF's archivist. The quote regarding the educational aim of the school appears in the *St. Ignatius College Prospectus, 1919–1920*, pages 7–8. The quote about developing character appears in the *St. Ignatius College Catalogue, 1925–1926*, page 11. The current Vision, Mission, and Values Statement of USF is available through the USF Web site at www.usfca.edu/mission/index.html.

Vignette #68 The first references to business-related classes at St. Ignatius College are found in the *St. Ignatius College Prospectus, 1861*, page 1, and in *The First Half Century: St. Ignatius Church and College* by Joseph Riordan, S.J., page 344. The quote regarding the addition of a College of Commerce and Finance appears in the *Ignatian*, 1925, page 36. Details on the entrance requirements and curriculum for the new College of Commerce and Finance are in the *Catalogue of St. Ignatius College, 1925–1926*, pages 70–72. The quote about the first graduates of the College of Commerce and Finance appears in the *Ignatian*, 1928, page 162.

Vignette #69 The first references to evening classes at St. Ignatius Academy are found in *The First Half Century: St. Ignatius Church and College* by Joseph Riordan, S.J., page 88. Details on the first evening programs in the 1920s appear in the *St. Ignatius College Catalogue, 1925–1926*, pages 70–71. Enrollment statistics on the evening programs during the late 1920s were furnished by Academic Services at USF, courtesy of Fred Baldwin, database manager.

Vignette #70 The School of Law during the 1920s is described in *The University of San Francisco School of Law: A History, 1912–1987* by Eric Abrahamson, pages 23–45. Details on the curriculum in the 1920s appear in the *St. Ignatius College Catalogue, 1925–1926*, pages 47–65. The quote about the future of the School of Law appears in the *Ignatian*, 1913, page 75. Enrollment statistics for the School of Law during the 1920s were furnished by Academic Services at USF, courtesy of Fred Baldwin, database manager.

Vignette #71 The first references to public speaking classes at St. Ignatius College are found in the *St. Ignatius College Prospectus, 1861*, page 1. The earliest examples of debating societies at the college are found in *The First Half Century: St. Ignatius Church and College* by Joseph Riordan, S.J., pages 122, 353, and 359. The quote regarding the success of the St. Ignatius

College debating team in the early 1920s appears in the *Ignatian*, June 1922, page 89. Details on the debates with other colleges held in 1927 are found in the *Ignatian*, 1927, pages 56–57. The McKinley Gold Medal Debate of 1925 is described in the *Ignatian*, 1925, page 38.

Vignette #72 The earliest descriptions of a drama program at St. Ignatius College are found in *The First Half Century: St Ignatius Church and College* by Joseph Riordan, S.J., page 343, and in *Jesuits by the Golden Gate: The Society of Jesus in San Francisco, 1849–1969* by John McGloin, S.J., page 25. The description and quotes regarding the *Pageant of Youth* appear in the *Ignatian*, 1925, pages 45–47. Details on the 1927–28 drama season, including the quote about the performances held in the new "little theater" of the Liberal Arts Building, are found in the *Ignatian*, 1928, pages 68–72. Information on the 1928–29 season is found in the *Ignatian*, 1929, pages 92–112. The quotation about James Gill appears on page 92 of that issue.

Vignette #73 Information about the first years of the intercollegiate basketball program at St. Ignatius College can be found in various issues of the *Ignatian*, beginning with the 1911 issue, pages 62–65. Other issues of the *Ignatian* that have been especially helpful were published in April 1916, pages 61–66; June 1918, pages 83–89; June 1920, pages 89–94; June 1921, pages 89–95; June 1922, pages 93–101; June 1923, pages 82–88; June 1924, pages 109–122; 1925, pages 58–70; 1926, pages 66–77; and 1927, pages 95–105.

Vignette #74 Details and quotes about the St. Ignatius College basketball championship teams of 1928 and 1929 can be found in the 1928 issue of the *Ignatian*, pages 117–130, and the 1929 issue, pages 202–221.

Vignette #75 Information about the first years of rugby and of the intercollegiate football program at St. Ignatius College can be found in various issues of the *Ignatian*, beginning with the 1912 issue, page 63. Other issues of the *Ignatian* that have been especially helpful were published in December 1914, pages 41–44; December 1915, pages 62–66; December 1917, pages 71–75; June 1924, page 110; 1925, pages 50–57; 1926, pages 56–65; and 1927, pages 83–93.

Vignette #76 Details about the St. Ignatius College football teams of 1927, 1928, and 1929 can be found in the following issues of the *Ignatian:* the 1928 issue, pages 91–113; the 1929 issue, pages 177–198; and the 1930 issue, pages not numbered.

Vignette #77 A brief history of baseball in the United States in the 19th century can be found in *100 Years of Major League Baseball* by David Nemec and Saul Wisnia, pages 6–21. The line from Walt Whitman is from a letter he wrote in 1889 and is reprinted in *100 Years of Major League Baseball*, page 6. Information about the early years of baseball at St. Ignatius College can be found in various issues of the *Ignatian*, beginning

with the 1912 issue, pages 71 and 72. Other issues of the *Ignatian* that have been especially helpful, and from which quotes were drawn, are the issues of December 1914, pages 45 and 46; March 1913, pages 71 and 72; April 1916, page 66; June 1916, pages 81–85; and June 1923, page 88.

Vignette #78 Details about the St. Ignatius College baseball teams from 1925 through 1929 can be found in the following issues of the *Ignatian:* the 1925 issue, pages 71–78; the 1926 issue, pages 80–84; the 1927 issue, pages 106–109; the 1928 issue, pages 132–136; and the 1929 issue, pages 228–233.

Vignette #79 The lives of Joseph Sasia, S.J., and Albert Trivelli, S.J., are described in *The Fifth St. Ignatius Church in San Francisco, California, 1910–1950* (an unpublished USF master's thesis) by Terrance Mahan, S.J., pages 36–37 and 49–50, and in files kept at the Jesuit community at USF, furnished by Edward Stackpoole, S.J., former rector of the Jesuit community and USF professor emeritus of English. Specific accomplishments and challenges during their respective administrations can be found in *Jesuits by the Golden Gate: The Society of Jesus in San Francisco, 1849–1969* by John McGloin, S.J., pages 95–100, 102, and 176. The quote about Fr. Trivelli can be found in the December 1911 issue of the *Ignatian,* page 54.

Vignette #80 The lives of Patrick Foote, S.J., and Pius Moore, S.J., are described in files kept at the Jesuit community at USF, furnished by Edward Stackpoole, S.J., former rector of the Jesuit community and USF professor emeritus of English. Specific accomplishments and challenges during their respective administrations can be found in *Jesuits by the Golden Gate: The Society of Jesus in San Francisco, 1849–1969* by John McGloin, S.J., pages 103–110. The quote about Fr. Foote can be found in the December 1915 issue of the *Ignatian*, page 47. Enrollment statistics for St. Ignatius College during the 1920s were furnished by Academic Services at USF, courtesy of Fred Baldwin, database manager.

Vignette #81 The planning and building of Campion Hall is described in *Jesuits by the Golden Gate: The Society of Jesus in San Francisco, 1849–1969* by John McGloin, S.J., pages 110–112. The depiction of the groundbreaking ceremony for the new building, including the quotes from the speakers at the event, can be found in the 1927 issue of the *Ignatian*, page 45. A description of the dedication can be found in the *San Francisco Monitor,* October 16, 1927, courtesy of Michael Kotlanger, USF's archivist.

Vignette #82 The social service and community outreach activities by the Jesuits of San Francisco during the 1920s are described in *Jesuits by the Golden Gate: The Society of Jesus in San Francisco, 1849–1969* by John McGloin, S.J., pages 179–181, and in *The Fifth St.*

Ignatius Church in San Francisco, California, 1910–1950 (an unpublished USF master's thesis) by Terrance Mahan, S.J., pages 97–99. Further details on the community outreach activities by the Jesuits of USF and St. Ignatius Church were furnished by Michael Kotlanger, S.J., university archivist, who personally knew many of the Jesuits described in this vignette, and who participated in some of the more recent outreach activities initiated by those men.

Vignette #83 The life and work of Richard Gleeson, S.J., is described in *Jesuits by the Golden Gate: The Society of Jesus in San Francisco, 1849–1969* by John McGloin, S.J., pages 79, 108, 128, and 212; in *The Fifth St. Ignatius Church in San Francisco, California, 1910–1950* (an unpublished USF master's thesis) by Terrance Mahan, S.J., pages 107 and 108; and the *Ignatian,* 1928, page 161.

Vignette #84 The stock market crash of 1929 and the Depression of the 1930s are described in most standard texts on U.S. history, including *The United States: An Experiment in Democracy* by Avery Craven and Walter Johnson, pages 704–708. A good summary of the 1930s in San Francisco appears in *The San Francisco Almanac* by Gladys Hansen, pages 49–53, and in *Fire and Gold: The San Francisco Story* by Charles Fracchia. The 1930s at the University of San Francisco are detailed in *Jesuits by the Golden Gate: The Society of Jesus in San Francisco, 1849–1969* by John McGloin, S.J., pages 152–170, and in the limited number of issues of the *Ignatian* published during that decade (1930–1932, 1937). Enrollment statistics from 1920 to 1939 were furnished by academic services at USF, courtesy of Fred Baldwin, database manager.

Vignette #85 Events surrounding the institution's name change from St. Ignatius College to the University of San Francisco are described in *Jesuits by the Golden Gate: The Society of Jesus in San Francisco, 1849–1969* by John McGloin, S.J., pages 152–154, and in the *Ignatian,* 1931, pages unnumbered.

Vignette #86 The Diamond Jubilee Celebration is described in *Jesuits by the Golden Gate: The Society of Jesus in San Francisco, 1849–1969* by John McGloin, S.J., pages 154–160, and in the *Ignatian,* 1931, pages unnumbered.

Vignette #87 The purchase of the Masonic Cemetery by USF is described in *Jesuits by the Golden Gate: The Society of Jesus in San Francisco, 1849–1969* by John McGloin, S.J., pages 160–163. The quote from the announcement about the cemetery's purchase is from page 160 of that book. An announcement about the purchase during the Golden Jubilee celebration is found in the *Ignatian,* 1931, pages unnumbered.

Vignette #88 Background information on the early years of the *Foghorn* is found in *Jesuits by the Golden Gate: The Society of Jesus in San Francisco, 1849–1969* by John McGloin, S.J., pages 164–165; in the *Ignatian,*

1927. page 44; in the *Foghorn,* May 10, 1961; and in an article by Gry Moren in *University of San Francisco Magazine,* spring 1997, pages 18–19.

Vignette #89 Background information on USF's intercollegiate athletic teams from 1930 to 1932 can be found in the *Ignatian,* 1930, pages unnumbered; the *Ignatian,* 1931, pages unnumbered; and the *University of San Francisco Annual, 1932,* pages 165–227. A discussion of the name change from the Grey Fog to the Dons appears in the *University of San Francisco Annual, 1932,* page 165, and in *Jesuits by the Golden Gate: The Society of Jesus in San Francisco, 1849–1969* by John McGloin, S.J., pages 164–165.

Vignette #90 Much of the biographical material on Fr. Flynn is in the form of curriculum vitae, a questionnaire completed by Fr. Flynn in 1944, class syllabi, and an alumni letter and sermon on the occasion of his Golden Jubilee. These documents were supplied by Daniel Peterson, S.J., archivist of the California Province of the Society of Jesus. Other information can be found in *Jesuits by the Golden Gate: The Society of Jesus in San Francisco, 1849–1969* by John McGloin, S.J., pages 164–165. Enrollment statistics from 1925 to 1934 were furnished by Academic Services at USF, courtesy of Fred Baldwin, database manager.

Vignette #91 Much of the biographical material on Fr. Whelan is in the form of a curriculum vitae, a questionnaire completed by Fr. Whelan in 1944, and various articles and personal letters. These documents were supplied by Daniel Peterson, S.J., archivist of the California Province of the Society of Jesus, and by Edward Stackpoole, S.J., former rector of the Jesuit community and USF professor emeritus of English. Other information can be found in *Jesuits by the Golden Gate: The Society of Jesus in San Francisco, 1849–1969* by John McGloin, S.J., pages 152–166.

Vignette #92 The impact of the Depression on USF is covered in *Jesuits by the Golden Gate: The Society of Jesus in San Francisco, 1849–1969* by John McGloin, S.J., pages 164–168; and in *The University of San Francisco School of Law: A History, 1912–1987* by Eric Abrahamson, pages 53–56. Much of the material on Fr. Ring was supplied by Daniel Peterson, S.J., archivist of the California Province of the Society of Jesus, and by Edward Stackpoole, S.J., former rector of the Jesuit community and USF professor emeritus of English. Enrollment statistics from 1929 to 1939 were furnished by Academic Services at USF, courtesy of Fred Baldwin, database manager. Co-curricular activities at USF during 1936 and 1937 are described in the 1937 edition of *The Don,* pages 30–65.

Vignette #93 Events leading up to World War II are described in most standard texts on United States history, such as *The United States: An Experiment in Democracy,* by Avery Craven and Walter Johnson, pages 783–802. A good summary of the Golden Gate International Exposition appears in *Fire and Gold: The San Francisco Story* by Charles Fracchia, pages 155 and 156. "USF Day" at the exposition is described in the *Foghorn*, May 10, 1961, page 11.

Vignette #94 The political situation in Europe on the eve of World War II is covered in most standard textbooks, including *A History of the Modern World* by R.R. Palmer and Joel Colton, pages 815–827. The context for the USF Credo, along with a full copy of the document, can be found in *Jesuits by the Golden Gate: The Society of Jesus in San Francisco, 1849–1969* by John McGloin, S.J., page 170. Biographical information about Fr. Feely can also be found in Fr. McGloin's book, on pages 205–221; and in *The University of San Francisco School of Law: A History, 1912–1987* by Eric Abrahamson, page 43. Much of the material on Fr. Feely was supplied by Edward Stackpoole, S.J., former rector of the Jesuit community and USF professor emeritus of English. Daniel Peterson, S.J., archivist of the California Province of the Society of Jesus also supplied many important documents about Fr. Feely.

Vignette #95 World War II is described in most standard texts on United States history, including *The United States: An Experiment in Democracy,* by Avery Craven and Walter Johnson, pages 803–843. A good summary of the reactions of San Franciscans to the onset of war appears in *Fire and Gold: The San Francisco Story* by Charles Fracchia, pages 156–159. The impact of the war on USF is covered in *Jesuits by the Golden Gate: The Society of Jesus in San Francisco, 1849–1969* by John McGloin, S.J., pages 170–174; and in *The University of San Francisco School of Law: A History, 1912–1987* by Eric Abrahamson, pages 62–64.

Vignette #96 The World War II naval engagement near Guadalcanal that cost Admiral Callaghan his life is described in *The History of United States Naval Operations in World War II, Volume V, The Struggle for Guadalcanal,* by Samuel Eliot Morison, pages 235-258. Descriptions of the memorial Masses in St. Ignatius Church are given in *Jesuits by the Golden Gate: The Society of Jesus in San Francisco, 1849–1969* by John McGloin, S.J., page 122, and pages 202–203.

Vignette #97 The information and direct quotes drawn from the letters written by World War II servicemen to Alexander Cody, S.J., appear in several issues of the *St. Ignatius Church Bulletin,* dated November 16, 1943; November 20, 1943; August 21, 1944; March 18, 1945; and April 26, 1945. The letters were made available by Daniel Peterson, S.J., archivist of the California Province of the Society of Jesus. Copies of the *Don Patrol* and the citation for Jerome Sullivan, S.J., were furnished by Michael Kotlanger, S.J., USF's archivist.

Vignette #98 The most moving and detailed account of the battle of Iwo Jima, including the famous flag-raising

ceremony on Mount Suribachi, the background to Joseph Rosenthal's photo, and the lives of the six men (Rene Gagnon, Harlon Block, Franklin Sousley, Mike Strank, Ira Hayes, and John Bradley) who were immortalized in the photograph, can be found in the book *Flags of Our Fathers* by James Bradley, son of corpsman John Bradley, who was one on the six who raised the flag. The quote from Rosenthal is found on page 157 of this book. A briefer account of the battle for Iwo Jima and Joe Rosenthal's photographic coverage of that event appears in an article by Christine Techky in *American History,* June 2000, pages 22–27, and in an article by Mel Taylor in *University of San Francisco Magazine,* spring 1995, pages 16–17. A description of the bronze plaque and service flag honoring the war dead from USF and St. Ignatius College is in *Jesuits by the Golden Gate: The Society of Jesus in San Francisco, 1849–1969* by John McGloin, S.J., pages 202–203.

Vignette #99 The final months of World War II are described in most texts on United States history, including *The United States: An Experiment in Democracy,* by Avery Craven and Walter Johnson, pages 836–841. A good summary of the reactions of San Franciscans to the end of war appears in *Fire and Gold: The San Francisco Story* by Charles Fracchia, page 159. The welcome by USF to the United Nations delegates is covered in Jesuits by the *Golden Gate: The Society of Jesus in San Francisco, 1849–1969* by John McGloin, S.J., page 189. The United Nations Conference held in San Francisco is detailed in *San Francisco: The Story of a City* by John McGloin, S.J., pages 346–349.

Vignette #100 The immediate postwar years at USF are detailed in *Jesuits by the Golden Gate: The Society of Jesus in San Francisco, 1849–1969* by John McGloin, S.J., pages 189–196; and in the *Alumni Bulletin* of November 1947, which carries an especially evocative account of the Memorial Mass of November 14, 1947. Enrollment statistics from the 1940s were furnished by Academic Services at USF, courtesy of Fred Baldwin, database manager.

Vignette #101 President Dunne's building plans, including quotes from his letter to the provincial, are given in *Jesuits by the Golden Gate: The Society of Jesus in San Francisco, 1849–1969* by John McGloin, S.J., pages 192–196. The document "The Future of Your University" is on file in the USF Office of Institutional Research. Enrollment statistics for 1946 were furnished by Academic Services at USF, courtesy of Fred Baldwin, database manager.

Vignette #102 A description of USF's first board of regents, including the quote from the *San Francisco Chronicle* about their work, is found in *Jesuits by the Golden Gate: The Society of Jesus in San Francisco, 1849–1969* by John McGloin, S.J., pages 196–200. A description of the kick-off dinner for the Greater University of San Francisco Fund, including the speech by Timothy Fitzpatrick, appears in the *USF Alumnus,* September 1949, pages 4 and 14. A biographical sketch of William McCarthy, chair of the first board of regents, appears in the *USF Alumnus,* April 1949, page 4.

Vignette #103 Information on the building of Gleeson Library can be found in *Jesuits by the Golden Gate: The Society of Jesus in San Francisco, 1849–1969* by John McGloin, S.J., pages 212–215. The dedication of Gleeson Library is described in the November 1950 issue of the *USF Alumnus,* page 3; facts, figures, and key people associated with Gleeson Library appear in a series of articles in the spring 1995 issue of *University of San Francisco Magazine,* pages 18–23; the dedication of the Geschke Center is described by Mel Taylor in the fall 1997 issue of *University of San Francisco Magazine,* pages 18–19; and the current statistics on library holdings come from the office of Tyrone Cannon, dean of the library, and his assistant, Carmen Fernandez-Baybay. The USF graduating student survey is administered by the USF Office of Institutional Research.

Vignette #104 The 1948–1949 championship basketball season is described in *Jesuits by the Golden Gate: The Society of Jesus in San Francisco, 1849–1969* by John McGloin, S.J., pages 211–212. Other details about the athletic accomplishments of the Dons during this Golden Year can be found in the following issues of the *USF Alumnus:* May 1949, page 13; June 1949, pages 8–9; and August 1949, pages 12–13. The May 10, 1961, issue of the *Foghorn,* page 15, also carries a detailed summary of this championship year. A shorter summary of the athletic accomplishments for the year, including photographs of the basketball team and of tennis star Harry Likas, can be found on the back cover of the *USF Magazine,* fall 2002.

Vignette #105 The highly segregated nature of the United States in 1951 is well documented in numerous sources, including *African American History: Primary Sources,* edited by Thomas Frazier, pages 365–386, and *Reporting Civil Rights, American Journalism, 1941–1963.* The definitive study of the 1951 USF football team is found in the book, *Undefeated, Untied, and Uninvited: A Documentary of the 1951 University of San Francisco Dons Football Team* by Kristine Setting Clark. Excellent short summaries of the team and the season can also be found in an article by Ryan Callan on the USF Dons Web site at usfdons.ocsn.com/trads/football_trad.html, and in the pages of the *San Francisco Chronicle,* including articles by Ken Garcia on July 8, 2000, and by Dwight Chapin on June 17, 2002. A description of the team's 50th anniversary celebration dinner, including the quote from Fr. Privett, appears in *USFnews,* October 23, 2001.

Vignette #106 Most of the material for this vignette was drawn from reports and letters housed in the offices of the provost, vice president for planning and budget, and institutional research at USF. The WASC *Handbook of Accreditation,* and an "Overview of U.S. Accreditation," published by the Council for Higher Education Accreditation and written by Judith Eaton, were also helpful. The first accreditation visits at USF in the early 1950s are described in *Jesuits by the Golden Gate: The Society of Jesus in San Francisco, 1849–1969* by John McGloin, S.J., pages 219–221.

Vignette #107 The first references to liberal arts and science classes at St. Ignatius Academy and St. Ignatius College are found in the *St. Ignatius College Prospectus, 1861,* page 1, and in *The First Half Century: St Ignatius Church and College* by Joseph Riordan, S.J., pages 88–89. Information regarding the beginning of the College of Arts and Sciences appears in the *Catalogue of St. Ignatius College, 1925–1926,* pages 14–43. The general catalogs of the University of San Francisco, especially the 1946–1947 and 1948–1949 issues, have been helpful in understanding the College of Arts and Sciences in the immediate postwar years. More recent catalogs were also consulted for information on curricula changes over the past 50 years. The immediate postwar years at USF are detailed in *Jesuits by the Golden Gate: The Society of Jesus in San Francisco, 1849–1969* by John McGloin, S.J., pages 189–196. Notes on faculty members who began their careers at USF in the postwar era appear in numerous publications, including the *USF Monday Bulletin* of June 20, 1988, page 1, and *University of San Francisco Magazine,* fall 2002, in an article by Mira Schwirtz, pages 16–23. Enrollment statistics from the 1940s were furnished by Academic Services at USF, courtesy of Fred Baldwin, database manager.

Vignette #108 The history of the USF School of Law during the immediate postwar years is detailed in *The University of San Francisco School of Law: A History, 1912–1987* by Eric Abrahamson, pages 67–98. Biographical information on law school faculty can be found in the annual publication, *University of San Francisco School of Law.* For this vignette, the 2000–2001 issue was especially helpful.

Vignette #109 Information regarding the beginning of the College of Business and Finance appears in the *Ignatian,* 1925, page 36, and details on the entrance requirements and curriculum for that college are in the *Catalogue of St. Ignatius College, 1925–1926,* pages 70–72. The general catalogs of the University of San Francisco, especially the 1946–1947 and 1948–1949 issues, have been helpful in understanding the business school in the immediate postwar years. More recent catalogs were also consulted for information on curricula changes over the past 50 years. Enrollment statistics for the business school were furnished by Fred Baldwin, database manager in Academic Services. Nicholas Imparato, professor in the School of Business and Management, provided valuable information about the school during the 1970s.

Vignette #110 The origins of the School of Education are recounted in *Jesuits by the Golden Gate: The Society of Jesus in San Francisco, 1849–1969* by John McGloin, S.J., pages 203–204. Other useful information about the development of the School of Education can be found in the general catalogs of the university, especially the editions of 1947–1948, 1949–1950, 1950–1951, 1976–1978, and 2003–2005, and in the annual reports of the USF School of Education. Enrollment statistics were furnished by Academic Services at USF, courtesy of Fred Baldwin, database manager. Michael O'Neill, former dean in the School of Education, and Robi Woody, former associate dean, also provided many important details about the history of the school.

Vignette #111 Much of the background material on the founding and development of the USF School of Nursing during its first 30 years is in an unpublished manuscript developed by Sarah Abrams and others and furnished by Roberta Romeo, associate professor emerita of nursing. Other details on the origins of the School of Nursing are found in *Jesuits by the Golden Gate: The Society of Jesus in San Francisco, 1849–1969* by John McGloin, S.J., pages 209–210; in the *USF Alumnus,* January 1955, page 7; and in a file of primary documents housed in the Office of Institutional Research at USF. Details on the first curriculum in the School of Nursing appear in the general catalog of the University of San Francisco, 1948–1949 issue. Important details on the history of the School of Nursing were also furnished by Jane Corbett, professor of nursing at USF; Michael Kotlanger, S.J., USF's archivist; and John Lo Schiavo, S.J., former president and current chancellor of USF.

Vignette #112 A list of the 28 students of St. Ignatius College who received graduate degrees from 1867 to 1905 is provided in *The First Half Century: St. Ignatius Church and College* by Joseph Riordan, S.J., page 382. The origins of the graduate division in 1949 is recounted in *Jesuits by the Golden Gate: The Society of Jesus in San Francisco, 1849–1969* by John McGloin, S.J., pages 215–216. Other useful information about the development of the graduate division can be found in the general catalogs of the university, especially the editions of 1948–1949, 1949–1950, and 1978–1979. Statistics on graduate enrollment since 1949 were furnished by Academic Services at USF, courtesy of Fred Baldwin, database manager.

Vignette #113 Information about the development of the evening division and college can be found in the general catalogs of the university, especially the editions of 1951–1952, 1952–1953, 1976–1978, and 1979–1980. Materials on the evening college, including back issues of *The Night Owl,* were supplied by Edward Stackpoole, S.J., former rector of the Jesuit Community

and USF professor emeritus of English. A description of the Labor Management School can be found in *Jesuits by the Golden Gate: The Society of Jesus in San Francisco, 1849–1969* by John McGloin, S.J., pages 200–201. Statistics on evening enrollment were furnished by Academic Services at USF, courtesy of Fred Baldwin, database manager.

Vignette #114 The life and times of William Dunne, S.J., is documented in a large selection of primary documents (letters, photos, newspaper articles) kept at the Jesuit Community at USF, furnished by Edward Stackpoole, S.J., former rector of the Jesuit Community and USF professor emeritus of English. Specific accomplishments and challenges during Fr. Dunne's presidency of USF can be found in *Jesuits by the Golden Gate: The Society of Jesus in San Francisco, 1849–1969* by John McGloin, S.J., pages 122–213.

Vignette #115 Among the many articles that have been written about the USF basketball teams of 1954 through 1957, two of the most detailed are by Bernie Schneider, USF class of 1959 and member of the 1955–1956 freshman basketball team as well as the 1958–1959 varsity team. His articles can be found at usfdons.ocsn.com/trads/russell years.html. Dwight Chapin, senior writer for the *San Francisco Examiner,* devoted an article in the March 27, 1996, issue of that paper to the racial barriers that were broken by the USF basketball teams of the era. Chapin's article includes several quotes from the players. In addition, the entire April 1955 issue of the *USF Alumnus* is devoted to the 1954–1955 basketball championship season. Finally, the importance of the 1955 and 1956 basketball championship teams for the institutional history of USF is underscored in *Jesuits by the Golden Gate: The Society of Jesus in San Francisco, 1849–1969* by John McGloin, S.J., pages 233–235.

Vignette #116 USF's centennial celebration is described in *Jesuits by the Golden Gate: The Society of Jesus in San Francisco, 1849–1969* by John McGloin, S.J., pages 237–241. Other details about the series of celebratory events can be found in the *USF Alumnus,* October 1955, pages 8–9.

Vignette #117 Much of the history of the USF soccer program is detailed in *Dynasty: The Story of USF Soccer, 1931–1997* by Joseph Eagan, S.J. The 1950 soccer season, during which Steve Negoesco received All-American honors and the team tied for the national championship, is described in the *USF Alumnus:* January 1950, page 16, and February 1950, page 17. Other details about the life and accomplishments of Steve Negoesco appear in *USFnews Online* (February 4, 2003), and in *University of San Francisco Magazine:* Winter 1996, page 29, and Summer 2000, page 33. The current soccer programs at USF, as well as many details about its history, are also portrayed in the 2003 media guide on the USF soccer program, *Back for More,* written and edited by Peter Simon, associate director of athletics/external relations at USF.

Vignette #118 The life and times of John Connolly, S.J., is documented in a large selection of primary documents (letters, memos, reports, photos, newspaper articles) kept at the Jesuit Community at USF, furnished by Edward Stackpoole, S.J., former rector of the Jesuit Community and USF professor emeritus of English. Specific accomplishments and challenges during Fr. Connolly's presidency of USF can be found in *Jesuits by the Golden Gate: The Society of Jesus in San Francisco, 1849–1969* by John McGloin, S.J., pages 207–281.

Vignette #119 A large number of primary documents covering United States history during the 1960s can be found in *Eyewitness to America,* edited by David Colbert, pages 110–200. Events at USF and at the institution's School of Law during the 1960s are described in *The University of San Francisco School of Law: A History, 1912–1987* by Eric Abrahamson, pages 88–99. Information on some of the relatively small protest movements at USF during the late 1960s was obtained from a video tape made of a presentation by John LePlante, a student leader during the late 1960s, to a class on the 1960s taught by Roberta Johnson and Scott McElwain in 1990.

Vignette #120 Events surrounding the building and dedication of Kendrick Hall are described in *The University of San Francisco School of Law: A History, 1912–1987* by Eric Abrahamson, pages 88–97. Information on the addition of the Dorraine Zief Law Library appears in several issues of *University of San Francisco Magazine,* including Fall 1998, pages 8–11; Summer 1999, pages 2–3; and Summer 2000, page 2. Details on the Koret Foundation grant to the School of Law for the Koret Law Center, including the quote from Dean Jeffrey Brand on the significance of that grant, appear in the spring 2002 issue of *University of San Francisco Magazine,* page 8. The dedication ceremony for the Koret Law Center is covered is *USFnews Online,* February 3, 2004. Michael Kotlanger, S.J., USF's archivist, also supplied several important details on the topic and provided a transcript of Robert Kennedy's telephone speech on the evening of September 29, 1962.

Vignettes #121 and #122 The long road to full coeducational status for USF is recounted in *Jesuits by the Golden Gate: The Society of Jesus in San Francisco, 1849–1969* by John McGloin, S.J., pages 204–210. Information about the first women students at St. Ignatius College can be found in the *Ignatian,* 1928, pages 53 and 55; the Ignatian, 1929, page 78; and *The University of San Francisco School of Law: A History, 1912–1987* by Eric Abrahamson, pages 39–42. Reflections by Anne Dolan, Fr. Dullea, and some of the first women in the classes that began in 1964 and 1965 appear in *Alumnus,* Winter 1990, pages 1 and 7. Dress

code regulations in the 1960s are listed in the student handbook, *The Hilltopper,* 68–69, page 33. Statistics on enrollment at USF were furnished by Academic Services at USF, courtesy of Fred Baldwin, database manager.

Vignette #123 The SWAP, Upward Bound, and legal aid programs at USF are described in *Jesuits by the Golden Gate: The Society of Jesus in San Francisco, 1849–1969* by John McGloin, S.J., pages 263–279. Details on the SWAP program were also supplied by Ralph Lane, USF professor of sociology, emeritus, and are in the USF Alumnus, July 1964, pages 3–6. Information about Upward Bound was also provided by Janice Dirden-Cook, the current director of the program and former instructor. Details of the USF Street Law program and its 25th anniversary celebration featuring Robert F. Kennedy Jr., appeared in the USF School of Law magazine, *The Lawyer,* Spring 2002, pages 6–8.

Vignette #124 An overview of the development of academic programs in the College of Arts and Sciences during the 1960s can be found in the *USF Report for the Accreditation Committees of the Western Association of Schools and Colleges,* October, 1970, pages 3–145. The general catalogs of the University of San Francisco during the 1960s were also useful in understanding the college during the decade. The early 1960s at USF, including developments in the College of Arts and Sciences, are detailed in *Jesuits by the Golden Gate: The Society of Jesus in San Francisco, 1849–1969* by John McGloin, S.J., pages 252–283. Notes on faculty members who began their careers at USF during the 1960s appear in numerous issues of the *USF Monday Bulletin* and *University of San Francisco Magazine. The New York Times* carried a front-page story on USF's "flash mob supercomputer" on February 23, 2004, and the event was described in *USF Magazine,* Spring 2004, page 4.

Vignette #125 The life and presidency of Charles Dullea, S.J., is documented in a large selection of primary documents (letters, photos, newspaper articles) kept at the Jesuit Community at USF, furnished by Edward Stackpoole, S.J., former rector of the Jesuit Community and USF professor emeritus of English. The quote from Fr. Dullea on assuming the presidency appears in the *USF Alumnus,* March–April 1963, page 2. Specific accomplishments and challenges during Fr. Dullea's presidency of USF can be found in *Jesuits by the Golden Gate: The Society of Jesus in San Francisco, 1849–1969* by John McGloin, S.J., pages 148–283. Statistics on enrollment from 1963 to 1969 were furnished by Academic Services at USF, courtesy of Fred Baldwin, database manager.

Vignette #126 A large number of primary documents covering United States history during the 1970s can be found in *Eyewitness to America,* edited by David Colbert, pages 110–200. Events at USF and at the institution's School of Law are described in *The University of San Francisco School of Law: A History, 1912–1987* by Eric Abrahamson, pages 109–116. USF's response in May of 1970 to the U.S. incursion into Cambodia was covered in an interview of Albert Jonsen conducted by the author on February 3, 2004. Details about the Vietnam Baby Airlift organized by faculty, staff, and students at USF appear in the *USF Bulletin,* April 18, 1975, page 1.

Vignette #127 The administrations of Fr. Jonsen and Fr. McInnes are documented in a large selection of primary documents (letters, memos, reports, photos, newspaper articles) kept at the Jesuit community at USF, furnished by Edward Stackpoole, S.J., former rector of the Jesuit community and USF professor emeritus of English. Specific challenges during their presidencies can be found in *The University of San Francisco School of Law: A History, 1912–1987* by Eric Abrahamson, pages 109–116. Additional information for the vignette was obtained in an interview of Albert Jonsen conducted by the author on February 3, 2004, and from the response of Fr. McInnes to a draft of the vignette sent to him in June 2004.

Vignettes #128 and #129 The comments by former USF President Albert Jonsen, S.J., in 1971 regarding the thrust toward unionization by USF faculty are on an audio tape supplied by John Lo Schiavo, S.J., former USF president and current chancellor. The historical context of faculty unionization in the United States during the early 1970s is provided in *Faculty Bargaining: Change and Conflict,* a report prepared by Joseph Garbarino and Bill Aussieker for the Carnegie Commission on Higher Education in 1975, and in an article in the *New York Times* on November 16, 1975. Details regarding the formation of the USF Faculty Association and the first round of negotiations under the collective bargaining agreement are found in a series of articles that appeared in the journal *Panel,* published by the USF Labor-Management School and written by Michael Lehmann in 1977 and 1978; letters written by the faculty welfare committee to the USF faculty and to the USF Board of Trustees in 1975; an article that appeared in December 1976 in *Catalyst,* a faculty association newsletter written by Joseph Simini, USF professor of accounting and information systems and member of the faculty welfare committee; articles that appeared in the *San Francisco Chronicle* on December 12 and 13, 1975, and March 31, 1976; and an article in the *USF Monday Bulletin,* on June 28, 1976. These primary documents were furnished by James Rose, a visiting assistant professor for one year in the USF history department. Rose, who is currently working on a book on the USF Faculty Association, read a draft of the vignettes on the formation of the union and supplied many important details on the topic. Fr. McInnes and Alan Heineman also read the vignettes in draft form and offered their

insights. The comments by Fr. Privett on the anniversary of the USF Part-Time Faculty Association appeared on *USFconnect* on September 26, 2003.

Vignette #130 An extensive article on Alfred and Hanna Fromm and the Fromm Institute, written by Robert Fordham, appeared in the spring 1995 issue of *University of San Francisco Magazine,* pages 10–11. Other information on the Fromms and the Fromm Institute is highlighted in the spring 2003 issue of that magazine, page 7; in *USFnews Online,* in its February 4, 2003 issue; and throughout numerous issues of *From the Rooftop,* the newsletter of the Fromm Institute.

Vignette #131 Information on the history of Lone Mountain can be found in *San Francisco: Magic City,* by Fremont Older, pages 37–38; in the spring 1990 issue of *USF Alumnus,* page 1; in an article in the *San Francisco Chronicle,* February 12, 1984; in the *Foghorn,* October 9, 1991; and in *USFnews Online,* in its February 4, 2003, June 1, 2004, and August 8, 2004 issues (www.usfca.edu/usfnews). The quote from John Lo Schiavo, S.J., former president and current chancellor of USF, on USF's purchase of Lone Mountain appears in the *USF Alumnus,* July 1978, page 2. Others details on the history of Lone Mountain were furnished by Michael Kotlanger, S.J., USF's archivist, and Fr. Lo Schiavo.

Vignette #132 The first efforts at developing a radio station at USF are documented in files maintained by USF's Office of Institutional Research. A good history of the early years of KUSF, written by Jim Muyo, appeared in the *USF Alumnus,* fall 1990, page 1. Articles on KUSF can also be found in *University of San Francisco Magazine,* including the Spring 1997 issue, pages 16-17, and the Spring 2002 issue, page 6. *USFnews Online* also highlighted the history of KUSF in its October 23, 2001, and April 4, 2002, issues (www.usfca.edu/usfnews). The *San Francisco Chronicle* carried an article on KUSF in its May 12, 2002, issue. Current programming information about KUSF appears in pamphlets issued by the station, such as *KUSF 90.3 FM Stereo Social Justice Programming* (the station's free quarterly program guide) and on the station's Web site, www.kusf.org. In addition, KUSF maintains an extensive archive of historical material. Important details for this vignette were also furnished by Steve Runyon, KUSF's station manager, and by Michael Kotlanger, S.J., USF's archivist.

Vignette #133 The development of the Koret Health and Recreation Center is described in several publications, including the December 1987 issue of the *Campaign Chronicle,* the Fall 1987 issue of *USF Welcome Line,* and the Autumn 1994 issue of *University of San Francisco Magazine,* page 23. The current programs offered by the Koret Health and Recreation Center are detailed in the *Fogcutter, The Student Handbook of 2003–2004,* pages 39–40.

Vignette #134 The origins of the College of Professional Studies can be found in various USF reports and memos housed in CPS and furnished by David Robinson, S.J., CPS director of Jesuit mission and Ignatian humanities. Other useful information about the development of CPS can be found in the general catalogs of the university, especially the editions of 1976 through 1987. Colin Silverthorne and David Fox, former deans of CPS, supplied a great deal of useful information about the beginning of CPS, as did Stan Buller, former associate dean and director. Hartmut Fischer, former associate dean and acting dean of the School of Continuing Education, was especially helpful in outlining the transition from the Office of Continuing Education to the College of Professional Studies. Michael O'Neill, founding director of the Institute for Nonprofit Organization Management in CPS, also provided many important details about the history of the school, as did William McInnes, S.J., USF's president from 1972 to 1976.

Vignette #135 The life, times, and administration of John Lo Schiavo, S.J., are documented in a large selection of primary documents (letters, photos, reports) kept at the Jesuit Community at USF, furnished by Edward Stackpoole, S.J., former rector of the Jesuit Community and USF professor emeritus of English. Information about Fr. Lo Schiavo's presidency at USF can be found in numerous publications, including the *USF Alumnus,* Spring 1990; the *USF Monday Bulletin,* January 26, 1987; *University of San Francisco Magazine,* Summer 1999; *USFnews Online,* June 1, 2004; the *San Francisco Chronicle,* October 17, 1982, January 9, 1983, April 7, 1983, November 29, 1983, February 2, 1990, and March 10, 1998; and the *Chronicle of Higher Education,* June 6, 1983 and April 4, 1990. The author taped three interviews with Fr. Lo Schiavo during 2002.

Vignette #136 The general catalogs of the University of San Francisco, beginning with the 1969–1971 issue, continuing through the 1989–1991 issue, have been helpful in understanding the College of Arts and Sciences during the 1970s and 1980s. More recent catalogs were also consulted for information on curricula changes over the past 35 years. Also useful was the *University of San Francisco Report for the Accreditation Committee of the Western Association of Schools and Colleges* of 1970. Notes on faculty members who began their careers at USF during the 1970s and 1980s appear in numerous publications, including the *USF Monday Bulletin,* published throughout the two decades. The names of all USF faculty members who received the Distinguished Teaching Award or the Distinguished Research Award appear on a plaque in Parina Lounge on the third floor of University Center. Enrollment statistics from the 1970s and 1980s were furnished by academic services at USF, courtesy of Fred Baldwin, database manager.

Vignette #137 Information on the Swig Judaic Studies Program at USF is found in several USF publications, including *USFnews,* June 8, 1992, and October 15, 1997, and *University of San Francisco Magazine,* Summer 2000, page 6. Background on the Davies Forum appears in the USF magazine *View,* Summer 1982, pages 4–8. Developments in the St. Ignatius Institute are traced in *USFnews,* April 11, 2001 and in *University of San Francisco Magazine,* Spring 2001, page 2. A summary of the Center for the Pacific Rim and the Ricci Institute appears in *University of San Francisco Magazine,* Winter 1996, pages 12–15. Primary documents related to these programs in the form of reports and memos are housed in the Office of Institutional Research. Current information about the programs can be found on the USF web site at www.pacificrim.usfca.edu, www.usfca.edu/judaicstudies, and www.usfca.edu/acadserv/catalog/instits_and_enrich_davies.html

Vignette #138 The history of the USF women's athletic program is chronicled in various articles, reports, and publications. Among the most important for this vignette was the *2003–2004 Media Guide for the University of San Francisco Lady Dons Basketball,* written by Ryan McCary, USF's associate media relations director; "USF Athletics in 2003, a Report to the Board of Trustees" by William Hogan, USF's executive director of athletics; "USF Athletics: Reaching New Heights on the Hilltop" by William Hogan and Sandee Hill, USF's senior associate athletic director; the "Dons' Ambition" by Dwight Chapin, in the November 4, 2002, issue of the *San Francisco Chronicle;* and several articles in *University of San Francisco Magazine,* including the issues of Spring 1997, Fall 1997, Spring 1998, Winter 2000, Summer 2000, Fall 2001, and Spring 2002. Fr. Niehoff's speech to USF's women's athletes appeared on USFconnect on April 28, 2003.

Vignettes #139 and #140 The history of USF's athletic program is detailed in *Jesuits by the Golden Gate: The Society of Jesus in San Francisco, 1849–1969* by John McGloin, S.J., pages 211–212 and pages 233–235; *Dynasty: The Story of USF Soccer, 1931–1997* by Joseph Egan, S.J.; the *2003–2004 Media Guide for the University of San Francisco Lady Dons Basketball,* written by Ryan McCary, USF's associate media relations director; the *2003–2004 USF Basketball Media Guide,* written and edited by Peter Simon, associate director of athletics/external relations at USF; "USF Athletics in 2003, a Report to the Board of Trustees" by William Hogan, USF's executive director of athletics; "USF Athletics: Reaching New Heights on the Hilltop" by William Hogan and Sandee Hill, USF's senior associate athletic director; the "Dons' Ambition" by Dwight Chapin, in the November 4, 2002, issue of the *San Francisco Chronicle;* and several articles in *University of San Francisco Magazine,* including the issues of Winter

1996, Spring 1997, Fall 1997, Spring 1998, Winter 2000, Summer 2000, Fall 2001, Spring 2002, and Fall 2004.

Vignette #141 *The College of Arts and Sciences Review 2003,* prepared by Dean Jennifer Turpin and her staff for the USF Board of Trustees, was especially helpful for this vignette. The general catalogs of the University of San Francisco, beginning with the 1990–91 issue and continuing through the 2003–2005 issue, have also been useful in understanding the College of Arts and Sciences during the past 15 years. Notes on faculty members who began their careers at USF since 1990 appear in numerous publications, including the *USF Monday Bulletin,* USFnews, and *USFnews Online.* Especially helpful was an article by Marlon Villa, "Affirmative Action to Supercomputers," that appeared in the Spring 1997 issue of *University of San Francisco Magazine,* pages 20–23, and an article by Mira Schwirtz, "The Art of Teaching," that appeared in the Fall 2002 issue of *USF Magazine,* pages 16–23. The names of all USF faculty members who received the Distinguished Teaching Award or the Distinguished Research Award appear on a plaque in Parina Lounge on the third floor of University Center. Enrollment statistics were furnished by Academic Services at USF, courtesy of Fred Baldwin, database manager.

Vignette #142 The history of the USF School of Law from 1970 to 1987 is detailed in *The University of San Francisco School of Law: A History, 1912–1987* by Eric Abrahamson, pages 99–119. Biographical information on law school faculty can be found in the annual publication, *University of San Francisco School of Law.* Additional details on the current School of Law can be found in the following issues of *University of San Francisco Magazine:* Fall 1998, pages 8–11; Summer 1999, pages 2–3; Winter 2000, page 2; and Spring 2002, page 8. The entire Spring 2002 issue of *The Lawyer,* a publication of the USF School of Law, provided a significant amount of background information for this vignette. The Fall 2004 issue of that magazine, pages 28–29, included an updated list of all of the school's graduates who became judges, and an article on the former admissions director, Ken Lloyd, pages 18–19. Jeffrey Brand's speech on the goal of the USF School of Law to promote a quest for justice among its students was given on October 13, 2003, at a conference titled *Western Conversations,* held on the USF campus. The comments were adapted from an article he wrote for the Jesuit national magazine, *Conversations,* Spring 2001, pages 28–35.

Vignette #143 Back issues of the *School of Business and Management Report* (formerly *McLaren Report*), expertly edited by Christine Raher, have been enormously helpful in tracing developments in the business school at USF. The general catalogs of the University of San Francisco, including the 1976–1978, 1979–1980, 2000–2002, and 2003–2005 issues, have been especially useful in understanding the business school over the past 35 years. Articles on recent developments in the School of Business and Management appear in numerous issues of *University of San Francisco Magazine,* including Autumn 1994, pages 22–23; Summer 1998, page 6; and Winter 2000, page 7. Enrollment statistics for the business school were furnished by Fred Baldwin, database manager in Academic Services. Information on business schools that currently are accredited by AACSB International at both the undergraduate and graduate level was obtained directly from that accrediting association. Important details on the recent history of the business school were also provided by Gary Williams, dean of the School of Business and Management; Eugene Muscat, senior associate dean of the School of Business and Management; and Michael Kotlanger, S.J., USF's archivist.

Vignette #144 Much of the background material on the development of the USF School of Nursing is in an unpublished manuscript developed by Sarah Abrams and others and furnished by Roberta Romeo, associate professor emerita of nursing. Romeo also personally supplied many important details about the past 15 years of the school. Other details on the development of the School of Nursing since 1980 are found in the *University of San Francisco Magazine,* Autumn 1994, pages 22–23; and in the general catalogs of the University of San Francisco, beginning with the 1978–1980 issue and including the most recent (2003–2005) issue. Enrollment statistics for the School of Nursing were furnished by Fred Baldwin, database manager in Academic Services. Important information on the history of the School of Nursing was also furnished by Jane Corbett, professor of nursing at USF, and by Michael Kotlanger, S.J., USF's archivist.

Vignette #145 The development of the School of Education during the last 27 years is described in numerous publications. Especially helpful were the following issues of the *USF Monday Bulletin:* February 23, 1987; December 21, 1987; June 6, 1988; May 10, 1993; December 5, 1994; May 22, 1995; June 26, 1995; April 8, 1996; November 18, 1998; July 16, 1999; and November 10, 1997. *USF News Online* carried useful articles on April 2, 2002, and May 6, 2003. Other information about the development of the School of Education can be found in the general catalogs of the university, especially the editions of 1978–1979, 1979–1980, 1981–1982, 1987–1989, 1994–1996, 2000–2003, and 2003–2005, and in the annual reports of the USF School of Education. Enrollment statistics were furnished by Academic Services at USF, courtesy of Fred Baldwin, database manager. Michael O'Neill and William Garner, former deans of the School of Education, and Robi Woody, former associate dean, also provided many important details about the history of the school, as did Michael Kotlanger, S.J., USF's archivist.

Vignette #146 The development of the College of Professional Studies from 1987 to the present can be traced in the general catalogs of the university, from 1987 through 2005. David Fox, former dean of CPS, supplied a great deal of useful information about the college, as did Stan Buller, former associate dean and director. Michael O'Neill, founding director of the Institute for Nonprofit Organization Management in CPS, also provided many important details about the college. The current dean, Larry Brewster, added valuable information about CPS since he became dean in 1999, and he provided a copy of the college's most recent annual report. From 1987 to 2004, numerous articles have appeared in *USFnews, USFnews Online,* and *University of San Francisco Magazine* about the College of Professional Studies. Especially useful were articles in *USFnews* that appeared on January 28, 1991; January 27, 1992; December 7, 1992; August 2, 1994; September 26, 1994; June 24, 1996; July 21, 1997; May 18, 1999; and February 16, 2000. *University of San Francisco Magazine* carried articles about various programs in CPS in the following issues: Autumn 1994, Spring 1995, Winter 1996, and Fall 2001. *USFnews Online* highlighted CPS in its issues of May 6, 2003 and June 1, 2004. Other important details about the college were furnished by David Robinson, S.J., CPS director of Jesuit mission and Ignatian humanities, and Michael Kotlanger, S.J., USF's archivist.

Vignette #147 All of Fr. Schlegel's major speeches, most of his reports to the USF community, and many of his letters, memoranda, and news clippings are housed in the USF Office of Institutional Research. Other information on his presidency is found throughout USFnews from 1991 to 2000. Especially useful articles appeared in the following issues of *University of San Francisco Magazine:* Spring 1994, page 22, Fall 1996, pages 8–11, and Winter 1999, page 2. An overview of Fr. Schlegel's term as president, "A Lasting Impression," was written by Donna Rosenthal, and was published in *University of San Francisco Magazine,* Summer 2000, pages 19–28.

Vignette #148 The entire Spring 2002 issue of *The Lawyer,* a publication of the USF School of Law, was devoted to international education at USF. The quote from Fr. Privett appears on page 21 of that issue. Articles on the importance of international education at USF by Fr. Privett and by Jeff Brand, dean of the USF School of Law, also appear in the spring issue of *Conversations on Jesuit Higher Education,* pages 12–16 and pages 32–39. Information on specific international programs at USF was collected from the deans' offices in the USF College of Arts and Sciences, the School of Business and Management, the School of Nursing, the School of Education, and the School of Law. Other important details about the university's international programs were furnished by Gerardo Marín, associate provost at USF. Survey results from USF study abroad students are available from the USF Office of

Institutional Research, as are current figures on USF students who have joined the Peace Corps.

Vignette #149 Information on Fr. Privett and his administration is found throughout *USFnews Online,* and *University of San Francisco Magazine,* beginning in the spring of 2000. Background on his life and tenure at Santa Clara University appeared in *USFnews* on May 5, 2000, and his series of town hall meetings with USF alumni was described in *USFnews Online* on March 5, 2002. Especially useful articles also appeared in the following issues of *University of San Francisco Magazine:* Summer 2000, page 2; Winter 2000, pages 8–13; Fall 2001, page 4; Fall 2003, pages 22–28; and Fall 2004, pages 18–29. All of Fr. Privett's speeches, homilies, many of his articles, and considerable biographical information are available at www.usfca.edu/president/genInfo/bio.html. Additional information for this vignette was obtained in an interview with Fr. Privett conducted by the author on March 4, 2004.

Vignette #150 The Vision, Mission, and Values Statement of the University of San Francisco is printed in several USF publications, including the most current university catalog. It is also available on the USF Web site at www.usfca.edu/mission/index.html. Background on the development of the statement is discussed in *USFnews Online,* September 21, 2001, and in *University of San Francisco Magazine,* Fall 2001, page 4. Further details about the approval of the new statement on September 11, 2001, and the events of that day, came from an interview with Fr. Privett conducted by the author on March 4, 2004. An article describing the trip to El Salvador by the USF executive officers in the summer of 2003 was written by David Macmillan, USF's vice president for university advancement, and appeared in the November 2003 issue of the Association of Jesuit Colleges and Universities online magazine, *Connections.*

Bibliography

Abrahamson, Eric. *The University of San Francisco School of Law: A History, 1912–1987.* San Francisco: The University of San Francisco School of Law, 1987.

Bean, Walter. *Boss Ruef's San Francisco: The Story of the Union Labor Party, Big Business, and the Graft Prosecution.* Berkeley, California: University of California Press, 1952.

Bradley, James. *Flags of Our Fathers.* New York: Bantam Books, 2000.

Brands, H. W. *The Age of Gold: The California Gold Rush and the New American Dream.* New York: Doubleday, 2002.

Buckley, Cornelius M. "Joseph Bixio, Furtive Founder of the University of San Francisco," *California History.* Vol. LXXVIII, No. 1 (Spring 1999): 14–25.

Byington, Lewis. *The History of San Francisco.* San Francisco: S.J. Clarke, 1931.

Clark, Kristine Setting. *Undefeated, Untied, and Uninvited: A Documentary of the 1951 University of San Francisco Dons Football Team.* Irvine, California: Griffin Publishing Group, 2002.

Colbert, David, Editor. *Eyewitness to America: 500 Years of America in the Words of Those Who Saw it Happen.* New York: Pantheon Books, 1997.

Craven, Avery and Walter Johnson. *The United States: Experiment in Democracy.* Boston: Ginn and Company, 1947.

Dalmases, Candido de. *Ignatius of Loyola, Founder of the Jesuits.* Translated by Jerome Aixalá. Saint Louis: The Institute of Jesuit Sources, 1985.

Davis, Angie. "Furst Aid in the Fight Against Cancer," *University of San Francisco Magazine,* Vol. 8, No. 2 (Fall 2001): 12–17.

Diamond, Jared, "The Latest on the Earliest," *Discover,* Vol. 11, No. 1 (January 1990): 50.

Eagan, Joseph F. "Dynasty: The Story of USF Soccer, 1931–1997." (Monograph from the University of San Francisco Athletics Department, San Francisco, n.d.).

Eaton, Judith S., "An Overview of U.S. Accreditation," in *Higher Education in the United States: An Encyclopedia,* edited by James Forest and Kevin Kinser. Santa Barbara, California: ABC-CLIO, 2002.

Fordham, Robert. "Turning the Golden Years to Platinum." *University of San Francisco Magazine.* Vol. 2, No.1 (Spring 1995): 10–11.

Fracchia, Charles A. *Fire and Gold: The San Francisco Story.* Encinitas, California: Heritage, 1994.

Fradkin, Philip L. *The Great Earthquake and Firestorms of 1906.* Berkeley, California: University of California Press, 2005.

Frazier, Thomas. *African American History: Primary Sources.* New York: Harcourt, Brace, and World, 1970.

Garbarino, Joseph and Bill Aussieker. *Faculty Bargaining: Change and Conflict.* New York: McGraw-Hill, 1975.

Handlin, Oscar. *The Uprooted.* Boston: Little Brown, 1973.

Hansen, Gladys. *San Francisco Almanac.* San Rafael, California: Presidio Press, 1980.

Hansen, Gladys and Emmet Condon. *Denial of Disaster: The Untold Story and Photographs of the San Francisco Earthquake and Fire of 1906.* San Francisco: Cameron and Company, 1989.

Hansen, Marcus Lee. *The Atlantic Migration 1607–1860.* Cambridge, Massachusetts: Harvard University Press, 1940.

Hatton, Nigel. "Humanitarians for Life," *University of San Francisco Magazine,* Vol. 7, No. 2 (Winter 2000): 18–24.

The *Ignatian* of St. Ignatius College. Volume 1. San Francisco: Students of St. Ignatius College, 1911.

The *Ignatian* of St. Ignatius College. Volumes 10–20. San Francisco: Associated Students of St. Ignatius College, 1920–1930.

The *Ignatian* of St. Ignatius University. Volumes 2–9. San Francisco: Students of St. Ignatius University, 1912–1919.

The *Ignatian* of the University of San Francisco. Volume 21. San Francisco: Associated Students of the University of San Francisco, 1931.

Jack, Homer A. "To Preserve White Neighborhoods," in *Reporting Civil Rights: American Journalism 1941–1963.* New York: The Library of America, 2003, 130–133.

Jennings, Peter and Todd Brewster. *The Century.* New York: Doubleday, 1998.

Lehmann, Michael, "Faculty Bargaining at the University of San Francisco," *Panel,* Vols. 27–29, Nos. 1 and 2 (March 1977–July 1978).

Lowney, Chris. *Heroic Leadership: Best Practices from a 450-Year-Old Company that Changed the World.* Chicago: Loyola Press, 2003.

Lucas, Thomas M. *Landmarking: City, Church, & Jesuit Urban Strategy.* Chicago: Loyola Press, 1997.

Mahan, Terrence L. "The Fifth St. Ignatius Church in San Francisco, California, 1910–1950" (master's thesis, University of San Francisco, 1951).

Mann, Charles. "1491," *Atlantic Monthly,* Vol. 289, No. 3 (March 2002): 41–53.

McCrary, Ryan. *2003–2004 Media Guide for the University of San Francisco Lady Dons Basketball.* San Francisco: USF Media Relations, 2003.

McCrary, Ryan and Peter Dunkle. *2005 USF Baseball Media Guide.* San Francisco: USF Media Relations, 2005.

McGloin, John B. *Eloquent Indian: The Life of James Bouchard, California Jesuit.* Stanford, California: Stanford University Press, 1949.

McGloin, John B. *Jesuits by the Golden Gate: The Society of Jesus in San Francisco, 1849–1969.* San Francisco: University of San Francisco, 1972.

McGloin, John B. *San Francisco: The Story of a City.* San Rafael, California: Presidio Press, 1978.

McKevitt, Gerald. "Across the Rockies: Italian Jesuits in the American West." *Company,* Vol. 18, No. 4 (Summer 2004): 17–21.

Meltzer, David. "Coming to America," *Discover,* Vol. 14, No. 10 (October 1993): 90–97.

Morison, Samuel Eliot. *The Struggle for Guadalcanal, August 1942–February 1943: History of the United States Naval Operations in World War II.* Boston: Little, Brown, and Company, 1949.

Muyo, Jim. "From Humble Beginnings, KUSF Now Stands as a Model Station," *University of San Francisco Alumnus,* Vol. 5, No. 2 (Fall 1990): 1.

Nemec, David, and Saul Wisnia. *100 Years of Major League Baseball.* Lincolnwood, Illinois: Publications International, 1999.

Older, Cora. *San Francisco: Magic City.* New York: Longmans, Green, and Company, 1961.

O'Malley, John W. *The First Jesuits.* Cambridge, Massachusetts: Harvard University Press, 1993.

Richards, Rand. *Historic San Francisco: A Concise History and Guide.* San Francisco: Heritage House Publishers, 1997.

Riordan, Joseph W. *The First Half Century of St. Ignatius Church and College.* San Francisco: H.S. Crocker Company, 1905.

Simon, Peter. *2003–2004 USF Basketball Media Guide.* San Francisco: USF Media Relations, 2003.

Simon, Peter. *2003 USF Soccer Media Guide.* San Francisco: USF Media Relations, 2003.

St. Ignatius College. *Bulletin of the Division of Arts and Sciences, 1930.* San Francisco: Alex. Dulfer Printing Co., 1930.

St. Ignatius College. *Catalogue of St. Ignatius College, 1925–1926.* San Francisco: Alex. Dulfer Printing Co., 1925.

St. Ignatius University. *Bulletin, 1918–1919.* San Francisco: James H. Barry Company, 1919.

Schermeister, Phil. *The University of San Francisco.* Louisville, Kentucky: Harmony House Publishers, 1987.

Schwirtz, Mira. "The Art of Teaching," *University of San Francisco Magazine,* Vol. 9, No. 2 (Fall 2002): 16–23.

Simini, Joseph. "To Set the Record Straight," *The Catalyst: A USF Faculty Association Newsletter,* Vol. 1, No. 2 (December 1976): 3.

Smith, Page. *America Enters the World: A People's History of the Progressive Era and World War I.* New York: McGraw-Hill Book Company, 1985.

Smith, Page. *The Rise of Industrial America: A People's History of the Post-Reconstruction Era.* New York: McGraw-Hill Book Company, 1984.

Smith, Page. *Trial by Fire: A People's History of the Civil War and Reconstruction.* New York: McGraw-Hill Book Company, 1982.

Starr, Kevin. *Americans and the California Dream, 1850-1915.* New York: Oxford University Press, 1973.

Taylor, Mel. "Joe Rosenthal, '46, Captures Universal Image of Courage," *University of San Francisco Magazine,* Vol. 2, No. 1 (Spring 1995), 16-17.

Totah, Paul. *Spiritus 'Magis': 150 Years of St. Ignatius College Preparatory.* San Francisco: St. Ignatius College Preparatory, 2005.

Tuchman, Barbara. *The Guns of August.* New York: Macmillan, 1962.

University of San Francisco *Adios, 1942.* San Francisco: The University of San Francisco Senior Class, 1942.

University of San Francisco *Alumnus*. San Francisco: The Alumni Association of the University of San Francisco, 1949–1993.

University of San Francisco *Annual, 1932*. San Francisco: Associated Students of the University of San Francisco, 1932.

University of San Francisco *Don, 1937*. San Francisco: Associated Students of the University of San Francisco, 1937.

University of San Francisco Catalog. San Francisco: University of San Francisco, 1945–2005.

University of San Francisco Magazine. Volumes 1–11. San Francisco: University of San Francisco, 1994–2004.

University of San Francisco *Monday Bulletin*. San Francisco: University of San Francisco, 1983–1991.

University of San Francisco Report for the Accreditation Committee of the Western Association of Schools and Colleges. San Francisco: University of San Francisco, 1970.

USFnews. San Francisco: University of San Francisco, 1991–2001.

USFnews Online. San Francisco: University of San Francisco, 2001–2004.

Villa, Marlon. "Affirmative Action to Supercomputers," *University of San Francisco Magazine*, Vol. 4, No. 1 (Spring 1997): 20–23.

Index